KT-210-262

gardening
success

gardening
success

A comprehensive step-by-step guide to creating
and maintaining the perfect garden

peter mchoy

with susan berry and steve bradley

TED SMART

This edition produced for
The Book People Ltd
Hall Wood Avenue
Haydock
St Helens WA11 9UL

© Anness Publishing Limited 1999, 2003
Hermes House, 88–89 Blackfriars Road, London SE1 8HA

All rights reserved. No part of this publication may be reproduced, stored in a retrieval
system, or transmitted in any way or by any means, electronic, mechanical, photocopying,
recording or otherwise, without the prior written permission of the copyright holder.

A CIP catalogue record for this book is available from the British Library

Publisher: Joanna Lorenz
Project Editors: Antony Atha, Judith Simons, Clare Nicholson
Assistant Editor: Sarah Ainley
Plant Consultant: Peter Lord
Commissioned Photography: Sue Atkinson and John Freeman
Design: Patrick McLeavey & Partners

Previously published as *The Complete Book of Practical Gardening*

1 3 5 7 9 10 8 6 4 2

CONTENTS

3 GARDENING THROUGH THE YEAR

4 INDOOR GARDENING

INTRODUCTION

SUCCESSFUL GARDENING DEPENDS UPON A combination of thorough planning and skilled execution as well as certain knowledge and understanding of plants. This book offers creative ideas for every shape and size of garden, indoors and out, and gives practical solutions to common gardening problems. It explains how to plan and furnish your garden and, just as importantly, when to do it.

To get the best from your garden, you must first decide what you want from it and then work out how this can be achieved, bearing in mind the constraints of terrain, soil and local climate. Devoted to all aspects of garden planning, the first section of the book explains what considerations must be taken into account when creating a garden design. Whether you wish to adapt a section of

an existing garden or rework an entire plot, there is plenty of information here to help you plan the structure, the hard and soft landscaping and the boundaries. Those finishing touches such as focal points, pergolas and lighting which can totally transform views and aspect, are also highlighted.

The second part of the book consists of a plant compendium. Arranged according to specific preferences or general characteristics, this section will prove an invaluable guide for choosing plants to thrive in the particular conditions of your garden. It will enable you to choose the right plants for just the right position – there is nothing worse than trying to grow a cherished plant in the wrong environment and watching it die. And if a desired plant will not be able to survive in the conditions you can offer, then the listings here will help you find a suitable alternative. Advice for soil and moisture requirements will enable you to improve conditions locally for particularly sensitive or demanding plants. Plants good for scent and winter colour are also featured.

The most careful planning and preparation will count for little unless complemented by practical knowledge of when the vital tasks should be undertaken. The third section of the book charts the specific needs of the kitchen and flower garden, the greenhouse and the conservatory through the entire gardening year. As gardening is so dependent on the weather, these tasks are arranged by season rather than precise weeks so that you can adjust your schedule according to the vagaries of the climate.

For those whose passion for plants means that they must be grown indoors as well as out, the final section of the book is devoted to the description and care of houseplants. Every category of indoor plant is discussed. Whether you have just a few potted plants around the house or aspire to a conversatory crammed with containers, this section will be invaluable.

This book has been designed to provide the kind of down-to-earth practical help and expert advice needed by all gardeners, whatever their experience and their gardening environment. It is a considerable source of information and guidance that you will return to time and again.

Top: Syringa X henryi *(Lilac).*

Above: Hemerocallis *'Burning Daylight' (Day lily).*

Left: Cornus canadensis.

Opposite page: Impatiens *New Guinea Hybrid.*

PLANNING *the* GARDEN

INTRODUCTION

MAKING THE MOST OF A GARDEN SPACE DEPENDS partly on design and partly on planting. If you want a low-maintenance garden the emphasis should be on hard landscaping and the use of ground cover and low-maintenance plants. If you are a plant collector, a design with the emphasis on planting space will be important . . . but choosing the right plants in proportion to the available space is vital.

You will find lots of ideas for redesigning a garden, from initial ideas to execution. But sometimes only minor modifications to your existing garden are necessary for a transformation, and the chapter on features and structures has plenty of thought-provoking ideas that you might like to consider.

Choosing appropriate plants can be the key to ensuring a garden design works well. In the third chapter of the section you will find hundreds of recommended plants, arranged by use or purpose – from plants for colour theme beds and borders, to those providing colour in the cold months. Many plants have more than a single role, of course, so to avoid repetition and to make space for more plants, multiple entries have been thoroughly cross-referenced.

Size is especially important in a smaller garden, so we have given an indication of likely heights and spreads. In the case of herbaceous plants these are typical dimensions after a couple of years, but for slower-growing trees and shrubs they are the probable size after 10–15 years. Bear in mind, however, that dimensions can be no more than a crude guide. Heights can vary greatly, according to soil, position, and local climate. Some trees and shrubs can be kept compact by regular pruning – for example, buddleias and eucalpytus are both too tall for a small garden if left unpruned, but will make compact shrubs with a good shape if cut back severely each spring.

Although you will find plenty of suggestions in the following pages, attractive gardens are not designed to a rigid formula, and there is always room for individual interpretation – and even eccentricity. Some gardens are designed to shock, some are traditional in concept, a few are strictly formal, and many are a compromise between formality and informality. There are as many garden styles as there are tastes, and the only criterion for success is whether the result pleases you personally.

ELEMENTS *of* DESIGN

Attractive gardens seldom just happen, they are designed. And despite the apparent contradiction, design does not become easier with decreasing size: rather it becomes more difficult and demanding. A large garden tends to look good anyway, with the odd weedy bed going almost unnoticed among the overall impression of lawns, stately trees and shrubs. In a small garden long vistas are out of the question and the use of trees and shrubs is often severely limited. Keep the design simple, stick to a style, and follow the suggestions in this section for making a plan to scale. Then check the effect by marking out the shapes in the garden before you start work. This way you will be assured of success.

ABOVE: *Sometimes accommodating essentials, such as this tool shed, attractively can become a problem. Careful screening can help minimize their impact.*

OPPOSITE: *A small garden should not lack impact. Provided it is well planted and has some strong focal points, it becomes easy to ignore the limitations of size.*

PLANNING YOUR GARDEN

SOME SUCCESSFUL GARDENS ARE WORKED OUT on the ground, in the mind's eye, perhaps visualized during a walk around the garden, or conceived in stages as construction takes place. This approach is for the gifted or very experienced, and it is far better to make your mistakes on paper first.

A major redesign can be time-consuming and expensive, especially if it involves hard landscaping (paving, walls, steps, etc). However, simply moving a few plants is rarely enough to transform an uninspiring garden into something special. It is worth having a goal, a plan to work to, even if you have to compromise along the way. Bear in mind that you may be able to stagger the work and cost over several seasons,

but having a well thought out design ensures the garden evolves in a structured way.

Use the checklist opposite to clarify your 'needs', then decide in your own mind the *style* of garden you want. Make a note of mundane and practical considerations, like where to dry the clothes and put the refuse, plus objects that need to be screened, such as a compost area, or an unpleasant view.

Unattractive views, and necessary but unsightly objects within the garden, such as toolsheds, are a particular problem because they can dominate a small garden. Well-positioned shrubs and small trees can act as a screen. To improve the outlook instantly use a large plant in a tub.

ABOVE: *In this garden the bird table helps to draw the eye away from the practical corner of the garden.*

LEFT: *Make a small garden look larger than it really is by ensuring the sides are well planted and creating a striking focal point.*

OPPOSITE: *Shape and form can be as important as colour in creating a stylish garden.*

LABOUR-SAVING TIPS

● To minimize cost and labour, retain as many paths and areas of paving as possible, but only if they don't compromise the design.
● If you want to enlarge an area of paving, or improve its appearance, it may be possible to pave over the top and thus avoid the arduous task of removing the original.
● Modifying the shape of your lawn is easier than digging it up and relaying a new one. It is simple to trim it to a smaller shape if you want a lawn of the same area, and if you wish to change the angle or shape, it may be possible to leave most of it intact, and simply lift and relay some of the turf.

LEFT: Strong lines and several changes of level give this small garden plenty of interest. In this kind of design, the hard landscaping is more important than the soft landscaping (the plants).

CHOICES CHECKLIST

Before you draw up your design, make a list of requirements for your ideal garden. You will almost certainly have to abandon or defer some of them, but at least you will realize which features are most important to you.

Use this checklist at the rough plan stage, when decisions have to be made . . . and it is easy to change your mind!

Features

Barbecue ☐
Beds ☐
Borders, for herbaceous ☐
Borders, for shrubs ☐
Borders, mixed ☐
Birdbath ☐
Changes of level ☐
Fruit garden ☐
Gravelled area ☐
Greenhouse/conservatory ☐
Herb garden ☐
Lawn (mainly for decoration) ☐
Lawn (mainly for recreation) ☐
Ornaments ☐
Patio/terrace ☐
Pergola ☐
Pond ☐
Raised beds ☐
Summerhouse ☐
Sundial ☐
Vegetable plot ☐
Plus .... ☐

Functional features

Compost area ☐
Garage ☐
Toolshed ☐
Plus .... ☐

Necessities

Children's play area ☐
   Climbing frame ☐
   Sandpit ☐
   Swing ☐
Clothes dryer ☐
Dustbin area ☐
Plus .... ☐

CHOOSING A STYLE

Before sitting down with pencil and paper to sketch out your garden, spend a little time thinking about the style that you want to achieve. In many gardens plants and features are used for no other reason than that they appeal; an excellent reason, perhaps, but not the way to create an overall design that will make your garden stand out from others in the street.

The styles shown in the following six pages are not exhaustive, and probably none will be exactly right for your own garden, but they will help you to clarify your thoughts. You should know roughly what you want from your garden before you start to design it.

FORMAL APPROACH

Formal gardens appeal to those who delight in crisp, neat edges, straight lines and a sense of order. Many traditional suburban gardens are formal in outline, with rectangular lawns flanked by straight flower borders, and perhaps rectangular or circular flower beds cut into them. Such rigid designs are often dictated by the drive for the car and straight paths laid by the house builder.

Although the gardens shown here are all very different, what they have in common is a structure as important as the plants contained within it. The designs are largely symmetrical, with no pretence at creating a natural-looking environment for the plants.

The very size and shape of most small gardens limits the opportunities for natural-looking landscapes, so a formal style is a popular choice.

Parterres and knot gardens

Parterres and knot gardens often appeal to those with a sense of garden history, though in a small garden the effect can only ever be a shadow of the grand designs used by sixteenth-century French and Italian gardeners.

Parterres are areas consisting of a series of shaped beds, or compart-

ABOVE: *A knot garden. This kind of garden is not colourful, but the strong lines and formal shape, backed by a variety of greens, make it a restful place to relax.*

LEFT: *This small, enclosed courtyard garden balances a central focal point with a boundary that features this dramatic entrance.*

ments, that fit together to form a pattern, often quite complex, on the ground. They were designed, often, to be viewed from the upper windows of grand houses.

Knot gardens, originally designed to be viewed from above, are similar but low-growing clipped hedges are used to form the geometric and often interwoven designs. The space between hedges can be filled with flowers or, more historically correct, coloured sands or gravel, or even crushed coal if black appeals.

These are expensive gardens to create, slow to establish, and labour-intensive to maintain, but the results can be stunning. This kind of garden is unsuitable for a young family.

Formal herb gardens

Herb gardens are popular features and are much easier to create than knot gardens. Illustrations of both old and new herb gardens in books will often give you ideas for designs.

Rose gardens

A formal rose garden is easy to create, and it will look good even in its first season. To provide interest throughout the year, edge the beds with seasonal flowers and underplant the roses with spring bulbs or low-growing summer flowers.

Paved gardens

A small garden lends itself to being paved throughout. By growing most plants in raised beds or in containers, less bending is involved and many of the smaller plants are more easily appreciated. Climbers can be used to make the most of vertical space, and if you plant in open areas left in the paving, the garden can still look green.

Courtyard gardens

Space can be at a real premium in the heart of a town, but you can turn your backyard into an oasis-like courtyard garden, with floor tiles and white walls that reflect the light. Add some lush green foliage, an 'architectural' tree or large shrub, and the sound of running water. Although the plants may be few, the impact is strong.

Traditional designs

A small formal garden, with a rectangular lawn, straight herbaceous border, and rose and flower beds is still a popular choice with gardeners looking for the opportunity to grow a wide variety of plants such as summer bedding, herbaceous plants, and popular favourites such as roses. The design element is less important than the plants.

LEFT: *The use of white masonry paint can help to lighten a dark basement garden or one enclosed by high walls.*

BELOW: *This long, narrow plot has been broken up by strong lines: a useful design technique.*

INFORMAL EFFECTS

The informality of the cottage garden and the 'wilderness' atmosphere of a wild garden are difficult to achieve in a small space, especially in a town. However, with fences well clothed with plants so that modern buildings do not intrude, an informal garden can work even here.

Cottage gardens

The cottage garden style is created partly by design and the use of suitable paving materials (bricks for paths instead of modern paving slabs), and also by the choice of plants.

Relatively little hard landscaping is necessary for a cottage garden – brick paths and perhaps stepping-stones through the beds may be enough. It is the juxtaposition of 'old-fashioned' plants and vegetables that creates the casual but colourful look associated with this type of garden.

Mix annuals with perennials – especially those that will self-seed such as calendulas and *Limnanthes douglasii*, which will grow everywhere and create a colourful chaos. If flowers self-sow at the edge of the path, or between other plants, leave most of them to grow where they have chosen to put down roots.

Plant some vegetables among the flowers, and perhaps grow decorative runner beans up canes at the back of the border.

Wildlife gardens

A small wildlife garden seems almost a contradiction in terms, but even a tiny plot can offer a refuge for all kinds of creatures if you design and plant with wildlife in mind.

Wildlife enthusiasts sometimes let their gardens 'go wild'. However, this is not necessary. A garden like this one looks well kept and pretty, yet it provides long vegetation where animals and insects can hide and find

RIGHT: *The house itself will inevitably dominate a small garden, especially when you look back towards it. Covering the walls with climbers will help it to blend in unobtrusively.*

food. There is water to attract aquatic life, and flowers and shrubs to bring the butterflies and seeds for the birds.

An orchard can also be a magnet for wildlife of many kinds.

Woodland gardens

A woodland effect is clearly impractical for a very tiny garden, but if you have a long, narrow back garden, trees and shrubs can be used very effectively. Choose quick-growing deciduous trees with a light canopy (birch trees, *Betula* species, are a good choice where there's space,

RIGHT: *The woodland effect can be delightfully refreshing on a warm spring or summer day, but works best with trees that have a tall canopy that allows plenty of light to filter through. Although a pond is attractive in this situation, care will have to be taken to remove leaves in the autumn.*
BELOW: *A pretty pond is a super way to attract wildlife, and looks especially good if well integrated into the garden like this one.*

but they can grow tall). Avoid evergreens, otherwise you will lose the benefit of the spring flowers and ferns that are so much a feature of the traditional woodland garden.

Use small-growing rhododendrons and azaleas to provide colour beneath the tree canopy, and fill in with ground cover plants, naturalized bulbs such as wood anemones and bluebells, and plant woodland plants such as ferns and primroses.

Use the woodland effect to block out an unattractive view or overlooking houses. As an added bonus it is low-maintenance too.

Rocks and streams

Rock or water features alone seldom work as a 'design'. They are usually most effective planned as part of a larger scheme. Combined, however, rocks and water can be used as the central theme of a design that attempts to create a natural style in an informal garden.

Meandering meadows

Instead of the rectangular lawn usually associated with small gardens, try broadening the borders with gentle sweeps, meandering to merge with an unobstructed boundary if there is an attractive view beyond. If the distant view is unappealing, take the border round so that the lawn curves to extend beyond the point of view. Use shrubs and lower-growing border plants to create the kind of border that you might find at the edge of a strip of woodland.

Bright beds and borders

If plants are more important than the elements of design, use plenty of sweeping beds and borders, and concentrate heavily on shrubs and herbaceous plants to give the garden shape. Allow plants to tumble over edges and let them grow informally among paving.

If you want to create a strong sense of design within such a plant-oriented small garden, use focal points such as ornaments, garden seats or birdbaths.

DISTANT INFLUENCES

Professional garden designers are frequently influenced by classic styles from other countries, especially Japan, but amateurs are often nervous of trying such designs themselves. Provided you start with the clear premise that what pleases you is the only real criterion of whether something works, creating a particular 'foreign' style can be great fun. Adapt the chosen style to suit climate, landscape and the availability of suitable plants and materials.

Japanese gardens

'Real' Japanese gardens are for the purist who is prepared to give the subject much study. Raked sand and grouped stones have special meaning for those briefed in the Japanese traditions, but can be enigmatic to untrained Western eyes.

Many elements from the Japanese style can be adapted for Western tastes, however, and many gardeners are happy to introduce the essential visual elements without concern for deeper meanings. This style is easily adapted to a small space, and the uncluttered appearance makes a confined area appear larger.

Stone and gravel gardens

Although stones and rocks are widely used in Japanese gardens, they can also be key components in creating a garden which is more reminiscent of a dry river bed in an arid region – the sort of garden that you might find in a rocky, semi-desert area.

This kind of garden needs minimal maintenance, and if you choose drought-tolerant plants it should look good even in a very dry summer.

Stone gardens appeal to those with a strong sense of design, and an adventurous spirit, rather than to plant-lovers. Although the plants play a vital role in the drama of the scene, opportunities for using a wide range of plants is limited.

Gravel gardens are also a practical choice where space is limited. You can add some large boulders or rocks as focal points, and plants can be used much more freely. It is easy to plant through the gravel, and a wide range of plants can be grown in groups or as isolated specimens.

LEFT: *You don't need a lot of plants to create a Japanese-style garden. Strong hard landscaping and the restrained use of plants is a hallmark of the Japanese garden style.*

OPPOSITE TOP: *The use of formal water, painted wall and patio overhead gives this garden a Mediterranean atmosphere.*

OPPOSITE: *The dry gravel slope and the use of plants like yuccas help to create the illusion of a garden in a warm, dry climate.*

Mediterranean gardens

The illusion of a Mediterranean garden is most easily achieved in a backyard or tiny walled garden. The effect is difficult to achieve if you view neighbouring homes and gardens over a low fence – guaranteed to kill any self-deception as to location!

Paint the walls white, or a pale colour, to reflect the light and create a bright, airy feeling. If possible include alcoves in which you can place plants, or build ledges on which you can stand pots.

Pave the area with bricks, terracotta-coloured pavers or tiles – but steer clear of paving slabs. Use plenty of decorative terracotta pots and tubs.

The illusion is completed by using plenty of appropriate plants, such as pelargoniums, oleanders, bougainvilleas, and daturas (brugmansias). Stand pots of large cacti and succulents outdoors too.

The success of this kind of garden owes less to its structural design than to the use of appropriate plants, ornaments, and garden furniture.

Exotic effects

You can give your garden an exotic appearance by concentrating on exotic-looking plants that are hardier than

their appearance might suggest. Grow them in pots on the patio (which will enable you to move the tender kinds to a greenhouse or conservatory, or just a sheltered position, if you garden in a cold area), or in a gravel garden.

Tough, spiky plants to consider for this kind of garden are many of the hardy yuccas, and phormiums if they grow in your area without protection. Add some agaves such as *A. americana* if you live in a very mild area.

Palms are associated with warm climates, but some are tough enough to withstand moderately severe winters. *Trachycarpus fortunei* is particularly reliable. Just a few well-chosen plants can create images of far-away places.

BASIC PATTERNS

Having decided on the *style* of garden that you want, and the *features* that you need to incorporate, it is time to tackle the much more difficult task of applying them to your own garden. The chances are that your garden will be the wrong size or shape, or the situation or outlook is inappropriate to the style of garden that you have admired. The way round this impasse is to keep in mind a style without attempting to recreate it closely.

If you can't visualize the whole of your back or front garden as, say, a stone or Japanese garden, it may be possible to include the feature as an element within a more general design.

STARTING POINTS
If you analyse successful garden designs, most fall into one of the three basic patterns described below, though clever planting and variations on the themes almost always result in individual designs.

Circular theme
Circular themes are very effective at disguising the predictable shape of a rectangular garden. Circular lawns, circular patios, and circular beds are all options, and you only need to overlap and interlock a few circles to create a stylish garden. Plants fill the gaps between the curved areas and the straight edges.

Using a compass, try various combinations of circles to see whether you can create an attractive pattern. Be prepared to vary the radii and to overlap the circles if necessary.

Diagonal theme
This device creates a sense of space by taking the eye along and across the garden. Start by drawing grid lines at 45 degrees to the house or main fence. Then draw in the design, using the grid as a guide.

Rectangular theme
Most people designing use a rectangular theme – even though they may not make a conscious effort to do so. The device is effective if you want to create a formal look, or wish to divide a long, narrow garden up into smaller sections.

Circular theme

Diagonal theme

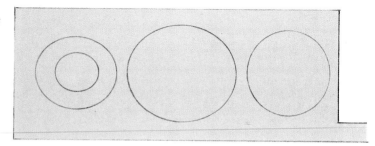

Rectangular theme

Circular theme

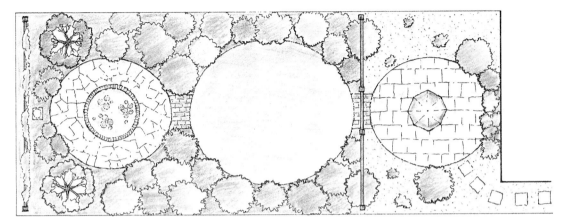

Diagonal theme

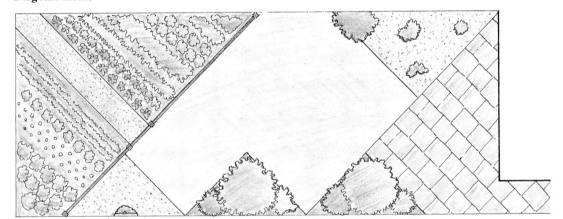

Rectangular theme

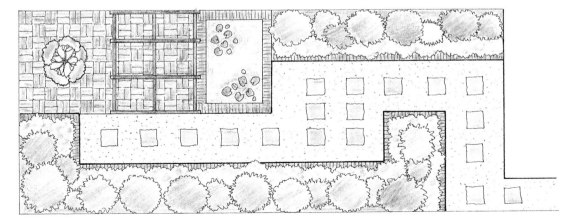

MEASURING UP

Whether designing a garden from scratch or simply modifying what you already have, you need to draw a plan of the garden as it is. A drawn plan will enable you to see the overall design clearly, and to experiment with different ideas before committing yourself to a definite option.

HOW TO MEASURE THE SITE

YOU WILL NEED:

- One, or ideally two, 30m (100ft) tape measures (unless your garden is very short). Plasticized fabric is the best material as linen stretches and steel is difficult to manipulate.
- A steel rule about 1.8m (6ft) long (to measure short distances).
- Pegs to mark out positions, and meat skewers to hold one end of the tape in position if working alone.
- Clip-board and pad or graph paper.
- A couple of pencils, sharpener and an eraser.

1 Make a rough visual sketch by eye. It does not have to be accurate, but try to keep existing important features roughly in proportion. Leave plenty of space on the plan for adding dimensions. If necessary, use several sheets of paper, and indicate where they join.

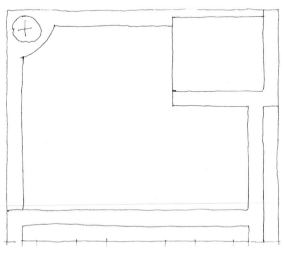

2 Choose a base line from which to start measuring. Make it a long, straight edge from which the majority of other points can be measured. A long fence or a house wall are often convenient starting points. From the straight edge or base line, measure off key points, such as the positions of windows, doors, any outbuildings, and so on. Measure out at right angles to establish the distances from the base line to the important features so that you can build the outline plan. Most key points on your plan can be established by measuring again at right angles from these right angles if necessary.

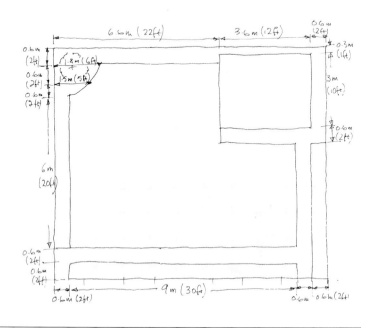

HOW TO MAKE
A SCALE DRAWING

1 To make a scale drawing, choose
a scale that enables you to fit the
garden (or at least a self-contained
section of it) onto the one sheet of
graph paper. Buy large sheets of
graph paper if necessary. For most
small gardens, a scale of 1:50 (2cm to
a metre or ¼in to 1ft) is about right.
If your garden is large, try a scale of
1:100. Draw your base line in first,
then transfer the scale measurements.
When the right-angle measurements
have been transferred, draw in the
relevant outlines.

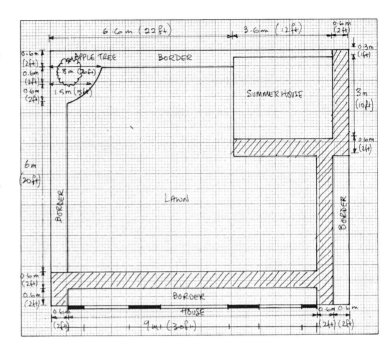

DON'T MAKE WORK

When measuring your plot, don't
waste time measuring and plotting
the position of features that you
have no intention of retaining in
your replanned garden. If you
intend to remove an unsightly tree
or large shrub, or to pull down a
garden shed that has seen better
days, leave them off your plan –
they will only clutter and confuse.

SLOPES AND
CONTOURS

In a large garden, slopes are often
significant and may have to be
taken into account. You can
generally ignore gentle slopes in
a small garden, or make a mental
note of them.

HOW TO USE TRIANGULATION

It may not be possible to position
some features or key points simply
by measuring a series of right
angles. These are best determined
by a process known as triangula-
tion. Using a known base, perhaps
the corners of the house, simply
measure the distance from two
points to the position to be
established. By transferring the

scale distances from the two
known points later, the exact
position can be established. To
transfer the triangulated measurements, set a compass to each of
the scale distances in turn, and
scribe an arc in the approximate
position. Where the second arc
intersects the first one, your point
is established.

*To fix position of tree,
measure to A, then to B.
Strike arcs on a scale
drawing with compasses
set at these measurements.
Where the arcs cross shows
the position of the tree in
relation to the house.*

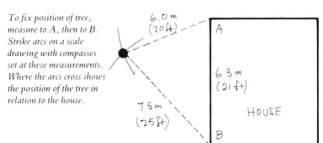

CREATING THE DESIGN

The most off-putting part of drawing up the design is the blank sheet of paper. Once this is overcome, producing alternative plans becomes fun, and there is the satisfaction of marking out the space to see the final effect in the garden. Just follow the stages below.

Stage 1: the basic grid
With the measurements transferred to graph paper you should already have a plan of your garden, showing any permanent structures and features that you want to retain.

Now superimpose onto this grid the type of design you have in mind – one based on circles, rectangles or diagonals, for example. If you are sure of the type of layout you want, draw these directly onto your plan in a second colour. If you think you might change your mind, draw the grid on a transparent overlay. For most small gardens, grid lines 1.8–2.4m (6–8ft) apart are about right.

Using an overlay, or a photocopy of your plan complete with grid, mark on the new features that you would like to include, in their approximate positions. You might find it helpful to cut out pieces of paper to an appropriate size and shape so that you can move them around.

Stage 2: the rough
Using an overlay or a photocopy, start sketching in your plan. If you can visualize an overall design, sketch this in first, then move around your features to fit into it. If you have not reached this stage, start by sketching in the features you have provisionally positioned – but be prepared to adjust them as the design evolves.

You will need to make many attempts. Don't be satisfied with the first one – it may be the best, but you won't know this unless you explore other options.

Don't worry about planting details at this stage, except perhaps for a few important plants that form focal points in the design.

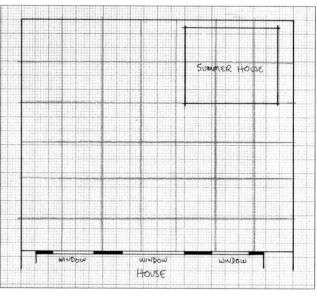

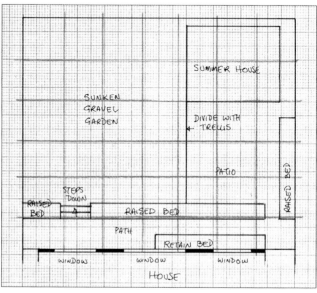

Stage 3: the detailed drawing

Details such as the type of paving should be decided now – not only because it will help you to see the final effect, but also because you need to work to areas that use multiples of full blocks, slabs or bricks if possible. Draw in key plants, especially large trees and shrubs, but omit detailed planting plans at this stage.

Trying it out

Before ordering materials or starting construction, mark out as much of the design as possible in the garden. Use string and pegs to indicate the areas, then walk around them. If possible take a look from an upstairs window. This will give a much better idea of the overall design and whether paths and sitting areas are large enough.

Use tall canes to indicate the positions of important plants and new trees. This will show how much screening they are likely to offer, and whether they may become a problem in time. By observing the shadow cast at various parts of the day, you'll also know whether shade will be a problem – for other plants or for a sitting-out area.

CONSTRUCTION

You can employ a contractor to construct the garden for you, but many gardeners prefer to get help with the main structural features, such as patios and raised beds, and do the rest of the work themselves to keep the cost down. Even the 'heavy' jobs are well within the ability of most gardeners with modest DIY skills. For more information see the next section.

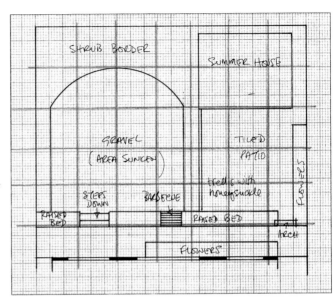

DIFFICULT SITES

DIFFICULT SITES AND PROBLEM SHAPES CAN BE A challenge, but one that can be met with a little determination and a touch of inspiration. Some ways to tackle a selection of special areas are suggested in the following pages.

If your garden is little more than a roof or a balcony, or your house has been wedged in on a building plot that is perhaps L-shaped, or even triangular, traditional garden design techniques might seem difficult to apply.

Many of the design ideas outlined in the previous chapter can still be applied, however, although you may require an alternative design strategy for specific areas.

Patios usually feature as an element in a larger overall design, but in turn have to be designed themselves. Difficult sites like slopes, windy

ABOVE: *When your front garden is as tiny as this, compensate by making the most of vertical space with climbers and windowboxes.*

LEFT: *High walls, which would otherwise have dominated this garden, are balanced by strong vertical lines. Even the tops of the walls have been put to good use!*

alleys and passageways between houses demand thoughtful planning and appropriate plants.

Front gardens present a special problem, not because of size or shape, but because a large portion of the garden is usually dedicated to the car – often there is a broad drive to the garage or a hard standing area where the vehicle is left for long periods. Legal restrictions about what you can do with your front garden can be another potential problem – especially on estates where the developers or local authority want to maintain an 'open plan' style.

If conditions really are too inhospitable for permanent plants, or the space too limited for a 'proper' garden, containers can provide the answer. Use them creatively, and be prepared to replant or rotate frequently so that they always look good, whatever the time of year.

Unpromising backyards and basements can be transformed as much by a coat of masonry paint, a few choice plants, and some elegant garden furniture and tubs, as by an extensive – and expensive – redesign. Imagination and inspiration are the keynotes for this type of garden design.

In this chapter you will find many solutions to specific problems like these, and even if your particular difficulty is not covered exactly, you should be able to find useful ideas to adapt.

ABOVE: *This long, narrow plot has been broken up into sections, with an angled path so that you don't walk along the garden in a straight line.*

LEFT: *Roof gardens are always cramped, but by keeping most of the pots around the edge it is possible to create a sense of space in the centre.*

UNUSUAL SHAPES

Turn a problem shape to your advantage by using its unusual outline to create a garden that stands out from others in your street. What was once a difficult area to fill will soon become the object of other gardeners' envy because of its originality.

Long and narrow – based on a circular theme

This plan shows a design based on a circular theme. The paved area near the house can be used as a patio, and the one at the far end for drying the. washing, largely out of sight from the house. Alternatively, if the end of the garden receives more sun, change the roles of the patios.

Taking the connecting path across the garden at an angle, and using small trees or large shrubs to prevent the eye going straight along the sides, creates the impression of a garden to be explored.

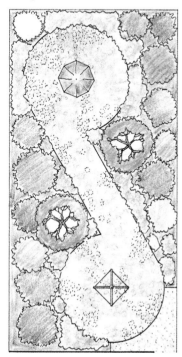

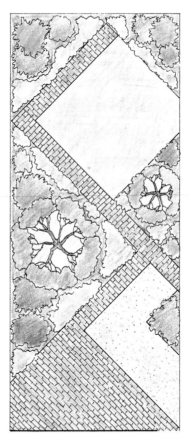

Long and narrow – based on diagonal lines

This garden uses diagonals to divide the garden into sections, but the objective is the same as the circular design. It avoids a straight path from one end of the garden to the other, and brings beds towards the centre to produce a series of mini-gardens.

Long and tapered to a point

If the garden is long as well as pointed, consider screening off the main area, leaving a gateway or arch to create the impression of more beyond while not revealing the actual shape. In this plan the narrowing area has been used as an orchard, but it could be a vegetable garden.

Staggering the three paved areas, with small changes of level too, adds interest and prevents the garden looking too long and boring. At the same time, a long view has been retained to give the impression of size.

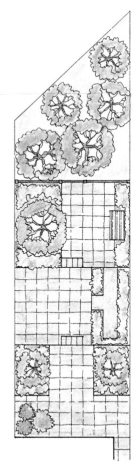

Corner sites

Corner sites are often larger than other plots in the road, and offer scope for some interesting designs. This one has been planned to make the most of the extra space at the side of the house, which has become the main feature rather than the more usual back or front areas.

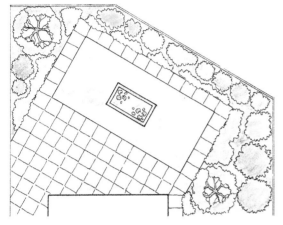

Square and squat

A small square site like this offers little scope for elaborate design, so keep to a few simple elements. To give the impression of greater space the viewpoint has been angled diagonally across the garden. For additional interest, the timber decking is slightly raised creating a change of level. In a tiny garden a small lawn can be difficult to cut, but you could try an alternative to grass, such as chamomile, which only needs mowing infrequently.

A variety of styles have been used in this plan, a combination of diagonals and circles – both of which counter the basic rectangle of the garden itself.

Curved corner sites

Curved corner gardens are more difficult to design effectively. In this plan the house is surrounded by a patio on the left-hand side, and a low wall partitions the patio from the rest of the garden, making it more private. For additional interest, the drive is separated from the gravel garden by a path. Gravel and boulders, punctuated by striking plants such as phormiums and yuccas, effectively marry the straight edges with the bold curve created by the corner site.

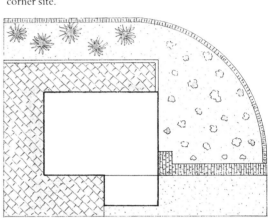

L-shaped

L-shaped gardens offer plenty of scope. Even in a small garden, the opportunity to walk around and explore an area that cannot be seen from one place is a considerable plus-point. This plan shows the clever use of focal points – a tree seat and a seat at the far end – to create a reason to explore the garden. The patio area is partially covered with overhead beams and separated from the rest of the garden by raised flowerbeds.

PLANNING PATIOS

The majority of small garden patios are little more than a paved area adjoining the back of the house, usually with little sense of design and often boring for most of the year. Your patio can be a key focal point that looks good in all seasons. A patio needs careful designing. It should be an attractive feature in its own right yet still form an integrated part of the total garden design.

Siting a patio

The natural choice for a sitting-out area is close to the house, especially if you plan a lot of outdoor eating. It's convenient, and forms an extra 'room', a kind of extension to the home, with a good view of the rest of the garden.

However, this spot may be shady for much of the day, in a wind tunnel created by adjacent buildings, or simply not fit in with your overall garden design.

Be prepared to move the patio away from the main building to gain

ABOVE: *Consider alternatives to paving slabs – bricks, clay and concrete pavers.*
BELOW: *The clever patio overhead makes this area function like an extra room.*

shelter or sun or if it suits your design. Using a position at one side of the garden, or even at the end, may give you more privacy from neighbours or a better view of the garden.

Choosing a shape

Most patios are rectangular – the logical shape for most gardens – but feel free to express yourself in a way that suits the overall design. A circular or semi-circular patio can form part of a circular theme. However, a round patio in a small garden designed around rectangles is likely to look incongruous.

Setting the patio at an angle to the house retains the convenience of straight lines, yet creates a strong sense of design. Consider using this shape on a corner of the house.

Patio boundaries

A clearly defined boundary will emphasize the lines of a design based on a rectangular grid. A low wall, designed with a planting cavity, will soften the hard line between paving and lawn.

High walls should be used with caution as a patio boundary, but occasionally they can be useful on one or perhaps two sides of the patio as a windbreak or privacy screen. A screen block wall will break up the space less than a solid wall, blocks or bricks. Planting suitable shrubs in front of the wall will soften the impact and help to filter the wind.

Changes of level

If the garden slopes towards the house a change of level helps to make a feature of a patio. Use a few shallow

LEFT: *Patios don't
have to be by the
house. A cosy corner
of the garden can even
be more appealing.*

steps to act like a 'doorway' to the rest
of the garden.

A raised patio is a practical solution
if your garden slopes away from the
house. This creates a vantage point, a
terrace from which you can overlook
the rest of the garden. On a flat site,
simply raising the level by perhaps
15cm (6in) can be enough to give the
patio another dimension.

Paving materials
The choice of paving sets the tone of
the patio: brash and colourful, muted
but tasteful, integrated or otherwise.
Do not be afraid to mix materials.
Single rows of bricks will break up a
large area of slabs. Choose any
combination of materials that is
appropriate for the setting.

If the patio is close to the house,
choose bricks or pavers that match the
house bricks closely. The facing
bricks used for the house may be
unsuitable for paving, but you should
be able to achieve a close match.

BELOW: *A patio at its
best where plants and
people meet. The use
of bricks instead of
large slabs gives the
illusion of size.*

FINISHING TOUCHES TO PATIO

It is the finishing touches that turn a patio from a hard, flat and uninteresting area into a spot where you can enjoy relaxing.

Patio pergola

The overhead beams of a pergola help to give the patio an enclosed, integrated appearance that effectively extends the home. They provide excellent support for climbers that can bring useful shade as well as beauty. Avoid covering the whole patio with a thick canopy of climbers, however, or you will be searching for the sun, and spattered in drips after a summer shower.

Grape vines are good climbers for an overhead, particularly as their leaves fall so you will get full winter sun. A relative with much larger leaves and gorgeous autumn colour is *Vitis coignettiae*.

You can attach overhead beams to a brick wall with joist hangers (remove some of the mortar, insert the hanger, and refill with mortar). Use ground anchors and supports for the posts to keep the timber out of contact with damp ground and prolong its life.

RIGHT: *If you position your patio away from the house, it may be necessary to construct a free-standing overhead feature.*

ABOVE: *Joist hangers are used to secure sawn timber to the house for a patio overhead.*

Built-in features

A built-in barbecue blends with the garden in a way that a free-standing one cannot, and it will probably be used more often. Built-in seats save space and, like the barbecue, give the patio a well-designed look. A few bright cushions give hard bench seats comfort and colour.

Planting spaces

Most people pack their patio with containers, but planting directly into the ground makes watering less of a chore. Permanent plants such as shrubs and small trees are best grown in the ground whenever possible. Some manufacturers make paving slabs that are designed to form a series of planting holes.

GETTING THE HEIGHT RIGHT

Patio beams should always be high enough to give plenty of clearance beneath them when clothed with plants. Even plants trained and tied in regularly may have shoots that cascade downwards, and this is especially hazardous with thorny plants such as climbing roses. If the beams are used as hanging basket supports in an area where you will be walking, make sure the bottom of the basket will be above head height. As a guide, a clearance of about 2.4m (8ft) should be the minimum in most instances.

ROOF GARDENS

Despite the handicaps, people manage to create verdant areas on top of tower blocks. If they are not overlooked, roof gardens can prove to be very private. However, there are potential structural limitations that must be checked out first. Never construct a roof garden without seeking professional advice from a structural engineer on whether the roof is able to take the weight.

You might be advised that it is safe, or told to keep the weight to certain areas, perhaps to the parapet wall, but you should abandon any idea of a roof garden if advised that it would be unsafe. Sometimes additional strengthening can be added, but this is a major and potentially expensive job.

The shape of the roof will largely determine your design. Usually raised beds are built in around the edge, with a sitting area in the centre. Pots can be used to provide variety within the paved area.

The roof is one place where artificial grass does have a place in the garden. Paving is heavy, artificial grass light. And it adds a touch of much-needed colour.

Suitable plants

Most plants simply won't stand the winds and cold winter temperatures on a roof. Choose a framework of wind- and cold-tolerant shrubs, which will provide shelter for the more vulnerable perennial plants and summer bedding.

Windbreak screens

Screens are useful windbreaks but also invaluable in masking many of the unattractive features that a rooftop presents. Use a trellis and cover it with tough climbers such as ivy.

Keeping weight down

Do everything possible to keep down the weight. Avoid thick, heavy paving stones – if you do use paving, choose the thinnest. Use lightweight, loam-free soil mixtures, and plastic or glass-fibre containers instead of terracotta or wood.

ABOVE: *A roof garden can be quite spectacular, especially if the building is strong enough to take structural features such as those shown in this picture.*

RIGHT: *Trellises provide privacy and shelter from the wind and can be fairly light which avoids increasing the weight.*

Watering

Plants in containers need frequent watering in warm weather. Carrying water to the rooftop in cans soon becomes unappealing, and getting out a hosepipe to connect to a tap indoors is also cumbersome. Give serious thought to installing an automatic watering system.

FRONT GARDENS

Front gardens greet visitors and can give delight to passers-by. Unfortunately they are difficult to design well if you have to accommodate a driveway for the car, and possibly a separate path to the front door. Even enthusiastic gardeners with delightful back gardens are often let down by an uninspired front garden. We have taken four typical front gardens and shown how they can be improved. Pick ideas from any of these that you think could enhance your own space.

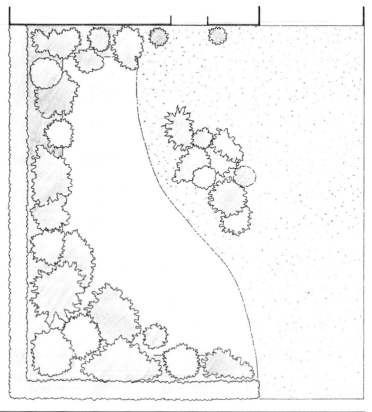

EXAMPLE ONE

This is a typical design for a front garden: a rectangular lawn is edged with a flower border used mainly for seasonal bedding, and bordered by a hedge. The redesigned garden concentrates on softening the harsh demarcation between drive and ornamental section. Plants now play a more prominent role, and the emphasis is on informality instead of angular lines.

Problems

• The drive isn't part of the garden design, and this makes the area left for plants and grass look even smaller.
• The soil close to the base of a hedge is often dry and impoverished, so bedding plants don't thrive.

Solutions

• Most of the lawn has been dispensed with, and the flower beds enlarged and planted with low-maintenance shrubs. Plenty of evergreens have been used to provide year-round interest.
• Gravel has been used for the drive, and extended to form a broad and informal sweep to the front door. Not everyone likes gravel as a surface to walk on, however, and pavers could have been used instead. If plenty of plants cascade over the edge, the widening sweep would still look soft and attractive.

EXAMPLE TWO

Tall conifers along the drive dominate the garden and will continue to do so even after redesigning it. Remove trees that are too large rather than attempt to design around them.

Problems

• Tall hedges offer privacy, but here the scale is out of proportion, and depending on the aspect may keep out too much light.

• Rose beds are popular, but the small circular bed in the lawn looks incongruous with the rectangular design and can be difficult to mow around.

• Narrow, straight-edged beds around the edges make the lawn seem even smaller.

Solutions

• The concrete drive has been paved with bricks or brick-like pavers.

• A central planting strip has been left to break up the expanse of paving.

• The tall, dark hedge has been replaced with an attractive white ranch fence. The gravelled area beneath is planted with alpines.

• Climbing roses replace the central weeping rose. Trained against the house they provide a fragrant welcome in summer.

• Existing borders remain to minimize the reconstruction.

• Small shrubs such as hebes and lavenders have been used, along with low-growing perennials like *Stachys lanata* (syn. *S. byzantina* or *S. olympica*) and *Bergenia cordifolia*, instead of seasonal bedding plants.

• A small deciduous tree, a crab apple, replaces the large conifer in the bottom corner. The area beneath can be planted with spring–flowering bulbs such as crocuses and snowdrops.

• The small circular bed has been enlarged and filled with gravel, as a base on which to stand pots.

• The narrow bed has been filled in with grass removed when the new paving in front of the house was laid. Bricks or blocks form a crisp edge.

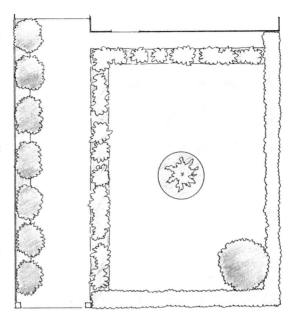

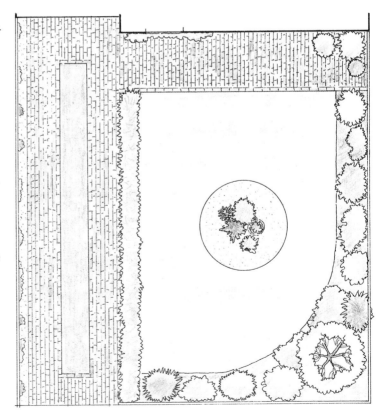

FRONT GARDENS

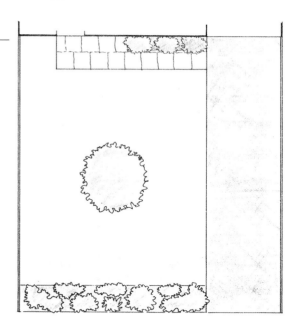

EXAMPLE THREE

Gardens don't come much more boring than this: a concrete drive, small narrow flower bed in front of the window and along the edge of the garden, and a single flowering cherry tree.

The solution for this garden was a simple one, as the redesigned garden shows. The cottage-garden style includes plants of all kinds which grow and mingle happily together with minimum intervention.

Besides being a short cut to the front door, the stepping stones encourage exploration of the garden and its plants. You actually walk through the planting, which cascades and tumbles around the paving slabs. The garden design has been reversed, with plants forming the heart of the garden rather than peripherals around the edge.

Problems

• Although the cherry is spectacular in flower, and provides a show of autumn colour, it is only attractive for a few weeks of the year. Its present position precludes any major redesign and so it is best removed.
• Unclothed wooden fences add to the drab appearance.
• Small flower beds like these lack impact, and are too small for the imaginative use of shrubs or herbaceous perennials.

Solutions

• The lawn and tree have been removed, and the whole area planted with a mixture of dwarf shrubs, herbaceous perennials, hardy annuals, and lots of bulbs for spring interest.
• Stepping-stones have been provided for those who want to take a short-cut (they also make access for weeding easier).
• The fences have been replaced with low walls so that the garden seems less confined.

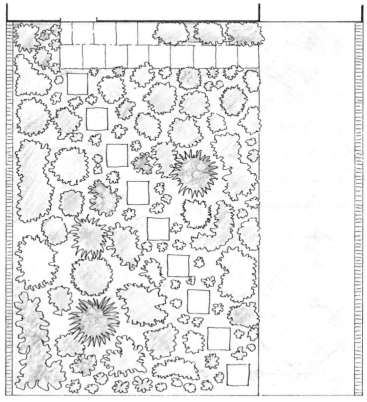

EXAMPLE FOUR

This garden is a jumble of shapes and angles, and lacks any sense of design. With its new look, the old curved path has been retained because its thick concrete base and the drain inspection covers within it would have made it difficult to move, but all the other lines have been simplified and more appropriate plants used.

Problems

• Rock gardens are seldom successful on a flat site, and although small rock beds in a lawn can be made to resemble a natural rock outcrop, in this position the rocks can never look convincing.

• The tree here is young but will grow large and eventually cast considerable shade and dominate the garden.

• Small beds like this, used for seasonal bedding, are colourful in summer but can lack interest in winter. This curve sits uneasily with the straight edge at one end and the curve of the path at the other.

Solutions

• The rock garden has been paved so that the cultivated area is not separated by the drive.

• Gravel replaces the lawn. This needs minimal maintenance and acts as a good foil for the plants.

• Dwarf and medium-sized conifers create height and cover. By using species and varieties in many shades of green and gold, and choosing a range of shapes, this part of the garden now looks interesting throughout the year.

• Stepping-stones add further interest. Because it isn't possible to see where the stepping stones lead to from either end (the conifers hide the route), a sense of mystery is added and this tempts the visitor to explore.

• The existing path has been retained but covered with slate crazy-paving it looks more interesting.

• A pond creates a water feature.

• The awkward, narrow curving strip has been turned into a 'stream', with circulating water flowing over a cascade into the pond at one end.

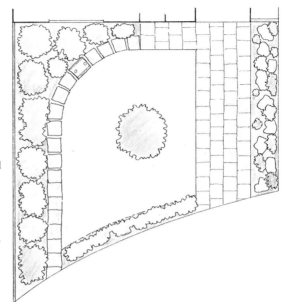

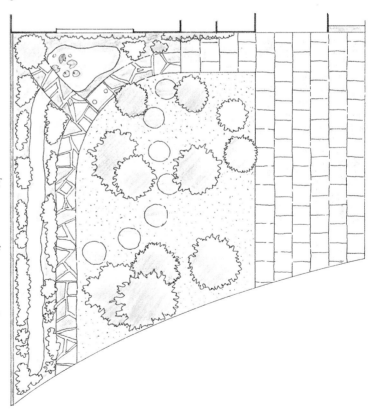

BASEMENT GARDENS AND BACKYARDS

Some gardens are not just small, they are gloomy too because they are below street level, or hemmed in by tall walls. Because there is little that can be done to alter this sort of garden structurally, it is best to direct any efforts towards improving the environment and devising a strategy that helps plants survive, or at least ensure lots of lush-looking plants to flourish despite the handicaps. Not all of the techniques shown here will be applicable to your own garden, but most of them can be adapted to suit even the most unpromising site.

Using lighting
Garden lights can extend the hours of enjoyment you derive from your garden, and you don't need many of them for a lot of impact in a small area. You can illuminate most of the space – useful if you often entertain in the evening – or use just one or two spotlights to pick out dramatic elements in the design. Some can be swivelled so that you can highlight different features. For subtle lighting, a cheaper and pretty option is to use lanterns which hold candles.

Painting the walls
In a garden enclosed by walls or fences, you need to do everything possible to reflect light and make the background bright and cheerful. Painting the walls a pale colour will improve things dramatically.

Using trellis
Trellis can be used as a decorative feature in its own right, or as a plant support. If you want to make a feature of it, paint it white, but if it is used primarily as a plant support, make sure it has been treated with a non-toxic preservative. Enclose unsightly downpipes in a trellis 'box' over which you can grow an evergreen climber such as ivy.

Adding water features
The sound of running water is refreshing on a summer's day, and in a small area you only need a trickle to do the job. A wall spout (with a tiny pool at ground level, from which the

ABOVE: *Ferns thrive in shady positions where many other plants would languish. If you can provide moisture from a water feature, so much the better.*
RIGHT: *Even the tiniest basement garden or backyard has space for a water feature.*

water is recirculated) or a self-contained wall fountain is ideal.

Introducing wind chimes
Wind chimes both look and sound good. Choose one primarily for the sound it makes.

Training wall shrubs
Cover some of the walls with climbers, but try espalier or fan-trained fruit trees or espalier pyracanthas too.

Furnishing in style
White-painted furniture looks bright in a small, enclosed garden, but don't add too much furniture or the area will look cluttered rather than elegant.

Using containers with character
If the area is small, make everything work for its space. Instead of plastic containers, use interesting old kitchen utensils, or other unexpected holders, but be sure to add drainage holes to prevent waterlogging.

Focal points in shade
Basement areas and enclosed backyards are often inhospitable for plants – the light is poor and the walls keep off much of the rain. If, in addition, you have a tree that casts shade, even the shade-loving plants will struggle. Use these positions for ornaments or make them into focal points.

Planting ferns
Ferns do well in a cool, shady spot, so use them freely in those areas too dull for bright summer flowers. Try a collection of hardy ferns – they won't look dull if you nestle an attractive ornament among them, or include white flowers, perhaps backed by a white wall. On a hot summer's day the space will be an oasis of coolness and tranquillity.

Growing white-flowered plants
Use pale flowers if the area lacks direct sun. You won't be able to use plants that need strong sun light, but fortunately some of the best white-flowering plants are shade-tolerant. Try white varieties of impatiens and white nicotianas, for example. White flowers will show up more brilliantly than coloured ones in a dull spot.

Introducing exotics
Gardens enclosed by walls can be hot and sunny too, and being sheltered provides the ideal environment for many exotic plants to grow successfully. Try a few bold houseplants to create a tropical effect.

LEFT: *Use wall pots and half baskets to make a dominant wall more interesting. They will be more effective staggered rather than in straight rows.*

LEFT BELOW: *White flowers, like this nicotiana, show up well in darker corners.*

Making the most of steps
Open railings can be used as supports for attractive climbers, planted in pots at the base of the steps, but always keep them trimmed so that slippery leaves do not trail across the steps or obstruct the hand-rail. If the steps are very wide, place pots of bright flowers on the steps themselves to produce a ribbon of colour. Do not obstruct the steps. If there is no space on the steps, use a group of containers filled with flowers at the top and bottom of the stairway.

Fixing windowboxes and wall baskets
Use windowboxes lavishly – not only beneath windows but fixed to walls too. Windowboxes, wall pots and half-baskets can all bring cascades of colour to a bare wall. Stagger the rows instead of placing them in neat and tidy lines.

Capturing the scents
An enclosed garden is an ideal place in which to grow scented plants – the fragrances are held in the air instead of being carried off on the wind. Use plenty of aromatic plants, especially big and bold plants like daturas, and those with a heavy perfume such as evening-scented nicotianas and night-scented stocks.

BALCONIES AND VERANDAS

For someone without a garden, a balcony may be their entire 'outdoor room', a 'garden' to enjoy from indoors when the weather is inclement. Even more than a patio, the balcony or veranda is an outdoor extension of the home.

The area is usually small, so the money you are prepared to spend on gardening will go a long way. Splash out on quality flooring and furniture, and ornate containers, which will create a classy setting for your plants.

Choosing flooring

The floor will help to set the tone and style, and it can make or mar a tiny 'garden' like this.

Paving slabs are best avoided: they are heavy, frequently lack the kind of refinement that you can achieve with tiles, and the size of individual slabs may be too large to look 'in scale' for the small area being covered.

Think of the veranda or balcony floor as you might the kitchen or conservatory floor – and use materials that you might use indoors. Quarry tiles and decorative ceramic tiles work well, and produce a good visual link with the house. Make sure ceramic tiles are frostproof however. Tiles are relatively light in weight, and their small size is in proportion to the area.

Timber decking is another good choice for a veranda.

The problem of aspect

Aspect is an important consideration. Unlike a normal garden, or even a roof garden, the light may be strong and intense all day, or there may be constant shade, depending on position. Balconies above may also cast shade.

If the aspect is sunny, some shade from above can be helpful. Consider installing an adjustable awning that you can pull down to provide shade for a hot spot. Choose sun-loving plants adapted to dry conditions for this situation – your indoor cacti and

RIGHT: *Roof gardens and balconies are often improved if you lay a wooden floor and create a timber overhead.*

succulents will be happy to go outside for the summer.

If the aspect is shady for most of the day a lot of flowering plants won't thrive. You may have to concentrate on foliage plants, though some bright flowers, such as impatiens and nicotiana, do well in shade.

Countering the wind

Like roof gardens, balconies are often exposed to cold and damaging winds. The higher a balcony the greater problem wind is likely to be.

To grow tender and exotic plants, provide a screen that will filter the wind without causing turbulent eddies. A trellis clothed with a tough evergreen such as an ivy is useful, or use screens of woven bamboo or reeds on the windiest side – these not only provide useful shelter and privacy, but make an attractive backdrop for plants in containers.

Adding colour round the year

Create a framework of tough evergreens to clothe the balcony or veranda throughout the year, and provide a backdrop for the more colourful seasonal flowers.

Use plenty of bright seasonal flowers in windowboxes or troughs along the edge, with trailers that cascade down over the edge.

In the more sheltered positions, grow lots of exotic-looking plants, and don't be afraid to give lots of your tough-leaved houseplants a summer holiday outside.

Pots of spring-flowering bulbs extend the season of bright flowers, but choose compact varieties – tall daffodils, for example, will almost certainly be bent forward as wind bounces back off the walls.

Add splashes of colour with cut flowers. In summer choose long-lasting 'exotics' such as strelitzias and anthuriums.

ABOVE: *In mild areas or a sheltered position, you can turn your balcony into a tropical garden.*

RIGHT: *Turn your balcony into an outdoor room where many indoor plants thrive in summer.*

FEATURES
and STRUCTURES

Overall garden design is important, but it is individual features that make a garden special. Major structural decisions, such as the type of paving to use, the shape of the lawn, or how to define the boundaries, have a significant impact, but even small details like ornaments and garden lights can lift a small garden above the ordinary. The use of containers is especially important in a small garden – on a tiny balcony they may be the garden. Use them imaginatively, choosing containers that are decorative, and grouping them for added interest.

ABOVE: *Create the urge to explore with small paths that lead to features such as seats and ornaments.*

OPPOSITE: *The garden floor is important, whether paving or a lawn, but it is features, like this arbour and its seat, that give the garden character.*

the GARDEN FLOOR

THE GARDEN FLOOR – LAWN, PAVING, PATHS, even areas of gravel or ground cover plants – can make or mar your garden. These surfaces are likely to account for more area than the beds and borders. Although they recede in importance when the garden is in full bloom, for much of the year they probably hold centre stage.

Removing existing paths and paved areas presents a practical problem. If they are laid on a thick bed of concrete you will probably have to hire equipment to break up the surface. Provided these areas do not compromise your design too much, it is much easier to leave as many as you can in position. Consider paving over the top with a more sympathetic material. It should be relatively easy to extend the area if you want to.

Lawns are more easily modified than paths and paved areas. At worst you can dig them up and resow or relay them. If you simply want to change the shape, you can trim off surplus grass or lift and relay just part of the lawn.

ABOVE: *Paths can be both functional and attractive, often giving the garden shape and form.*

OPPOSITE: *Hard landscaping, such as bricks, combined with soft landscaping, such as lawns, can look very harmonious if designed with integration in mind.*

OPPOSITE ABOVE: *A brick edging marks the boundary between lawn and border, and serves the practical purpose of making mowing easier.*

LEFT: *Areas like this would soon become weedy if not densely planted. Here hostas suppress the weeds, and Soleirolia soleirolii spills over onto the path.*

Timber decking is very popular in some countries, seldom used in others. Much depends on the price of timber locally, and to some extent the climate, but decking should always be on your list of options.

There are useful alternatives to grass for areas that are not used for recreation or are seldom trodden on. Ground cover plants not only suppress weeds in flower beds, but can replace a lawn where the surface does not have to take the wear and tear of trampling feet. Inset stepping-stones to protect the plants. Where the garden is *very* small, low-growing ground cover may be much more practical than a lawn that is almost too tiny to cut with a mower.

LAWNS

The lawn is often the centrepiece of a garden, the canvas against which the rest of the garden is painted. For many gardeners this makes it worth all the mowing, feeding and grooming that a good lawn demands. If your lawn has to serve as a play area too, be realistic and sow tough grasses, and settle for a hard-wearing lawn rather than a showpiece. It can still look green and lush – the important consideration from a design viewpoint. Instead of aiming for a bowling-green finish, the shape of the lawn or a striking edging could be its strong visual message.

Working with circles

Circular lawns can be very effective. Several circular lawns, linked by areas of paving, such as cobbles, work well in a long, narrow garden.

If the garden is very small, all you will have space for is a single circular lawn. If you make it the centrepoint with beds around it that become deeper towards the corner of the garden, you will be able to combine small trees and tall shrubs at the back with smaller shrubs and herbaceous plants in front. To add interest, include a couple of stepping-stone paths that lead to a hidden corner.

Using rectangles

Rectangular lawns can look boring, but sometimes they can be made more interesting by extending another garden feature – such as a patio or flower bed – into them to produce an L-shaped lawn.

Alternatively, include an interesting feature such as a birdbath or sundial (often better towards one side or end of the lawn than in the middle). A water feature is another good way to break up a boring rectangle of grass.

An angled lawn

If you have chosen a diagonal theme for your design, you will probably want to set your lawn at an angle to the house so that it fits in with the

ABOVE RIGHT: *A sweeping lawn can help to create a sense of perspective.*
RIGHT: *This lawn would look boring with straight edges. The curves add style.*

other features. The same rectangle of lawn becomes much more interesting when set at an angle of about 45 degrees. By lifting and patching the lawn, you may be able to achieve this without having to start from scratch.

Creating curves

A sweeping lawn with bays and curves where the flower borders ebb and flow is very attractive. It is difficult to achieve in a small garden. However, you can bring out a border in a large curve so the grass disappears around the back. You may be able to do this by extending the border into an existing rectangular lawn.

Changing height

If you have to create an impression in a small space, try a raised or sunken lawn. The step does not have to be large – 15–23cm (6–9in) is often enough. If making a sunken lawn, always include a mowing edge so that you can use the mower right up to the edge of the grass.

ABOVE: *Sunken lawns make a bold feature.*

KEEPING A TRIM EDGE

Circular lawns must be edged properly. Nothing looks worse than a circle that isn't circular, and of course constant trimming back will eat into the lawn over the years. To avoid this, incorporate a firm edging, such as bricks placed on end and mortared into position, when you make the lawn.

Where the edges are straight use proprietary lawn edging strips.

HOW TO CREATE A MOWING EDGE

If flowers tumble out of your borders, or there is a steep edge that makes mowing difficult, lay a mowing edge of bricks or paving slabs.

1 Mark out the area of grass to be lifted using the paving as a guide. Lift the grass where you want to lay the paved edge. To keep the new edge straight, use a half-moon edger against the paving slab. Then lift the grass to be removed by slicing it off with a spade.

2 Make a firm base by compacting gravel or a mixture of sand and gravel where the paving is to be laid. Use a plank of wood to ensure it is level. Allow for the thickness of the paving and a few blobs of mortar.

3 It is best to bed the edging on mortar for stability, but as it will not be taking a heavy weight just press the slabs onto blobs of mortar and tap level (use a spirit-level to double-check).

GRASS SUBSTITUTES

Grass is still the best form of living carpet for a large lawn subject to wear, but small areas are ideal for experimenting with those alternatives to grass that will give your garden a highly individual touch.

None of the plants described will form such a hard-wearing lawn as grass, but they have their own attractions. Bear in mind that you can't use a normal selective lawn weedkiller on these broad-leaved plants, so be prepared for some hand weeding. On a small-scale, however, this is manageable, and a price worth paying if you fancy a lawn with a difference.

RIGHT: *For an attractive-looking lawn in a small area not subject to heavy wear, chamomile is ideal.*

BELOW: *Thyme is tough enough to grow between paving, where it is often crushed underfoot.*

Scent with chamomile

This classic grass substitute has been used for centuries to make an attractive, pale green lawn. The fact that it is aromatic when walked on combined with an ability to tolerate a reasonable amount of wear, makes it an excellent choice for a small, ornamental area. But, like the other plants suggested here, chamomile is not a practical proposition for a children's play area.

What it looks like Chamomile has small, feathery, aromatic leaves and white daisy flowers, though the non-flowering 'Treneague' is preferable as flowers spoil the close carpeted effect. It spreads rapidly by creeping stems, which is one reason that it makes such a good substitute for grass.

How to sow or plant You can sow seed, but the best lawns are established from young offshoots or cuttings of a non-flowering variety. If you buy seed, start them off in seed trays to produce young plants to put out later. If you buy young plants or offshoots by post they will probably arrive in a plastic bag – larger specimens from a garden centre will

be pot-grown but you will pay more.

Plant 23cm (9in) apart – closer if you have a lot of seed-raised plants or cuttings of your own. Close spacing will achieve quicker cover, but the final result is unlikely to be any better. If you are growing from seed, start off under glass in early spring, and plant out in late spring, rather than sow directly in the open ground like grass.

Trim with the mower set high to encourage the development of sideshoots if the plants do not seem to be making enough bushy side growth. You will have to mow flowering forms occasionally to keep the plants compact.

You may find chamomile under

one of its two widely used Latin names *Chamaemelum nobile* or *Anthemis nobilis.*

Thyme

Thyme is another popular alternative to grass for a small area, but be sure to choose the right kind of thyme. The culinary species is too tall and bushy for this purpose. Choose the more prostrate *Thymus serpyllum.*

Thymes are good for dry soils, and do well in alkaline (chalky) areas. Unfortunately they tend to become woody and straggly after about four or five years. Cuttings are easy to root, however, so periodic replanting should not be an expensive task.

What it looks like Thymes have small, aromatic leaves, and *T. serpyllum* has low, spreading growth 5cm (2in) high. Clusters of tiny purple, white, pink, red, or lavender flowers appear in summer.

How to sow or plant Plant about 23cm (9in) apart. You can raise your own plants from seed (sow in trays, not directly into the soil).

HOW TO PLANT A THYME LAWN

1 Prepare the ground thoroughly by digging over the area and levelling it at least a month before planting. Dig out any weeds that appear. Hoe off seedlings. Rake level.

2 Water the plants in their pots, then set them out about 20cm (8in) apart, in staggered rows (a little closer for quicker cover, a little further apart for economy but slower cover).

3 Knock the plant from its pot and carefully tease out a few of the roots if they are running tightly around the edge of the pot.

5 Water the ground thoroughly and keep well watered for the first season.

4 Plant at their original depth, and firm the soil around the roots before planting the next one.

ABOVE: *Clover – in this case wild white – makes a novel lawn, as gardeners usually spend so much time trying to eliminate it.*

Clover

If clovers seem to thrive better than the grass in your existing lawn, eliminate the grass and try a clover lawn – it will probably look greener than grass in dry weather! You will, of course, still have to weed, to remove non-clover seedlings.

What it looks like The three-lobed leaves of the clover are well known. The white or purple flowers should not be a feature of a clover lawn – mow the plants before they are tall enough to flower.

How to sow or plant Clover is sown in-situ, on ground cleared of weeds, ideally in spring. You can sometimes buy clover seed from companies specializing in wild flower seeds. White clover (*Trifolium repens*) is a good one to sow for a lawn.

Cotula

There are several low-growing species of cotula that can be used for a lawn. In some countries they are regarded as lawn weeds, in others lawns are sometimes created for them. They are worth a try if you are prepared for a rampant plant that may need curtailing.

What it looks like Cotulas are low-growing plants, with divided, fern-like leaves. The creeping stems root as they grow. Masses of small yellow flowers are produced in mid summer.

How to sow or plant Plant about 10–15cm (4–6in) apart. *Cotula coronopifolia* is the one usually used as a grass substitute. The cheapest way is to sow seed, but this is only likely to be available from suppliers dealing in the less common plants.

IMAGINATIVE PAVING

Most gardens have a patio or at least a paved area close to the house. Often it is the main feature around which the remainder of the back garden is arranged. It can be the link that integrates home and garden, creating an outdoor room. At its worst, paving can be boring and off-putting; at its best it can make a real contribution to the overall impact of the garden.

On the following pages you will find a selection of popular paving materials, with suggestions for use, and their advantanges and dis-advantages. Always shop around because the availability and price of natural stones vary enormously, not only from country to country, but also from area to area.

Even the availability of man-made paving will vary from one area to another. Choosing the material is only part of the secret of successful paving – how you use it, alone or combined with other materials, is what can make an area of paving mundane or something special.

Colour combinations
Your liking for bright and brash colour combinations will depend on the effect you want to create. Be wary of bright colours though – they can detract from the plants, although they will mellow with age.

Sizing up the problem
In a small garden, large-sized paving units can destroy the sense of scale. Try small-sized paving slabs (which are also easier to handle), or go for bricks, pavers, or cobbles.

Mix and match
Mixing different paving materials can work well, even in a small space. Try areas or rows of bricks or clay pavers with paving slabs, railway sleepers with bricks, in fact any combination that looks good together and blends with the setting. Avoid using more than three different materials, however, as this can look too fussy in a small garden.

LEFT: *Bricks and pavers often look more attractive if laid to a pattern such as this herringbone style.*

Paving patterns
You can go for a completely random pattern – crazy-paving is a perfect example – but most paving is laid to a pre-planned pattern using rectangular paving slabs or bricks. Look at the brochures for paving slabs. These usually suggest a variety of ways in which the slabs can be laid.

Although a large area laid with slabs of the same size can look boring, avoid too many different sizes, or complex patterns in a small space. Simplicity is often more effective.

Bricks and clay pavers are often the best choice for a small area, because their small size is more likely to be in harmony with the scale of the garden. The way they are laid makes a significant visual difference, however, so choose carefully.

The stretcher bond is usually most effective for a small area, and for paths. The herringbone pattern is suitable for both large and small areas, but the basket weave needs a reasonably large expanse for the pattern to be appreciated.

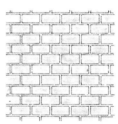

Stretcher bond

Herringbone

Basket weave

HOW TO LAY PAVING

1 Excavate the area to a depth that will allow for about 5cm (2in) of compacted hardcore topped with about 3–5cm (1–2in) of ballast, plus the thickness of the paving and mortar. As an alternative to hardcore topped with ballast, you can use 5cm (2in) of scalpings. Check the depth of the foundation before laying the paving. If adjoining the house, make sure that the paving will end up below the damp-proof course.

2 Put five blobs of mortar where the slab is to be placed – one at each corner, and the other in the middle.

3 Alternatively, cover the area where the paving is to be laid with mortar, then level.

4 Position the slab carefully, bedding it on the mortar.

5 Use a spirit-level to ensure that the slab is level, but use a small wedge of wood under one end to create a slight slope over a large area of paving so that rainwater runs off freely. Tap the slab down further, or raise it by lifting and packing in a little more mortar. Position the level over more than one slab (place it on a straight-edged piece of wood if necessary).

6 Use spacers of an even thickness to ensure regular spacing. Remove these later, before the joints are filled with mortar.

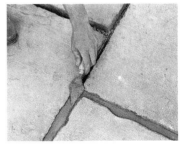

7 A day or two after laying the paving, go over it again to fill in the joints. Use a small pointing trowel and a dryish mortar mix to do this. Finish off with a smooth stroke that leaves the mortar slightly recessed. This produces an attractive, crisp look. Wash any surplus mortar off the slabs before it dries.

PAVING MATERIALS

There are plenty of paving materials from which to choose, so spend time looking through brochures and visit garden centres and builders' merchants before you come to a decision.

RIGHT: Bricks, unlike clay pavers, are laid with mortared joints. This can emphasize the design.

PAVING SLABS
Rectangular paving slabs

The majority of paving slabs are based on a full-sized slab 45 × 45cm (18 × 18in) or 45 × 60cm (18 × 24in). Half and quarter slabs may be a little smaller in proportion to allow for mortar joints. Thickness may vary according to make, but provided you mix only those made by the same manufacturer this won't matter.

A *smooth* surface can be boring, slippery, and a little too much like public paving, but many have a *textured* finish. Textures vary. A riven finish usually looks like natural stone, an exposed aggregate finish has exposed gravel to give a natural-looking non-slip finish.

Slabs imprinted with a section of a larger pattern are usually unsatisfactory in a small area. As quite a large area of paving is usually required to complete the pattern, they only emphasize the space limitations.

Shaped paving slabs

Use shaped slabs with caution. Circular slabs are useful for stepping-stones, but are difficult to design into a small patio. Hexagonal slabs also need a fairly large area to be appreciated. Special half-block edging pieces are usually available to produce a straight edge.

Paved and cobbled finish slabs

Some designs are stamped with an impression to resemble groups of pavers or bricks, some containing as many as eight basket-weave 'bricks' within the one slab. They create the illusion of smaller paving units, and are very effective in a small area.

TOP LEFT: Slabs like this are particularly useful for a small area because they give the illusion of smaller paving units.
TOP RIGHT: Paving slabs with a riven finish look convincingly like real weathered stone.
MIDDLE LEFT: Paving slabs will always weather. Pale colours like this will soon look darker, while bright colours will become muted.
MIDDLE RIGHT: Hexagonal paving slabs can be attractive, but are not usually satisfactory in a very small area.
BOTTOM: Rectangular shapes like this can be used alone, or integrated with other sizes to build up an attractive design.

Planting circles

A few manufacturers produce paving slabs with an arc taken out of one corner. Four of these placed together leave a circular planting area for a tree or other specimen plant.

BRICKS AND PAVERS

Bricks and pavers are especially useful for a small garden. You can create an attractive design even in a small area, and you may be able to obtain them in a colour and finish that matches your home, which will produce a more integrated effect.

Always check that the bricks are suitable for paving, however, as some intended for house building will not withstand the frequent saturation and freezing that paths and patios are subjected to. After a few seasons they will begin to crumble. Clay pavers, on the other hand, have been fired in a way that makes them suitable for paving. Concrete pavers and blocks are another option, though these are usually more suitable for a drive than a small patio.

Rectangular pavers

Clay pavers look superficially like bricks but are designed to lock together without mortar. They are also thinner than most bricks, though this is not obvious once they have been laid. Concrete pavers or paving blocks are laid in a similar way and are more attractive than concrete laid in-situ for a drive. They can look a little 'municipal'.

Interlocking pavers and blocks

Concrete pavers or blocks are often shaped so that they interlock. Interlocking clay pavers may also be available.

Bricks

Bricks require mortar joints – they won't interlock snugly like clay pavers. On the other hand you may be able to use the same bricks for raised beds and low walls, giving the whole design a more planned and well-integrated appearance.

To use bricks economically, lay them with their largest surface exposed, not on edge. This excludes the use of pierced bricks (which have holes through them). It does not matter if they have a frog (depression) on one side, provided this is placed face-down.

Setts and cobbles

Imitation granite setts, which are made from reconstituted stone, and cobbles, which are natural, large, rounded stones shaped by the sea or glaciers, are both excellent for small areas of irregular shape. Their size makes them much easier to lay to a curve. Bed them into a mortar mix on a firm base.

Tiles

Quarry and ceramic tiles are appropriate for small areas near the house, or to create a patio that looks just that little bit different. Always make sure ceramic tiles are frostproof. Lay them on a concrete base that has been allowed to set, and fix them with an adhesive recommended by the supplier or manufacturer.

LEFT: *Hard paving comes in many forms. The top row shows (from left to right) natural stone sett, clay paver, clay brick, artificial sett. The centre row shows a typical range of concrete paving blocks. The bottom row illustrates some of the colours available in concrete paving slabs.*

PATHS AND PATH MATERIALS

As with any other garden structure, paths should be designed to suit the purpose they are to serve. There are a wide range of materials on the market to suit every need so shop around before deciding which you require.

Practical paths should be functional first and attractive second. Drives for cars and paths to the front door must be firmly laid on proper foundations. And don't skimp on width – it is extremely frustrating for visitors if they have to approach your door in single file. It might be better for the route to take a detour, perhaps forming an L-shape with the drive, if there isn't enough space for a wide path directly to the door.

Internal paths, used to connect one part of the garden to another, can be more lightly constructed, and are softened with plants.

Casual paths, which often lead nowhere and are created for effect, such as stepping-stones through a flower bed, can be lightly constructed and much less formal in style.

Bricks and pavers
These are ideal materials for internal garden paths that have to be both practical and pretty. Complex bonding patterns are best avoided unless the path is very wide.

Paving slabs
By mixing them with other materials the look of paving slabs can be much improved. A narrow gravel strip either side can look smart, and the gravel can be extended between the joints to space out the slabs. The slab-and-gravel combination is ideal if you need a curved path.

A straight path can be broken up with strips of beach pebbles mortared between the slabs. Tamp them in so that they are flush with the surrounding paving.

RIGHT: *Although the gaps between these paving slabs have been filled with chipped bark in this example, you could also use gravel.*

BELOW: *Paving can reflect artistic ambitions.*
BELOW RIGHT: *Victorian-style rope edging.*

Crazy-paving

Use this with caution. In the right place, and using a natural stone, the effect can be mellow, and harmonize well with the plants. Be more wary of using broken paving slabs – even though they are cheap. Coloured ones can look garish, and even neutral slabs still look angular and lack the softness of natural stone.

Path edgings

Paths always make a smarter feature with a neat or interesting edging. If you have an older-style property, try a Victorian-style edging. If it is a country cottage, try something both subtle and unusual, like green glass bottles sunk into the ground so that just the bottoms are visible. Or use bricks: on their sides, on end, or set at an angle of about 45 degrees.

CREVICE PLANTS

Plants look attractive and soften the harsh outline of a rigid or straight path. They are easy to use with crazy-paving or any path edged with gravel. It may be necessary to excavate small holes. Fill them with a good potting mixture. Sow or plant into these prepared pockets.

Some of the best plants to use for areas likely to be trodden on are chamomile, *Thymus serpyllum* and *Cotula squalida*. For areas not likely to be trodden there are many more good candidates, such as *Ajuga reptans* and *Armeria maritima*.

HOW TO LAY CLAY OR CONCRETE PAVERS

The method of laying clay or concrete pavers described in the following steps can be used for a drive or a patio as well as a path.

1 Excavate the area and prepare a sub-base of about 5cm (2in) of compacted hardcore or sand and gravel mix. Set an edging along one end and side first, mortaring into position, before laying the pavers.

2 Lay a 5cm (2in) bed of sharp sand over the area, then use a straight-edged piece of wood stretched between two height gauges (battens fixed at the height of the sand bed) to strike off surplus sand and provide a level surface.

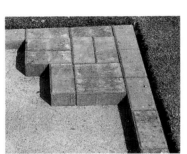

3 Position the pavers, laying 2m (6½ft) at a time. Make sure they butt up to each other, and are firm against the edging. Mortar further edging strips into place as you proceed.

5 Brush more sand into the joints, then vibrate or tamp again. It may be necessary to repeat this once more.

4 Hire a flat-plate vibrator to consolidate the sand. Alternatively, tamp the pavers down with a club hammer over a piece of wood. Do not go too close to an unsupported edge with the vibrator.

TIMBER DECKING

Timber decking creates a distinctive effect, and will make a refreshing change from ordinary paving for the patio area. As with paving, the material used should be in proportion to the size of the garden, so the width of the planks is important. Wide planks look best in a large garden, but in a small, enclosed area narrower planks are usually preferable.

Different designs can be achieved by using planks of different widths and fixing them in different directions, as illustrated here, but on the whole it is best to keep any pattern fairly simple. Leave a small gap between each plank, but not so large that high-heeled shoes can slip into it.

The construction method and timber sizes must reflect the size of the overall structure and its design – especially if built up over sloping ground. In some countries there are building codes and regulations that may have to be met. If in doubt, seek professional help with the design, even if you construct it yourself.

All timber used for decking must be thoroughly treated with a wood preservative. Some preservatives and wood stains are available in a range of colours, and this provides the opportunity for a little creativity. Dark browns and black always look good and weather well, but if you want to be more adventurous choose from reds, greens and greys.

If you want your decking to have a long life, special pressure-treated timber is the best choice. However, the range of colours available is bound to be less extensive.

Parquet decking
The easiest way to use timber as a surface is to make or buy parquet decking. Provided the ground is flat panels are easy to lay and can look very pleasing. Bed them on about 5cm (2in) of sand over a layer of gravel, to ensure free drainage beneath. If you already have a suitable concrete base to use, you can lay them directly onto this.

LEFT: *Timber decking makes a refreshing change from paving slabs or bricks, and can give the garden a touch of class.*

Patterns of Timber Decking

GROUND COVER WITH PLANTS

If you want to cover an area of ground with a living carpet simply for texture, and don't expect to walk on the area, suitable ground cover plants are the answer.

To use ground cover plants like this, rather than simply as a means to suppress weeds in a flower bed, they must be evergreen, compact, and grow to a low, even height.

HOW TO PLANT CLUMP-FORMING GROUND COVER

1 Clear the ground of weeds first, and be especially careful to remove any deep-rooted or difficult perennial weeds.

2 Add plenty of garden compost or rotted manure, then rake in a controlled-release fertilizer. Add these before laying a mulching sheet.

3 Cover the area with a weed-suppressing mulching sheet. You can use a polythene sheet, but a special woven mulching sheet is much better.

4 Make crossed slits through the sheet where you want to plant. Avoid making the slits too large.

5 Excavate planting holes and firm in the plants. If necessary tease a few of the roots apart first.

6 Water thoroughly, and keep well watered. Remove the sheet once the plants are well established.

GROUND COVER PLANTS

Some of the best plants for the job are *Armeria maritima*, bergenias, *Cotoneaster dammeri*, *Euonymus fortunei* varieties, *Hypericum calycinum*, and *Pachysandra terminalis*. If you want flowers as the main feature, heathers are difficult to better.

HOW TO PLANT CREEPING GROUND COVER

The mulching sheet method is a good way to get clump-forming plants such as heathers off to a good start, but don't use it for those that creep and root, such as ajugas and *Hypericum calycinum*. Plant these normally but apply a loose mulch about 5cm (2in) thick to cover the soil.

GRAVEL GARDENS

Gravel is an inexpensive and flexible alternative to paving or a lawn, although it is not suitable for a patio. It blends beautifully with plants, needs little maintenance, and can be used in both formal and informal designs. It is also a useful 'filler' material to use among other hard surfaces, or in irregularly shaped areas where paving will not easily fit and a lawn would be difficult to mow.

LEFT: *Gravels naturally vary considerably in colour.*

Types of gravel

Gravel comes in many different shapes, sizes and colours. Some types are angular, others rounded, some are white, others assorted shades of green or red. All of them will look different in sun or shade, when wet or dry. The subtle change of colour and mood is one of the appeals of gravel. The gravels available will depend on where you live, and which ones can be transported economically from further afield. Shop around first going to garden centres and builders merchants to see what is available in your area before making your choice.

Gravel paths

Gravel is often used for drives, but it is also a good choice for informal paths within the garden. It conforms to any shape so is useful for paths that meander. However, it is not a good choice for paths where you will have to wheel the mower.

HOW TO LAY A GRAVEL PATH

1 Excavate the area to a depth of about 15cm (6in), and ram the base firm.

2 Provide a stout edge to retain the gravel. For a straight path, battens secured by pegs about 1m (3ft) apart is an easy and inexpensive method.

3 First place a layer of compacted hardcore. Add a mixture of sand and coarse gravel (you can use sand and gravel mixture sold as ballast). Rake level and tamp or roll until firm.

4 Top up to the required height with the final grade of gravel. In small gardens, the size often known as pea gravel looks good and is easy to walk on. Rake and roll repeatedly until the surface is firm and stable.

If the path is wide, it is a good idea to build the gravel up towards the centre slightly so that puddles do not form after heavy rain.

Gravel beds

Gravel can be used as a straight substitute for grass and requires much less maintenance. You can even convert an existing lawn very simply by applying a weedkiller to the grass, laying edging blocks around the edge, then topping up with gravel.

Informal gravel beds still require some kind of edging restraint to prevent the gravel from spreading. If the bed is surrounded by a lawn, simply make sure that the gravelled area is about 5cm (2in) below the surrounding grass.

Other practical ways to prevent the gravel from scattering onto beds and other unwanted areas are to create a slightly sunken garden or to raise the surround slightly with a suitable edging.

Informal gravel areas often look especially effective if some plants are grown through the gravel – either in beds with seamless edges where the gravel goes over them, or as individual specimen plants.

HOW TO LAY A GRAVEL BED

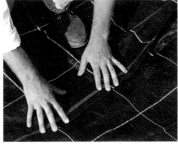

1 Excavate the area to the required depth – about 5cm (2in) of gravel is sufficient in most cases.

2 Level the ground. Lay heavy-duty black polythene or a mulching sheet over the area. Overlap strips by about 5cm (2in).

3 Then tip the gravel on top and rake level.

4 To plant through the gravel, draw it back from the planting area and make a slit in the polythene. Plant normally, enriching the soil beneath if necessary.

5 Firm in and pull back the polythene before re-covering with gravel.

FORMING BOUNDARIES

Most of us have an instinctive desire to mark our territory with a very visible boundary. It gives us a sense of privacy and the illusion of security, but above all it marks out our plot of land, the area in which we create our own very special paradise.

The problem with a small garden is that the boundary forms a large part of the garden, and the chances are that you will see it from whichever direction you look. In a large garden the boundary often merges into the background, but in a small one it can easily dominate.

Tall walls can be an asset – the walled town garden has many of the treasured attributes of an old walled country garden – but drab wooden fences and large overgrown hedges pose real problems if you want to make your garden look smart and stylish.

Don't take your boundary for granted, and never assume it can't be improved. Replacing a fence or grubbing up a long-established hedge are not projects to be tackled lightly – they can be expensive or labour-intensive. Never make changes until you have consulted neighbours that

LEFT: *This is an excellent example of a combination boundary – a wooden picket fence supported on a low wall, with an escallonia flowering hedge growing through it.*

OPPOSITE ABOVE: *Walls make secure boundaries, but to prevent them looking oppressive cover with climbers, and if possible create a view beyond, as this attractive gate has done.*

OPPOSITE: *A wall as tall as this can easily dominate a small garden, but by treating it boldly and using it as a feature it becomes an asset.*

are affected. The boundary may belong to them, in which case it is not yours to change unilaterally. Even if it is legally yours to replace, the courtesy of discussing changes with others affected will go a long way to helping you remain on good terms with your neighbours.

Although you are unlikely to want to exceed them in a small garden, there may be legal limitations on boundary height, perhaps laid down in the terms of the contract when you bought the property. In some countries there may be restrictions placed by the highways authority on road safety grounds.

Restrictions are most likely in front gardens – some 'open plan' estates, for example, may have limitations on anything that might infringe the integrated structure of the gardens.

None of these restrictions need inhibit good garden design, but it is always worth checking whether any restrictions exist before erecting or planting a new boundary.

HEDGES FOR GARDENS

Many of the classic hedges, like beech, yew, and tall conifers like × *Cupressocyparis leylandii*, and even the privet (*Ligustrum ovalifolium*) have strictly limited use in a small garden. In small gardens the emphasis should be on plants that have much to offer or compact growth. The hedges suggested here are just some of the plants that could be used to mark your boundary without being dull or oppressive. Be prepared to experiment with others.

Clipped formality

The classic box hedge (*Buxus sempervirens*) is still one of the best. It clips well and can be kept compact, but choose the variety 'Suffruticosa' if you want a really dwarf hedge like those seen in knot gardens. A quick-growing substitute is *Lonicera nitida*, and there's a golden form that always looks bright – but be prepared to cut frequently. Some of the dwarf berberis stand close clipping – try the red-leaved *Berberis thunbergii* 'Atropurpurea Nana'. Yew (*Taxus baccata*) is also excellent for formal clipping, and it can be kept compact enough for a small garden.

Colourful informal hedges

If you want to cut down on clipping, and want something brighter and more colourful than most foliage hedges, try the grey-leaved *Senecio* 'Sunshine' or the golden *Philadelphus coronarius* 'Aureus' (unfortunately sheds its leaves in winter). *Viburnum tinus* can also be kept to a reasonable height, and provided you avoid pruning out the new flowers it will bloom in winter. Many of the flowering and foliage berberis also make good 'shrubby' hedges. These will lack a neatly clipped profile, but pruning and shaping is normally only an annual job.

ABOVE: *Although Lonicera nitida needs frequent clipping, it makes a neat formal hedge.*

LEFT: *Many shrub roses can make an attractive flowering hedge in summer, but do not plant them too close to the edge of a path otherwise their thorny stems may be a nuisance.*

Using roses

Roses make delightful – and often fragrant – boundaries, but they have shortcomings. Their summer beauty is matched by winter ugliness, and they are not a good choice for a boundary where passers-by may be scratched by thorns. You can use a row of floribunda (cluster-flowered) roses, but the shrubby type are usually preferred for this job.

Old-fashioned lavender and rosemary dividers

Both these herbs make excellent informal flowering hedges, with the merit of being evergreen too. You could try the shorter lavender in front of the taller rosemary. Both become untidy with age, so replace the plants when it becomes necessary.

Other flowering hedges

Forsythia is one of the most popular flowering hedges, but careful pruning is required to achieve consistent flowering on a compact hedge. There are plenty of alternatives, including the shrubby potentillas, berberis like *B. × stenophylla*, with bold flowers, though this one can take up a lot of space, and even tall varieties of heathers if you just want a boundary marker rather than a barrier.

ABOVE: *Box is one of the classic plants to use for clipped formality. This is a glaucous form.*

HOW TO PLANT A NEW HEDGE

1 Prepare the ground very thoroughly. Excavate a trench – ideally about 60cm (2ft) wide – and fork in plenty of rotten manure or garden compost.

2 Add a balanced fertilizer at the rate recommended by the manufacturer. Use a controlled-release fertilizer if planting in the autumn.

3 Use a garden line, stretched along the centre of the trench, as a positioning guide. If the area is windy or you need a particularly dense hedge, plant a double row of trees. Bare-root plants are cheaper than container-grown plants, but only separate them and expose the roots once you are ready to plant. Only the most popular hedging plants are likely to be available bare-root, and for many of the plants suggested you will have to plant a single row of container-grown plants.

4 Use a piece of wood or a cane cut to the appropriate length as a guide for even spacing. Make sure the roots are well spread out. If planting container-grown plants, tease out some of the roots that are running around the edge of the root-ball.

5 Firm the plants in well and water thoroughly. Be prepared to water the hedge regularly in dry weather for the first season. Keep down weeds until the hedge is well established, then it should suppress the weeds naturally.

GARDEN WALLS

Except for special cases, such as basement flats and the need for privacy or screening in a difficult neighbourhood, high walls are inappropriate for a small garden. However, low walls up to about 1–1.2m (3–4ft) are a useful alternative to a hedge, particularly if you want to avoid regular trimming. Although the rain shadow and shade problems remain the same for a wall as a hedge, a wall will not impoverish the soil in the same way as a hedge.

Low walls

A low wall, say 30–60cm (1–2ft) tall, will serve the same demarcation function as a taller one, but in more appropriate scale for a small garden, and shrubs planted behind it are more likely to thrive. Modest garden walls like this are much easier to construct than tall ones, which may need substantial reinforcing piers, and are well within the scope of a competent garden handyman to build. ·

Brick walls

Plain brick walls can harmonize with the house, but generally look dull from a design viewpoint. A skilled bricklayer can often add interest by laying panels or strips to a different pattern. The choice of brick and the capping will also alter the appearance. Some are capped with bricks, others have special coping tiles. These all add to the subtle variety of brick walls.

Block walls

Many manufacturers of concrete paving slabs also produce walling blocks made from the same material. These are especially useful for internal garden walls and raised beds. They are often coloured to resemble natural stone, but brighter colours are available if you want to match the colour scheme used for the paving. Bear in mind that colours will weather and become much more muted within a couple of years.

ABOVE: *An interesting brick wall.*
RIGHT: *A wall like this makes a solid and secure boundary without making the garden appear too enclosed.*

Screen block walls

Screen block walls (sometimes called pierced block) are most frequently used for internal walls, perhaps around the patio or to divide one part of the garden from another, but they can also be used to create a striking boundary wall too.

These blocks have to be used with special piers and topped with the appropriate coping. They are useful if you want to create a modern image, or perhaps the atmosphere of a Mediterranean garden.

Mixing materials

Some of the smartest boundary walls are made from more than one material. Screen blocks look good as panels within a concrete walling block framework. Screen blocks can also be incorporated into a brick wall, and help to let light through and to filter some of the wind. Panels of flint or other stone can be set into an otherwise boring tall brick wall.

BELOW: *Walls can be colourful . . . if you create planting areas. The summer bedding plants used here are replaced at the end of the season with bulbs and spring bedding plants to use the planting areas to their full advantage.*

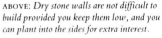
ABOVE: *Dry stone walls are not difficult to build provided you keep them low, and you can plant into the sides for extra interest.*

Cavity walls

Low cavity walls that can be lined with plants soon become an eye-catching feature. Pack them with colourful summer flowers, or plant with permanent perennials such as dwarf conifers, which maintain interest throughout the year (but be sure to choose truly dwarf conifers for this). If you plant cascading forms such as nasturtium or trailing lobelia, the effect can be really stunning. For a spring display, try aubrietia and the yellow *Alyssum saxatile*, with a few dwarf spring-flowering bulbs.

Dry stone walling

Dry stone walls are more often used for retaining banks or as internal dividers, but in an appropriate setting this kind of wall makes an attractive boundary. This type of wall looks best where dry stone walls are part of the natural landscape.

The great advantage of a dry stone wall – which is assembled without mortar – is the ability to plant in the sides. This can provide a home for many kinds of alpines.

Walls with a difference

The larger and taller the wall, the more imaginative you should be when designing it. Try incorporating an alcove for an ornament, or a panel into which you can set an artistic piece of wrought-iron that can be viewed against the green of a neighbouring field or garden.

WALL BUILDING MATERIALS

Most builders' merchants stock a good range of bricks, the majority are suitable for garden walls, but if you need a lot of bricks – enough to justify ordering direct – get in touch with a few brick companies. Their expertise can be invaluable, and most will be able to offer you a wide choice.

Buying bricks is something most of us do only rarely, so professional advice is especially useful. The author's experience, however, suggests that you can't always depend on the advice of a builder's merchant. Shop around until you find someone who really appears to have a knowledgeable passion for bricks – they will tell you about all the different finishes and colours available, and most importantly will know whether a particular brick is suitable for the job you have in mind. *Always* explain what you want your bricks for: a building, a garden wall, wall of a raised bed, or for paving. Some bricks which are perfectly suitable for house walls may be very unsuitable for paths or garden walls.

If you need a lot of bricks (many hundreds), it may be better, and cheaper, to buy direct from a brick manufacturer if they will deal with the general public.

ABOVE: *Bricks come in many colours and finishes, and these are just a small selection from the many kinds available. Names of bricks vary from country to country, but whatever names are used you are likely to have a good choice.*

MASONRY MORTAR

A suitable mortar for bricklaying can be made from 1 part cement to 3 parts soft sand. Parts are by volume and not weight. Cement dyes can be added to create special effects, but use coloured mortar cautiously.

Common bonds

Expert brick-layers may use more complicated bonds, but for ordinary garden walls – and especially those that you are likely to lay yourself, perhaps for a low boundary wall or for a raised bed within the garden – it is best to choose one of the three bonds illustrated below.

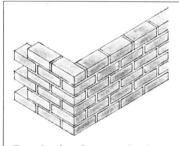

Running bond or stretcher bond
This is the simplest form of bonding, and is used for walls a single brick wide – or where you want to create a cavity, such as a low wall with a planting space.

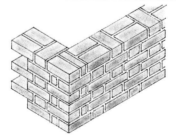

Flemish bond This is another way to create a strong bond in a wall two bricks wide. The bricks are laid both lengthways and across the wall within the same course.

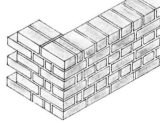

English bond This is used for a thick wall the width of two bricks laid side by side – useful where strength is needed for a high wall. Alternate courses are laid lengthways then across the wall.

HOW TO LAY BRICKS AND BLOCKS

Although bricks are being laid here, the same principles apply to laying walling blocks.

1 All walls require a footing. The one shown here is for a low wall just one brick wide: for larger and thicker walls the dimensions of the footing will have to be increased.

Excavate a trench about 30cm (12in) deep, and place about 13cm (5in) of consolidated hardcore in the bottom. Drive pegs in so that the tops are at the final height of the base. Use a spirit-level to check levels.

2 Fill with a concrete mix of 1 part cement, 2½ parts sharp sand and 3½ parts 2cm(¾in) aggregate, and level it off with the peg tops.

3 When the concrete has hardened for a few days, lay the bricks on a bed of mortar, also place a wedge of mortar at one end of each brick to be laid. For stability, always make a pier at each end, and at intervals of about 1.8–2.4m (6–8ft) if the wall is long. Here two bricks have been laid crossways for this purpose.

4 For subsequent courses, lay a ribbon of mortar on top of the previous row, then 'butter' one end of the brick to be laid.

5 Tap level, checking constantly with a spirit-level.

6 The wall must be finished off with a coping of suitable bricks or with special coping sold for the purpose.

BOUNDARY FENCES

Fences have the great merit of being more instant than hedges and less expensive than walls. That is the reason they are so often chosen by builders for new properties, and why they are frequently chosen again when the original fences come to the end of their useful life.

Closeboard and panel fences are popular, but predictable and a little boring. There are plenty of styles to choose from, however, so select a fence appropriate to your garden design yet practical for the purposes you have in mind.

If you want privacy or animal-proofing, you will have to opt for one of the solid styles, but if it is just a boundary-marker that is needed there are many attractive fences that look stylish and won't appear oppressive in a small garden.

The names of particular fence types can vary from country to country. If you do not recognize any of the names here check with the illustrations.

Closeboard

Closeboard fencing is erected on site by nailing overlapping feather-edged boards to horizontal rails already secured to stout upright posts. It is a strong, secure fence, but not particularly attractive – especially viewed from the side with the rails.

Panels

Prefabricated panels are quick and easy to erect and a popular choice for that reason. Panels are usually about 1.8m (6ft) long and range in height from about 60cm (2ft) to 1.8m (6ft), generally in 30cm (1ft) steps. The interwoven or overlapping boards are sandwiched between a frame of sawn timber. The woven style is not as peep-proof as overlapping boards.

Interlap or hit-and-miss

This combines strength and a solid appearance with better wind-filtering than a solid fence (which can create turbulent eddies that can be damaging

ABOVE: *Closeboard fencing well covered with climbing roses.*

ABOVE: *Wattle or woven fences make an attractive background for plants.*

ABOVE: *A low wooden fence is not obtrusive and can look very attractive.*

to plants). It is constructed from square-edged boards that are nailed to the horizontal rails on alternate sides. Overlapping the edges gives more privacy, while spacing them further apart can look more decorative.

Picket

Picket fences look good in country gardens, but can also be a smart choice for a small town garden. Narrow, vertical pales are nailed to horizontal timbers, spaced about 5cm (2in) apart. You can make them yourself or buy kits with some of the laborious work done for you. The simplest shape for the top of each pale is a point, but you can make them rounded or choose a more ornate finial shape. A picket fence can be left in natural wood colour, but they look particularly smart painted white. Because they are usually relatively low, and you can see plenty of garden through the well-spaced pales, they don't dominate the garden in the same way as a tall, solid fence.

Ranch-style

Ranch-style fences consist of broad horizontal rails fixed to stout upright posts. They are usually quite low, and frequently consist of just two or three rails. White-painted wood is a popular material, but wipe-down plastic equivalents are very convincing and easy to maintain. For a small garden

they provide a clear boundary without becoming a visual obstruction. Also, rain and sun shadows are not created in the way that occurs with more solid fences.

Post and chain

This is the least obtrusive of all fences. Purely a boundary marker, it will do nothing to deter animals or children, or keep balls out of the garden, but it is a good choice if you want a fence that is hardly noticeable. You can use wooden, concrete or plastic posts and metal or plastic chains. Choose a white plastic chain if you want to make a feature of the fence, black if you want the chain to recede and blend into the background.

Chain link

Chain link is not an aesthetic choice, but it is highly practical and an effective barrier for animals. It is probably best to have a contractor erect a chain link fence, as it needs to be tensioned properly. You may like the fact that you can see through it, especially if the view beyond is attractive, but you may prefer to plant

climbers beside it to provide a better screen. Choose tough evergreens such as ivy if you want year-round screening.

Bamboo

Bamboo is a natural choice if you've created an oriental-style garden, but don't be afraid to use this type of fence for any garden style if it looks right. Bamboo fences come in many shapes and sizes, and the one you adopt will depend partly on the availability and cost of the material and partly on your creativity and skill in building this kind of fence.

ABOVE: *A fence like this just needs a supply of bamboo and skill at tying knots!*

LEFT: *A white picket fence can make the boundary a feature of the garden.*

HOW TO ERECT A FENCE

Many gardeners prefer to employ a contractor to erect or replace a fence. They will certainly make lighter work of it with their professional tools for excavating post holes, and a speed that comes with expertise, but some fences are very easy to erect yourself. Two of the easiest are panel and ranch-type fences, which are illustrated in simple steps below.

HOW TO ERECT A PANEL FENCE

1 Post spikes are an easier option than excavating holes and concreting the post in position. The cost saving on using a shorter post and no concrete will go some way towards the cost of the spike.

Use a special tool to protect the spike top, then drive it in with a sledge-hammer. Check periodically with a spirit-level to ensure it is absolutely vertical.

2 Once the spike has been driven in, insert the post and check the vertical again.

3 Lay the panel in position on the ground and mark the position of the next post. Drive in the next spike, testing for the vertical again.

4 There are various ways to fix the panels to the posts, but panel brackets are easy to use.

5 Insert the panel and nail in position, through the brackets. Insert the post at the other end and nail the panel in position at that end.

6 Check the horizontal level both before and after nailing, and make any necessary adjustments before moving on to the next panel.

7 Finish off by nailing a post cap to the top of each post. This will keep water out of the end grain of the timber and extend its life.

HOW TO ERECT A RANCH-STYLE FENCE

1 Although ranch-style fences are easy to erect the posts must be well secured in the ground. For a wooden fence, use 12.5 × 10cm (5 × 4in) posts, set at about 2m (6½ft) intervals. For additional strength add intermediate posts. A size of 9cm (3½in) square is adequate for these.

Make sure the posts go at least 45cm (18in) into the ground.

2 Concrete the posts into position, then screw or nail the planks in position, making sure fixings are rust-proof. Use a spirit-level to make sure the planks are horizontal. Butt-join the planks in the centre of a post, but try to stagger the joints on each row so that there is not a weak point in the fence.

3 Fit a post cap. This improves the appearance and also protects the posts. Paint with a good quality paint recommended for outdoor use.

ABOVE LEFT: *Panel fences are easily erected and provide a peep-proof barrier, but are best clothed with plants to soften the effect.*
ABOVE: *Ranch-style fences make an unobtrusive barrier – ideal where the garden merges into the countryside.*

THE PLASTIC ALTERNATIVE

There are many plastic ranch-style fences. They will vary slightly in the way they are assembled. Detailed instructions should come with them, however, and you should have no difficulty.

The 'planks' are sometimes available in different widths – 10cm (4in) and 15cm (6in) for example – and these help to create different visual appearances. Gates made from the same material are also available from some manufacturers.

Posts are usually concreted into the ground, and the cellular plastic planks are push-fitted into slots or special fittings. Special union pieces are used to join lengths, and post caps are usually glued and pushed into position.

White ranch fencing needs to be kept clean to look good, and plastic can simply be washed when it looks grubby.

SEE-THROUGH BOUNDARIES

The best boundary of all might be no boundary . . . at least none that you can see. The ha-ha, once popular with the great landscape gardeners of the past, was a successful way of achieving this. The boundary is a deep, wide ditch that can't easily be seen from within the garden, so the garden appears to continue into the rolling countryside beyond.

The ha-ha is not a technique easily adapted to a small modern garden, and totally inappropriate if you overlook a townscape instead of pleasant green fields. However, the principle of being able to blur the margin between your garden and your neighbour's garden, or perhaps open countryside if you are fortunate enough to have the option, is one worth pursuing.

Ditches

A ditch sounds an unattractive feature. However, if one happens to run along one of your boundaries it might be possible to make a feature of it, rather than trying to hide it. Try planting it with bog plants, and landscape it into your garden, perhaps with a pond and an extended bog garden linking the two.

Some people even try to create a ditch, using a liner that restricts water loss and flooding it with water periodically. Provided the view of the garden beyond is attractive, this is a sure-fire way to give your small garden an open style only normally associated with larger gardens.

Shared gardens

Like-minded gardening enthusiasts sometimes design their gardens so that they appear to be linked. Usually this is done by taking the lawn through a gap in the boundary and using shrubs or mixed borders that start in one garden and end in the next. This can work surprisingly well, and although each is responsible for his own area the illusion is that the garden goes on beyond.

If this seems too 'communal', the same effect can be achieved by making lawns and borders meet yet still retain an unobtrusive fence, such as a widely spaced post and rail fence, or even a few simple strands of wire – which can be almost invisible from a distance.

Alternatively, consider linking gardens with an attractive gate. You don't have to use it, but it will look as though there is more garden beyond to be explored.

Shrubby solutions

Although a continuous lawn is the best way to link adjoining gardens and make them look larger, you can instead agree to abolish the fence and both plant shrubs in a bed along the boundary. Even if a relatively narrow strip is used in each garden, the

ABOVE: *A window in the wall can immediately transform a potentially boring area of brick into a real focus point.*

impression will be of a much larger and more substantial shrub border with no sign of obtrusive fences.

Claire-voyée

The term means literally 'clear view', and came into use after the lawless Middle Ages in Europe when it became less necessary to enclose one's property with a solid wall, and apertures were cut in walls to allow the countryside beyond to be viewed from within.

If you have a view that is worth framing, you can introduce a claire-voyée 'window' in the wall of even a tiny garden.

BRIGHTENING UP FENCES AND WALLS

If replacing an existing old fence or wall simply isn't practical because of the time and expense involved, consider ways to camouflage or brighten up the old one.

Climbers

Climbers present one of the most pleasing ways to cover an unsightly wall or fence, but always make sure the fence is firm in its foundations first . . . otherwise the extra weight and wind resistance will just bring it down sooner and you will have to untangle the climber and repair the fence anyway.

For year-round cover, tough evergreens such as ivies are justifiably popular. They can be slow to establish, but ultimately provide dense cover and can easily be clipped back once or twice a year to prevent the shoots encroaching beyond their territory.

For summer-only cover, try the vigorous hop (*Humulus lupulus*), especially in its very attractive golden form 'Aureus'. Once established one plant will cover a large area of fence.

For flowers some of the clematis can be very successful, though winter's an unattractive time. Tall-growing species such as *Clematis montana* sound unlikely candidates, but they will run along the fence and cascade down each side instead of climbing, and the pink *C. m. rubens* looks particularly splendid.

Trained trees

Trained fruit trees can transform a tall wall or fence and turn it into a real feature when laden with flowers or fruit. Even in winter the bare stems of a fan or espalier tree can look dramatic, especially if picked out against a white-painted wall.

Training from scratch is difficult and time-consuming, and it is worth buying ready-trained trees.

RIGHT: *Old fences discolour and look drab and shabby with age. This is one way to transform a dull fence.*

BELOW: *Vigorous clematis such as C. montana will cover a fence with blooms in late spring and early summer.*

A coat of paint

A drab old wall can be transformed with a coat of masonry paint. White reflects the light well, but any pale colour can look pleasing, particularly when contrasted with greenery.

Grow striking plants like phormiums or yuccas in front so that their strong profiles are picked out against the background, or stand groups of containers so that they are backed by the painted wall.

Framed effects

Fences are more difficult to paint as a backdrop for plants, and you must be careful about paint seeping through to your neighbour's side, but a little localized painting could work well.

Try a large white circle within which you can frame a striking plant as a focal point. Instead of painting the actual fence, try cutting out a large wooden circle and painting that – then pin it to the fence.

FINISHING TOUCHES

Every garden should be full of surprises, packed with finishing touches that complete the overall effect.

Many of the focal point techniques used in large gardens can be scaled down and applied on a small scale, and even in a small space the garden can express the owner's sense of fun and personality in the little extras that are grafted onto the basic design.

The whole area can be made to work, every corner can be exploited with devices if not plants, and a degree of flexibility can be built in that makes variety a real possibility.

ABOVE: *A seat like this suggests a gardener with a strong sense of design.*

OPPOSITE ABOVE: *Ornaments have been used to excellent effect here. A sundial commands centre stage and the eye is taken across the garden to a figure which adds light and life.*

OPPOSITE BELOW: *Figures usually look best framed by plants.*

LEFT: *This quiet corner has been transformed by white-painted trellis and seat.*

In a large garden most ornaments, furniture and fixtures like garden lights are a static part of the design. In a small garden a slight rearrangement of the furniture, the changed position of a light, or the simple exchange of one ornament for another according to mood and season means that the garden need never be predictable despite limitations of size.

Ornaments in particular can set a tone for the garden: serious or frivolous, classic or modern. They suggest the owner's taste . . . and even sense of humour. Just as the painting on the living-room wall or the ornaments on the sideboard can tell you a lot about the occupier, so garden ornaments reveal the personality of the garden maker.

Garden lighting can be practical and even a useful security measure, but it also offers scope for artistic interpretation. Experiment with spotlights in various positions and discover the dramatically different effects created by the use of light and shadows from different angles.

Arches and pergolas are a more permanent element of the garden's design, but they don't have to be planned in at the design stage and are easily added to an existing garden.

PERGOLAS AND ARCHES

A sense of height is important even in a small garden. Unless there is vertical use of plants or upright garden features, the centre of the garden will be flat. Attention will pass over the centre and go instead to the edges of the garden: exactly the lifeless effect you want to avoid.

Small trees, wall shrubs and climbers can provide the necessary verticals, but if these are in short supply an arch or pergola may be the answer.

Traditionally, and especially in cottage gardens, they have been made from rustic poles, but where they adjoin the house or link home with patio, sawn timber is a better choice. The various constructions described here are free-standing, and usually used as plant supports. Their visual effect is to take the eye to further down the garden.

If a pergola or arch seems inappropriate, similar construction techniques can be used to create an intimate arbour.

HOW TO ASSEMBLE AN ARCH

The simplest way to make an arch is to use a kit, which only needs assembling.

1 First establish the post positions, allowing 30cm (1ft) between the edge of the path and post, so that plants do not obstruct the path.

2 Fence spikes are the easiest way to fix the posts. Drive them in using a protective dolly. Check frequently with a spirit-level. Insert the posts and tighten the spikes around them. Alternatively, excavate four holes, each to the depth of 60cm (2ft).

3 Position the legs of the arch in the holes. Fill in with the excavated earth, and compact.

4 Lay the halves of the overhead beams on a flat surface, and carefully screw the joint together with rust-proof screws.

5 Fit the overhead beams to the posts – in this example they slot into the tops of the posts and are nailed in place.

HOW TO JOIN RUSTIC POLES

Rustic arches and pergolas look particularly attractive covered with roses or other climbers. You can be creative with the designs, but the same few basic joints shown here are all that you will need.

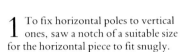

1 To fix horizontal poles to vertical ones, saw a notch of a suitable size for the horizontal piece to fit snugly.

2 If you have to join two horizontal pieces, saw two opposing and matching notches so that one sits over the other, and secure them.

3 To fix cross-pieces to horizontals or uprights, remove a V-shaped notch using a chisel if necessary to achieve a snug fit, then nail into place with rust-proof nails.

4 Use halving joints where two pieces cross. Make two saw cuts half way through the pole, then remove the waste timber with a chisel.

5 Secure the joint with a nail. For extra strength, paint the joint with woodworking adhesive first.

6 Bird's mouth joints are useful for connecting horizontal or diagonal pieces to uprights. Cut out a V-shaped notch about 3cm (1in) deep, and saw the other piece to match. Use a chisel to achieve a good fit.

7 Try out the assembly on the ground, then insert the uprights in prepared holes and make sure these are secure before adding any horizontal or top pieces. Most pieces can be nailed together, but screw any sections subject to stress.

ABOVE: *Rustic poles are an appropriate choice for a feature such as this.*

USING ORNAMENTS

Ornaments can be used around the garden in much the same way as around the house. Choose them simply because you like them, because they will look good in a particular position, or as a device for attracting attention and admiration.

In a small garden their use as a focal point is paramount. Large focal points are impractical or can only ever be few in number, but small ornaments, birdbaths, sundials, and attractive urns can be used liberally. The only 'rule' is not to have more than a couple in view at once, as they will then compete for attention rather than taking centre stage. There is no limit to the number you can use in a small garden provided they form part of a journey of discovery. Use them among plants that you only discover from a particular viewpoint, or around a corner that is not visible from where you viewed the previous focal point.

Never let ornaments detract from major focal points that form part of the basic design, and don't allow the garden to look cluttered. Aim for simplicity with surprises.

Sundials

Whole books are written about sundials, and purists expect them to be functional. Setting them up accurately not only demands a sunny spot but quite a lot of calculations too, with compensation for geographical position. Most of us, using the sundial simply as an ornament, are happy to go out at noon on a sunny day in summer and align the gnomon to give the appropriate reading. It won't be accurate as the seasons change, but then you are unlikely to be using it to decide when it is time to leave for the office.

Accuracy may not be important, but a sunny position is. The whole object of a sundial is lost in a shady

RIGHT: A bird bath is a better choice than a sundial for a position often in shade.

BELOW: A chimney pot makes an unusual plinth for a sundial.

spot, where a birdbath would serve a similar design function without looking incongruous.

Choose the plinth carefully – they vary in style and height (you could even build your own from bricks) and go for a fairly low plinth if the area available is quite small.

The best place for a sundial is as a centrepiece for a formal garden, perhaps in the centre of a herb garden with paths radiating out from the centre. The lawn is another practical choice, but if the lawn is small, consider placing the sundial to one side rather than in the centre.

Birdbaths

The positions suggested for a sundial are also appropriate for a birdbath, but birdbaths are much more useful for shady positions – though not too close to trees, otherwise they become filled with leaves and debris. A birdbath can even look effective in a flower border, with much of the plinth covered by flowers, or try it as a patio ornament if you want the pleasures of watching the birds drinking from it and bathing.

Sculptures

The use of sculptures and artistic objects demands confidence. Few people react adversely to a sundial or birdbath, but sculptures or artistic ornaments that generate admiration in one person can be abhorrent to another. This should never deter anyone from using ornaments that please them, but they are bound to be somewhat more difficult to place in a small garden.

Human figures

Busts sound unlikely ornaments for a small garden, but provided they aren't too large they can look great in an alcove or on a plinth in a dull corner. Small figures can sometimes work well if surrounded by clever planting.

Animal figures

Animal figures are always a safe bet, especially if set among the plants, or even on the lawn.

Abstract ornaments

Abstract ornaments should be used with restraint – they make a considerable impact. Too many will tend to make the area look more like an art gallery than a garden.

Wall masks, plaque and gargoyles

These are great for relieving a dull wall, but are almost always best set amid the leaves of a climber such as ivy. The foliage frames the feature, and emphasizes its role as an unusual focal point.

Gnomes

You probably love them or hate them, and that is the problem with using gnomes. One or two little people cleverly used with restraint can be very effective and add a sense of fun, but usually either they are banished from the garden or there is a whole army of them. The problem with the latter approach is that the garden will simply appear as a setting for a gnome collection.

Plinths and pedestals

Plinths are essential for raising a sundial, birdbath or bust to an appropriate height, but they can look stark in a small garden. Make more of a feature of a plinth by planting some low-growing plants around the base, and then use a few tall ground cover plants that can gradually stretch up around the base.

A plinth can look severe on a lawn and mowing around it can be difficult. Try setting one in a gravel bed with alpines around the base, or leave the bed as soil and plant thymes or other low-growing aromatic herbs.

ABOVE: *Small animal figures creeping out from the plants add a sense of fun.*

ABOVE: *This kind of ornament needs careful placing in a small garden – always take time to consider position.*

RIGHT: *Figures are often more exciting when they are discovered among the plants.*

GARDEN LIGHTING

Garden lights not only make your garden look more dramatic as dusk falls, they also extend the hours during which you can enjoy it. If you like entertaining in the garden on summer evenings, or just want to sit and relax, lights will add another dimension to the space.

When illuminating your garden you are not attempting to fill the garden with floodlights, but rather to use spotlights to pick out a particular tree, highlight an ornament, or bring to life the droplets of a cascade or fountain.

You don't even need elaborate mains lighting. Low-voltage lighting supplied from a transformer indoors is perfectly adequate for most lighting jobs in a small garden.

Lighting beds
Summer bedding looks good with pools of light thrown downwards onto the beds. If you find the lights obtrusive during the day, choose a low-voltage type that is easy to move around. Simply push the spiked supports into the bed when you want to use the garden in the evening.

Picking out plants
Use a spotlight to pick out one or two striking plants that will form focal points in the evening. The white bark of a birch tree, perhaps underplanted with white impatiens, the tall ramrod spikes of red hot pokers (kniphofias), or a spiky yucca, make excellent focal points picked out in a spotlight. Tall feathery plants, such as fennel, also illuminate well.

Spotlighting ornaments
Ornaments and containers full of plants also make striking features to pick out in a spotlight.

Before highlighting an ornament, try moving the beam around. Quite different effects can be achieved by directing it upwards or downwards, and side lighting creates a very different effect to straight-on illumination.

ABOVE: *An illuminated garden can become magical as dusk falls, and you will derive many more hours of pleasure from being able to sit out in the evening.*

Illuminating water
Underwater lighting is popular and you can buy special sealed lamps designed to be submerged or to float, but the effect can be disappointing if the water is murky or if algae grows thickly on the lenses. A simple white spotlight playing on moving water is often the most effective.

THINKING OF THE NEIGHBOURS
There is a problem with using garden lights in a small garden: you have to consider neighbours. It is unsociable to fix a spotlight where the beam not only illuminates your favourite tree but also falls on the windows of your neighbour's house. If you direct beams downwards rather than upwards, the pools of light should not obtrude.

WHEN PROFESSIONAL ADVICE IS NEEDED . . .

Low voltage lighting is designed for DIY installation, but mains voltage demands special care. If you know how to wire up your garden, using special outdoor fittings, and are aware of any regulations concerning the depth cables have to be buried and the protection required, you may be able to do the wiring yourself. But if in the slightest doubt use a professional electrician. If you want to keep the cost down, offer to do the labouring, such as digging trenches, yourself.

LEFT: *The best garden lighting is not obtrusive or unattractive during the day, and throws off white light when illuminated.*

HOW TO INSTALL LOW-VOLTAGE LIGHTING

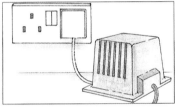

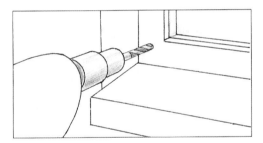

2 Drill a hole through the window frame or wall, just wide enough to take the cable. Fill in any gaps afterwards, using a mastic or other waterproof filler.

1 A low-voltage lighting kit will come with a transformer. This must always be positioned in a dry place indoors or in a garage or outbuilding.

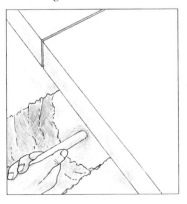

3 Although the cable carries a low voltage and you will not be electrocuted, it is still a potential hazard if left lying on the surface where someone might trip over it. Unless the lights are to be positioned close to where the cable emerges from indoors, run it underground in a conduit

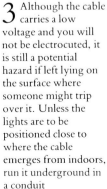

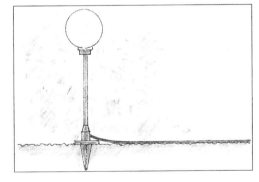

4 Most low-voltage lighting systems are designed so that the lamps are easy to position and to move around. Many of them can just be pushed into the ground wherever you choose to place them.

FURNISHING THE GARDEN

A few seats and a table make the garden an inviting place to eat, or to sit and relax. Unfortunately where space is at a premium every item has to be chosen and placed with care. Built-in seats, and especially tree seats, are a good choice for a small garden.

Portable furniture
Furniture that can be moved is useful for a quick scene change and helps to prevent your garden becoming predictable. It is surprising how effective a canvas 'director's chair' can look on a summer's day, and it is quick and easy to fold up and store when not in use.

Built-in
Built-in furniture saves space and helps prevent a small garden looking cluttered. The best place for built-in seating is the patio, where it can often be designed along with the rest of the structure. White-painted planks look smart, and can quickly be transformed with cushions to look elegant as well as feel comfortable.

Built-round
A tree seat makes an eye-catching garden feature, and this is one occasion when the advice not to have a seat beneath a tree can be ignored! White paint will help the seat to stand out in the shade of its branches.

Wrought and cast iron
Genuine cast and wrought iron furniture is expensive and very heavy, but alloy imitations are available with all the charm of the original but at a more manageable price and weight. White is again a popular colour, but bear in mind that although this type of furniture can stand outside throughout the year, it will soon become dirty. Cleaning the intricate patterns isn't easy. Colours such as green look smart yet don't show the dirt.

Use cushions to add patches of colour, and to make the chairs less uncomfortable to sit on!

LEFT: *White-painted metal furniture looks tasteful and can help enliven a dull corner of the garden.*

BELOW: *A charming wooden seat.*

BELOW LEFT: *A reconstituted stone seat has a timeless appeal that beckons you to sit and rest.*

Wooden seats and benches
Timber seats can be left in natural wood colour to blend with the background or painted so that they become a focal point. White is popular, but green and even red can look very smart. Yacht paint is weather-resistant.

Plastic
Don't dismiss plastic. Certainly there are plenty of cheap and nasty pieces of garden furniture made from this material, but the better pieces can look very stylish for a patio in the setting of a modern garden.

HOW TO MAKE A TREE SEAT

1 Start by securing the legs in position. Use 3.8cm × 7.5cm (1½in × 3in) softwood, treated with a preservative. You will need eight lengths about 68cm (27in) long. Concrete them into position.

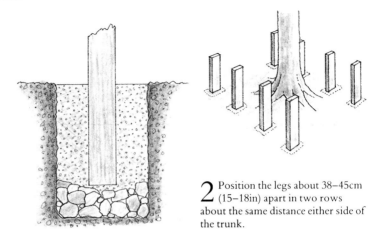

2 Position the legs about 38–45cm (15–18in) apart in two rows about the same distance either side of the trunk.

3 Cut four pieces of 2.5cm × 5cm (1in × 2in) softwood for the cross-bars. Allow 7.5cm (3in) overhang at each end.

4 Drill and screw these to the posts. Then, cut slats to the required length (the number will depend on the size of your seat). Allow for a 2.5cm (1in) space between each slat. Paint the slats and cross-bars with white paint (or a wood preservative or stain if you prefer), and allow to dry before final assembly. Test the spacing, using an offcut of wood as a guide, and when satisfied that they are evenly spaced on the cross-bars, mark the positions with a pencil. Then glue and nail into position.

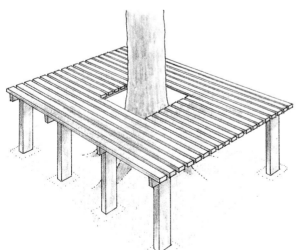

CONTAINER CHOICES

MANY PLANT CONTAINERS ARE PURELY
practical: plain clay pots, unadorned plastic
windowboxes, wooden troughs that are
functional but not inspiring. There is nothing
wrong with any of these if they are to be covered
with trailers and cascading blooms, but most
plants have an upright habit and an interesting
container forms part of the display and becomes
an important feature.

Containers are especially useful in a small
garden because they bring life and colour, or just
subtle shades of green, to corners that might
otherwise remain bare. By hanging interesting or
colourful containers on bleak walls, by using
them alongside the steps to a basement garden, or
simply using tubs by the front door, containers
make the most of all the available space.

LEFT: *Don't discard the old metal watering-can. It can be painted and pressed into use for plants such as ivies.*

FAR LEFT: *This old copper boiler has found new life as a container for tulips and pansies.*

OPPOSITE ABOVE: *Although a clematis seems an unlikely choice for these old chimney pots, it will eventually cascade down over the edge.*

OPPOSITE BELOW: *Containers are invaluable in a small garden as they can be used to take advantage of any spare space.*

BELOW: *It is surprising how much you can do with a roof garden, by growing a wide range of plants in containers.*

Don't confine your choice of container plants to summer bedding and spring bulbs, however. If you do, your containers will look like monuments to past glories for many months of the year. Plant evergreen shrubs, or groups of evergreen border plants. Use short-term pot plants in the winter and don't be afraid to discard them after a few weeks.

Houseplants can be used in summer to add a touch of the exotic to your patio. Provided they are carefully acclimatized first (placed in a sheltered position, and protected from winds and strong sun, perhaps with a covering of horticultural fleece for the first week), you can use them to create tropical corners. It's best to use only those plants with thick or fleshy leaves.

Be bold. Use kitchen utensils such as pots and pans as containers, old chimney pots, drainpipes, boots and shoes, but always make sure that there are drainage holes.

You can even make large clay pots more interesting by painting on an attractive design with masonry paint. Use a stencil if you are not artistically inclined.

POTS FOR DOORWAY DECORATION

Always choose an imposing plant in an attractive container to go by the front door, and if possible one that looks good for a long period.

This is the place for a clipped bay in an ornate pot or Versailles tub, or an attractive bamboo in an oriental-style container.

If you have chosen imposing plants to go by the front door supplement these with a group of smaller containers that add seasonal colour, and perhaps scent. Don't be afraid to move pots around to maintain interest. Keep a small lilac in a tub or grow pots of hyacinths to move them to the front door as they come into flower to add a heady perfume.

Formal shrubs
If space really is limited and the rest of the garden has a formal style, a couple of clipped or trained evergreens can look elegant throughout the year. Clipped bays are good, but in cold areas are likely to suffer from damaged leaves in winter, but many conifers have a naturally formal outline and remain attractive throughout the year with minimal attention. Box can be bought clipped into topiary shapes, and though expensive to buy will add instant impact. You can easily buy a box plant and clip it into a ball or pyramid

LEFT: Remember to appeal to the sense of smell as well as sight. Here lavender not only colour co-ordinates, it adds a touch of fragrance as well.

BELOW LEFT: Formally clipped box can be expensive to buy, but with patience you can train your own. They are ideal for a formal setting.

BELOW: Don't forget that pots can always be used to grow well-trained shrubs.

shape over the course of a couple of years, if you are happy with a simple geometric shape.

Scented delights
Scent always arouses comment from visitors to the door. In winter you will have to rely on bulbs like hyacinths and *Iris danfordiae*. In spring follow these with daphne and then lilac (both indifferent for the rest of the year, so be prepared to move them to a less conspicuous part of the garden after flowering).

Summer brings the opportunity to use scented bedding plants such as flowering tobacco plants and stocks.

Climbers in pots
A climber round the door always looks attractive, and you can usually erect a trellis for support. If there is a choice, plant directly into the ground, but if that is not possible, pot a climber in a tub. Large-flowered

clematis will do well, and even a honeysuckle. You can try a climbing or rambling rose, but these are more demanding in pots.

GROUPING POTS AND PLANTS

If isolated pots seem to lack impact, try grouping them together – the mutual support they lend each other gives them a strength that they lack individually. If the pots are rather plain, placing smaller ones in front will mask those behind and bring the display almost to ground level.

Groups in the porch

Make a bold display in a porch by using tall plants, especially evergreen shrubs, at the back and smaller flowering plants in front.

If space is limited, instead of going for a lush effect with lots of foliage and flowers, concentrate on the containers rather than the plants. Decorative pots are often available as matching sets. Grouping these together looks good even if the plants they contain are only mediocre.

Groups in corners

Difficult corners are an ideal place in which to use containers to create colour, filling in a spare piece of ground where nothing much seems to do well. Patios usually have corners that would otherwise remain unused. Group shrubs or tall houseplants at the back and colourful summer bedding plants in front, along with bright-leaved indoor plants for the warmest months.

Alternatively, choose a small group of elegant containers and use the plants in a more restrained way. A trailer growing from a pedestal container with a cluster of distinctive small pots around the base can be as eye-catching as a large group.

In a dull corner, perhaps formed where two wooden fences join, or where house joins fence in a sunless position, try making a bed of small-sized gravel on which to place a group of terracotta pots. Red gravel will help to bring colour. Fill the pots with bright annuals for the summer, and winter-flowering pansies and bulbs for winter and spring. Try spacing the pots out and adding a few interesting pieces of rock among them.

ABOVE LEFT: *Grouping plants in a porch makes a high-impact feature. Replace plants when they have passed their best, to keep it looking good.*

ABOVE: *Feature groups of plants in containers where the garden needs an uplift. The beach pebbles add an individual touch.*

LEFT: *Individually, these containers would not look special, but grouping them makes a focal point.*

Groups on the lawn

Clusters of pots are an ideal means to breaking up a large expanse of lawn. Don't stand them directly on the grass, but use a bed of sand or gravel – this will stand out well from the grass, and make mowing round the containers easier.

YEAR-ROUND CONTAINERS

In a large garden containers are usually used for splashes of summer colour. The voids left in winter when the plants have died are not so noticeable among the many other garden features. In a small garden, and especially on a patio, bare containers in winter look positively off-putting, and only emphasize the lack of year-round plants.

The choice for summer is limitless, so the emphasis here is on autumn and winter – the seasons for which most effort has to be made.

Year-round troughs and boxes

Dwarf evergreen shrubs and dwarf conifers, in their many shapes and colours, will provide year-round interest. But to prevent them becoming so much background greenery, leave space in front to plant a few bulbs or small bedding plants. Allow for a space the size of a small pot for these seasonal plantings, so that you can easily replace the small flowers as they finish. Grow a reserve of them in pots to fit the space.

Autumn highlights

Grow one or two autumn-glory shrubs in tubs that you can bring out of their place of hiding when you need a final burst of colour.

Ceratostigma willmottianum has compact growth and lovely autumn foliage tints while still producing blue flowers. Berries can also be used as a feature, and you can usually buy compact pernettyas already bearing berries in your garden centre.

Winter colour

Some winter-flowering shrubs can be used in tubs, such as *Viburnum tinus* and *Mahonia* 'Charity'. But try being bold with short-term pot plants like Cape heathers (*Erica x hyemalis* and *E. gracilis*) and winter cherries (*Solanum capsicastrum* and similar species and hybrids). You will have to throw them away afterwards, but they will look respectable for a few weeks even in cold and frosty winter weather.

LEFT: Solanum capsicastrum *is widely sold as a houseplant in the winter months, but you can use it as a short-term plant to add a touch of colour to permanent plantings of evergreens in outdoor containers. Those pictured were still happy in late winter. Discard once the berries shrivel.*
BELOW: *The intense blue flowers of ceratostigma last well into autumn, when there is the bonus of rich foliage colour before the leaves fall.*

HOW TO PROTECT PLANTS FROM FROST

Many of the most dramatic summer patio shrubs – like daturas and oleanders – must be taken into a frost-free place for the winter. Others that are frost-tolerant but of borderline hardiness in cold areas, like the bay (*Laurus nobilis*), or that are vulnerable to frost and wind damage to the leaves that is disfiguring even though not fatal (such as *Choisya ternata* 'Sundance') need a degree of winter protection. It is a pity to lose these magnificent patio plants for the sake of a little forethought as autumn draws to a close.

A MOVING BUSINESS

Those shrubs that won't tolerate winter outdoors, even with protection, must be taken into a greenhouse or conservatory. Moving a heavy container is difficult, but the following tips are useful.

Try rolling the pot on its edge. Even a heavy container can be moved quite easily like this. Alternatively, 'walk' the container onto a low trolley. If one person pushes the trolley while another holds the container, even large trees and shrubs can be moved.

1 Shrubs that are fairly tough and need a little protection from the worst weather, can be covered with horticultural fleece, or bubble polythene. Insert four or five canes around the edge of the pot.

3 If in a sleeve, slip it over the canes; if in a sheet, wrap it round the plant, allowing a generous overlap. For particularly vulnerable plants, use more than one layer.

2 Cut the fleece or polythene to size first. If you use fleece, you may be able to buy it as a sleeve (ideal for winter protection for shrubs in tubs). Allow for an overlap over the pot.

4 Securely tie the protection around the pot. For very delicate plants, it is a good idea to bring the material well down over the pot, to keep the root-ball warm.

5 Tie the top closed if covering with fleece (moisture will be able to penetrate and tying the top will help to conserve warmth). If using polythene, it is best to leave the top open for ventilation and to permit watering if necessary.

ROCK AND WATER GARDENS

ROCK AND WATER FEATURES ADD AN EXTRA
dimension to any garden, but imagination is
needed to get the best from them in a small area.
The vast majority of rock and water plants thrive
best in a sunny position, and it may be difficult to
find a suitable site in a small garden. If you can't
find a spot that is in the sun for at least half the
day – and preferably longer – it might be better to
choose a water feature that depends less on plants
for its effect, and to grow your rock plants in
other ways, such as between paving and in raised
beds or a gravel garden.

Very small ponds are much more difficult to
'balance' biologically than large ones, and green
water is often a problem for much of the year. If
the garden is very tiny choose a bubble fountain,
wall spout, or container pond instead.

Rock gardens look best on a natural slope or built to look like a natural outcrop of rocks in a large lawn. Most small gardens offer neither opportunity. Combining a rock feature with the pond is often the most satisfactory solution. You can create the raised ground from the soil excavated for the pond.

Rock plants – or alpines if you prefer the label – offer huge scope for an enthusiastic gardener with a passion for plants but without the space to grow many. You can plant dozens in the space taken by just one medium-sized shrub, and even the tiniest garden can be home for hundreds of plants.

Be careful with the choice of water plants. Some irises and rushes are compact, others are rampant and will soon make a take-over bid. There are waterlilies that need deep water and a large surface area, others that will be happy in 23cm (9in) of water and will make do with a much smaller surface area.

TOP: Sedum spurium *'Atropurpureum'*.
ABOVE: *Campanulas – here growing through* Asplenium scolopendrium *– are popular rock plants.*
RIGHT: *This sink garden contains more than half a dozen different plants in less space than a single shrub would normally occupy.*
OPPOSITE: *Raising the edges of this pond has emphasized its role as the centre of attention.*
OPPOSITE ABOVE: *Various species of dianthus do well in a rock garden and always have a special appeal.*

PONDS AND WATER FEATURES

Making a pond is very easy nowadays – most flexible liners are strong and long-lasting, and pre-formed pools are as near as you can get to buying an instant pond off the shelf. If you don't have space for a 'proper' pond, make one in a barrel or shrub tub.

If you want to grow plants and keep fish, choose a bright position for your pond, one that receives sun for at least half the day. Avoid overhanging trees, they not only cast shade but shed leaves too, which can pollute the water.

Fountains and cascades

Introduce a cascade if you build a rock garden with your pond. A simple low-voltage submersible pump linking the head of the cascade with a hose is usually adequate for a small cascade with a modest flow of water.

Fountains need a large area of water, otherwise drift will cause a gradual drop in the water level. Be aware that the disturbed surface does not suit waterlilies and some other aquatic plants. A simple bubble or geyser type of jet is often more appropriate than a high, ornate jet in a small garden.

ABOVE: *You don't need a large garden to enjoy the sight and sound of moving water, as this attractive feature shows.*

Wall features

In a courtyard or a basement garden enclosed by walls, a wall fountain is often the best choice. You don't need a great gush of water.

You can fix a spout that pours water into a reservoir at the base of the wall to be recirculated through a hidden pump; alternatively buy one that is self-contained with water simply trickling into an integrated dish beneath the spout.

Miniature ponds

If you've no room for a proper pond, make one in a half-barrel or even a plastic shrub tub. Sink it into the ground, half-sink it into the soil, or have it free-standing, perhaps on a paved area such as the patio. Container ponds are not suitable for fish, but you can grow an interesting small collection of aquatic plants in them, including miniature waterlilies.

HOW TO MAKE A POND USING A LINER

1 Mark out the shape of your pond with a piece of rope, hosepipe or by sprinkling sand. Then remove the grass and excavate the soil to the required depth, leaving a shallow ledge about 23cm (9in) wide at about that depth from the top.

2 Remove the grass or soil around the edge if you plan to pave it. Allow for the thickness of the paving plus a bed of mortar. Check levels and remove extra soil from one side if necessary. The water surface needs to be level to the sides of the pond.

3 Remove sharp stones and large roots, then line the pool with about 1cm (½in) of damp sand – it should stick to the sides if they slope slightly. Use a polyester mat (from water garden specialists) or old carpet instead of sand if the soil is stony.

HOW TO INSTALL A PRE-FORMED POND

1 Transfer the shape of your pool to the ground by inserting canes around the edge. Use a hosepipe or rope to define the shape.

2 Excavate the hole to approximately the right depth, and following the profile of the shelves as accurately as possible.

3 Place a straight-edged piece of wood across the top and check that the edges are level. Measure down to check the depths.

4 Place the pool in the hole and add or remove more soil if it does not sit snugly. Also remove any sharp stones. Check that it is absolutely straight with a spirit-level.

5 Remove the pond and line the shape with sand. Backfill so that the pond shape fits the hole snugly.

6 Run water in from a hose, and backfill and firm again as the water rises. Check the levels frequently as the backfilling often tends to lift the pool slightly.

4 Drape the liner over the hole, anchoring the edges with bricks. Run water into the pool from a hose. As the weight of water takes the liner into the hole, release the bricks occasionally. Some creases will form but are not usually noticeable.

5 Trim the liner, leaving an overlap around the edge of about 15cm (6in), to be covered by the paving.

6 Bed the paving on mortar, covering the edge of the liner. The paving should overlap the edge of the pool by about 3cm (1in). Finish off by pointing the joints with mortar.

WAYS TO GROW ROCK PLANTS

If you have a sunny corner, a rock garden could be an attractive way to fill it. Alternatively, introduce rocks with a pond. A steeply sloped rock garden provides an opportunity to include a series of cascades that run through the rock garden to the pool beneath. It also solves the problem of what to do with the soil excavated during pond construction!

If your interests lie more with the exquisite beauty of the plants than with the landscaping aspects of a rock garden, there are plenty of ways to include alpines in areas other than a rock garden.

Combined with water
Rock gardens and ponds both require a sunny position to do well, and they associate well together. It is often possible to introduce a series of cascades linking a small pool at the top with the main pool below. Bury the connecting hose when constructing the rock garden, and use plenty of rocks to make the cascades look as natural as possible.

Very pleasing combined rock and water gardens can also be constructed without running water.

Island rock beds
Provided the lawn is reasonably large, and informal in shape, small rock outcrops can be created. You don't need many rocks for this kind of rock garden, just a few bold ones, carefully positioned so that they look as though they are protruding through the ground. For rocks to look convincing it is important to slope them into the ground, and for the strata to lie in one direction.

Rock plants in gravel gardens
Rock plants look good in gravel, so include them in a gravel garden or create a small flat gravel bed just for rock plants. Provide the same soil conditions as for a raised rockery, but on the flat. In addition, you can include a few rocks to create the impression of a scree.

ABOVE: *If you like alpines but don't want a rock garden, why not have a whole collection of sink gardens?*

LEFT: *A low rock bank is another easy way to grow rock plants, and is very simple to construct.*

Sink gardens
Alpines are perfect for sink gardens. Genuine stone sinks are ideal, but these are scarce and expensive. Perfectly attractive gardens can be created in imitation stone sinks.

Although you can simply plant 'on the flat' within the trough or sink, much more effective are 'landscaped' displays in which a section of rock face is created.

Raised beds
The great advantage of a raised bed for alpines is that you are better able to appreciate their beauty in miniature. You can build the beds with bricks or walling blocks, but natural stone is much better, especially if you can leave plenty of planting holes in the sides.

Peat beds
The vast majority of alpines grow happily in ordinary or alkaline soil, but a few require acid conditions. If these plants appeal, build a peat bed from peat blocks, bonding the blocks like bricks. Fill with a peaty mixture or an ericaceous potting soil and plant the alpines in your chosen arrangemen

HOW TO MAKE A ROCK GARDEN

1 The base is a good place to dispose of rubble, which you can then cover with garden soil – the ideal place for soil excavated from the pond.

2 It is best to use a special soil mixture for the top 15–23cm (6–9in), especially if soil excavated from the pond is used. Mix together equal parts soil, coarse grit and peat (or peat substitute), and spread this evenly over the mound.

3 Lay the first rocks at the base, trying to keep the strata running in the same direction.

4 Lever the next row of rocks into position. Use rollers and levers to move them.

5 As each layer is built up, add more of the soil mixture, and consolidate it around the rocks.

6 Ensure that the sides all slope inwards, and make the top reasonably flat rather than building it into a pinnacle. Position the plants, then cover the exposed soil with a thin layer of horticultural grit.

CHOOSING AND PLANTING

A visit to any garden centre will reveal a huge selection of plants for your rock garden. One of the delights of collecting alpines is the constant surprises as new treasures are encountered, and the ability to indulge in a wide range of plants that won't take up much space.

The plants suggested here can only be an arbitrary selection of some of the best, with the emphasis on plants that are fairly widely available.

Useful for a wall
- *Acaena microphylla* (top or face)
- *Achillea tomentosa* (top)
- *Alyssum montanum* (top)
- *Alyssum saxatile* (top or face)
- *Arabis caucasica* (top or face)
- *Arenaria balearica* (top or face)
- *Aubrietia* (face)
- *Campanula garganica* (face)
- *Cerastium tomentosum* (face)
- *Corydalis lutea* (face)
- *Dianthus deltoides* (top or face)
- *Erinus alpinus* (top or face)
- *Gypsophila repens* (top or face)
- *Sedum*, many (face)
- *Sempervivum*, many (face)

Try these in a trough
- *Arabis ferdinandi-coburgi* 'Variegata'
- *Aster alpinus*
- *Gentiana acaulis*
- *Hypericum olympicum*
- *Phlox douglasii*
- *Potentilla tabernaemontani*
- *Raoulia australis*
- *Rhodohypoxis baurii*
- *Sedum lydium*
- *Sempervivum* (various)

Good starter plants for a rock garden
Some of these plants are quite rampant or large – *Alyssum saxatile* and helianthemums, for example. If you are not familiar with particular plants, look them up in an encyclopedia.

- *Acaena microphylla*
- *Alyssum saxatile*

LEFT: Alyssum saxatile.

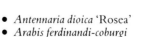

BELOW LEFT: Dianthus deltoides *'Electra'*.
BELOW: Helianthemum *'Fire Dragon'*.

- *Antennaria dioica* 'Rosea'
- *Arabis ferdinandi-coburgi* 'Variegata'
- *Armeria maritima*
- *Campanula carpatica*
- *Campanula cochleariifolia*
- *Dianthus deltoides*
- *Dryas octopetala*

- *Erinus alpinus*
- *Gentiana acaulis*
- *Gentiana septemfida*
- *Gentiana sino-ornata*
- *Geranium subcaulescens* 'Splendens'
- *Gypsophila repens*
- *Helianthemum*

- *Hypericum olympicum*
- *Iberis sempervirens* 'Snowflake'
- *Oxalis adenophylla*
- *Phlox douglasii*
- *Phlox subulata*
- *Pulsatilla vulgaris*
- *Raoulia australis*
- *Saxifraga* (mossy type)
- *Sedum spathulifolium* 'Cape Blanco'
- *Sedum spurium*
- *Sempervivums* (various)
- *Silene schafta*
- *Thymus serpyllum* (various)
- *Veronica prostrata*

LEFT: Sempervivum ballsii.

HOW TO PLANT ALPINES

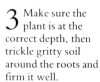

1 Position the plants while still in their pots so that you can see how they look and can move them around easily if necessary.

2 Use a trowel to take out a hole a little larger than the root-ball. You can buy narrow trowels that are particularly useful for planting in the crevices between rocks.

3 Make sure the plant is at the correct depth, then trickle gritty soil around the roots and firm it well.

4 Finish off by covering the exposed surface with more grit.

CHOOSING PLANTS

Hard landscaping (paving, walls, fences, pergolas, and so on)
is what gives a garden a strong sense of design, and provides the skeleton
that gives the garden its shape. But it is the soft landscaping – the plants –
that provides the flesh, shape and texture of the garden.
The same basic design can look very different in the hands of
gardeners with different ideas on the use of plants.

ABOVE: *Mixing different types of plant can*
be very effective. This border contains shrubs,
herbaceous plants, bulbs, and grasses.

OPPOSITE: *No matter how attractive the*
design of a garden, it is the plants
that make it pretty.

BEDS AND BORDERS

BEDS AND BORDERS NEED TO BE PLANNED. THE shape will affect the overall appearance, of course, but there are also practical considerations such as the amount of maintenance required, the theme to be created, as well as the crucial question of the actual plants to be used.

Formal beds and borders are normally dictated by the basic design concept, which will often determine the type of plants you can use. A formal rose garden will clearly feature roses, and only the 'filler' plants might have to be debated. A classic style with neat asymmetrical beds cut into the lawn, or edged by clipped box, demands the type of formal bedding associated with this type of garden.

Herbaceous and shrub borders are much more open to interpretation, and the actual plants used will have as much affect on the overall impression created as the shape or size of the border.

In traditional large gardens there is a clear distinction between herbaceous borders and shrub borders, but few small gardens can afford this luxury and the inclusion of a 'mixed border' is the usual compromise. Here shrubs jostle for

LEFT: *By curving the corners of borders in a small garden you can generate extra planting space that helps to make the garden more interesting.*

OPPOSITE ABOVE: *A garden like this, with plenty of shrubs such as roses, require little maintenance and because the hard landscaping is minimal is relatively inexpensive to create.*

OPPOSITE BELOW: *Single-sided herbaceous borders can look right in a rural setting if you have enough space. A border like this can be colourful for many months.*

position with herbaceous plants and annuals, while summer bedding plants and spring bulbs make bids for any areas of inhabitable space left. There is nothing wrong with this type of gardening: the border looks clothed long after the herbaceous plants have died down, and there will be flowers and pockets of changing interest for a much longer period than could be achieved with shrubs alone.

Colour themes are also difficult to achieve in a small garden, and although single-colour borders can be planted in a small garden, it is best to be a little more flexible. Settle for a 'golden corner' rather than a golden border, or a blue-and-silver theme for just part of a border rather than a more extensive area.

Small beds cut into the lawn do not have to be filled with summer bedding and then replaced by spring bulbs and spring bedding. Instead plant them with blocks of perennial ground cover, or use a perennial edging and plant seasonal flowers within it.

ISLAND BEDS

Traditionally, low-growing seasonal plants have been grown in beds cut into the lawn – island beds – and taller herbaceous plants and shrubs placed in long borders designed to be viewed from one side. Island beds planted with herbaceous plants and shrubs bridge this divide, and provide planting opportunities that can be put to good use in a small garden.

Planting principles

Island beds are intended to be viewed from all sides, so the tallest plants usually go in the centre and the smaller ones around the edge. Don't be too rigid, however. Concentrate on creating a bed that you have to walk around to see the other side, rather than simply planting tall summer flowers like delphiniums in the centre. Shrubby plants, even medium-sized evergreens, might be better for the centre of the bed, with other lower-growing shrubs creating bays that can be filled with plants that die down for the winter. Your bed will then retain its function of breaking up a lawn and creating a

diversion that has to be explored.

Don't be afraid to plant a small tree, such as *Malus floribunda*, in an island bed, to create much-needed height.

If seasonal bedding appeals more than shrubs and border perennials, then island beds can still be used creatively for these.

The question of shape

Most people think of island beds as informal in outline, but you can introduce rectangular beds if this suits the style of your garden.

Curved beds generally look much more pleasing, however, especially if you introduce broad and narrow areas so that there are gentle bays.

Design considerations

Use an island bed to break the line of sight. By taking it across the garden, an island bed may distract attention from an uninspiring view – whether beyond the garden or simply the fence itself. Attention is directed to the sides, and as you walk around the bed, the eye is taken into the bed rather than to the perimeters.

A series of island beds can be used to divide up a long, narrow garden. Instead of the eye being taken in a straight line to the end, the beds become a series of diversions.

BELOW: *Island beds help to break up a large lawn, and create a sense of height.*

ONE-SIDED BORDERS

Single-sided borders are useful if you want to create flowery boundaries around the perimeter and emphasize an open space within the garden, turning the garden in on itself. These borders are also useful for taking the eye to a distant focal point, and, by varying the width of the border, you can create a false sense of perspective that can appear to alter the size of the garden.

Straight and narrow beds
Most gardens have at least some straight and narrow borders around the edge of the lawn, a favourite spot for roses or seasonal bedding. If you want to cut down on the regular replanting work, plant with dwarf shrubs as backbone plants then include flowering ground cover herbaceous plants such as hardy geraniums and spring bulbs to provide flowers over a long period.

Make a border look wider by laying a mowing edge. Then use plants that will sprawl over the edge, softening the hard line and giving the impression of a wider border.

The advantages of curved borders
Straight edges are easier to mow and trim, but unless the border is wide and variation is created with the use of shrubs of various sizes, they can appear unimaginative and may take the eye too quickly along the garden, making it seem smaller. Gentle curves that create bays enable the plants to be brought further out into the garden and provide much more adventurous planting scope.

It may be possible to modify an existing straight border by cutting into the lawn. Bear in mind that mowing time is likely to be increased rather than decreased, however.

ABOVE: *Single-sided borders are the best choice for small town gardens that have high enclosing walls, especially if you can use climbers or tall plants to hide the wall.*
LEFT: *A single-sided mixed border.*

Turning corners
Don't forget that borders can turn corners. Right-angled turns seldom look satisfactory, however, so add a curve to the corner. This will give it greater depth at that point.

You can even take the border right round the garden in a continuous strip. A small square garden with a circular central lawn surrounded by border can look quite spectacular if well planted with a wide range of plants that hold interest throughout the seasons.

HOW TO MAKE BEDS AND BORDERS

If you are making a garden from scratch, areas allocated to lawns, beds and borders will be laid out accordingly, but you can often improve an existing garden by altering the shape of a border, or creating beds in what is currently a large and uninspiring lawn.

HOW TO MARK OUT AN OVAL BED

For small formal beds, such as ovals and circles, it is best to sow or lay the grass over the whole area first, then cut out the beds once the grass has become established.

Start by marking out a rectangle that will contain the oval. Afterwards you can check that it is square by measuring across the diagonals, which should be the same length.

Place a peg half way along each side, and stretch a string between them. The two strings will cross at the centre point. Then cut a piece of string half the *length* of the oval and using a side peg as a pivot, insert pegs where it intersects the long string along the centre.

Make a loop from a piece of string twice the distance between one of these two pegs and the top or bottom of the oval (whichever is the furthest away).

With the loop draped over the inner pegs, scribe a line in the grass while keeping the string taut. You can make the line more visible by using a narrow-necked bottle filled with dry sand instead of a stick.

Use an edging iron to cut out the shape, then lift the grass with a spade.

HOW TO MAKE A CURVED BORDER

1 If you want a quick and easy method, and can trust your eye for an even curve, lay hosepipe where you think the new edge should be. Run warm water through it first if the weather is cold, otherwise it may not be flexible enough to lie on the ground without awkward kinks.

2 The best way to judge whether the curves are satisfactory is to view the garden from an upstairs window, and have someone on the ground who can make further adjustments if necessary.

3 When the profile is satisfactory, run sand along the marker (dry sand in a wine bottle is a convenient method). Use an edging iron to cut the new edge, then lift the surplus grass and dig the soil thoroughly before attempting to replant.

4 An alternative and a more accurate way to achieve smooth curves is to use a stick or bottle fixed to a string attached to a peg. Use this as a pivot. By adjusting the length of the string and the position of the pivot, a series of curves can be achieved. Cut the edge as before.

HOW TO GET A NEAT EDGE

Emphasize the profile of your beds and borders, as well as your paths, by giving them a crisp or interesting edge. A mowing edge is a practical solution for a straight-edged border. Curved beds and borders usually have to be edged in other ways.

Some methods, like the corrugated edging strip and the wooden edge shown below are not particularly elegant, but they help to prevent the gradual erosion of the lawn through constant trimming and cutting back, and they maintain a crisp profile.

Using ornate or unusual edgings
For a period garden, choose a suitable edging. Victorian-style rope edging tiles are appropriate. If you live in a coastal area, consider using large seashells. If you enjoy your wine as well as your garden, why not put the empty bottles to use by forming an edging with them? Bury them neck-down in a single or double row, with just a portion showing.

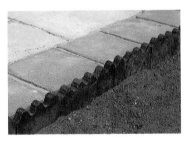

TOP: *It is possible to buy a modern version of Victorian rope-edging.*
ABOVE: *Edgings such as this are useful if you want to create a formal or old-fashioned effect.*

HOW TO FIT EDGING STRIPS

Edging strips like this are available in a thin metal, soft enough to cut with old scissors, or in plastic. These strips help stop erosion of the grass through frequent edge clipping and cutting back. Although these may not be the most decorative edging strips, they are quick and easy to fit.

1 Make a slit trench along the lawn edge with a spade, then lay the strip alongside the trench and cut to length. Place the edging strip loosely into it.

2 Backfill with soil for a firm fit. Press the strip in gently as you proceed. Finish off by tapping it level with a hammer over a straight-edged piece of wood.

HOW TO FIT WOODEN EDGING ROLL

Wired rolls of sawn logs can make a strong and attractive edging where you want the bed to be raised slightly above the lawn, but bear in mind that it may be difficult to mow right up to the edge.

1 Cut the roll to length using wire-cutters or strong pliers to cut through the wires, and insert the edging in a shallow trench. Join pieces by wiring them together. Backfill with soil for a firm fit. Make sure that the edging is level, first by eye. Use a hammer over a straight-edged piece of wood to tap it down. Then check the height with a spirit-level. Adjust as necessary.

PLANNING BORDERS

THE SECRET OF A SUCCESSFUL BORDER IS PLANNING for a long period of interest. However large a border, it probably will not remain attractive for more than about a month if you plan it only with plants that flower together. Planning should include not only plants that make pleasing associations when flowering, but that look good even out of bloom. Also incorporate plants that flower at different seasons.

The risk of planting a series of plants that bloom at different times is an uncoordinated appearance, with plants in flower dotted about amid a swathe of foliage in varying stages of

ABOVE: *Hydrangeas look good in shrub borders or mixed borders, but the flower colour may vary according to the acidity or alkalinity of the soil.*

LEFT: *Don't be afraid to use a focal point like a birdbath in a border. It will be eyecatching even when the plants are not at their best.*

growth. Sadly, in a small garden there isn't space to devote to a spring border, summer border, and autumn border.

Some of these shortcomings can be overcome by planting a mixed border that clearly incorporates many different kinds of plants, and by always planting in bold groups rather than using isolated specimens.

If starting from scratch, plan your borders on paper first. In an existing border you will obviously want to retain as many plants as possible, but be prepared to uproot and move or discard those that are out of place.

Choosing plants is always difficult, but in the following pages you will find suggestions of some of the most useful for a small garden. Space precludes mention of more than a small selection of suitable plants, so add special favourites and others that suit *your* garden and *your* taste.

TOP: *A border showing a good mix of shrubs and perennials.*
ABOVE: *Hollies are useful for the back of a shrub border.*

HOW TO PLANT A BORDER

Y ou don't have to be an artist to draw a functional planting plan. You can buy simple computer programs that will help you draw one up, but you still have to provide the plant knowledge that makes a border come alive and fulfil your own expectations. You can achieve results that are just as acceptable, and probably just as quickly, with pencil and paper.

A SCALE OUTLINE

1 Draw the outline shape of the bed and border, marking on the scale. Use graph paper so that you can easily estimate the size of a particular plant as you work.

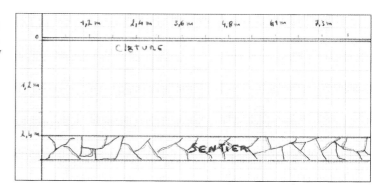

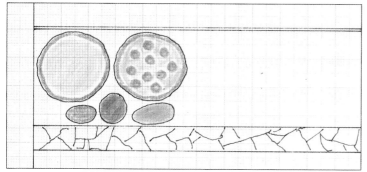

2 Make a list of plants that you want to include. Be sure to add essential details such as height, spread, and flowering season. If you find it easier to move around pieces of paper rather than use pencil and eraser initially, cut out several pieces of paper of appropriate size, with the height and flowering period marked on. You could colour them – evergreen greens, variegated green and gold stripes, and flowering plants in the colour of the blooms.

3 Either start with a basic plan with a series of spaces to be allocated (just indicate whether tall, medium or small), or shuffle around your cut-outs until they appear to form a pleasing pattern. Don't worry about whether the plants will fill the exact shape – with time they will all grow into each other, and in the meantime you can fill the gaps with annuals.

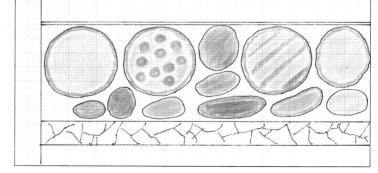

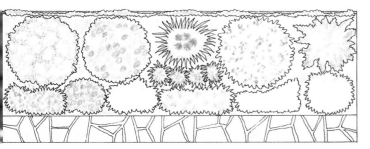

4 When satisfied with your key plants, draw these in on a more detailed planting plan. Then fill in the gaps with other plants, not necessarily on your priority list.

If you feel sufficiently artistically inclined, you can try a profile view that will give a better idea of how the border will look – though you can only make a snapshot of how it would look in one season.

HOW TO PLANT HERBACEOUS PLANTS

GUIDELINES TO GETTING IT RIGHT

• Unless the plants are large, plant in groups of about three – a bold spash usually looks better than single plants. Using single plants just because space is limited is a common mistake – the impact is often better if you use fewer kinds but more of each.

• Take into account the likely ultimate height, but remember that plants may grow taller in one garden than another.

• As a rule place the taller plants at the back (in the centre of an island bed), with the smallest at the front. But don't follow this too slavishly unless planting formal summer bedding. A few focal point plants that stand out from the rest can be very effective.

• Consider planting the border so that different parts are at their best at different times, perhaps starting with spring flowers at one end and working through to autumn at the other.

• Use foliage plants to maintain interest throughout the border.

1 Always prepare the soil first. Dig it deeply, remove weeds, and incorporate a fertilizer and garden compost if impoverished. Most herbaceous plants are sold in pots, so space them out according to your plan. Change positions if associations don't look right.

2 Water thoroughly about half an hour before knocking the plant from its pot, then remove a planting hole with a trowel. If the roots are wound tightly around the root-ball, carefully tease out a few of them first. Work methodically from the back of the border, or from one end.

3 Firm the soil around the roots to remove any large pockets of air.

4 Always water thoroughly after planting, and keep well watered in dry weather for the first few months.

PLANTING FOR TEXTURE

Quite dramatic plantings can be achieved simply by planting blocks of the same plant – whether summer bedding, herbaceous perennials or shrubs. If the garden is seen as an area of voids and masses, blocks of colours and textures, the overall impression can be as important as individual plants. Ground cover plants are ideal for this purpose.

ABOVE: *Thyme is a useful ground cover for a sunny position, and will even tolerate being walked upon occasionally.*

CONVENTIONAL PLANTING

Many ground cover plants spread by sideways growth, sending up new plants a short distance from the parent. These are best planted like normal herbaceous or shrubby plants. Suppress weeds initially with a 5cm (2in) layer of a mulch such as chipped bark. This is also the best way to plant any kind of ground cover that forms part of a mixed border.

HOW TO PLANT GROUND COVER

If planting ground cover plants as a 'texture block', or perhaps to cover an area of ground that is difficult to cultivate, such as a steep slope, it is best to plant through a mulching sheet. You can use black polythene, but a proper mulching sheet is better as it allows water to penetrate. However, do not use the sheet method for plants that colonize by spreading shoots that send up new plants, as the sheet will prevent growth by suppressing the shoots as effectively as the weeds.

1 Prepare the ground well, eliminating weeds. Add rotted manure or garden compost, and rake in fertilizer if the soil is impoverished.
   Secure the sheet around each edge. Tuck the edges firmly into the ground and cover with soil. Make two slits in the form of a cross where you want to plant.

2 Plant through the sheet as you would normally, firming the soil around the roots.
   If you use small plants, planting with a trowel will not be a problem. Water thoroughly.

3 Although the mulching sheet will suppress weeds very effectively while the ground cover is still young and not able to do the job itself, it does not look attractive, so cover it with an ornamental mulch, such as chipped bark.

HOW TO PLANT SHRUBS

1 Most shrubs are sold in pots, and can be planted at any time of the year when the ground is not frozen or waterlogged. Space them out in their pots first, then adjust if the spacing does not look even.

2 Prepare the ground thoroughly, making sure it is free of weeds. Dig in plenty of organic material such as well-rotted manure or garden compost. Otherwise use a proprietary planting mix.

3 Excavate the hole and try the plant for size. Use a garden cane or piece of wood across the hole to make sure the plant is at its original depth. Add or remove soil as necessary.

4 Remove the plant from the pot. If the roots are tightly wound around the root-ball, carefully tease some of them free, to encourage rapid rooting.

5 Firm the plant in well to eliminate large air pockets. Gentle pressure with the heel is an efficient way to do this, or alternatively you can do this by hand.

6 Rake or hoe in a balanced fertilizer to get the plant off to a good start. In autumn use one that is slow acting or has controlled release, to avoid stimulating growth during the cold months. If planting in winter, wait until spring before adding the fertilizer. Water well, then mulch with a 5cm (2in) layer of organic material such as garden compost, cocoa shells, or chipped bark.

COLOUR THEMES

Colour themes can be very effective, and although it may not be practical to plant whole borders like this in a small garden, you can often use a colour theme in part of a border, devote an island bed to shades of one or two colours, or perhaps cheer up a dull corner with yellow and gold.

Mixed borders

The plants suggested here will form the foundation of a colour theme for a mixed border, but you can add to them and broaden the scope by using bulbs and annuals in appropriate colours too.

Red borders are best avoided in a small garden. They need space and the relief of contrasting colours to be at their most affective.

Blue and silver

Agapanthus hybrids
Deciduous to evergreen perennial. Light to deep blue ball-shaped flower heads mid and late summer *45 × 75cm (18 × 30in).*

Artemisia absinthium
Deciduous sub-shrub. Deeply divided silvery-grey leaves. Yellow flowers in mid and late summer *1m × 60cm (3 × 2ft).*

Artemisia ludoviciana
Herbaceous perennial. Silver-grey foliage *1m × 45cm (3ft × 18in).*

Ceanothus x burkwoodii
Evergreen shrub. Clusters of bright blue flowers mid summer to mid autumn *2.4 × 2.1m (8 × 7ft).*

Delphinium hybrids
Herbaceous perennial. Tall flower spikes in various shades of blue *1.8m × 60cm (6 × 2ft).*

Festuca glauca
Grass. Dense tufts of blue-grey leaves *23 × 23cm (9 × 9in).*

Hibiscus syriacus 'Blue Bird'
Deciduous shrub. Lilac-blue flowers late summer to mid autumn *2.4 × 2.4m (8 × 8ft).*

LEFT: *Many ceanothus grow tall, so use them where you need bold plants for the back of a blue border. There are both evergreen and deciduous kinds of ceanothus.*

BELOW LEFT: *Grey-leaved plants are useful for filling in between blue flowers. This one is* Artemisia ludoviciana.

Nepeta x *faassenii*
Herbaceous perennial. Spike-like heads of lavender-blue flowers all summer. Grey-green leaves *45 × 45cm (18 × 18in).*

Perovskia atriplicifolia
Shrubby perennial. Feathery sprays of violet-blue flowers in late summer and early autumn. Grey-green leaves *1.2m × 45cm (4ft × 18in).*

ABOVE: *Delphiniums are some of the best blue herbaceous border plants.*

Santolina chamaecyparissus
Evergreen shrub. Silvery, woolly
leaves on mound-forming plant.
Small yellow flowers in mid summer
45 × 45cm (18 × 18in).

Senecio 'Sunshine' (syn.
Brachyglottis 'Sunshine')
Evergreen shrub. Silver-grey foliage.
Yellow daisy-type flowers in mid and
late summer *1 × 1.2m (3 × 4ft)*.

Stachys lanata (syn. *S. byzantina* or
S. olympica)
Almost evergreen herbaceous
perennial. Bold silvery leaves. Spikes
of purple flowers in mid summer
30 × 30cm (12 × 12in).

Yellow and gold

Achillea filipendulina
Herbaceous perennial. Flat heads of
lemon-yellow flowers in mid and late
summer *1 × 1m (3 × 3ft)*.

Alyssum saxatile
Evergreen shrubby perennial.
Golden-yellow flowers in mid and
late spring. Grey-green leaves
30 × 45cm (12 × 18in).

Anthemis tinctoria
Herbaceous perennial. Yellow daisy-
like flowers early to late summer.
'E. C. Buxton' is lemon-yellow,
'Grallagh Gold' is deep golden-yellow
75 × 45cm (2½ft × 18in).

ABOVE: Achillea filipendulina *'Gold Plate',*
one of the essential plants for a yellow border.

Berberis thunbergii 'Aurea'
Deciduous shrub. Yellow foliage,
pale yellow flowers in mid spring.
Red berries in autumn *1.2 × 1.2m
(4 × 4ft)*.

Choisya ternata 'Sundance'
Evergreen shrub that is generally
planted in a somewhat sheltered
position. Yellow foliage. White
flowers in mid and late spring *1.5 ×
1.5m (5 × 5ft)*.

Forsythia x *intermedia*
Deciduous shrub. Covered with
yellow flowers in early and mid
spring *2.4 × 2.1m (8 × 7ft)*.

Hemerocallis hybrids
Herbaceous perennial. There are
many yellow varieties, flowering
throughout summer *1m × 75cm
(3 × 2½ft)*.

Hypericum 'Hidcote'
Evergreen or semi-evergreen shrub.
Large yellow flowers from mid
summer to early autumn *1.5 × 1.5m
(5 × 5ft)*.

Ligustrum ovalifolium 'Aureum'
Evergreen or semi-evergreen shrub.
Green and gold foliage *2.4 × 2.4m
(8 × 8ft)*, but can be clipped to keep it
more compact.

LEFT: Hypericum
calycinum *can be a*
rampant partner for
other plants, but use
it wherever you need
to create a bold splash
of yellow in an
unpromising
position.

BELOW: *Hemerocallis*
come in a range of
colours, but there are
many good yellow
varieties, such as
'Dutch Beauty'.

Lonicera nitida 'Baggesen's Gold'
Evergreen shrub. Golden foliage
1.2 × 1.8m (4 × 6ft).

Philadelphus coronarius 'Aureus'
Deciduous shrub. Yellow leaves (can
become scorched in strong sun; turn
green by late summer). White flowers
in late spring and early summer *2.4 ×
1.8m (8 × 6ft)*.

Potentilla fruticosa
Deciduous shrub. Many varieties
with yellow flowers all summer
1.2 × 1.2m (4 × 4ft).

Solidago hybrids
Herbaceous perennial. Sprays of
bright yellow flowers in late summer
and early autumn *30cm–1.5m ×
30–60cm (12in–5ft × 12in–2ft)*,
according to variety.

EVERBRIGHT EVERGREENS

Evergreens alone can make a dull garden. They need to be relieved by plants that renew themselves, otherwise you miss the variety that comes with fresh green leaves newly emerged from their buds or the final fling of many shrubs as they go out in a blaze of colourful glory in the autumn. But a garden without evergreens is equally dull, and the clever use of them will ensure that your garden always looks good, whatever the season.

Use a few evergreens in mixed borders and beds, so that there is some height and texture in winter, or devote an area of the garden to evergreens – a heather and dwarf conifer garden can look superb. Try evergreens for focal points and specimen trees in the lawn.

When creating an evergreen bed or border, use plants in many different shades of green, and use variegated plants between plain ones.

Aucuba japonica
Large, glossy leaves. Flowers insignificant, but red berries sometimes a bonus. Choose one of the variegated varieties *1.8 × 1.8m (6 × 6ft)*.

Berberis darwinii
Small, holly-shaped leaves. Masses of attractive small orange-yellow flowers in mid and late spring *2.4 × 2.4m (8 × 8ft)*.

Bergenia hybrids
Evergreen non-woody perennial, useful as ground cover in front of shrubs. Large, rounded leaves, often tinged red or purple in winter. Pink, red or white flowers in spring *30 × 60cm (1 × 2ft)*.

Camellia hybrids
Glossy leaves and large single or double flowers, usually in shades of pink, red or white, in spring *2.4 × 1.8m (8 × 6ft)*.

Ceanothus x *'burkwoodii'*
See *Colour themes*.

Choisya ternata 'Sundance'
See *Colour themes*.

ABOVE: Erica carnea 'Myretoun Ruby' is just one of many attractive winter-flowering plants.

OPPOSITE: *Hebes are excellent compact, rounded plants (though some are tall). This is* Hebe × franciscana 'Variegata', *suitable for even the tiniest plot.*

LEFT: *Evergreens have the advantage of looking good all year, like this combination of* Elaeagnus pungens 'Maculata' *with* Hebe pinguifolia 'Pagei' *in front.*

Cotoneaster dammeri
Prostrate ground cover to use in front of other shrubs. Small leaves. White flowers in early summer, red berries in autumn and winter *5–8cm × 1.5m (2–3in × 5ft)*.

Elaeagnus pungens 'Maculata'
Green leaves boldly splashed with gold in the centre. Very striking in winter sun *2.4 × 2.4m (8 × 8ft)*.

Erica
There are many species and varieties – look especially for varieties of *Erica carnea* (syn. *E. herbacea*) and *E. x darleyensis*, both winter-flowering and lime-tolerant *30 × 60cm (1 × 2ft)*.

Escallonia macrantha
Small leaves, clusters of pink or red flowers in summer *1.8 × 1.8m (6 × 6ft)*.

Euonymus fortunei
Will grow along the ground or up against a wall. Choose one of the variegated varieties, such as 'Emerald 'n' Gold' (green and gold) *30cm × 1.2m (12in × 4ft)* on the ground.

Hebe
Hebes make nicely shaped, usually rounded, plants and often have attractive flowers and sometimes colourful or variegated foliage. Heights can range from *30cm–1.2m (12in–4ft)*, with similar spreads, depending on species. Many are of borderline hardiness where frosts can be severe, so check with your local garden centre to see which ones are reliable enough for your area.

Ilex
The holly needs little introduction, but for a small garden choose one trained as a bush and a variegated variety such as 'Golden King' or 'Golden Queen' (the King is female and has berries, the Queen's male and doesn't!) *3 × 2.4m (10 × 8ft)*.

Lonicera nitida 'Baggesen's Gold'
See *Colour themes*.

Mahonia 'Charity'
Fragrant clusters of yellow flowers in early and mid winter *2.4 × 1.8m (8 × 6ft)*.

Phormium hybrids
Tall, sword-shaped leaves arising from ground level. Usually variegated cream or shades of pink or purple, according to variety. Of borderline hardiness in areas where frosts can be severe, so check with your local garden centre about which ones are suitable for your garden *1.2–1.8m × 1–1.2m (4–6ft × 3–4ft)*.

Rosmarinus officinalis
Grey-green, aromatic leaves. Small blue flowers in spring *1.8 × 1.5m (6 × 5ft)*.

Santolina chamaecyparissus
See *Colour themes*.

Senecio 'Sunshine'
See *Colour themes*.

BELOW: *Rosemary is pretty in flower, and in mild areas will often start blooming in late winter.*
LEFT: *Hollies are usually so slow-growing that most people can find space for one. This one is* Ilex aquifolium *'Aurea Marginata'.*

Viburnum tinus
Deep to mid green leaves on tidy bush. White flowers (tinged pink in some varieties) from late autumn to early spring *2.4 × 1.8m (8 × 6ft)*.

Yucca filamentosa 'Variegata'
Sword-like leaves with broad cream and yellow margins. Large bell-shaped flowers on tall spikes in mid and late summer *1.2 × 1m (4 × 3ft)*.

DWARF CONIFERS

A good garden centre will have hundreds of dwarf conifers, in a huge range of shades, shapes, and sizes. The permutations are enormous, and the best way to choose them is to go along armed with a book or catalogue that will give you likely sizes after, say, 15 years, then choose combinations that will make a pleasing group.

COLOUR FOR THE COLD MONTHS

Evergreens provide winter clothes for the garden, but they don't look very dressy and they are best interspersed with plants that renew themselves. There is no substitute for flowers and fruits, which, though more transient, are all the more appreciated.

Autumn leaf colour can be as bold and bright as many flowers, but it is worth including some autumn blooms too. A few well-placed pools of late flowers will prolong summer and keep autumn at bay.

Don't overlook colourful barks and twigs in winter, which can become focal points on a sunny day.

Chimonanthus praecox
Deciduous shrub. Scented yellow flowers on bare stems in winter *2.4 × 2.4m (8 × 8ft)*.

Chrysanthemum
Look for varieties that flower late. Some flower well into late autumn and even early winter. Height varies with variety. Consult a specialist book or ask your garden centre for suitable varieties.

Colchicum speciosum and hybrids
Corms with large crocus-like flowers, mainly in shades of pink and mauve, single or double, in autumn. The foliage does not appear until spring *15 × 23cm (6 × 9in)*. The leaves can double the height.

Cornus mas
Deciduous shrub or small tree. Masses of tiny yellow flowers on bare branches in late winter and early spring *3 × 2.4m (10 × 8ft)*.

Crocus speciosus
Corm. Lilac-blue typical crocus flowers in mid autumn *10 × 8cm (4 × 3in)*.

Crocus tommasinianus
Corm, flowering between mid winter and early spring. Typical crocus flowers, usually lilac or purple in colour *8 × 8cm (3 × 3in)*.

Cyclamen coum
Corm. Miniature cyclamen-shaped flowers with reflexed petals. Mainly shades of pink, but also white. Flowers early winter to early spring. Leaves often marbled silver *8 × 15cm (3 × 6in)*.

Cyclamen hederifolium (syn. *C. neapolitanum*).
Similar to above but flowers from late summer to late autumn.

Erica
See *Everbright evergreens*.

Hamamelis mollis
Fragrant spidery yellow flowers on bare branches in mid and late winter *2.4 × 2.4m (8 × 8ft)*.

ABOVE: Chrysanthemum 'Ruby Mound'.

LEFT: *Long before spring crocuses are in flower, the blooms of* C. tommasinianus *will be putting in an appearance. These were photographed in late winter.*

Helleborus niger
Evergreen perennial border plant.
Large white flowers in mid winter
30 × 45cm (12 × 18in).

Helleborus orientalis
Evergreen perennial border plant.
Large white, pink, or purple flowers
in late winter and early spring *45 ×
60cm (18in × 2ft).*

Iris unguicularis (syn. *I. stylosa*)
Evergreen perennial border plant.
Large blue iris flowers in winter and
early spring *30 × 45cm (12 × 18in).*

Jasminum nudiflorum
Sprawling shrub, usually grown
against a wall or trellis. Bright yellow
flowers from late autumn to early
spring *2.4 × 2.4m (8 × 8ft).*

Mahonia 'Charity'
See *Everbright evergreens.*

Nerine bowdenii
Heads of pretty pink, spidery flowers
on leafless stems from late summer to
early winter. The foliage appears in
spring *60 × 30cm (2 × 1ft).*

Prunus subhirtella 'Pendula' (syn.
'Autumnalis Pendula')
Small to medium-sized drooping
deciduous tree. White flowers,
sometimes tinged pink, from late
autumn and throughout the winter in
mild spells *3 × 3m (10 × 10ft).*

Sternbergia lutea
Bulb. Crocus-like yellow flowers in
mid and late autumn *10 × 10cm
(4 × 4in).*

Viburnum x *bodnantense* 'Dawn'
Deciduous shrub. Small clusters of
white to pink flowers on bare stems
from late autumn to early spring
2.4 × 1.5m (8 × 5ft).

Viburnum tinus
See *Everbright evergreens.*

LEFT ABOVE: *The hellebores span winter and
spring. This is* H. orientalis guttatus.
LEFT: Iris unguicularis *can be in bloom in
mild spells right through the winter. The
plants take a few years to settle down before
flowering prolifically.*
BELOW: Nerine bowdenii *flowers in autumn,
but will sometimes continue into winter.*

COLOURFUL STEMS

A specimen tree with attractive
bark, perhaps placed in a lawn or
in an open position and
surrounded by winter-flowering
heathers, can be a winter focal
point. One of the white-bark
birches such as *Betula jacquemontii*
always looks good. If you need a
really small tree, however, try
B. pendula 'Youngii', a small
weeping tree.

In a small garden, shrubs are
more likely to be a practical
proposition, and two of the best
are *Cornus alba* 'Sibirica' (red
stems) and *C. stolonifera*
'Flaviramea' (green stems).

As a half-way house between
tree and shrub, pollard *Salix alba*
'Chermesina', a willow with
scarlet shoots. Cut the stems
hard back to a stump perhaps
1.2m/4ft tall; do this every
second year.

VARIETY WITH VARIEGATION

Variegated plants make a border look lighter and more interesting when flowers are scarce, and variegated evergreens are particularly useful at times when little is flowering.

Avoid planting too many variegated plants close together. Use them between other plants with plain foliage where the leaf colouring will be shown off to advantage.

Aralia elata 'Variegata'
Deciduous shrub or small tree. Leaflets margined and marked creamy-white ('Aureovariegata' has a broad, irregular gold margin). White flowers in late summer and early autumn *3 × 2.1m (10 × 7ft)*.

Arundinaria viridistriata (syn. *Pleioblastus auricomus, Pleioblastus viridistriatus*)
Bamboo. Dark green leaves broadly striped yellow. Purplish-green canes *1m × 60cm (3 × 2ft)*.

ABOVE: Hosta fortunei albopicta.
BELOW: *Only a few variegated trees are suitable. This is* Aralia elata *'Variegata'*.

Aucuba japonica (variegated varieties)
See *Everbright evergreens*.

Buxus sempervirens 'Aureovariegata'
Evergreen shrub with small leaves striped, splashed and mottled pale yellow. 'Elegantissima' has irregular creamy-white margins *1.2 × 1m (4 × 3ft)*.

Carex morrowii 'Evergold' Sedge
Clump-forming with grass-like leaves striped yellow along the centre *25 × 30cm (10 × 12in)*.

Cornus alba 'Elegantissima'
Deciduous suckering shrub with red stems and leaves margined and mottled with white. 'Spaethii' is similar but has gold variegation *2.1 × 1.8m (7 × 6ft)*.

Elaeagnus x *ebbingei* 'Limelight'
Evergreen shrub. Large green leaves with a central splash of deep yellow *2.4 × 2.1m (8 × 7ft)*.

Elaeagnus pungens 'Maculata'
See *Everbright evergreens*.

Euonymus fortunei (variegated varieties)
See *Everbright evergreens*.

Fuchsia magellanica 'Versicolor'
Deciduous shrub. Small fuchsia-type flower in summer and into autumn. Grey-green, white, yellow, and pink variegation. Hardy except in cold areas *1.2 × 1m (4 × 3ft)*.

Hebe x *franciscana* 'Variegata'
Evergreen shrub, not suitable for very cold areas. Small rounded leaves edged cream. Mauve-blue flowers in summer *60 × 60cm (2 × 2ft)*.

ABOVE: Pachysandra terminalis *is an excellent ground cover for shade, but the plain green form looks rather boring. 'Variegata' is much more interesting.*

LEFT: Houttuynia cordata *'Chameleon'.*

BELOW: Vinca minor *'Variegata'.*

Hostas (many variegated varieties)
Herbaceous perennial *30–60cm × 30–75cm (12in–2ft × 12in–2½ft).*

Houttuynia cordata 'Chameleon'
Herbaceous perennial. Outstandingly striking, heart-shaped foliage, variegated with shades of yellow, green, bronze and red. Small white flowers in summer *30 × 45cm (12 × 18in).*

Hypericum x moseranum 'Tricolor'
Evergreen shrub. Yellow flowers about 5cm (2in) across from mid summer to mid autumn. Green and white leaves edged pink *60 × 60cm (2 × 2ft).*

Ilex (variegated varieties)
See *Everbright evergreens.*

Iris pallida 'Variegata'
Sword-like leaves, striped creamy-white and green. Blue flowers in early summer *60 × 60cm (2 × 2ft).*

Iris pseudacorus 'Variegatus'
Sword-like leaves striped green and yellow while young, turning greener with age. Blue flowers in early summer. Although associated with water, it will grow in an ordinary border though it does best in damp soil *1m × 60cm (3 × 2ft).*

Ligustrum (variegated varieties)
See *Colour themes.*

Pachysandra terminalis 'Variegata'
Evergreen sub-shrub. Green and white leaves. Insignificant white flowers in late spring *30 × 45cm (12 × 18in).*

ABOVE: *Variegation is important in the herbaceous border. This is* Iris pallida *'Variegata'.*

Phormium hybrids
See *Everbright evergreens.*

Salvia officinalis 'Icterina'
Evergreen shrub. Grey-green leaves splashed with yellow *60 × 60cm (2 × 2ft).*

Vinca minor 'Variegata'
Evergreen prostrate shrub. Green and creamy-white leaves. Pale mauve flowers *20 × 60cm (8in × 2ft).*

Weigela florida 'Variegata'
Deciduous shrub. Leaves edged creamy-white. Pink flowers in early summer *1.5 × 1.2m (5 × 4ft).*

Yucca gloriosa 'Variegata'
See *Everbright evergreens.*

PLANTING FOR QUICK RESULTS

Annuals are almost instant – many are already in flower when you buy them – border perennials are respectable after a year, but shrubs can seem infuriatingly slow to mature.

Not all shrubs are slow-growers, however, so if you want your border to look well established in three years instead of five or even ten, try those suggested here.

Even those plants that grow quickly will leave gaps in the early years. In a mixed border, fill these gaps with the quicker-growing border perennials; in a shrub border add a few bushy annuals.

Bear in mind that some shrubs that grow quickly while young may continue to grow (over-enthusiastically) once they've reached what you consider a modest size. The height and spread estimates below are based on three years (though much depends on soil and climate), but the ones listed are only likely to grow a little more than this even by 10 years. Those that grow taller can be pruned back hard to restrict their size. *Buddleia davidii*, for example, will be much better if you cut it back hard each spring.

There are many more quick-growers, however, so don't assume that your scope for an almost instant border is limited solely to those listed below.

Aucuba japonica
See *Everbright evergreens*.

Buddleia davidii
Deciduous shrub. Fragrant, usually lilac-blue flower clusters at ends of arching branches, from mid summer to mid autumn. Other colours include shades of red, purple, and white *2.4 × 1.5m (8 × 5ft)*.

Caryopteris x *clandonensis*
Deciduous shrub. Narrow, grey-green leaves. Clusters of bright blue flowers in late summer and early autumn *1m × 60cm (3 × 2ft)*.

Choisya ternata
See *Colour themes*.

LEFT: *Tough, low-growing, quick to mature, and very bright in flower are qualities that make* Genista tinctoria *well worth considering. This variety is 'Royal Gold'.*

BELOW: Hypericum calycinum *grows and spreads rapidly, so don't plant it where these characteristics can become an embarrassment. The flowers are bold and beautiful.*

Cistus x *corbariensis*
Evergreen shrub. Dull green leaves wavy at the edge. Bold white flowers with a yellow mark at the base of each petal, in late spring and early summer *75 × 60cm (2½ × 2ft)*.

Cytisus x *kewensis*
Deciduous shrub. Pale yellow, pea-like flowers, in profusion in late spring. Spreading shape *45cm × 1m (18in × 3ft)*.

ABOVE: Leycesteria formosa *is quick-growing, and highly popular with birds. They love the dark purple berries.*
RIGHT: *Weigelas come in a range of colours, but mainly pinks and reds. They grow quickly and flower young and so make an excellent choice if you want fast results.*

Erica carnea
See *Everbright evergreens.*

Fuchsia magallanica
See *Variety with variegation.*

Genista tinctoria
Deciduous shrub. Deep yellow pea-type flowers all summer *75 × 60cm (2½ × 2ft)*, but height tends to be very variable.

Hebe 'Midsummer Beauty'
Evergreen shrub. Pale green leaves, slightly reddish beneath. Sprays of lavender-purple flowers from mid summer to mid autumn. Not reliably hardy in cold areas *1 × 1m (3 × 3ft).*

Hypericum calycinum
Evergreen shrub. Large yellow, cup-shaped flowers all summer. Can be invasive *45 × 60cm (18in × 2ft).*

Lavandula (various)
Evergreen shrub. The popular lavender. Grey-green leaves and flowers in shades of blue or purple *60 × 60cm (2 × 2ft).*

Leycesteria formosa
Deciduous shrub. Cane-like stems forming a bamboo-like clump. Drooping flower tassels containing white flowers with claret bracts, followed by purple-black fruits *1.5 × 1m (5 × 3ft).*

Lupinus arboreus
Short-lived deciduous shrub. Foliage and flower spikes resemble the herbaceous lupin, but the lightly fragrant flowers are much sparser. Usually yellow, but can be lilac to purple or blue. Good for a hot, dry site *1.2 × 1m (4 × 3ft).*

Mahonia 'Charity'
See *Everbright evergreens.*

Philadelphus coronarius 'Aureus'
See *Colour themes.*

Potentilla fruticosa
See *Colour themes.*

Senecio 'Sunshine'
See *Colour themes.*

Spiraea x *bumalda* (various varieties)
Twiggy deciduous shrub. Flat flower heads, usually crimson, in late summer. Some varieties have variegated foliage *75 × 45cm (2½ft × 18in).*

Weigela hybrids
Deciduous shrub. Funnel-shaped flowers in late spring and early summer. Mainly shades of red and pink *1.8 × 1.5m (6 × 5ft).*

BELOW: Spiraea × bumalda *(syn. S. japonica). This is 'Anthony Waterer'.*

NO FUSS, LOW-MAINTENANCE PLANTS

There are plenty of people who do not have a lot of time to tend to their gardens. If you want to save the cost and time involved in regularly replanting with seasonal plants, grow hardy perennials and shrubs. But if you really want to cut down on maintenance, grow only those that are undemanding, with no need to prune regularly, or to keep lifting, dividing, or hacking back.

Most shrubs will require very occasional pruning, perhaps to cut out a dead or diseased shoot, or to improve the shape if growth is not symmetrical, and sooner or later border perennials will benefit from being lifted and divided, but the plants suggested here can be left for many years without attention. They will almost thrive on neglect, yet will not get out of control.

Aucuba japonica
See *Everbright evergreens*.

Berberis thunbergii
There are many varieties, including variegated, purple-leaved and gold-leaved. Shape and height also vary with variety: *B.t. atropurpurea* 'Bagatelle', for example, makes a dwarf rounded ball of growth covered with coppery-red leaves, usually less than *45cm (18in)* tall and broad, 'Helmond Pillar' is dark purple but grows into a narrow column *1.2m (4ft)* or so high but only about *30cm (12in)* wide.

Bergenia hybrids
See *Everbright evergreens*.

ABOVE: Cotinus coggygria *is sometimes called the smoke bush because of its flower heads. It can make quite a large shrub in time, but requires minimal attention.*

Choisya ternata
Both green and golden forms (see *Colour themes*) are trouble-free plants if protected from cold winds in winter.

Cornus stolonifera 'Flaviramea'
Deciduous shrub. Green leaves turn yellow before falling. Yellowish-green winter stems *1.8 × 1.8m (6 × 6ft)*.

Cotinus coggygria
Deciduous shrub. Rounded shape with pale green leaves (there are also purple-leaved varieties) that have brilliant autumn colours. Feathery sprays of purple or pink flowers in mid summer *2.4 × 2.4m (8 × 8ft)*.

Cotoneaster
There are many cotoneasters, from ground-huggers to shrubs *3m (10ft)* or more tall. *C. horizontalis* (see *Autumn leaves and berries*) and *C. dammeri* (see *Everbright evergreens*), are popular ground-huggers, but many others are suitable for a small garden.

Elaeagnus pungens 'Maculata'
See *Everbright evergreens*.

Erica carnea
See *Everbright evergreens*.

ABOVE: Cotoneaster horizontalis *can be grown as ground cover or as a climber.*

Fatsia japonica
Evergreen shrub. Large, hand-shaped glossy green leaves (there is a variegated variety). White, ball-shaped flower heads that appear on mature plants in mid autumn *2.4 × 2.4m (8 × 8ft)*.

Griselinia littoralis
Evergreen shrub. Pale green leaves (there are variegated varieties). Not suitable for cold areas. Slow-growing *3 × 3m (10 × 10ft)*.

Hebes
See *Everbright evergreens*.

Hemerocallis hybrids
See *Colour themes*.

Hibiscus syriacus
See *Colour themes*, but there are other varieties in different shades of blue, pink, and white.

Ilex
See *Everbright evergreens*.

Kniphofia hybrids
Herbaceous perennial. Large, stiff, poker-like orange or yellow flower spikes. Flowering season extends from early summer to mid autumn, according to variety *60cm–1.2m × 60cm–1.2m (2–4 × 2–4ft)*.

Liriope muscari
Evergreen perennial. Clumps of broad, grassy leaves, and spikes of mauve-lilac flowers from late summer to mid autumn *45 × 30cm (18 × 12in)*.

Mahonia japonica
Evergreen shrub. Glossy, dark green leaves divided into leaflets. Fragrant, lemon-yellow flowers from early winter to early spring *2.4 × 2.4m (8 × 8ft)*.

Potentilla fruticosa
See *Colour themes*.

Ribes sanguineum
Deciduous shrub. Drooping clusters of small pink or red flowers in spring *1.8 × 1.8m (6 × 6ft)*.

Ulex europaeus
Evergreen shrub. Spiny growth, covered with deep yellow single or double flowers in spring. Flowers may also appear intermittently in winter *1.5 × 1.5m (5 × 5ft)*.

Viburnum davidii
Evergreen shrub. White flowers in early summer. Turquoise-blue berries later if both male and female plants are planted *1 × 1.2m (3 × 4ft)*.

Viburnum tinus
See *Everbright evergreens*.

Yucca
See *Everbright evergreens*, but the non-variegated form is equally suitable for a border or as a specimen plant.

ABOVE: *The kniphofias, sometimes called red-hot-pokers, are bold herbaceous border plants. Once well established they make large clumps. Some species are quite small, however, and different varieties flower at different times. Many kniphofias are unhappy in very cold areas and may need protection in some areas.*

DON'T FORGET THE DWARF CONIFERS

Conifers need negligible care, and if you choose dwarf species and varieties they will remain compact enough for a small garden. Be cautious about using them in a mixed border, however, as they seldom blend in as satisfactorily as ordinary shrubs.

PLANTS FOR A PURPOSE

ONE OF THE SECRETS OF SUCCESSFUL GARDENING IS the ability to choose the right plant for a particular position or use. Plants will always thrive more readily if they are suited to the conditions. Forcing an inappropriate plant into shade if it demands sun, or planting a shade-lover in scorching sunlight, is a recipe for disappointment.

You will find plenty of ideas for plants that relish problem areas like shade or sun in the pages that follow, but sometimes the question is less which plant suits particular conditions as which fulfils a particular purpose. In the following pages you will find plants that provide the right solution, whether you want a scented shrub, climber for a pergola, or an arresting

ABOVE: *Don't be afraid to grow shrubs and plants such as lilies in pots and tubs as well as the more ubiquitous seasonal summer flowers.*

LEFT: *Climbing and rambling roses are useful for summer screens, but bear in mind that it is only seasonal cover.*

LEFT: *Clematis can be planted in shade provided they can rise above it to flower in the sun.*

OPPOSITE ABOVE: *Ivies will grow almost anywhere, in sun or shade, along the ground or up a wall or tree. Green varieties can be a trifle boring, but variegated varieties are always bright.*

BELOW: *'Exotics' can be used as focal points to bring interest to an otherwise boring area during the summer, but will probably need winter protection.*

'architectural' plant as a focal point.

There are 'exotics', some of which are quite tough, other plants will only thrive during the summer months and you will either have to protect them in winter or treat them as expendable. There are also suggestions of plants to attract wildlife.

If a particular variety has been mentioned, other varieties, perhaps in different colours or with minor variations in size or shape, will almost certainly do well in the same situation. White and pale colours tend to show up better in shade, however, and where possible varieties particularly suited to the conditions have been mentioned.

Be prepared to experiment with plants, especially with those that seem to thrive in similar situations in your area, and concentrate on those that clearly do well. Do not be afraid to abandon plants that fail to live up to expectations.

PLANTS FOR THE TROPICAL LOOK

If you are trying to create a garden based on Mediterranean influences with white-painted walls and with the emphasis on hot climate flora, you will need to use plenty of plants that give the impression that they are exotic or tender when in fact they are quite frost-tolerant.

Some of the plants suggested here are only hardy enough for warm areas where frosts are light and seldom prolonged, others are really tough.

You can of course use many of them in an ordinary border, but the ones suggested here are primarily effective as part of an area reserved for the more striking plants.

If you live in a cold area and have a greenhouse, conservatory, or even a porch, grow the more vulnerable plants in large pots and move them to this protected area for winter.

Arundinaria viridistriata
See *Variety with variegation*.

Clianthus puniceus
Evergreen climbing shrub. Divided, feathery leaves, crimson-scarlet claw-shaped flowers in early summer. Will only survive outdoors in mild districts. Can reach about *3m (10ft)*.

Cordyline australis
Palm-like plant with strap-like leaves at top of plant. *C. a. purpurea* has brownish-purple leaves. Where winters are mild and frost not severe it can be left in the ground and may grow into a tall tree. Elsewhere grow in a pot, where it will remain much smaller. Protect for the winter.

Fatsia japonica
See *No fuss, low-maintenance plants*.

Gunnera manicata
Huge leaves, like a giant rhubarb. In the ground it is large even for a big garden, but you can grow it in a tub or a patio pot to restrict its size. Keep very moist, and protect during the winter.

Kniphofia hybrids
See *No fuss, low-maintenance plants*.

ABOVE: Cordyline australis *'Alberti'*.

Lilium hybrids
You can buy bulbs and pot up your own lilies, or buy them about to bloom. These may have been dwarfed chemically and will probably make better container plants. Heights vary.

Phormium hybrids
See *Everbright evergreens*.

Rheum palmatum
An ornamental rhubarb that reaches *2.4m (8ft)* tall in flower, but the leaves are less than half this height. White or red flowers in early summer.

ABOVE: *For the cost of a packet of seeds you can have a show like this* Ipomoea tricolor *'Heavenly Blue'*.

ABOVE: *Where winters are mild* Zantedeschia aethiopica *can be overwintered outside.*
TOP: *The big, bold leaves of* Rheum palmatum *look very exotic.*
LEFT: *Lilies are quite easy to grow in pots provided you choose suitable varieties.*

Yucca

See *Everbright evergreens*, but the green form can be just as effective as a variegated variety.

Zantedeschia aethiopica

Well-known white arum flowers, popular with florists. Can be kept outdoors where winters are mild, but is usually best grown in a pot and given winter protection. The growth dies down in winter.

Exotic annuals

Some annuals that are regarded as indoor plants can be grown in the garden for the summer.

Among the flowering plants, celosias are always eye-catching, whether you grow the plume-shaped varieties or those shaped like a cock's comb. A mixture will usually include shades of yellow, red, and pink. The coleus is one of the best foliage pot-plants to try outdoors *en-masse* – plants are very easy to raise cheaply from seed. The multi-coloured foliage matches the exotic croton in boldness and colour combinations. Make sure they are carefully acclimatized, and don't put them out too early.

Many half-hardy bedding plants are easily raised from seed – try large daisy-like flowers such as arctotis, with flowers in shades of red, orange and pink. Salpiglossis are always eye-catching, and with their velvety, funnel-shaped flowers in shades of red, purple, and yellow, usually prominently veined and marked, certainly have that 'exotic' look.

Portulacas and cleomes (with spidery-looking flower heads) are among the other half-hardy annuals to include. But be sure to make space for *Ipomoea tricolor*, with its big blue flowers often *10cm (4in)* or so across, which are bound to make a real feature climbing up a trellis.

Disposable houseplants

Use flowering pot-plants to add short-term colour to your patio. Plants like gerberas, and dwarfed chrysanthemums, are inexpensive and generally treated as disposable plants if used indoors. Sink the pot into the soil so that the plant is easily removed after flowering.

ARCHITECTURAL PLANTS

Architectural plants may seem a contradiction in terms, for one implies the rigidity of buildings and structures, the other the informality and fluidity of plant life. The term is often a puzzle to non-gardeners, yet a plant enthusiast will know instantly when he sees an 'architectural' plant.

'Sculptural' plants

'Sculptural' is perhaps a better way to describe those plants, which, though clearly possessing all the natural beauty of any first-rate plant, also have structure and stature, and above all a shape – and perhaps texture – that an architect might be pleased to use to enhance his buildings and structures in the same way as a piece of sculpture might be used.

Some herbaceous plants, such as the acanthus, have assumed architectural status – in this case because the acanthus leaf occurs so often as a pattern in classical architecture, but also because the plant has the bold stance and distinctive profile that makes it stand out from the ordinary. Most architectural plants are trees and shrubs, however, with height as well as a distinctive outline. Use architectural plants sparingly and with careful consideration, not as part of a mixed planting but rather as you would large ornaments, as punctuation points within the garden.

Use architectural plants to make a bold statement in paved and gravel gardens, or to break up an otherwise boring area of lawn.

Acanthus spinosus

Statuesque plant with large, deeply divided leaves that are both erect and arching. Mauve and white, hooded flowers on stiff spikes in mid and late summer *1 × 1m (3 × 3ft)*.

Angelica archangelica

Biennial or short-lived perennial. Large, deeply divided, aromatic leaves on stiff, upright plant. Ball-like head of smaller clusters of yellowish-green flowers in mid and late summer *2.4 × 1m (8 × 3ft)*.

LEFT: Acanthus spinosus *is one of those plants with dramatic leaves and equally imposing flowers, and not one that will be ignored.*

BELOW: Angelica archangelica *makes a bold plant about 1.8m (6ft) tall, with large leaves and striking globular flower heads. Use it as a focal-point plant in the herb garden.*

Catalpa bignonioides 'Aurea'

Deciduous tree. The green species is far too large for a small garden, but 'Aurea' is more compact, and can be bought trained as a shrub-like multi-stemmed tree. The golden leaves are very large and handsome *4.5 × 4.5m (15 × 15ft)*.

Cordyline australis

See *Plants for the tropical look.*

Cornus controversa 'Variegata'

A small tree with wide-spreading branches spaced out to give it a layered effect. Leaves have striking silver margins *4.5 × 4.5m (15 × 15ft)*.

LEFT: *Daturas (now more correctly called brugmansias) are ideal for the summer patio but they have to be taken indoors for winter frost protection.*

RIGHT: *'Charity' is one of the most imposing hybrid mahonias, with bold sprays of yellow flowers blooming through the coldest months of the year.*

Crambe cordifolia
Herbaceous perennial. Normally a plant for a large garden, but sparsely planted it will make a bold statement. Enormous leaves and huge clouds of gypsophila-like small white flowers in early and mid-summer *1.8 × 1.8m (6 × 6ft)*.

Datura (syn. *Brugmansia*)
Tender shrub. Must be overwintered in frost-proof place, but often grown on patio in a large tub for summer. Large drooping leaves, big bell-shaped very fragrant flowers – usually white or cream, but there are also red and pink kinds *1.8 × 1.2m (6 × 4ft)* in tub.

Fatsia japonica
See *No fuss, low maintenance plants*.

Gunnera manicata
See *Plants for the tropical look*.

Juniperus scopulorum 'Skyrocket'
Conifer. You may also find it sold under the name of *J. virginiana* 'Skyrocket'. Very narrow, pencil-like growth. Typical conifer foliage *4.5m × 75cm (15 × 2½ft)*.

Kniphofia
See *No fuss, low maintenance plants*.

Mahonia 'Charity'
See *Everbright evergreens*.

RIGHT: Salix matsudana *'Tortuosa' is a small tree that can be as fascinating in winter as it is in summer.*

Paulownia tomentosa
A large tree totally unsuitable for a small garden. It can be grown as a large shrub, however, by annual hard pruning close to ground level, when the leaves become huge. Treated like this height will be about *2.4–3m (8–10ft)* and spread about *1.8m (6ft)*.

Phormium hybrids
See *Everbright evergreens*.

Salix matsudana 'Tortuosa'
A small to medium-sized tree with spiralling and twisted stems as well as contorted leaves. Seen at its best in winter when the stems are bare *4.5 × 4.5m (15 × 15ft)*.

Yucca
See *Everbright evergreens*, but a green form is just as useful as a variegated variety as an architectural plant.

LIVING SCREENS

The screening plants described here are not rows of tall conifers or large windbreaks along the boundary, which are inappropriate in a small garden, but plants that you can use to screen objects within the garden and plants that you would be happy to grow as ornamentals too.

Generally, something that requires screening will need it the year round, so evergreens naturally predominate in any list of screening plants. But sometimes a summer-only screen is acceptable. For a summer screen within the vegetable plot, consider Jerusalem artichokes, which provide excellent summer cover and a crop to harvest at the end of the season!

When looking for a good screening shrub, check that it is well clothed at the base. If you are prepared to erect a trellis or internal fence, many of the plants described in Climbers, Wall Shrubs & Hedges, Section Two will also make excellent internal screens. A trellis covered with sweet-smelling honeysuckle will make a summer screen that is pleasing to the eye and the nose. The most popular – and best – honeysuckles are deciduous, so don't expect winter cover, but some fragrant climbing honeysuckles, such as *Lonicera japonica*, are evergreen or semi-evergreen so you will have winter cover as well as summer scent – though with less spectacular flowers.

Trellises and screen block walls
Sometimes it is possible to screen an unsightly object, such as a storage tank with just two or three well-chosen shrubs. Alternatively, erect a trellis or screen wall, carefully integrated as part of the garden design, then use climbers, wall shrubs or ordinary shrubs against these. This double-masking is often the most effective because you have a whole range of climbers that can be used on a trellis, including the ubiquitous but very practical and evergreen ivy, and wall shrubs such as pyracanthas.

Garage walls
Detached garages can dominate a small garden, so you probably need to soften the impact of the walls. Climbers are a natural choice, as are wall shrubs. But you could use a garage as an ideal backdrop for espalier or fan trained fruit trees.

Many evergreen shrubs will do an excellent masking job in front of a garage wall. Let hedging plants such

ABOVE: Griselinia littoralis *'Dixon's Cream'*.
LEFT: Griselinia littoralis.

as *Lonicera nitida* 'Baggesen's Gold' or a golden privet (such as *Ligustrum ovalifolium* 'Aureum') grow up untrimmed until the required height has been reached. Don't attempt to clip these like a formal hedge, but prune over-enthusiastic growth occasionally, and leave them with a natural shape.

LEFT: *For a fast-growing shrubby screen the climbing* Polygonum baldschuanicum *(syn.* Fallopia baldschuanica*) is difficult to beat.*

BELOW: Ligustrum ovalifolium *'Aureo-marginatum' (syn. 'Aureum') is a fast-growing hedging plant, much more attractive than the form with plain green leaves.*

Arundo donax
Grass. Forms tall, almost bamboo-like clump, with drooping blue-green leaves. There is also a variegated form *2.4 × 1.2m (8 × 4ft)*.

Buxus
Be careful not to choose a dwarf form if you want a taller screen. This is a classic shrub to clip to shape, and is much used for topiary as well as hedges. You could clip your screen to shape.

Griselinia littoralis
See *No fuss, low maintenance plants.*

Ilex
See *Everbright evergreens.*

Ligustrum ovalifolium 'Aureum'
See *Colour themes.*

Lonicera nitida 'Baggesen's Gold'
See *Colour themes.*

Miscanthus sacchariflorus
A large grass. Narrow, arching leaves, forming a dense clump *2.4 × 1m (8 × 3ft)*.

Polygonum baldschuanicum
Now more correctly *Fallopia baldschuanica*. Deciduous climbing shrub. A vigorous climber, but instead of using it as a screen up a trellis, try letting it grow over the eyesore itself, if it is an old shed, for example. Within a few years it will almost cover it. Profusion of small white or pale pink flowers in conspicuous sprays from mid summer to early autumn. Height and spread is usually dictated by its support.

PERMANENT PLANTS FOR CONTAINERS

The choices and permutations for summer bedding plants to use in containers are almost endless. Every year there are new varieties of seed-raised plants, and growers re-introduce some of the old and neglected tender perennials to keep up the supply of novelties.

On this page you will find ideas for permanent plants to try – those that will form part of the framework of the garden, summer and winter. Use them alongside, and not instead of, seasonal flowers. You might even be able to plant spring bulbs and summer annuals around the base of some of the shrubs suggested.

Agapanthus
See *Colour themes.*

Camellia
See *Everbright evergreens.*

Ceratostigma willmottianum
See Autumn & Winter Foliage, Section Two.

Choisya ternata 'Sundance'
See *Colour themes.*

Clematis, large–flowered
Deciduous climbing shrub. Large flowers in a wide range of colours. Avoid the rampant species in a container.

Cotoneaster 'Hybridus Pendulus'
Deciduous shrub, grafted to form a small weeping tree. Small white flowers in early summer. Red berries in autumn *1.8 × 1m (6 × 3ft).*

Laburnum
Small deciduous tree. Produces long tassels of yellow pea–like flowers in late spring and early summer *2.4 × 1.6m (8 × 6ft).*

Laurus nobilis
Evergreen shrub. The popular kitchen herb, sweet bay. Sometimes attractively trained and clipped into a formal shape. About *1.8m (6ft).*

Mahonia 'Charity'
See *Everbright evergreens.*

Miscanthus sinensis 'Zebrinus'
Grass. Forms a dense clump of vertical stems that unfurl at the top into narrow, reflexed leaves, with distinctive yellow bands. Grows to an approximate height of *1.2m (4ft)* when contained in a large tub or half-barrel.

Rhododendron
Evergreen shrub (some azaleas are deciduous). There are many rhododendrons and azaleas

ABOVE: Choisya ternata *'Sundance',* an excellent garden plant and attractive in a large container.
TOP: *Agapanthus are excellent tub plants, but need winter protection in cold areas. This variety is 'Delft'.*

RIGHT: Clematis *'Nelly Moser' (top) and 'Lasurstern'.*

(botanically types of rhododendron) dwarf enough to be grown in a container. An ericaceous compost is essential for good results. Colour and size depend on variety.

Rosmarinus officinalis
See *Everbright evergreens.*

Salix caprea 'Pendula'
Deciduous weeping tree. Also known as *Salix* 'Kilmarnock'. Small, umbrella-shaped tree with stiffly pendulous branches. Attractive catkins in spring.

Taxus baccata
Conifer. The popular yew, but choose a golden form such as 'Aurea'. This makes an irregular cone in outline. If you prefer a slimmer, more pencil-shaped profile, try *T. b.* 'Fastigiata Aurea'.

Viburnum tinus
See *Everbright evergreens.*

Yucca
See *Everbright evergreens.*

LEFT:
Rhododendron *'Loder's White' in a clay pot decorated with masonry paint.*

HOW TO PLANT A CLEMATIS BARREL

A clematis barrel can look really stunning when well established. You can choose several varieties to flower at the same time, or different ones that will flower at different times and so extend the period of interest, but bear in mind that this could make pruning more difficult.

1 Fill a half barrel or other large container with a loam-based compost. You need a large, deep container and heavy potting mixture which will support the canes as well as the plants.

2 Plant about three to four clematis in a barrel of this size. Angle the root-ball so that the plants point slightly inwards.

3 Secure the canes at the top. Tie them with string or use a proprietary plastic cane holder. Don't worry if the growth reaches the tops of the canes, it will just tumble down again and make the planting look even more dense.

ATTRACTING WILDLIFE

You don't have to turn your garden into something that resembles a meadow – some might say overgrown and weedy garden – to attract wildlife.

Lots of shrubs, border and rock plants, and annuals and biennials will attract wildlife of many kinds, from birds, bees and butterflies to wasps and weevils. Not all are welcome, of course, but for the few that you don't want to attract you will certainly gain many beautiful and beneficial animals that will help to control the pests.

You will, of course, need to create particular habitats if you want to encourage particular types of wildlife, such as a pond for aquatic creatures. And there is a lot to be said for leaving an area of grass long – perhaps where bulbs are naturalized if you want a horticultural justification – and if you let a few nettles grow behind the garden shed you will provide food plants for many kinds of caterpillars that will later grace your garden as butterflies.

Attracting wildlife in general often brings the bonus of more beneficial insects such as hoverflies and ladybirds, which will help to keep down pests such as aphids.

LEFT: Aucuba japonica *'Variegata'*.

ABOVE: Berberis thunbergii *'Atropurpurea Nana'*.

Shrubs

Aucuba (birds)
Berberis (birds, bees, butterflies)
Callicarpa (birds)
Ceanothus (bees)
Cistus (bees)
Cotoneaster (bees, birds)
Cytisus (bees)
Daphne (birds, bees)
Escallonia (bees)
Hebe (butterflies)
Hedera (bees, butterflies)
Hypericum (birds)
Ilex (birds)
Lavandula (bees, butterflies)
Leycesteria formosa (birds)
Ligustrum (bees, butterflies)
Lonicera periclymenum (butterflies)
Mahonia (birds)
Pernettya (birds)
Perovskia (bees)
Potentilla (bees)
Pyracantha (birds, bees)
Rhamnus frangula (bees, butterflies)
Ribes sanguineum (bees)
Skimmia (birds, bees)
Symphoricarpos (birds, bees)
Syringa (bees, butterflies)
Ulex (bees)
Viburnum (birds, bees)
Weigela (bees)

Border and rock plants
Achillea filipendulina (bees, butterflies)
Alyssum saxatile (butterflies)
Armeria maritima (bees, butterflies)
Aster novi-beglii (bees, butterflies)
Erigeron (bees, butterflies)
Nepeta (bees, butterflies)
Scabiosa caucasica (bees, butterflies)
Sedum spectabile (bees, butterflies)
Solidago (birds, bees, butterflies)
Thymus (bees, butterflies)

Annuals and biennials
Centaurea cyanus (bees, butterflies)
Dipsacus spp (birds)
Helianthus annuus (birds)
Hesperis matronalis (bees)
Limanthes douglasii (bees)
Lunaria annua (birds)
Scabious annual (bees, butterflies)

LEFT: Sedum *'Autumn Joy'*

BELOW: Solidago.

ABOVE: Alyssum saxatile.

OTHER WAYS TO ATTRACT WILDLIFE

A thick hedge attracts far more wildlife than a fence or wall. A prickly evergreen hedge like holly will provide good nest and roost sites for many birds.

An old log pile provides refuge for many beneficial insects and can make a nest site for small mammals.

the KITCHEN GARDEN

AMBITIOUS KITCHEN GARDENS ARE SELDOM achievable in a small space. Vegetables that are hungry for space such as potatoes and cabbages may lose out to flowers. But if you are content with smaller vegetables such as lettuces, carrots, beetroot, and dwarf beans, and can relegate tall climbing beans and expansive plants like globe artichokes to the mixed or herbaceous border, it is quite practical to grow a wide range of vegetables even where space is quite restricted.

Grow a whole range of vegetables, from lettuces to peas, in containers like windowboxes

ABOVE: *Raspberries are not an ideal crop for a small garden but they can be trained so that they don't take up too much space.*

TOP: *Fruit-growing is possible even on a roof or balcony garden . . . with a little imagination.*

OPPOSITE: *This picture shows an interesting way of providing supports for tall vegetables in a small kitchen garden.*

LEFT: *One of the upright-growing apple trees ideal for a small garden or limited space. This variety is 'Walz', planted in a bed of 'Surrey' ground cover roses.*

and growing bags. Even potatoes can be harvested from pots and growing bags and tomatoes of all types have been grown with great success in growing bags. This kind of small-scale vegetable gardening is demanding, and the yields always very modest for the effort involved, but if the idea of harvesting your own fresh vegetables just before you pop them into the pot appeals, you may find it worth the effort. It can certainly be fun.

If you have a reasonably sized garden – large enough to divide off a section for a kitchen garden – growing them in the ground is the most practical way to produce your vegetables, and much of the fruit.

Fruit trees and bushes are often ornamental and can be easily integrated into the flower garden. Trained fruit trees like espalier and fan apples look attractive even with bare branches in winter.

Herbs are much more easily accommodated than vegetables. Many are highly ornamental and lots of them make good container plants. Others look perfectly in place in a border. If you want to make a real feature of your herbs, make a herb garden a key part of your garden design.

ORNAMENTAL HERBS

Formal herb gardens look impressive, but can be difficult to accommodate in a small space.

However, as the illustrations below show, there are alternatives.

Bear in mind that though herb gardens are packed with interest in summer, in winter you will be left with just a few evergreen shrubs and a handful of herbs that retain their foliage and are tough enough to survive unprotected. Alternatively, incorporate your herbs in an overall garden design that carries interest through all the seasons. Here are some other ways to incorporate herbs in a small garden.

A collection in a container
A herb pot can hold half a dozen or more different herbs. Do not start to harvest until plants are growing strongly, then keep harvesting little and often to produce compact yet well-clothed plants.

Shrubby plants like bay and rosemary can be grown in tubs to decorate the patio or to display by the front or back door.

Windowbox herbs
Herbs can be grown in windowboxes and troughs provided you choose compact plants such as thymes and marjorams. Ornamental, variegated mints also look good.

Growing bags
Growing bags are not elegant, but they are useful for rampant plants like mints, which would otherwise make a take-over bid for the border.

In among the flowers
Many herbs are so decorative that they don't look amiss in beds and borders, and indeed some are planted more for their ornamental than culinary uses.

Among the herbs that look good with other border plants are chives, fennel, marjoram, and lemon balm.

ABOVE: *Have fun with your small herbs. They can be arranged informally in pots, or grouped together as in the small wheelbarrow.*

RIGHT: *An attractive herb collection can be grown in a small raised bed, but bear in mind that many of these plants will grow much larger.*

HOW TO MAKE A HERB WHEEL

If you have an old cartwheel, just paint or varnish that and set it into the ground ready to plant. Few of us have access to cartwheels, however, but an acceptable second best can be made from bricks. Adjust the size of the wheel to suit your garden. Bricks are a convenient way to make the 'spokes', but you could use dwarf dividing 'hedges' of hyssop or thyme. Place an attractive terracotta pot in the centre as the hub of the wheel, and plant with herbs, or place an upright rosemary in the centre. A rosemary may become too large after a few years, but either keep it clipped to shape and size or replace it every second or third year.

1 Mark a circle about 1.5–1.8m (5–6ft) across, using a line fixed to a peg to ensure an even shape. If it helps, use a wine bottle filled with dry sand instead of a stick to mark out the perimeter. Excavate the ground to a depth of about 15cm (6in).

2 Place the bricks on end, or at an angle, around the edge. If you place them at a 45 degree angle it will create a dog-tooth effect; bricks placed on end will look more formal. Either lay them loose in compacted earth, or bed them on mortar.

3 Lay rows of brick, cross-fashion, as shown. If the diameter does not allow for them to be laid without gaps in the centre, stand an ornament or pot in the middle if you are not planting directly into the soil in that position.

4 Top up the areas between the spokes with good garden or potting soil.

5 Plant up each section, using plants that will balance each other in size of growth if possible. You could, for instance, grow a collection of different thymes.

6 For a smart finish, carefully cover the soil with fine gravel.

FRUIT IN A SMALL SPACE

The most satisfactory way to grow tree fruits such as apples and pears in a small garden or a confined space is trained as a cordon, fan or espalier against a wall or fence. Even some bush fruits such as gooseberries can be trained as cordons or double cordons against a fence.

ABOVE: *Wall-trained fruit trees take up relatively little space.*
RIGHT: *If you want apples in a small garden it is best to use one of the columnar varieties or to grow an ordinary variety on a trained system like this espalier 'Lord Lambourne'.*

Blackberries and hybrid berries can be trained against a fence or over an arch, but keep the growth contained and avoid allowing thorny shoots to overhang pathways.

It is even possible to grow apples in pots on the patio, but with the new flagpole-type varieties available that grow in a narrow column, you may prefer to plant these where space is limited. They will require much less watering and attention than ordinary varieties on dwarfing rootstocks in pots.

The initial training of espaliers, fans and cordons demands patience and skill. Unless you particularly like the challenge and can wait for two or three years longer, it is best to buy a ready-trained tree.

BUYING FRUIT TREES

Whether a fruit tree such as an apple, peach or cherry is suitable for a small garden depends not so much on the variety of the fruit but on the rootstock. This has a profound affect on the size of the tree (as well as how soon it starts to fruit). Always check the root-stock before you buy, and if in doubt ask whether it is suitably dwarfing for a small garden.

TRAINED FRUIT TREES

Trained trees look attractive and produce a heavy crop from a restricted space. But they require regular and methodical training, sometimes twice a year. If in doubt about how to prune a particular trained fruit, consult an encyclopedia or fruit book.

Espaliers are more ornamental than cordons (some shrubs, such as pyracanthas, are occasionally trained as espaliers using the same methods).

Cordons are usually trained at an angle of about 45 degrees, secured to support canes and wires fixed to stout posts or to a fence. Many plants can be planted in a small space, and soft fruits such as gooseberries and red and white currants can be trained in this way, saving the space taken up by a bush form.

Fans can be free-standing, tied to wires supported by posts, but they are usually planted against a wall or fence. In time a fan can be trained to cover a large area, such as a garage wall.

Step-overs are single-tiered espaliers, used as a fruiting edging, perhaps within the kitchen garden.

Potted fruit

Apples can be grown in pots provided you choose a very dwarfing rootstock. The same applies to peaches. You can experiment with other bush and tree fruits, but bear in mind that this is second best to growing them in the ground.

Flagpole apples

You can buy a range of apple trees that rarely produce long sideshoots, but instead grow upright and produce most fruiting spurs along the main vertical stem. These take up little space and won't cast a heavy shadow, so they are ideal for growing in a flower bed. The blossom is pretty in spring, and the ripening fruits are ornamental later in the year.

Rhubarb

Rhubarb is ornamental enough to be grown in the flower border. You can even grow it in a large pot as a foliage plant for the patio, though this is not the best way to achieve a heavy crop.

ABOVE: *This rhubarb chard is growing in a flower bed.*

Strawberries

If you don't have much space for fruit, at least try growing strawberries. A strawberry barrel or a tower container will hold a lot of strawberries and provided you keep the container well watered it will be laden with fruit . . . which won't

ABOVE: *There is always space for a few strawberries if you grow them in a container like this.*

become splashed with mud if the weather is wet or awkward to pick. Also the fruit will be more difficult for slugs to reach.

FINDING ROOM FOR VEGETABLES

If you are really restricted for space, and the lure of fresh home-grown vegetables is strong, you can grow them in containers. Wherever possible, however, it is better to grow them in the ground.

If you simply don't have space for a vegetable plot, quite a lot of vegetables can be grown in beds and borders intermixed with ornamental plants.

The 'vegetable plot' should never be tucked away in a dull, sunless part of the garden. Most vegetables need good light and plenty of moisture to do well. Dry ground shaded by hedges and walls seldom produces succulent vegetables.

Among the flowers

It is quite possible to incorporate vegetables as part of a formal bedding scheme – red or purple rhubarb chard leaves contrast well with grey foliaged bedding plants, carrot foliage doesn't look unattractive as a foil for bright summer bedding plants, and even a red or green leaved cut-and-come-again (oak leaf) lettuce such as 'Salad Bowl' will make a pretty edging for a bed of summer bedding. Unfortunately the problem comes at harvest time. When gaps soon become rather conspicuous in a formal bedding scheme.

ABOVE: *This raised vegetable bed in a flower garden makes an interesting feature as well as a productive area.*

LEFT: *Ornamental kales are usually grown for their decorative effect, but they are edible if you get tired of looking at them! This variety is 'Coral Queen'.*

Vegetables are more acceptable as gap fillers in the herbaceous or mixed border. They fill the space admirably, and after harvesting the border is left no less attractive than it was originally. Suitable candidates are lettuces, radishes, beetroot, asparagus peas, carrots, leaf beet, and spinach, but much depends on the size of the space and your imagination.

Ornamental potagers

The term potager comes from *jardin potager*, simply being French for kitchen garden. But the term has come to refer primarily to a kitchen garden – usually with both fruit and vegetables – laid out ornamentally, perhaps with beds edged with low hedges like a parterre. Treated like this, your kitchen garden can become a prominent design element in the small garden.

Growing bags

Growing bags are excellent for vegetables if all you have is a balcony or patio on which to grow them. It is quite feasible to grow lettuces, spinach, radishes, cucumbers, tomatoes, turnips, even self-blanching celery and potatoes, in growing bags.

Clearly, you won't keep the family fed with potatoes from a couple of growing bags, and the economics don't make much sense. But it is worth planting an early variety (you can always move the bag into a protected area if frost threatens) so that you can enjoy those first few new potatoes straight from the garden . . . or patio . . . or balcony.

ABOVE: *These are 'Totem' tomatoes growing in a 25cm (10in) pot.*

BELOW: *You can even grow tomatoes in a hanging basket.*

Dwarf peas, another unlikely-sounding crop, can also be grown successfully in a growing bag.

Troughs, tubs and pots

Tomatoes are one of the most successful crops for a growing bag, and they are equally successful in pots provided you choose a suitable compact variety.

Courgettes and cucumbers are also a practical choice for a tub or large pot. Potatoes can be grown in a large pot for a bit of fun, but you might be better planting an aubergine or pepper in it.

Windowboxes and baskets

The only vegetable likely to do well in a hanging basket is the tomato, but you must choose a trailing or drooping variety, and maintain excellent control over both watering and feeding.

Windowboxes offer more scope, and apart from tomatoes (again, a dwarf or trailing variety is essential), stump-rooted carrots, radishes, onions, and lettuces are among the crops that do well.

Rather than grow a hearting lettuce, which leaves a gap as the whole head is harvested at once, try a non-hearting, cut-and-come-again variety that you can harvest in stages.

BEST PLANTS
for your
GARDEN

INTRODUCTION

A cottage-style border showing a blend of perennials and small shrubs including alliums, poppies, astrantia, elaeagnus, cistus and hostas.

For all gardeners, making the right selection of plants is the single most important ingredient for success in gardening. To do this, you need to be informed on several different levels: you need to be able to identify the overall look you are hoping to achieve and the kind of garden you want to create, and you also need to understand the conditions that determine which plants will grow successfully. One of the most important lessons for any novice gardener to grasp is that you cannot grow exactly what you want wherever you please.

Although you always want to try to manage nature, or at least influence it as much as you dare, the most successful gardeners are those who look at how plants grow in their natural habitat, and apply this to their own garden, working with nature wherever possible. The greater understanding you have of where plants grow best, and the more you understand their needs, the easier it becomes to grow them. The section on page 152 explains these requirements in more detail.

PLANNING YOUR GARDEN

When planning a garden you must have some understanding of what your soil is like – whether it is acid or alkaline, heavy clay or light sand – and whether the climate is hot or cool, wet or dry. Immense strides have been made in plant breeding, and recent innovations have allowed gardeners far greater freedom of choice than they had previously now that in many instances plants are bred to be both beautiful and tough. Even so, nature still plays by far the most important role, and a plant that naturally thrives in a damp or wet habitat will not flourish in hot dry sun as well. Its entire organism has evolved over thousands of years to cope with the particular conditions in which it originated, and usually it is only in similar conditions that it will continue to thrive.

Fortunately, some plants do withstand quite a wide range of climatic variations and are particularly well adapted, thriving surprisingly well in conditions very far removed from those of their natural habitat. The sensible gardener tries to pay attention to these needs, and to select his or her plants from within the range of those that are broadly suitable.

Whether planning an entire garden or just designing a border, you will probably want to include a range of different types to give height and variety to your plan. Try to remember that foliage is as important as flowers in the overall structure and shape of the garden, and make sure you pick a framework of plants with good shape or attractive foliage, on which the more ephemeral elements of the design such as perennials and annuals can be hung.

Flowers, while eye-catching, are not always the major element in the success of any garden design. It is also the way in which the garden is laid out and constructed: the organization of its hard surfaces including terraces and paths; any hedges and screens; the creation of a vertical element, in the form of climbing plants, shrubs and trees. These also give shelter and create pockets of dry shade which a further range of plants will enjoy. A selection of climbers, wall shrubs and hedges is listed in chapter 7. Nature often tends to provide these variations unaided, but if they do not exist in your garden, you will have to make your own varied but viable micro-climate, thereby increasing the range you can grow, and also your own enjoyment.

Not all gardens have a naturally damp area which could support moisture-loving plants, but a boggy patch or even a pond is easy to make and certainly gives you the opportunity to include these attractive plants.

Another important element when planning a garden is winter interest. Try to ensure you have a good number of evergreen shrubs or trees which will provide a structure for the garden during the winter months. Without them, the garden can look impossibly bleak and dull, when the foliage of most herbaceous perennials has disappeared, leaving you with bare stems and branches. In a new garden, ground cover can be an important element in the plan to help prevent the bare soil becoming engulfed in weeds. You can opt either for plants that naturally spread to cover the soil, or for those shrubs and perennials that have a spreading habit, thereby effectively suppressing weeds by their shady canopy. Chapter 8 suggests a range of plants that are suitable for ground cover.

CULTIVATION

Whatever plants you choose, you need to ensure that you look after them correctly. This means not only do you plant them where they are most likely to thrive, but you also attend to any special requirements, in terms of watering, feeding and pruning.

Most plants look far better when planted in largish groups rather than dotted about singly, and propagation is one of the easiest and cheapest ways to increase your stock of plants. When purchasing your plants initially, it is a good idea to pick plants that can be propagated easily and that are fairly fast to establish, so that building up your stock of plants and also furnishing the bare spaces in your garden are achieved relatively quickly.

Although many plants are more or less pest- and disease-free, others are singularly prone to various complaints and to attacks by a particular kind of insect. Hostas, for example, are notoriously easy prey to slugs, while tender young shoots, leaves and buds of many plants will quickly become infested with aphids in summer. You can do a lot to control these problems if you are forewarned when you select your plants. Hostas, for example, can be surrounded with a layer of grit, which deters slugs and snails, or, if you are not averse to chemical methods, you can use slug pellets. Particular problems for individual plants are indicated in each entry.

Like most humans, plants respond best to regular, systematic sensible care, and very rarely to the feast or famine principle of gardening. Try not to neglect your plants for a long period of time and then make up for it in one mammoth session of attention, whether it is feeding, watering, pruning or whatever. It is far better to keep a watchful eye on your plants, noting any problems as they arise, and nipping them in the bud, if you will forgive the expression, before they become more serious. Even the vexed problem of pruning is better if tackled after flowering on a week-by-week basis, rather than in one massive hit in late autumn or early spring.

HOW TO USE THIS SECTION

This section is divided into ten chapters which focus on some of the common conditions and basic needs of modern gardeners, with the idea that once you have identitifed these, you can then find some suitable plants for your purpose.

The plants we have selected in this section have been chosen on the basis of good overall performance: they are all reasonably easy to grow and have more than one good feature. Within the specific categories of need or condition identified, you will find a cross-section of the following types: trees, shrubs, herbaceous perennials, and climbers – the plants which usually make up the core planting of any garden, and bulbs, tuberous plants and roses which everyone will want to grow have their own sections. Annuals, which can be grown from seed in one season, and therefore are not a permanent feature in the garden, get only relatively minor coverage here.

At the end of each chapter there is a cross reference list which itemises other plants that might be grown. Most plants will tolerate differing soil types and the chart on page 153 shows you plants that can be chosen if you need to consider more than one feature.

WHAT PLANTS NEED

Knowledge of what a plant requires in terms of light, water, temperature, soil type and nutrients is essential for good gardening. In addition, you also need to identify which of these requirements your garden can naturally provide, and how you can change the micro-environment within your garden if the conditions are not suitable for the plants you aspire (and in many instances perspire) to grow. For instance, in a dark situation, thinning existing plants will allow in more light, and in a damp garden, improving the soil drainage will encourage plants which prefer drier conditions. Alternatively, you may prefer to use your garden's natural dampness and enjoy the range of moisture-loving plants listed in chapter 4.

The plants you may wish to grow originate from many different areas of the world, where very different growing conditions exist. In their natural environment, some will grow in dense shade on the forest floor while others are exposed to intense bright sunlight for long periods of time. This wide diversity of natural habitat explains why the many different ornamental plants we grow require different conditions. The ability to adapt to unfamiliar conditions is a major reason for the popularity of many common plants. Of course, some plants are much more adaptable than others; classic examples are the forsythia, which seems to be flowering everywhere in the spring, and *Buddleja davidii*, which has been so successful at colonizing areas that many people now regard it as a weed.

Salvias, lilies, sambucus and daisies emphasized by the white of
Geranium clarkei 'Kashmir White' make a quiet corner in a mixed border.

Plants pushing out onto gravel paths create a charming informality. Here Lavandula stoechas *and* Lychnis coronaria *catch the evening sun.*

LIGHT

Light is essential to all plants, as it provides the energy needed by the plant to manufacture food during daylight hours. Other activities within the plant are also influenced by light; for instance, the response to the hours of daylight within the 24-hour cycle will determine the time of year that flowers are produced. This response to the day-length is called photoperiodism, and explains why plants flower at specific times of the year, regardless of the prevailing weather conditions. As day-length appears to be a plant's main method of knowing which season is which, it is a factor which gardeners would love to be able to tamper with, but this can only realistically be done at great expense in a fully controlled environment, as in the production of pot plants such as poinsettias for Christmas.

The amount of light is also the main stimulus for autumn leaf fall in deciduous trees and shrubs, the trigger which starts this response being the shortening days of autumn. The various colour changes within the leaf are brought about by the chemical changes which occur when plant nutrients are drawn out of the leaf back into the stem. (See chapter 9 for autumn and winter foliage plants.) As a gardener you are able to influence (to some extent) the light intensity your plants receive by providing shade to reduce light levels. Alternatively, to raise light levels in a darkened corner, you could use mirrors and create light-reflective surfaces such as white gravel and paving . However, there is a selection of plants in chapter 5 that enjoy a shady situation, while plants that love sunny conditions are listed in chapter 6.

Generally speaking, most plants consist of roots, stems, leaves, flowers and usually fruits, many of which contain seeds. None of these parts functions in isolation. There is a close relationship between the individual parts of the plant and the plant's overall growth rate. Some plants are also scented and these are a particular favourite with gardeners. A selection of these is listed in chapter 10.

THE SOIL

Although it is not easy to describe what soil actually is, we know that plants grow better when planted in the right type of soil. A basic understanding can help to create a good root environment for the plants you wish to grow. Soil is required by the gardener to have certain properties: the ability to hold moisture and air so that the plant's roots are not deprived of oxygen; the correct balance of nutrients; and the appropriate level of lime or acidity.

What makes growing plants more of a challenge is that many garden soils play host to a number of unwanted 'additives' such as weed seeds, stones (and occasionally builder's debris), pests and diseases. Heavy, clay soils are also difficult to work with and choosing plants that thrive in this situation is essential. Chapter 3 suggests a range of plants for clay soils.

Acidity and alkalinity are measured on a scale of pH which ranges from 0 to 14, with 0 being the most acid and 14 being the most alkaline. The influence of pH affects the solubility of minerals and hence their availability to plants. Acid conditions tend to encourage phosphorus deficiency and sometimes contain excess manganese and aluminium, while alkaline conditions can lead to a lack of manganese, boron, and phosphorus. Soil pH can also influence the number and type of beneficial soil-borne organisms, as well as the incidence of pests and diseases. For example, worms dislike a low pH, but leatherjackets and wireworms are more commonly found in acid conditions. What is the optimum pH? Again, the pH range for good plant growth varies depending upon the preference of the individual plants. Some plants are more sensitive than others and have quite specific requirements: lime-loving plants that prefer chalky soil are known as calcicoles, and lime-haters that like an acid soil are called calcifuges. These plants are listed in chapter 1 for acid soils and chapter 2 for chalky soils.

Many gardeners wish to grow the widest range of plants possible and the temptation is to try to manipulate the pH of the soil. Although this may be possible, to lower the soil pH is difficult, costly, and usually only a short-term measure, whereas raising soil pH is relatively easy and, if done correctly, can have beneficial effects on a long-term basis. If you really cannot resist the temptation to grow lime-hating plants and your soil has a pH reading of 6.0 or over, then by far the best option is to grow them in containers. That way you can exercise complete control over the pH of the compost.

The question of what plants you can grow in your garden is now, therefore, a matter of turning to the appropriate chapter for your particular requirements.

Best Plants for a Variety of Conditions

The following selection of plants has been chosen from those featured in this section and represents the trees, shrubs, climbers and herbaceous perennials which have a range of useful features; they are, therefore, good all-rounders.

	Acid soil	Chalk soil	Clay soil	Moisture-loving	Shade	Dry/Sunny	Climbers/Hedges	Ground cover	Winter interest	Scent	Growth rate	Season of interest	Classification	Evergreen
Acanthus spinosus		•	•							•	F	2	HP	
Acer palmatum	•			•					•		S	3	T	
Actinidia kolomikta	•						•			•	M	2-3	C	
Agapanthus		•				•			•		M	2-3	HP	
Amelanchier			•						•		S	1-3	S	
Arbutus	•				•	•					M	1&3-4	T	
Aucuba	•	•		•							M	2-3	S	•
Berberis			•	•	•						M	2-3	S	•
Bergenia	•							•			S	1	HP	•
Buxus sempervirens		•	•			•	•				S	1-4	S	•
Calluna	•			•		•	•				S	2-4	S	•
Camellia	•			•		•					S	1-2	S	•
Campsis		•		•	•						F	2-3	C	
Cercidiphyllum	•				•		•	•			M	3	T	
Cercis		•	•	•	•						M	1-3	S	
Crataegus	•	•	•		•						F	2-3	T	
Eccremocarpus		•		•	•						F	2-3	C	•
Epimedium	•		•	•		•	•				M	2-3	HP	•
Escallonia	•	•	•	•	•						F	2-3	S	•
Festuca	•			•	•			•			M	1-4	HP	•
Ficus carica		•		•	•	•					S	2-3	S	
Filipendula		•	•	•							M	2-3	HP	
Garrya		•		•	•	•					M	1	S	•
Gaultheria	•			•	•		•				S	2-4	S	•
Gleditsia	•	•	•		•						M	2-3	T	
Hamamelis	•				•	•	•				M	1&3	S	
Hosta		•	•	•			•		•		F	2-3	HP	
Ilex		•		•		•					S	2-4	T	•
Imperata	•		•	•			•	•			M	3-4	HP	
Iris pseudacorus		•	•	•							M	1-2	HP	
Kalmia latifolia	•			•		•					M	1-2	S	•
Laburnum		•	•			•			•		M	2-3	T	
Lathyrus		•	•				•			•	F	2-3	CHP	
Lavandula		•			•	•	•	•	•		M	2	S	•
Lilium	•				•				•		F	1-2	HP	
Mahonia		•		•	•	•	•	•	•	•	M	3-4	S	•
Osmunda	•	•	•					•			M	3	HP	
Parrotia	•				•			•			S	1&3	T	
Parthenocissus		•	•		•		•	•			F	2-3	C	
Pieris	•			•		•					M	1-2	S	•
Prunus	•					•					M	1&3	T	
Pyracantha		•		•	•		•	•			M	2-3	S	•
Rhus hirta		•			•	•					M	3	S	
Rosa rugosa		•		•		•					F	2&3	S	
Rosmarinus		•			•			•			M	2	S	•
Salvia officinalis		•			•		•	•			M	2-3	S	
Senecio 'Sunshine'	•	•		•	•		•				M	2-3	S	•
Stachys	•	•			•		•	•			M	2	HP	
Stewartia	•			•	•				•		M	2	S	
Taxus		•			•		•				M	3-4	T	•
Viburnum		•	•	•		•	•	•	•	•	M	1&3-4	S	•
Vitis		•	•				•	•			F	3-4	C	
Wisteria		•	•				•	•		•	F	2-3	C	
Zenobia	•				•				•		S	2-3	S	

KEY

Growth rate
S – Slow
M – Medium
F – Fast

Season of interest
1 – Spring
2 – Summer
3 – Autumn
4 – Winter

Classification
T – Tree
S – Shrub
HP – Herbaceous Perennial
C – Climber
CHP – Climbing Hardy Perennial

Evergreen
• – Some varieties are evergreen

PLANTS
for ACID SOILS

For gardens, borders and containers with an acid soil, here is a
selection of the many excellent garden plants that prefer this
condition, of which camellias and rhododendrons are perhaps the best
known. Acid soil occurs frequently in areas of high rainfall but can
also be found under conifers where their needles drop.

ABOVE: Kalmia latifolia, *a magnificent rhododendron-like shrub*
which can only be grown successfully in acid soil.

OPPOSITE: *A mixed heather border. Heathers are ideal for planting in*
acid soil and require little upkeep once established.

ABOVE: *A rich mixture of magnolias and rhododendrons – two of the best candidates for acid soil – makes an enticing late spring display. Some magnolias, however, will grow satisfactorily in alkaline conditions.*

Plants that prefer to grow in an acid soil are often wrongly referred to as ericaceous plants, because many acid-loving plants belong to the family, *ericaceae*, including heathers (*erica*), arbutus, kalmia, pieris and, of course, rhododendrons. It is worth remembering that many other attractive plants such as camellia, eucryphia, hamamelis and some magnolias are also acid-loving but are not of the family *ericaceae*. The correct term for plants which prefer acid soil is calcifuges.

Some excellent garden plants grow only in acid soil, so if your garden has this condition, you can look forward to growing some real treasures. Acid-loving plants are often associated with the tendency to be spring flowering as are camellias and hamamelis, but many of these plants, for example fothergilla and stewartia, are renowned for their autumn foliage colour, and if you can grow a range of heathers it is possible to have plants in flower practically all year round.

You can check on the pH of your soil to determine its acidity by using a home soil testing kit. It is a matter of a few minutes to discover whether or not your soil is suitable. As a rough guide, if your soil measures more than 6.5 on the pH scale it is unsuitable for growing acid-lovers. Of course, even if this is the case, you can always grow the plants you want in containers where you have complete control over the growing medium.

In nature, the most acid soils are usually found on heather moorland, or in coniferous forests. Remember, soil type is not always directly linked to soil pH. Acid soils can be free-draining and sandy, or heavy and sticky, or even organic with a high peat content. Clay soils may be acid or alkaline, depending on their make-up. Peat-based soils are almost always acid. Some soils, even if originally alkaline, can gradually become more acid as a result of the lime being washed out of the upper layers, close to the soil surface. This is due to the fact that rainwater is slightly acidic, and the lime in the soil dissolves and is washed (leached) down through the soil. Soils in high rainfall areas are more likely to be acid than alkaline and many of the gardens famous for their rhododendrons are found in the west of the country.

Plants which grow naturally in acid soils, marked pH in the text, will usually struggle when grown in anything else. This is because of the different availability of plant nutrients at lower pH levels as plants vary in their ability to absorb these nutrients. Most acid-loving plants are unable to take up enough iron from the soil if the pH is too high. Initially, this shows as a yellowing (chlorosis) between the leaf veins, and in many cases is followed by the death of the plant unless additional iron is supplied.

LEFT: *Heathers are ideal subjects for acid soils, and when mixed together in a large bed, provide a wonderful tapestry of colour and shape. The best impact is gained when, as here, several different cultivars are combined in one area of the garden.*

Abies koreana

Korean fir
HEIGHT: 10ft (3m) • Hardy
FLOWERING SEASON: None

Commonly known as the Korean fir, this conifer is a small, slow-growing tree, with a broad-based, conical shape, the base of the tree being as wide as its overall height. Each leaf or 'needle' is an attractive dark green above with a silvery white underside. It produces striking, violet-purple cones 2-3in (5-7.5cm) long, even on young plants. Propagation is by seed, sown into pots and placed outdoors in February. Prone to attack by the adelgid, which distorts young growths.

Acer rubrum

Red maple
HEIGHT: 50ft (15m) • Hardy
FLOWERING SEASON: Spring

The red maple forms a large round-headed deciduous tree with dark green leaves which turn bright red in the autumn. There are tiny red flowers which appear on the branches in the spring but these are insignificant. Like all maples the best autumn colour is found when the tree is grown on acid soil but it is easy to cultivate and flourishes in any ordinary well-tilled soil.

Andromeda polifolia 'Compacta'

HEIGHT: 6-9in (15-23cm) • Hardy • pH
FLOWERING SEASON: Late summer/early autumn

This charming dwarf evergreen shrub has slender stems covered in narrow, bluish-green leaves each with a white underside. The soft pink flowers are produced in clusters on the tips of the shoots. It belongs to the heather family and grows wild in peat bogs in northern Europe. It does not flourish when there is lime in the soil. Propagate by semi-ripe cuttings taken in late summer. The plant may suffer from vine weevil grubs, which eat the roots and cause wilting and collapse if they attack in large numbers.

Arbutus × andrachnoides

HEIGHT: 50ft (15m) • Hardy
FLOWERING SEASON: Late autumn/early spring

A hybrid between *A. andrachos* and *A. unedo*, the Killarney strawberry tree, this attractive, slow-growing, broad-leafed evergreen forms an open spreading tree with striking orange-red bark which peels and flakes from the trunk and older branches to reveal the new bark beneath. The white, urn-shaped flowers, produced in large upright spikes in late autumn/early spring appear as the orange-red fruits of the previous year ripen. In a severe winter some of the leaves and shoots may be damaged. Propagation is by semi-ripe cuttings taken in late summer.

Arctostaphylos uva-ursi

Bearberry
HEIGHT: 4in (10cm) • Hardy • pH
FLOWERING SEASON: Summer

This is a low evergreen shrub with a spreading habit and small, oval, bright green leaves, that is ideal as a ground-cover plant. The small heather-like flowers are white flushed pink, followed by a display of small scarlet berries in autumn and winter. It likes acid soil and shelter from cold winds. A particularly interesting form is *A. u.* 'Point Reyes', which has pale pink flowers against a backdrop of grey-green leaves. Propagation is by semi-ripe cuttings with a heel taken in August and inserted into a cold frame.

Aristolochia durior

Birthwort/Dutchman's pipe
HEIGHT: 27ft (9m) • Not fully hardy
FLOWERING SEASON: Summer

A vigorous climber, its unusual tubular flowers are yellowish-green with a brownish-purple interior, they are 1.5-2in (3-5cm) long with the bottom half bent upwards to resemble a smoker's pipe, hence the common name Dutchman's pipe. The large, dull green leaves are heart-shaped and up to 12in (30cm) in length, borne on thin, woody twining stems. It provides a good wall covering when given support. Propagation is by softwood tip cuttings taken in July. Prune by thinning shoots in March.

Begonia × carrierei

Begonia
HEIGHT: 9in (23cm) • Half-hardy
FLOWERING SEASON: Summer/autumn

These plants, with their colourful leaves and attractive flowers, are popular for containers or summer bedding schemes. They are available with either green or bronze leaves, and produce masses of red, pink or white flowers from June until the first frosts. There are several mixed colour selections, including 'New Generation', which has shades of salmon, rose, pink, scarlet and white. Propagation is by seed sown in spring, or by softwood tip cuttings taken in summer.

Berberidopsis corallina

Coral plant
HEIGHT: 14ft (4.5m) • Moderately hardy
FLOWERING SEASON: Late summer

A beautiful evergreen climber with woody, twining stems, the heart-shaped, dark green leaves have a thick leathery texture, and a single row of spine-like teeth along the margin. The common name, coral plant, refers to the small, round, deep red flowers on thin red stalks that hang in bunches. This plant grows best in a shaded slightly sheltered situation with a moist soil. Propagation is by seed sown indoors in spring or semi-ripe stem cuttings taken in late summer.

Calluna vulgaris 'J H Hamilton'

Ling/Scottish heather
HEIGHT: 2ft (60cm) • Hardy • pH
FLOWERING SEASON: Midsummer/late autumn

A low-growing evergreen, bushy shrub with small, hairy leaves carried on thin, woody stems. The leaves may vary in colour from mid green or grey to yellow, orange or a bright reddish-brown, and many varieties, such as *C. v.* 'Sunrise', display their most attractive colours through the winter. The small bell-like flowers range from white to dark mauve, and are carried in spikes on the tips of shoots and branches. Propagate by cuttings taken in autumn after flowering.

Camellia japonica 'R L Wheeler'

Camellia
HEIGHT: 12ft (4m) • Moderately hardy • pH
FLOWERING SEASON: Spring

C. japonica, the common camellia, can grow as large as 30ft (10m) although it may take some years to attain this height. *C.j.* 'R L Wheeler' is one of the most popular cultivars with a robust upright growth habit and large dark-green leaves. The flowers are rose-pink, semi-double with striking circles of gold stamens. Camellias can be grown successfully in tubs where there is limited space in a small garden and they may require some shelter in very cold weather. Prune in the spring after flowering if they outgrow their space.

Camellia × williamsii 'Donation'

Camellia
HEIGHT: 10ft (3m) • Moderately hardy • pH
FLOWERING SEASON: Late winter/late spring

These shrubs or small trees are attractive, easy to grow, and valued highly for their spectacular flowers and glossy foliage. The flowers come in a wide range of shades of white, pink or red, and occasionally a combination of two or more colours in early spring. The flowers may be single, semi-double or double depending upon the cultivar. Camellias grow well in a sheltered situation. Propagation is by semi-ripe cuttings taken in early autumn.

Cassiope 'Muirhead'

HEIGHT: 12in (30cm) • Hardy • pH
FLOWERING SEASON: Spring

These dwarf evergreen shrubs have a low compact or spreading habit, and each shoot is covered in densely overlapping, scale-like dark green leaves. The small bell-like flowers, which vary from white to white-tinged red, hang singly or in pairs on the stems and branches. They need a damp sheltered site with some shade in order to establish and grow well and they do not like lime in the soil. The cultivar 'Edinburgh' is possibly the easiest to grow. Propagation is layering or semi-ripe cuttings taken in late summer or early autumn.

Cercidiphyllum japonicum

Katsura tree
HEIGHT: 25ft (8m) • Hardy
FLOWERING SEASON: Spring

This graceful tree is grown for the colour
and beauty of its unusual round or heart-
shaped leaves which are red as they unfold
and change to mid green within a few days.
The main display comes in autumn when
the leaves turn pale yellow before becoming
a soft pink. In addition, the plants give off an
aroma of 'candy floss' as these colour changes
occur. The young shoots may be damaged by
late frosts. Propagation is by seed sown in a
cold frame during the autumn and winter.

Clethra arborea

Lily-of-the-valley tree of Madeira
HEIGHT: 25ft (8m) • Half-hardy
FLOWERING SEASON: Mid-late summer

This handsome tree has a dense bushy habit,
and its oval, evergreen leaves are a rich green
with a toothed margin. The long clusters of
white, bell-shaped flowers are very fragrant
and look very similar to the blooms of lily-
of-the-valley. To produce its best display,
clethra should be grown in a moist peaty soil
in semi-shade. It also produces good autumn
colour. Propagation is by softwood cuttings
taken in summer or by freshly collected seed
sown in autumn.

Cornus canadensis

Creeping dogwood
HEIGHT: 6in (15cm) • Hardy • pH
FLOWERING SEASON: Summer

Strictly speaking, this low spreading plant is
not a shrub, as the shoots die down each
winter and are replaced by fresh shoots the
following spring. The mid green leaves are
carried in clusters at the tips of the thin
green stems. An ideal ground-cover plant, it
forms a carpet of small starry white flowers
followed by tight clusters of vivid red fruits
in the autumn. Propagation is by division of
established plants in winter. Late spring frosts
may damage the leaves.

Cornus kousa var. *chinensis*

Dogwood
HEIGHT: 10ft (3m) • Hardy
FLOWERING SEASON: Summer

This is a graceful shrubby plant, the dull
green, oval leaves have a pronounced wavy
margin and are carried along the branches in
opposite pairs. The multitude of flower-like
bracts which are carried on spreading
branches make a lovely display in early
summer and are followed by strawberry-like
fruits ripening in autumn and winter. The
attractive cultivar *C. k.* 'Satomi' has deep pink
bracts and leaves that turn reddish-purple in
early autumn. Propagation for species is from
fresh seed, sown in the autumn.

Cornus nuttallii

Mountain dogwood/Pacific dogwood
HEIGHT: 25ft (8m) • Hardy
FLOWERING SEASON: Late spring/early summer

This large, free-flowering plant has attractive
creamy-white bracts surrounding small
yellow-green flowers. The bracts become
flushed pink as they age. The roughly oval
leaves are a dull green throughout the
summer, changing to rich bronze and
crimson hues in the autumn. The cultivar
C. n. 'Gold Spot' has mottled yellow leaves.
It prefers a sheltered position in rich well-
drained soil. Propagation is from fresh seed,
sown in a cold frame in the autumn, but
germination may take eighteen months.

Corydalis cheilanthifolia

Fumitory
HEIGHT: 10in (25cm) • Hardy
FLOWERING SEASON: Late spring/early summer

This evergreen perennial forms a decorative
plant with its pretty fern-like olive-green
foliage which is initially produced in a low-
growing rosette. The dense spikes of light
yellow flowers are held erect above the leaves.
It can be an attractive feature in the border
for most of the year, and once established
will self-seed on an annual basis. It prefers
light well-drained soil and will tolerate some
shade. Propagation is by seed sown in
autumn, or by division of the thick fleshy
roots in winter when the plant is dormant.

Corylopsis pauciflora

HEIGHT: 6ft (1.8m) • Hardy • pH
FLOWERING SEASON: Spring

This beautiful flowering shrub produces
drooping strands of highly fragrant primrose-
yellow flowers which appear in spring before
the leaves. The broadly oval leaves have
bristled margins when they first appear and
are a pinkish-bronze, changing to bright
green as they mature. They like a sunny sheltered position and the delicate flowers may
be damaged by late spring frosts. Propagation
is by softwood cuttings in the summer or by
seed sown in a cold frame in the autumn to
root slowly during the winter.

Cryptomeria japonica

Japanese cedar
HEIGHT: 60ft (18m) • Hardy
FLOWERING SEASON: Spring

A large, fast-growing tree with a broad
conical habit and soft, orange-red bark
which shreds into fine strips as the tree ages.
The thin, needle-like leaves are mid green
deepening to dark green and densely packed
in spirals along the branches. The cultivar
C. j. 'Elegans', has decorative foliage which
changes from green to reddish-bronze in the
autumn and winter. To propagate, put semi-
ripe, heeled cuttings in early autumn in a
cold frame to root slowly over winter.

Cypripedium reginae

Showy lady's slipper orchid
HEIGHT: 2ft (60cm) • Hardy
FLOWERING SEASON: Spring/summer

This deciduous, hardy perennial is commonly referred to as the showy lady's slipper
orchid. It has pale green, deeply grooved,
long strap-like leaves, which look rather like
hosta leaves. The flowers are predominantly
white with a pink and white pouch forming
the 'toe' of the slipper. They are carried on
green stems or spikes, with as many as four
flowers to a spike. Although attractive when
flowering, these plants take time to establish.
Propagation is by division in the spring.

Daboecia cantabrica

St Dabeoc's heath
HEIGHT: 2ft (60cm) • Hardy
FLOWERING SEASON: Summer/autumn

This is one of the most charming dwarf
shrubs, with tough, thin stems. The small,
lance-shaped leaves are dark green above and
silvery-grey beneath. The small, urn-shaped,
rose-purple flowers are produced in long
strand-like bunches. The cultivar
D. c. 'Snowdrift' has white flowers. Young
soft growths may be damaged by late spring
frosts. The plant responds well to hard
pruning. Propagate by taking semi-
hardwood cuttings in late summer, or
layering year-old shoots in the spring.

Darlingtonia californica

Pitcher plant
HEIGHT: 3ft (1m) • Hardy
FLOWERING SEASON: Spring/summer

This pitcher plant has fleshy rhizomes below
ground and a dense rosette of yellowish-
green, white-spotted leaves, modified at the
tip to form a hooded tube or mouth, in
which insects are trapped. The solitary
flowers, a yellowish-green flushed with dark
red-purple, are carried above the pitchers on
long, leafless stalks. They are followed by a
small fruit which contains many seeds. This
plant prefers moist sheltered conditions such
as a bog garden. Propagate by seed or
division in the spring.

Desfontainia spinosa

HEIGHT: 5ft (1.5m) • Moderately hardy • pH
FLOWERING SEASON: Summer/autumn

A magnificent slow-growing evergreen
shrub, of dense growth and fairly erect habit,
with small, holly-like leaves which are a shiny
dark green. The flowers, which are carried
singly at the base of each leaf, are slender
scarlet tubes with a yellow mouth and a waxy
texture. This plant needs some shade and
likes moist, acid soil. It grows particularly
well in mild western areas of the country.
The cultivar *D. s.* 'Harold Comber', produces larger flowers that are a deeper red.
Propagation is by semi-ripe cuttings taken in
the summer and placed in a heated frame.

Embothrium coccineum

Chilean fire bush
HEIGHT: 18ft (6m) • Moderately hardy •pH
FLOWERING SEASON: Early summer

This semi-evergreen tree has a narrow
upright habit and stiff erect branches. The
glossy, deep green leaves are slightly elliptical
and have a leathery appearance. Clusters of
brilliant orange-red spiky flowers are produced in great profusion along the branches.
A hardier selection, the *E. c.* Lanceolatum
Group, has slightly larger flowers but it is
more deciduous. Propagate by sowing seeds
in spring or by taking root cuttings in winter
and putting them in a cold frame.

Enkianthus campanulatus

HEIGHT: 8ft (2.4m) • Hardy •pH
FLOWERING SEASON: Early summer

This is a deciduous shrub with dense, erect
branches and smooth red twigs. The finely
toothed leaves are a dull green, broadly elliptical and produced in clusters on the tips of
the branches. In the autumn they turn yellow
and then a brilliant red before falling. The
small, urn-shaped flowers are sulphur yellow
veined with red and are produced in small
hanging clusters. They often last for up to
three weeks. They like sun or semi-shade and
moist soil. Propagation is by semi-ripe cuttings taken in late summer or early autumn.

Epimedium grandiflorum

Barrenwort
HEIGHT: 12in (30cm) • Hardy
FLOWERING SEASON: Spring/summer

These attractive, low-growing perennials
make excellent ground cover, especially in
moist, well-drained soil in partial shade. The
heart-shaped leaves are bright green, tinted
pinky-red when young, changing to a darker
green as they mature. In the autumn these
leaves display vivid tints of yellow, orange,
red and bronze. The small, cup-shaped flowers are carried in clusters above the leaves;
colours vary depending upon the cultivar.
Propagation is by division in early spring.

Erica carnea
'Springwood White'

Heather/Alpine heath
HEIGHT: 12-18in (30-45cm) • Hardy
FLOWERING SEASON: All year round

Heathers are popular evergreen plants
because year-round flowering is possible if a
range of the different cultivars is planted.
Most heathers prefer full sun and acid soil
but *E. carnea* and its cultivars will tolerate
some lime and shade. 'Springwood White' is
the most vigorous white cultivar and bears
large flowers from late winter into spring.
Heathers look their best grown in a mass and
should be pruned immediately after flowering by removing the old flowers with shears.

Erica × darleyensis
'Darley Dale'

Heather
HEIGHT: 12-18in (30-45cm) • Hardy
FLOWERING SEASON: All year round

Many heathers have most attractive foliage
as well as their flowers: *E. cinerea* 'Golden
Drop' has golden foliage with copper-red
new growth and *E. carnea* 'Aurea' has golden-yellow leaves and pink flowers.
E. × d. 'Darley Dale' has pale mauve-pink
flowers which last from late autumn into
spring, *E. × d* 'Kramer's Red' has deep ruby
flowers and *E. × d.* 'Silberschmelze' is silver-
white. Propagate by hardwood cuttings
taken in September.

Eucryphia × nymansensis
'Nymansay'

Eucryphia
HEIGHT: 20ft (6m) • Moderately hardy
FLOWERING SEASON: Late summer/early autumn

The mid to dark green evergreen leaves have
a leathery texture and a crinkled margin; they
are carried singly or in groups on a short leaf
stalk. The most notable is *E. × nymansensis*,
a hybrid between *E. cordifolia × E. glutinosa*;
the cultivar 'Nymansay' forms a small tree of
erect habit, which matures quickly, producing
pure white flowers. *E. lucida* 'Pink Cloud' has
pale pink flowers with a thin white margin
to each petal. Propagate by taking semi-ripe
cuttings with a heel in September.

Fothergilla major

HEIGHT: 6ft (1.8m) • Hardy • pH
FLOWERING SEASON: Spring

This is a slow-growing shrub with a thin
straggly appearance. The broadly oval leaves
are a glossy dark-green on the upper surface,
with a bluish-white bloom beneath. In the
autumn they turn yellow and vivid orange-
red before the winter frosts. The flowers,
which are very fragrant and look like small,
white bottle-brushes, appear before the
leaves. They prefer sandy, lime-free soil and a
sheltered position. Propagation is by layering
young shoots in autumn. Prone to damage
and branch death by the coral spot fungus.

Gaultheria mucronata

HEIGHT: 3ft (1m) • Hardy • pH
FLOWERING SEASON: Late spring/early summer

Formerly known as pernettyas, gaultherias
are a genus of evergreen shrubs. *G. mucronata*
has small, glossy, dark green leaves which are
oval and end in a sharp point. The flowers
are generally white, followed by clusters of
small round fruit, which vary from white
and pink to purple and red. Cultivars
include: *G. m.* 'Bell's Seedling' which has
bright cherry-red fruits and *G. m.* 'Lilacina',
with pale lilac fruit. Both male and female
plants are needed for berries. Propagation is
by semi-ripe cuttings taken in September.

Gaultheria shallon

Shallon
HEIGHT: 4ft (1.2m) • Hardy • pH
FLOWERING SEASON: Late spring/early summer

This vigorous evergreen plant produces
broad, oval leaves which are thick, leathery
and borne on slender, upright, reddish-green
stems. The small, pinkish-white flowers
which are produced at the base of the leaves
and form large drooping clusters, are followed by dark purple fruits in the autumn.
This plant is very invasive and requires plenty
of room, but it is ideal for growing in shade,
and makes excellent ground cover. Propagate
by dividing established plants in winter.

Gentiana sino-ornata

Gentian
HEIGHT: 6in (15cm) • Hardy • pH
FLOWERING SEASON: Autumn

This evergreen perennial is possibly the best
autumn-flowering gentian. In the spring a
number of thin green trailing stems appear
which sprawl across the ground, each of
which, lengthening during the summer, produces in the autumn a brilliant blue flower,
handsomely striped on the outside. *G. sino-
ornata* needs moist, acid soil. Propagation is
by 'thongs', where the roots, complete with
a small segment of stem, are pulled from the
parent plant and potted on or replanted in
early spring.

Halesia monticola

Snowdrop tree/Silver bell tree
HEIGHT: 25ft (8m) • Hardy
FLOWERING SEASON: Spring

A hardy, deciduous tree which has a
spreading habit, this attractive plant is grown
primarily for its distinctive clusters of white,
bell-shaped flowers, which appear in spring
before the leaves. The flowers are usually
followed by small, green, winged and roughly pear-shaped fruit in the autumn. The
broadly oval leaves are a light to mid green.
The tree prefers moist acid to neutral soil
and propagation is by softwood cuttings
taken in summer or by seed sown in a cold
frame in autumn.

Hamamelis × intermedia

Witch hazel
HEIGHT: 10ft (3m) • Hardy
FLOWERING SEASON: Winter/spring

This very distinctive and beautiful deciduous
shrub produces its fragrant flowers in winter.
They have small strap-like petals chiefly in
shades of yellow, although some cultivars
have darker flowers: *H. × intermedia* 'Ruby
Glow' has copper-red flowers and *H. × i.*
'Diane' deep red ones. They prefer sun or
semi-shade and well-drained acid to neutral
soil. The large, mid green leaves are broadly
oval and give a magnificent autumn display.
Propagation is by softwood cuttings in late
summer or grafting in midwinter.

Holboellia coriacea

HEIGHT: 18ft (6m) • Moderately hardy
FLOWERING SEASON: Late spring

An evergreen climber that supports itself by means of twining woody stems carrying glossy green leaves composed of three sub-divided stalked leaflets. The flowers of both sexes are borne on the same plant; the male flowers are purple and the female ones are greenish-white with purple tints. As a result, in the autumn, blackish-purple, sausage-shaped fruits containing black seeds usually develop. It grows in any well-drained soil in sun or semi-shade. Propagate by semi-ripe stem cuttings taken in late summer.

Hydrangea macrophylla 'Générale Vicomtesse de Vibray'

HEIGHT: 5ft (1.5m) • Moderately hardy
FLOWERING SEASON: Summer/autumn

Mop-head (hortensias) and lace-cap hydrangeas have broad, flat blooms, which in lace-caps are surrounded by one or more rows of pink, white or blue sepals. They grow in most soils but the colour varies from pink to blue according to the amount of acid in the soil. As their name implies they like moisture. Remove the dead flower heads in spring after the frosts and cut up one third of the shoots on mature plants to ground level. Propagate by stem cuttings taken in August.

Indigofera heterantha

Indigo
HEIGHT: 5ft (1.5m) • Moderately hardy
FLOWERING SEASON: Early summer/autumn

A charming member of the pea family, this plant produces spikes of purplish-pink flowers on arching branches throughout the summer. It prefers well-drained loamy soil and a sunny position. The plant can be grown against a wall as a climber or in open ground where it should be cut back in the spring. If cut down by frosts it will regenerate. Propagate by cuttings of young shoots taken in July and inserted in a cold frame or by seed in May

Kalmia latifolia

Calico bush
HEIGHT: 10ft (3m) • Hardy • pH
FLOWERING SEASON: Summer

A magnificent rhododendron-like evergreen shrub with a dense bushy habit, the alternate leaves, which are a glossy dark green and have a tough leathery appearance, are borne on thin, whippy, green stems. The unusual crimped buds open to produce large clusters of bright pink, cup-shaped flowers in summer. The cultivars *K. l.* var. *alba* and *K. l.* 'Silver Dollar' have white flowers flushed pink. It prefers full sun and moist acid soil. Propagation is by semi-ripe stem cuttings taken in late summer.

Kirengeshoma palmata

HEIGHT: 3ft (1m) • Hardy • pH
FLOWERING SEASON: Late summer/autumn

An upright hardy herbaceous perennial which has lush, bright green, palm-like leaves. The creamy-yellow, shuttlecock-shaped flowers are produced in clusters above the large, roundish leaves on tall, erect purplish-maroon stems and appear in late summer. This plant does best in conditions where there is some light shade with protection from the wind, while a damp but well-drained, preferably lime-free, soil is essential. It should be planted in the spring and propagation is by division of the rootstock in early spring.

Koelreuteria paniculata

Golden-rain tree/Pride of India
HEIGHT: 30ft (9m) • Moderately hardy
FLOWERING SEASON: Late summer

A handsome deciduous tree with large mid green leaves divided into numerous leaflets which turn yellow in autumn. It has large terminal clusters of yellow flowers in late summer followed by inflated triangular pinkish-brown seed pods and requires a position in full sun and well-drained, fertile soil. It is best propagated by seeds sown when ripe in the autumn in sandy soil in a cold frame. The tree is named after Joseph G Koelreuter, a professor of natural history at Karlsruhe in the eighteenth century.

Leucothoe fontanesiana

HEIGHT: 5ft (1.5m) • Hardy • pH
FLOWERING SEASON: Spring

An elegant evergreen shrub which is ideal as
ground cover. The graceful, arching shoots
carry leathery, strap-like leaves, which are a
glossy dark green in the spring and summer,
becoming tinted a beetroot-red or bronze in
autumn and winter. The small white flowers
are urn-shaped and hang in small clusters
along the entire length of the stem.
L. f. 'Rainbow' has leaves splashed with
cream, yellow and pink. Likes moist acid soil
and shade or partial shade. Propagation is by
semi-ripe cuttings taken in late summer.

Liquidambar styraciflua 'Worplesdon'

Sweet gum
HEIGHT: 25ft (8m) • Hardy
FLOWERING SEASON: Spring

A large tree with maple-like, glossy, dark
green leaves which turn orange and yellow
in autumn. Initially forming a slender
pyramid with the lower branches having
upturned ends, it develops a broadly conical
shape with age. The trunk becomes deeply
grooved and fissured, changing from dark
brown to dark grey. Small green flowers
may be produced in spring. Propagation is
by grafting under protection in spring.

Lupinus luteus

Yellow lupin
HEIGHT: 2½ft (75cm) • Hardy
FLOWERING SEASON: Summer

This striking annual has mid green stems
thickly covered with soft hairs, the pale to
mid green oval leaves are narrower towards
the base and sparsely covered in a coating
of fine soft hair. The bright yellow flowers,
which are arranged in a circle or whorl at the
end of the stem, are followed by small, black,
hairy pods, each containing about five slightly flattened black seeds. Propagation is by
seed sown in situ in the spring; pre-soak the
seed in water for about twenty-four hours.

Magnolia × soulangeana 'Lennei'

Magnolia/Lily tree
HEIGHT: 20ft (6m) • Hardy
FLOWERING SEASON: Early spring

Contrary to perceived opinion there are a
number of magnolias which will tolerate
chalky soil, *M. delavayi*, *M. kobus* and *M.
wilsonii* are three of them. That said the
majority thrive best in neutral to acid soil
and like to be sheltered from east winds
which may otherwise damage the flowers
when they emerge in the spring. The
× *soulangeana* hybrids like 'Lennei' are
among the hardiest and have a colour range
of pink through rose-purple to white.

Magnolia stellata

Star magnolia
HEIGHT: 10ft (3m) • Hardy
FLOWERING SEASON: Spring

The star magnolia is a shapely bush which
carries many fragrant, star-like, white flowers
in great profusion in spring before coming
into leaf. The leaves are narrow and deep
green. Magnolias come from North
America, the Himalayas and Japan and are
named after Pierre Magnol. Among the
finest are *M. campbellii*, *M. acuminata* (the
cucumber tree), *M denudata* (the lily tree)
and *M. grandiflora* (page 148). They can be
propagated by semi-ripe cuttings taken in
summer or by seed sown in autumn.

Meconopsis betonicifolia

Blue poppy
HEIGHT: 4ft (1.2m) • Hardy
FLOWERING SEASON: Summer

The mid green leaves are oblong in shape
and covered with soft bristles. The vivid,
sky-blue flowers, with their central core of
golden-yellow stamens, are carried on tall,
slender stems, in hairy, pod-like buds. This
plant requires a deep, rich, preferably acid
compost and a cool, sheltered, shady site.
Propagate this perennial from seed, sown
into a cold frame in the autumn, and kept
sheltered over winter. Do not allow these
plants to flower in the first year after germination and divide them every four years.

Menziesia ciliicalyx 'Spring Morning'

HEIGHT: 3-5ft (1-1.5m) • Hardy • pH
FLOWERING SEASON: Early summer

This very attractive flowering shrub is a native of Japan and is a real treasure when grown in association with rhododendrons. The leaves are pale to mid green in colour and have a bristled margin. *M. c.* 'Spring Morning' has pale creamy urn-shaped flowers while *M. c.* var. *purpurea* has purple ones. They appear during May and June. It likes semi-shade and moist acid soil. Propagation is by semi-ripe cuttings taken with a heel during mid to late summer.

Ourisia macrophylla

HEIGHT: 10in (25cm) • Hardy
FLOWERING SEASON: Midsummer

A low-growing plant with creeping rhizomatous rootstocks below ground, and mid green rounded leaves with a notched margin that form dense mats. This plant produces erect, slender stems, which carry white (sometimes streaked with pink) tubular flowers up to 1in (2.5cm) long, very like those of a miniature penstemon, on a spike above the leaves. This plant must have partial shade and a well-drained soil. Propagation is by division in spring or by seed sown in late spring.

Oxydendrum arboreum

Sorrel tree
HEIGHT: 27ft (9m) • Hardy • pH
FLOWERING SEASON: Summer

This deciduous spreading tree is grown mainly for its spectacular yellow and crimson autumn leaf colours. In spring and summer they are elliptical in shape and a glossy dark green. The white flowers are produced in long, dangling clusters on the tips of the shoots in summer. In winter the bark is an attractive rusty-red, which turns to grey as it ages. It likes sun and moist acid soil. Propagation is by softwood cuttings taken in summer or by fresh seed sown in autumn.

Picea pungens 'Koster'

Colorado spruce
HEIGHT: 50ft (15m) • Hardy
FLOWERING SEASON: Spring

The type forms a medium-sized tree with a conical profile. New growth is orange-brown, while the sharply pointed mature 'needles' are greyish-green. The dangling light-brown cones are bluish-green when young. The most popular cultivar, *P. p.* 'Koster', forms a small tree with silvery-blue leaves. Most species can be propagated by seed sown outdoors in the spring, the named selections are grafted under cover in early spring. Prone to attack by the adelgid, which sucks sap and distorts young growths.

Pieris japonica 'Firecrest'

HEIGHT: 10ft (3m) • Hardy • pH
FLOWERING SEASON: Spring

These compact evergreen shrubs have narrow leaves and white or pink bell-shaped flowers that look much like lily-of-the-valley. Most are grown for their spring display of bright foliage, ranging from lime-green to crimson or bronze. They like a shady site and moist acid soil. The cultivar *Pieris* 'Forest Flame' has young leaves which start red, change through pink and cream before turning green. *P. j.* 'Variegata' is a slow-growing cultivar with white and green variegated leaves, flushed pink when young. Propagation is by semi-ripe cuttings in August.

Pseudolarix amabilis

Golden larch
HEIGHT: 45ft (15m) • Hardy • pH
FLOWERING SEASON: Insignificant

This is a beautiful, deciduous and open-crowned tree that is very slow-growing, partly because the growing tips of young trees are often killed by late spring frosts, yet will eventually make a good height. The long, larch-like leaves are light green and turn a clear golden-yellow, orange and then reddish-brown in autumn. It bears erect cones with spreading scales which carry the seeds. This plant is particularly sensitive to lime in the soil. Propagation is by seed sown under protection in spring.

Pseudotsuga menziesii

Douglas fir
HEIGHT: 75ft (25m) • Hardy
FLOWERING SEASON: Insignificant

This large vigorous tree develops a deeply grooved, corky bark as it ages, and a flat, broadly spreading crown also develops as the tree reaches maturity. The broad 'needle' leaves are aromatic and arranged in two horizontal lines along the branchlets, they are a rich dark green above with two silvery lines on the underside. The blue-leaved variety, *P. m.* var. *glauca,* will tolerate drier soils. Propagate by seed sown under protection in spring.

Rhododendron 'Kirin'

Azalea
HEIGHT: 5ft (1.5m) • Hardy • pH
FLOWERING SEASON: Spring

Botanically speaking all azaleas are classified as rhododendrons but most gardeners commonly reserve the name of azalea for those species which lose their leaves in winter. Just to complicate things a number of azaleas are evergreen and 'Kirin' is one of those. All rhododendrons and azaleas prefer moist, neutral to acid soil, with some dappled shade. Propagate by half-ripe cuttings taken with a thin heel from the current year's growth in July or by layering.

Rhododendron davidsonianum

Rhododendron
HEIGHT: 5-10ft (1.5-3m) • Hardy • pH
FLOWERING SEASON: Late spring

Rhododendrons in full bloom are one of the most glorious sights of spring and the best known gardens, Kew, the Savill Garden, Exbury and Bodnant are well worth visiting to appreciate the massed blooms.
R. davidsonianum is a relatively slow growing species with clusters of pale pink to pale mauve funnel-shaped flowers. As all rhododendrons are shallow rooting it is a good idea to mulch with half-decayed leaves in May to keep the soil moist in summer.

Rhodohypoxis baurii

HEIGHT: 4in (10cm) • Not fully hardy
FLOWERING SEASON: Spring/summer

This low-growing herbaceous perennial has a tufty habit and a crown of erect, spear-shaped hairy leaves. The small, flattish, six-petalled flowers, which vary from white to pale pink or red, are carried on slender, erect stems, each flower has six petals which meet at the centre so the flower has no eye. The ideal conditions for this plant are full sun and a moist, sandy, peaty soil. Propagation can be achieved by seed sown in spring for the species, but named cultivars, such as *R. b.* 'Douglas', must be propagated by division in early spring.

Staphylea colchica

Bladder nut
HEIGHT: 11ft (3.5m) • Hardy
FLOWERING SEASON: Late spring

A large deciduous shrub which comes from the Causasus which bears handsome clusters of white flowers in May. These are followed by inflated seed pods up to 2in (5cm) long. It has bright green leaves each having three to five oval leaflets, and requires sun or semi-shade and moist fertile soil. *S. holocarpa* 'Rosea' has pink flowers. The species can be propagated by seed sown in autumn and selected forms by softwood cuttings taken with a slight heel of old wood in July. Trim young plants to encourage a bushy habit.

Stewartia sinensis

HEIGHT: 20ft (6m) • Hardy
FLOWERING SEASON: Summer

This small deciduous tree has attractive brown stems and unusually peeling ornamental bark; it belongs to the camellia family. The broad, spear-shaped, mid green leaves have a leathery texture and provide a vivid display of red and yellow in the autumn. The pure white, cup-shaped flowers have prominent yellow anthers in the centre. These plants grow best in a sunny spot with their roots shaded, and are very intolerant of root disturbance. Propagation is by softwood cuttings taken in the summer, or by seed sown in a cold frame in autumn.

Styrax officinalis

Storax
HEIGHT: 12ft (4m) • Hardy • pH
FLOWERING SEASON: Early summer

This attractive deciduous shrub has a loose, open habit and spear-shaped leaves that are dark green on the upper surface and silver-white beneath. The short drooping clusters of large, white, fragrant, bell-shaped flowers are carried on the tips of the shoots in early summer. This plant prefers a sheltered position in full sun or partial shade, and a moist well-drained soil. Propagation is by softwood cuttings taken in summer, or by seed sown in a cold frame in autumn.

Taxodium distichum

Bald cypress/Swamp cypress
HEIGHT: 75ft (25m) • Hardy
FLOWERING SEASON: Winter

A strikingly beautiful, slow-growing deciduous tree which has fibrous, reddish-brown, peeling bark. The branches are a bright orange-brown with grey-green young shoots. The bright yellow-green leaves are small and narrow, turning a russet brown in autumn. This tree is ideal for growing close to water, so that the beautiful autumn colours are reflected on the surface. Propagation is by seed sown in spring or by hardwood cuttings taken in autumn.

Trillium grandiflorum

Trinity flower/Wood lily/Wake robin
HEIGHT: 18in (45cm) • Hardy
FLOWERING SEASON: Spring/summer

This clump-forming perennial develops into a dome-shaped plant with large, oval, deeply veined, dark green leaves. The pure white, funnel-shaped flowers, which gradually become flushed pink as the flower ages, are produced singly on short arching stems from spring until summer. There are also species with pink flowers and double white flowers. It likes shade and moist soil. Propagation is by division of the rhizomes after the leaves have died down.

Tropaeolum speciosum

Flame creeper
HEIGHT: 15ft (4.5m) • Hardy
FLOWERING SEASON: Summer/autumn

This deciduous herbaceous perennial climber has long-stalked, brilliant scarlet, trumpet-shaped flowers which are made up of five rounded wavy petals opening out flat, produced singly on curling stems. The stems, with their notched and circular mid green leaves, form an attractive plant even before the flowers start to appear. These plants are slow to establish but are worth the wait and like to have their roots in the shade. Prune in spring by cutting out the dead stems. Propagate by division in March.

Tsuga heterophylla

Western hemlock
HEIGHT: 70-100ft (20-30m) • Hardy
FLOWERING SEASON: None

A large, fast-growing tree with drooping branches and shoot tips. The young shoots are white and hairy bearing leaves which are dark green above and silver on the underside. The dark brown bark is scaly and deeply grooved. These trees perform best in sheltered areas with a heavy rainfall and in a partially shaded position. Propagation is by seed sown under protection in the spring, or for named cultivars, by semi-ripe cuttings taken in autumn. Other species are smaller. They dislike urban pollution.

Uvularia grandiflora

Bellwort/Merry-bells
HEIGHT: 18in (45cm) • Hardy • pH
FLOWERING SEASON: Spring

This clump-forming herbaceous perennial has narrow, pointed leaves which appear in the spring and only partially unfold to reveal clusters of graceful, bell-shaped, yellow flowers. These are carried on olive-green, succulent-looking stems, and after flowering the leaves unroll completely. A slower-growing species, *U. perfoliata*, has yellow flowers with twisted petals. Semi-shade is essential for this plant and it prefers moist peaty soil. Propagation is by division in early spring before flowering.

Vaccinium corymbosum

Blueberry/Whortleberry/Cowberry/Bilberry
HEIGHT: 5ft (1.5m) • Hardy • pH
FLOWERING SEASON: Spring

This small deciduous shrub forms a dense suckering thicket of upright multi-branched shoots, covered in bright green, spear-shaped leaves, which turn to bronze and scarlet in the autumn. The flowers are urn-shaped and vary in colour from white to white-blushed-pink. They are followed in the autumn by sweet, edible, black berries which are covered by blue bloom. *V. c.* 'Pioneer' is grown for its vivid red autumn foliage. Propagation is by semi-ripe cuttings taken in late summer.

Viburnum plicatum 'Mariesii'

HEIGHT: 6ft (1.8m) • Hardy
FLOWERING SEASON: Spring/summer

This is a spectacular, large, wide-spreading shrub with a tendency to produce its branches in stacked layers, which gives a tiered effect. The oval leaves, which are deeply crinkled and a bright green through the summer, change to yellow and reddish-purple in autumn. The white flowers are carried in large flat heads, making the shrub look as if a layer of snow has just fallen on it. Propagation is by semi-ripe cuttings taken in late summer or by layering young shoots in early autumn.

Zenobia pulverulenta

Zenobia
HEIGHT: 6ft (1.8m) • Hardy • pH
FLOWERING SEASON: Summer

This is a beautiful small deciduous or semi-evergreen shrub with an open habit and thin, twiggy stems that are covered in a bluish-white bloom. The strap-like leaves are a glossy blue-green with a bluish-white underside when young. Large white flowers, very similar to those of the lily-of-the-valley, that hang in clusters from the leaf joints are produced in summer. The blooms give off a faint scent of aniseed. Propagation is by semi-ripe cuttings taken in late summer.

More Plants for Acid Soils

It is important to distinguish between those plants which are lime-haters and have to have acid soil to thrive and other plants which are quite tolerant of some acidity in the soil. The lime-haters are marked pH in the plant details and if you garden on clay or chalk it really is a waste of time trying to grow them.

Otherwise if your soil is not too acid and your climate isn't too wet then there is very little restriction on what you can grow. Your roses may not be quite as bountiful, and your stone fruit may not yeild quite as much as someone who lives a hundred miles away and is lucky enough to garden on the best loam but they will be fine for the average gardener. You may be best to avoid the Mediterranean plants like cistus and lavender. Acid soil can always be sweetened by adding lime and the productivity improved by digging in compost or manure.

The following plants included in other chapters in this book are just some of those that can also be grown in acid soils. Space prevents the inclusion of roses and bulbs which are also perfectly viable.

TREES

Acers (in variety)
Alnus incana
Amelanchier canadensis
Carpinus betulus
Chamaecyparis lawsoniana (and most conifers)
Crataegus (in variety)
Fagus (in variety)
Hamamelis mollis
Larix decidua
Liriodendron tulipifera
Magnolia grandiflora
Sorbus (in variety)

SHRUBS

Aucuba japonica
Berberis (in variety)
Ceanothus (in variety)
Choisya ternata
Cornus (in variety)
Cotinus coggygria
Euonymus fortunei cvs
Forsythia suspensa
Lavatera 'Barnsley'
Ligustrum ovalifolium
Mahonia (in variety)
Osmanthus (in variety)
Rhododendron – including *azaleas* (in variety)
Sambucus (in variety)
Sarcococca (in variety)
Syringa (in variety)
Vaccinium glaucoalbum
Viburnum (in variety)

PERENNIALS, GROUND COVER PLANTS & CLIMBERS

Aconitum 'Bressingham Spire'
Alchemilla mollis
Aquilegia alpina
Aronia arbutifolia
Artemesia absinthium
Aruncus dioicus
Astrantia major
Bergenia cordifolia
Buddleja (in variety)
Campanula (in variety)
Centhranthus ruber
Ceratostigma willmottianum
Echinops bannaticus
Filipendula palmata
Galium odoratum
Geranium (in variety)
Gunnera manicata
Iris germanica
Jasminum officinale
Lamium maculatum
Lapageria rosea
Ligularia (in variety)
Myosotis sylvestris
Phlomis fruticosa
Polygonatum × hybridum
Primula (in variety)
Santolina chamaecyparissus
Tradescantia (in variety)
Veronica prostrata
Vinca minor 'Argenteovariegata'
Viola (in variety)

Plants *for* Chalk Soils

Chalky soil occurs naturally in limestone areas, but is also created by the inclusion of builder's rubble in the soil, often around the bases of walls, where clematis thrives. Although gardeners with this soil are fortunate in that lime-loving plants are more numerous than acid-loving plants, chalky dry soil does need added leaf mould and compost to increase the nutrient content and water-retaining capacity.

ABOVE: Saponaria ocymoides, *with the charming common name of 'Tumbling Ted', is an ideal mat-forming perennial for a dry bank.*

OPPOSITE: *An informal border of yarrow, violas, geraniums and iris makes an attractive display. Most of the summer-flowering perennials do well on chalky soil, giving the gardener a wide range to choose from.*

ABOVE: Linum narbonense *is a charming, small, clump-forming perennial with flowers ranging from light to deep blue in summer. It likes light soil.*

It is understandable that those gardeners who can grow rhododendrons, and the many other lovely plants needing similar soil, think they are so lucky, but if you look at the vast range of lime-loving plants available, you will soon realize that as a group they can provide interest and beauty at least on a par with the acid-loving plants.

Plants that prefer to grow in an alkaline soil, that is, with a pH of 7.0 or higher, are called Calcicole plants. Use a soil-testing kit to check your soil's pH. If you look at the number of plants which grow well on alkaline soils, you will see that there is a wide range of attractive trees and shrubs, including clematis, lonicera (honeysuckle), sorbus and viburnums, that like these conditions. The list of plants also includes many herbaceous perennials, and many members of the pea family often excel on these soils, including cytisus and genista (broom), gleditsia, lathyrus (the sweet pea), and robinia.

In some areas, gardens made up of a shallow layer of soil over solid chalk or limestone have several characteristic features which make them difficult to garden. The presence of the base rock so near the surface of the soil makes it difficult to position plants at any depth without resorting to the use of a pickaxe or other heavy-duty implement. Even this does not alter the fact that you are planting into rock and not soil, so that plant roots will have great difficulty penetrating it. This can lead to poor anchorage, particularly of trees, although some trees like beech (*Fagus sylvatica*), which does grow on shallow, chalky soil, have developed a naturally broad, shallow root system in order to cope with the lack of soil.

During dry periods, these thin layers of soil can hold only limited reserves of water, and the upper levels of the rock become extremely dry. However, once established, many plants will produce an extensive root system which penetrates the soft rock, so that when rain does fall, they can absorb the maximum amount before it drains through the soil. Adding bulky organic matter to improve the soil is usually best done soon after a period of rain.

Many gardens have certain areas with more chalky soil than other parts, in particular where builder's rubble has accumulated, often near house walls or patios. This is particularly true of many town gardens in areas around garden walls where old lime mortar may turn the soil from acid to alkaline. In a case like this, move plants if they do not do well in the position chosen for them originally. These are ideal situations for chalk-loving plants, especially clematis, but it is essential when growing clematis that you shelter their roots from hot sun. Many gardeners are frightened of moving plants, particularly in summer. Even if it is not recommended, if you take plenty of soil with the plant, dig a deep hole, and puddle the plant in thoroughly, it is usually perfectly satisfactory.

ABOVE: *An informal woodland walk in spring in a garden with chalky soil. Hellebores seen on the left do best in partial shade.*

LEFT: *The glorious rugosa rose, R. 'Roseraie de L'Haÿ' will flourish in chalky soil. It is sometimes grown successfully as a low hedge.*

Acanthus spinosus

Bear's breeches
HEIGHT: 3ft (1m) • Hardy
FLOWERING SEASON: Summer

This herbaceous perennial is often described as an 'architectural' plant. It has large arching leaves, which are a glossy dark-green and strap-like, with sharp spines on the points of the toothed margins. The tall spikes of white and purple tubular flowers, which alternate between layers of green spiny bracts, are borne throughout summer. The dead flowerheads look attractive during winter when frost-covered. Propagate by root cuttings in early spring, or division in winter.

Acer negundo 'Flamingo'

Ash-leaved maple/Box elder
HEIGHT: 50ft (15m) • Hardy
FLOWERING SEASON: Spring

A vigorous tree with ash-like leaves that are bright green in summer, turning to golden-yellow in autumn. In the spring, bright greenish-yellow flowers are produced in flat clusters on the branches before the leaves. *A. n.* var. *violaceum* has purple leaves and shoots, and the cultivar *A. n.* 'Variegatum' has mid green leaves marbled with creamy-white flecks and pink shoot tips in the spring. Propagation is by seed sown in the spring or budding in the summer (for cultivars).

Achillea filipendulina 'Gold Plate'

Yarrow
HEIGHT: 3ft (1m) • Hardy
FLOWERING SEASON: Late summer/early autumn

This herbaceous perennial has a compact upright habit, with broad, finely divided, slightly hairy, dull green leaves. The lemon-yellow flowers are held erect above the foliage in bold flat clusters 5-6in (12-15cm) across. The cultivar *A. f.* 'Gold Plate' has deep golden-yellow flowers. Propagate by lifting the clumps in March, dividing them into smaller portions of 4-5 shoots and replanting them in the growing site.

Actinidia kolomikta

HEIGHT: 12ft (4m) • Hardy
FLOWERING SEASON: Late summer

This deciduous climbing shrub with twining stems has heart-shaped, dark green leaves marked with pink and white at the tip. Actinidias generally prefer shade but *A. kolomikta* will grow well on a sheltered fence or wall in full sun and preferably a neutral, well-drained soil. It has small white, slightly fragrant flowers in June. The young leaves are prone to damage by late spring frosts. Propagation is by semi-ripe cuttings in July and August. In February prune by thinning out overcrowded growths, and shorten excessively vigorous shoots.

Aesculus pavia

Red buckeye/Horse chestnut
HEIGHT: 10ft (3m) • Hardy
FLOWERING SEASON: Early summer

This is a round-headed shrub, with large, mid green, palm-like leaves made up of five leaflets. The snapdragon-like flowers are bright red with a yellow throat, and carried on erect spikes up to 6in (15cm) long. There are two good cultivars: *A. p.* 'Atrosanguinea', which has deeper red flowers, and *A. p.* 'Humilis', which has a low, spreading habit. *A. hippocastanum* is the common horse chestnut or conker tree. Propagation is by seed sown in spring, budding in summer or grafting indoors in spring (for named cultivars).

Amelanchier canadensis

Snowy mespilus
HEIGHT: 20ft (6m) • Hardy
FLOWERING SEASON: Late spring

This is a deciduous, suckering shrub or small tree with a dense, upright habit and dark whippy shoots. The oval, mid to dark green leaves with toothed margins are woolly when young, and turn vivid shades of yellow, orange and red in autumn. Brilliant white, star-shaped flowers, are carried in bold erect spikes in spring before the leaves have developed, followed by small, purple, currant-like fruits in late summer. Propagation is by seed sown in early autumn. Fireblight may cause shrivelling of young shoots and flowers.

Anchusa azurea

Blue alkanet
HEIGHT: 3ft (1m) • Hardy
FLOWERING SEASON: Mid/late summer

A hardy herbaceous perennial with mid green, strap-like leaves covered in fine bristly hairs. The small, dish-shaped flowers are produced in long blunt spikes carried high above the foliage. Among the most popular cultivars are: 'Loddon Royalist', with rich gentian-blue flowers or the sky-blue variety 'Opal'. This plant thrives in full sun or partial shade, but must have a well-drained site. Propagation is by root cuttings 2in (5cm) long in February.

Aquilegia alpina

Columbine/Alpine columbine
HEIGHT: 18in (45cm) • Hardy
FLOWERING SEASON: Spring/early summer

Aquilegias are hardy perennial plants which bear long-spurred beautifully-coloured flowers from late spring throughout the summer. *A. alpina* has clear violet-blue flowers while *A. vulgaris*, 'Granny's bonnets', has flowers ranging from white through pink to purple. They prefer sun or partial shade and thrive in most garden soils provided that they do not dry out. Propagate by seed sown in spring or autumn but named forms seldom come true from seed and they cross freely.

Astrantia major

Masterwort
HEIGHT: 2ft (60cm) • Hardy
FLOWERING SEASON: Summer

One of the most under-rated garden perennials astrantias are easy to grow and tolerant of most soils and conditions provided the soil does not become waterlogged. They prefer slight shade. The flowers are pinkish-white and are borne in profusion throughout the summer above mid green leaves. Cut the plants down to soil level in late autumn and divide every three or four years. Propagate by dividing the plants into rooted pieces in March or October.

Aucuba japonica

HEIGHT: 6-12ft (2-4m) • Hardy
FLOWERING SEASON: Late spring

This evergreen shrub is easy to grow and will tolerate both dense shade and atmospheric pollution. The leaves, which are narrow, oval and have several teeth or notches at the tip, are glossy, leathery and a rich dark green. Of the various coloured leaf cultivars, *A. j.* 'Crotonifolia', with green and yellow mottled leaves, and *A. j.* 'Picturata' with a vivid golden splash in the centre of each leaf, are the most popular. To obtain fruits both male and female plants have to be grown. Propagation is by semi-ripe cuttings in September and October.

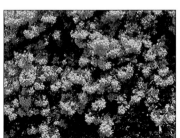

Berberis darwinii

Darwin's barberry
HEIGHT: 10ft (3m) • Hardy
FLOWERING SEASON: Late spring

This berberis is one of the hardiest of shrubs originating from Chile. It has an upright habit. Its dark, shining evergreen leaves have three spiny points, which make it look like a miniature holly in winter. In spring the leaves are almost lost beneath a shower of brilliant orange-yellow blossom, which is followed by small, blue-black fruits which have a grey bloom to them. It prefers full sun and moist well-drained soil. Propagate by taking heel cuttings in late summer or by semi-ripe cuttings taken in the autumn.

Brunnera macrophylla

Siberian bugloss
HEIGHT: 18in (45cm) • Hardy
FLOWERING SEASON: Late spring

This is a low-growing woodland plant which prefers at least partial shade. In the late spring it bears delicate sprays of small, star-shaped, bright blue flowers with an orange-yellow eye in the centre. The flowers are followed by roughly textured heart-shaped, slightly hairy, matt green leaves. The cultivar *B. m.* 'Dawson's White' has ivory-white margins to the dark green leaves. It needs shade to keep its colour. Propagation is by division in the spring or, for species, seed sown in the autumn.

Campanula lactiflora

Bellflower
HEIGHT: 4ft (1.2m) • Hardy
FLOWERING SEASON: Summer

This herbaceous perennial has light green, oval leaves carried on strong, upright green stems. Bell-shaped flowers of light lavender-blue are produced on branching stems in summer. There are a number of named cultivars: *C. l.* 'Prichard's Variety' has deep lavender-blue flowers and *C. l.* 'Loddon Anna' soft pink ones. Propagation is by division in the early spring. The stems of these plants are so strong that they very rarely require staking. They like some shade.

Campsis × *tagliabuana* 'Mme Galen'

HEIGHT: 30ft (9m) • Moderately hardy
FLOWERING SEASON: Late summer/early autumn

This vigorous free-flowering hybrid is ideal for sunny walls and fences, and pergolas or other similar structures. It has up to twelve trumpet-like, salmon-red flowers, carried in clusters on the shoot tips from late summer until the first frosts. The light to mid green foliage consists of oval leaflets with toothed margins. Good yellow autumn colour. The stem is light grey-green when young, ageing to creamy-brown. Propagation is by root cuttings taken in early spring.

Caryopteris × *clandonensis* 'Heavenly Blue'

HEIGHT: 3ft (1m) • Moderately hardy
FLOWERING SEASON: Late summer/autumn

A perennial sub-shrub caryopteris produce masses of small blue flowers at the end of the summer above silvery, grey-green, lance-shaped leaves. They prefer full sun and light well-drained soil with the addition of some peat to the soil and appreciate the shelter of a wall if grown in colder parts of the country. Cut the plant back hard in the spring. *C. incana* has deeper more purple flowers. Propagate by taking cuttings from non-flowering shoots at the ends of July.

Ceanothus impressus

Californian lilac
HEIGHT: 6ft (1.8m) • Moderately hardy
FLOWERING SEASON: Mid spring/early summer

This colourful, bushy evergreen shrub has small, dark green leaves which are slightly paler and downy on the underside. It produces many dense clusters of tiny, deep blue flowers. An excellent plant for its vibrant blue colour, for the best effect it should be grown as a wall shrub. This is one of the hardiest of the evergreen ceanothus that can be grown in cooler climates, it likes a sheltered sunny position and well-drained soil. Propagation is by semi-ripe cuttings taken in summer or autumn.

Centranthus ruber

Red valerian
HEIGHT: 2½ft (75cm) • Hardy
FLOWERING SEASON: Mid/late summer

This perennial has thick, oval, grey-green leaves, carried on erect, fleshy, stems with the flowers developing at the tip. Branching heads of fierce red or deep pink, star-shaped flowers are borne in slightly domed clusters. There is a white-flowered form, *C. r. albus*, which also has pale green leaves. This plant will grow in virtually any soil: almost pure chalk, brick dust or even builder's rubble. Propagation is by seed sown in autumn or spring, or by division in spring. Valerian is very invasive and must be controlled.

Cercis siliquastrum

Judas tree/Redbud tree
HEIGHT: 20ft (6m) • Hardy
FLOWERING SEASON: Late spring/early summer

This is a large, slow-growing shrub or small tree, which has deeply veined, broad, heart-shaped leaves, often purple-green when young with a blue sheen later, and turning yellow in autumn. The pretty, small, purple-pink, pea-shaped flowers are produced in vast quantities on both old and new wood from late spring to early summer. Small dark-brown, pod-like fruits are produced in autumn. It has been cultivated in British gardens since 1596. Propagation is by seed which is sown in spring.

Cistus × cyprius

Rock rose/Gum cistus
Height: 5ft (1.5m) • Moderately hardy
Flowering Season: Early summer

Beautiful half-hardy evergreen shrubby plants, rock roses like full sun, a warm sheltered position and light well-drained soil. Each flower lasts for one day but the plants carry flowers in succession throughout June and July. *C. × cyprius* has white flowers with a prominent red spot at the base of each petal, *C. albidus* has pale pink flowers and *C. creticus* has bright pink flowers. Propagate by semi-ripe cuttings in summer or hardwood cuttings in winter.

Clematis texensis

Height: 7ft (2m) • Hardy
Flowering Season: Late summer/early autumn

This is one of the less vigorous clematis and is ideal for growing into trees, bushy shrubs or hedges. The blue-green leaves have up to eight oval leaflets with the leaf stalk being the part of the plant which twines to support the plant. In the late summer single, scarlet-red, tulip-shaped flowers are produced. The hybrid *C.* 'The Princess of Wales' has attractive deep pink blooms. Like all clematis it prefers rich well-drained soil with its roots in the shade. Propagation is by semi-ripe cuttings taken in midsummer.

Corydalis lutea

Fumitory
Height: 8in (20cm) • Hardy
Flowering Season: Spring/autumn

This low-growing, clump-forming herbaceous perennial has grey-green, evergreen leaves, which are finely dissected and fern-like. The leaves of this plant often hang limply, giving the impression that the plant is wilting. From late spring spikes of yellow tubular flowers which open out to form a split funnel shape are carried above the leaves on thin green stems. Propagation is by seed sown in autumn or by division in early spring when the plants are dormant.

Crataegus laevigata 'Paul's Scarlet'

Hawthorn
Height: 15ft (4.5m) • Hardy
Flowering Season: Spring

The native tree, often called 'may', has grey-green, twiggy stems with small, very sharp spines, and an open spreading habit. The deeply lobed oval leaves are mid green in the summer, turning yellow in autumn. The clusters of white flowers which have a musky scent are followed by clusters of small red fruits in autumn and winter. The cultivar *C. l.* 'Paul's Scarlet' has double red flowers. Propagation is by budding in summer or grafting in spring.

Cupressus arizonica var. glabra 'Blue Ice'

Arizona cypress
Height: 60ft (18m) • Hardy
Flowering Season: Early autumn

This is a large coniferous tree of broadly conical habit. It has smooth, purple bark which flakes off to reveal yellow patches of new bark beneath. The blue-grey leaves are short, stubby and closely packed together, completely hiding the twigs. There are a number of slow-growing forms with attractive foliage. The cultivar *C. a.* var. *g.* 'Compacta' is a true dwarf conifer. Propagation is by semi-ripe cuttings, taken with a heel in September and October.

Delphinium 'Lord Butler'

Delphinium/Perennial larkspur
Height: 5ft (1.5m) • Hardy/half hardy
Flowering Season: Summer

Hardy perennials which bloom in mid-summer with tall spikes of flowers which are, by tradition, blue, but are available in a colour range from white, through mauve to indigo. They do best in deep well-drained soil enriched with compost or manure and full sun. They require staking which must be done early and it is a good idea to thin out the shoots. Cut down the flower spikes after flowering and divide every four years in spring. Raise from seed or take basal cuttings in spring.

Deutzia scabra 'Plena'

HEIGHT: 8ft (2.5m) • Hardy
FLOWERING SEASON: Early/midsummer

This is a bushy deciduous shrub with an erect habit and attractive peeling nut-brown bark on the older stems. The narrow, oval leaves are mid to dark green in colour. Dense spikes of scented, cup-shaped white flowers are produced in summer. Of the cultivars *D. s.* 'Candidissima' has white, double flowers, and *D. s.* 'Plena' has white blooms flushed rose-pink. Prefers full sun and fertile well-drained soil. Propagation is by semi-ripe cuttings taken in late summer, or by hardwood cuttings taken in winter.

Dianthus 'Doris'

Carnation/Pink
HEIGHT: 16in (40cm) • Hardy
FLOWERING SEASON: Summer/autumn

These plants have tufted, cushion-forming mounds of silver-grey foliage, with the leaves arranged in pairs on the silver-grey stems. They are ideal for the front of a border as they produce flushes of delicately scented, brightly coloured blooms, in colours ranging from white, through pink to dark red, in summer and again in autumn. They like sun and well-drained soil. Propagation is by division every three years, or by layering or cuttings in late summer.

Doronicum plantagineum

Leopard's bane
HEIGHT: 3ft (1m) • Hardy
FLOWERING SEASON: Spring/summer

This is a sturdy little plant with bright green, heart-shaped leaves. Above the leaves rise the stems, each carrying up to four large, bright yellow, daisy-like flowers. Three popular hybrids are: *D. × excelsum* 'Harpur Crewe' which has larger golden-yellow flowers, *D. × e.* 'Miss Mason', which is shorter and more compact, and the double-flowered *D. × e.* 'Spring Beauty'. They grow in sun or shade and any well-drained soil. Propagation is by division in the autumn or early spring.

Dryas octopetala

Mountain avens
HEIGHT: 3in (7.5cm) • Hardy
FLOWERING SEASON: Late spring/early summer

This tough, evergreen perennial, has a prostrate, spreading habit, and it develops into a dense mat of dark green, leathery leaves, the underneath of which is grey. The leaves are deeply lobed, giving them an oak-like appearance. The small, cup-shaped flowers are creamy-white and carried on stems just above the leaves from April. They are followed by attractive silvery-grey seed-heads: a good plant for ground cover in a rock garden. Propagation is by seed sown fresh or semi-ripe cuttings in midsummer.

Eccremocarpus scaber

Chilean glory flower
HEIGHT: 8-10ft (2.5-3m) • Moderately hardy
FLOWERING SEASON: Summer/autumn

This plant makes a vigorous climber when established, quickly covering whatever support it can find with its green slender stems. It supports itself with tendrils which are modifications of the dull green leaves. The small, orange, tubular flowers appear in large bunches from June onwards. *E. s. roseus* is a pink form, and *E. s. aurantiacus* a yellow one. Often grown as an annual it likes full sun and any well-drained soil but parts of the plant will die back each winter. Propagation is by seed sown in March.

Eremurus himalaicus

Foxtail lily/King's spear
HEIGHT: 8ft (2.5m) • Hardy
FLOWERING SEASON: Early summer

This is a truly majestic perennial. The bright green, narrow, strap-like leaves are produced in spring, but die down in summer as the flower spike develops. Tall spikes of white, cup-shaped flowers are produced from May onwards. *E. robusta* has soft pink flowers and *E. × isabellinus* Shelford Hybrids produce pink, orange or white flowers. Propagation is by seed sown in autumn, or by division in spring. These plants prefer sun and well-drained soil and come into growth early in spring, so may suffer some frost damage.

Erysimum cheiri

Wallflower
HEIGHT: 2ft (60cm) • Hardy
FLOWERING SEASON: Spring

Evergreen shrubby perennial, with woody stems forming a low mound. The strap-like leaves are dark green and slightly paler on the underside. The flat, four-petalled flowers are carried above the leaves in dense spikes. Of several named cultivars the most popular is *E. c.* 'Harpur Crewe', with double, mustard-yellow, fragrant flowers; this lasts about five years. Propagation is by softwood cuttings taken in summer. Clubroot causes stunted top growth and death.

Exochorda × macrantha 'The Bride'

Pearl bush/Bride bush
HEIGHT: 5ft (1.5m) • Hardy
FLOWERING SEASON: Late spring/early summer

A deciduous, arching, free-flowering shrub that flourishes in sun. It likes loamy soil and should have a top dressing of farmyard compost every other year. It eventually forms a thick mound covered with large, attractively-shaped, white flowers in late spring. Pruning is not really necessary but the plant benefits from thinning the old shoots after flowering. Exochordas are spectacular enough to merit an isolated place in the garden. Propagation is by cuttings of young shoots taken in late summer.

Forsythia suspensa

Golden bell
HEIGHT: 8ft (2.5m) • Hardy
FLOWERING SEASON: Spring

These ubiquitous shrubs, with their open, spreading habit and long, gently arching, grey-brown branches are a familiar sight in spring. The light to mid green leaves which are roughly oval in shape, turn butter-yellow in autumn. Delicate, pale to golden yellow flowers are produced abundantly in spring on the previous year's growth before the leaves emerge. They should be pruned after flowering. Propagation is by hardwood cuttings taken in the winter.

Geranium 'Johnson's Blue'

Cranesbill
HEIGHT: 2½ft (75cm) • Hardy (most)
FLOWERING SEASON: Late spring

The leaves of many of these versatile herbaceous perennials are their main attraction. Deeply notched to form a palm-like shape, they are carried on tough, thin leaf stalks and in many varieties turn orange-scarlet in autumn. The flowers appear as large clusters of small, saucer-shaped blooms. There are a large number of geraniums and among the easiest to grow are: *G.* 'Johnson's Blue' and *G. endressii*. They prefer a sunny position in well-drained garden soil. Propagation is by division in early spring.

Geranium pratense

Meadow cranesbill
HEIGHT: 2ft (60cm) • Hardy
FLOWERING SEASON: Midsummer

This low-growing perennial is another popular member of the large genus of hardy cranesbills. It has mid green, deeply lobed leaves with a scalloped margin, held above the ground on thin green leaf stalks. The saucer-shaped flowers have five petals, and are violet-blue with clearly marked red veins on each petal. The cultivar 'Mrs Kendall Clark', is very free flowering, with clear blue flowers. Propagation is by division in early spring. In autumn the leaves of these plants turn orange before dying down for winter.

Gypsophila 'Rosenschleier' syn. 'Rosy Veil'

Baby's breath/Chalk plant
HEIGHT: 3ft (1m) • Hardy
FLOWERING SEASON: Summer

These cottage garden favourites have thin, strap-like, grey-green leaves very like those of the carnation, carried on thick, grey-green stems. Masses of very small flowers are produced in large clusters. Dwarf and pink-flowered cultivars are available as well as a double cultivar, *G. paniculata* 'Bristol Fairy'. *G. repens* 'Rosea' is very low-growing, 4-6in (10-15cm), and spreads to form a dense mat, with small, rose-pink flowers produced in abundance. Propagation is by root cuttings.

Hydrangea aspera
Villosa Group

Hydrangea
HEIGHT: 10ft (3m) • Hardy
FLOWERING SEASON: Late summer/autumn

The Villosa Group hydrangeas are rather gaunt shrubs with narrow bluish green leaves above and grey down underneath. In late summer they carry large flower heads with a mass of small purple-pink flowers in the centre surrounded by larger pinkish–white flowers on the outside. The whole effect is most striking and attractive. They prefer partial shade and moist soil. Propagation is by softwood cuttings taken in summer.

Iris germanica

Common German flag
HEIGHT: 2½ft (75cm) • Hardy
FLOWERING SEASON: Spring/summer

This tough evergreen plant has dark green, strap-like leaves up to 2ft (60cm) in length. The primrose-scented flowers have silky purple petals with a yellow centre. They are carried on short stems in late spring. Among many good hybrids are: *I.* 'Black Swan', with deep, blue-black flowers with a dark blue beard, and the free-flowering *I.* 'Wabash', which has white standards and violet-blue falls. Bearded irises of which this is one will grow in most ordinary soils enriched by compost. Propagation is by division of established plants immediately after flowering.

Juniperus virginiana
'Sulphur Spray'

Pencil cedar
HEIGHT: 21ft (7m) • Hardy
FLOWERING SEASON: Spring

These versatile hardy conifers come in a vast array of cultivars. The low-growing, 'prostrate' cultivars make very good ground cover for low maintenance gardens. In contrast, *J. scopulorum* 'Skyrocket', with its silvery blue-green foliage, is probably the most narrow and upright conifer in cultivation. The wood of *J. virginiana* was used to make lead pencils. Propagation is by semi-ripe cuttings with a heel taken in September.

Kerria japonica 'Pleniflora'

Jew's mallow
HEIGHT: 10ft (3m) • Hardy
FLOWERING SEASON: Spring

A hardy leaf losing shrub with bright green leaves and arching shoots with yellow, spiky, pompom-type flowers carried on the branches in spring. They are often grown against a wall where they may have to be tied back. Kerria is one of the easiest shrubs to grow and tolerates all soil conditions but does best in sun where the soil has been deeply dug and enriched by compost or manure. Mature plants form clumps and propagation is by dividing the clumps in late autumn.

Kolkwitzia amabilis

Beauty bush
HEIGHT: 10ft (3m) • Hardy
FLOWERING SEASON: Late spring/early summer

This medium-sized shrub is commonly known as the beauty bush, a name it thoroughly deserves. The small, bell-shaped flowers, which are a soft-pink with a trace of yellow in the open throat, hang in small clusters on the thin twiggy branches. The light olive-green leaves are tinged red when young. The thin, twiggy shoots are erect when young but develop a drooping habit as they become older. Prefers full sun and fertile well-drained soil. Propagated from semi-ripe cuttings taken in midsummer.

Lavatera 'Barnsley'

Tree mallow
HEIGHT: 6ft(1.8m) • Moderately hardy
FLOWERING SEASON: Summer/autumn

A popular vigorous garden plant which may keep its leaves in mild winters, in the summer it carries a multitude of pinkish–white flowers with a deeper pink circle at the centre. The leaves are a greyish green. *L.* 'Rosea' is bright pink. Lavateras must have well-drained soil and do not do well in heavy clay or soil that is very acidic. They like a sunny position. Cut the whole plant down to within 1ft (30cm) of the ground in the spring. Propagate by semi-ripe cuttings in summer or hardwood cuttings in winter.

Lonicera × brownii 'Dropmore Scarlet'

Scarlet trumpet honeysuckle
HEIGHT: 10ft (3m) • Hardy
FLOWERING SEASON: Mid/late summer

These attractive twining climbers have fragrant flowers which are tubular, opening out to a broad mouth, carried individually or in clusters. The colours range from white through pale yellow to gold, pink and scarlet. The pale to mid green leaves vary in shape from broadly oval to almost circular. *L. periclymenum* cultivars are very popular. Propagation is by semi-ripe cuttings taken in autumn.

Lupinus Russell Hybrids

Lupin
HEIGHT: 4ft (1.2m) • Hardy
FLOWERING SEASON: Summer

One of the delights of the herbaceous border in high summer, lupins are easy to grow and flourish in most soils. They prefer a sunny position. They come in a variety of colours which range from yellow to purple, blue and red. They are best raised from seed sown in the spring and planted out in position in the autumn, or they can be propagated by basal cuttings taken in the spring. The plants are not long-lived and will require replacing every 3 or 4 years. Prone to attack by aphids.

Morus nigra

Black mulberry
HEIGHT: 24ft (7.5m) • Hardy
FLOWERING SEASON: Early spring

This remarkable tree has large, grey-green pointed leaves, with a coarsely toothed margin and a coarse texture. The leaves give a striking display of autumn colour. The catkin-like flowers are of little significance and often go unnoticed, but are followed in autumn by reddish-purple, blackberry-like fruit, almost black when ripe, which is juicy and very tasty. Propagation is by hardwood cuttings taken in early winter and rooted out in the open ground.

Nigella damascena

Love-in-a-mist/Devil-in-a-bush
HEIGHT: 2ft (60cm) • Hardy
Flowering Season: Summer

A hardy annual grown for its attractive blue flowers, the flowers are set among very finely divided leaf stems which add considerably to their charms. *N. d.* 'Miss Jekyll' has darker blue flowers and *N. d.* 'Persian Jewels' has white, pink or blue flowers. The flowers are followed by decorative seed pods much used in flower arranging but if these are not required it is best to dead head the plant as this prolongs the flowering period. Likes sun and fertile well-drained soil. Sow seed in spring for flowers that summer.

Osmanthus delavayi

HEIGHT: 8ft (2.5m) • Hardy
FLOWERING SEASON: Spring

An evergreen shrub, *O. delavayi* is from China and was originally introduced in 1890. It has oval, toothed leaves which are a dark, glossy green. It produces clusters of small tubular white flowers which are highly fragrant. It will grow in sun or partial shade and prefers well-drained soil, but ideally needs a site sheltered from cold winds. The species, *O. heterophyllus*, makes a good hedging plant. If growing *O. heterophyllus* as a hedge, trim it regularly. To propagate take half-ripe cuttings in summer or layer branches in autumn.

Ostrya carpinifolia

Hop hornbeam
HEIGHT: 50ft (15m) • Hardy
FLOWERING SEASON: Mid spring

This attractive tree has greyish-purple bark on the main trunk and reddish-brown shoots which carry the glossy, dark green, oval leaves, which turn butter-yellow in the autumn. The flowers are long yellow catkins which hang from the bare branches in large quantities in spring. Green, hop-like fruits appear in autumn which later turn brown, they have a small nut-type seed under each 'hop' scale. For small gardens, the smaller *O. virginiana* is more useful. Propagation is by seed sown in late autumn or early spring.

Paeonia delavayi

Tree peony
HEIGHT: 6ft (1.8m) • Hardy
FLOWERING SEASON: Summer

The tree peony is a deciduous shrub with erect branches and an open suckering habit, the pale-brown bark flakes from the stems as they age. Large, oval leaves are finely divided into pointed sections with reddish-green stalks. The small, cup-shaped, single red flowers have golden stamens in the centre, and are followed by green, black-seeded fruits in autumn. Propagation is by seed sown in autumn or semi-ripe cuttings taken in summer.

Philadelphus coronarius 'Variegatus'

Mock orange
HEIGHT: 6ft (1.8m) • Hardy
FLOWERING SEASON: Summer

This deciduous, bushy shrub has a dense, upright habit and mid green, oval leaves. The small, creamy-white flowers are noted for their heady fragrance. A number of cultivars have coloured leaves: *P. c.* 'Aureus' has golden-yellow leaves, which turn lemon-green as they age, and *P. c.* 'Variegatus' green leaves edged with white. Propagation is by softwood cuttings taken in summer or hard-wood cuttings taken in autumn and winter.

Phillyrea latifolia

HEIGHT: 10ft (3m) • Hardy
FLOWERING SEASON: Late spring/early summer

An evergreen shrub which has small but very fragrant flowers. The small, elliptical strap-like leaves are a shiny dark green and leathery. The small, scented white flowers are carried in clusters at the end of the young, branching stems. They are sometimes followed by blackcurrant-like fruits in autumn. Many of the branches tend to arch over so that a loose mound-like shrub is formed. It likes a sunny position and well-drained soil. Propagation is by semi-ripe cuttings taken in early summer.

Phlomis fruticosa

Jerusalem sage
HEIGHT: 3ft (1m) • Hardy
FLOWERING SEASON: Summer

An attractive, summer-flowering shrub, which forms a dense evergreen mound of straggly twiggy branches. The unusually shaped yellow flowers are produced in large ball-shaped trusses on the shoot tips. Broadly oval grey-green, coarsely textured leaves have a felty surface which turns slightly yellow in autumn. The young erect stems are also covered in felt, which disappears by the end of the first year of growth. Prune in late spring after the last frosts. Propagation is by softwood cuttings taken in late summer.

Populus alba 'Raket'

White poplar
HEIGHT: 80ft (25m) • Hardy
FLOWERING SEASON: Early spring

A deciduous tree with a broad, spreading habit, dark grey-green fissured bark, and young shoots which are covered with a thick white felt. The main attraction is the foliage: dark green leaves which have a silver down on the underside turn golden yellow in autumn. The cultivar *P. a.* 'Richardii' is much slower-growing and has small golden leaves which are white beneath. Poplar trees like coastal districts. Propagation is by hard-wood cuttings taken in autumn. Silver leaf fungus kills large branches.

Potentilla fruticosa 'Hopley's Orange'

HEIGHT: 4ft (1.2m) • Hardy
FLOWERING SEASON: Spring/summer

This is a compact, bushy shrub with masses of spindly branches, with orange-brown bark which turns grey-brown and flakes with age. Deeply lobed, mid green leaves are in dense clusters over the younger branches. Flowers are small, buttercup-yellow and borne in clusters of no more than three blooms. Numerous named cultivars include the low-growing, *P. f.* 'Red Ace', with vermilion flowers and *P. f.* 'Abbotswood', with dark green foliage and white flowers. Propagation is by semi-ripe cuttings taken in autumn.

Prunus sargentii

Sargent cherry
HEIGHT: 25ft (8m) • Hardy
FLOWERING SEASON: Early/mid spring

This tree produces vast quantities of clear, single, shell-pink flowers in large clusters, which are complemented by the emerging glossy, bronze-red foliage of the new season's growth. Even more striking is the dramatic change of foliage colour in early autumn when the leaves turn yellow, orange and crimson shades before falling. Most ornamental cherries are propagated by budding or grafting in commercial nurseries, and offered for sale as young trees.

Robinia hispida

Rose acacia
HEIGHT: 6ft (1.8m) • Hardy
FLOWERING SEASON: Late spring/early summer

This attractive deciduous shrub has a loose, open habit and slightly arching branches, which are brittle and break very easily. The dark green leaves, which consist of up to thirteen small, oval leaflets arranged along a green central leaf stalk, turn butter-yellow in autumn. The large, sweet pea-like flowers are deep rose-pink, and are borne in long dangling clusters. It is ideal for training up against a wall or fence. The shrub tolerates most soils except for waterlogged sites and prefers full sun. Propagation is by seed sown in spring.

Romneya coulteri

Californian tree poppy
HEIGHT: 6ft (1.8m) • Moderately hardy
FLOWERING SEASON: Late summer

A striking and beautiful summer flowering perennial which needs the shelter of a south or south-west wall. It has large fragrant white flowers with prominent centres of golden-yellow stamens which appear in late summer. The leaves are deeply divided and grey-green in colour. It needs well-drained soil enriched by compost or leaf mould. Cut back the stems in the spring. Propagation is by root cuttings taken in the spring or by seed sown in the autumn.

Rosmarinus officinalis

Rosemary
HEIGHT: 6ft (1.8m) • Moderately hardy
FLOWERING SEASON: Spring/autumn

This popular aromatic shrub has an erect open habit, with narrow, aromatic, evergreen leaves that are mid to dark green in colour with pale green undersides. The tubular flowers, which range in colour from white to blues, pinks and mauves, are produced in small clusters at the leaf joints. These plants do not respond favourably to hard pruning, just trim back any straggling shoots. They grow best in well-drained soil and full sun. Propagation is by semi-ripe cuttings taken in August and September.

Sambucus racemosa

Red-berried elder
HEIGHT: 9ft (3m) • Hardy
FLOWERING SEASON: Late spring

This is a large deciduous shrub with a broad, spreading habit. It is grown for its lush foliage and colourful fruits. The leaves are mid green and divided into five oval leaflets joined at the base to form a 'hand'. They turn pale yellow in autumn. In spring, large flat heads of white flowers are produced, to be followed by huge clusters of bright red berries in autumn. The cultivar *S. r.* 'Plumosa Aurea' has golden, finely-cut leaves. Elders grow almost anywhere. Propagation is by hardwood cuttings taken in winter.

Scabiosa 'Butterfly Blue'

Scabious
HEIGHT: 2ft (60cm) • Hardy
FLOWERING SEASON: Summer/autumn

A clump-forming herbaceous perennial with leaves that are divided into narrow segments. The large flowers, which range from white through blue to mauves and pinks, are borne on long, slender, leafless stems. *S. caucasica* 'Clive Greaves' is a rich mauve; 'Miss Willmott' is the best white cultivar. Two recent introductions are the more compact species 'Butterfly Blue' and 'Pink Mist'. It likes a sunny position and well-drained soil. Propagation is by softwood cuttings taken in spring and summer, or division in spring.

Spiraea betulifolia

Meadowsweet
HEIGHT: 3ft (1m) • Hardy
FLOWERING SEASON: Spring

Spiraeas are hardy deciduous shrubs grown for their leaf colour and the masses of small flowers that appear in spring and summer. *S.* 'Arguta' known as the 'Bridal wreath', has arched branches covered with white flowers in May as has *S. betulifolia. S. japonica* 'Goldflame' is a more upright arching shrub with orange-red young leaves in the spring and heads of deep rose-pink flowers. Spiraeas can be grown in most soils and semi-shade. Propagate by semi-ripe cuttings in summer.

Stachyurus chinensis

HEIGHT: 12ft (4m) • Hardy
FLOWERING SEASON: Winter

These winter-flowering shrubs do well on most soils and deserve to be more common than they are. When young, the plant has an upright habit, later forming a network of branching, purple-green shoots. The dark green, purple-tinged leaves are deeply veined, large, oval and end in a point. The small, pale yellow flowers, which are in long catkin-like structures, are borne freely along the bare branches in winter and spring. Propagation is by layering of low branches or semi-ripe cuttings taken in summer.

Symphoricarpos × *doorenbosii* 'Mother of Pearl'

Snowberry
HEIGHT: 5ft (1.5m) • Hardy
FLOWERING SEASON: Summer

The common snowberry, *S. albus* has small pink flowers in summer followed by white round berries which can be seen on bushes all winter as they are often ignored by the birds. *S.* × *d.* 'Mother of Pearl' has pink berries and *S. orbiculatus*, the coral berry, has white flowers and red berries. They can be grown in all soils and in shade as well as sun. They can make a useful informal hedge. Propagate by semi-ripe cuttings in summer.

Syringa × *henryi*

Lilac
HEIGHT: 5-15ft (1.5-4.5m) • Moderately hardy
FLOWERING SEASON: Summer

Attractive, deciduous shrubs, lilacs have mid green leaves, arranged along the twiggy branches in opposite pairs. The small flowers are carried in spikes at the tips of shoots, they are very fragrant, tubular and range in colour from deep pink through mauve to white. There are a number of species and cultivars available and care should be taken to select one that does not grow too large. They flourish in light or heavy fertile soil and prefer a sunny site. Propagation is by semi-ripe cuttings taken in mid to late summer.

Teucrium fruticans

Shrubby germander
Height: 6ft (1.8m) • Moderately hardy
Flowering Season: Summer

An evergreen shrub sometimes called the tree germander which has rather untidy pointing branches. These carry blue-grey silvery aromatic leaves which are white underneath. In the summer blue flowers appear along the length of each branch. It likes full sun and fertile well-drained soil and is a useful addition to any mixed border. It does not require pruning except to remove straggly branches and any dead wood in the spring. Propagate by semi-ripe cuttings taken in the summer.

Thuja occidentalis 'Sunkist'

Eastern white cedar
HEIGHT: 60ft (18m) • Hardy
FLOWERING SEASON: Early spring

This is a vigorous, long-lived tree with a neat conical shape. The bark, which is light to reddish-brown, peels and flakes off as the tree ages. The flat leaves are made up of many small, scale-like sections, and have a strong 'pineapple' aroma which is released when the leaves are crushed. The cones are small and brown. *T. plicata* 'Zebrina' has yellow bands on the leaves which are so close together that the plant appears to be golden. Propagation is by semi-ripe cuttings taken in spring or autumn.

Viburnum tinus

Laurustinus
HEIGHT: 5ft (1.5m) • Hardy
FLOWERING SEASON: Winter

Verbascum chaixii

Mullein
HEIGHT: 3ft (1m) • Hardy
FLOWERING SEASON: Summer

This evergreen perennial has large, nettle-like leaves which are grey-green in colour and covered with a fine, grey felt. The slender spires of yellow flowers with purple centres are produced in July and August and the white-flowered cultivar *V. c.* 'Album', is even more striking. Propagation is by seed in spring or late summer or by root cuttings in winter. Blackfly are often a problem but mullein moth caterpillars are possibly the most devastating pest.

This evergreen shrub has an upright habit when young but becomes a rather open, round-topped, spreading plant as it ages. The broadly oval, dark green leaves have paler undersides and are arranged in pairs along the dark, greenish-brown stems which end in flat clusters of small, white, slightly fragrant tubular flowers. Possibly the best plant is *V. t.* 'Eve Price', which has flowers that are deep rose-pink in bud, opening to white flushed with pink. It tolerates most soils and some shade. Propagation is by semi-ripe cuttings taken in early summer.

Weigela florida 'Foliis Purpureis'

Bush honeysuckle
HEIGHT: 3ft (1m) Hardy
FLOWERING SEASON: Spring/early summer

A deciduous, low-growing, bushy shrub which has funnel-shaped flowers, bright pink on the outside and a paler pink shading to white within. The leaves are a dullish dark green. Weigelas will grow in almost any soil and while they prefer sun they will tolerate some shade. Prune established plants after flowering by cutting out up to one third of the branches to ground level. Propagate by semi-ripe cuttings in summer.

More Plants for Chalk Soil

Many plants can be grown on chalk soil. The list is very large and we can only give a small selection of the most suitable plants but it should be noted that most bulbs (see pages 282–289) do well on chalk.

Gardening on chalk is governed by the depth of soil over the underlying chalk or limestone strata, chalk soil is inclined to be dry and hungry. It can be improved by adding copious quantities of farmyard manure, leaf mould, garden compost and turf and the fertility can be improved by adding dried blood and balanced artificial fertilisers such as Growmore.

TREES
Abies koreana
Acer (in variety)
Betula (in variety)
Carpinus betulus
Catalpa bignonioides
Cercidiphyllum japonicum
Chimonanthus praecox
Corylus (in variety)
Crataegus (in variety)
Davidia involucrata
Fagus (in variety)
Ficus carica
Fraxinus angustifolia

Koelreuteria paniculata
Larix decidua
Liquidambar styraciflua 'Worplesdon'
Malus (in variety)
Pyrus (in variety)
Sorbus (in variety)

SHRUBS
Aronia arbutifolia
Artemesia absinthium
Berberis (in variety)
Buddleja (in variety)
Chaenomeles japonica
Choisya ternata
Cornus (in variety)
Cotinus coggygria
Escallonia (in variety)
Euonymus fortunei cvs.
Jasminum officinale
Lavandula (in variety)
Ligustrum ovalifolium
Mahonia (in variety)
Myrtus communis
Osmanthus (in variety)
Philadelphus (in variety)
Ribes laurifolium
Rosa 'Königin von Dänemark'
R. 'Madame Legras de Saint Germain'
(Old-fashioned and Alba roses are particularly suitable for poor soil and conditions)
Salvia officinalis
Sarcococca hookeriana
Senecio (Brachyglottis) 'Sunshine'
Stepanandra tanakae

Syringa (in variety)
Viburnum (in variety)

PERENNIALS & GROUND COVER PLANTS
Alchemilla mollis
Anemone × hybrida
Aruncus dioicus
Aster novi-belgii
Astilbe (in variety)
Bergenia (in variety)
Campanula carpatica
Catananche caerulea
Ceratostigma willmottianum
Crambe cordifolia
Dianthus (in variety)
Dicentra (in variety)
Digitalis (in variety)
Echinops bannaticus
Geranium (in variety)
Helianthemum (in variety)
Iris (in variety)
Lamium maculatum
Leucanthemum × superbum
Nepeta × faassenii
Penstemon (in variety)
Perovskia atriplicifolia
Phlox paniculata
Polygonatum × hybridum
Primula auricula 'Adrian'
Pulmonaria saccharata
Santolina chamaecyparissus
Veronica prostrata
Vinca (in variety)

PLANTS
for CLAY SOILS

Although part of the garden landscape in many areas, clay soil can be difficult to deal with, becoming waterlogged in winter and baked hard in summer. Plants suffer alternately from too much water or from drought. Here is a selection of plants that are attractive and tough enough to cope with these far from ideal conditions.

ABOVE: Houttuynia cordata 'Chameleon', a robust ground-covering perennial with lovely leaf colour that likes moisture and appreciates some sun. It grows well beside water.

OPPOSITE: Foxgloves make an impressive bank at the back of a border with yellow hemerocallis, geranium and lady's mantle at the front.

ABOVE: *Big clump-forming hostas, such as* Hosta crispula *with its wavy-edged, cream-splashed leaves, are successful on clay, as are the drifts of* Persicaria bistorta, *with its spires of pink flowers in summer.*

Clay is one of those substances that is wonderful in small quantities, but a real nuisance if you have too much of it. It is an essential part of a good soil, because it holds onto the nutrients that plants need for healthy growth, and retains moisture, so that plants growing in it suffer less from drought in all but the driest of summers. Unfortunately, despite these advantages, really heavy, wet, sticky clay soil is often totally unworkable, and it is also cold in spring, which can quickly rot delicate plants.

These difficulties come about as a direct result of the composition of the soil. The particles that make up a clay soil are the smallest found in mineral soils, with the result that the water retained in the tiny spaces between the particles binds them together into an unresponsive mass. Physically working this soil is largely a matter of timing; try to do it when it is too wet and it will smear and form a 'pan' at the depth you go down to, forming an impenetrable layer for plant roots and draining water alike. Leave it until it is too dry, on the other hand, and you are working with what feels like lumps of rock. Once you have experienced both situations, it will become apparent that you must establish the ideal state in which to tackle your soil.

Clay soils have a tendency to either become sticky and greasy when they are wet, or to bake hard and crack open when they dry out. This cracking process leaves deep crevices which speed up the drying-out process by exposing a greater surface area from which the moisture can evaporate. Any rain which falls then simply runs off without soaking in. At this stage, you would expect the plants to wilt and die, but even though the soil seems to be rock hard, enough water is still being held by the soil particles to sustain the plants for a while.

While water retention is a distinct advantage in summer, it is usually just the opposite in winter. So much water may be retained in the soil, and for such long periods, that plant roots have to be able to tolerate very damp conditions, often with little air to help compensate. Many members of the rose family thrive in these conditions; and aronia, chaenomeles (quince), cotoneaster, crataegus (hawthorn), malus (crab apple) and pyracantha do particularly well.

If the soil can be improved to make it more workable by the addition of organic matter to loosen it up, it will retain plant nutrients for longer periods than other soils, so that plants are able to use more of them before they are leached away by rain. Fertiliser applications are then more effective and the nutrients released by organic matter as it rots are used more effectively.

Finally, clay soils can be acid, neutral or alkaline, which will also affect your choice of plants, so a soil test is helpful if the vegetation in the immediate surroundings fail to give any clues. Although clay soils are more stable in their acidity and alkalinity, they are much more difficult to change. More often than not the limiting factor as to what you can grow on a clay soil will in fact be the soil pH reading rather than the clay content of your soil.

There are many bulbs, herbaceous perennials and marginal plants such as aruncus, lysimachia, mimulus, and tradescantia which prefer the cool, moist conditions that clay soils offer. As with any situation where one condition overrides the others, once you have chosen the plants which thrive under those circumstances, you can have as good a display as anywhere else. Grow plants with a vigorous constitution as those are the ones likely to do best.

BELOW: Persicaria bistorta, *at the front of the border, with iris, geranium phaeum and philadelphus behind are all plants that will flourish in heavy soil. Roses are particularly suitable plants to grow if you garden on clay.*

Abelia × *grandiflora*

HEIGHT: 5ft (1.5m) • Hardy
FLOWERING SEASON: Late summer/late autumn

This hybrid shrub has glossy green, oval leaves carried on thin branches, giving the plant a loose, spreading appearance. The tubular flowers, borne in open clusters on the shoot tips, are slightly fragrant and a soft pink, which fades to white with age. Regular pruning is not required. It likes well-drained soil and a sheltered sunny position, some protection may be necessary in severe winters. This plant is easy to propagate from 4in (10cm) tip cuttings placed in a cold frame in August.

Acer platanoides

Norway maple
HEIGHT: 100ft (30m) • Hardy
FLOWERING SEASON: Spring

This is a vigorous tree with typical, palmate maple leaves. Bright green in summer, they turn a bright golden-yellow in the autumn. In the spring bright golden flowers are produced in broad flat clusters on the branches before the leaves. Two good cultivars are the purple-leaved *A. p.* 'Crimson King' and *A. p.* 'Drummondii', which has mid green leaves with a creamy-white margin. Propagation is by seed sown in the spring or, for named cultivars, budding in the summer.

Alcea rosea Chater's Double Group

Hollyhock
HEIGHT: 8ft (2.5m) • Hardy
FLOWERING SEASON: Summer

Hollyhocks are hardy biennial plants although in some cases they are short lived perennials. They are a familiar sight throughout cottage gardens in the country and their large upright flower spikes make a focal point in any border. They should be raised from seed sown in a prepared bed in May and planted out in position in October. Hollyhocks like well-drained soil and a sunny position. Rust may be a problem.

Alnus incana

Grey alder
HEIGHT: 60ft (18m) • Hardy
FLOWERING SEASON: Early spring

This is a deciduous tree with reddish-brown shoots and a wide conical habit. The broadly oval leaves are dark green on the upper surface, grey beneath and deeply veined, with slightly puckered margins. In late winter and early spring, dangling yellow catkins are produced close to the shoot tips. Alders grow in most conditions and this tree is ideal for poor soils and cold exposed sites. There is a golden-leafed cultivar *A. i.* 'Aurea'. Propagation is by seed sown in spring, or, for named cultivars, grafting.

Amaranthus caudatus

Love-lies-bleeding/Joseph's coat
HEIGHT: 3-4ft (1-1.2m) • Half-hardy
FLOWERING SEASON: Summer/autumn

This popular plant has broadly oval, light green leaves and crimson drooping, rope-like flowers up to 18in (45cm) long. The stems of the plant often turn crimson in the autumn. *A. c.* 'Viridis' has attractive pale green tassels, while a very striking variety, *A. tricolor* var. *salicifolius* is grown for its drooping, willow-like leaves which are shades of orange, reddish-pink and bronze. This easy-going plant will grow in any light, from full sun through to partial shade. Propagation is by seeds sown in March.

Anemone × *hybrida* 'Königin Charlotte'

Japanese anemone
HEIGHT: 3ft (1m) • Hardy
FLOWERING SEASON: Late summer/early autumn

This vigorous branching plant thrives in moist soils, in a partially shaded situation. The mid to deep green leaves are deeply cut and almost trifoliate. The shallowly cup-shaped flowers, which range from white to deep rose-pink with a bright core of yellow stamens, are carried on tall, thin, green stems Among the cultivars are *A.* × *h.* 'Honorine Jobert' with white flowers, and the semi-double-flowered *A. hupehensis* var. *japonica* 'Bressingham Glow' with rosy-red blooms.

Aralia elata

Japanese angelica tree
HEIGHT: 25ft (8m) • Hardy
FLOWERING SEASON: Late summer

This large suckering shrub has sparse, angular branches clad with short, broad-based prickles. It is grown for the beauty of its large clusters of dark green leaves which are arranged in a whorl on the end of each branch. Large spikes of small white flowers are carried on the tip of each branch from late August. A very attractive cultivar, *A.e.* 'Aureovariegata', has irregular, golden-yellow edged leaves. Propagate by root cuttings taken in February.

Aronia arbutifolia

Chokeberry
HEIGHT: 8ft (2.5m) • Hardy
FLOWERING SEASON: Spring

A colourful, deciduous shrub which has a rather erect habit when young, but becomes lax and spreading with age. It is grown for its flowers, fruits and autumn colour. The leaves are narrowly oval, dark green with a grey-green underside, and turn shades of brilliant orange, crimson and purple in autumn. In spring, small, white, hawthorn-like flowers are produced in flat clusters, followed by small red berries. It prefers sun or semi-shade and moist well-drained soil. Propagation is by semi-ripe cuttings in summer or seed sown in spring.

Aruncus dioicus

Goat's beard
HEIGHT: 5ft (1.5m) • Hardy
FLOWERING SEASON: Summer

This hummock-forming perennial has large, light green, deeply-veined leaves which are made up of several strap-like leaflets, held on tough sturdy stems. In the summer, large feathery plumes of creamy-white flowers are carried on strong thin reddish-green stems. In the autumn the female plants bear chest-nut brown seed-heads, but it is the male plants that produce the best flowers. It will grow in any well-drained soil and likes full sun. Propagation is by division in winter.

Astilbe × arendsii

Goat's beard
HEIGHT: 3ft (1m) • Hardy
FLOWERING SEASON: Midsummer

This hardy herbaceous perennial has deep green, finely cut, fern-like foliage, carried on thin wiry reddish-green stems; some of the red-flowered cultivars have bronze-green foliage in the spring. In the summer large, pointed spikes of plume-like blooms appear. A large number of cultivars are now available: *A.* 'Bressingham Beauty' has spikes of rich pink flowers, and *A.* 'Feuer', has salmon-red blooms. They like moist rich soil and at least partial shade. Propagation is by division in the winter.

Berberis × stenophylla

Barberry
HEIGHT: 8ft (2.5m) • Hardy
FLOWERING SEASON: Late spring

This evergreen shrub has gracefully arching, slender branches, with small, orange-yellow flowers, which are followed by small, blue fruits. The small, glossy, dark green leaves are narrow and tipped with sharp spines. It is effective as an impenetrable, informal hedge, but also as an individual specimen plant. The dwarf cultivar *B.* × *s.* 'Crawley Gem', has a low, bushy habit and orange flowers which are red when in bud. They are soil tolerant and grow in sun or semi-shade. Propagation is by semi-ripe cuttings taken in summer.

Campsis radicans

Trumpet flower/Trumpet vine
HEIGHT: 30ft (9m) • Moderately hardy
FLOWERING SEASON: Late summer/early autumn

A fast-growing plant ideal for sunny walls and fences, pergolas and gazebos, or other, similar structures. Four to twelve trumpet-like orange/red flowers are carried in clusters on the shoot tips. There are also red- and yellow-flowered cultivars. The light to mid green foliage consists of oval leaflets which form pinnate leaves. Good yellow autumn colour. Fast rate of growth. Likes sun and fertile, well-drained soil, water in the summer in dry spells. Propagation is by root cuttings taken in early spring.

Cardamine pratensis 'Flore Pleno'

Cuckoo flower/Lady's smock/Bitter cress
HEIGHT: 18in (45cm) • Hardy
FLOWERING SEASON: Late spring

This neat, clump-forming plant has mid green leaves divided into many small, rounded leaflets arranged in neat basal rosettes. *C. p.* 'Flore Pleno', produces loose, open clusters of double lilac flowers in late spring. This plant does not produce seed but is very easy to propagate: leaves in contact with a moist surface produce adventitious roots, and later shoots which can be divided up to produce more plants.

Celastrus orbiculatus

Oriental bittersweet/Staff vine
HEIGHT: 22ft (7m) • Hardy
FLOWERING SEASON: Summer

A large, vigorous, useful climber with oval, mid green leaves on short stalks and tiny greenish flowers carried on the female plant in summer. The leaves turn a good yellow in autumn. The twining stems are light grey-green, changing to light creamy-brown with age in early summer, followed by bright orange capsules containing a scarlet-coated seed if a male plant is available as a pollinator. Prefers shade and grows in most soils. Propagation is from seed sown in autumn.

Chaenomeles japonica

Japonica/Japanese quince
HEIGHT: 4ft (1.2m) • Hardy
FLOWERING SEASON: Spring

A colourful, slow-growing shrub with a lax spreading habit. The single flowers, orange-red with a golden centre, are produced in profusion along the older wood in spring, followed by bright yellow quince fruits. Elliptical leaves are green, changing to pale yellow in autumn. Often grown on walls it prefers sun and well-drained soil. Prune after flowering. Propagation is by semi-ripe cuttings taken with a heel in late summer. Coral spot fungus can cause problems.

Crambe cordifolia

Ornamental sea kale
HEIGHT: 6ft (1.8m) • Hardy
FLOWERING SEASON: Summer

A large spreading plant which forms a great clump when established and in the summer is covered with masses of small white fragrant flowers rather like a giant gypsophila. They are carried above large dark green crinkled leaves. *C. maritima* is a smaller plant more generally found in the kitchen garden where it can be grown as a spring vegetable. Kale is easy to cultivate in ordinary well-drained garden soil and tolerates some shade. Propagate by dividing up the clumps in the spring.

Darmera peltata

Umbrella plant
HEIGHT: 4ft (1.2m) • Hardy
FLOWERING SEASON: Spring

This is a spreading perennial with large, disc-like leaves which turn an interesting bronze-pink in the autumn. The pale pink flowers, which have a white reverse to the petals, are carried in large round clusters on dark greenish-brown stems, which are covered in fine white hairs. The flowers and stems appear before the leaves. It needs moist conditions and makes a fine water plant beside a pool. Grows in sun or shade. Propagation is by division of the rhizomes in spring or by seed in autumn.

Digitalis grandiflora

Foxglove
HEIGHT: 3ft (1m) • Hardy
FLOWERING SEASON: Late summer

This superb perennial foxglove forms a clump of strap-like leaves which are mid green and covered with soft hairs particularly on the underside. The clear, pale yellow flowers have a pattern of brown, net-like markings on the inside, and are carried on tall flower spikes up to 3ft (1m) or more in height. Foxgloves grow best in moist well-drained soil and semi-shade. This plant is relatively short-lived and must be replaced every third or fourth year. Propagation is by seed sown in late spring or early summer.

Dodecatheon pulchellum

Shooting star/American cowslip
HEIGHT: 18in (45cm) • Hardy
FLOWERING SEASON: Early summer

These clump-forming hardy herbaceous perennials have light green, elliptical leaves arranged in flat, spreading rosettes growing close to the ground. In the summer the nodding flowers appear on strong slender stems, each bloom is a circle of rose-purple petals which are swept back away from the bright yellow anthers in the centre of the flower. They prefer a shady position in moist soil. Propagation is by seed sown in autumn, or by division in winter.

Filipendula palmata 'Alba'

Meadowsweet/Dropwort
HEIGHT: 3ft (1m) • Hardy
FLOWERING SEASON: Midsummer

This attractive perennial has mid green, deeply cut foliage, giving the leaves a fern-like appearance. There is a double-flowered cultivar *F. vulgaris* 'Multiplex' which produces large spikes of creamy-white, plumes of flowers in summer which remain attractive for a long period. They grow best in a cool, moist situation with partial shade, and do not like too much disturbance. *F. rubra* has pink flowers and will grow in boggy ground. Propagation is by division in the winter.

Ginkgo biloba

Maidenhair tree
HEIGHT: 70ft (21m) • Hardy
FLOWERING SEASON: Spring

A most interesting and ornamental deciduous tree it has peculiarly shaped leaves with crinkled edges. They turn brilliant yellow and gold before falling in the autumn. The tree also carries fruits in the autumn, but it requires both male and female trees to be grown together for the flowers to become fertile. It prefers well-drained soil and tolerates some shade. The tree has been found in fossil beds millions of years old. It was often planted near temples.

Hemerocallis 'Burning Daylight'

Day lily
HEIGHT: 3ft (1m) • Hardy
FLOWERING SEASON: Summer

These are colourful, clump-forming plants, with leaves that are pale to mid green, strap-shaped, ending in a point at the tip. The brightly coloured, lily-like flowers only last for a day, but are produced in such abundance that this is hardly noticeable. The popular Kwanso cultivars include the orange, double-flowered *H. fulva* 'Flore Pleno' and the variegated *H. f.* 'Kwanso Variegata'. They like full sun and moist soil. Propagation is by division in early spring.

Hosta 'Spinners'

Plantain lily
HEIGHT: 2ft (60cm) • Hardy
FLOWERING SEASON: Late summer/early autumn

These hardy herbaceous perennials are grown for their attractive foliage. Leaf shapes range from long and narrow to oval with a pointed tip. Leaf colours can vary from blue to rich combinations of silver or golden variegations. The flowers are carried on spikes above the leaves. *H. sieboldiana* var. *elegans* has broadly spear-shaped, glossy, bluish-green leaves with prominent veins, and soft lilac-blue flowers. Propagation is by division in early spring, but replant immediately. The leaves are very prone to slug and snail damage.

Houttuynia cordata 'Chameleon'

HEIGHT: 18in (45cm) • Hardy
FLOWERING SEASON: Spring

This is a vigorous, spreading perennial with dark blue-green, aromatic, heart-shaped leaves, carried on reddish-green leaf stalks, and fleshy erect stems. This plant spreads rapidly by means of underground runners just below the soil surface. The white flowers are carried on the tips of erect stems just above the leaves. There is a double white cultivar *H. c.* 'Flore Pleno'. *H. c.* 'Chameleon' has leaves splashed with yellow and red on a dark green base. Propagation is by division in late autumn or early spring.

Humulus lupulus 'Aureus'

Golden hop
HEIGHT: 25ft (8m) • Hardy
FLOWERING SEASON: Late summer

An attractive self-supporting, perennial climber with thin bristly twining stems. The bristly leaves are toothed around the margins and are deeply lobed. The flowers are insignificant, but the fruit clusters are quite attractive in the autumn. *H. l.* 'Aureus' has soft, golden-yellow leaves, stems and fruits. There is a less vigorous variegated sort with creamy-white and green variegated leaves. Propagation is by semi-ripe cuttings taken in June and July.

Iris pseudacorus

Yellow flag
HEIGHT: 3ft (1m) • Hardy
FLOWERING SEASON: Spring/summer

This popular hardy herbaceous perennial known as yellow flag has buttercup yellow flowers and broad, strap-like, bluish-green foliage arranged in a fan. A very striking plant is *I. p.* 'Variegata', with its gold and green striped foliage. It will grow in a range of conditions but it really thrives in semi-shade, heavy soil and waterlogged conditions, and even in water up to 18in (45cm) deep. Propagation is by division immediately after the plant has flowered.

Lathyrus grandiflorus

Everlasting pea
HEIGHT: 10ft (3m) • Hardy
FLOWERING SEASON: Summer/autumn

Originally from Italy, this tall, self-supporting climber has curling tendrils at the tip of each of the mid green leaflets. The flowers are scented (especially in the evening) and come in a variety of colours, with pink, white and deep purple being the most popular. The cultivar *L. latifolius* 'White Pearl' gives a lovely cottage garden effect. Propagation is by seed sown in September or March. Harden off before planting out. New growth is very prone to slug damage in wet seasons.

Leucanthemum × superbum

Shasta daisy
HEIGHT: 3ft (1m) • Hardy
FLOWERING SEASON: Mid/late summer

Formerly known as *Chrysanthemum × superbum* this is a valued perennial, with strap-shaped, dark green leaves. The single flowers are white with a golden centre, carried on tall green stems. The species is rarely grown, as cultivars with improved flowers have been introduced. These include *L. × s.* 'Snowcap', with a dwarfing habit and white daisy-like flowers, and *L. × s.* 'Wirral Supreme', with large double flowers with a golden centre. Propagation is by division in winter or by basal cuttings taken in spring.

Mimulus × burnetii

Musk/Monkey flower
HEIGHT: 12in (30cm) • Hardy
FLOWERING SEASON: Early/late summer

This low, spreading plant thrives in cool, damp soil, but likes to have its head in the sunshine. They can be good plants for the bog garden and waterside. The elliptical, mid green leaves are carried on square stems and often have a green bract-like leaf at the point where the leaf stalk is attached to the stem. Yellow, snapdragon-like flowers open to reveal a throat mottled with brown and purple markings. Propagation is by division in the spring or seed sown in the autumn or spring, but it will often layer itself in wet soil.

Myosotis scorpioides

Water forget-me-not
HEIGHT: 10in (25cm) • Hardy
FLOWERING SEASON: Late spring/midsummer

This is a moisture-loving evergreen perennial with a long flowering period in summer when it produces branching green stems of minute blue flowers with a yellow-orange 'eye'. Spoon-shaped leaves are carried on thin green stems and covered with fine hairs when young. It is often grown as a marginal water plant. A cultivar with larger flowers is *M. s.* 'Mermaid', which has a sprawling habit and forms a loose mound. These plants last only for three or four years. Propagate by semi-ripe basal cuttings taken in spring.

Persicaria bistorta 'Superba'

Knotweed/Snakeweed
HEIGHT: 4ft (1.2m) • Hardy
FLOWERING SEASON: Summer

Persicarias were formerly known as polygonums and have the common name of knotweed. *P .b.* 'Superba' which is sometimes called snakeweed, can be invasive, but makes an attractive drift beside a water feature. It forms large clumps of arrow-shaped, centrally ribbed, mid green leaves and spires of soft pink flowers throughout the summer. It will cope with sun or partial shade, but needs moist soil. Propagate by division in spring or autumn or raise from seed.

Phlox paniculata 'Fujiyama'

HEIGHT: 3ft (1m) • Hardy
FLOWERING SEASON: Late summer

Colourful upright perennials *P. paniculata* cultivars have tubular, five-lobed flowers, generally pink in colour, carried on conical heads: among the best known are 'Amethyst', violet, 'Norah Leigh', pale lilac, and 'Franz Schubert', pink. They like deep rich soil that does not dry out, and semi-shade. Cut down to soil level after flowering and propagate by division in spring or semi-ripe cuttings in summer.

Phormium tenax

New Zealand flax
HEIGHT: 4ft (1.2m) • Moderately hardy
FLOWERING SEASON: Summer

This clump-forming, evergreen perennial has bold, sword-shaped leaves which have a tough, leathery texture and are deep green in colour. When the plant has established, dull orange flowers are borne on large, erect spikes. These are followed by scimitar-shaped seed capsules. Among the cultivars with variegated foliage, *P.* 'Dazzler' has leaves with shades of yellow, salmon-pink, orange-red and bronze. Propagation is by seed sown in the spring or division in spring.

Populus × *candicans* 'Aurora'

Ontario poplar/Balm of Gilead
HEIGHT: 80ft (25m) • Hardy
FLOWERING SEASON: Spring

A large tree with a broad crown and broad, almost heart-shaped, leaves which have a strong scent of balsam in the spring. The attractive *P. × c.* 'Aurora' has variegated foliage, the dark green leaves being splashed with pale green, creamy-white and pink. It must be pruned very hard each spring to maintain this striking effect. Poplars prefers full sun and deep moist well-drained soil. They have extensive root systems and are not suitable for planting close to buildings. Propagation is by hardwood cuttings taken in autumn.

Pterocarya fraxinifolia

Caucasian wing nut
HEIGHT: 80ft (25m) • Hardy
FLOWERING SEASON: Summer

A moisture-loving, spreading, deciduous tree, with a characteristic short trunk and deeply grooved bark. The glossy, dark green ash-like leaves are made up of many finely toothed leaflets and turn yellow in autumn. The flowers consist of long green catkins up to 18in (45cm) long, which are followed by greenish-brown winged fruits in autumn. It likes a sunny position and moist well-drained soil. Propagation is by softwood cuttings in summer, by seed sown outdoors in spring or by removing the suckers.

Pyracantha 'Orange Glow'

Firethorn
HEIGHT: 10ft (3m) • Hardy
FLOWERING SEASON: Early summer

Versatile evergreen shrubs, with attractive foliage, fruit and flowers, these are useful for hedging, as wall shrubs or free-standing specimens. The large clusters of small white, or pale pink blooms are followed by clusters of round fruits in autumn, coloured yellow, orange or red depending upon the cultivar. Oval, glossy, dark evergreen leaves with a finely toothed margin, are carried on brown stems with sharp spines. Propagation is by semi-ripe cuttings taken in summer. Pyracantha scab may cause premature leaf drop.

Pyrus calleryana

Callery pear
HEIGHT: 50ft (15m) • Hardy
FLOWERING SEASON: Mid/late spring

This is a medium-sized, deciduous tree with a broadly conical habit and slightly erect thorny branches. The glossy green leaves are broadly oval. Clusters of single white, cup-shaped flowers are produced in spring, and are followed by small brown fruits in autumn. The cultivar *P. c.* 'Chanticleer' has a narrow conical habit and is particularly attractive in autumn when the leaves turn a reddish-purple. Propagation is by budding in summer or by grafting in winter.

Quercus palustris

Pin oak
HEIGHT: 50ft (15m) • Hardy
FLOWERING SEASON: Late spring/early summer

A fast-growing, dense-headed, deciduous tree with a spreading habit and slender branches that droop gracefully at the tips. As this tree ages, the bark becomes purplish-grey and deeply grooved. The leaves, which are a shining dark green on the upper surface and pale green below, have deeply lobed margins, turn a rich scarlet in autumn. The small flowers are produced in late spring, and greenish-brown 'acorns' follow in autumn. Propagation is by seed sown outdoors in spring.

Rheum palmatum

Rhubarb
HEIGHT: 6ft (1.8m) • Hardy
FLOWERING SEASON: Summer

Most ornamental rhubarbs have large, glossy, mid green leaves which are held above the crown on thick fleshy stalks. The small flowers are carried above the leaves on tall spikes. *R. alexandrae* is grown for its 3ft (1m) flower spikes. These have large papery bracts like drooping tongues covering the small, inconspicuous flowers. *R. palmatum* has deeply cut, hand-shaped leaves and greenish-yellow flowers. They prefer moist conditions. Propagation is by division in winter.

Rodgersia pinnata 'Superba'

HEIGHT: 3ft (1m) • Moderately hardy
FLOWERING SEASON: Summer

This clump-forming herbaceous perennial is usually grown for its foliage. The deeply-veined leaves are made up of as many as nine deep green leaflets joined together by a thin, green, central leaf stalk. In the summer plumes of small pinkish-red, star-like flowers are produced on erect, bare, multi-branched stalks. The bronze-leaved *R. p.* 'Superba', is very good for autumn colour. It prefers some shade and a sheltered site but will grow in sun as long as the soil does not dry out. Propagation is by division of the rhizomes in spring.

Salix babylonica var. pekinensis 'Tortuosa'

Dragon's claw willow
HEIGHT: 50ft (15m) • Hardy
FLOWERING SEASON: Spring

This large shrub or small tree has unusual, corkscrew-shaped branches and green winter bark. A vigorous plant, initially it has a narrow shape, but spreads from the centre with age. The bright green leaves are narrow and strap-like, and may be quite straight or as twisted and contorted as the branches, with some leaves being curled up like a watch spring. Propagation is by hardwood cuttings, taken in November and December when the plant is dormant.

Salix caprea

Goat willow/Pussy willow
HEIGHT: 30ft (9m) • Hardy
FLOWERING SEASON: Spring

This familiar large shrub or small tree is most noticeable in spring when male trees produce large, yellow catkins later becoming soft, silvery-grey 'pussy-willow' catkins. The fluffy seeds shed in early summer. The elliptical leaves are dark green on the upper surface and grey-green and hairy on the underside. As the shrub ages the grey-brown bark becomes deeply fissured. Propagation is by hardwood cuttings taken in winter and planted outside. The disease anthracnose often causes brown spots on leaves and stem die-back.

Sorbaria aitchisonii

HEIGHT: 9ft (3m) • Hardy
FLOWERING SEASON: Late summer

This very hardy, deciduous shrub makes
a broad dome shape, with reddish-brown
shoots and long spreading branches. The
fern-like, mid green leaves are made up of
many small leaflets, evenly arranged along a
slender leaf stalk. In autumn the leaves turn
golden-yellow and orange. Small, creamy-
white blooms are produced in large flower
spikes in late summer. Prefers sun and deep
moist soil. This plant can be very invasive.
Propagation is by semi-ripe cuttings with a
heel taken in summer.

Tradescantia × andersoniana 'Purple Dome'

Spiderwort/Flower-of-a-day
HEIGHT: 2ft (60cm) • Hardy
FLOWERING SEASON: Summer/autumn

This herbaceous perennial is a popular plant
for the mixed border, as it requires very little
care and attention and flowers throughout
the summer. It is attractive with dull green,
strap-like leaves which taper to a narrow
point. The flowers consist of three petals and
are produced in small clusters. Among the
hybrids are 'Blue Stone', with deep blue
flowers, and 'Isis', with rich purple ones.
Propagate by division in March or April.

Viburnum opulus

Guelder rose
HEIGHT: 15ft (4.5m) • Hardy
FLOWERING SEASON: Mid/late summer

A large deciduous popular shrub which
has a vigorous, spreading habit. The dark
green, sycamore-like leaves, which are
carried on reddish-green leaf stalks, turn
orange and yellow in autumn. The large,
white, elder-like flowers are followed by
translucent red berries. Striking cultivars
include *V. o.* 'Xanthocarpum', which has
all the characteristics of the type but golden-
yellow berries, and the golden-leaved
V. o. 'Aureum'.

More Plants for Clay Soil

Gardening on very heavy clay can be
extremely difficult. If the sub-soil is
moderately porous then, through cultivation, clay can usually be transformed into
good garden soil on which most plants can
be grown. If the sub-soil is incapable of
carrying away water then the list of trees
and plants that will survive is limited. To
improve heavy clay the land should first be
drained and then it should be dug roughly
and the soil allowed to lie in clumps over
winter. Don't attempt to cultivate the soil
in wet periods and dug in grit, ashes and
leaf mold when planting. Choose plants
that have a vigorous constitution and which
can look after themselves. Roses do
particularly well on clay soil and a section
on roses has been included in this chapter.
Bulbs can be grown they may not do so
well if the soil becomes waterlogged.

TREES

Acer (in variety)
Amelanchier canadensis
Arbutus × andrachnoides
Betula ermanii
Catalpa bignonioides

Cercidiphyllum japonicum
Chimonanthus praecox
Corylus avellana 'Contorta'
Crataegus (in variety)
Ficus carica
Fraxinus angustifolia
Liquidambar styraciflua
Malus (in variety)
Pyrus (in variety)
Sambucus racemosa
Taxodium distichum

SHRUBS

Artemesia absinthium
Berberis (in variety)
Chaenomeles (in variety)
Choisya ternata
Cornus (in variety)
Cotinus coggygria
Exochorda × macrantha 'The Bride'
Forsythia suspensa
Lavandula (in variety)
Lavatera 'Barnsley'
Ligustrum ovalifolium
Mahonia (in variety)
Philadelphus (in variety)
Roses
Salvia officinalis
Santolina chamaecyparissus
Sarcococca hookeriana
Stepanandra tanakae
Syringa (in variety)
Viburnum (in variety)

PERENNIALS & GROUND COVER PLANTS

Alchemilla mollis
Anenome × hybrida
Aquilegia alpina
Aster novi-belgii
Astrantia major
Aucuba japonica
Bergenia (in variety)
Buddleja (in variety)
Campanula carpatica
Centranthus ruber
Dianthus (in variety)
Dicentra (in variety)
Digitalis (in variety)
Echinops bannaticus
Erysimum cheiri
Geranium (in variety)
Gunnera manicata
Hemerocallis (in variety)
Inula magnifica
Iris laevigata
Lamium maculatum
Ligularia (in variety)
Nepeta × faassenii
Penstemon (in variety)
Polygonatum × hybridum
Primula florindae
Pulmonaria saccharata
Scabiosa (in variety)
Tradescantia (in variety)
Trollius europaeus
Veronica prostrata
Vinca minor

Rosa 'Abraham Darby'

TYPE: English rose
HEIGHT: 5ft (1.5m) • Hardy
FLOWERING SEASON: Summer/autumn

One of the English roses bred by David
Austin in the 1970s, *R.* 'Abraham Darby' has
deeply cupped blooms, yellow and apricot in
colour, combined with a rich fragrance.
English roses are a cross between certain old-
fashioned roses and modern hybrid tea and
floribunda roses. They combine the scent
and form of the old-fashioned roses with the
ability to repeat flower throughout the
season. They can be grown in borders or as
shrubs making a focal point in the garden.

Roses

Roses are among the commonest and best
loved of all garden plants. They are hardy,
generally soil tolerant, many have glorious
scent and, with care, some can be found
which will grow in shade, even as climbers
on a north wall. The choice and variety is
confusing but it can be simplified if you
decide on the job you want the rose to do.
Rambler and climber roses are self-explicit,
climbers should be grown up walls and
fences while ramblers should be grown
through another plant such as a tree.
Ramblers are very vigorous and you can
only grow them successfully if you have a
fair amount of room.

If you to make a formal rose bed then
you should choose a hybrid tea, floribunda
or English rose. If you want a shrub, choose
a shrub or bush rose and to create an old-
fashioned look in your garden plant a
selection from the numerous old roses available which are wonderful in scent and
bloom but usually flower only once a year.
Many roses are also grown as standards
which can make a focal point in any border
and there are also roses which can be
planted as ground coverers.

Rosa 'Albéric Barbier'

TYPE: Rambler (Wichuriana hybrid)
HEIGHT: 25ft (8m) • Hardy
FLOWERING SEASON: Early summer

'Albéric Barbier' is one of the most popular
ramblers, less vigorous than some but it has
strong growth and thick foliage which is
almost evergreen. It is an ideal rose for
growing up an unsightly wall. It has yellow
buds which open into fully double creamy
white flowers with a fruity fragrance. There
is often a good second crop of flowers. Other
good roses of this type are, 'Albertine', pink
and deliciously scented, 'Crimson Shower',
red and 'May Queen', pale pink.

Rosa banksiae 'Lutea'

TYPE: Climber • The Banksian rose
HEIGHT: 30ft (9m) • Half-hardy
FLOWERING SEASON: Summer

The species rose, known as the Banksian rose
or Banks's rose, is tender and best grown up a
south or south-west wall in the warmer parts
of the country. It can also be grown along
the ground. It has very fragrant, pure white,
single flowers about 2.5cm (1in). More
commonly, the double yellow cultivar
'Lutea' is grown which is not fragrant or the
single yellow 'Lutescens'. The rose is thornless and requires the removal of spent wood
after flowering as it flowers on the wood
made in the previous year.

Rosa 'Cottage Rose'

TYPE: English rose
HEIGHT: 3½ft (1m) • Hardy
FLOWERING SEASON: Summer

A rose of true character with medium-sized,
fragrant, cupped blooms in a lovely warm
pink colour which repeat flowers through
the summer. It is a good idea to give English
roses a good mulch in the spring followed
by another after the first flush of flowers. Do
not prune them in the first year but in the
second year and after cut back the shoots by
a third or a half of their length. David Austin
recommends that they are planted in groups
of three, 18in (45cm) apart, and allowed to
develop into one large shrub.

Rosa 'English Miss'

TYPE; Floribunda
HEIGHT: 2½ft (75cm) • Hardy
FLOWERING SEASON: Summer

Floribunda roses carry large sprays of flowers
and then have repeat shows throughout the
summer. The flowers may not be so large or
perfectly formed as hybrid tea roses but they
are more graceful. Among the best known
are 'Evelyn Fison' and 'Glad Tidings', red,
'Paddy McGredy' and 'Pink Parfait', pink,
'Apricot Nectar' and 'Summer Dream',
apricot-yellow, 'Korresia' and 'Mount-
batten', yellow, 'Iceberg' and 'Margaret
Merrill' white and 'Masquerade' multi-
coloured, yellow, pink, red.

Rosa filipes 'Kiftsgate'

TYPE: Rambler
HEIGHT: 30-50ft (9-15m) • Hardy
FLOWERING SEASON: Midsummer

This is one of the biggest, most vigorous of rambler roses. It is literally covered with trusses of single, white, scented flowers in midsummer, followed by small red hips in autumn. It makes an ideal climber to grow over banks or trees but beware once established it is almost impossible to control. To prune, cut about a third of any stems that have flowered down to ground level. Its near relative *R*. 'Rambling Rector' with a yellow eye in the flower is slightly less vigorous.

Rosa 'Fragrant Cloud'

TYPE: Hybrid tea
HEIGHT: 4ft (1.2m) • Hardy
FLOWERING SEASON: Summer

This is one of the highly scented hybrid tea roses. Its deep rich red flowers fade after opening. Hybrid tea roses have the advantage of a long flowering season from mid to late summer. They do well in sun or partial shade, and like all roses need plenty of well-rotted manure as feed. Prune in winter, taking back the current year's growth to about four buds. 'Pascali' and 'Polar Star' are good white roses while 'Peace', light-yellow flushed with pink is an old favourite.

Rosa 'Iceberg'

TYPE: Floribunda
HEIGHT: 4ft (1.2m) • Hardy
FLOWERING SEASON: Summer/autumn

One of the best of the floribundas, 'Iceberg' has medium-sized double flowers, pure white in the summer and often tinged with pink in the autumn. It often flowers on into the winter. It is sometimes grown as a standard where it can make a focal point in a herbaceous border and there is a climbing form. The flowers, as with many of the floribundas, are fragrant. Prune in the winter cutting back shoots by about a half and removing any weak shoots.

Rosa 'Königin von Dänemark'

TYPE: Alba
HEIGHT: 5ft (1.5m) • Hardy
FLOWERING SEASON: Midsummer

Alba roses date back to the Middle Ages. They are restricted in colour to white and shades of pink but they are amongst the hardiest roses there are and will survive and flower in shade. The 'Queen of Denmark' is one of the finest, with beautifully formed quartered flowers and grey-green leaves. Other well known roses of this type are 'Félicité Parmentier', a very delicate pale pink , *R*. × *alba* 'Alba Maxima', the Jacobite rose, which is white, tinted pink and 'Maiden's Blush' which is pink.

Rosa 'L D Braithwaite'

TYPE: English rose
HEIGHT: 3½ft (1m) • Hardy
FLOWERING SEASON: Summer

An English rose of the most brilliant crimson colour and form, the flowers are produced over a long period and are very fragrant. When planting all roses the ground should be well prepared, and thoroughly dug with the addition of a good amount of farmyard manure or compost. If this is not available incorporate plenty of peat and bonemeal. Do not plant roses when the soil is very wet heel them in and wait for a dry period and do not plant roses in soil where roses have been growing in the last two years.

Rosa 'Madame Legras de Saint Germain'

TYPE: Alba
HEIGHT: 6ft (1.8m) • Very hardy
FLOWERING SEASON: Summer

One of the best of the alba roses the flowers open flat and then fill out with petals giving a pompom effect. They are carried on long, lax branches and are beautifully fragrant. Two other groups of old roses, all grown as garden shrubs, are gallica roses, often deep red in colour, which date back to Roman times and damask roses, a group supposedly brought back from the Middle East by the Crusaders. Nearly all of these are fragrant but they only flower once.

Rosa 'Maigold'

TYPE: Climber
HEIGHT: 12ft (4m) • Hardy
FLOWERING SEASON: Midsummer

This is one of the most attractive yellow-flowered climbers with double flowers and prominent golden stamens. It is a rose which tolerates poor conditions and will flower when grown as a climber on a north wall. A number of roses have been bred as modern climbers which repeat flower well and are often shorter in growth making them suitable for town gardens: among them are 'Compassion', pink, 'Schoolgirl', orange, 'White Cockade' and 'Golden Showers'.

Rosa 'Nevada'

TYPE: Shrub
HEIGHT: 7ft (2m) • Hardy
FLOWERING SEASON: Early summer

'Nevada' grows into a large shrub, 7ft (2m) across which is smothered in early summer with semi-double, 4in (10cm), creamy-white blooms carried on arching red-brown branches. The leaves are light green. It has smaller crops of flowers later in the year. A spectacular rose, it makes an ideal shrub grown in the center of a lawn. Other well-known shrub roses are 'Ballerina', pink, 'Frühlingsgold', pale yellow, 'Scarlet Fire', red, and 'Zigeunerknabe', dark purple.

Rosa nitida

TYPE: Shrub
HEIGHT: 3ft (1m) • Hardy
FLOWERING SEASON: Summer

This is a low-growing, shrub rose with thin stems covered in small, hair-like thorns. The mid green leaves, which are small and almost fern-like are held on reddish-brown, erect stems, and turn crimson in autumn. Small, deep-pink, single flowers are followed by small, crimson fruits in the autumn. This rose spreads by rhizome-like roots and can be very invasive. It makes good ground cover. Propagation is by softwood cuttings in summer or by division in late winter.

Rosa 'Pascali'

TYPE: Hybrid tea
HEIGHT: 3ft (1m) • Hardy
FLOWERING SEASON: Summer

'Pascali' is a strong healthy rose which has beautifully shaped white flowers ideal for cutting. They have a slight fragrance. Prune in the winter by cutting back to an outer bud about 12in (30cm) from the ground, alternately cut through the whole bush regardless of the condition of the wood at that height. This rather drastic method has been adopted after trials by the Rose Society. Other well known hybrid tea roses are 'Elizabeth Harkness', buff-pink, 'Ophelia', pink, and 'Blue Moon', silver-lilac.

Rosa 'Paul's Himalayan Musk'

TYPE: Rambler
Height: 30ft (9m) • Hardy
Flowering Season: Summer

This rose has been called the most beautiful of the ramblers and makes an unforgettable sight when established, epitomising the best of an English summer. It carries hanging open sprays of blush-pink rosettes on long trailing branches and is an ideal rose for growing into a tree or over a pergola. Like all ramblers, once established it is difficult to control, and the sharp arched spines which many of these roses possess make any pruning a trial. Eventually some of the old growth will need thinning.

Rosa primula

TYPE: Shrub • The incense rose
HEIGHT: 8ft (2.5m) • Hardy
FLOWERING SEASON: Spring

This species rose, also known as the incense rose, is unusual in the rose family in having aromatic foliage which releases a strong, spicy scent when crushed. The pale yellow, single flowers, with prominent golden stamens, are borne in late spring, and are also fragrant. They will cope with most conditions and can be trained against a trellis. In a hard winter the foliage may die back but it will regenerate in the spring. Prune in early spring. Prone to black spot, rust and various mildews.

Rosa 'Roseraie de l'Haÿ'

Type: Rugosa
Height: 6ft (1.8m) • Hardy
Flowering Season: Summer

Rugosa roses have sturdy stems, prickly branches and fresh green foliage, glossy on top and downy beneath. They grow under poor conditions and most repeat flower with a vivid display of hips in the autumn. They make good hedges although some flowers may be lost if they are kept closely trimmed: 'Roseraie de l'Haÿ', wine-red, 'Blanche Double de Coubert', white, 'Sarah van Fleet', pink, and 'Mrs Anthony Waterer', deep-red are among the best known.

Rosa rugosa

Type: Rugosa
Height: 6ft (1.8m) • Hardy
Flowering Season: Summer/autumn

This is a very tough, vigorous rose with light grey-brown shoots densely covered in fine bristly thorns. The leathery, deeply veined, glossy dark green leaves turn yellow in autumn. It is one of the few wild roses which repeat flowers. The large, single, cup-shaped flowers are a deep pink with a golden-yellow centre. These are followed, in autumn, by large, round, bright red hips. *R. r.* 'Alba' has white flowers and *R. r. rubra* has red ones. They all make good hedges.

Rosa 'Tour de Malakoff'

Type: Centifolia rose • The Rose of Provence
Height: 6ft (1.8m) • Hardy
Flowering Season: Summer

Centifolia roses make lax open shrubs with many thorns and rather coarse leaves. Often they carry so many flowers that they hang their heads facing towards the ground. Nearly all have large cabbage-like flowers and heavy fragrance. Among the best are: 'Tour de Malakoff', richly purple and often grown as a climber, × *centifolia* 'Cristata', pink, 'Fantin-Latour', blush-pink and 'Robert le Diable' a mixture of many colours, purple, scarlet and cerise.

Rosa 'Whisky Mac'

Type: Hybrid tea
Height: 4ft (1.2m) • Hardy
Flowering Season: Summer

One of the most striking of the hybrid tea roses with yellow flowers which open copper-orange and then fade to a clear pale yellow. The flowers are very fragrant and are carried on very upright stems. Hybrid tea and floribunda roses look best grown in a beds devoted to a single variety and a rose garden can be planned with varying colours passing from deep red to yellow, pale orange, white and pink. Ideas can be gathered by visiting some of the best rose gardens or consulting rose breeders for advice.

Rosa 'Winchester Cathedral'

Type: English rose
Height: 4ft (1.2m) • Hardy
Flowering Season: Summer

A brilliant white rose with multi-petalled flowers 'Winchester Cathedral' forms a robust bushy shrub which produces new branches throughout the summer carrying a succession of flowers. When deciding to plant any rose the most important thing is to consider the situation in your garden and the effect that you are trying to achieve. Three similar plants grouped together, or small beds planted with the same variety of rose make a better and more effective statement than a number of individual plants.

Rosa 'Zéphirine Drouhin'

Type: Climber
Height: 12ft (4m) • Hardy
Flowering Season: Summer and autumn

This rose is particularly renowned for the fact that it is thornless. It is a Bourbon climber, with bronze-red tinted foliage and bright pink, semi-double flowers that are sweetly scented. It will flower again in autumn if deadheaded. It is extremely hardy and is particularly suitable for growing on a north wall. It can also be planted as a hedge or shrub. Bourbon roses are a cross between China and Portland roses and other old roses. They were first bred in the 1840s and 'Zéphirine Drouhin' was bred in 1868.

MOISTURE-LOVING PLANTS

Many gardens have a damp, slightly waterlogged area or perhaps a small pond which can be turned to advantage to grow a wide range of moisture-loving plants. Some, such as bog plants, prefer just a moist soil, others, called aquatics, thrive with their roots actually in water or are grown fully submerged.

ABOVE: Ranunculus acris *'Flore Pleno', the meadow buttercup, growing beside water.*

OPPOSITE: *A shady pond crammed with variegated irises, water and arum lilies and surrounded by ferns, pulmonaria, alchemilla, clematis and hostas. Agapanthus grow in a pot beside the pool.*

ABOVE: *Some irises will grow in water, and some prefer damp soil. They are ideal pool and poolside plants, their tall strappy leaves as important a contribution as their delicate papery flowers. Large-leaved, lush-looking plants like gunnera are spectacular, while, in this planting, ferns and ivy tumble down the brickwork.*

Moisture-loving plants have some special virtues. They are easily grown if you have a permanently damp corner in your garden or a small stream or pond, but for many they provide the incentive to make a pond in the garden or just a boggy area, to convert into a bog garden so that the range of plants in the garden can be extended.

These plants fall into different categories: those that thrive in moist soil, those that thrive in wet soil, and those that actually grow best in water. The plants listed in this section fall into all three categories, but where they actually do well in a depth of water, this is indicated in the entry.

If you already have a damp area of the garden, it is a question of choosing suitable plants for the existing conditions. Quite often, these damp corners are also shady, and any attempt on your part to grow the usual sun-loving perennials will be doomed to disappointment. Analyse the conditions in your garden, and try to learn some lessons from what naturally thrives. Very few bulbs like very wet soil (except those specifically listed here) and will simply rot if waterlogged. Plants from dry, rocky areas or from the hot dry areas around the Mediterranean will also fail to cope. Foliage is a good indication of a plant's natural habitat and often plants with larger, greener, lusher leaves have acquired these characteristics from exposure to moist or shady conditions.

A damp garden or corner, therefore, is an opportunity to grow some exciting large foliage plants such as gunneras, rodgersias, rheums and ligularias. If you are making a pond, you can increase your range of plants to those that enjoy being in water, including some of the irises and marsh

LEFT: *This stream has a wealth of damp-loving plants surrounding it, including different kinds of primula (such as the unusual P.* vialii *with its poker-like flowers), irises, water buttercups, hostas, and the interestingly marked leaves of the* Houttuynia cordata *'Chameleon' with big-leaved ligularias planted behind.*

BELOW: *In a raised pool and bog garden, irises, primulas and the handsome white spathes of the arum lily (zantedeschia) make the most of a small space.*

marigolds, and if the water is deep enough, the exotic-looking water lilies as well.

Even if your garden is not naturally damp, you can create a small area of bog garden by digging out a section and lining it with black plastic liner, with a few perforations in it for drainage and returning the soil on top. This will act like a layer of natural clay, helping to retain the moisture in the soil for longer periods, and allowing you to grow those plants that enjoy wet soil. You will have to be prepared to keep the soil moist by watering in periods of drought.

Garden ponds do not have to be large, and even a 3ft x 3ft (1m x 1m) pond, created with a butyl liner, will provide the correct environment for a good selection of water-loving plants. It is also rewarding to encourage wildlife by providing a suitable ledge so that animals and birds can drink. Create more than one level in the pond, so that both marginal plants (those that like shallow water) such as marsh marigolds and rushes, as well as aquatics (those that float in deep water), including water lilies and the water hawthorn, can be grown successfully.

Acorus calamus 'Variegatus'

Sweet flag/Myrtle flag
HEIGHT: 2½ft (75cm) • Hardy
FLOWERING SEASON: Insignificant

This marginal water plant, commonly called sweet or myrtle flag, grows at the water's edge in water up to 10in (25cm) deep. It is grown for its particularly handsome, sword-shaped foliage, with its neatly cream-edged border. The young leaves are flushed pink in spring. It is sweetly scented, hence the common name. This plant is fairly prolific therefore to control its spread, divide the clumps every few years. Propagation is by division of the rhizomes.

Acorus gramineus 'Variegatus'

HEIGHT: 10in (25cm) • Hardy
FLOWERING SEASON: Insignificant

This is a much smaller plant than *A. calamus*. A semi-evergreen perennial it grows at the water's edge, or with its roots submerged in shallow water. Its fine, grass-like leaves are held stiffly upright. This particular form has cream-edged foliage, and produces insignificant greenish yellow flowers in summer. To propagate and to keep it under control, divide the clumps every couple of years in the spring or autumn.

Aponogeton distachyos

Cape pondweed/Water hawthorn
HEIGHT: 2in (5cm) • Half-hardy
FLOWERING SEASON: Late spring/autumn

The water hawthorn, as this deep-water aquatic plant is known, originates in South Africa and has large, oval, slender leaves that float like a water lily's on the surface of the water. They are deep green, occasionally splashed with purple. The flowers, which are white and waxy, are carried in a forked spire and are hawthorn-scented. This plant does best in a sunny position but will also cope with partial shade. Propagation is by division of the tubers.

Asplenium scolopendrium

Hart's tongue fern
HEIGHT: 2ft (60cm) • Hardy
FLOWERING SEASON: Insignificant

The hart's tongue fern is so-called because it produces long, curling leaves, which are bright green and evergreen. *A. s.* Crispum Group has wavy margins to the leaves while cultivars of *A. s.* Cristatum Group have crested tips to the fronds. *A. scolopendrium* does best in moisture-retentive soil in shade, and will seed itself from spores in the right conditions. Propagate by sowing the spores in spring, or divide plants at the same time of year. Generally problem free, although rust can develop on young fronds.

Astilboides tabularis

HEIGHT: 3ft (1m) • Hardy
FLOWERING SEASON: Midsummer

This plant was formerly known as *Rodgersia tabularis*. It is a large-leaved perennial and makes a handsome foliage plant for the bog garden, with its huge, umbrella-shaped, bright green leaves. It bears creamy panicles of flowers in midsummer. Plant the crowns about 1in (2.5cm) below the soil surface in spring, ensuring that it contains plenty of decayed vegetable matter. The plant will grow in sun or semi-shade and is propagated by division of the crowns in the spring. It may require some protection in very hard weather.

Butomus umbellatus

Flowering rush
HEIGHT: 3ft (1m) • Hardy
FLOWERING SEASON: Summer

Known as the flowering rush, *B. umbellatus* is a most attractive deciduous perennial that bears umbels of rose-pink flowers in midsummer. It quickly makes large spreading clumps of strappy foliage, which is bronze-purple when young and becomes green later, and it grows in depths of water up to 10in (5cm). It prefers a sunny position and is best suited to large ponds. Divide the clumps in spring to keep its spread under control. Propagation is also by division in spring.

Calla palustris

Bog arum
HEIGHT: 10in (25cm) • Hardy
FLOWERING SEASON: Spring

Known as the bog arum, *C. palustris* is a deciduous or semi-evergreen perennial that makes a spreading clump at the water's edge. It has large, heart-shaped, bright green, glossy leaves, and the typical arum flowers with a white spathe, followed by a bright orange spire of fruits. Plant in full sun, either in the bog garden, or into water a few inches deep. It likes good soil enriched by leaf mould or compost. Propagate by division of the rhizomes in spring.

Caltha palustris

Marsh marigold
HEIGHT: 2ft (60cm) • Hardy
FLOWERING SEASON: Late spring

The marsh marigold or kingcup flourishes in water of up to 6in (15cm). It has attractively rounded rich green leaves and the profuse large yellow flowers are cup-shaped. There is a white variety with yellow stamens, *C. p. var. alba*, which is not as free-flowering. It does best as a marginal plant, in slightly acid soil with plenty of humus, in sun or light shade. Divide and replant after flowering.

Cornus alba 'Sibirica'

Red-barked dogwood
HEIGHT: 10ft (3m) • Hardy
FLOWERING SEASON: Summer

The dogwoods, to which this suckering deciduous shrub belongs, do well in moist soil in sun or partial shade, and look particularly good as the backdrop to a water feature. *C. a.* 'Sibirica' has coral-red stems in winter and small clusters of creamy white flowers in summer, followed by white berries. The leaves are green and turn a bright scarlet in autumn. Cut hard back in spring to promote the growth of colourful stems. Propagate from rooted suckers, or layer shoots in autumn.

Cyperus involucratus

Umbrella grass
HEIGHT: 2ft (60cm) • Tender
FLOWERING SEASON: Summer

Known as umbrella grass, this moisture-loving rush-like perennial carries umbrella spoke-like leaves at the top of long arching stems. Very small flowers are borne in summer. It will grow in shallow water or at the water's edge in mild climates, or in harsher ones can be grown in containers in shallow water and overwintered indoors. 'Variegatus' has white-striped leaves. Remove the dead stems from plants grown out of doors in the spring. Propagate by detaching and replanting young growths.

Filipendula palmata

Meadowsweet
HEIGHT: 3ft (1m) • Hardy
FLOWERING SEASON: Summer

F. palmata, which is related to the European wild meadowsweet, is a good subject for a bog garden, thriving in rich, moist soil in sun. The leaves are divided, with five lobes, dark green, and hairy underneath. The pale rose-pink flowers rise well above the leaves, in multi-branched heads. Grow it in a large garden in drifts, with lythrum and lysimachia. Cut the stems back hard in autumn. To propagate, divide and replant crowns in autumn or early spring. It is sometimes prone to mildews, but is usually pest-free.

Gunnera manicata

Prickly rhubarb
HEIGHT: 10ft (3m) • Half-hardy
FLOWERING SEASON: Spring

This huge bruiser of a herbaceous perennial hails from Brazil. It has massive, rhubarb-like leaves, up to 4ft (1.2m) across borne on tall prickly stems and bears conical, light green flower spikes in early summer. It needs moist soil with plenty of humus incorporated, and it is an admirable architectural plant for the bog garden. It dies down in autumn, and the remaining crown should be protected with sacking, straw or bubble plastic in frosts. Increase by removing small crowns and replanting in spring.

Hemerocallis dumortieri

Day lily
HEIGHT: 2ft (60cm) • Hardy
FLOWERING SEASON: Early summer

This robust day lily produces large numbers of highly scented, yellow, typical lily flowers which last only a day or two, but several flowerheads are borne on one stem, set among the strap-shaped leaves. A clump-forming, spreading perennial, it will quickly establish a large drift given the right conditions: preferably sun and moist soil. *H. lilioasphodelus* has flowers of a brighter yellow. Propagate by division in autumn. Slugs and snails may attack young foliage.

Hottonia palustris

Water violet
HEIGHT: Irrelevant • Hardy
FLOWERING SEASON: Summer

This submerged water plant, which is known as the water violet, is an oxygenating plant and does best in deep water in a sunny pool. The leaves form a dense mass of spreading foliage, from which the pinkish-lilac or whitish flowers rise above the water's surface in summer. It may be necessary to divide the plant occasionally to control its spread. Propagation is by division.

Hydrocharis morsus-ranae

Frogbit
HEIGHT: 2in (5cm) • Hardy
FLOWERING SEASON: Summer

This delightful floating water plant is known sometimes as frogbit and has small water-lily-like leaves that are waxy and pale olive green. It bears small, white, flowers with yellow stamens which rise slightly above the water's surface and are produced in summer. *H. morsus-ranae* is a plant which prefers to be positioned in full sun. Propagate by detaching any young plantlets from the main plant in spring and then replanting them immediately.

Inula magnifica

Fleabane
HEIGHT: 6ft (1.8m) • Hardy
FLOWERING SEASON: Late summer

This is the largest of the most commonly grown species in this genus of daisy-like herbaceous perennials. The smallest, which is *I. acaulis*, is only about 6in (15cm) tall. *I. magnifica* forms large clumps of lance-shaped, hairy leaves above which rise tall stems bearing bright yellow, daisy flowers that are up to 4in (10cm) across. It does well in large drifts in moisture-retentive soil in sun but it will require staking. Plant in autumn and spring, and divide plants from autumn to spring.

Iris ensata

Bog iris/Japanese flag
HEIGHT: 12in (30cm) • Hardy
FLOWERING SEASON: Late spring

This is one of the beardless irises which belongs to a sub-section known as Apogon irises, popularly called bog irises. It does well in sun in very moist soil and will cope with shallow water. It comes from Tibet and China and is characterized by its fine, grass-like leaves and delicate mauve flowers. There are numerous cultivars in shades of white, violet, pink, blue and red. 'Alba' is an elegant white cultivar and 'Variegata' has hand-somely striped leaves. Divide in autumn to propagate. Prone to various viruses.

Iris laevigata

Japanese iris
HEIGHT: 2ft (60cm) • Hardy
FLOWERING SEASON: Early summer

This Japanese iris is a true water iris, thriving in water up to 6in (15cm) deep. It has decid-uous, pale green leaves and bears three deep blue flowers, with a white streak on the falls, on each stem. There are several named cultivars, including the pure white 'Alba', 'Variegata' with striped leaves and pale blue flowers which sometimes flowers for a second time in the autumn, 'Atropurpurea' with reddish-purple flowers and 'Regal' with red flowers. It does best in sun or semi-shade. Propagate by division in autumn.

Ligularia dentata 'Desdemona'

Giant groundsel
HEIGHT: 4ft (1.2m) • Hardy
FLOWERING SEASON: Mid/late summer

This big herbaceous perennial forms a hand-some mound of large, heart-shaped, deep green leaves, with rusty red undersides, borne on the end of long stalks. Big, bright orange, daisy flowers appear in late summer, making a striking contrast with the leaves. In addition to being suited to bog gardens, it makes a good container plant provided the soil is kept moist. It needs humus-rich retentive soil and a sunny or partially shaded site. Divide in spring. Prone to attacks by slugs and snails.

Ligularia stenocephala

Giant groundsel
HEIGHT: 6ft (1.8m) • Hardy
FLOWERING SEASON: Late summer

This cultivar forms similar clumps to *L. dentata* (left), but the leaves are rounded and toothed, and paler green. The yellow-orange daisy-like flowers are borne in long spires on purplish stems. It likes the same conditions as *L. dentata* and looks best when planted in groups of five to seven, in the moist soil around the edge of a water feature. It needs humus-rich retentive soil.

Lobelia cardinalis

Cardinal flower
HEIGHT: 3ft (1m) • Half hardy
FLOWERING SEASON: Summer

This unlikely-looking lobelia bears tall spires of bright red, five-lobed flowers in mid to late summer. The foliage is carried on erect, branching stems. It makes a good border plant in moist soil in partial shade but is not very long-lasting. Grows best in a mild, moist climate with shelter from cold winds and it will grow close to water. Cut down the dead spikes after flowering. Propagate by division in spring. Can be affected by a virus which causes the leaves to mottle and distort.

Lysimachia clethroides

Loosestrife
HEIGHT: 3ft (1m) • Hardy
FLOWERING SEASON: Mid to late summer

This native of China and Japan is a tall summer-flowering perennial with elongated green leaves that turn colour in autumn. It carries small, starry, white flowers with pronounced eyes in long arching spires. It does well in moist soil in sun or partial shade and is most suitable for naturalising by the waterside or in a bog garden. The name comes from the Greek, *lusimachion*, *lysis* meaning concluding or ending, and *mache*, strife, from the reputedly soothing properties of the plant. Divide and replant in autumn.

Lysimachia nummularia

Creeping Jenny/Moneywort
HEIGHT: 2in (5cm) • Hardy
FLOWERING SEASON: Summer

This small creeping perennial, known as moneywort or creeping Jenny, has rounded soft leaves and bright yellow flowers that form in the leaf axils. A cultivar known as 'Aurea' has yellowish-green leaves. It prefers partial shade, and a moist, retentive soil but it is one of the easiest garden plants and can be grown in almost any soil or situation. It is ideal for planting near the borders of a garden pond. Propagate by division in spring or by planting short lengths of the stem in spring or autumn.

Lysimachia punctata

Garden loosestrife
HEIGHT: 3ft (1m) • Hardy
FLOWERING SEASON: Summer

This garden loosestrife is a rapidly spreading, clump-forming, herbaceous perennial. In summer it will produce large drifts of tall, bright golden-yellow flower spires, rising on erect stems above the oval, lance-shaped leaves. *L. punctata* blends well with ligularias in informal bog garden plantings. It prefers moist well-drained soil in partial shade although it will tolerate some sun. It may need staking occasionally. Propagate by division in spring or by seed sown in the open or in a cold frame.

Lysichiton americanus

Yellow skunk cabbage
HEIGHT: 4ft (1.2m) • Hardy
FLOWERING SEASON: Spring

This big-leaved perennial flourishes in the
very moist soil alongside streams and ponds.
It will spread rapidly in the right conditions,
making an eye-catching feature with its
huge, ribbed, mid green leaves and bright
yellow flower spathes about 18in (45cm) tall.
A smaller species, *L. camtschatcensis*, has white
flower spathes. Plant in wet soil or shallow
water, and ensure that the plants have plenty
of humus. Copes with sun or partial shade.
Propagate by division in early spring.

Mertensia pulmonarioides

Virginian cowslip
HEIGHT: 2ft (60cm) • Hardy
FLOWERING SEASON: Late spring

The Virginian cowslip has bluish-grey leaves
and attractive terminal clusters of hanging
purple-blue bells in late spring. It needs a
rich, moist soil in shade to do well. Cut the
plants back in autumn. These plants are
suitable for growing in the shady side of a
rock garden, under deciduous trees or at the
edge of a shrubbery. They do not like being
disturbed but when the clumps grow too
large they can be divided and the roots
replanted in autumn or spring.

Miscanthus sinensis

Zebra grass
HEIGHT: 5ft (1.5m) • Hardy
FLOWERING SEASON: Insignificant

This attractive vigorous giant grass is a hardy
perennial that will serve as a windbreak, its
narrow bluish-green leaves arching over.
There are a number of different cultivars
'Zebrinus' has a yellow band on the leaves,
while 'Gracillimus' has particularly narrow
leaves. It may bear fan-shaped panicles of
hairy white spikelets in the autumn. Plant
in moist garden soil in sun. Cut down to
ground level in late spring. Divide and
replant roots in spring.

Nuphar lutea

Yellow water lily/Brandy bottle
HEIGHT: 2in (5cm) • Hardy
FLOWERING SEASON: Summer

This deep-water aquatic perennial is a good
subject for a large pool. It is vigorous and not
as fussy about sun as the real water lily, and
will grow in running water, which water
lilies will not. The flat, water lily-like leaves
float on the water's surface. In summer it
produces yellow flowers, which are bottle-
shaped, giving rise to the common name
of brandy bottle. Plant in good garden loam
in a sack which is then lowered into the
water. Divide in spring to control its spread.
Propagation is by division in spring.

Nymphaea alba

Water lily
HEIGHT: 2in (5cm) • Hardy
FLOWERING SEASON: Summer

A large water lily, *N. alba*, as the name
implies, has large, pure white flowers which
are semi-double and cup-shaped, with
bright gold stamens. They measure about
4in (10cm) across. Water lilies are deciduous,
perennial, deep water plants and generally
need a 3ft (90cm) depth of water, which
must be still and in sunshine, preferably away
from overhanging trees. It is necessary to
divide the plants every few years in spring or
summer to keep them under control.
Propagation is also by division of rhizomes.

Nymphaea × helvola

Water lily
HEIGHT: 2in (5cm) • Hardy
FLOWERING SEASON: Summer

This small water lily has dark green leaves
which are purple beneath and float on the
surface of the water. It will grow in 12in
(30cm) of water. It bears small, star-shaped,
semi-double yellow flowers in summer. For
best results plant in good loam in a wicker
basket or old-fashioned sack. Like all water
lilies it must be grown in still water and in
sunshine. It is best to remove the foliage of
all water lilies as it dies back. Propagate by
dividing and replanting the rhizomes every
few years.

Nymphaea 'James Brydon'

Water lily
HEIGHT: 2in (5cm) • Hardy
FLOWERING SEASON: Summer

Dark green leaves and fragrant, cup-shaped, rose-coloured, semi-double flowers are the hallmarks of this water lily. White, pink, yellow and purple cultivars are also available, all with characteristically large, semi-double flowers. It needs about a 3ft (1m) depth of water, which must be still and in sunshine. If you want to grow water lilies in a concrete pool you need two barrow loads of soil for each plant. Divide every few years in spring or summer and to propagate.

Nymphoides peltata

Fringed water lily/Water fringe
HEIGHT: 2in (5cm) • Hardy
FLOWERING SEASON: Summer

This deciduous perennial deep-water plant is similar to the water lily, and has the common name fringed water lily. It has dark green, floating, rounded leaves with brown splashed markings and produces small, fringed, yellow flowers throughout the summer. It needs sun and a sheltered site and, like water lilies, likes deep, still water. To propagate, or control its spread, divide in spring or summer.

Osmunda regalis

Royal fern
HEIGHT: 5ft (1.5m) • Hardy
FLOWERING SEASON: Insignificant

This, the royal fern, is an extremely handsome fern, with large, yellowish-green fronds arching over gracefully, growing out of a crown that gradually becomes like a small trunk. There are a couple of interesting varieties, *O. r.* Cristata Group has crested pinnae, and *O. r. purpurascens* has young fronds which are bronzy-pink. The royal fern does well in very damp soil near pond margins. Propagate by dividing well-separated crowns in spring.

Polystichum setiferum

Soft shield fern
HEIGHT: 3ft (1m) • Hardy
FLOWERING SEASON: Insignificant

The soft shield fern, a native of temperate and tropical regions throughout the world, has large soft-textured fronds which are finely divided and mid green in colour. It will naturalize in damp conditions. There are several named cultivars, including 'Divisilobum Laxum' which has huge fronds with white scales when young, these arch initially and become prostrate later. It is best to grow these ferns in shade in humus-rich, moisture-retentive soil. Propagate by dividing the crowns in spring.

Pontederia cordata

Pickerel weed
HEIGHT: 2ft (60cm) • Hardy
FLOWERING SEASON: Late summer

The pickerel weed, as it is commonly known, is a vigorous, aquatic perennial that will grow in up to 9in (23cm) of water. It has glossy green, heart-shaped leaves, rather like those of an arum lily, and produces small, bright blue flowers with a yellow eye in late summer. It needs full sun, and should be planted in loam. It is a good idea to remove the flower heads as they fade to encourage further flowering. Divide the plant in late spring and replant in shallow water until the plants are established.

Populus × canadensis 'Serotina'

Canadian poplar
HEIGHT: 36ft (11m) • Hardy
FLOWERING SEASON: Spring

This is a quick-growing tree with oval, pointed leaves that are coppery red when juvenile, turning dark green later. There is a golden-leaved cultivar, 'Aurea', which turns a very bright yellow in autumn. It bears long red catkins in the spring and should be planted well away from buildings as the branches are somewhat brittle and often break off in very strong winds. Propagate from hardwood cuttings in autumn. May be attacked by aphids and suffer various fungal disorders.

Primula florindae

Giant cowslip/Himalayan cowslip
HEIGHT: 6ft (1.8m) • Hardy
FLOWERING SEASON: Spring

This giant cowslip, also known as the
Himalayan cowslip, originates in Tibet and
China. It has large, heart-shaped leaves with
serrated edges on a fairly long leaf stalk. In
spring, tall stems bear umbels of scented,
bell-shaped, pale lemon flowers on drooping
stalks. Forms are also available with orange
or red flowers. These primulas prefer sun or
partial shade and moist soil but may require
protection from winter wet. Divide to
propagate. Prone to rots and moulds.

Primula pulverulenta

Candelabra primula
HEIGHT: 3ft (1m) • Hardy
FLOWERING SEASON: Summer

These tall, candelabra-type primulas look
attractive in large drifts near a pond or a
stream. They have the typical oval, primrose-
type leaves in pale green while the flowers
are deep reddish-purple carried in a whorl
at the top of long white stems. *P. p.* Bartley
Hybrids and *P. p.* 'Bartley Pink' are soft pink
in colour with a deeper crimson eye.
P. pulverulenta does best in sun or partial
shade and prefers rich loamy soil. Propagate
named forms by dividing crowns or by
removing offsets in spring. They are prone to
attacks by aphids and various moulds.

Ranunculus acris 'Flore Pleno'

Double meadow buttercup
HEIGHT: 18in (45cm) • Hardy
FLOWERING SEASON: Summer

This is double-flowered buttercup is
sometimes also known as yellow bachelor's
buttons. It produces large, bright yellow,
saucer-shaped flowers in sprays and has
deeply cut, lobed, mid green leaves. This
widely grown species is mat-forming but
not invasive. It thrives in moist, well-drained
soil and prefers to be in sun or partial shade.
Once established, it needs little attention.
To propagate, divide and replant the clumps
in autumn or in spring.

Ranunculus aquatilis

Water crowfoot
HEIGHT: 2ft (60cm) • Hardy
FLOWERING SEASON: Spring/midsummer

This water crowfoot is an aquatic plant
which can be grown in water up to 12in
(30cm) deep and will grow in slow-moving
streams. It has myriads of white blossoms in
the spring which cover the surface of the
water, looking like miniature water lilies. It
has two types of leaf, floating leaves carried
on long stems which are smooth and round
and submerged leaves which are finely divided and hair-like. Plant in the sun. *R. aquatilis*
is very vigorous and will need to be divided
and thinned annually.

Rheum palmatum

Ornamental rhubarb
HEIGHT: 6ft (1.8m) • Hardy
FLOWERING SEASON: Summer

This ornamental rhubarb is an excellent
large perennial for a bog garden and forms a
huge and spectacular plant. It produces a
pyramid-shaped clump of large, deeply cut,
rhubarb-like leaves that open reddish purple
and turn green. The flowers, which are rusty
pink, are carried at the end of tall spires in
midsummer. Plant in humus-rich soil in
partial shade and mulch each autumn. Do
not let the soil dry out in the growing season. Generally pest and disease-free, but can
be prone to aphid attacks.

Sagittaria sagittifolia

Common arrowhead
HEIGHT: 3ft (1m) • Hardy
FLOWERING SEASON: Summer

The common arrowhead can be planted in
water of depths up to 3ft (90cm). A hardy
perennial, it has arrow-shaped, light green
leaves and whorls of white flowers in
summer. *S. s.* 'Flore Pleno' is a double-
flowered variety. Plant in March or October
in any good garden soil enriched with well-
rotted manure. Put the soil in an old-
fashioned sack or wicker basket, plant the
tubers, weigh the soil down with a large
stone and then drop it into the pool. It likes
full sun. Thin in the summer.

Stratiotes aloides

Water soldier/Crab's claw
HEIGHT: 6in (15cm) • Hardy
FLOWERING SEASON: Summer

This semi-evergreen perennial, known as the water soldier, is a submerged aquatic, which floats freely in any depth of water. It has strappy, fleshy, olive-green leaves in a rosette formation, and produces small, cup-shaped, white flowers in summer. During winter the plants lie dormant on the pool bottom. The plant spreads quickly and may well need to be controlled in a garden pool. Propagation is by division of the plants in spring.

Trapa natans

Jesuit's nut/Water chestnut
HEIGHT: 1in (2.5cm) • Half-hardy
FLOWERING SEASON: Summer

This annual aquatic plant,which is some-times known as the Jesuit's nut or water chestnut, has pretty triangular leaves, with serrated edges,that are marked with bronze-purple splashes. It produces white flowers in summer. It is not reliably frost-hardy so the young plants will require some degree of protection if planted in early spring, or plant when the last frosts have passed. Propagation is by division of the plants in spring or by seed.

Typha latifolia

Reed mace/Bulrush
HEIGHT: 6ft (1.8m) • Hardy
FLOWERING SEASON: Summer

This marginal reed is grown for its long, strappy, mid green leaves and its decorative dark brown cylinders of seed heads in autumn. The beige flowers which emerge in midsummer are not particularly significant but the seed heads are spectacular and a com-mon sight, often used by flower arrangers. It is invasive, and is often used to colonize large ponds and lakes. To control its spread plant it in a tub. It will do well in sun or shade, and can be propagated by division in spring.

More Plants for Moisture

AQUATICS

Examples of the majority of aquatic plants, plants that like growing with their roots in water, have been included in this chapter. There is a wide choice of water lilies and if you plan to make a pond, it is best to visit a nursery which specializes in plants for the water garden. It is worth stressing that water lilies must be grown in deep, still water and a sunny position.

Other suitable aquatic plants worth considering include:

Alisma plantago-aquatica (Water plantain)
Azolla filiculoides (Water fern)
Lagarosiphon major
Myosotis scorpioides (Water forget-me-not)
Myriophyllum aquaticum (Parrot's feather)
M. verticillatum (Water milfoil)
Orontium aquaticum (Golden club)
Potamogeton crispus (Curled pondweed)

PLANTS FOR MOISTURE

If you have a very wet area of your garden then you have to grown plants that will tolerate these conditions. All plants need water but a relatively small number will survive in conditions of constant moisture.

Bog garden plants are obvious examples. Plants that will survive in swampy sites are marked (S).

TREES

Abies (in variety)
Acer negundo
Alnus (in variety)
Amelanchier canadensis
Betula nigra
Crataegus (in variety)
Embothrium coccineum
Fraxinus angustifolia
Liquidambar styraciflua
Liriodendron tulipifera
Parrotia persica
Populus (in variety) (S)
Prunus padus
Pterocarya fraxinifolia (S)
Salix (in variety) (S)
Sambucus (in variety) (S)
Taxodium distichum (S)
Tsuga heterophylla

SHRUBS

Aucuba japonica
Camellia (in variety)
Clethra arborea
Cornus (in variety)
Desfontainia spinosa
Elaeagnus × ebbingei
Fatsia japonica
Hydrangea (in variety)
Osmanthus (in variety)
Sarcococca hookeriana
Skimmia japonica
Symphoricarpos × doorenbosii
Viburnum davidii
Zenobia pulverulenta

PERENNIALS & GROUND COVER PLANTS

Ajuga reptans
Alchemilla mollis
Anemone × hybrida cvs
Aruncus dioicus
Astilbe (in variety)
Bergenia (in variety)
Campanula persicifolia
Cardamine pratensis
Convallaria majalis
Darmera peltata (S)
Dodecatheon pulchellum
Enkianthus campanulatus
Filipendula palmata
Helleborus orientalis
Hosta (in variety)
Houttuynia cordata (S)
Iris pseudacorus (S)
Kirengeshoma palmata
Mentha (in variety)
Menziesia ciliicalyx
Persicaria bistorta
Polypodium vulgare (S)
Rheum palmatum
Rodgersia pinnata (S)
Trillium grandiflorum

Plants *for* Shade

Shade-loving plants are essential in most gardens as few are completely without a dark corner or spot under trees. In this selection you can find plants that like damp or dry shade, and also different degrees of shade, from heavy shade to only partial shade.

ABOVE: Alchemilla mollis, *lady's mantle, an invaluable standby for all gardens, was a plant much used by the great Gertrude Jekyll.*

OPPOSITE: *A shady corner is brightened with gold-splashed varieties of holly with the yellow flowers of the perennials like coreopsis and genista (broom) blending in with the yellow rose.*

ABOVE: *A small woodland garden has a handsome* Acer palmatum *var.* dissectum *'Ornatum' as a prominent feature which is underplanted with bluebells.*

RIGHT: Aucuba japonica, *with its yellow-splashed, evergreen leaves, on the right of the picture, will grow even in deep shade, as will the ivies covering the walls and steps. Camellias, on the left, are another plant that grows well in partial shade.*

Very few gardens are completely without shade in some form, but before planting you need to work out whether the shade is dry or damp, since not all plants that do well in damp shade will do well in dry shade and vice versa. Only a tiny number of plants will cope with almost total shade – ivies among them – since all plants require light in some form to create the food they need to survive.

On the whole, shade-loving plants appear rather different from sun-loving ones. They tend to have large foliage – nature's way of ensuring that the maximum amount of chlorophyll is exposed to the light to help photosynthesis (food manufacture) – and with smaller and paler flowers, quite often white. It is possible to create sophisticated and attractive shade gardens using only foliage and white-flowered plants.

This lack of colour was at one time, regarded as a disadvantage particularly by the Victorians and Edwardians who preferred the brightest, biggest flowers they could grow in rigidly controlled bedding formations. Gardens that are heavily shaded will not support a bright array of flowering plants – begonias and busy lizzies are among the very few flowering annuals that will survive in shade. They will, however, provide a successful home for many handsome architectural foliage plants and one of the best is *Fatsia japonica* with its big, glossy, evergreen, hand-shaped leaves. Another good performer in quite deep shade is the mottled, green-leaved *Aucuba japonica*. Rhododendrons and azaleas prefer partial shade (but they also like acid soil, so refer to this section as well). Remember that there are many varieties of ivy, with a whole range of different leaf colours and formations

that will grow in even the deepest shade, as will some ferns.

Usually shady areas are to be found under a tree, for example, or beneath a wall. These, because of the canopy of the tree or the shelter of the wall, will also tend to be dry and you must therefore look for plants that like dry shade. Ivies, of course, cope extremely well with dry shade, as do some hostas, foxgloves, hellebores and alchemilla (lady's mantle).

In moist soil in shade you can grow many of the woodland plants, as well as the Welsh poppy (*Meconopsis cambrica*) and some ferns, such as the shuttlecock fern (*Matteuccia struthiopteris*) and the soft shield fern (*Polystichum setiferum*)

Ideally, when creating areas of shade-loving foliage plants, try to contrast the different types, colours and forms of foliage, to make a green tapestry of leaves. Tall, strappy leaves of irises can be contrasted with soft feathery fronds of ferns and the big pleated leaves of veratrums, for example. If you have a wide selection of different foliage forms and colours, the garden will acquire just as much interest as a more colourful sunny flower border, and will last throughout the growing season, and into winter if you select a few evergreens as well.

Among good evergreens for the shade garden are the ivies, aucuba and fatsia, mahonia (some of which have the bonus of scented flowers), yew (taxus) and skimmias (again with scented flowers), skimmias are particularly good for town gardens as they grow slowly.

Many of the plants listed in other sections will flourish in partial shade as well and a comprehensive cross index to the other plants in the book can be found at the end of the chapter.

Above: A shady border, with the front edge in sun, provides a home for ligularias and aucuba, with nasturtiums (tropaeolum) providing front of the border colour. Anthemis tinctoria with its yellow daisy-like heads is on the left.

Aconitum 'Bressingham Spire'

Monkshood/Wolfbane
HEIGHT: 3-5ft (1-1.5m) • Hardy
FLOWERING SEASON: Summer

Known as monkshood or wolfbane, from
its hooded flowers, all parts of this plant,
from the tuberous roots to the finely divided
leaves, are very poisonous. Various aconitum
cultivars include: 'Blue Sceptre' and
'Bressingham Spire' which have straight spires
about 3ft (1m) tall with deep mauve blue
flowers in summer. Needs a moist soil. Cut
the flowers down after flowering to encourage flowering stems. Cut down all stems in
autumn. Propagate by division in autumn.

Adiantum pedatum

Northern maidenhair fern
HEIGHT: 12in (30cm) • Hardy
FLOWERING SEASON: None

This attractive small fern is native to North
America and Japan and is fully hardy in the
British Isles, although it dies down soon after
the first frosts. The light green fronds with
purple stalks arch gracefully from a central
rosette. There are several variants: *A. p.* var.
subpumilum, which is only 5in (12cm) high,
is ideal for a rock garden; *A. p.* Asiatic form
has copper-coloured fronds in spring, which
turn green as they mature. Propagate by
sowing the spores in spring, or by dividing
the rhizomes in spring. May be attacked by
woodlice and root mealy bugs.

Ajuga reptans

Bugle
HEIGHT: 5in (12cm) • Hardy
FLOWERING SEASON: Spring

Known as bugle, this small, vigorous
perennial likes shade, although it will grow
quite well in sun. It makes good ground
cover for damp soil. The dark-leaved cultivars,
such as 'Atropurpurea' and 'Braunherz', are
among the most attractive. The little spikes
of brilliant blue flowers rise above the leaves
in spring. It spreads by means of runners.
Another cultivar, 'Burgundy Glow', has light
blue flowers and cream-edged leaves.
Propagate by dividing clumps in winter.

Alchemilla mollis

Lady's mantle
HEIGHT: 18in (45cm) • Hardy
FLOWERING SEASON: Summer

Known as lady's mantle, this perennial has
rounded leaves about 5in (13cm) across, with
a serrated edge in a downy bluish-green, and
it is the foliage which is the plant's chief
glory. The lime-green flowers appear in tall
sprays in midsummer. It will normally self
seed easily, particularly in cracks in paving
and grows in all but very boggy soil. A
smaller species, *A. alpina*, grows to about
5in (13cm). To propagate, sow seeds under
cover in early spring, or divide clumps and
replant in autumn and winter.

Begonia rex hybrids

Begonia
HEIGHT: 18-24in (45-60cm) • Tender
FLOWERING SEASON: Insignificant

These evergreen begonias are grown principally for their attractive leaf forms. In general,
the leaves are heart-shaped with purple-
tinged edges, but different hybrids all have
particular characteristics: 'Merry Christmas'
has red leaves with an emerald green outer
band, while 'Princess of Hanover' has large
emerald green leaves with silver and dark red
bands. They are ideal for hanging baskets.
They require a minimum temperature of
13-15°C (55-59°F), humid conditions,
partial shade and moist, slightly acid soil.

Brunnera macrophylla

Siberian bugloss
HEIGHT: 18in (45cm) • Hardy
FLOWERING SEASON: Late spring

The Siberian bugloss bears delicate sprays
of small, brilliant, blue flowers, very similar
to forget-me-nots, in late spring. These are
followed by hairy, heart-shaped, green leaves.
The cultivar, *B. m.* 'Hadspen Cream' has
green and cream leaves, which tend to
colour best in the shady conditions which
the plant prefers. Divide the plants in autumn.
They are generally trouble-free, but do best
in soil that does not dry out in summer.
They are fully hardy and make good ground
cover plants.

Carex elata 'Aurea'

Bowles' golden sedge
HEIGHT: 3ft (1m) • Hardy
FLOWERING SEASON: Summer

Bowles' golden sedge is a selection of the tufted sedge, a perennial needing very moist soil or, ideally, its feet in water. It is one of the most graceful sedges with very fine golden-yellow leaves that arch attractively and, if planted in the right position, reflect the sunlight beautifully. Blackish-brown flower spikes are borne in summer. Divide in spring. *C. buchananii* from New Zealand has reddish leaves and *C. pendula* likes moist conditions and partial shade.

Choisya ternata

Mexican orange blossom
HEIGHT: 6ft (l.8m) or more • Hardy
FLOWERING SEASON: Early summer

This evergreen shrub, which is sometimes known as Mexican orange blossom, with its distinct foxy scent, is supposed to like sun, but, in fact, does extremely well in partial shade. The glossy evergreen leaves grow in a whorl, and the plant naturally makes an attractive dome-shaped bush. Many clusters of small, white, scented flowers are borne in late spring and early summer. It propagates easily from semi-ripe cuttings simply struck in ordinary garden soil in late summer.

Crataegus laevigata 'Punicea'

Hawthorn/May
HEIGHT: 20ft (6m) • Hardy
FLOWERING SEASON: Spring

This hawthorn is deciduous. In spring the small, oval, dark green leaves provide a foil for the clusters of deep crimson flowers, which are then followed by round bright red fruit. It copes well with urban pollution, and partial shade, and makes an excellent tree for a small garden. Some species of hawthorn have very good autumn colour, notably *C. crus-galli, C. × lavalleei* and *C. persimilis* 'Prunifolia'. Hawthorns make very good hedging plants.

Dicentra spectabilis 'Alba'

Bleeding heart/Dutchman's trousers
HEIGHT: 2½ft (75cm) • Hardy
FLOWERING SEASON: Late spring/summer

Known as Dutchman's trousers, or bleeding heart, this perennial has arching, pendant sprays of clear white, heart-shaped flowers with white inner petals, rather like a locket on a necklace. The leaves are grey-green and dissected, like those of ferns. *D. spectabilis* has pinkish-red flowers. *D. formosa* is a much smaller species with spreading blue-grey foliage and heart shaped purple flowers held aloft on stems 12in (30cm) high. It makes a good ground cover plant. They like moist soil, semi-shade and resent being moved.

Dicksonia antarctica

Australian tree fern
HEIGHT: 10ft (3m) or more • Half-hardy
FLOWERING SEASON: None

These handsome tree-like ferns come from Australia and do best in partial shade and soil which is moist and humus-rich. In temperate climates they are usually grown in containers, so that they can be overwintered indoors as they require a minimum temperature of 41°F (5°C). The fern makes a stout trunk, topped with huge, feathery, palm-like fronds which arise from the centre of the trunk in a curled spear. Remove the external, brown fronds as they fade. In its native state it will reach a height of 30ft (10m) or more.

Digitalis purpurea

Foxglove
HEIGHT: 3ft (1m) • Hardy
FLOWERING SEASON: Summer

The native foxglove is biennial (although it is sometimes perennial in ideal conditions). Its distinctive spire of tubular flowers rises high above a rosette of large, soft, green leaves and the flowers are noticeably speckled on the inside. There are many garden varieties and colours, including cream and pinkish-purple. Remove the main flower spike after flowering to encourage secondary, but smaller, flower spikes. Propagate by sowing seed in early summer. The crowns may rot in very damp or wet soil.

Dryopteris filix-mas

Male fern
HEIGHT: 3ft (1m) • Hardy
FLOWERING SEASON: None

The male fern, as it is commonly known, is the most common native fern and self-seeds itself freely, often popping up in crevices in pavings, but it is none the less welcome, having pretty, finely-divided, deep green fronds. It is unfussy as to soil but does best in plenty of shade – in the shadow of a wall for example – and looks best planted in small colonies, perhaps with other ferns, as a ribbon planting at the foot of a wall or under trees.

Elaeagnus × ebbingei 'Gilt Edge'

HEIGHT: 10ft (3m) or more • Hardy
FLOWERING SEASON: Autumn

This evergreen shrub is grown for its attractively silvered, small, oval leaves. It forms a large, densely covered, mounded shrub which makes a good screen and is also useful for hedging. The very small, bell-shaped and hard-to-spot flowers are very sweetly scented and fill the autumn air with unexpected fragrance. Small, egg-shaped, orange or red fruits follow the flowers. Plant in spring or early autumn, and prune by one-third after planting to promote bushy growth.

Epimedium grandiflorum

Barrenwort
HEIGHT: 9-12in (23-30cm) • Hardy
FLOWERING SEASON: Spring

This smallish perennial is native to Japan, and is grown for its foliage, which it retains throughout the winter, making good ground cover in partial shade. The leaves turn attractive shades of gold, scarlet and copper in autumn. The flowers come in shades of white, pink and yellow during a short season in spring. A cultivar known as 'Rose Queen' has bright pink flowers. It does best in a sandy soil with plenty of leaf-mould. To propagate, divide and replant in autumn.

Euphorbia amygdaloides var. *robbiae*

Milkwort/Wood spurge
HEIGHT: 18in (45cm) • Hardy
FLOWERING SEASON: Midsummer

There are more than 2,000 species in this genus. *E. amygdaloides* var. *robbiae* is a tough perennial that does particularly well in shade. It has the typical whorl-like euphorbia leaves in a dark glossy green, and the bright lime-yellow bracts are borne in quite large heads. Propagate by dividing clumps in autumn or by taking cuttings in early summer. May be subject to grey mould if damaged by frost. Note: the white sap is a skin irritant and care must be taken when handling the plants.

Fatsia japonica

Rice paper plant
HEIGHT: 15ft (4.5m) • Half-hardy
FLOWERING SEASON: Autumn

This plant, which hails from Japan, is grown principally for its handsome, glossy, evergreen leaves, which are hand-shaped with seven to nine lobes. It is particularly good for town gardens and it will grow under the shade of trees, where it will rapidly make a large spreading bush. It prefers fertile well-drained soil. In cold areas, give it the shelter of a south or west wall. There is also an autumn display of white panicles of flowers. Generally trouble-free, although young growth can be prey to blackfly.

Fuchsia 'Golden Dawn'

HEIGHT: 5ft (1.5m) • Half-hardy
FLOWERING SEASON: Summer/autumn

Fuchsia is a large genus with over 2000 plants in cultivation. These range from fully hardy to half-hardy and come in a bewildering range of colours and shapes mainly white, pink, red and purple. The flowers are variations on a bell-shaped theme and hang gracefully from the branches. They prefer a sheltered, shaded position and like moist well-drained soil. The top growth can often be damaged by frost and this can be cut back to ground level each spring. It is often necessary to cut back the hardiest varieties too, to keep them within their allotted bounds.

Gentiana asclepiadea

Willow gentian
HEIGHT: 2ft (60cm) • Hardy
FLOWERING SEASON: Mid/late summer

The willow gentian is not at all like its more familiar Swiss cousin, the trumpet gentian. This perennial also has blue, trumpet-shaped flowers, but there the similarity ends, as the willow gentian is a large perennial with slender, arching stems along which small, bright blue flowers are borne in mid to late summer, a good plant will throw up twelve or more shoots a year. It needs moist soil and partial shade to thrive. Can be grown from seed or cuttings, and is usually pest free.

Geranium phaeum

Mourning widow
HEIGHT: 18in (45cm) • Half-hardy
FLOWERING SEASON: Late spring/summer

This clump-forming geranium has lobed soft green leaves and carries its single dark-purple flowers on arching stems in late spring. In the right conditions it will self-seed freely. *G. palmatum* with its purplish-pink flowers, is another good geranium for growing in shade and has larger leaves than most geraniums with good autumn colour. Hardy geraniums or cranesbills are among the best garden plants, flowering for long periods in the summer and generally tolerant of a wide range of soils and conditions. Propagate by division in autumn or spring.

Hedera canariensis 'Gloire de Marengo'

Canary Island ivy
HEIGHT: 20ft (6m) • Half-hardy
FLOWERING SEASON: Insignificant

The Canary Island ivy is one of the less hardy ivies, but will grow quickly against a wall in a sheltered spot. If cut down by frost, it will regrow. The leaves are oval and without the usual lobes. 'Gloire de Marengo' has silver-splashed leaves; *H. algeriensis* 'Ravensholst' has large, mid green ones. To propagate, grow from softwood cuttings or rooted layers. Generally pest and disease free, but may be attacked by red spider mite.

Helleborus orientalis

Christmas rose/Lenten rose
HEIGHT: 18in (45cm) • Hardy
FLOWERING SEASON: Early spring

This particular hellebore, known as the Lenten rose because of its flowering time, is a native of the eastern Mediterranean, and in mild climates the leaves, which are broad and dark green, are evergreen. The nodding heads of cup-shaped flowers are the plant's chief attraction. The flowers can be mauve, purple, pink or white; all have prominent central stamens. It prefers moist, well-drained soil and partial shade. Grow from seed or divide in spring after flowering. Prone to aphid attacks in early summer.

Hepatica nobilis

Hepatica anemone
HEIGHT: 4in (10cm) • Hardy
FLOWERING SEASON: Spring

This little woodland plant, formerly *Anemone hepatica*, is ideal for a shady corner of a rock garden. The leaves which are mid green have three lobes, and the anemone-like flowers with their many petals come in various shades of white through pale pink to deep carmine, pale blue and purple to mauve. There are also fully double forms. It does best in partial shade in deep moist soil to which plenty of leaf mould has been added. The plants resent being disturbed. Generally pest and disease free.

Hosta fortunei

Plantain lily
HEIGHT: 2ft (60cm) • Hardy
FLOWERING SEASON: Early summer

The plantain lily, as the hosta is sometimes called, is particularly good for moist soil and partial shade. *H. fortunei* is a robust, vigorous hosta, that usually forms large clumps. Pale violet flowers are carried in a spire above the leaves. *H. f.* var. *aureomarginata* has yellow-edged leaves and is widely available, and *H. f.* var. *albopicta* has pale green leaves, with a yellow centre. Propagate by dividing mature clumps in early spring. All hostas are prone to attacks by slugs and snails and for this reason are often grown in containers.

Hosta sieboldiana var. elegans

Plantain lily
HEIGHT: 3ft (1m) • Hardy
FLOWERING SEASON: Summer

This hosta has huge, thickly ribbed leaves in an unusual shade of grey-green, and forms an impressively large clump when fully grown. Off-white flowers are tinged with lilac, and are borne in a tall spire, appearing in late summer. The variety *H. s.* var. *elegans* has waxy leaves, and lilac-coloured flowers in mid to late summer. Propagate by dividing mature clumps in early spring. If you don't use slug pellets, protect from slugs by circles of ash, or lime and soot around the plants.

Hydrangea anomala subsp. petiolaris

Climbing hydrangea
HEIGHT: 33ft (10m) or more • Hardy
FLOWERING SEASON: Summer

The climbing hydrangea is one of the few climbers that do well in shade; it climbs by means of aerial roots and will cling unaided. It is particularly useful for cool, north-facing walls. It has toothed green leaves and distinctive large flat heads of white flowers in summer. Like all hydrangeas, it needs a moisture-retentive soil and plenty of well-decayed manure. Prune out weak or damaged shoots in early spring and cut back to keep within bounds. Propagate it by tip cuttings taken after flowering.

Hypericum × inodorum 'Elstead'

St John's wort
HEIGHT: 4ft (1.2m) • Moderately hardy
FLOWERING SEASON: Summer

This particular species of St. John's wort comes from the Canary Islands. It is a semi-evergreen shrub with the typical golden yellow, cup-shaped flowers, borne on the ends of the branches right through the summer. These are followed by brilliant red large clusters of berries that are slightly oval in shape. It makes a good ground cover plant in the milder parts of the country. Take cuttings from non-flowering shoots in summer. Can be prone to rust.

Impatiens New Guinea Hybrids

Busy lizzies
HEIGHT: 12in (30cm) • Tender
FLOWERING SEASON: Summer

Busy lizzies, as they are often known, are an extremely popular tender plant, grown as an annual in cold climates, and used for hanging baskets, window boxes and summer bedding. They are one of the few brightly coloured flowering plants that do well in shade. The New Guinea hybrids have handsome deep red leaves and strongly coloured flowers, in pinks, reds and whites. Frequent watering is required in hot weather. Propagate named cultivars from cuttings or grow from seed sown in spring in warmth.

Mahonia aquifolium 'Atropurpurea'

Oregon grape
HEIGHT: 4ft (1.2m) • Hardy
FLOWERING SEASON: Spring

This evergreen shrub, known as the Oregon grape, has distinctive spiny, glossy, dark green foliage, each leaf composed of five to nine spiny leaflets. Richly scented bright yellow flowers are borne in dense clusters in spring, followed by blue berries. It has attractively coloured leaves which turn wine-red in winter. Plant mahonias in spring or autumn, in a soil rich in leaf-mould, ideally in partial shade. Take tip cuttings in summer. Troubled by rust, powdery mildew and leaf spot.

Matteuccia struthiopteris

Ostrich feather fern/Shuttlecock fern
HEIGHT: 3ft (1m) • Hardy
FLOWERING SEASON: None

The shuttlecock fern, as it is often known, is one of the most elegant ferns, with an attractive arching habit. The name shuttlecock fern describes the plant clearly with its crown of shorter, dark brown fronds surrounded by a circle of paler green ones. It needs moisture-retentive soil, with plenty of humus added to it, and does best in partial shade. It also requires plenty of room for the roots to expand. To increase the stock, remove any offsets in spring, and plant at least 4ft (1.2m) from the parent plant.

Meconopsis cambrica

Welsh poppy
HEIGHT: 12in (30cm) • Hardy
FLOWERING SEASON: Summer

This perennial, known as the Welsh poppy, produces large, bright, yellow or orange, papery flowers, rather like a large buttercup, all summer long. The plant grows 12-18in (30-45cm) tall and sends up a clump of fresh, green, fern-like foliage surmounted by a number of poppy-like flowers. It flourishes in shady places and needs a light rich soil, preferably neutral to acid, and plenty of water in summer but not very much in winter. It will usually seed itself.

Paeonia lactiflora hybrids

Peony
HEIGHT: 2ft (60cm) • Hardy
FLOWERING SEASON: Summer

There are both single and double-flowered forms of this herbaceous perennial and some are scented. Although the double cultivars are more showy, the single cultivars have a particular beauty, especially the pure white cultivars such as *P. l.* 'White Wings' and *P. l.* 'Whitleyi Major'. Grow peonies in a situation sheltered from morning sun, and humus-rich soil. Deadhead after flowering.

Paeonia mlokosewitschii

Peony
HEIGHT: 2ft (60cm) • Hardy
FLOWERING SEASON: Spring

This perennial peony has large, bright, lemon-yellow, single flowers with prominent stamens. The pale green leaves sometimes turn colour in autumn. It also has attractive seedpods. Peonies can be grown in moist, well-drained, well-manured soil in partial shade, ideally sheltered from the morning sun. Plant in early autumn or spring, making sure the crowns are not planted too deep. Prone to some viral disorders and damage from dry soil conditions or root disturbance.

Phyllostachys viridiglaucescens

Bamboo
HEIGHT: 20-25ft (6-8m) • Moderately hardy
FLOWERING SEASON: None

Phyllostachys are useful clump-forming bamboos which come from East Asia and Himalaya. They like moist rich soil which is on the light side and they must have a sheltered position. They flower about once every 30-40 years and after planting the whole plant dies so it is important to save seed when it is available. Propagation is normally by division which should be done in May when the new shoots are only an inch or two long. Cut the old shoots right down to the ground in spring.

Polygonatum × hybridum

Solomon's seal
HEIGHT: 4ft (1.2m) • Hardy
FLOWERING SEASON: Summer

Solomon's seal (or David's harp) is a large herbaceous perennial which is tough and very hardy. It will grow almost anywhere in both shade and sun. It makes an attractive arching plant with its thickly ribbed, mid green leaves and tubular white flowers dangling the length of the stems in summer. Give it plenty of leaf-mould, and cut the stems down in autumn. Propagate by division in autumn or spring. Generally disease-free, but sawfly caterpillars may damage leaves.

Schizophragma integrifolium

Hydrangea vine
HEIGHT: 20ft (6m) • Hardy
FLOWERING SEASON: Summer/autumn

This climber will attach itself to a wall or tree trunk using its aerial roots, so it needs no tying in. Closely related to its more vigorous cousin, *S. hydrangeoides*, it has the same large, flat, white, hydrangea-like florets from summer through to autumn, and bright green leaves with silvery backs. The plant will grow against a north wall but does better with some sun. It prefers moist well-drained soil. Propagate by taking short cuttings of the side shoots made with a slight heel of old wood inserted in sandy soil in July.

Skimmia japonica

Skimmia
HEIGHT: 4ft (1.2m) • Hardy
FLOWERING SEASON: Early summer

This handsome, rounded, bushy shrub is an
excellent plant for a small urban garden. It
has the bonus not only of neat, glossy evergreen leaves, but of scented, creamy-white
flower panicles, followed by bright scarlet
berries. It does well in partial shade in good
garden soil. The cultivar *S. j.* 'Rubella' with
its red rimmed aromatic leaves and red
flower buds which open to white flowers in
spring is particularly popular. Propagate from
semi-ripe cuttings in late summer.

Smilacina racemosa

False spikenard/False Solomon's seal
HEIGHT: 3ft (1m) • Hardy
FLOWERING SEASON: Summer

Known as the false spikenard, or false
Solomon's seal, this herbaceous perennial
likes lightly shaded woodland and moist,
neutral to acid soil. The white scented
flowers are carried on the ends of the stems.
Cut back the plants in autumn. To
propagate, lift the plant in spring and divide
the rhizomatous rootstock once the plant
has been established for a few years.

Stewartia pseudocamellia

HEIGHT: 16ft (5m) • Hardy
FLOWERING SEASON: Late summer

S. pseudocamellia is a small tree that makes a
good subject for planting in part shade in
neutral to acid soil. It has single large white
cup-shaped flowers in summer and the mid
green ovate leaves turn attractive shades of
gold and scarlet in autumn, while in winter
the peeling bark is a bonus. *S. p.* Koreana
Group is similar with flowers that open out
flat. *S. sinensis*, has fragrant saucer-shaped
flowers. The plant will not flourish against
an east wall. Propagate from half-ripe cuttings in late summer.

Symphytum × uplandicum 'Variegatum'

Comfrey
HEIGHT: 10in (25cm) • Hardy
FLOWERING SEASON: Spring

This is a vigorous perennial, which does best
in partial shade and fairly moist conditions.
They are, perhaps, best suited to a wild
garden and generally will self-seed freely.
The leaves, which are lance-shaped, are
bristly and tough, cream and green splashed,
and the flowers are blue or pink.
S. grandiflorum has small creamy-white
flowers and makes good ground cover,
S. 'Hidcote Blue', is similar with pale blue
flowers. Propagate by division in autumn.

Tellima grandiflora

Fringe cup
HEIGHT: 2ft (60cm) • Hardy
FLOWERING SEASON: Early summer

This evergreen perennial is easy to grow and
a very good subject for shade. It is a
particularly good weed suppressor and
makes a good ground cover plant in a shrubbery. The leaves, which form a dense crown
close to the ground, are fairly large, maple-
like and rough in texture. The tall flower
spires carry rather insignificant greenish-
yellow flowers in early summer. The
Tellima grandiflora Rubra Group cultivars
have attractive bronze purple leaves.
Propagate by dividing the plants or by seed.

Thalictrum aquilegiifolium var. album

Meadow rue/Maidenhair fern
HEIGHT: 3-4 ft (1-1.2m) • Hardy
FLOWERING SEASON: Summer

This elegant, clump-forming perennial has
particularly attractive foliage, very similar to
that of the aquilegia. In summer it carries
branching heads of small, white, starry
flowers. There is another good white cultivar
called 'White Cloud'. *T. aquilegiifolium* has
attractive lilac-purple flowers. This plant
prefers moist soil, and flourishes in partial
shade, although it will also cope with sun. It
looks well grown at the edge of woodland.
Propagate by division in spring.

Trollius europaeus

Globe flower
HEIGHT: 2ft (60cm) • Hardy
FLOWERING SEASON: Early summer

The globe flower has attractive bright yellow or orange tightly petalled flowers, some 2in (5cm) across. The leaves are deeply divided, lobed and toothed. It does well as a marginal plant for streams or ponds or in any moist soil in sun or partial shade. Good hybrids include the pale yellow *T.* × *cultorum* 'Canary Bird', or the bright orange *T.* × *c.* 'Orange Princess'. Cut the flowers back after flowering to produce a second flush of blooms. Divide and replant fibrous roots in autumn.

Veratrum nigrum

Black false hellebore
HEIGHT: 4ft (1.2m) • Hardy
FLOWERING SEASON: Late summer

These big, hardy perennials make handsome spires of deep purple, star-shaped flowers above large, dark green, pleated leaves. They are good imposing plants for the back of a shady border. *V. nigrum* likes moist soil to which peat has been added, and benefits from being cut down in autumn. Propagate by dividing the clumps in autumn or spring. A greenish-white flowered species, *V. album*, makes a similar height and can be treated in the same way.

Viola riviniana Purpurea Group

Sweet violet
HEIGHT: 5in (12cm) • Hardy
FLOWERING SEASON: Spring

This small woodland plant formerly known as *V. labradorica purpurea* is ideal for shade. It has attractively coloured purplish-bronze leaves and the typical small, mauve violet flowers in spring. It does well on any light fertile soil which does not dry out. Plant in autumn or spring, and deadhead the flowers as they fade, to encourage a longer flowering season. Can be grown from seed. Pest-free, but prone to a variety of viral disorders.

More Plants for Shade

All gardens have some shade and we have divided the plants that grow best in shade into three groups: plants that will grow in dry shade; plants that will grow in moist shade, of which a number are listed under moisture on page 213; and plants that will grow on a north wall. These lists are only a selection and there are a number of other plants that are suitable for these problem positions.

PLANTS FOR DRY SHADE

TREES

Acer campestre
  A. platanoides & cvs
Alnus (in variety)
Betula (in variety)
Gleditsia triacanthos
Ilex aquifolium
Robinia pseudoacacia & cvs
Sorbus aucuparia

SHRUBS

Aucuba japonica
Bashania syn. *Arundinaria* (in variety)
Berberis (in variety)
Buxus sempervirens
Cotoneaster horizontalis
Euonymus fortunei cvs

Hippophae rhamnoides
Lonicera pileata
Osmanthus (in variety)
Prunus laurocerasus

PERENNIALS & GROUND COVER PLANTS

Bergenia (in variety)
Iris foetidissima
Lamium maculatum
Pachysandra terminalis
Pulmonaria saccharata

PLANTS FOR MOIST SHADE

TREES

Acers (in variety)
Alnus incana
Betula nigra
  B. pendula
Crataegus (in variety)
Embothrium coccineum
Salix (in variety)
Sorbus aucuparia

SHRUBS

Aucuba japonica
Camellia (in variety)
Clethra arborea
Cornus (in variety)
Desfontainia spinosa
Gaultheria (in variety)
Kalmia latifolia
Leucothoe fontanesiana
Rhododendron (in variety)
Symphoricarpus × *doorenbosii*

PERENNIALS, GROUND COVER PLANTS & CLIMBERS

Astilbe (in variety)
Begonia rex Hybrids
Campanula lactiflora
Dicentra (in variety)
Dodecatheon pulchellum
Epimedium grandiflorum
Galium odoratum
Houttuynia cordata
Iris pseudacorus
Mentha suavolens
Oxalis acetosella
Polypodium vulgare
Tradescantia (in variety)
Trillium grandiflorum
Tropaeolum speciosum

CLIMBERS & PLANTS FOR NORTH WALLS

Berberidopsis corallina
Clematis (large-flowered varieties)
Cotoneaster horizontalis
Forsythia suspensa
Garrya elliptica
Hydrangea petiolaris
Jasminum nudiflorum (Winter jasmine)
Kerria japonica
Parthenocissus (in variety)
Pyracantha (in variety)
Rosa 'Königin von Dänemark'
  R. 'Madame Legras de Saint German'
  R. 'Maigold'
Schizophragma hydrangeoides

PLANTS *for* DRY SUN

For sunny, dry areas in your garden, plants from the hotter areas of the world are a good choice because they thrive in these conditions. Many are distinguished by divided, waxy or felted leaves. Grey-leaved plants, such as lavender and senecio, are typical examples.

ABOVE: Convolvulus cneorum, *a grey-leaved sub-shrub, thrives in hot dry conditions and produces a profusion of delicate white flowers.*

OPPOSITE: *A garden in summer with the climbing roses just coming into bloom. The roses give additional height to the border and the mixed colours of the herbaceous perennials provide a splendid contrast.*

ABOVE: *A mixed border, with the front edge in sun, provides a home for a cottage-garden style planting of opium poppies in the front, contrasting with the silvery-grey Miss Willmott's Ghost* (Eryngium giganteum) *and the spires of the purple form of the burning bush,* (Dictamnus albus *var.* purpureus) *behind.*

Anyone who has travelled abroad to the Mediterranean, California or Australia, especially in the spring, will realize that a hot and dry site is by no means a problem in a garden. If you select your plants carefully, you can create a fine display which will provide colour and interest. Start with some of the best known plants from the Mediterranean: lavender, rosemary, sage, salvia and santolina, rock roses (cistus), helichrysum (the everlasting flower) and marigolds. These are just some of the plants that like a position in full sun and dry soil.

The plants which survive these conditions tend to have evolved and adapted in order to cope with high temperatures and low rainfall. These adaptations are often what make the plants so attractive. *Convolvulus cneorum*, with its silver and grey foliage, appears this colour because it has developed a coating of fine hairs on the leaf surface, which has the effect of reducing moisture loss and reflecting sunlight. Other plants, such as *Senecio* 'Sunshine' (now properly called *Brachyglottis*), have modified their leaves by thickening them to protect the inside, while the underside of the leaf remains felted. Brooms, such as *Genista aetnensis*, reduce moisture loss by having hardly any leaves at all, but thin tough stems.

The soil in which these plants grow in the wild is often poor and impoverished. It may be almost pure sand or gravel, which makes it very quick to drain, and in summer there is very little natural moisture. There is little organic matter too, as any fallen leaves burn up quickly, or there may be just a very shallow scraping of soil over solid rock, the roots clinging on for life by penetrating cracks and crevices.

In the garden, these conditions can exist naturally or can be created artificially; where the garden is of thin shallow soil overlying solid rock, for example, or where the subsoil is pure sand or gravel which has found its way to the surface, as can happen in a new garden if the topsoil has been removed during building works. Perhaps you have a south-facing border against a house wall, particularly if there is a path or patio to the other side, or a south-facing, sloping garden; these also tend towards dryness, and more so if the soil is also sandy.

The main problem with such soils is lack of moisture for the plants. Improving the soil is difficult, as any organic matter you try to incorporate is quickly burnt up, and the plant nutrients you do apply will be washed through the soil along with the water. On the positive side, however, dry soils are quick to warm up in spring, and if you can achieve a cover of plants that like this environment, they will soon start to help themselves by using their natural adaptations to conserve moisture.

RIGHT: *The brilliant white flowers of* Anthemis punctata *ssp.* cupaniana *with their yellow eyes make it an ideal subject to plant at the edge of a gravel garden.*

BELOW: *A gravel garden provides a home for alpines that enjoy both sun and free draining soil: here the yellow flowers of the helianthemum and the pink spreading saponaria, tumbling Ted, provide a foil for the French lavender.*

Acantholimon glumaceum

Prickly thrift
HEIGHT: 6in (15cm) • Hardy
FLOWERING SEASON: Summer

An evergreen perennial with a low, cushion-forming habit; the stems often root into the soil as the plant spreads across the ground. The flowers are produced in small, short spikes of up to eight star-shaped, pink blooms which are carried above the spiny, spear-shaped, bluish-green leaves, and arranged in tight rosettes on the stems. Propagation is by softwood cuttings taken from non-flowering shoots in spring and summer and rooted in a cold frame.

Aethionema 'Warley Ruber'

Persian candytuft
HEIGHT: 6in (15cm) • Hardy
FLOWERING SEASON: Spring/summer

This colourful evergreen sub-shrub has tiny strap-like leaves which are a bluish-green colour. It has a naturally spreading habit and forms a dense mat of foliage over the soil. The small cross-shaped flowers are a deep rose-pink and grow in loose clusters on the tips of the shoots. Often grown in the rock garden, this plant needs an open, free-draining soil to grow well. Trim the plants in July after the flowers are over and propagate by taking softwood cuttings from the new growth, either in the late summer, or in the spring.

Agapanthus Headbourne Hybrids

African lily
HEIGHT: 3ft (1m) • Moderately hardy
FLOWERING SEASON: Mid/late summer

A clump-forming herbaceous perennial with deep green strap-like leaves up to 2½ft (75cm) long and large clusters of deep blue flowers produced from July onwards. Cultivars, such as Headbourne Hybrids, are usually hardier than many of the species. They like full sun, and have thick fleshy roots which provide a good water store and drought tolerance. In northern areas they require winter protection. Propagate by division in spring.

Anthemis punctata ssp. *cupaniana*

Chamomile/Dog fennel
HEIGHT: 12in (30cm) • Hardy
FLOWERING SEASON: Early summer

An evergreen herbaceous perennial that is invaluable for a dry sunny garden. It forms a loose cushion of finely cut, silvery-grey, aromatic foliage, which turns green in winter. The white daisy-like flowers have a golden centre, or 'eye', and are carried singly above the leaves on short erect stems. No regular pruning is required but the dead flower heads are usually removed in autumn. Propagation is by semi-ripe basal cuttings taken in summer.

Aster novi-belgii 'Jenny'

Michaelmas daisy
HEIGHT: 2½ft (75cm) • Hardy
FLOWERING SEASON: Early autumn

This popular herbaceous perennial has mid to deep green leaves carried on sturdy erect green stems, they are roughly elliptical but terminate in a sharp point. The colourful daisy-like flowers are produced in large quantities in autumn. Many reliable named cultivars are available: *A. n-b.* 'Royal Ruby' has deep red flowers, and 'White Ladies' has white flowers and dark foliage. They flourish in sun or part shade and are generally soil tolerant. Propagate by softwood cuttings in summer, or division in early spring.

Buddleja alternifolia

Butterfly bush
HEIGHT: 15ft (4.5m) • Hardy
FLOWERING SEASON: Summer

A large deciduous shrub with graceful arching stems covered in grey-green, narrow strap-like leaves, which have a bluish underside. Clusters of small, delicately fragrant, lilac-blue flowers are produced in June on the previous year's wood. Prune after flowering but if left unpruned the shrub develops into a sprawling plant with a semi-weeping habit. An interesting cultivar, *B. a.* 'Argentea', has hairy silver-grey leaves. This plant is easy to propagate by softwood cuttings in summer or hardwood cuttings in winter.

Campanula persicifolia

Peach-leaved bellflower
HEIGHT: 3ft (1m) • Hardy
FLOWERING SEASON: Mid-late summer

This clump-forming, evergreen, herbaceous perennial has long, narrow, mid green, leathery leaves which grow in tight rosettes. The bell-shaped flowers are produced close to the main stem, and range in colour from bluish-purple to pure white. A number of cultivars are available: 'Telham Beauty' has deep blue flowers and *C. p.* var. *planiflora* f. *alba,* pure white ones. Propagate by seed sown in March and April, cuttings taken in April and May, or dividing the plants in October.

Catalpa bignonioides

Indian bean tree
HEIGHT: 50ft (15m) • Hardy
FLOWERING SEASON: Summer

This outstanding deciduous tree has an open, spreading habit and, in mature specimens, a deeply grooved bark. It is valued for its tolerance of urban pollution. The large, heart-shaped leaves are tinged with purple as they open, turning light-green as they mature.In summer white, bell-shaped flowers with yellow and purple markings are produced, followed by long hanging pods which stay throughout winter. There is a striking golden-leaved cultivar: *C. b.* 'Aurea'. Propagate in summer using softwood tip cuttings.

Catananche caerulea

Cupid's dart/Blue cupidone
HEIGHT: 2ft (60cm) • Hardy
FLOWERING SEASON: Summer

This clump forming perennial known as cupid's dart, has narrow, grey-green, strap-like leaves carried on tall erect mid green stems and masses of daisy-like, purple-blue flowers throughout the summer. They like a sunny, open position and light, well-drained soil. There are a number of named cultivars: *C. c.* 'Major', has lavender blue flowers, *C. c.* 'Perry's White', is the most popular white cultivar. Named cultivars must be propagated by root cuttings taken in winter.

Clarkia elegans

Clarkia
HEIGHT: 2ft (60cm) • Hardy
FLOWERING SEASON: Late summer/autumn

This popular annual is grown for its colourful display of summer flowers, the leaves are narrow, oval and mid green in colour. The flowers are produced in bold spikes on erect green stems in colours which range through white, salmon, orange, purple, scarlet and lavender. In addition, double-flowered forms are also available; *C. e.* Love Affair, is a mixed colour strain with large double flowers and compact growth. Propagation is by seed sown outdoors in early spring. Thin the seedlings to 9-12in (20-30cm) apart.

Convolvulus cneorum

HEIGHT: 2½ft (75cm) • Moderately hardy
FLOWERING SEASON: Late spring/early autumn

A rather surprising member of the same genus as the pernicious bindweed, this is a slightly tender evergreen shrub of compact and low-growing bushy habit, with silvery, silky, narrow pointed leaves, on silver hairy stems. The short-lived flowers, produced at the tips of the shoots from May to September, are a soft pink in tight bud, opening to pure white with a small golden-yellow eye in the centre. It prefers a sheltered position in well-drained but nutrient-poor soil in full sun. Propagation is by semi-ripe cuttings, taken in July.

Cortaderia selloana 'Aureolineata'

Pampas grass
HEIGHT: 8ft (2.5m) • Moderately hardy
FLOWERING SEASON: Summer/autumn

A bold, showy, clump-forming ornamental grass, with narrow, pale to mid green, spear-shaped, evergreen leaves, which have razor sharp edges. The flowers, which are carried in majestic silvery-white plumes tinged red or purple in autumn, are held high above the arching leaves on erect almost white stems. A popular cultivar is *C. s.* 'Sunningdale Silver', which has long-lasting, large, silver flower-plumes. Propagation is by division in spring; select female plants for a better flower display.

Corylus avellana 'Contorta'

Cobnut/Hazelnut
HEIGHT: 10ft (3m) • Hardy
FLOWERING SEASON: Early spring

This large deciduous shrub is grown for its curiously twisted branches and twigs. The broadly oval, mid green leaves have a noticeably toothed margin and turn a deep gold in autumn. The female flowers are very small, but the long yellow male catkins are very attractive in February. It likes well-drained limy soil and mortar rubble may be added before planting if the soil is lime-deficient. It is best to propagate by layering one-year-old shoots, but rooting will take up to a year.

Crataegus laciniata

Hawthorn
HEIGHT: 22ft (7m) • Hardy
FLOWERING SEASON: Spring

A beautiful small ornamental tree, with sparsely thorned, lax branches covered in felt when young. The deeply cut, downy leaves are dark green above and grey-green beneath. The large fruits are a pinkish-yellow later turning red and hang on the tree most of the winter. Propagation is by budding in summer or grafting in early spring. The bacterial disease fireblight causes withering and progressive die-back of young shoots.

Cytisus battandieri

Pineapple broom/Moroccan broom
HEIGHT: 12ft (4m) • Moderately hardy
FLOWERING SEASON: Early summer

A spectacular semi-evergreen open shrub best grown against the shelter of a west- or south-facing wall, the pineapple bush carries large racemes of the pineapple-scented flowers which give it its name from early to midsummer. Like all brooms it prefers light well-drained soil but it can be grown successfully on heavier land provided plenty of sand and leaf mould are worked into the ground before planting. Propagate by semi-ripe cuttings taken in late summer.

Cytisus × kewensis

Broom
HEIGHT: 2ft (60cm) • Hardy
FLOWERING SEASON: Late spring

This attractive, low-growing shrub was raised at Kew Gardens in 1891 and has been popular ever since. In spring, cascades of creamy-yellow, sweet-pea-shaped blooms cover the bush, obscuring the stems and leaves. The mid green leaves are small, strap-like, covered in fine hairs and grow sparsely along the lax, twiggy, green stems. This plant should be pruned after flowering but it does not respond well to hard pruning or being moved. Propagation is by semi-ripe cuttings with a heel taken in summer.

Davidia involucrata

Dove tree/Handkerchief tree
HEIGHT: 50ft (15m) • Hardy
FLOWERING SEASON: Late spring

This beautiful tree is grown for the striking display of large, white, modified leaf bracts, from which it gets its common name 'hand-kerchief tree'. The insignificant flowers appear in small clusters on mature plants in May. The mid green, heart-shaped leaves have dense hairs on the underside, and in autumn turn a bright golden-yellow with a red tinge at the margin. It likes a sunny position and deep well-drained soil. Propagation is by seed sown in autumn or semi-ripe cuttings taken in early summer.

Diascia fetcaniensis

HEIGHT: 12in (30cm) • Half-hardy
FLOWERING SEASON: Summer

These plants are slender, low-growing annuals or short-lived perennials with dark green, glossy, broadly oval leaves, with a toothed margin. The tube-shaped, rosy-pink, lilac or apricot flowers open out into a shell-like bloom with spotted throat. They are produced in large flushes on the tips of slender green shoots. A popular cultivar, *D.* 'Ruby Field', has salmon-pink flowers. They like sun and rich, moist, well-drained soil that does not dry out. Propagate by cuttings taken in late summer. (This plant is often mistakenly identified as nemesia.)

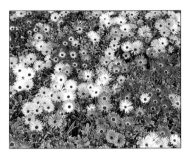

Dorotheanthus bellidiformis

Livingstone daisy/Ice plant/Fig marigold
HEIGHT: 4in (10cm) • Tender
FLOWERING SEASON: Summer/autumn

Some mesembryanthemums have become dorotheanthus, but this is still the Livingstone daisy, which is well adapted to surviving in dry, arid conditions. Low and spreading in habit, its narrow, light green, tube-like leaves have a glistening appearance. In a dry sunny position it produces masses of brightly coloured, small, daisy-like flowers. The colour range includes white, pink, carmine, salmon, apricot and orange. Propagate by sowing seeds indoors in March.

Echinops bannaticus 'Taplow Blue'

Globe thistle
HEIGHT: 4ft (1.2m) • Hardy
FLOWERING SEASON: Late summer

An attractive upright perennial with narrow leaves and palish-blue thistle-like heads carried on branching stems in late summer. Globe thistles flourish in ordinary garden soil and like a sunny position. They are useful plants for the herbaceous border as their pale, neutral colour provides a good foil for brighter plants. Propagate by division in the autumn or by root cuttings taken in mild weather in winter.

Eryngium bourgatii

Sea holly
HEIGHT: 2½ft (75cm) • Hardy
FLOWERING SEASON: Summer/autumn

At first glance, these tough herbaceous perennials look like a cross between a holly and a thistle, but they are not related to either. The tough, spiny, coarsely toothed leaves vary in colour from dark green to silvery-blue. The flowers, which often look very like teasel heads, are metallic silvery-blue, darkening with age, with a collar of broad spines at the base; they are held on strong wiry stems above the leaves. Propagation is by division or root cuttings in spring.

Escallonia 'Slieve Donard'

Escallonia
HEIGHT: 14ft (4.5m) • Not fully hardy
FLOWERING SEASON: Late spring/early summer

Escallonias are handsome evergreen shrubs which can be grown either as hedges, in the shrubbery, or against a wall. They have an attractive range of flower colours from white through pink to scarlet. The small, bell-shaped flowers are produced in clusters on short spur-like branches above the glossy oval leaves, dark green above and pale green beneath. They like sun and well-drained soil and are an excellent plant for southern coastal regions. Propagates very easily from softwood cuttings taken in midsummer.

Eucalyptus gunnii

Cider gum
HEIGHT: 35ft (10.5m) • Moderately hardy
FLOWERING SEASON: Autumn/winter

The cider gum is an evergreen tree that comes from Australia and is grown mainly for its blue-grey, leathery-textured leaves and stems. The leaf shape varies with the age of the plant: the juvenile leaves are almost circular and appear to clasp the short stems on which they are produced, but as the plant matures the new leaves are strap-like and hang down vertically. Young trees have a blue-grey bark. Eucalyptus can be cut to the ground each spring and grown as shrubs. Propagation is by seed sown in spring.

Galtonia candicans

Summer hyacinth
HEIGHT: 4ft (1.2m) • Moderately hardy
FLOWERING SEASON: Late summer/early autumn

These outstanding late-flowering bulbs have leaves which are a bluish grey-green, widely strap-shaped and quite thick and fleshy. Single stems carry a head of large, slightly scented, drooping, white bells, with pale green markings at the base of each petal. These bulbs make an attractive display at a time when many other plants are looking jaded. They like a sheltered sunny site. They produce seed very freely and may become invasive. Propagation is by seed sown in spring or bulblets in autumn.

Genista aetnensis

Mount Etna broom
HEIGHT: 25ft (8m) • Hardy
FLOWERING SEASON: Summer

This is a large elegant shrub, with many slender drooping, bright green branches, which are practically leafless. The tough, sparse leaves are mid green and strap-like, with fine, white, silky hairs. The golden-yellow, heavily scented, pea-like flowers are produced in large quantities at the tips of the shoots in midsummer. It likes full sun and will tolerate almost any soil conditions except waterlogging. Propagation is by seed sown in spring.

Gleditsia triacanthos 'Sunburst'

Honey locust
HEIGHT: 30ft (9m) • Moderately hardy
FLOWERING SEASON: Midsummer

A beautiful small tree ideal for giving light shade in the garden, provided the site is not exposed. The small, delicate leaflets are arranged in large numbers (up to 32) along a tough green leaf stalk, although a glossy mid green, the most popular cultivar is the golden-leaved *G. t.* 'Sunburst', and there is a purple-leaved cultivar, *G. t.* 'Rubylace'. Propagation is by seed sown under protection in spring or the named cultivars are increased by grafting in early spring.

Gypsophila repens 'Rosa Schönheit'

Chalk plant
HEIGHT: 3ft (1m) • Hardy
FLOWERING SEASON: Summer

These cottage garden favourites have thin, strap-like grey-green leaves very similar to those of the carnation, carried on thick, grey-green stems. Masses of very small, usually white, flowers are produced in large clusters. There are dwarf and pink-flowered forms. *G. repens* 'Rosea' is low-growing, 4-6in (10-15cm), and spreads to form a dense mat, with rose-pink flowers. Propagate by root cuttings taken when dormant.

× Halimiocistus wintonensis

HEIGHT: 2ft (60cm) • Not fully hardy
FLOWERING SEASON: Summer

This hybrid evergreen plant makes a low, spreading bush with small tough, slightly hairy, grey-green leaves supported on thin, grey-green, semi-prostrate stems. The small, saucer-shaped flowers are white with a red blotch at the base of each petal and a yellow centre to the bloom. The flowers open early in the morning and die the same day, leaving a carpet of petals around the plant. It likes full sun and fertile well-drained soil but will require shelter if grown in colder areas. Propagation is by small semi-ripe cuttings taken in summer.

Helianthemum 'Amy Baring'

Rock rose/Sun rose
HEIGHT: 3-4in (7.5-10cm) • Hardy
FLOWERING SEASON: Late summer/autumn

A dwarf and very drought-resistant evergreen shrub with small, oval, pale green leaves covered in fine hairs. The small, saucer-shaped flowers are produced in massed flushes, close to the ground on short stems. Good cultivars are *H.* 'Rhodanthe Carneum' with pink flowers emerging through grey foliage, 'Wisley Primrose', soft golden-yellow flowers, and 'Wisley White', pure white flowers and grey foliage. Cut back lightly after flowering. Propagate by semi-ripe heel cuttings taken in August.

Helichrysum italicum

Curry plant
HEIGHT: 15in (35cm) • Moderately hardy
FLOWERING SEASON: Summer

This dwarf shrub has a dense, bushy habit and short, narrow silvery-grey, aromatic leaves which smell of curry when they are crushed or when the weather is very hot and sunny. The flowers grow in broad clusters of small, oblong, mustard-yellow flower-heads on long upright white shoots. It likes sun and well-drained soil. If not pruned with shears immediately after flowering, this shrub will spread, leaving an open, bare centre. Propagation is by semi-ripe cuttings taken with a heel in summer.

Hibiscus syriacus 'Red Heart'

Hibiscus
HEIGHT: 10ft (3m) • Moderately hardy
FLOWERING SEASON: Late summer

Another popular cultivar of *H. syriacus*, 'Red Heart' has large white flowers with conspicuous red centres. Hibiscus should be planted in March or November and are useful as background plants in a herbaceous border in the milder parts of the country. Little pruning is required but they can be thinned out in spring if the shrub is becoming overcrowded. Propagated by semi-ripe cuttings taken in summer and inserted in sandy soil in a cold frame.

Hibiscus syriacus 'Oiseau Bleu'

Hibiscus
HEIGHT: 10ft (3m) • Moderately hardy
FLOWERING SEASON: Late summer

A large upright deciduous shrub with deeply notched dark green leaves. *H. s.* 'Oiseau Blue' carries large lilac-blue flowers with a red centre from late summer to mid autumn. Hibiscus come from the mallow family, *malvaceae*, and vary from hardy to frost tender. They like full sun and rich well-drained soil. Among the best garden plants are the species, *H. syriacus* which is white with a red centre, and its cultivar *H. s.* 'Woodbridge' which is deep pink with a dark red centre.

Hypericum 'Hidcote'

St John's wort
HEIGHT: 4ft (1.2m) • Hardy
FLOWERING SEASON: Late summer/early autumn

This is a deciduous to semi-evergreen shrub with a dense bushy habit and thin, grey-green stems which turn pale-brown as they age. The small strap-like leaves are deep green on the upper surface with a slight blue-green sheen on the underside. The golden yellow saucer-shaped flowers are produced in clusters from late summer to early autumn. *H.* 'Hidcote Variegated' has a white margin to the leaf. Propagation is by semi-ripe cuttings taken with a heel in summer and autumn.

Ilex aquifolium 'Silver Queen'

Holly
HEIGHT: 15ft (4.5m) • Hardy
FLOWERING SEASON: Spring/summer

The hollies, the evergreen shrubs associated with Christmas, all have small, white, star-shaped flowers, with red, orange, yellow or even white berries produced on the female plants in winter. The leaves vary in colour but have sharp spines around the margin. Popular cultivars are *I. aquifolium* 'Silver Queen' with dark green leaves and a silver margin and *I.* × *altaclerensis* 'Golden King', with a golden margin. All of them prefer well-drained soil. Propagation is by semi-ripe cuttings taken in summer.

Kniphofia 'Royal Standard'

Red-hot poker/Torch lily
HEIGHT: 3ft (1m) • Moderately hardy
FLOWERING SEASON: Late summer

A familiar sight in many borders in late summer red-hot pokers carry their spears of red-tipped buds opening to yellow flowers above grass-like tufts of leaves. They prefer full sun and fertile well-drained soil and they do not do well in soil that becomes water-logged. The crowns may need protection in winter in hard weather. *K.* 'Little Maid' carries pale creamy-yellow, whitish flowers and *K.* 'Samuel's Sensation' deep orange ones. The plants resent being disturbed. Propagate by division in spring.

Laburnum × *watereri* 'Vossii'

Voss's laburnum
HEIGHT: 28ft (9m) • Hardy
FLOWERING SEASON: Late spring

A well-known flowering tree which produces large quantities of long, trailing clusters (racemes) of deep golden-yellow, pea-like flowers in late spring. In autumn the small, grey-brown pods split open to release small black seeds, which are poisonous. The grey-green leaves, which have a glossy upper surface and paler underside, are made up of three small leaflets. Laburnums grow in any but waterlogged soil but have a brittle root system and must be permanently staked. Propagate by grafting in spring.

Lavandula angustifolia

Lavender
HEIGHT: 3ft (1m) • Hardy
FLOWERING SEASON: Mid/late summer

This evergreen perennial has long, narrow, aromatic, silver-grey leaves covered with fine, felt-like hairs which are very effective in reducing moisture loss. The small, tube-like flowers are carried in narrow clusters, on tough, square stems. The most commonly grown cultivar, *L. a.* 'Hidcote', has strongly scented, deep purple-blue flowers and a compact bushy habit. *L. a.* 'Alba' is white and *L. a.* 'Rosea', pink. Propagation is by semi-ripe cuttings with a heel in summer.

Liriope muscari

Lilyturf
HEIGHT: 18in (45cm) • Hardy
FLOWERING SEASON: Late summer/late autumn

This clump-forming perennial has glossy, deep green, grass-like leaves. A network of rhizomes below ground provides a spreading habit which makes it ideal for ground cover. The thick clusters of flower spikes bear violet-blue, bell-shaped flowers.
L. m. 'Curly Twist' has lilac flowers flushed with burgundy and spirally twisting leaves.
L. m. 'Variegata' has a bold yellow stripe along the leaf margin. Propagation is by division in early spring.

Lithodora diffusa
'Heavenly Blue'

Gromwell
HEIGHT: 4in (10cm) • Hardy • pH
FLOWERING SEASON: Summer/late autumn

This prostrate, spreading plant is perfect for a hot, dry position, the slender stems are covered with small, dull green leaves which are spear-shaped and covered with fine hairs to reduce moisture loss. Small, deep-blue, funnel-shaped flowers are produced in vast quantities from early June onwards. Hard pruning in spring will prevent the plant becoming straggly. Propagation is by semi-ripe cuttings taken in midsummer.

Lychnis chalcedonica

Jerusalem cross/Maltese cross
HEIGHT: 3ft (1m) • Hardy
FLOWERING SEASON: Summer

A neat clump-forming perennial which bears large clustered heads of flowers of an intense pure scarlet colour in early summer. It is easily grown and does best in full sun in fertile well-drained soil but it prefers soil which does not dry out. The cultivar *L. c.* 'Alba' is white. Other species include *L. flos-cuculi*, the ragged robin or cuckoo flower, which grows wild in Europe and Great Britain, its rose-pink flowers are extremely showy. Propagate by division of the roots in March.

Macleaya microcarpa

Plume poppy
HEIGHT: 6ft (1.8m) • Hardy
FLOWERING SEASON: Summer

Known as the plume poppy, this is an invasive herbaceous perennial which is particulary useful for the back of the border or for areas of woodland garden, since it does well in dappled shade as well as sun. The leaves are handsome, grey-green in colour, large and deeply lobed, the rather insignificant flowers are carried in tall plumes, in a soft bronze-pink shade. It grows in any soil but prefers soil that is well-manured and does not dry out. Divide and replant in autumn.

Nepeta × faassenii

Catmint
HEIGHT: 18in (45cm) • Hardy
FLOWERING SEASON: Late spring/autumn

This low-growing, bushy perennial is used for ground cover or as an edging plant for borders. The mounds of narrowly oval, grey-green leaves are arranged on short, square, grey stems, the tips terminating in tubular lavender-blue, salvia-like flowers which are held above the foliage. The cultivar *N.* 'Six Hills Giant', which is generally grown, is larger, with flower spikes up to 3ft (1m) high. It prefers a light soil and sunny position. Propagate by division in winter or by stem cutting in spring.

Oenothera missouriensis

Evening primrose
HEIGHT: 8in (20cm) • Hardy
FLOWERING SEASON: Mid/late summer

An excellent perennial for a hot, sunny spot. The spear-shaped, mid green leaves are carried on reddish-green, prostrate stems with upward-turning growing tips. The large, golden-yellow, bell-shaped flowers which open in the evening are produced continuously from June until August. It prefers a well-drained soil in sun or light shade. Cut the plant down to ground level in autumn. Propagation is by seed sown in spring or by division in late winter.

Osteospermum 'Buttermilk'

HEIGHT: 2ft (60cm) • Half hardy
FLOWERING SEASON: Summer/autumn

Evergreen semi-woody perennials which will require protection in cold areas, osteospermums flower continually from midsummer through to the autumn carrying their daisy-like flowers on single stems above narrow deep green foliage. The most popular cultivars are 'Buttermilk', 'Cannington Roy', pink with dark eyes, 'Silver Sparkler', 'Tresco Purple', deep purple-red, and 'Whirligig', bluish-white with flower heads that look like the spokes of a wheel with drops on the end. They prefer sun and well-drained soil. Propagate by cuttings of non-flowering shoots in midsummer.

Papaver orientale 'Mrs Perry'

Oriental poppy
HEIGHT: 3ft (1m) • Hardy
FLOWERING SEASON: Summer

The oriental poppy bears large cup-shaped flowers in a variety of brilliant colours in early summer and is one of the most striking border plants. The species plant has deep orange flowers and good cultivars are 'Black and White' and 'Mrs Perry'. Poppies like sun and deep rich soil although they will flower in semi-shade. They are unruly plants and need careful siting. Propagate by taking root cuttings in mild weather in winter although they will all self-seed freely.

Parrotia persica

Persian ironwood
HEIGHT: 15ft (4.5m) • Hardy
FLOWERING SEASON: Late winter/early spring

A small deciduous tree with a wide-spreading habit and attractive autumn leaf colours. The leaves, which are roughly oval with a rounded base, are mid green until turning crimson-red and gold in the autumn. Small crimson flowers appear before the leaves, and the bark of mature plants flakes off in patches to reveal interesting patterns in the winter. The flowers may be killed by late frosts. There is also a weeping cultivar, *P. p.* 'Pendula'. Propagation is by softwood cuttings taken in summer or by seed sown in autumn.

Penstemon 'Apple Blossom'

Beard tongue
HEIGHT: 18in (45cm) • Moderately hardy
FLOWERING SEASON: Midsummer

A large genus of annuals, perennials, sub-shrubs and shrubs, the most popular are the semi-evergreen perennials which carry sprays of flowers above narrow green foliage throughout the summer. Among the best known cultivars are 'Alice Hindley', 'Apple Blossom' and 'Andenken an Friedrich Hahn' syn. 'Garnet'. They must have a sunny position in rich well-drained soil and will not flourish in poor conditions. Propagate by taking semi-ripe cuttings in summer or division in spring.

Perovskia atriplicifolia

Azure sage/Russian sage
HEIGHT: 4ft (1.2m) • Hardy
FLOWERING SEASON: Late summer/mid autumn

This deciduous shrub has thin grey-white stems which carry the narrowly oval, coarsely toothed, grey-green, aromatic foliage. The violet-blue, salvia-like flowers are produced in long slender spikes at the tips of the shoots. The best-known hybrid is *P.* 'Blue Spire', which has larger blue flowers and deeply cut grey-green leaves. Average winter frosts will cut the plant down to the ground, but it grows up again from the base in spring. Propagation is by softwood cuttings taken in late spring.

Ruta graveolens 'Jackman's Blue'

Rue
HEIGHT: 4ft (1.2m) • Hardy
FLOWERING SEASON: Summer/autumn

This is a bushy sub-shrub with leaves which are blue-green, oval and deeply divided to give a fern-like appearance with small, mustard-yellow flowers on the tip of each shoot. *R. g.* 'Jackman's Blue' has a more compact habit and brighter, blue-grey foliage. *R. g.* 'Variegata' has creamy-white and green variegated leaves. Propagation is by semi-ripe cuttings taken in late summer. This plant has sap which is a skin irritant.

Salvia officinalis Purpurascens Group

Sage
HEIGHT: 4ft (1.2m) • Hardy perennial
FLOWERING SEASON: Late summer/autumn

The true sage has dull green leaves with a roughly textured surface, arranged in pairs on erect, square stems, which often have a reddish tinge to them. The tubular flowers open into a funnel shape, and are produced in clusters at the tips of the stems or from the leaf joints. The Purpurascens Group have purple leaves and *S. o.* 'Icterina' variegated yellow ones. Propagation is by semi-ripe cuttings taken in May or August.

Senecio 'Sunshine'

Daisy bush
HEIGHT: 3ft (1m) • Hardy
FLOWERING SEASON: Summer

The correct name for this shrub is now *Brachyglottis* Dunedin Hybrids Group 'Sunshine'. It forms a dense, broad-based mound and the leaves are silvery-grey at first, turning grey-green on the upper surface as they age. Sprays of silvery buds open to reveal yellow daisy-like flowers which are arranged in broad flat clusters. Prune after flowering to prevent the plant becoming straggly. Propagation is by semi-ripe cuttings taken with a heel in summer.

Sophora tetraptera

New Zealand laburnum
HEIGHT: 10ft (3m) • Not fully hardy
FLOWERING SEASON: Late spring

This large evergreen shrub or small tree will only grow well in a sheltered location. The foliage consists of rows of small, oblong, light green leaves which are held together by a tough, greenish-brown leafstalk. In spring a profusion of small, yellow, tubular flowers are produced in pendant clusters on the shoot tips, followed by winged fruits containing the seeds. The cultivar *S. microphylla* 'Early Gold' has pale yellow flowers and fern-like foliage. Propagation is by semi-ripe cuttings taken in early summer.

Spartium junceum

Spanish broom
HEIGHT: 10ft (3m) • Hardy
FLOWERING SEASON: Summer/early autumn

This deciduous flowering shrub has thin, tubular straggling branches which have a weeping appearance, the green stems make the plant seem evergreen. The small, inconspicuous leaves are short-lived, oval, mid green and covered in fine hairs. The large, pea-like flowers are bright golden-yellow and fragrant, they are carried at the tips of the new growth. It likes fairly poor soil and should be trimmed in early spring but does not respond well to hard pruning into old wood. Propagation is by seed sown in spring.

Stachys byzantina

Rabbit's ears/Lamb's tongue
HEIGHT: 16in (40cm) • Hardy
FLOWERING SEASON: Summer

This low growing, evergreen perennial is one of the most attractive and useful ground-cover plants for light soil and a hot sunny position. Its furry leaves which are covered in silvery hairs, give the plant a silver, grey or blue appearance, according to the light. The small, mauve flowers appear on white fluffy spikes up to about 16in (40cm) high. The cultivar *S. b.* 'Silver Carpet' is excellent ground cover. Propagation is by division in spring, although in summer it may be possible to find stems that have already rooted.

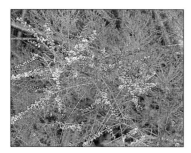

Yucca filamentosa

Adam's needle
HEIGHT: 2-3ft (60-90cm) • Moderately hardy
FLOWERING SEASON: Late summer

Tamarix ramosissima

Tamarisk
HEIGHT: 15ft (4.5m) • Hardy
FLOWERING SEASON: Late summer

An excellent plant for hot exposed sites, or coastal regions because it tolerates salt spray. The slender, gracefully arching, reddish-brown branches carry plumes of narrow, conifer-like foliage. The pink flowers are produced on long thin spikes during the summer. There are cultivars with darker flowers: the rose-pink, *T. r.* 'Rosea', the pale red *T. r.* 'Rubra'. Propagation is by semi-ripe cuttings taken with a heel in summer or hardwood cuttings in winter.

A striking evergreen shrub, generally grown as an architectural plant that thrives in poor, sandy conditions. The long, strap-like, bluish-green leaves are usually dried and brown at the tip, forming a sharp spine-like point and they are edged with white threads. The reddish-brown flower spikes are often 5-6ft (1.5-1.8m) high and covered with white, bell-shaped blooms. *Y. f.* 'Bright Edge' has a narrow golden margin to the leaf edges, and *Y. f.* 'Variegata' has creamy white ones. Propagate by division, removing and planting rooted suckers in spring.

Zauschneria californica

Californian fuchsia
HEIGHT: 18in (45cm) • Half-hardy
FLOWERING SEASON: Summer/autumn

This clump-forming perennial with a dense, bushy habit, produces an attractive display of bright scarlet, funnel-shaped flowers in clusters at the tips of slender green shoots from August onwards. The grey-green leaves are narrow, strap-like and end in a sharp point. The cultivar *Z. c.* ssp. *cana* 'Dublin' has deep, orange-scarlet flowers. Propagation is by division in the spring or semi-ripe cuttings in the summer. Prone to attack by aphids, which cause distorted growth.

More Plants for Dry Sun

There is a wide choice of plants that will thrive in hot dry conditions, particularly those plants which come from the Mediterranean. If you have a south-facing aspect and dry beds in your garden the main problem will be moisture loss during the hot summer months. It is a good idea to dig plenty of garden compost and leaf mould into the soil and it is also a help to mulch the bed in summer with wood bark or shavings. Both these measures help the soil to retain moisture and the mulch also suppresses the weeds.

TREES

Carpinus betulus
Juniperus communis
Populus alba

SHRUBS

Abelia × grandiflora
Berberis (in variety)
Buxus sempervirens
Carpentaria californica
Caryopteris × clandonensis
Ceanothus (in variety)
Ceratostigma willmottiana
Cistus × cyprius

Coronilla valentina ssp. *glauca*
Cotoneaster horizontalis
Euonymus fortunei cvs
Fremontodendron 'California Glory'
Hebe pinguifolia 'Pagei'
Hippophae rhamnoides
Indigofera heterantha
Myrtus communis
Olearia × haastii
Philadelphus (in variety)
Phlomis fruticosa
Phygelius capensis (Cape figwort)
Potentilla fruticosa
Rhus typhina
Rosmarinus officinalis
Sambucus (in variety)
Santolina chamaecyparissus
Spirea (in variety)
Symphoricarpus × doorenbosii
Teucrium fruticans

PERENNIALS, GROUND COVER PLANTS & CLIMBERS

Acanthus spinosus
Achillea filipendulina
Anchusa azurea
Artemesia absinthium
Campsis radicans
Carex elata
Catananche centaurea
Centhranthus ruber
Centaurea cyanus (Cornflower)
Clematis tangutica

Crambe cordifolia
Crocosmia 'Lucifer'
Dianthus (in variety)
Eccremocarpus scaber
Euphorbia (in variety)
Geranium (in variety)
Gypsophila (in variety)
Ipomea hederacea
Iris germanica
Kniphofia 'Sunningdale Yellow'
Lamium maculatum
Lonicera japonica 'Halliana'
Lysimachia punctata
Nepeta 'Six Hills Giant'
Nerine (in variety)
Parthenocissus tricuspidata
Phlox paniculata
Phormium tenax
Osteospermum (in variety)
Romneya coulteri
Saponaria ocymoides
Sisyrinchium striatum
Stipa gigantea (Golden Oats)
Thymus herba-barona
Verbascum nigrum
Veronica prostrata
Viola (in variety)
Vitis coignetiae

CLIMBERS, WALL SHRUBS & HEDGES

To get the best from your garden, do not overlook the potential of walls, which can be used to provide a home for a wide range of colourful flowering climbers and wall shrubs, and plants with attractive foliage. Climbers and hedges with dense foliage also provide screening and a much-needed shelter in the garden.

ABOVE: Carpenteria californica, *with its attractive glossy green leaves and scented white flowers, is one of the best wall shrubs for a south- or west-facing wall.*

OPPOSITE: *This little walled garden has a rich array of perennials including lavender, rock roses, agapanthus, Canterbury bells and pansies in the borders with clematis and roses on the walls.*

ABOVE: *Clematis, both species and hybrids, are among the best climbing plants, and can be grown either over a trellis or scrambling through other plants.*

The plants used for hedges or as wall shrubs either define or decorate the boundaries of a garden and, if they are used within the garden in this way, they provide areas of privacy or shelter.

Choose the right plants for their purpose. If you want, for example, to create a boundary hedge, then you will almost certainly want plants that provide an impenetrable, permanent barrier. Some of the evergreen, spiny plants are ideal; tough berberis, for example, or Rugosa roses and beech, yew and hawthorn are excellent choices. Ideally, plants for hedges should be fairly easy to maintain, not being so fast growing that they need constant clipping, as well as resistant to pests, diseases and pollution. In another situation, you may be looking for quick cover of an unsightly fence or wall or an unattractive view, and then you will want a really rampant grower that will put on several feet in one season, and, for permanent cover, choose an evergreen.

In small gardens, it is good sense to include climbing plants and wall shrubs, since they will display their assets at a high level, effectively leaving the ground space for small perennials and annuals. You can get a lot of flower power from a relatively small number of flowering climbers trained up a wall. Plants such as clematis and climbing roses are invaluable for this, although bear in mind that their flowering season is relatively short, and that it pays to choose several with different flowering seasons, to prolong the period of attraction. A couple of handsome foliage plants, such as an ornamental vine (*Vitis coignetiae*), or an attractive ivy such as *Hedera canariensis*, will help lengthen the season. Always pay attention to the foliage attributes of any climber because a few have more than one virtue to their name, and are particularly valuable as a result. Take a good look first at the site and the kind of soil you have, since many climbers are fussy and require a particular soil or situation.

If you wish, you can use some of the evergreen hedging plants to create ornamental shapes, known as topiary. This simply involves clipping an evergreen, small-leaved shrub or perennial into a shaped structure – at its simplest, a ball, pyramid or cone. It provides a growing form of garden sculpture, and when combined in matched pairs, for example, at the entrance to an area of the garden, or on a doorstep in containers, it gives the garden the equivalent of a punctuation mark in a sentence. Box (*Buxus sempervirens*), yew (*Taxus baccata*) and privet (*Ligustrum*) are among the best subjects for topiary.

Hedges can also be used at a low level to section off parts of the garden; you can opt for informal, loose tapestry-type hedging of mixed plants, per-haps flowering ones such as Rugosa roses, or much more geometric, clipped forms, from small-leaved evergreens, again the box, yew or privet. If you opt for the latter, bear in mind that they must be kept in good condition by reg-ular feeding and watering so they grow well, and clipped regularly to maintain a neat appearance.

BELOW: *A corner of a small walled garden uses climbing plants to good effect, mixing roses and clematis to provide both colour and scent behind a classic wrought-iron bench.*

Bear in mind that when creat-ing a hedge, the plants must be closely planted to form a solid, dense mass of foliage. Pinching out the growing tips of young plants will encourage bushiness, and although the hedge will take longer to reach the required height, it will form an appropri-ately impenetrable barrier. Normally, planting at about 12in (30cm) apart is the right spacing.

The plants listed in this chap-ter are a selection of large and small, evergreen and deciduous, flowering and foliage plants for a variety of situations: sun and shade, damp and dry, acid and alkaline soil. There are many, many others and the cross refer-ence section at the end of the chapter lists other plants which are suitable alternatives for these purposes.

Abutilon megapotamicum

HEIGHT: 10ft (3m) • Half-hardy
FLOWERING SEASON: Late spring/autumn

This is an attractive evergreen shrub, suitable for sheltered sites in mild climates, that should be trained on wires for support. It has dark green, oval leaves, heart-shaped at the base, and bell-shaped, drooping, yellow and red flowers. It does best in humus-enriched, well-drained soil with plenty of water during the growing season and likes full sun or partial shade. Prune the tips of young plants to promote a more bushy shape. Propagate by semi-ripe cuttings in summer. May be attacked by whitefly and red spider mite.

Acca sellowiana

Pineapple guava
HEIGHT: 10ft (3m) • Half-hardy
FLOWERING SEASON: Midsummer

The pineapple guava is not particularly common, but is a valuable evergreen shrub, with dark green leaves, white felted on the undersides. The dark red flowers have silvery edges and are followed (if male and female plants are grown) by reddish-green, edible fruits. Plant in full sun in light, well-drained soil. Propagate by softwood cuttings in summer.

Actinidia deliciosa

Chinese gooseberry/Kiwi fruit
HEIGHT: 30ft (9m) • Moderately hardy
FLOWERING SEASON: Summer

The kiwi fruit, or Chinese gooseberry, is grown in warmer climates for its fruits, but in colder climates it can be grown for its foliage and flowers. It has large, heart-shaped leaves which are attractive in their own right, and cup-shaped, white flowers, borne in clusters, followed by the fruit (if both male and female plants are grown). Plant in partial shade and moist soil but it may need protection in the winter. Propagate by semi-ripe cuttings in summer or by layering in autumn.

Akebia quinata

Chocolate vine
HEIGHT: 30ft (9m) • Half-hardy
FLOWERING SEASON: Late spring/early summer

Known as the chocolate vine, on account of its small, brownish, vanilla-scented flowers, this twining climber is a good subject for a sheltered east- or north-facing position in good, well-drained soil but it does prefer a sunnier position. Sausage-shaped fruits follow the flowers if both male and female plants are grown. It is semi-evergreen in mild winters or sheltered areas. Propagate by seed sown in autumn or spring, from semi-ripe cuttings taken after flowering or by layering in the autumn.

Bignonia capreolata

Cross vine/Trumpet flower
HEIGHT: 30ft (9m) • Half-hardy
FLOWERING SEASON: Summer

An evergreen tendril climber, each leaf has two oblong leaflets and a tendril. In the summer large reddish-orange trumpet-shaped flowers emerge in clusters held on the leaf axis. The fruits appear in the autumn and are rather like long pea-pods about 6in (15cm) long. It is best grown against a south wall in the milder parts of the country and it flourishes in any well-drained garden soil. Prune in early spring by cutting back weak shoots. Propagate by cuttings taken from new growth with three buds in spring.

Buxus sempervirens

Box
HEIGHT: 13ft (4m) • Hardy
FLOWERING SEASON: Insignificant

This is one of the most popular shrubs for low hedges, such as those in knot gardens and parterres, as it is very dense, with small evergreen leaves, and very slow growing. It can be clipped into formal shapes (topiary) which need trimming about twice a year. Does best in sun but tolerates semi-shade (but beware of the shade being on one side of the plant – it will become lopsided) and in most soils except waterlogged. It will cope well with dry conditions. Propagate by semi-ripe cuttings in spring, summer or autumn.

Carpenteria californica

Californian mock orange
HEIGHT: 10ft (3m) • Half-hardy
FLOWERING SEASON: Summer

This evergreen shrub is one of the best wall shrubs for a south- or west-facing wall. It has attractive, glossy green leaves all year round and its pristine white, anemone-like flowers are deliciously scented. It prefers a sunny site and moist, well-drained soil enriched with compost or leaf mould. No pruning is usually needed, except for trimming any straggly shoots after flowering. Propagate by green-wood cuttings of the non-flowering shoots in summer or layering the lower branches.

Carpinus betulus

Hornbeam
HEIGHT: 80ft (25m) in wild • Hardy
FLOWERING SEASON: Late spring

The common hornbeam, which makes a huge spreading tree in the wild, can also be used to create good hedging. Produces catkins in late spring. Although deciduous, it will form a tightly twisted mass of branches, and it retains its leaves through the winter. For a hedge, plant 12in (30cm) apart and feed well while establishing. Trim or clip to shape it in early summer.

Ceanothus 'Autumnal Blue'

Californian lilac
HEIGHT: 8ft (2.5m) • Hardy
FLOWERING SEASON: Summer/autumn

This is a spreading, evergreen shrub with small, glossy, dark green leaves. Long panicles of little, powder blue flowers are carried for a long flowering season, from summer through to autumn. Will grow against a sheltered wall in colder climates, although it does best in a sunny site in good garden soil that is free from lime. Prune in March by thinning out the weak shoots. Propagate from cuttings taken from lateral shoots in midsummer. Can be prone to attacks by scale insects.

Ceanothus 'Gloire de Versailles'

Californian lilac
HEIGHT: 6ft (1.8m) • Hardy
FLOWERING SEASON: Summer/autumn

This deciduous ceanothus is smaller than C. 'Autumnal Blue' and makes a good specimen for formal plantings, if kept hard pruned in early spring. The flowers, which are borne in long panicles, are similarly soft blue but are also fragrant and the leaves are larger and a paler green than most of the other forms. It does best in a sunny site in good garden soil that is free from lime but it may require some protection in cold spells. Propagate from cuttings taken from lateral shoots in midsummer.

Chaenomeles speciosa

Flowering quince/Japonica
HEIGHT: 6ft (1.8m) • Hardy
FLOWERING SEASON: Late winter/early spring

A vigorous deciduous shrub with spiky thorns, it has dark green, glossy leaves and small clusters of bowl-shaped red flowers, followed by yellow quince fruits. There is a wide range of different cultivars, with flowers that range from white, through pink, to scarlet, some with double flowers.
C. s. 'Moerloosei' has pale, pinkish-white flowers and C. s. 'Crimson and Gold' has deep red flowers with bright yellow stamens. Plant in sun against a wall or fence. Propagate by cuttings taken in summer.

Clematis 'Comtesse de Bouchaud'

Large late-flowering clematis
HEIGHT: 10ft (3m) • Moderately hardy
FLOWERING SEASON: Midsummer

Clematis are divided into three groups: the early flowering species, alpina, macropetala and montana types, all of which should be pruned after flowering; early large-flowering cultivars which should be pruned in early spring; and the late-flowering cultivars. C. 'Comtesse de Bouchaud' belongs to the third group. It carries large pinkish-purple flowers with yellow anthers in late summer. All clematis like their feet in the shade and prefer moist well-drained soil.

Clematis 'Etoile Violette'

Late-flowering clematis (viticella)
HEIGHT: 13ft (4m) • Hardy
FLOWERING SEASON: Late summer

Late-flowering clematis are divided into three sub-groups: the large-flowering cultivars, the late-flowering species and small-flowered cultivars, and the herbaceous types. The species, *C. viticella* has purple-mauve flowers. Its cultivars are among the most delicate-looking of all clematis, with small hanging, open, bell-shaped flowers, that are also fragrant. 'Abundance' is rose-pink, 'Alba Luxurians' is white, flushed with mauve and 'Etoile Violette' is deep purple.

Clematis 'Jackmanii'

Large late-flowering clematis
HEIGHT: 10ft (3m) • Moderately hardy
FLOWERING SEASON: Midsummer

The epitome of the large late-flowering types, *C.* 'Jackmanii' carries large violet-purple flowers which fade slightly as they age. They have light brown anthers and the flowers appear from midsummer onwards. Other good late-flowering cultivars are 'Star of India', purple-blue, 'Hagley Hybrid', rosy-mauve, 'Perle d'Azur' blue, amd 'John Huxtable', white. All these should be pruned hard in February to within 12in (30cm), or three buds, of the ground.

Clematis montana var. rubens

Early-flowering clematis (montana)
HEIGHT: 40ft (12m) • Hardy
FLOWERING SEASON: Late spring

C. montana is one of the easiest clematis to grow, being vigorous and unfussy as to aspect. It is one of the few that does well on a north-facing wall. It is deciduous, with tri-foliate, dark green leaves and four-petalled white flowers with prominent stamens. There are various named forms, including *C. m.* var. *rubens* which has bronze-coloured leaves and *C. m.* var. *wilsonii* which is later-flowering and has large white flowers. Plant in alkaline soil with the roots in shade.

Clematis 'Nelly Moser'

Early large-flowered clematis
HEIGHT: 12ft (4m) • Moderately hardy
FLOWERING SEASON: Early summer

One of the best-known of all clematis, 'Nelly Moser' has large single mauvy-pink flowers in early summer. The flowers are fully 6in (15cm) across and have a prominent red stripe down the centre of each petal. They do not like too much sun and do better in a reasonably shady position. Other well known cultivars in the same group are 'Marie Boisselet', white, 'Mrs Cholmondley', pale-blue, and 'The President', purple. Propagate from softwood or semi-ripe cuttings taken in summer.

Clematis tangutica

Late-flowering clematis
HEIGHT: 16ft (5m) • Hardy
FLOWERING SEASON: Late summer/autumn

This autumn flowering clematis, carries small, yellow bell-shaped flowers. It is deciduous, with a slender habit and is best grown scrambling over a low wall or tree stump. The leaves are greyish-green, and the bright yellow flowers are followed by silvery seed heads. Train the young shoots horizontally so that the flowering shoots grow vertically. In spring prune back to a pair of buds near the base of the vertical shoots. Aphids, mildew and clematis wilt may give problems with all clematis plants.

Cobaea scandens

Cup-and-saucer vine
HEIGHT: 20ft (6m) • Half-hardy
FLOWERING SEASON: Summer/autumn

The cup and saucer plant, as this is commonly known, is a vigorous climber, treated as an annual in colder climates. It produces large flowers (the cup) set in a green calyx (the saucer). The flowers open green and change via pink to purple. It supports itself with tendrils growing from the ends of leaf stalks. There is a white-flowered form, *C. s. alba*. Plant in a sunny site in well-drained soil. Sow seeds in spring. May be attacked by a variety of pests, including aphids and red spider mite, but it is usually disease-free.

Euonymus japonicus 'Ovatus Aureus'

Japanese spindle/Spindle tree
HEIGHT: 12ft (4m) • Moderately hardy
FLOWERING SEASON: Summer

An excellent evergreen shrub grown mainly for its variegated foliage, often used for hedging in the milder parts of the country. It is popular in coastal districts as it tolerates poor soil conditions. It carries clusters of small greenish-white flowers in spring followed by small fruits. *E.j.* 'Latifolius Albomarginatus' has leaves edged with white. If grown as a hedge clip in midsummer and again in autumn.

Fagus sylvatica

Beech
HEIGHT: 20ft (6m) (As a hedge) • Hardy
FLOWERING SEASON: Insignificant

Beech trees are among the most graceful of the hardy deciduous native trees, growing to a height of 100ft (30m) or more. They make one of the best hedges, retaining the old leaves throughout the winter, and as such should be planted about 2ft (60cm) apart in soil that has been well dug and enriched by manure and compost. They will grow in any soil but do not like waterlogged conditions. A beech hedge can be almost any height and width but 6-12ft (1.8-4m) high and 2ft (60cm) wide is usually enough. Clip in midsummer and again in early autumn.

Fagus sylvatica Atropurpurea Group

Copper beech
HEIGHT: 38ft (12m) • Hardy
FLOWERING SEASON: Insignificant

A purple-leaved form of the beech, this beautiful tree can be used effectively for hedging and some gardeners plant mixed groups of copper and ordinary beech to give the hedge added variety. There is no difference in cultivation. Remove the upper shoots after planting to encourage branching and mulch the hedge in the spring to encourage growth. Prone to scale insects and aphids and sometimes to coral spot.

Fallopia baldschuanica

Russian vine
HEIGHT: 33ft (10m) • Hardy
FLOWERING SEASON: Summer/autumn

Formerly known as *Polygonum baldschuanicum* this is a singularly rampant, tough climber, generally called the Russian vine. It is not easy to eradicate once planted, and will grow very fast, up to 15ft (4.5m) a year, so beware of planting it in restricted situations. It is ideal for covering an unsightly wall or fence but it is deciduous so dies down in winter. The leaves are mid green, pointed ovals. The flowers, borne in long fluffy panicles, are creamy white. Plant in sun or partial shade in any soil.

Fremontodendron 'California Glory'

Flannel flower
HEIGHT: 20ft (6m) • Half-hardy
FLOWERING SEASON: Spring/autumn

This is a tall, fairly upright, vigorous evergreen or semi-evergreen shrub. Its chief glory is the profusion of large, brilliant yellow flowers borne from late spring to early autumn. The leaves are dark green, rounded and lobed. It makes an excellent wall shrub on a south- or west-facing wall in full sun in well-drained soil, to which humus has been added. Propagate by semi-ripe cuttings in summer. Generally trouble-free, but dislikes being moved.

Garrya elliptica

Silk-tassel bush
HEIGHT: 8ft (2.5m) • Hardy
FLOWERING SEASON: Late spring

An ideal wall shrub, *G. elliptica* has thick, oval evergreen leaves with a slightly crinkled margin, dark green, with a glossy upper surface, and a slightly blue sheen on the underside. In spring long strands of small bell-like flowers on the male plants form attractive catkins. Tolerates poor soil but likes a sunny position and may require protection in prolonged cold spells. The cultivar *G. e.* 'James Roof', has the longest, most colourful catkins. Propagate by semi-ripe cuttings taken in midsummer.

Griselinia littoralis 'Variegata'

HEIGHT: 25ft (8m) • Half-hardy
FLOWERING SEASON: Insignificant

This evergreen shrub, a native of New
Zealand, makes an excellent hedging plant,
especially for the milder coastal areas of the
country as it is both wind and salt resistant. It
has leathery, glossy, white-variegated leaves.
The species plant, *G. littoralis,* is the hardier
and has yellow-green leaves. Plant in sun or
shade in any well-drained garden soil but
protect young plants from frost. Remove tips
to encourage bushiness and trim hedges with
secateurs to avoid damaging the leaves.
Propagate from heel cuttings in autumn.

Hedera colchica 'Sulphur Heart'

Ivy/Paddy's pride
HEIGHT: Unlimited • Hardy
FLOWERING SEASON: Insignificant

This particular ivy, also known as 'Paddy's
Pride', has unusually large leaves with
strongly marked yellow and green colouring
and a slightly drooping habit. It is a self-
clinging climber and will cope with partial
shade and dry soil, but the variegated cultivars of ivy are less shade-tolerant than the
green cultivars. It can be propagated from
rooted layers or softwood cuttings.

Hedera helix 'Königer's Auslese'

Common English ivy
HEIGHT: 4ft (1.2m) • Hardy
FLOWERING SEASON: Insignificant

This is a particularly pretty ivy with the usual
three-lobed leaf formation, but with finger-
like, deeply cut leaves. Another cultivar of
H. helix, 'Pedata', known as the bird's foot ivy,
is similar with narrow leaves of which the
central lobe forms a long finger. It is more
vigorous, growing to 10ft (3m) or more. Ivies
will grow in poor soil, in shade. Propagate
from softwood cuttings or rooted layers.
Generally pest- and disease-free but may be
attacked by red spider mite.

Hippophae rhamnoides

Sea buckthorn
HEIGHT: 8ft (2.5m) • Hardy
FLOWERING SEASON: Insignificant

The sea buckthorn is an excellent subject
for hedges in coastal areas as it will withstand
seaspray and makes a good windbreak. It is
deciduous with thin, silvery leaves and sharp
spines on the branches. Very small yellow
flowers appear before the leaves in April and
if both male and female plants are planted,
small orange berries will ripen along the
branches in the autumn and hang all through
the winter to the spring. Grow in any good
garden soil in sunny or part-shaded situations. Trim hedges in late summer.

Ipomoea hederacea

Morning glory
HEIGHT: 13ft (4m) • Tender
FLOWERING SEASON: Summer

Morning glory, as this tender twining
climber is known, has three-lobed, mid
green leaves and showy, funnel-shaped
flowers in shades from white through pink
and blue to purple, from summer through to
early autumn. It needs a sunny site and well-
drained soil to which plenty of leaf mould
has been added. Grow it up a trellis or let it
scramble through a shrub. Propagate from
seed sown in spring or from semi-ripe cuttings in summer. Red spider mite and
whitefly can be a problem.

Jasminum officinale

Common jasmine
HEIGHT: 40ft (12m) • Hardy
FLOWERING SEASON: Summer/autumn

The common jasmine is one of the most
attractive climbing plants. It has prettily
divided leaves and clusters of highly fragrant,
small, white flowers, with pink buds, over a
long season. It is semi-evergreen and supports
itself by twining. The cultivar known as
'Aureum' has yellow-splashed leaves and
J. o. f. *affine* has larger flowers. It needs full
sun and a rich, well-drained soil. It is very
vigorous and must be pruned after flowering.
Propagate from semi-ripe cuttings in
summer. May be attacked by aphids.

Lapageria rosea

Chilean bellflower
HEIGHT: 15ft (4.5m) • Half-hardy
FLOWERING SEASON: Summer/autumn

The Chilean bellflower is a climber that will twine itself around a support. Its dark green, slightly pointed, oval leaves are evergreen, and throughout the summer hanging bells of rosy red flowers, about 3in (7.5cm) long, are carried either singly or in small clusters. There is also a white-flowered variety, *L. r.* var. *albiflora*. It likes a slightly acid soil and a warm sheltered wall. Protect the roots in winter in colder climates. Propagate by layering in spring or autumn.

Lathyrus latifolius

Everlasting pea/Perennial pea
HEIGHT: 6ft (1.8m) • Hardy
FLOWERING SEASON: Summer/autumn

This everlasting pea is another perennial sweet pea, which grows vigorously and can be trained over a support like a climber. It has rather dull green leaves but a profusion of flowers in shades of red or pink. There is also a white-flowered cultivar 'White Pearl'. Grow in good garden soil, preferably slightly chalky, but put in lots of manure as the plants are very greedy. Pinch out tips of young plants to promote bushiness. Deadhead to encourage a longer flowering season and cut down the plants in late autumn. Sow from chipped seed in spring.

Ligustrum ovalifolium

Privet
HEIGHT: 12ft (4m) • Hardy
FLOWERING SEASON: Midsummer

This privet comes from Japan, and has evergreen, glossy, oval leaves and is very good for hedging or clipped into topiary shapes. The white flowers are attractive to bees. Black berries follow the flowers in autumn. There is a golden-leaved cultivar, 'Aureum', known as the golden privet. Grow in sun or shade in any soil. For hedging, prune hard in the first year to encourage bushy growth. Propagate from hardwood cuttings in autumn. Can be attacked by honey fungus.

Lonicera nitida

Honeysuckle
HEIGHT: 5ft (1.5m) • Hardy
FLOWERING SEASON: Insignificant

This dense evergreen shrub is a native of China. It makes excellent hedging, or can be used for topiary, and is a good subject for shade. The leaves are small, glossy and dark green. There is also a golden-leaved cultivar, 'Baggesen's Gold', which must be planted in sun. For a hedge, plant in rich soil about 12in (30cm) apart. Cut new hedges hard back in the first year and pinch out growing tips to establish bushy plants. Clip in late spring and early autumn to maintain. Prone to aphid attacks and to leaf spot.

Lonicera periclymenum 'Belgica'

Early Dutch honeysuckle
HEIGHT: 12ft (4m) • Hardy
FLOWERING SEASON: Summer

L. p. 'Belgica' is a cultivar of the common honeysuckle or woodbine, *L. periclymenum,* whose orangy yellow-white flowers are a common sight in hedges in summer. It has reddish-yellow fragrant flowers and is one of the best garden forms. Other good cultivars are 'Graham Thomas', whitish-yellow and 'Serotina', deeper red. All honeysuckles like moist well-drained soil and full sun to moderate shade. Cut back hard in the spring to prevent them becoming straggly.

Lonicera × tellmanniana

Honeysuckle
HEIGHT: 15ft (4.5m) • Moderately hardy
FLOWERING SEASON: Summer

A favourite deciduous woody-stemmed climber which bears a profusion of fragrant orange-yellow flowers from late spring through the summer. As all honeysuckles tend to be unkempt it is a good idea to grow them as climbers over an old tree or a large fence as they do not appear at their best if they are confined to a trellis or a wall. They do not like very wet or very dry conditions. Propagate by taking semi-ripe cuttings in summer but some varieties are difficult to strike. Layering is often successful.

Malus domestica

Apple
HEIGHT: 10ft (3m) • Hardy
FLOWERING SEASON: Spring

Apples make good wall shrubs if trained as espaliers or cordons. 'Egremont Russet' is a good garden variety which keeps reasonably well, is hardy, and has compact growth. Espalier apples should be planted about 10ft (3m) apart; cordons about 6ft (1.8m) apart, against a supporting network of posts and wires, and the young plants are then pruned to develop fruiting branches along the wires. They need enriched garden soil and plenty of watering while setting fruit.

Olearia × haastii

Daisy bush
HEIGHT: 5ft (1.5m) • Hardy
FLOWERING SEASON: Summer

An evergreen dense shrub with thick leathery leaves, dark green above and silvery beneath. The branches and undersides of the leaves are covered with a thick greyish down. It has numerous clusters of fragrant star-like daisy flowers in late summer. It makes a good hedge in milder parts of the country and by the seaside. It should be trimmed as soon as the flowers fade. Dislikes soil which contains a lot of lime. Propagate by semi-ripe cuttings taken in late summer.

Parthenocissus henryana

HEIGHT: 30ft (9m) • Hardy
FLOWERING SEASON: Spring/summer

An attractive self-clinging climber closely related to *P. quinquefolia*, the Virginia creeper. It has five-parted leaves which are a deep velvety-green marked with white and pink along the midrib and veins. The leaves turn a brilliant red in the autumn and the colour is best if it is grown on a north- or east-facing wall. Likes well-drained soil. Do not let the tendrils of the climber get into gutters or under slates or tiles on the roof. It has bluish-black berries in the autumn. Propagate by softwood cuttings in summer.

Parthenocissus tricuspidata

Boston ivy/Japanese ivy
HEIGHT: 40ft (12m) • Hardy
FLOWERING SEASON: Summer

The Boston ivy is a hardy deciduous climber that clings by means of aerial roots, so needs no tying in. It is grown primarily for its brilliantly coloured autumn foliage, the three-lobed leaves of which turn a rich, bronze-red in autumn. Small, yellowish flowers are borne in summer, followed by dark blue fruits in some years. Grow in any good garden soil in sun or partial shade. Propagate by layering or by half-ripe cuttings taken in late summer. Prone to scale insects and to aphids.

Passiflora caerulea

Common passion flower
HEIGHT: 20ft (6m) • Not fully hardy
FLOWERING SEASON: Mid/late summer

The passion flower is really a climbing perennial, but although frequently dying down in winter, it will emerge as vigorous as ever the following spring. The large, beautiful flowers are fragrant, and have big pinky-white sepals and petals, with spiky blue filaments tinged white and purple in the centre of the bloom. The palm shaped-leaves are mid green and carried on square, green stems which are supported by thin green tendrils. Propagation is by semi-ripe cuttings taken in summer or by seed.

Passiflora caerulea 'Constance Elliott'

White passion flower
HEIGHT: 25ft (8m) • Half hardy
FLOWERING SEASON: Early summer/autumn

The best known white passion flower *P. c.* 'Constance Elliott' is a tough, vigorous evergreen climber, with palmate, mid green leaves. It produces quite extraordinary flowers with a surrounding saucer of petals and prominent corolla and stamens in clear white. Oval yellow fruits are sometimes borne after the flowers. Will grow in sun or partial shade. Protect young plants in winter. Thin out overgrown plants in early spring. Propagate from stem sections in late summer.

Prunus laurocerasus 'Otto Luyken'

Cherry laurel/Laurel
HEIGHT: 6ft (1.8m) • Hardy
FLOWERING SEASON: Summer

This ornamental cherry laurel makes a good specimen for a low hedge. It has the usual glossy, evergreen, dark green leaves that are oval and slender and borne slightly upright. Long spires of white flowers are borne in summer, followed by small black fruits. Grows in shade or sun. *P. l.* 'Zabeliana' is almost prostrate, making good ground cover. Plant in autumn in chalky soil. Propagate from half-ripe cuttings in summer.

Pyracantha 'Mohave'

Firethorn
HEIGHT: 8ft (2.5m) • Hardy
FLOWERING SEASON: Midsummer

This hybrid firethorn, as it is known, is a tough, evergreen shrub that is grown either as a wall shrub or as hedging. It has spiny branches, small, glossy, dark green leaves, and clusters of small white five-petalled flowers in summer followed by bright orange-red berries in autumn. Grow in any well-drained garden soil in sun or partial shade, against wires, to which it should be tied. For hedging, pinch out young plants to encourage bushiness and clip in summer. Take cuttings of new shoots in summer to propagate. Can be troubled by scale insects.

Pyracantha 'Watereri'

Firethorn
HEIGHT: 10ft (3m) • Hardy
FLOWERING SEASON: Early summer

This particular hybrid firethorn makes a tallish evergreen shrub, with arching, spiny branches and dense, glossy, bright green leaves. The flowers are white, cup-shaped, and borne in fattish clusters, followed by big clusters of bright red berries in autumn. For hedging, pinch out young plants to encourage bushiness and clip once a year in summer. Take cuttings of current year's shoots in summer to propagate. Can be troubled by scale insects.

Pyrus 'Conference'

Conference pear
HEIGHT: 24ft (7.5m) • Hardy
FLOWERING SEASON: Spring

Pear trees are slightly easier to grow than apple trees, provided the situation is fairly warm and sheltered. They grow best in full sun, in fertile loam with adequate moisture. They can be trained against a wall either as cordons or espaliers. Pears must be planted with or near a cross-pollinator to produce fruit. Two which do this are 'Conference' and 'Williams' Bon Chrétien'. Plant in autumn, about 6ft (1.8m) apart for cordons, and 8ft (2.5m) for espaliers and tie in to supports. Prone to the usual pests and diseases.

Schizophragma hydrangeoides

Japanese hydrangea vine
HEIGHT: 25ft (8m) • Hardy
FLOWERING SEASON: Summer

This deciduous climber is very similar to *Hydrangea anomala* ssp. *petiolaris* and will attach itself to a support by means of aerial roots. It has broad, hairy leaves almost 5in (12cm) long that are deep green above and silvery beneath. The large, flat flowerheads are small, creamy flowers surrounded by pale lemon-coloured bracts in summer. Does best in semi-shade in a soil with plenty of leaf mould. Deadhead after flowering. Propagate by half-ripe cuttings in late summer or layering in autumn.

Solanum crispum 'Glasnevin'

Chilean potato tree
HEIGHT: 19ft (6m) • Almost hardy
FLOWERING SEASON: Summer/autumn

Known as the Chilean potato tree (the edible potato belongs to the same genus), this semi-evergreen, almost hardy scrambler has dark green, oval, pointed leaves and produces trusses of star-shaped, violet-blue flowers with bright yellow centres throughout the summer. 'Glasnevin' has a longer flowering season than the species. Grow in any good garden soil against a south- or west-facing wall, and tie in to trellis or wires. Propagate from cuttings of side shoots in late summer. Can be prone to attacks by aphids or mould.

Solanum jasminoides 'Album'

Jasmine nightshade/Potato vine
HEIGHT: 10ft (3m) • Half-hardy
FLOWERING SEASON: Summer/autumn

Known as the jasmine nightshade, the species of this almost hardy climber has clear blue star-shaped flowers with golden anthers, but this variety is a white-flowered form that has a yellow eye. The leaves are evergreen, and a glossy pale green. Unlike *S. crispum* this plant is usually self-clinging, but it may need support occasionally. Propagate from cuttings of side shoots taken in late summer. Can be prone to attacks by aphids and to various moulds.

Taxus baccata

Common yew
HEIGHT: 16ft (5m) • Hardy
FLOWERING SEASON: Insignificant

This is one of the best, if slow growing, hedging and topiary plants, its dark green, needle-like leaves forming a dense, impenetrable thicket. It copes well with wind, pollution and drought, and makes a good boundary hedge. The flowers are barely visible, and are followed by small, cup-shaped, red fruits. All parts of the plant are highly poisonous. It grows in any good well-drained garden soil in sun or deep shade. Plant hedging plants about 2ft (60cm) apart and mulch each spring. Pinch out leading shoots to encourage bushiness.

Thuja plicata 'Atrovirens'

Arbor-vitae/Red cedar
HEIGHT: 20ft (6m) • Hardy
FLOWERING SEASON: Insignificant

A cultivar of the giant red cedar, *T.p.* 'Atrovirens' makes a quick growing, dark green hedge which will grow well in any soil and tolerates full shade when established. The leaves give off a tansy-like aroma when crushed. If grown as a hedge, thujas should not be clipped hard in the same way as a yew hedge. They should be looked over carefully and long branches shortened with secateurs. Other useful cultivars are *T. p.* 'Aurea' and *T. p.* 'Stoneham Gold'.

Thunbergia alata

Black-eyed Susan
HEIGHT: 10ft (3m) • Half-hardy
FLOWERING SEASON: Summer/autumn

Known as black-eyed Susan, this is one of the few orange-yellow flowered climbers. The flowers have flat heads and a long purplish tube, with a dark brown eye, hence the common name. It flowers from early summer until the autumn. In sheltered areas it can be grown out of doors, but in colder regions it must be overwintered indoors, so grow it in a container with its own support system in normal potting compost or against a sunny wall in a sheltered spot. It will twine around a trellis. Sow seed in spring.

Trachelospermum jasminoides

Confederate jasmine/Chinese jasmine
HEIGHT: 10ft (3m) • Hardy • pH
FLOWERING SEASON: Summer

This is a handsome evergreen, self-clinging, twining climber, with dark green, oval, leathery leaves and very fragrant white, five-petalled, starry flowers with a yellow eye, profusely borne in summer, followed by seed pods up to 6in (15cm) long. The cultivar *T. j.* 'Variegatum', has cream-splashed leaves. Plant it against a sunny wall in acid soil. Deadhead after flowering. Propagate from cuttings taken from side shoots, or by layering in autumn. Generally disease-free, but may be subject to attacks by aphids.

Tropaeolum speciosum

Flame creeper/Scottish flame flower
HEIGHT: 10ft (3m) • Hardy
FLOWERING SEASON: Summer/autumn

This perennial nasturtium is a twining climber with apple-green, lobed, waxy leaves and bright scarlet flowers, held erect on long, reddish stems. It flowers from late summer onwards and the flowers are followed by dull red seed capsules exposing lovely turquoise blue seeds as large as peas. It should be planted in peaty soil in at least partial shade preferably on the north side of a yew hedge. Once established it will scramble over trees and shrubs although in some gardens it can prove difficult.

Vitis coignetiae

Crimson glory vine
HEIGHT: 70ft (21m) • Hardy
FLOWERING SEASON: Spring

This Japanese crimson glory vine is one of the best foliage climbers, clinging by means of tendrils. It is deciduous and in autumn the large, heart-shaped leaves turn a glorious mixture of orange, crimson and gold. The greenish flowers are born in spring in panicles, followed by inedible black 'grapes'. Grow in sun or partial shade in limy, moist soil. Prune back hard after planting and tie in young shoots. Propagate by layering in autumn. Prone to attacks by scale insects.

Vitis vinifera 'Purpurea'

Grape vine
HEIGHT: 20ft (6m) • Hardy
FLOWERING SEASON: Summer

This ornamental form of the grape vine is known as the Teinturier grape. It is grown for its handsome, dark foliage which turns purple in autumn. The leaves are large, serrated and lobed. Tiny green flowers are borne in summer in short panicles, followed by blue-black fruits. Grow in moist loamy soil in sun or partial shade. Grow in sun or partial shade in limy, moist soil. Prune back hard after planting and tie in young shoots. Propagate by layering in autumn.

Wisteria floribunda

Japanese wisteria
HEIGHT: 22ft (7m) • Hardy
FLOWERING SEASON: Early summer

This vigorous climber, which will twine around a support, has attractive, light green leaves, composed of many small leaflets, and scented, blue-mauve flowers, in long, drooping racemes. There is a white cultivar, 'Alba', and one with very long, lilac-blue flowers, 'Macrobotrys'. Plant in sun in rich, moist soil, ideally against a south- or west-facing wall. Tie it in to supports until established. Propagate from heel cuttings of current growth in late summer.

More Climbers, Wall Shrubs and Hedging Plants

We have divided the additional plants for this section into the three groups and sub-divided the climbers and wall shrubs into those which are suitable for north- and east-facing walls and those which should be grown on south- or west-facing walls. A letter after the plant means that where there is a choice it should only be grown on that wall.

CLIMBERS FOR NORTH- AND EAST-FACING WALLS

Aristolochia durior (N)
Berberidopsis corallina
Celastrus scandens
Clematis armandii
  C. texensis
Hedera helix 'Buttercup'
Holboella coriacea (N or W)
Hydrangea petiolaris
Kerria japonica
Rosa 'Gloire de Dijon'
  R. Golden Showers
  R. 'Guinée'
  R. 'Madame Alfred Carrière'
  R. 'Madame Grégoire Staechelin'
  R. 'Maigold'

  R. 'New Dawn'
  R. 'Zéphirine Drouhin'
Schizophragma integrifolium (N or W)
(see also *Climbers for North Walls* on page 81)

SHRUBS FOR NORTH- AND EAST-FACING WALLS

Cotoneaster horizontalis
Escallonia (in variety) (N)
Elaeagnus × ebbingei 'Gilt Edge'
Euonymus fortunei cvs
Forsythia suspensa
Pyracantha (in variety)

CLIMBERS FOR SOUTH- AND WEST-FACING WALLS

Abeliophyllum distichum
Actinidia kolomikta
Ampelopsis glandulosa
Campsis radicans
  C. × tagliabuana 'Mme Galen'
Clematis (in variety)
Cytisus battandieri
Dregea sinensis
Eccremocarpus scaber
Hedera canariensis 'Gloire de Marengo'
  H. colchica 'Dentata'
Humulus lupulus 'Aureus'
Hydrangea petiolaris
Lathyrus odoratus
Lonicera (in variety)
Rosa 'Albéric Barbier'
  R. banksiae 'Lutea'
  R. 'Mermaid'

  R. 'Paul's Himalayan Musk'
Wisteria sinensis

SHRUBS FOR SOUTH- AND WEST-FACING WALLS

Berberis darwinii
Ceanothus (in variety)
Chaenomeles japonica
Chimonanthus preacox
Magnolia grandiflora
Osmanthus × burkwoodii
Prunus incisa
Tamarix ramosissima

HEDGES

Berberis (in variety)
Chamaecyparis lawsoniana
Crataegus (in variety)
Cupressocyparis × leylandii
Escallonia (in variety)
Ilex aquifolium
Juniperus communis
Lavandula (in variety)
Laurus nobilis
Osmanthus × burkwoodii
Pittosporum tenuifolium
Potentilla fruticosa
Pseudotsuga menziesii
Pyracantha (in variety)
Rosa 'Roseraie de l'Haÿ'
  R. rugosa
Rosmarinus officinalis
Symphoricarpus (in variety)
Syringa (in variety)
Thuja occidentalis 'Sunkist'

PLANTS *for* GROUND COVER

In large gardens, or where gardening time is at a premium, ground-cover plants are a valuable asset because they suppress weeds while creating an attractive carpet of colour and texture. This selection includes spreading plants and those that self-seed to make large drifts.

ABOVE: Myosotis alpestris, *the Alpine forget-me-not, makes a spreading mound covered with light blue flowers.*

OPPOSITE: *The silver-splashed leaves of lungwort* (Pulmonaria longifolia) *with its purple-blue flowers held erect on stems are one of the loveliest sights in a spring garden.*

ABOVE: *Ground cover plants can be allowed to encroach onto a gravel path to soften the edges and provide an informality that would otherwise be lacking. There is a wide choice available: alchemilla, geraniums, forget-me-nots, pansies and stachys (lamb's ears) can all be used to break up the edge of a path or lawn.*

For many gardeners, particularly those with large gardens or who are too busy to spend a great deal of time looking after their plants, ground-covering plants are essential. They come in various forms – those that spread to create large areas of weed-suppressing cover and those, by virtue of their habit of growth, that create enough shade to make it difficult for weeds to grow under their canopy.

Removal of light is one of the most effective means of controlling weeds, and if you do not want to do it with plants, you can, of course, use black plastic covered with bark chippings instead – a system now often used by gardeners for municipal parks. This is often a useful means of covering the ground while waiting for your ground cover plants to do their job and is also useful while establishing larger plants or a shrub border, for example.

As with all plants, the natural habitat determines how successfully they will perform in any given situation. If your garden has a shady area that gets very little moisture, then you will have to pick ground-cover plants that thrive naturally in these conditions – ivy is an obvious choice. If, on the other hand, your garden is open and sunny, then the ground cover you seek must be able to withstand heat and drought. This is a bit more difficult, since ground-covering plants in nature tend to be woodland carpeting plants, that flourish under the shade of a taller canopy of leaves, so for dry sunny sites you are better picking perennials with a mound-forming habits, such as geraniums, which fan out to cover quite a large area of ground. If you pick plants that can be propagated easily, you can soon build up a sizable collection of plants for these situations without spending a fortune.

Plants that spread by runners or layering will quickly create large drifts of ground cover, but be aware that they will not necessarily confine themselves to the areas you have chosen, so that some measure of control will be necessary to prevent invasive behaviour. This may mean simply uprooting any additional growth in autumn. Plants that spread by root runners, however, can be more difficult to control – mint is one example – and these are sometimes best situated in a controlled space. You could use slates sunk into the soil to stop any such unwanted spread.

Try to pick ground-cover plants that look appropriate for the situation and, for interest, avoid very large expanses of the same plant, unless covering a bank, or creating ground cover in a small woodland area. To provide variation in colour and texture, use several different mound-forming plants that will gradually spread and knit together to make an interesting tapestry of foliage.

Although evergreen plants will cover the ground throughout the year, most weed growth is in the growing season, so even deciduous plants can make effective ground cover.

BELOW: *A dense cottage-style planting of herbaceous perennials many of which will self-seed. Prominent in these borders is the purple knapweed (centaurea) with its thistle-like head.*

Acaena microphylla

New Zealand burr
HEIGHT: 2in (5cm) • Hardy
FLOWERING SEASON: Insignificant

This herbaceous carpeting perennial, which comes from New Zealand, makes good ground cover for growing between paving stones in patios or terraces and in rockeries. It forms dense mats of grey-green leaves, and russet-coloured 'burrs' from early to late summer. It does well in sun or partial shade and likes well-drained soil. It will spread rapidly in the right conditions. Propagate by sowing seed in spring, or by dividing the plants in the autumn.

Adiantum venustum

Maidenhair fern
HEIGHT: 6in (15cm) • Hardy
FLOWERING SEASON: None

This little fern, which hails from the Himalayas, has delicately formed fronds which change colour over the year. Pink when they first appear in spring, they change to pale green, becoming a russet brown after the first frosts. Does well in soil rich in leaf mould in partial shade. Propagate in autumn from rhizomes cut into pieces with a growing point on each piece. Prone to attacks by wood lice and root mealy bugs, but generally disease-free.

Aegopodium podagraria 'Variegatum'

Variegated bishop's weed/Variegated gout weed
HEIGHT: 4in (10cm) • Hardy
FLOWERING SEASON: Summer (insignificant)

This vigorous, creeping perennial, which is known as variegated bishop's weed, or variegated gout weed, is a fast-growing plant that is useful for ground cover. It has creamy-white splashed green leaves that are lobed and insignificant flowers in summer. It does well in either a sunny or a shady site with well-drained soil. Its spread may need restricting occasionally. Propagate by division of the rhizomes in spring or in autumn.

Anaphalis triplinervis

Pearl everlasting/Immortelle
HEIGHT: 12in (30cm) • Hardy
FLOWERING SEASON: Late summer

A. triplinervis makes an attractive mound of silvery-green divided foliage, topped with tightly packed heads of white flowers in late summer. They are known as pearl everlasting flowers or immortelle, and are popular with flower arrangers as the heads can be both dried and dyed. They are used for winter decoration. Plant in the autumn in well-drained soil in sun or dry shade. Cut the plants back in autumn if they start to sprawl too much. Propagate from cuttings of basal shoots in spring or sow seed in spring.

Aurinia saxatile var. citrina

Gold dust/Gold tuft
HEIGHT: 12in (30cm) • Hardy
FLOWERING SEASON: Late spring/early summer

This clump-forming shrubby perennial which was formerly known as *Alyssum saxatile* provides excellent cover on terraces and rockeries. Densely packed heads of yellow flowers create a golden carpet of colour from late spring to summer. There are many different varieties with flowers varying in colour from lemon to gold. Grow in a sunny site in well-drained soil. Propagate from cuttings in summer or from seed in spring. Prone to attacks by slugs and to downy mildew.

Bergenia cordifolia

Elephant's ears
HEIGHT: 12in (30cm) • Hardy
FLOWERING SEASON: Spring

Bergenia, sometimes known as elephant's ears, makes extremely good ground cover, its huge, leathery, evergreen leaves effectively suppressing any weeds beneath their canopy. *B. cordifolia* has pinkish-purple flower spires in spring, and *B. c.* 'Purpurea' has leaves that are purple-tinged. *B.* 'Silberlicht' has white flowers, and the leaves turn an attractive bronzy-red in autumn. The leaf colour is often best in poorer soils. It is soil tolerant, and grows in sun or partial shade. Propagate by division in autumn. Prone to leaf spot.

Campanula carpatica

Carpathian bellflower
HEIGHT: 9in (23cm) • Hardy
FLOWERING SEASON: Summer

This little bellflower comes from the Carp-athian mountains of eastern Europe. It makes clumps of toothed green leaves, surmounted with a sea of large, bright blue, cup-shaped flowers in summer. It self-seeds freely. There are a number of named cultivars in shades from deep indigo to white. *C. carpatica* will thrive in sun or partial shade, and does par-ticularly well in crevices in pavings. Sow seed in spring or divide crowns in autumn. Prone to attacks by slugs and also leaf spot and rust.

Cotoneaster horizontalis

Wall-spray
HEIGHT: 2ft (60cm) • Hardy
FLOWERING SEASON: Summer

This widely spreading deciduous shrub has long slender branches which grow laterally from the main stem. The small, glossy, dark green leaves turn scarlet in autumn, and the small pinkish flowers in early summer are followed by clusters of bright red berries in autumn. It makes good ground cover for banks but it can also be trained as a wall shrub. Likes a sunny site and well-drained soil.

Epilobium glabellum

Willow herb
HEIGHT: 9in (23cm) • Hardy
FLOWERING SEASON: Summer/autumn

This little perennial, which is a form of willow herb, forms attractive low mounds of small, mid green, oval leaves and produces cup-shaped, white flowers on taller stems throughout the summer. It does best when grown in a sunny position or in partial shade in moist well-drained soil. *E. fleischeri* is taller – about 12in (30cm) – with narrow greyish leaves and rosy-pink flowers. Propagate from seed sown in spring, or from cuttings taken from basal shoots in spring.

Epimedium × youngianum 'Niveum'

Barrenwort/Bishop's hat
HEIGHT: 8in (20cm) • Hardy
FLOWERING SEASON: Spring

This little woodland plant, with the common name of barrenwort or bishop's hat, makes excellent ground cover in the partial shade provided by deciduous trees. The leaves turn an attractive bronze-red in autumn. The flowers of the species, appear-ing in spring, are pink, but 'Niveum' is a white cultivar. *E. × warleyense* is another carpeting hybrid, about 12in (30cm) high, with heart-shaped, chocolate-tinted leaves and orange flowers in spring.

Erigeron karvinskianus

Fleabane/Summer starwort
HEIGHT: 9in (23cm) • Hardy
FLOWERING SEASON: Summer

This herbaceous perennial self-seeds freely, particularly in cracks in pavings, and is there-fore suitable for softening hard surfaces. It prefers a sunny site and grows in any well-drained soil but it must not be allowed to dry out in the growing season. Its sprawling stems bear narrow, lance-shaped leaves and clouds of small daisy-like flowers that open white, turn pink, then fade to a deepening purple. It can scramble up to 2ft (60cm) or more with support. Propagate by division in autumn or sow seed in spring.

Euphorbia characias ssp. *wulfenii*

Spurge
HEIGHT: 4ft (1.2m) • Moderately hardy
FLOWERING SEASON: Early summer

This is one of the largest euphorbias, with bluish-grey glaucous leaves that are ever-green in mild climates. The sulphur yellow, bottlebrush-like flowerheads rise above the leaves in early summer. Grow within the shelter of a wall to protect from cool easterly winds in spring. Cutting flowering stems down after flowering will help to promote bushiness. Propagate from cuttings of basal shoots in spring. Pest-free, but susceptible to moulds. The sap is an irritant.

Galium odoratum

Bedstraw/Woodruff
HEIGHT: 6in (15cm) • Hardy
FLOWERING SEASON: Spring

The little woodruff is a carpeting perennial
with attractive lupin-like leaves and small,
starry, white flowers that stud the plant in
summer. All parts of the plant are aromatic
and the leaves used to be picked and dried
to scent clothes. It grows very well in partial
shade, making excellent ground cover in the
right conditions. It prefers well-drained
slightly acid soil with plenty of leaf mould.
Propagate by lifting and dividing the plants
in early spring or autumn.

Geranium × oxonianum 'Winscombe'

Cranesbill
HEIGHT: 18in (45cm) • Hardy
FLOWERING SEASON: Summer/autumn

Known as cranesbill, hardy geraniums
(not to be confused with pelargoniums,
commonly called geraniums) often make
good ground cover. G. endressii does so in
lightly shaded situations. There are many
hybrids, of which G. × o. 'Wargrave Pink'
has particularly bright pink flowers.
G. × o. 'Winscombe' has mauve flowers. Cut
back the old flowering stems to
encourage new growth. Propagate by
division in autumn. May be attacked by
slugs and prone to rust.

Glechoma hederacea 'Variegata'

Ground ivy
HEIGHT: 6in (15cm) • Hardy
FLOWERING SEASON: Insignificant

This variegated ground ivy is a rapidly
spreading, carpeting perennial that has small,
rounded leaves with lobed edges that are
marbled with white. G. hederacea does well
grown in sun or in partial shade so it can be
planted under trees but does not like deep
shade. It prefers moist well-drained soil. It
can be invasive so it is best planted where its
spread can be controlled. Propagate by
division in autumn or from cuttings taken
in spring.

Hebe pinguifolia 'Pagei'

Disc-leaved hebe
HEIGHT: 9in (23cm) • Hardy
FLOWERING SEASON: Early summer

This little hebe, which forms a spreading
mound up to 3ft (90cm) across, has small,
grey-green, waxy leaves and spires of pure-
white, star-shaped flowers in late spring or
early summer. It does best in full sun and
flourishes in most garden soils. Propagate
from cuttings taken in late summer or by
layering. If the plant suffers frost damage cut
right down almost to soil level in the spring.
This hebe is usually pest-free, but it is sometimes prone to downy mildew or leaf spot in
wetter areas.

Hedera colchica 'Dentata'

Persian ivy/Elephant's ears
HEIGHT: 20ft (6m) • Hardy
FLOWERING SEASON: Insignificant

This large-leaved ivy grows vigorously in
sun or shade. The leaves, which are dark
green, have toothed edges. Another cultivar,
'Dentata Variegata', has yellow-splashed,
lighter green leaves. Ivies are not fussy about
soil or situation, and climb by aerial roots
over any surface. Take cuttings of runners
for climbing ivies and from adult growth
for bushes. Prune it back hard in the spring
to prevent it becoming unruly. Prone to
attack by scale insects and to leaf spot, red
spider mite may also be a problem.

× Heucherella tiarelloides

HEIGHT: 18in (45cm) • Hardy
FLOWERING SEASON: Early summer

From a hybrid genus (Heuchera × Tiarella) this
evergreen perennial makes good ground
cover, with the advantage of attractive spires
of small, rose-pink, bell-shaped little flowers
in early summer. The leaves form a dense
mound of heart-shaped leaves from which
the flower spires rise. This plant prefers semi-
shade and must have fertile well-drained soil.
It will not flourish in hot dry conditions.
× H. alba 'Bridget Bloom' has taller, lighter-
pink flower spikes which last for many
weeks. Divide the crowns in early autumn to
propagate or take basal cuttings in spring.

Hypericum calycinum

Aaron's beard/Rose of Sharon
HEIGHT: 18in (45cm) • Hardy
FLOWERING SEASON: Summer

The rose of Sharon, as this is sometimes known, is a vigorous sub-shrub that forms widely spreading mounds, making good ground cover via its spreading stolons. The leaves are bright green and oval and the brilliant gold flowers are borne on the end of the flowering shoots all summer long. It will cope with dry shade, but flowers better in sun. Propagate by division of roots in autumn. Cut hard back every couple of years to keep it in shape. Sometimes prone to rust.

Juniperus communis 'Prostrata'

Common juniper
HEIGHT: 8in (20cm) • Hardy
FLOWERING SEASON: Insignificant

A carpeting form of the common juniper, *J. c.* 'Prostrata' is a conifer that spreads across the ground to about 5ft (1.5m). It has typical, needle-like, aromatic foliage and bears small berries that ripen from blue to black. It thrives in sun or light shade and in any garden soil although it will do better in soil that is not too heavy or alkaline. Prone to attacks by scale insects and to rust.

Lamium maculatum

Dead nettle
HEIGHT: 12in (30cm) • Hardy
FLOWERING SEASON: Early summer

This dead nettle has typical, small, nettle-like leaves but with a broad silver stripe running down the centre rib. The pinkish-purple flowers are borne in spikes in early summer. There is a white-flowered form, *L. m. album*, and a cultivar with golden foliage, 'Aureum', which is not as vigorous and also needs shade and moist soil. Shear the plants after flowering to increase the ground-covering capacity of the leaves. Propagation is by division in autumn.

Leptospermum rupestre

HEIGHT: 6in (15cm) • Half-hardy
FLOWERING SEASON: Early summer

An evergreen flowering shrub, formerly known as *L. humifusum*, this particular species is semi-prostrate with arching branches and therefore makes good ground cover in a sunny sheltered spot, spreading up to 5ft (1.5m) across. The dark green leaves are narrow and oblong and turn bronze in winter, and the white flowers, flushed with red when in bud, are borne in great profusion in summer. It likes well-drained loamy soil to which some peat and sand have been added. Propagate from half-ripe cuttings in late summer, take care not to overwater.

Lonicera pileata

Honeysuckle
HEIGHT: 2ft (60cm) • Hardy
FLOWERING SEASON: Spring

An evergreen low dense shrub, this is by no means the prettiest of honeysuckles, but this particular lonicera has the advantage of a spreading habit even in heavy shade that makes it a good ground-cover plant. The leaves are pale green and narrowly oval, and the small, yellowish-green flowers are followed by small violet-blue fruits. Propagate from hardwood cuttings in autumn or by layering in autumn. Prone to attacks by aphids and to suffer from leaf spot and powdery mildew.

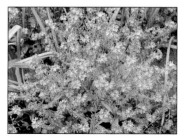

Myosotis sylvestris

Forget-me-not
HEIGHT: 12in (30cm) • Hardy
FLOWERING SEASON: Spring/early summer

This woodland herbaceous biennial will self-seed easily and quickly in the right conditions – partial shade and plenty of leaf mould, plus adequate moisture – to create useful ground cover. It makes bushy clumps of mid green, hairy leaves, surmounted by a profusion of tiny blue flowers carried in open sprays. To propagate, sow the seeds in spring and transfer young plants into their flowering position in autumn. Generally pest- and trouble-free free, but sometimes prone to moulds and mildews.

Oxalis acetosella f. rosea

Wood sorrel/Shamrock
HEIGHT: 4in (10cm) • Hardy
FLOWERING SEASON: Mid/late spring

The little wood sorrel will naturalize well
in a shady area of the garden, it is very
invasive and self-seeds freely. It makes small
clumps of pale green shamrock-like leaves
with five-petalled pink flowers with a white
centre and golden eye. The species plant,
O. *acetosella* has white flowers with purple
veined leaves. This plant prefers a moist well-
drained soil that contains plenty of leaf
mould. Propagate by dividing and
replanting in spring.

Pachysandra terminalis

Allegheny spruce
HEIGHT: 12in (30cm) • Hardy
FLOWERING SEASON: Spring

This sub-shrub spreads vigorously and is
excellent for ground cover in the shade,
since it is one of the few plants that will
thrive even in deep dry shade beneath trees.
It has neat, oval, shiny evergreen leaves and
tiny greenish-white flowers with prominent
purple-tinged stamens. P. s. 'Variegata' has
creamy edges to the leaves, and is slightly less
vigorous than the species. Divide in spring.

Petasites japonicus

Japanese butter burr
HEIGHT: 18in (45cm) • Hardy
FLOWERING SEASON: Early spring

This spreading perennial can be invasive, but
it makes an excellent ground-cover plant and
weed suppressor thanks to its huge dinner-
plate-like leaves. Cones of yellowish-white,
star-shaped flowers are produced in early
spring before the leaves appear. P. *japonicus*
does best in partial shade, and in moist but
well-drained soil. P. *fragrans*, the winter
heliotrope, has small vanilla-scented pinkish-
white flowers. Propagate by division of the
roots in autumn.

Phlomis russeliana

Jerusalem sage
HEIGHT: 4ft (1.2m) • Half-hardy
FLOWERING SEASON: Summer

One of a genus of more than 100 perennials,
shrubs and sub-shrubs, this particular species
originates in Syria. It has large, hairy, heart-
shaped leaves and tiers of yellow, hooded
flowers in summer. It does best in sun and in
any good garden soil. It is a good idea to
transplant the herbaceous kinds of phlomis
every two or three years. Cut the flowers
down after flowering is finished unless seeds
are wanted and cut back quite hard in
autumn. To propagate, divide the roots in
autumn or spring.

Phlox stolonifera

Creeping phlox
HEIGHT: 6in (15cm) • Hardy
FLOWERING SEASON: Early summer

This little phlox spreads to about 12in
(30cm). It is evergreen and more or less
prostrate, producing a profusion of small,
cup-shaped, azure blue flowers in early
summer. It prefers moist rather acid soil with
plenty of peat and is a good plant for a peat
bed. There are cultivars with different
coloured flowers: 'Ariane' has pure white
ones and 'Blue Ridge' pale mauve ones. Cut
back after flowering. Take cuttings of non-
flowering shoots in summer. Prone to attacks
by eelworm and to powdery mildew.

Polypodium vulgare 'Bifidocristatum'

Polypody fern/Oak fern
HEIGHT: 6in (15cm) • Hardy
FLOWERING SEASON: None

This little fern spreads by means of creeping
rhizomes. Being hardy, evergreen and easy
to grow, it is ideal for ground cover in a
partially shaded spot such as under trees.
Plant with the rhizomes more or less on the
surface of the soil to which plenty of humus
has been added as it likes soil that is fertile
but well-drained. The cultivar
P. *v.* 'Cornubiense' is a particularly pretty
form and has deeply divided fronds. Divide
in spring to propagate. Generally pest-free.

Pulmonaria saccharata

Lungwort/Blue cowslip
HEIGHT: 12in (30cm) • Hardy
FLOWERING SEASON: Spring

This early-flowering, semi-evergreen, clump-forming perennial has long, broadly oval leaves, which are flecked with silvery-white on a dark green base. The small, tubular flowers are borne in clusters on the ends of short, erect stems just above the leaves. The flowers open pink but change to purple after pollination. *P. officinalis* 'Sissinghurst White' has large white blooms, and *P. rubra* 'Bowles' Red' has red ones. These plants are good for ground cover, but must have some shade.

Raoulia australis

HEIGHT: 2in (5cm) • Hardy
FLOWERING SEASON: Spring/summer

A small, carpeting evergreen perennial originating in New Zealand, which spreads to about 10in (25cm), this is a good subject for a sunny rock garden. Tiny greenish-yellow flowerheads, with a fluffy appearance, are borne in early summer. *R. glabra* is similarly mat-forming with bright green leaves and white flowers. and *R. haastii* has minute leaves that change from pale green in spring to brown in winter. It does well in sun or partial shade, but needs free-draining peaty soil. Propagate by division in late summer.

Ribes laurifolium

Currant
HEIGHT: 2ft (60cm) • Hardy
FLOWERING SEASON: Early spring

This attractive evergreen shrub will spread up to 4ft (1.2m). It has small, tough; leathery, dark green leaves and dangling racemes of greenish-yellow flowers in early spring. It does well in both shade and sun in well-drained soil. If both male and female plants are grown, the female plants will bear edible black berries. Propagate by cuttings in autumn. Prune out any old wood after flowering. Occasionally subject to aphid attacks and leaf spot.

Salix repens

Creeping willow
HEIGHT: up to 6ft (1.8m) • Hardy
FLOWERING SEASON: Insignificant

Known appropriately enough as the creeping willow, this deciduous prostrate shrub bears attractive silvery-grey leaves which gradually darken to mid green by summer. The catkins, which are about 1in (2.5cm) long and also silvery-grey, are produced in spring. On dry soil, it is smaller and less vigorous than in moist loam. It does best in a sunny position. Take hardwood cuttings in autumn. Like all willows it is prone to several pests, including scale insects, and to a variety of fungal disorders.

Sarcococca humilis

Christmas box/Sweet box
HEIGHT: 3ft (1m) • Hardy
FLOWERING SEASON: Late winter

Christmas box, or sweet box, as it is sometimes known, is grown both for its elegant, glossy, evergreen foliage and for its fragrant flowers which appear in winter. *S. humilis* grows in neat clumps, but because it spreads by underground stems it provides good ground cover. The tiny, white, scented flowers are followed by spherical fruits. This plant does well in sun or in partial shade, in good soil that does not dry out. It can be propagated by semi-ripe cuttings taken in summer.

Saxifraga cuneifolia

Saxifrage
HEIGHT: 8in (20cm) • Hardy
FLOWERING SEASON: Late spring

This evergreen perennial makes a good carpeting plant, the rosettes of rounded leaves covering the soil surface. Rising high above them in late spring and early summer are clouds of white flowers borne on delicate stems. It is rather like a small 'London pride', *S. × urbium,* and is a charming little plant for shady places in a rock garden. Does best in moist soil in partial shade and belongs to the group of saxifrages which needs protection from the midday sun. Propagate by sowing seed in autumn or division in winter.

Soleirolia soleirolii

Mind-your-own-business/Baby's tears
HEIGHT: 2in (5cm) • Half-hardy
FLOWERING SEASON: Insignificant

Known as mother of thousands, mind-your-own-business or baby's tears, this little carpeting plant spreads very rapidly in sun or partial shade. Its leaves are killed by frost but it grows again quickly in spring. It is ideal ground cover for patios and terrace but may need fairly ruthless control for it spreads rapidly. It has inconspicuous flowers in summer. It used to be grown in formal greenhouses as edging to the stagings. Propagate by division.

Tiarella cordifolia

Foam flower/False mitrewort
HEIGHT: 8in (20cm) • Hardy
FLOWERING SEASON: Early summer

The foam flower, so-called because it produces clouds of tiny white flowers on tallish stems in early spring, does well even in deep shade, provided the soil is moist. It spreads vigorously by runners. The evergreen leaves are heart-shaped, bright green and serrated and they have darker veins which turn red in winter. The plant is easy to grow and may be divided at almost any time in the year.

Tolmiea menziesii 'Taff's Gold'

Pick-a-back plant
HEIGHT: 18in (45cm) • Hardy
FLOWERING SEASON: Spring

This is known as the pick-a-back plant or youth-on-age from its habit of producing plantlets where the leaves join the stem. It is semi-evergreen and has ivy-shaped leaves with crinkled edges. Small, bell-shaped, green and brown flowers appear in spring. *T. menziesii* is fully hardy and does well in shade and well-drained, neutral to acid soil. It is a suitable plant for the woodland area in any garden. Propagate by removing young plantlets and replanting.

Trifolium repens 'Purpurascens Quadrifolium'

Clover trefoil/Dutch clover
HEIGHT: 5in (12cm) • Hardy
FLOWERING SEASON: All summer

This little clover has very attractively marked leaves, bright green on the edge with purplish-bronze centres, the leaves on this cultivar are held in groups of four, hence the name. Small, white, typical pea flowers are borne in summer. *T. r.* 'Purpurascens' often does duty as the shamrock on St Patrick's Day but the true shamrock is the wood sorrel (page 118). It does well in sun and well-drained soil, and is ideal for covering a bank, because it can spread to about 12in (30cm). ·

Vaccinium glaucoalbum

Ornamental blueberry
HEIGHT: 4ft (1.2m) • Moderately hardy • pH
FLOWERING SEASON: Early summer

This is an ornamental form of the common bilberry or blueberry which hails from the Himalayas. An evergreen, it makes a good spreading bush about 5ft (1.5m) wide. It has dark green leaves that are paler when young and whitish underneath. The short racemes of white-tinted pink flowers are borne in early summer, followed by fine blue-black edible fruits. It should be planted in an acid, peaty soil in a sunny position or in partial shade. Propagate by layering, division in autumn, or half-ripe cuttings in summer.

Veronica prostrata

Prostrate speedwell
HEIGHT: 12in (30cm) • Hardy
FLOWERING SEASON: Early summer

This speedwell forms a dense mat of narrow green leaves, above which are borne a profusion of saucer-shaped, bright blue flowers in early summer. Two cultivars, 'Spode Blue' and 'Trehane', have taller spires of blue flowers. They do best in full sun and well-drained soil. Other good ground covering speedwells are *V. austriaca*, *V. pectinata* and *V. reptans*. Propagate by division in spring or by semi-ripe cuttings in late summer. It is pest-free, but prone to mildew.

Viburnum davidii

HEIGHT: 4ft (1.2m) • Hardy
FLOWERING SEASON: Summer

This evergreen viburnum makes good ground cover, because its spreading, neat mound of foliage which forms a dome effectively blankets out any weeds. It is also grown for its decorative leaves. Flat white flowerheads, about 3in (7.5cm) across are produced in summer, followed by greenish-blue berries if both male and female plants are grown. It prefers a moist soil and full sun. Prune in late summer if necessary. Propagate by taking cuttings in late summer or by layering in autumn.

Vinca minor 'Argenteovariegata'

Lesser periwinkle
HEIGHT: 4in (10cm) • Hardy
FLOWERING SEASON: Spring/autumn

This vigorously spreading sub-shrub makes ideal ground cover and is slightly less invasive than the larger, but similar, *V. major*. *V. minor* 'Argenteovariegata' has leaves attractively splashed with white and the typical pale blue periwinkle flowers. It grows in any soil that does not dry out completely and will grown in shade but it prefers some sun. Propagate by semi-ripe cuttings in summer or division in autumn. It is pest-free, but sometimes prone to cucumber mosaic virus.

Waldsteinia ternata

HEIGHT: 4in (10cm) • Hardy
FLOWERING SEASON: Early summer

This spreading semi-evergreen perennial has attractive three-lobed, bright green leaves and small, yellow, saucer-shaped, five-petalled flowers in late spring to early summer. It spreads via runners, making good ground cover. It grows best in sun although it will tolerate some shade and does best in well-drained soil. It will not flourish in heavy soils. Another species, *W. fragariodes* has similar characteristics and carries yellow flowers in spring to late summer. Propagate by division in early spring.

More Ground Cover Plants

Good ground cover plants are essential to any garden both for their own sake and to help suppress the weeds; the bigger the garden the more important they become. Take care to choose plants to fit the situation, be it dry or moist, sunny or shady, and remember that many clump-forming perennial plants spread, so that a vigorous hardy perennial like one of the geraniums or *Alchemilla mollis* makes a good ground cover plant over a period and the same applies to low-growing, prostrate shrubs.

There are also a number of roses available which have been bred specifically to provide ground cover. Generally these are in two forms: the prostrate creeping varieties – *Rosa* 'Max Graf' and *R.* Partridge are good varieties – and the low-growing shrubs up to 3ft (1m) in height with a spread wider than their height; *R.* Bonica and *R.* Fiona are two of these.

If you are creating a new garden and have largish areas of soil where you need to control the weeds, you can buy or hire one of the chipper/shredder machines. They produce an instant fine mulch of wood or leaves which can be spread on the garden. This not only suppresses the weeds but helps to improve the soil. Mulching with garden compost is even more beneficial to the soil but is not quite so good at suppressing the weeds.

Evergreen plants are marked (E) and semi-evergreen, (S-E).

SHRUBS

Arctostaphylos uva-ursi (E)
Calluna vulgaris (E)
Cassiope 'Muirhead' (E)
Cornus canadensis
Daboecia cantabrica (E)
Erica carnea 'Springwood White' (E)
  E. × darleyensis 'Darley Dale' (E)
Euonymus fortunei cvs (E)
Gaultheria shallon (E)
Gypsophila repens 'Rosa Schönheit' (S-E)
Hebe pinguifolia 'Pagei'
Hypericum 'Hidcote' (S-E)
Hypericum × inodorum 'Elstead' (S-E)
Juniperus virginiana 'Sulphur Spray' (E)
Leucothoe fontanesiana (E)
Lithodora diffusa 'Heavenly Blue' (E)
Rosmarinus officinalis 'Jackman's Prostrate' (E)
Rubus tricolor (E)
Senecio (syn. *Brachyglottis*) 'Sunshine' (E)
Stephanandra tanakae
Zauschneria californica

PERENNIALS

Acantholimon glumaceum (E)
Ajuga reptans (E)
Alchemilla mollis
Aubrieta (in variety)
Brunnera macrophylla
Cardamine pratensis 'Flore Pleno'
Convallaria majalis (in variety)
Corydalis cheilanthifolia
  C. lutea
Darmera peltata
Dryas octopetala
Epimedium grandiflorum
Geranium (in variety) (S-E)
Hosta fortunei
Iberis sempervirens
Lysimachia nummularia
Mertensia pulmonarioides
Mimulus × burnetii
Nepeta × faassenii
Ourisia macrophylla (E)
Persicaria affinis (E)
Stachys byzantina (E)
Symphytum grandiflorum
Tellima grandiflora (S-E)
Thalictrum aquilegiifolium
Veronica prostrata

Autumn &
Winter Foliage

*Even after the main flowering season is over in summer, gardens
retain much interest. Many shrubs and trees are grown for their
autumn colour and often it is the most beautiful time of the year.
Trees and shrubs native to the eastern states of the US and to China,
especially the maples, are particularly striking.*

ABOVE: *The buff coloured bark of* Acer griseum *rolls off in large
pieces to reveal striking orange-brown new bark beneath.*

OPPOSITE: *The red maple (*Acer rubrum*) in the autumn sunlight. If
you have room in your garden it is worth planting some autumn foliage
trees: maples, cherries, hawthorn and rowans are all good choices.*

ABOVE: *Autumn colour can be found in perennials and shrubs as well as trees – in fact any plants that lose their leaves in winter. The deep purple of* Cotinus coggygria Purpureus Group *makes an excellent foil for the winter-flowering heather below.*

Autumn is a time of year when many deciduous plants, and a few evergreen ones, will make you appreciate their presence. Their brilliant and dramatic hues are highly prized and many gardeners select them to extend the season of interest. Among the most popular plants for small gardens are the Japanese maples (*Acer palmatum*), some of which have brilliant autumn colour, as well as several climbers, including various creepers and ornamental vines.

The vivid colour changes of autumn foliage are part of the natural processes which begin well before the leaves fall and are usually a response to the shortening autumn days, rather than to lower temperatures or frost. The brilliance of autumn colour differs considerably in any one area from year to year and there can be marked differences in the intensity of the colour. This is usually due to the prevailing weather conditions. The ideal conditions for a good autumn display are a cool wet autumn, with very little wind and no frost, as these give slow colour changes, with the leaves hanging on the trees for the longest possible time. Autumn colour is, therefore, somewhat elusive.

The chemistry of autumn leaf colour is mainly concerned with the irregular rate at which ageing takes place in different parts of the leaf. Natural pigments within the leaf of the carotene (red/orange) group persist after the chlorophyll (green) has almost gone. This is augmented in some plants by the presence of tannins which account for the brilliant yellow characteristic of birches, ginkgos, the tulip tree (*Liriodendron tulipifera*) and poplars. The red or purple colours of acers (maples), liquidambar and many others are caused by anthocyanins, a result of accumulations of sugars in the leaves caused by photosynthesis continuing after the transportation of sugars to other parts of the plant has stopped.

When considering where to position trees that are to be grown for the

beauty of their autumn foliage, choose a site which is
well drained, but not too dry, especially in late summer
or this may result in premature colouring and early leaf-
drop. Exposure to full sun, however, especially in the
second half of the day, will give you the best effect, and
contribute to the production of the brightest colours.

A number of the best plants for autumn colour are
illustrated in this chapter and in a sense it is invidious to
single out one rather than another. Much will depend
on the situation, soil and the weather in any particular
year but, for the connoisseur, *Fothergilla major* (page 163)
has particularly striking autumn colour, as has *Parrotia
persica* (page 237) and many of the maples, while the
Virginia creepers (parthenocissus) make a brilliant if
rather short-lived splash of colour against the wall of a
house. Everyone will have their own favourites. There
is a comprehensive list of all plants that provide good
colour at the end of this chapter, and one or two
suggestions of other plants that there was not room for
in this section, which can be found in most well-
stocked nurseries and garden centres.

ABOVE: *Perennial borders assume
attractive tints before they die down, at
which point the plants can be cut right
back, and the debris cleared away.
Many gardeners prefer to leave this
task until early spring as the form of
the foliage is often attractive in winter,
particularly in a hard frost.*

LEFT: *The tinted leaves of a golden
hop (Humulus lupulus 'Aureus')
and Virginia creeper, turning rusty
red, combined with the variegated
evergreen leaves of ivy make an
attractive autumn picture.*

Acer cappadocicum

Cappadocian maple
HEIGHT: 30ft (9m) • Hardy
FLOWERING SEASON: Spring

This exquisite tree has very striking five- to seven-lobed palmate leaves held by scarlet-red leaf stalks. A glossy dark green in spring and summer, the leaves turn a rich golden yellow in autumn. There are some attractive cultivars: *A. c.* 'Rubrum', has young leaves which are tinged red around the margin, and *A. c.* 'Aureum' has leaves which are yellow in spring, lime-green in summer, and yellow again in autumn. Propagation is by softwood cuttings in early summer or by layering.

Acer griseum

Paper-bark maple
HEIGHT: 20ft (6m) • Hardy
FLOWERING SEASON: Spring

This slow-growing tree has trifoliate leaves which are dark green on the upper surface and blue-green beneath, before turning red and scarlet in the autumn. On young trees some leaves remain in place all winter. The buff-coloured bark on the trunk and branches rolls off in large pieces to reveal light, orange-brown, new bark beneath. The fruits are grey-green and covered in soft, downy felt. Propagation is difficult, but seed sown in autumn is the most successful method.

Acer palmatum var. dissectum

Japanese maple
HEIGHT: 15ft (4.5m) • Hardy
FLOWERING SEASON: Spring

A slow-growing large shrub or small tree grown for the delicate palm-like leaves deeply divided into five or seven lobes, which can range in colour from pale green to deep reddish-purple. Most forms produce vivid autumn leaves, and some are also prized for their brightly coloured bark. The thin, delicate leaves are prone to wind damage. Propagate from seed sown in early spring or, for named varieties, from softwood cuttings in June.

Ampelopsis glandulosa var. brevipedunculata 'Elegans'

HEIGHT: 20ft (6m) • Hardy
FLOWERING SEASON: Mid/late spring

Vigorous climbers grown mainly for their attractive autumn foliage, they are ideal for growing against walls and fences or up a pergola. The broadly oval, coarse-textured leaves are three- to five-lobed, bright green with prominent purple veins in the summer, before turning a golden orange-yellow in autumn. The plant supports itself with curling tendrils, and has small insignificant flowers which are followed by small fruits. Propagation is by semi-ripe cuttings taken in summer.

Azolla filiculoides

Floating water fern
HEIGHT: 1in (2.5cm) • Moderately hardy
FLOWERING SEASON: Summer

This deciduous perennial, floating water fern is grown for its decorative foliage. The finely divided leaves or fronds vary from pink to bronze-red in full sun, and from pale green to blue-green in shade, particularly in autumn when they can make the surface of the water look as if it is on fire. It is ideal for controlling algae by reducing light beneath water, but if it is not kept in check it may be invasive. Remove portions with a net if necessary. Propagate by redistributing clusters of the new plantlets when they appear.

Bassia scoparia f. trichophylla

Burning bush
HEIGHT: 3ft (1m) • Half-hardy
FLOWERING SEASON: Late summer

A popular annual which is usually grown for its masses of pale green, pointed, narrow and strap-shaped leaves. In autumn the leaves turn a vivid crimson red which lasts until the plant is killed by the autumn frosts. Indeed, it is this autumn colour which gives the plant its common name of burning bush. The small green flowers are quite insignificant. It likes sun and is soil tolerant. The cultivar, *B. s.* 'Childsii', has a neater habit. Propagation is by seed sown under glass in spring and planted out in position.

Berberis dictyophylla

Barberry
HEIGHT: 6ft (1.8m) • Hardy
FLOWERING SEASON: Late spring

A deciduous, upright shrub with thin erect stems. When young the new shoots are covered with a waxy, grey bloom giving an attractive 'whitewash' effect. In spring yellow flowers are produced in small clusters on the previous year's shoots, to be followed in autumn by small red berries. The elliptical leaves, which are pale green on the upper surface and bluish-green beneath, turn scarlet in autumn. Propagation is by semi-ripe cuttings taken with a heel in late summer.

Betula ermanii

Birch
HEIGHT: 25ft (8m) • Hardy
FLOWERING SEASON: Late spring

This graceful tree has beautiful, peeling bark which is orange-brown changing to a pinkish creamy-white. A vigorous tree, it comes into growth early in the year, producing oval, mid green leaves which are heart-shaped and deeply veined. They are liable to damage from late spring frosts if the site is exposed. *B. e.* 'Blush' syn. *B. costata* and *B. e.* 'Grayswood Hill' are fine cultivars. The leaves produce good autumn colour. Propagate by grafting under protection in early spring.

Cercis canadensis 'Forest Pansy'

Eastern redbud/Judas tree
HEIGHT: 10ft (3m) • Moderately hardy
FLOWERING SEASON: Late spring

An outstanding slow-growing large shrub or small tree. The deeply veined, broad, heart-shaped leaves which are glossy green when young develop a slight blue sheen later and turn red and yellow in the autumn. The pretty, small, bright-pink, pea-shaped flowers are produced in vast quantities, followed by small pod-like fruits in autumn. The tree often leans over because the root system is very brittle. Propagation is by seed sown in spring.Coral spot may cause death of leaves.

Celastrus orbiculatus

Oriental bittersweet/Staff vine
HEIGHT: 30 ft (9m) • Hardy
FLOWERING SEASON: Summer

A vigorous climber useful for growing over buildings such as garages and sheds, or through large trees and shrubs. The oval leaves have a pointed tip and are carried on short stalks, they are mid green, with good yellow autumn colour. The twining stems are light grey-green changing to light creamy-brown with age. Small green flowers are carried in clusters of up to four in early summer. Propagation is from semi-ripe cuttings taken in summer.

Chiastophyllum oppositifolium

HEIGHT: 8in (20cm) • Hardy
FLOWERING SEASON: Late spring/early summer

A hardy evergreen perennial which consists of clusters of creeping rosettes with a lax, trailing habit. The mid green, large, broadly oblong and succulent leaves have serrated edges and bronzed margins in autumn. In late spring and early summer there are sprays of small, yellow flowers which hang like strings of beads from erect, slender red stems rising 6in (15cm) above the leaves. This plant needs shade and a moist, well-drained soil that does not dry out completely. Propagate by soft tip cuttings in early summer or seed sown in autumn.

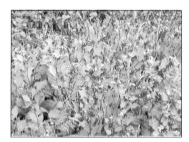

Ceratostigma willmottianum

HEIGHT: 3ft (1m) • Moderately hardy
FLOWERING SEASON: Midsummer

This deciduous shrub forms a dome of dense twiggy growth. In spring the first sign of new growth are the tiny coral-red buds that open into dark green, diamond-shaped, narrow leaves along the stems, pink at first, later turning green. In early July the small, clear blue flowers show in rather tight heads at the end of the shoots, and flowering continues over a long period. In autumn the leaves turn a rich fiery red. It likes full sun and grows best in well-drained soil. Cut out dead wood in the spring. Propagate from heel cuttings taken in late summer.

Coronilla valentina ssp. *glauca*

Crown vetch
HEIGHT: 3ft (1m) • Not reliably hardy
FLOWERING SEASON: Spring/summer

This evergreen shrub has a dense, bushy habit, with a mass of gently arching, greenish-brown, woody stems. The bluish-grey leaves are divided into five or seven round leaflets. The small, fragrant flowers are yellow, pea-like and are carried in small clusters above the leaves on thin green stalks. The cultivar *C. v.* ssp. *g.* 'Variegata' has creamy-white splashes on the leaves. Propagation is by soft-wood cuttings in summer. In some years this plant may be severely attacked by blackfly.

Cotinus coggygria

Smoke plant/Venetian sumach
HEIGHT: 8ft (2.5m) • Hardy
FLOWERING SEASON: Summer

A rounded shrub with a tangle of thin, whippy, grey-green branches which bear round leaves carried in thin leaf stalks (petioles). The light green leaves colour brilliantly in shades of yellow, orange and red in autumn. The small, fawn-coloured flowers are carried in loose, feathery panicles. *C. c.* 'Royal Purple', has dark, plum-purple foliage and produces light red autumn tints. Propagate by layering long shoots in late summer, or semi-ripe heeled cuttings.

Crataegus crus-galli

Cockspur thorn
HEIGHT: 15ft (4.5m) • Hardy
FLOWERING SEASON: Summer

A wide-spreading, small tree, with wicked-looking thorns often up to 3in (8cm) long. The broadly oval leaves are glossy green and produce an attractive display of autumn colour, with shades of yellow, orange, and brilliant scarlet. The large clusters of white flowers are followed by scarlet fruits which last on the tree well into winter. There is also a thornless variety, *C. c-g.* var. *pyracanthifolia*. Propagation is by seed sown in autumn, but germination may take up to two years.

Decaisnea fargesii

HEIGHT: 20ft (6m) • Moderately hardy
FLOWERING SEASON: Spring/summer

This large deciduous shrub with an erect, open habit, has branches which are semi-arching. The large leaves, which are a light grey-green and made up of up to twelve small, spear-shaped leaflets, turn an attractive yellow in the autumn. Large clusters of lime-green flowers are followed in autumn by strange pod-like fruits. These are metallic blue in colour and contain black seeds suspended in a thick clear mucilage. It likes a sheltered sunny position and good soil that does not dry out. Propagation is by sowing the fresh seed in autumn.

Disanthus cercidifolius

HEIGHT: 10ft (3m) • Hardy
FLOWERING SEASON: Autumn

This is a medium-sized deciduous shrub with a rounded habit and dense, twiggy branches. The bluish-green leaves are broadly oval and almost heart-shaped. In autumn they turn yellow, orange, soft crim-son and claret-red before falling. The flowers, which have small, strap-like, dark-red petals, are produced in pairs just as the leaves start to fall. It needs partial shade and moist, rich, neutral to acid soil for the colours to be at their best. Propagation is by layering in spring or by fresh seed sown in winter and placed in a cold frame.

Dregea sinensis

HEIGHT: 10ft (3m) • Not reliably frost hardy
FLOWERING SEASON: Summer

Formerly known as *Wattakaka sinensis,* this is a woody-stemmed climber with a loose, twining habit. The mid green, heart-shaped leaves, which are grey-green on the under side, turn yellow along the margins in autumn. The small, trumpet-like, fragrant flowers appear in clusters and have star-shaped openings that are creamy-white with red dots and splashes followed by slender seed pods. This plant must have a sheltered site to survive. Propagation is by softwood cuttings in summer, or seed sown under protection in spring.

Festuca glauca

Blue fescue
HEIGHT: 10in (25cm) • Hardy
FLOWERING SEASON: Summer

Euonymus fortunei 'Emerald 'n' Gold'

HEIGHT: 6–10ft (1.8–3m) • Hardy
FLOWERING SEASON: Early summer

These popular plants often have narrow, oval, mid green leaves which produce very attractive autumn colours. The flowers are insignificant but the winged fruits can be brightly coloured and very striking. *E. europaeus* 'Red Cascade' has leaves which turn a rich scarlet in autumn and produces large quantities of rosy-red fruits which hang on the plant all winter. Propagation is by semi-ripe cuttings with a heel, taken in August. No regular pruning is required.

This is a low-growing, tussock-forming little grass with tufts of bristle-like, blue-grey leaves. It maintains its pattern and colour throughout the winter and copes well on exposed, windy sites. The purple flower spikes are carried above the leaves in summer and remain to provide decoration long after flowering has finished. It is easy to grow in any sunny position and likes well-drained soil. It is lime tolerant. Propagate by division and replanting in spring.

Ficus carica

Common fig
HEIGHT: 5ft (1.5m) • Moderately hardy
FLOWERING SEASON: Summer

This is a small tree or large shrub, with light green stems when young, turning grey-green as they age. The large, deciduous, palm-like leaves are mid to grey-green turning butter-yellow in the autumn. A versatile plant, it can be grown on a fence, or as a free-standing bush, but a wall which gives some frost protection is best. The cultivar *F. c.* 'Brown Turkey' regularly produces brown-green fruits in late summer. Propagation is by semi-ripe cuttings taken in summer.

Fraxinus angustifolia 'Raywood'

Narrow-leaved ash
HEIGHT: 45ft (15m) • Hardy
FLOWERING SEASON: Spring

This is a fast-growing deciduous tree of dense, fairly upright habit, and a bark which is dark grey, with closely networked ridges, which become deep and knobbly with age. The leaves are usually blue-green, pinnate and opposite, with up to thirteen spear-shaped leaflets joined by a strong central midrib. In autumn the leaves become plum-purple before falling. Likes sun and fertile well-drained soil that does not dry out. Propagate by seed or grafting, but named cultivars must be grafted in March.

Hakonechloa macra 'Alboaurea'

HEIGHT: 2½ft (75cm) • Hardy
FLOWERING SEASON: Autumn

This lovely clump-forming grass has long narrow, ribbon-shaped leaves growing alternately along a red-tinted stem and giving a light, arching 'mop head' effect. The leaves are very striking, being a combination of warm golden-yellow, finely striped with narrow green lines, and sometimes tinged bronze along the edges. In autumn they become tinged with bronze-red along the margins and makes a spectacular sight. It bears insignificant flower spikes in autumn. It prefers a cool site. Propagate by division in early spring.

Hamamelis mollis

Chinese witch hazel
HEIGHT: 7ft (2m) • Hardy • pH
FLOWERING SEASON: Winter/spring

This distinctive deciduous shrub produces its wonderfully fragrant flowers in winter. The frost-hardy flowers are spidery in appearance, with small, strap-like petals chiefly in shades of yellow, although some cultivars have darker flowers. The large mid green leaves are broadly oval and make a magnificent display in autumn, turning yellow and copper before falling. Likes sun or semi-shade and fertile, well-drained, peaty, acid soil. Propagation is by softwood cuttings taken in late summer or by grafting in midwinter.

Imperata cylindrica

HEIGHT: 2½ft (75cm) • Hardy
FLOWERING SEASON: Autumn

Helleborus argutifolius

Christmas rose/Lenten rose
HEIGHT: 2½ft (75cm) • Hardy
FLOWERING SEASON: Winter/spring

This hardy evergreen perennial forms a compact mound of tough, leathery leaves which are mid to pale green with a spiny margin. In autumn the older leaves turn bronze-yellow along the margins. The large flower heads are made up of many cup-shaped, yellow-green blooms. The weight of these heads often causes the stems to collapse.
Cut back such stems after flowering. Propagation is by seed sown in summer and placed in a cold frame.

A hardy perennial grass with erect, slender stems. In autumn it produces light, wispy, silvery-white flower spikes up to 8in (20cm) long, which often persist throughout the winter. The mid to dark green leaves are flat and narrow, tapering gradually to a pointed tip. The cultivar *I. c.* 'Rubra' which is the plant most widely available in nurseries, has leaves which are flushed with bright ruby red changing to dark burgundy in autumn and winter. Will flourish in any well-drained soil and prefers some sun. Propagation, like all grasses, is by division and replanting in early spring.

Lagerstroemia indica

Crape myrtle
HEIGHT: 5ft (1.5m) • Not reliably hardy
FLOWERING SEASON: Summer/early autumn

This very attractive shrub has rigid, erect branches, which are grey-green when young, turning duller with age. The foliage consists of broad, spear-like leaves arranged in groups of three on short stalks, they are mid green with very prominent veins, and turn a vivid yellow in autumn. In summer and autumn trusses of white, pink or purple flowers are produced. This plant must have some protection during winter. Propagation is by semi-ripe cuttings taken in summer.

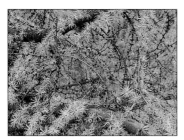

Larix decidua

European larch
HEIGHT: 55ft (18m) • Hardy
FLOWERING SEASON: Spring

This vigorous, deciduous conifer has rosettes of light green, needle-like leaves which become darker through the summer and change to a golden yellow before falling. The bark is a greenish grey-brown and fairly smooth when the tree is young, often becoming deeply ridged and an attractive pinkish-brown with age. Grows in almost all soils and conditions. Though easily propagated by seed sown outdoors in the spring, this tree is really too large for all but the very biggest gardens.

Lindera obtusiloba

Spice bush
HEIGHT: 20ft (6m) • Hardy
FLOWERING SEASON: Early spring

A large deciduous shrub that comes from Japan that is grown for its broadly oval, glossy, dark green, three-lobed aromatic leaves which turn butter yellow with rich pink tints in autumn. The small, deep yellow, star-shaped flowers are produced in spring before the leaves emerge and are followed by small round black berries. Likes semi-shade and moist acid soil. Propagation is by seed sown in spring or by layering in early summer, although rooting may take up to eighteen months.

Liriodendron tulipifera

Tulip tree
HEIGHT: 100ft (30m) • Hardy
FLOWERING SEASON: Summer

A large, vigorous tree with a spreading habit, and grey-green bark. The large, deep green leaves are very distinctive, with deep lobes and a very square tip. In the autumn they turn a bright golden-yellow. The large, magnolia-like flowers are tulip-shaped, greenish-white and splashed with orange markings. The cultivar *L. t.* 'Aureomargina-tum' has deep green leaves with a golden-yellow margin. It likes fertile well-drained slightly acid soil. Propagation is by seed sown in spring or by summer budding.

Malus tschonoskii

Crab apple
HEIGHT: 40ft (12m) • Hardy
FLOWERING SEASON: Late spring

This attractive tree has a strong, vigorous, and characteristically erect, conical habit. The mid green leaves are broadly oval and covered with a dense felt of grey hairs on the underside and along the young shoots as they develop. In autumn the tree produces a magnificent display of yellow, orange, scarlet and purple colours. The small, single flowers are white flushed pink. Propagation is by budding in summer or grafting in spring. Apple canker can infect the tree.

Miscanthus sinensis 'Strictus'

Zebra grass
HEIGHT: 4ft (1.2m) • Hardy
FLOWERING SEASON: Summer

This vigorous, clump-forming ornamental grass has bold, glossy leaves with golden bands running across them. They turn yellow and later bronze in autumn. The flower-heads will only form in a hot summer and are useful for drying and using in floral arrangements. The usual method of propagation is by division in March, when the clump is split into smaller portions of 4-5 shoots. Though generally pest- and disease-free, over-feeding can cause soft weak growth to develop.

Nyssa sylvatica

Tupelo
HEIGHT: 25ft (8m) • Hardy
FLOWERING SEASON: Summer

A handsome, slow-growing, deciduous tree from north America that is broadly conical in shape with horizontal branches upturned at the tip. The oval leaves taper to a point, they are a dark, glossy green in summer, turning to shades of rich scarlet, orange and yellow in autumn. This tree rarely comes into leaf before May, when the risk of a frost is all but gone. Unsuitable for limy or dry soils. Propagation is by seed sown in autumn and overwintered in a cold frame.

Ophiopogon planiscapus 'Nigrescens'

Snake's beard
HEIGHT: 10in (25cm) • Hardy
FLOWERING SEASON: Late summer

This evergreen perennial has arching, strap-like, spidery clusters of leaves which are almost black and remain throughout winter. The flowers appear in short sprays of tiny mauve bells tucked between the leaves, to be followed by shiny black berries in autumn. Creeping underground stolons gradually establish this plant as a dense thicket. Grows in sun or partial shade and fertile well-drained soil. Propagate by fresh seed sown in autumn or by division in spring.

Paliurus spina-christi

Christ's thorn
HEIGHT: 12ft (4m) • Moderately hardy
FLOWERING SEASON: Summer

This large, deciduous shrub makes a dense thicket of slender, green, thorny shoots. The leaves are broadly oval, glossy and bright green. Tiny, greeny-yellow flowers are produced in short, dangling clusters, to be followed by woody, winged, yellow-green fruits in autumn. Propagation is by softwood cuttings in summer or seed sown under protection in autumn. This plant is slow to establish, and may require some winter protection. It also needs full sun, and a light, free-draining soil.

Persicaria affinis

Knotweed
HEIGHT: 10in (25cm) • Hardy
FLOWERING SEASON: Summer/autumn

The short, mat-forming knotweeds, such as this one, give a low, bold flash of colour at the front of the border. The plant makes a wide clump of creeping stems with narrow, dark green leaves, and in late summer and autumn produces spikes of rose-pink or red flowers. There are a number of cultivars: *P. a.* 'Dimity' has white flowers flushed pink and scarlet foliage in the autumn; *P. a.* 'Donald Lowndes' has deep pink flowers all summer long. Propagation is by division in early spring.

Prunus incisa

Fuji cherry
HEIGHT: 15ft (4.5m) • Hardy
FLOWERING SEASON: Spring

This is a shrubby deciduous species with slender erect branches. The mid green leaves are small, prominently toothed around the margins and turn beautiful shades of yellow and orange in autumn. The flowers, which appear before the leaves, are deep pink in the bud, opening to form small pink-tinged white blooms. This tree makes an excellent hedge. Propagation is by softwood cuttings taken in early summer. The bacterial fireblight may cause young shoots to shrivel.

Ptelea trifoliata

Hop tree
HEIGHT: 22ft (7m) • Hardy
FLOWERING SEASON: Early/midsummer

A deciduous, large shrub or small tree, with a bushy, low-spreading habit and a tangle of thin, grey-green branches. The dark green aromatic leaves are made up of three narrow oval leaflets, which turn butter yellow in autumn. In summer, clusters of very fragrant, small, star-shaped, yellowish-green flowers appear, followed by bunches of pale green winged fruits. Propagation is by seed sown in autumn, or by softwood cuttings taken in summer for cultivars.

Rhus typhina

Stag's horn sumach
HEIGHT: 15ft (4.5m) • Hardy
FLOWERING SEASON: Summer

This wide-spreading, suckering shrub, develops a scrawny, flat-topped appearance as it ages. The young shoots are a furry velvety-brown. The large, dark green leaves are made up of many small leaflets, evenly arranged along a slender leaf stalk. In autumn the leaves turn a rich orange and reddish-purple. The flower spikes are reddish-brown in colour and are carried like candles on the shoot tips. They last throughout the winter. Propagation is by root cuttings taken in late winter.

Rubus phoenicolasius

Japanese wineberry
HEIGHT: 6ft (1.8m) • Hardy
FLOWERING SEASON: Early summer

An attractive shrub with an open habit and gently arching, orange-red stems, which look very pretty in winter. The mid green leaves, which are sub-divided into three leaflets, have a slightly felty texture with a silvery-green undersurface. They turn a soft yellow in autumn. Clusters of single, pink, rose-like flowers are followed by bright red, edible fruits in autumn. Prune out flowering shoots in winter to encourage new shoots to develop from the plant base. Propagation is by semi-ripe cuttings taken in early summer.

Rubus tricolor

Bramble
HEIGHT: 2ft (60cm) • Hardy
FLOWERING SEASON: Summer

This evergreen bramble makes an excellent ground-cover plant that is fairly low-growing. It has glossy, dark green leaves, and produces cup-shaped, papery white flowers in summer. The raspberry-like fruits are scarlet and edible. Will grow under most conditions but does best in fertile well-drained soil in sun or in partial shade. Propagate by tip layering or by taking semi-hardwood cuttings in late summer. Generally pest-free, but it is sometimes prone to grey mould and rust.

Sorbus 'Joseph Rock'

Mountain ash/Rowan tree
HEIGHT: 25ft (8m) • Hardy
FLOWERING SEASON: Early summer

A deciduous upright tree with ascending branches and long pointed buds which are bright red and sticky in spring. The leaves consist of up to seventeen small, light green oval leaflets, which turn yellow and orange in autumn. The small, creamy-white flowers are produced in dense clusters in summer, followed by densely packed bunches of bright yellow fruits. These would last into late winter but are generally eaten by the birds. Propagation is by seed sown in spring or budding in summer.

Stephanandra tanakae

HEIGHT: 7ft (2m) • Hardy
FLOWERING SEASON: Midsummer

A medium-sized shrub that produces a wealth of long, arching branches which are a rich nut-brown. The broadly oval, mid green leaves are sharply toothed and turn deep yellow and orange in early autumn. In winter the bare, brown stems are very showy. The tiny yellow and white flowers appear at the tip of each shoot in June and July. Likes sun or semi-shade and moist well-drained soil. Propagation is by hardwood cuttings taken in winter, or by digging up rooted suckers when the plant is dormant.

Tiarella wherryi

Foam flower
HEIGHT: 12in (30cm) • Hardy
FLOWERING SEASON: Spring/summer

This is an excellent evergreen ground-cover perennial with masses of pretty maple-shaped leaves that form a dense mat over the soil. In summer the leaves are pale to mid green, but take on coppery tints through autumn and winter. It is rather slow grow-ing. In spring clusters of creamy-white or pink flowers are carried above the leaves on spikes. This plant does well in a semi-shaded position and is perfect for the woodland gar-den. It gows in any soil but likes soil that is moist and does not dry out. Propagation is by division in early autumn or spring.

Toona sinensis 'Flamingo'

HEIGHT: 65ft (20m) • Hardy
FLOWERING SEASON: Spring/summer

This is a fairly fast-growing deciduous tree, with attractive pinnate leaves which are a bronzy-pink in spring, deep green through the summer and butter yellow in autumn. The white, fragrant flowers are produced in spikes up to 12in (30cm) in length. The cultivar *T. s.* 'Flamingo' has vivid pink young leaves which turn cream and eventually bright green. Propagation is by root cuttings taken in late winter and placed in a cold frame or by seed sown in autumn. 'Flamingo' must be grafted.

More Plants for Autumn and Winter Interest

Many deciduous shrubs and trees are grown especially for their autumn colour. For many people the colours of autumn are the loveliest in the whole year and the plants listed in this chapter and below are just a few of those that will give pleasure to everyone as the year comes to its close. A number of trees produce their best colour when grown in slightly acid soil and some plants, particularly those which have variegated leaves, are best grown in sun. These details are given in the plant descriptions. Plants that flower in winter are another of nature's bonuses and every garden should contain at least two, they are often beautifully fragrant.

TREES

Acer negundo 'Flamingo'
    A. platanoides
(Most acers produce brilliant autumn hues)
Aesculus pavia
Amelanchier canadensis
Arbutus × *andrachnoides*
Cercidiphyllum japonicum
Crataegus (in variety)

Cryptomeria japonica
Ginkgo biloba
Hamamelis × *intermedia*
Koelreuteria paniculata
Liquidambar styraciflua 'Worplesdon'
Malus hupehensis
Ostrya carpinifolia
Oxydendrum arboreum
Parrotia persica
Populus alba
    P. × *canadensis* 'Serotina'
Prunus (in variety)
    P. sargentii
Pseudolarix amabilis
Pterocarya fraxinifolia
Pyrus calleryana
Robinia pseudoacacia
Sorbus (in variety)
Stewartia sinensis
Taxodium distichum

SHRUBS

Berberis (in variety)
Calluna vulgaris
Cornus kousa var. *chinensis*
    C. nuttallii
Daboecia cantabrica
Enkianthus campanulatus
Erica carnea 'Springwood White'
    E. × *darleyensis* 'Darley Dale'
Euonymus fortunei cvs
Fothergilla major
Pyracantha 'Mohave'

Pyracantha 'Watereri'
Rhododendron (azaleas – deciduous varieties)
Spireae japonica 'Goldflame'
Symphoricarpos × *doorenbosii*
Vaccinium corymbosum
Viburnum opulus
    V. plicatum 'Lanarth'
    V. tinus

PERENNIALS & CLIMBERS

Epimedium grandiflorum
Holboella coriacea
Humulus lupulus 'Aureus'
Miscanthus sinensis
Parthenocissus henryana
    P. tricuspidata
Vitis coignetiae
    V. vinifera 'Purpurea'

SCENTED PLANTS

No garden is complete without a number of scented plants. Ideally, there should be a selection that provides the garden with scent at all seasons of the year. Both aromatic plants, with pungent foliage, and scented flowering perennials and shrubs, are included in this chapter.

ABOVE: Verbena 'Novalis', one of a large group of colourful, scented plants generally grown as annuals.

OPPOSITE: A pink azalea contrasts with the blue of the forget-me-nots to make a scented corner in a spring border. Many of the best garden effects like this corner happen by chance and are not planned.

ABOVE: *Old-fashioned and species roses are among the best of the scented roses, but most of them only flower once a year. Growing roses among other plants will help to extend the appeal of the scented garden. Here the shrub rose R. 'Zigeunerknabe' is grown with salvias.*

Luckily for gardeners many plants have a delicious scent but some plants are especially prized for their fragrance and no garden should be without some of these, ideally with one or two flowering at the different seasons of the year. Appreciation of fragrance is subjective and there is a wide range of types of scent from sweet and cloying, like that of hyacinths, to spicy and musky like that of sage.

It is not always the flower that is the scented part of the plant. With some plants, as with the incense rose (*Rosa primula*), Russian sage (*Perovskia atriplicifolia*), or mint for example, it is the foliage that is the principal provider of scent. Usually foliage is at its most aromatic when crushed, and it is a good idea therefore to position plants with aromatic foliage close to a path or, if they are small enough, in cracks in paving stones so that they are crushed underfoot or brushed as you walk past. A bush of scented viburnum or mock orange (philadelphus) just outside a window will fill the whole house with scent, as will any of the scented climbers such as the fragrant honeysuckles (only some are scented), jasmine, wisteria or the evergreen *Trachelospermum jasminoides*.

Most herbs are aromatic: lavender, santolina, sage, nepeta and artemisia, in particular, and they can all be planted in a silver-leaved border.

The flowers of many scented plants are well known to all. Everyone immediately thinks of roses when they think of scented plants, but some varieties are not so well-scented. There are many varieties available which are, so avoid the non-scented ones if this is important to you. The old-fashioned roses, including the Albas, are among the most fragrant roses and have recently become extremely fashionable, although they only flower once a year. New breeds of rose, like the 'English' roses, developed by David Austin, have the attributes of old roses in form and scent with some of the repeat-flowering habits of modern roses. There are literally hundreds of roses available and the rose section (pages 198-201) includes a selection of most of the varieties available.

If the garden is large enough, it is well worth growing some of the scented flowers and foliage for drying, either for flower arrangements or to incorporate as pot pourri. In this way you extend the enjoyment you get from the scent over a very long season. Flowers that pick and dry well for pot pourri are roses, most of the herbs, and a number of the perennials, in particular helichrysum, the everlasting flower.

If you are planning a big summer border in which colour is the main objective do not forget to include some of the scented perennials as well. It will increase your enjoyment of the border immeasurably. Alternatively, a few of the scented shrubs can be grown at the back of the border, if the scented perennials do not fit in with your plan. All gardens should contain a philadelphus for its wonderful summer scent if there is room.

Some plants are winter-flowering and although your opportunity for appreciating their scent outdoors may be less, you can pick them for indoor use. Chinese witch hazel (hamamelis) is one such subject, as are some of the daphnes. *Elaeagnus × ebbingei* is another winter-flowering scented plant, and although the flowers are too small to notice, the scent is surprisingly strong, so it may take some time to work out where it is coming from.

BELOW: *A corner of a charming cottage garden full of scented plants. Salvias and rock roses mingle with the purple broom while lavender makes a fragrant edging in the background.*

Bulbs & Tubers

Bulbs and tubers are among the easiest and most rewarding of all garden plants. Once planted they can, and indeed often are, forgotten, until they emerge the next year. This section covers tubers as well as the favourite bulbs of spring and there is a number of plants which should be found in all gardens. They will increase and provide pleasure for many years repaying the initial outlay many times over.

Most bulbs are reasonably tolerant as to soil and position but if you can only give them heavy, rather waterlogged, conditions, it is a good idea to lift bulbs like tulips and replant them again the following spring. Treat them in the same way as tuberous plants like dahlias. Buy good quality bulbs from a good supplier and don't plant mixed lots as they will all flower at slightly different times and look pretty odd. All bulbs will benefit from a foliar feed when they have finished flowering to help them build up their strength and they should all be planted deeply, at least three times the depth of the bulb. And if they are grown in grass let all the foliage die down before you cut the grass.

Allium caeruleum

Ornamental onion/Ornamental garlic
HEIGHT: 2ft (60cm) • Hardy
FLOWERING SEASON: Summer

A clump-forming, summer-flowering bulb which has small, bright blue, flowers held together in a tight ball on the tops of long stems. It has narrow dark green leaves. Alliums grow in any soil although they do best in soil that is well-drained and does not become waterlogged. They like a sunny position. The colours range from white through pink to blue. Plant the bulbs in the autumn and propagate by sowing seed in autumn or division in spring.

Allium giganteum

Ornamental onion/Ornamental garlic
HEIGHT: 4ft (1.2m) • Hardy
FLOWERING SEASON: Summer

A spectacular sight when grown in a herbaceous border, *A. giganteum* can reach a height of 6ft (2m) when grown in favourable conditions. It carries its distinctive mauvy-purple flowers in a dense spherical ball and is robust and clump-forming. Other good species are, *A. rosenbachianum*, pink, and *A. multibulbosum*, which has unusual whitish florets held on a flat head. *A. flavum*, which is yellow, and *A. ostrowskyanum*, deep pink, are small alliums suitable for the rockery.

Alstromeria aurea

Peruvian lily
HEIGHT: 2½ft (80cm) • Hardy
FLOWERING SEASON: Summer

A genus of summer-flowering tuberous perennials known as Peruvian lilies which have showy, multi-coloured flowers in summer. *A. aurea* has orange flowers with short dark red markings and narrow lance-shaped, dark green leaves. The most popular sort are *A.* Ligtu Hybrids which have widely flared flowers in varying shades of pink, orange, peach, pale-red and creamy-white often marked with contrasting colours. Likes sun and well-drained soil. Plant the tubers 10in (25cm) deep and mulch in the autumn.

Amaryllis belladonna

Belladonna lily
HEIGHT: 2½ft (80cm) • Moderately hardy★★
FLOWERING SEASON: Autumn

An autumn-flowering bulb which has a stout deep red stem and carries funnel-shaped, fragrant, pink flowers. The leaves appear after the flowers and are mid green, long, strap-like and semi-erect. Most people associate the name amaryllis with the large bulbs grown in pots but they are correctly known as hippeastrums. *A. belladonna* needs a sheltered position in sun and likes light, fertile, well-drained soil. The bulbs must be planted at least 8in (20cm) deep. It must not be disturbed and likes a mulch in autumn.

Anemone ranunculoides

Wood anemone
HEIGHT: 8in (20cm) • Hardy
FLOWERING SEASON: Summer

This little wood anemone will naturalize and spread in the right conditions. The leaves are deep green, and lobed. The flowers are about 1in (2.5cm) across, and bright yellow. *A. nemorosa*, the true wild wood anemone of Great Britain, is white and *A. n.* 'Robinsoniana' is blue. They grow best in humus-rich soil in light shade. Plant the tubers in autumn about 1in (2.5cm) deep. Propagate by division in late summer. Prone to attacks from flea beetles, caterpillars and aphids, and to various viral disorders.

Arum italicum

Cuckoo pint/Lords and Ladies
HEIGHT: 18in (45cm) • Half-hardy
FLOWERING SEASON: Insignificant

This handsome foliage plant, a native of
Europe and North Africa, is ideal for the
winter garden. The spear-shaped, dark green
leaves are attractively marbled with cream
and it has a yellowish-green flower spathe in
early spring. The leaves are much used by
flower arrangers. By summer the foliage has
vanished, leaving a spear of bright scarlet
berries. They grow best in sun or semi-shade
and moist well-drained soil. Propagate by
dividing the tubers in autumn.

Arum italicum 'Marmoratum'

Cuckoo pint/Lords and Ladies
HEIGHT: 12in (30cm) • Hardy
FLOWERING SEASON: Spring

This plant appears in autumn when glossy
green, cream and grey veined spear-shaped
leaves are thrust up on mid green stalks. The
leaves die down in late summer. The flower
spathes, which appear in April or May, are
pale yellow-green and hooded, terminating
in a pointed tip. In early autumn a short
yellow-green stem is all that remains and on
the top third is a dense cluster of glowing
(poisonous) red berries. Propagate in
autumn by division and separating offsets.

Camassia leichtlinii

Quamash
HEIGHT: 3ft (1m) • Hardy
FLOWERING SEASON: Summer

This is one of five species in a genus of bulbs
that were originally imported from North
America. Known as the quamash, it was used
by the Indians for food. It has strappy green
leaves and flower stems bearing spires of
bright lavender-blue or white flowers in
summer. *C. l.* Caerulea Group have purple-
blue flowers. Plant in heavy moist soil in
autumn, about 4in (10cm) deep. The plants
like sun or partial shade. Propagate from offsets in autumn or by seed sown in autumn.

Camassia quamash

Common camassia/Quamash
HEIGHT: 2½ft (75cm) • Hardy
FLOWERING SEASON: Midsummer

This is an attractive, clump-forming, summer-flowering bulb with mid green leaves
which are tall, erect and strap-shaped, and
end in a sharp point. The small, star-shaped
flowers are carried in large showy spikes on
tall, leafless, stalks. The flowers vary from
white through blue to purple. This bulb is
perfect for growing in damp areas close to
streams and water courses. Divide the plants
when dormant to prevent overcrowding.
Propagate by removing the offsets from the
sides of the parent bulb in September.

Canna indica 'Indian Shot'

Indian shot
HEIGHT: 3ft (1m) • Tender
FLOWERING SEASON: Midsummer

Robust, showy, rhizomatous perennials,
which are grown out of doors in the summer
as bedding plants in the milder parts of the
country. They have bold, oval, pointed,
green or reddish-bronze leaves with showy
flowers generally red, orange or yellow in
colour. Put the plants in a cold frame in May
and plant out in June. They like well-
cultivated rich soil and require frequent
watering during the growing period. Lift
and store tubers when the leaves die down.
To propagate divide the tubers in winter.

Cardiocrinum giganteum

Giant lily
HEIGHT: 6ft (1.8m) • Hardy
FLOWERING SEASON: Summer

Known as the giant lily, *C. giganteum* makes
an eye-catching addition to any bog garden.
Plant the bulbs just below the soil's surface
in humus-rich moist soil in partial shade.
The slightly drooping, creamy white, funnel-
shaped fragrant flowers can be up to 6in
(15cm) long. Each flower stem, which may
have several flowers, is borne aloft on stout
leafy stems in summer. The flowers are
followed by decorative seed-heads. After
flowering the bulb dies, but offsets of the
main bulb will flower eventually.

Chionodoxa luciliae Gigantea Group

Glory of the Snow
HEIGHT: 6in (15cm) • Hardy
FLOWERING SEASON: Spring

Spring flowering bulbs which are suitable for naturalising in rock gardens or in woodland areas. They are effective colonisers. The bulbs have two leaves and the six-petalled starry flowers which grow on a leafless stem are blue with a white centre. There are white and pink forms. *C. sardensis* has deep blue flowers. Plant the bulbs in August in ordinary garden soil 3in (7.5cm) deep and about the same distance apart.

Clivia miniata

HEIGHT: 16in (40cm) • Frost tender
FLOWERING SEASON: Spring/summer

This handsome evergreen grows from a rhizome. Both leaves and flowers are striking: the leaves are long, strap-shaped and a glossy dark green. They form a rosette around the flower stem which bears waxy red or orange flowers in a dense cluster in late spring or early summer. Generally grown as a house plant. It needs protection in winter – grow it in containers and wrap the container base in bubble plastic or something similar to overwinter it outdoors. Propagate by seed or division.

Colchycum speciosum 'Album'

Meadow saffron
HEIGHT: 8in (20cm) • Hardy
FLOWERING SEASON: Spring/autumn

Colchycums are charming plants, mainly autumn flowering, sometimes wrongly called the autumn crocus. *C.s.* 'Album', a rare, beautiful species, is pure white. Large semi-erect basal leaves develop in late winter or spring. *C. luteum* is a spring flowering species with yellow flowers. *C. autumnale*, the meadow saffron, has purple, pink or white flowers in September. They like an open sunny position and well-drained garden soil. Propagate by seed or division in the autumn.

Crinum × *powellii*

Cape lily
HEIGHT: 3ft (1m) • Moderately hardy
FLOWERING SEASON: Late summer

A large late-summer flowering bulb with a long neck which produces a group of strap-shaped leaves and fragrant, funnel-shaped, pink flowers held on leafless stems. *C. bulbispermum* has white or pinkish-red flowers and *C. moorei* is deeper pink. They should be planted 6in (15cm) deep in April in well-drained soil in a sheltered sunny position, preferably a south-facing wall. In the winter cover with 3-4in (7.5-10cm) of ash. Propagate by offsets taken in the spring but these will take 3-4 years to flower.

Crocosmia 'Lucifer'

Montbretia
HEIGHT: 2½ft (75cm) • Hardy
FLOWERING SEASON: Late summer

These colourful plants have a dense, clump-forming habit, and spread by producing corms on the end of long underground stems. They have erect, deeply-veined, sword-like, mid green leaves and, in late summer, the upright green stems carry two rows of small tubular flowers. Cultivars include *C.* × *crocosmiiflora* 'Emily MacKenzie', with deep orange and crimson flowers, and the early flowering, *C.* 'Lucifer', with flame red flowers. Likes well-drained soil and a sunny open site. Propagate by division in spring.

Crocus chrysanthus 'E A Bowles'

Crocus
HEIGHT: 4in (10cm) • Hardy
FLOWERING SEASON: Early spring

Crocuses are one of the most spectacular harbingers of early spring, flowering from February onwards. 'E A Bowles' is one of the most beautiful, with old gold petals and a dark bronzy throat. There a large number of cultivars, *C. vernus* ssp. *albiflorus* 'Remembrance' is the deepest purple and *C. c.* 'Snow Bunting' has creamy white outer petals with a mustard yellow throat. Plant in a sunny open site 2in (5cm) deep. Propagate by sowing seed or division in autumn.

Crocus laevigatus

Crocus
HEIGHT: 3in (7.5cm) • Hardy
FLOWERING SEASON: Autumn/winter

There are many different species of crocus
from different parts of Europe and Asia
Minor, but this particular species is a native
of Greece. It has pale mauve to whitish
flowers with purple veins and an orange
throat; unusually, it is highly scented. There
is a cultivar, *C. l.* 'Fontenayi', which has
deep mauve and buff flowers, slightly later in
the year. Crocuses benefit from shelter from
the wind and do well in the rock garden.
Prone to damage by birds and mice.

Crocus vernus ssp. *albiflorus* 'Pickwick'

Crocus
HEIGHT: 3in (7.5cm) • Hardy
FLOWERING SEASON: Early spring

A common sight in early spring, this is one
of the most popular crocuses with long
pale purple flowers. Crocuses will grow
and flower freely in ordinary garden soil
and prefer leaf mould to be added to the
soil rather than manure. Plant new bulbs in
August or September in a sunny position
in informal groups with small clusters at
the end of larger plantings. Do not disturb
the plants once they are established.

Cyclamen coum

Hardy cyclamen/Sowbread
HEIGHT: 3in (7.5cm) • Hardy
FLOWERING SEASON: Winter/early spring

Tuberous perennials which have small delicate flowers in varying shades of white, pink,
mauve and red. They flower in late winter
and early spring. *C. c.* ssp. *coum album* is
white. The leaves are plain or marbled and
rounded in shape. There are a number of
hybrids available. Although they do best in
moist organic soil, cyclamen thrive in thin
soil under deciduous trees as long as they are
given some mulch or top dressing. They self-
seed and may need dividing every five years.

Cyclamen hederifolium

Hardy cyclamen/Ivy-leaved cyclamen
HEIGHT: 6in (15cm) • Hardy
FLOWERING SEASON: Autumn

The autumn flowering species of the hardy
cyclamen, these little perennials have
attractively marked rounded leaves and small,
shuttlecock-shaped, pink flowers borne aloft
on short stems. There is also a white form,
C. h. f. album. They do well in the shade of
trees or large shrubs in light, humus-rich
soil, and, in the right conditions, may form
extensive colonies through the spread of
seeds. They are prone to quite a few pests
and diseases, and the corms are particularly
attractive to mice.

Dahlia 'Bluesette'

Water lily dahlia
HEIGHT: 4ft (1.2m) • Half hardy
FLOWERING SEASON: Summer

Dahlias are a large and popular genus of
plants which provide vivid colour in the border. 'Bluesette' has glossy dark green leaves
and dark pink coloured flowers with a gold
centre. Other popular forms of dahlia are
cactus, decorative, ball and pompom, all of
which refer to the shape of the flower heads.
There are ten in all. They grow best in a
sunny position and fertile well-drained soil.
All forms except dwarf dahlias require
staking. Lift the tubers when the flowers die
and store in a frost-free place over winter.

Dierama pendulum

Angel's fishing rod/Wandflower
HEIGHT: 4ft (1.2m) • Moderately hardy
FLOWERING SEASON: Summer

An evergreen summer-flowering corm
D. pendulum has long pendulous stems from
which hang deep pink bell-shaped flowers in
long racemes. The leaves are long and grass-
like and die down partially in winter. The
plants look best beside water but prefer a
sunny position. They like moist well-drained
soil. *D. pulcherrimum* has pink flowers with
white stripes. Propagate by dividing the
corms in spring or sowing seed in autumn.
The corms resent being disturbed and may
take two years to flower after transplanting.

Eranthis hyemalis

Winter aconite
HEIGHT: 4in (10cm) • Hardy
FLOWERING SEASON: Early spring

The winter aconite, much valued for its early flowering, is a tuberous-rooted, hardy perennial, with pale green, deeply cut leaves. In the early spring it produces small, buttercup-like, yellow flowers which are surrounded by a collar of green, frilled leaves. This is an excellent plant naturalising in a shaded or semi-shaded situation. It does best in moist woodland conditions. Divide in spring as soon as the flowers have died down and replant immediately.

Erythronium dens-canis

Dog's tooth violet
HEIGHT: 6in (15cm) • Hardy
FLOWERING SEASON: Spring

Dwarf bulbous plants which are normally found in woodland gardens and have recently been revived as a garden species. The flowers of the species are purple-pink. Of the best-known cultivars, *E. d-c.* 'Purple King' is pink with blue anthers and *E. d-c.* 'Rose Queen' is rose-pink while *E. californicum* 'White Beauty' is white and *E.* 'Pagoda' a clear yellow. They need moist soil with plenty of organic matter, and some shade. If left undisturbed, they will colonize.

Freesia

HEIGHT: 2ft (60cm) • Half hardy
FLOWERING SEASON: Summer

The sweetly scented freesia, long popular as a cut flower, can be grown outdoors in the garden from specially prepared corms. These should be planted in mid-spring, and will then flower in the summer of the same year. After the leaves have died down the corms must be lifted and overwintered for replanting the following year. Plant in light sandy soil in a sunny and sheltered site. Propagate from offsets or grow from seed. Aphids and caterpillars will sometimes attack plants grown outdoors.

Fritillaria meleagris

Snake's head fritillary/Meadow fritillary
HEIGHT: 12in (30cm) • Hardy
FLOWERING SEASON: Spring

A spring flowering bulb which has narrow grey-green leaves and solitary bell-shaped flowers prominently marked with checks in colours varying from pink to purple and white. It grows best in moisture-retentive soil and is good for naturalizing in grass meadowland where it will self-seed freely. They like some shade. There is a lovely white cultivar *F. m.* 'Aphrodite'. Plant bulbs 4in (10cm) deep in the autumn and propagate by sowing seed in autumn or taking offsets in the summer.

Galanthus elwesii

The giant snowdrop
HEIGHT: 8in (20cm) • Hardy
FLOWERING SEASON: Late spring

This snowdrop differs from the common snowdrop in being slightly taller with broader leaves and larger flowers that are deep green on the inner petals and it appears later in late spring. *G. elwesii* does well under deciduous trees as it benefits from light in the winter, but is happier in shade the rest of the year. It likes rich moist soil. Always plant or move snowdrops just after flowering. They are occasionally affected by narcissi-fly maggots, and by eelworms, and they can also succumb to grey mould.

Galanthus nivalis

Common snowdrop/Fair maids of February
HEIGHT: 8in (20cm) • Hardy
FLOWERING SEASON: Spring

Late winter- or early spring- flowering bulbs which have narrow strap-like leaves and small white flowers with a green tip at the end of each inner petal. Snowdrops colonize freely and establish themselves under trees and in grassland. Plant the bulbs 2in (5cm) deep in September and, if they are grown in grassland, do not mow until the leaves have died down completely. Like all bulbs they will benefit by the application of liquid manure or fertiliser to the leaves after the flowers have died.

Galtonia viridiflora

Cape hyacinth
HEIGHT: 4ft (1.2m) • Moderately hardy
FLOWERING SEASON: Spring

A clump-forming, summer-flowering, bulb which has large, grey-green, semi-erect, tulip-like leaves, and tall spikes which carry up to thirty, hanging, funnel-shaped, pale green, whitish-tinged flowers. They need a sunny, sheltered site and fertile moist well-drained soil that does not dry out in summer. The plants die down in the winter and are propagated by lifting and division in spring. Plant the bulbs in spring at least 5in (12.5cm) deep and 15in (35cm) apart.

Hippeastrum 'Apple Blossom'

Amaryllis
HEIGHT: 18in (45cm) • Tender
FLOWERING SEASON: Winter/spring

While it is technically incorrect to call hippeastrums, amaryllis, so many people do that this is the name they are known by and sold under. They are spectacular greenhouse bulbs which come from tropical America and Brazil. There are many kinds in colours varying from white through pale pink to orange and red. Feed the bulbs when flowering has finished and then place the pots on their sides in winter to dry off when the leaves have died down.

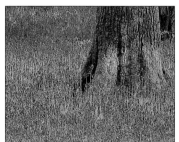

Hyacinthoides non-scriptus

Common bluebell
HEIGHT: 10in (25cm) • Hardy
FLOWERING SEASON: Spring

The common bluebell does best in partial shade, at the outer edge of a tree canopy, for example, in humus-rich soil. In the right conditions it will naturalize well and is ideal for planting in a small woodland area of the garden. Bluebells can be grown from seed scattered on a bed of leaf-mould, where they will not be disturbed, but they will take several years to develop into flowering bulbs. Generally pest- and disease-free, although they can be attacked by rust.

Hyacinthus orientalis

Hyacinth
HEIGHT: 8in (20cm) or more • Hardy
FLOWERING SEASON: Spring

Hyacinths are among the most strongly scented of all garden flowers, giving off a rich fragrance from their spires of densely packed tubular flowers in various shades of white, cream, blue, mauve and pink. Apple-green, strappy foliage surrounds the flower spires. There are many good named cultivars including 'Delft Blue', a strong cerulean blue, and 'L'Innocence' which is a clump-forming pure white hyacinth whose leaves appear after flowering. Propagate by offsets in autumn.

Leucojum vernum

Snowflake
HEIGHT: 6in (15cm) • Hardy
FLOWERING SEASON: Spring

Snowflakes are closely related to snowdrops which they much resemble. The favourite kind is *L. vernum* which has rather large drooping flowers, white with green tips at the end of each petal. It flowers in March. The summer snowflake, *L. aestivum,* reaches a height of 20in (50cm) and flowers in May and *L. autumnale,* which has pink tips on the end of the flowers, flowers in September. They prefer sandy loamy soil. Plant in September at least 3in (7.5cm) deep but they may take some time to get established.

Lilium 'Casa Blanca'

Lily – Asiatic hybrid
HEIGHT: 3ft (1m) • Hardy
FLOWERING SEASON: Summer/autumn

These colourful bulbous plants have shapely, trumpet-like blooms with six petals which curl open to produce flowers ranging in size from 1in (2.5cm) to 10in (25cm) across depending upon the variety. In addition to the brilliant display of colour, many lilies are very fragrant and make excellent cut flowers. The leaves are pale to dark green, some are narrow, almost grass-like and grouped at the base of the plant, while others produce leaves in clusters (whorls) at intervals along the stem. Propagate from scales in autumn.

Lilium regale

Regal lily
HEIGHT: 5ft (1.5m) • Hardy
FLOWERING SEASON: Summer

This handsome lily has large, highly-scented, funnel-shaped flowers in midsummer, borne in clusters on top of tall stems. It has large, bright yellow stamens and pinkish-tinged backs to the petals. It does best in full sun, in ordinary soil, but makes an excellent container plant. Ideally, the stems should be discreetly staked. Plant the bulbs in autumn at three times the depth of the bulb. Propagate from offset bulblets in autumn. Prone to attack by aphids and lily beetle.

Muscari armeniacum

Grape hyacinth
HEIGHT: 6in (15cm) • Hardy
FLOWERING SEASON: Spring

Very attractive little spring-flowering bulbs which have semi-erect basal leaves and tight heads of deep blue flowers carried on spikes. The flowers have a musky fragrance. They like ordinary well-drained garden soil and a sunny position. As plants they do best in the less formal parts of the garden as the leaves become an untidy mass. Plant the bulbs as early as possible covered by at least 2in (5cm) of soil. Once planted they can be left undisturbed for several years.

Narcissus 'Golden Ducat'

Daffodil
HEIGHT: 15in (35cm) • Hardy
FLOWERING SEASON: Spring

Daffodils are botanically known as narcissus. They appeal to everyone with their bright promise of spring and the golden sunshine of summer to come. The varieties are bewildering and the genus is classified into twelve divisions. 'Golden Ducat' is a bright yellow, double-flowered form from group 4 which flowers in mid-spring. All daffodils need to be planted as early in the year as possible, with at least 6in (15cm) of soil on top of the bulbs.

Narcissus 'Ice Follies'

Daffodil
HEIGHT: 15in (35cm) • Hardy
FLOWERING SEASON: Spring

One of the group 2 large-cupped narcissi, 'Ice Follies' has slightly pointed perianth (the outer part of the flower) petals and a large flat crown or cup which opens pale lemon and ages to an ivory white. It produces a large number of lovely flowers. All daffodils should be dead-headed after flowering and they benefit from an application of liquid fertiliser to the leaves after the flowers have died. They will flourish in all soils and like sun or light shade but they do best in fertile well-drained soil.

Narcissus 'Kilworth'

Daffodil
HEIGHT: 15in (35cm) • Hardy
FLOWERING SEASON: Spring

'Kilworth' is another group 2 daffodil with large pale white perianth and a vivid orange red cup with a spot of intense green in the eye. All daffodils are fragrant but the sweetest smelling come from the jonquil, tazetta and poeticus groups with smaller, less showy, flowers often borne in clusters on the stem. It is important not to cut daffodils down before the foliage has died away as this will weaken the bulbs. If they are not planted deeply enough or cut down too soon they may well be 'blind' the following year.

Nerine bowdenii

Guernsey lily
HEIGHT: 15in (35cm) • Moderately hardy
FLOWERING SEASON: Autumn

A autumn-flowering bulb which carries its head of five or six bright pink flowers on an upright stem. The leaves are strap-like and mid green. They used to be considered plants for the greenhouse only as they come from South Africa but they are perfectly hardy in the milder parts of the country given the shelter of a south- or west-facing wall. They like light sandy soil and full sun. Propagate by seed sown in autumn or by offsets detached in August. Plant these in small pots and treat as newly potted plants.

Nerine sarniensis var. *curvifolia* f. *fothergillii*

Guernsey lily
HEIGHT: 2ft (60cm) • Moderately hardy
FLOWERING SEASON: Autumn

Varieties of *N. sarniensis* have up to ten heads of flowers in colours ranging from orange through pink to white. They are not so hardy as *N. bowdenii* and need more protection in hard winters. Once planted nerines should not be disturbed as they grow best when they are pot-bound. They take some time to establish themselves but they make a wonderful sight in autumn when the garden is looking rather bare.

Scilla siberica

Siberian squill
HEIGHT: 4in (10cm) • Hardy
FLOWERING SEASON: Spring

An early spring-flowering bulb which has four strap-like glossy mid green leaves and bell-shaped, lilac-blue flowers carried on a short spike. Scillas will grow in any garden soil but prefer sandy well-drained loam and sun or partial shade. Plant them in rockeries or at the edge of the lawn in the shrubbery where they will colonize and make a display of bright blue colour early in the year. Propagate by division in late summer or by sowing seed in the autumn.

Triteleia hyacintha

Spring star flower/Missouri hyacinth
HEIGHT: 15in (35cm) • Hardy
FLOWERING SEASON: Late spring/early summer

A late spring- or early summer-flowering bulb which carries large heads of white flowers like alliums, tinged with blue or purple early in summer. It has long narrow semi-erect spreading basal leaves which are mid green. They must have light well-drained soil and will not flourish in heavy clay unless the soil is very carefully prepared. They die down at the end of summer. Propagate by sowing seeds or by taking offsets in the autumn.

Tulipa 'Golden Age'

Late-flowering tulip (Group 5)
HEIGHT: 18in (45cm) • Hardy
FLOWERING SEASON: Spring

Botanically speaking, tulips have been classified into fourteen divisions, which can be divided into early flowering, mid-season flowering, and late flowering kinds (these make up the first eleven divisions) and the species *Kaufmanniana*, *Fosteriana* and *Greigii* and their hybrids. The mid-season tulips which flower in April and May are the most suitable for exposed positions as they are weather resistant. 'Douglas Bader' is a lovely pale-pink variety and 'Prominence', deep red, but the colour range is extensive.

Tulipa 'Pink Impression'

Darwin Hybrid tulip (Group 4)
HEIGHT: 2ft (60cm) • Hardy
FLOWERING SEASON: Spring

Tulips are the most tolerant bulbs and will grow in all types of soil as long as there is reasonable drainage. They are best when they are planted in groups and like daffodils it is a mistake to plant mixtures as they will all flower at slightly different times. 'Pink Impression' is a Darwin Hybrid which flowers at the end of April. They are the largest tulips yet produced. Tulips will colonize freely and are increased by lifting and dividing the bulbs in the autumn. In very wet areas lift and store the bulbs in winter.

Zantedeschia aethiopica

Arum lily/Calla lily
HEIGHT: 2½ft (75cm) • Moderately hardy
FLOWERING SEASON: Summer

The epitome of the garden lily which carries large white flower spathes in midsummer each enclosing a club-shaped spadix above large, evergreen, arrow-shaped, semi-erect, deep green leaves. *Z. aethiopica* likes sun or partial shade and moist, free-draining soil. It will grow beside a pool as a marginal water plant in up to 6in (15cm) of water. It needs to be sheltered from strong winds and in cold areas is best grown in pots and lifted in winter. Plant the tubers 6in (15cm) deep and propagate by taking offsets in winter.

Artemisia absinthium

Wormwood
HEIGHT: 3ft (1m) • Hardy
FLOWERING SEASON: Summer

This shrubby species of wormwood has the typical silvery-grey, aromatic leaves of the genus, which are finely dissected and feathery. The cultivar 'Lambrook Silver', as its name implies, is particularly silvery. The small, button-like, yellow flowers are borne in late summer. It does well in any sunny position in good garden soil. Propagate from semi-hardwood cuttings in late summer. Can be prone to root aphids and blackfly, leaf miner, and rust.

Buddleja 'Pink Delight'

Butterfly bush
HEIGHT: 10ft (3m) • Hardy
FLOWERING SEASON: Summer

The butterfly bush, so-called because its flower spikes are attractive to butterflies, is a deciduous shrub with light green leaves and a spreading habit. The species plant, B. davidii has pale-purple flowers borne at the end of arching branches. Cultivars have a range of flower colours from the purple 'Black Knight' to the pure white 'White Cloud'. It benefits from tough pruning in early spring. Propagate from half-ripe cuttings in late summer or from hardwood cuttings in autumn.

Chamaecyparis lawsoniana

Lawson's cypress
HEIGHT: 50-80ft (15-25m) • Hardy
FLOWERING SEASON: Insignificant

Known as false cypress, the genus Chamaecyparis are widely used trees with aromatic foliage. Some species make excellent hedging and there are also dwarf forms that are ideal for window boxes and rock gardens. C. l. 'Gnome' is a small 20in (50cm) cultivar which is bun-shaped with bluish foliage, but in the main false cypresses are tall and erect. C. l. 'Lane' is about 47ft (15m) high, with golden-yellow aromatic foliage. Does well in acid soil in sun or shade.

Chimonanthus praecox

Wintersweet
HEIGHT: 8ft (2.5m) • Hardy
FLOWERING SEASON: Winter

Known as wintersweet, from the season in which its richly fragrant flowers appear, this shrub has glossy, oval, dark green leaves. The yellow, cup-shaped, purple-centred flowers, which are highly scented, bloom on bare branches. 'Grandiflorus' has larger, deep yellow flowers; 'Luteus' has bright yellow ones. Ideally it should be grown on a south- or west-facing wall or fence, and it needs full sun and rich well-drained soil. Propagate by cuttings, taken from softwood in summer or by layering a shoot in autumn.

Clematis armandii

Early-flowering clematis
HEIGHT: 10-15ft (3-4.5m) • Frost hardy
FLOWERING SEASON: Early spring

This twining climber is both evergreen and scented. The leaves are long, oval and glossy, and the flowers are white, six-petalled, small and star-like with yellow stamens. It should be pruned after flowering, to ripen wood for the next season's flowers. It will need support on trellis or on wires, a sheltered south- or west-facing site, and does best in rich, well-drained soil with the roots shaded. It is very vigorous when established. Propagate from seed sown in autumn. May be troubled by aphids, mildew and clematis wilt.

Convallaria majalis 'Albostriata'

Lily-of-the-valley
HEIGHT: 8in (20cm) • Hardy
FLOWERING SEASON: Late spring

Lily-of-the-valley is very fragrant, the perfume filling the air in spring wherever large drifts have naturalized. A herbaceous perennial, it will spread quickly in cool shade and while it will grow in any soil it prefers moist soil that has plenty of leaf mould. The leaves are broad, dark green and grow in pairs, and the spires of white, scented bell-shaped flowers rise between them. 'Albostriata' has a white-striped leaf. Divide well-grown clumps from autumn to spring.

Convallaria majalis var. rosea

Lily-of-the-valley
HEIGHT: 8in (20cm) • Hardy
FLOWERING SEASON: Spring

The lily-of-the-valley is an excellent plant for creating drifts of scent in shady corners of the garden. It should naturalize well given the right conditions: partial shade, soil containing plenty of leaf-mould and ample moisture. The little bells of white flowers are deliciously scented. There are a number of cultivars including *C. m.* 'Fortin's Giant' which has slightly larger flowers and the variety, *C. m.* var. *rosea* which is pink. Divide well-grown clumps from autumn to spring.

Daphne odora

HEIGHT: 5ft (1.5m) • Frost hardy
FLOWERING SEASON: Midwinter/early spring

A good shrub to scent the winter garden, this particular daphne has very fragrant, deep pinky-purple and white flowers borne in clusters between the glossy evergreen oval leaves. 'Aureomarginata', a more hardy cultivar, has cream margins to the leaves. This shrub propagates easily from cuttings taken with a heel in autumn, and can also be grown from seed sown in autumn. Prefers fertile well-drained moist soil and does not like being moved. Prone to mottling and distortion of the leaves from virus disorders, which may affect flowering as well. Aphids may sometimes attack the young shoots.

Dianthus 'Pink Mrs Sinkins'

Pink
HEIGHT: 12in (30cm) • Hardy
FLOWERING SEASON: Summer

Old-fashioned pinks, of which 'Pink Mrs Sinkins' and 'Mrs Sinkins' are two, are among the most strongly scented of all pinks. 'Mrs Sinkins' is fully double with white, fringed petals. Pinks have a low, spreading habit and produce large numbers of flowers. The stems and foliage are silvery green. They do best in sun and in an alkaline soil. Pinch out the flowers in their first year to build a strong plant. Propagate from seed, by taking cuttings in summer or by layering.

Hyssopus officinalis

Hyssop
HEIGHT: 18in (45cm) • Hardy
FLOWERING SEASON: Summer

Hyssop is a herb from the eastern Mediterranean region. The thin pointed leaves, which are aromatic, are arranged in pairs up the stems; the small, purplish-blue flowers are also borne along the length of the stems. There is a white form *H. o. f. albus* and a pink form, *roseus*. It likes full sun and fertile well-drained soil. Can be grown as a low hedge, in which case pinch out the growing tips to encourage bushy growth and trim lightly in spring. Propagate from seed or from basal cuttings, taken in spring.

Iris graminea

Spuria iris
HEIGHT: 8in (20cm) • Hardy
FLOWERING SEASON: Summer

I. graminea belongs to the group known as Spuria irises, which are beardless irises with a rhizomatous rootstock. It has grassy leaves that are about a foot tall, and the flowers, which are plum-scented, have red-purple standards (the raised part of the flower) and bluish-purple veined white falls (the lower part of the flower). Plant in autumn in a sunny position or semi-shade in good garden soil. Do not disturb after planting. Propagate by dividing and cutting the rhizomes. Prone to various viral disorders.

Iris unguicularis

Algerian iris
HEIGHT: 9in (23cm) • Hardy
FLOWERING SEASON: Autumn/winter

This beardless iris, known as the Algerian iris, has delicately scented lavender flowers with a yellow flash on the fall (lower part), and long dark green strappy leaves. It usually starts flowering early in autumn and continues until the following spring. It does best in a sunny, sheltered situation in well-drained, sandy soil but it is tolerant both of acid and alkaline conditions. Propagate by dividing and cutting the rhizomes in early autumn. Prone to attack by slugs and snails, and to a range of viral disorders.

Lathyrus odoratus

Sweet pea
HEIGHT: 4ft (1.2m) • Hardy
FLOWERING SEASON: Summer

The sweet pea species will grow up to 10ft (3m) high but the dwarf sweet pea Knee-hi will grow to about 4ft (1.2m) and the Bijou series grows to about 18in (45cm). Sweet peas will twine their leaf tendrils around a support, producing the delicate, sweetly scented flowers in a range of colours. The very small strain Little Sweetheart is ideal for edgings. Give them a sunny site and lots of organic matter in the soil. Prone to attacks by slugs and aphids, and to viral disorders.

Laurus nobilis

Sweet bay tree
HEIGHT: 18ft (6m) • Hardy
FLOWERING SEASON: Inconspicuous

The sweet bay, a native of the Mediterranean, has glossy, dark green, lance-shaped leaves that are highly aromatic, and used in cooking particularly for flavouring soups and stews. Bays make excellent formal standards for containers and tubs, and can be clipped into geometric shapes. The variety 'Aurea' has golden-yellow leaves. Small greenish-yellow flowers are borne in spring, but usually go unnoticed. Propagate from heel cuttings taken in late summer. Prune container-grown bay trees in summer. Bays can be infested by scale insects.

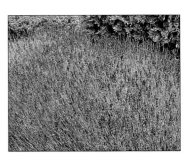

Lavandula angustifolia 'Hidcote'

Lavender
HEIGHT: 2ft (60cm) • Hardy
FLOWERING SEASON: Summer

An evergreen bushy shrub with dark purple flowers which are very fragrant and narrow, aromatic, silver-grey leaves. It makes an excellent low hedge. Lavenders come from the Mediterranean and do best in light soil that contains plenty of leaf mould or manure and full sun. They may well be damaged by frost if grown on heavy soil and they do not like being waterlogged. To propagate take cuttings from the side shoots in late summer.

Lavandula × intermedia

Old English Lavender
HEIGHT: 2-3ft (60-90cm) • Hardy
FLOWERING SEASON: Summer

Lavender is one of the best scented plants with its highly fragrant flowers and foliage. Old English lavender is a variant of *L. × intermedia*. It is a vigorous plant with greyish-green leaves. Dutch lavender (also *L. × intermedia*) has wider, whiter leaves. The stems, with silvery-green narrow leaves, form a dense clump which can be clipped into shapes. It does best in full sun in light soil. *L. stoechas*, the French lavender has deep purple flowers surmounted by violet bracts. Propagate from cuttings in early autumn after flowering.

Lonicera japonica

Japanese honeysuckle/Burmese honeysuckle
HEIGHT: 30ft (9m) • Hardy
FLOWERING SEASON: Summer/autumn

Known as the giant Burmese honeysuckle, this is one of the most vigorous species, of which two cultivars are most often grown: 'Aureoreticulata' has yellow-veined green leaves and long-tubed fragrant white flowers, which yellow as they age. The other popular cultivar, 'Halliana', also has very fragrant flowers. As twining climbers, honeysuckles need a suitable support, and they do well in either sun or partial shade, in any good garden soil. Prune after flowering. Propagate from semi-ripe cuttings in summer.

Magnolia grandiflora

Laurel magnolia/Bull bay
HEIGHT: 13ft (4m) or more • Moderately hardy
FLOWERING SEASON: Summer

This big evergreen shrub is one of the best magnolias – there are more than 120 species in the genus. It has large, handsome, glossy green leaves that have russet felting on the underside. It bears huge, highly scented, dish-like flowers in a creamy white, from mid- to late-summer. It is almost always grown as a wall shrub, where it has protection from cold winds. Prefers neutral to acid soil. Propagate from heeled semi-ripe cuttings in summer. Generally pest-free, but prone to some viral disorders.

Mahonia × media 'Charity'

Oregon grape
HEIGHT: 10ft (3m) • Hardy
FLOWERING SEASON: Late autumn/early spring

This evergreen shrub is particularly good value for winter, with its strongly scented racemes of bright yellow flowers. There are several species and cultivars that are worth growing for scent, of which 'Charity' is just one: others are *M. lomariifolia* and *M. japonica* Bealei Group. Mahonias do well in shade or partial shade, and prefer fertile, moist soil. Propagate by sowing seeds when ripe, layering the branches in spring or from semi-ripe cuttings in summer.

Malus hupehensis

Hupeh crab
HEIGHT: 33ft (10m) • Hardy
FLOWERING SEASON: Early summer

This crab apple, which has a vigorous habit, is unusual in that it has scented flowers, which are quite large – about 1in (2.5cm) across and single followed by reddish-tinged, yellow fruits in early autumn. *M.* 'John Downie' is another excellent crab apple with orange-red fruits in autumn. Plant new trees in the autumn or spring, and keep the area around the trunk grass-free until the tree is established. Will cope with partial shade, but feed well in spring. Prone to attacks by caterpillars, and to the same diseases as ordinary apple trees, in particular apple scab.

Mentha suavolens 'Variegata'

Mint
HEIGHT: 2ft (60cm) • Hardy
FLOWERING SEASON: Summer

Common mint, or *M. spicata*, is the one most often used in cookery, but apple mint, *M. suavolens* has the most highly scented leaves. The attractively variegated cultivar, *M. suavolens* 'Variegata', has creamy-white margins to the leaves, and small, bluish-mauve flowers in summer. All forms of mint are best grown in moist, slightly shaded conditions, and in a place where their root run can be constricted. Propagate by division in the dormant season.

Myrtus communis

Common myrtle
Height: 10ft (3m) • Tender
Flowering SEASON: Summer

The common myrtle is a Mediterranean shrub that is normally grown in containers in cooler climates. It is grown for its neat, evergreen leaves, which are also aromatic. White flowers, about 1in (2.5cm) across, are borne in summer, and occasionally blue-black fruits follow in autumn. There are other sorts: 'Variegata' has creamy-tinted leaves, and *M. c.* ssp. *tarentina* is more dwarf. In warmer areas it can be grown against a sheltered wall. Propagate from heeled cuttings of non-flowering shoots in summer.

Nicotiana × sanderae

Tobacco plant
HEIGHT: 3ft (1m) • Half-hardy
FLOWERING SEASON: Summer

The tobacco plant has wonderfully scented flowers, which fill the evening air with their fragrance. *N. × sanderae* has several cultivars, among them 'Sensation Mixed' in colours including white, cream, carmine and yellow; the flowers stay open all day instead of opening only in the evening, as the species does. The cultivar 'Lime Green', has almost fluorescent looking yellowish-green flowers. Sow seed in spring under glass. Prefers sun and well-drained soil. Generally disease-free, but may be liable to attack by aphids.

Nicotiana sylvestris

Flowering tobacco
HEIGHT: 5ft (1.5m) • Half-hardy
FLOWERING SEASON: Late summer

This large perennial is often grown as an annual, principally for its small white tubular flowers at the end of long stems which give off a heady perfume in the evening in the late summer. The flowers form in sprays at the ends of the stems, above the mid green, rough oval leaves. It is easily grown from seed in early spring. Like all tobacco plants it does best in sun and fertile, well-drained soil. Generally pest- and disease-free, although slugs may attack the young shoots.

Origanum vulgare

Wild marjoram
HEIGHT: 12in (30cm) • Hardy
FLOWERING SEASON: Summer

The common marjoram grows in the wild on hillsides around the Mediterranean. Its aromatic leaves are used to flavour soups and stews. The pinkish-purple flowers are borne in dense clusters at the end of the flowering stems in summer. There is a golden-leaved cultivar, 'Aureum'. Likes a sunny position and well-drained soil. Sow from seed or take cuttings of basal shoots in late spring. Marjoram for drying for culinary use should be picked before the flowers open.

Osmanthus × burkwoodii

HEIGHT: 6ft (1.8m) • Hardy
FLOWERING SEASON: Late spring

A hybrid between *Osmanthus delavayi* and *O. deconis*, this makes a good hedging plant. It has evergreen mid green leaves and clusters of tubular, white, very fragrant flowers in late spring. It is more compact in habit than *O. delavayi*. For hedging, plant about 18in (45cm) apart in sun or partial shade. It prefers fertile well-drained soil that contains some peat and has some leaf mould or compost added when planting. If planted as a hedge trim in midsummer, prune shrubs when the flowers fade. To propagate, take half-ripe cuttings in summer or layer branches in autumn.

Pelargonium crispum

Geranium
HEIGHT: 2ft (60cm) • Tender
FLOWERING SEASON: Summer/autumn

This pelargonium is grown primarily for its foliage, which is small, dense and almost frilly in appearance. The leaves have a subtle lemon scent. The delicate pale pink flowers are relatively small, and are borne in clusters all summer. The cultivar, 'Variegatum', with silvery edges to the leaves, is particularly attractive. Plant out after the last frosts in a sunny position. Feed during flowering. Propagate from tip cuttings in late summer. Prone to mould and rust.

Pelargonium tomentosum

Peppermint geranium
HEIGHT: 1-2ft (30-60cm) • Frost tender
FLOWERING SEASON: Summer

This pelargonium is grown for its large, grey-green, fragrant peppermint-scented leaves, hence its common name, peppermint geranium. The flowers are borne in clusters, and are small and white. The leaves can be used to flavour drinks and fruit tarts. It should be grown in partial shade, not full sun like other pelargoniums, and the growing tips should be pinched out to keep a neat, bushy shape. Prefers well-drained neutral to alkaline soil. Propagate from cuttings from spring to autumn. Dislikes over-watering.

Philadelphus 'Beauclerk'

Mock orange
HEIGHT: 6ft (1.8m) • Hardy
FLOWERING SEASON: Summer

This hybrid mock orange is a hardy, deciduous, spreading shrub. The flowers are single, fragrant and creamy-white with a dark red blotch. The leaves are light green and pointed. Plant in sun or part shade between autumn and spring. Generally soil tolerant but prefers fertile well-drained loam. Prune after flowering, taking care not to remove young shoots, which will bear flowers next year. Propagate by taking half-ripe cuttings in late summer or hardwood cuttings in autumn. Sometimes prone to leaf spot.

Philadelphus coronarius

Mock orange
HEIGHT: 10ft (3m) • Hardy
FLOWERING SEASON: Summer

Often called, mock orange, this free-flowering shrub is covered in large, white cup-shaped flowers in summer, which have a wonderfully heady scent. It is a spreading shrub, almost as wide as it is tall, and does well in dry situations. A golden-leaved cultivar, 'Aureus', is very popular but needs to be grown in partial shade. Prune out old wood after flowering. Propagate from half-ripe cuttings in late summer or from hardwood cuttings in winter. Generally pest-resistant, but can be prone to leaf spot.

Primula auricula 'Adrian'

Alpine auricula
HEIGHT: 6in (15cm) • Hardy
FLOWERING SEASON: Spring

Native to the European Alps, the flowers of this species of primula have distinctly marked golden centres, which are carried in branching heads on an upright stem. The leaves are greyish-green and form a cluster around the stems. There are a number of different cultivars in a variety of colours. These primulas do best in well-drained soil with plenty of humus, in sun or partial shade. Take cuttings in summer. Prone to attack from caterpillars and cutworms.

Rhododendron luteum

Azalea
HEIGHT: 10ft (3m) • Hardy • pH
FLOWERING SEASON: Late spring

This species was formerly classified as an azalea, but it is now classed as a rhododendron. One of a huge genus of over 800 species, ranging from the massive to the miniscule, *R. luteum* is one of the very fragrant species. It has bright, yellow, tubular flowers about 5cm (2in) wide, which are borne in large trusses. It is the parent of numerous hybrids. Rhododendrons need peaty, acid soil and some shade. Propagate by layering. Prone to attacks by leafhoppers, and azalea gall.

Rosmarinus officinalis 'Jackman's Prostrate'

Rosemary
HEIGHT: 6ft (1.8m) • Frost hardy
FLOWERING SEASON: Summer

The foliage of rosemary, a culinary herb, is richly aromatic. The leaves are small and spiny, and the small, bright, pale-blue flowers are borne along the length of the stems. 'Miss Jessopp's Upright' is a compact, upright shrub, while the Prostratus Group hybrids are very low growing. Rosemary benefits from regular trimming and if grown as a hedge, trim after flowering. Propagates easily from heeled cuttings in summer.

Santolina chamaecyparissus

Cotton lavender
HEIGHT: 2ft (60cm) • Hardy
FLOWERING SEASON: Summer

Cotton lavender, as santolina is also known, makes attractive mounds of silvery-grey aromatic foliage. It can be treated as a low hedging plant or grown as a border edging. Small yellow flower buttons are borne profusely in midsummer. A smaller variety, *S. c.* var. *nana*, is sometimes grown in the rock garden. Santolina needs full sun and well-drained soil that is not too rich. For hedging, pinch out the growing tips to encourage bushiness. Propagate from cuttings in midsummer.

Sarcococca hookeriana

Christmas box/Sweet box
HEIGHT: 5ft (1.5m) • Hardy
FLOWERING SEASON: Winter

This sweetly scented evergreen shrub is another useful addition to the winter garden, flowering as it does in winter. The small white flowers are not very significant; they appear in the leaf axils, almost obscured by them. The leaves themselves are narrow, pointed and glossy green. Black fruits are borne after flowering. It can be grown in shade or sun, but it needs a fertile soil that does not dry out. Propagate by taking semi-ripe cuttings in summer or by sowing seed in autumn.

Syringa × *chinensis*

Rouen lilac
HEIGHT: 8ft (2.5m) • Hardy
FLOWERING SEASON: Late spring

This bushy lilac, known as Rouen lilac, makes a useful informal deciduous hedge in a town garden. A hybrid between *S. persica* and *S. vulgaris*, it makes a dense shrub with the typical fragrant lilac-purple flowers borne in upright panicles and the typical oval, tapering, mid green leaves. Plant in sun or part shade in fertile, preferably alkaline, soil. Remove the flowers in the first season to create a stronger shrub. Propagate from half-ripe cuttings in late summer. Prone to scale insects and to forms of blight.

Syringa vulgaris 'Congo'

Common lilac
HEIGHT: 15ft (5m) • Hardy
FLOWERING SEASON: Late spring

Lilac, as this deciduous shrub is also known, bears large panicles of scented flowers in a range of colours from white to deep purple. This cultivar has deep purplish-pink flowers which open from paler buds. The leaves are heart-shaped and dark green. Lilacs need alkaline soil and sun to flourish, and prefer the soil fertile and well-drained. If required prune after flowering. Propagate from softwood cuttings in summer. Susceptible to leaf miners, leaf spot and lilac blight.

Tagetes patula

French marigold
HEIGHT: 12in (30cm) • Half-hardy
FLOWERING SEASON: Summer

This marigold, known as the French marigold has rust-coloured or bright yellow single or double flowers, and there is a wide range of varieties, some dwarf. The feathery, deep green foliage gives off a pungent scent when crushed. A half-hardy annual, it is normally grown from seed sown in warmth in early spring. Plant out the seedlings after the last frosts. Does best in rich soil, but will cope with poor soil. Deadhead to encourage a longer flowering period.

Verbena × hybrida

HEIGHT: 12in (30cm) • Tender
FLOWERING SEASON: Summer/autumn

These hybrids are treated as summer-flowering annuals, much in favour for window-boxes and hanging baskets, as they produce a wealth of flowerheads in many bright colours ranging from white, pink, purple and red to blue. There are tall and dwarf types, and cultivars that comprise several colours, such as Sparkle Mixed which is bushier and more dwarf in habit. Likes sun and well-drained soil. Pinch out the leading shoots of young plants for bushier growth. Susceptible to aphids.

Viburnum × burkwoodii

HEIGHT: 8ft (2.4m) • Hardy
FLOWERING SEASON: Spring

This evergreen viburnum has bronze-tinged foliage and very highly scented flowers, which are pink when in bud, opening to wide flat heads of white flowers throughout spring. There is a variety, 'Park Farm Hybrid', which has larger flowers and 'Anne Russell' has very fragrant flowers. The older leaves turn bright red in the autumn. Grows in most garden soils but prefers slightly acid soil which does not dry out and full sun. Thin out old wood in late spring. Propagate from lateral shoots in summer. Can be prone to aphid and whitefly attacks and scale insect.

Viburnum carlesii

HEIGHT: 4ft (1.2m) • Hardy
FLOWERING SEASON: Late spring

This deciduous viburnum has ovate mid green leaves that are slightly rough and produces highly fragrant rounded heads of waxy pink flowers which turn to white in late spring. There are cultivars with different characteristics: 'Aurora' has pale pink flowers, opening from reddish buds, as does 'Diana', which also has a more compact habit. Grow in full sun, in moist garden soil. It is a good idea to grow a number of viburnums together. Propagate from heel cuttings in late summer or layer shoots in autumn. Prone to aphid attacks.

Viburnum farreri

HEIGHT: 8ft (2.4m) • Hardy
FLOWERING SEASON: Winter

Formerly known as *V. fragrans* this is one of the relatively few scented winter-flowering shrubs, it has bright green oval toothed leaves that are bronze-tinged when young. The heavily scented white flowers with a pink tinge are borne in hanging clusters from autumn through mild periods in the winter to the spring. The cultivar 'Candissimum' has light green foliage and pure white flowers. Grow in full sun, in moist garden soil. Propagate from heel cuttings in late summer or layer shoots in autumn. Prone to aphid attacks.

Viola odorata

Sweet violet
HEIGHT: 6in (15cm) • Hardy
FLOWERING SEASON: Spring

Known as the sweet violet, and native to many temperate parts of the world, this small plant spreads quickly by means of runners, to form colonies. It has small, heart-shaped, mid green leaves and lightly scented, violet-blue, pansy-like flowers in early spring. There are a number of cultivars, including *V. o.* 'Alba' which is a winter-flowering white violet and *V.* 'Czar' which is a dark purple. Plant in autumn or spring in partial shade. Sow from seed in spring.

Wisteria sinensis

Chinese wisteria
HEIGHT: 100ft (30m) • Hardy
FLOWERING SEASON: Late spring

This wisteria, known as Chinese wisteria, is one of the most vigorous climbers. It has long drooping racemes of pale violet flowers that are lightly scented and cover the whole plant profusely. The leaves are attractive, light green, with about twelve leaflets. There is a white cultivar, 'Alba' and *W. venusta* var. *violacea* has violet flowers. Plant in moist, rich soil on a south- or west-facing wall if possible. Can also be trained into a standard. Propagate from heel cuttings in late summer.

Wisteria sinensis 'Alba'

Chinese wisteria
HEIGHT: 100ft (30m) • Hardy
FLOWERING SEASON: Late spring

The white cultivar of the Chinese wisteria, *W. s.* 'Alba' shares the characteristics of the species plant. New plants require careful training and pruning. After the first year select three to five shoots to form the main frame of the plant, cut them back by half and tie them to support wires. At the end of the summer cut all the thin whippy shoots back to five buds and in winter, shorten all growths to two buds. Wisterias seldom flower within the first five years.

More Scented Plants

Large numbers of garden plants are scented and in many ways it might be easier to make a list of those which are not. The only plants to avoid are perhaps, ligustrum (privet) whose flowers have an overpower-ing, rather nasty, smell in the summer and those plants aptly called *foetidissima* (fetid – stinking). Many roses, but not all, have a lovely scent as do the majority of bulbs and tuberous plants which appear in their own section at the beginning of this chapter. We have therefore not included any roses or bulbs in the lists below nor have we added any plants as there simply isn't room to list more than a tiny fraction of those available. We have included plants with fragrant foliage like salvias as well as those with fragrant flowers.

TREES AND SHRUBS

Abelia × grandiflora
Carpenteria californica
Caryopteris × clandonensis
Cercidiphyllum japonicum
Choisya ternata
Clethra arborea
Coronilla valentina ssp. *glauca*

Corylopsis pauciflora
Crataegus (in variety)
Cytisus battandieri
Deutzia scabra 'Plena'
Eucalyptus gunnii
Fothergilla major
Genista aetnensis
Hamamelis × intermedia
Laburnum × watereri 'Vossii'
Lavandula angustifolia
Lonicera nitida
Osmanthus delavayi
Philadelphus coronarius 'Variegatus'
Phillyrea latifolia
Phlomis fruticosa
Populus balsamifera
  P. × candicans 'Aurora'
Prunus (in variety)
Rhododendron – azaleas (in variety)
Robinia pseudoacacia
Ruta graveolens 'Jackman's Blue'
Salvia officinalis Purpurascens Group
Skimmia japonica
Spartium junceum
Styrax officinalis
Syringa × henryi

PERENNIALS AND CLIMBERS

Centaurea moschata
Crambe cordifolia
Dianthus 'Doris'
Erysimum cheiri
Galium odoratum

Jasminum officinale
Lathyrus grandiflorus
  L. latifolius
Lonicera × brownii 'Dropmore Scarlet'
  L. periclymenum 'Belgica'
  L. × tellmanniana
Petasites japonicus
Romneya coulteri
Saxifraga cuneifolia
Trachelospermum jasminoides
Wisteria floribunda

GARDENING
through the
YEAR

NTRODUCTION

CCESS DOES NOT COME WITHOUT EFFORT OR
w-how, however, even for the experienced
lener. For the beginner, success depends
ely on sound advice for all those essential
s that lie behind the well-kept garden that we
dmire.

you are not sure what you should be doing
y, this book will tell you *and* show you. Jobs
e been arranged by seasons rather than precise
rks, as gardening is very much dependent on
weather, and precise dates can be misleading
even potentially hazardous to your plants.
ou cannot garden successfully by the calendar
ne. Frosts can come early in autumn or occur
xpectedly in early summer. The ground may
rozen when you would like to be planting, or
dry when you want to sow your summer
ls. Use the suggested timings as a guide, but
repared to bring things forward or put them
k to suit your own area and the particular
on.

he most time-critical jobs are likely to be in
ng and autumn, and when frost-tender plants
put outside or taken in. If in doubt about the
t time, it is always worth making a note of
en your local parks department does the job.
Vinter jobs, on the other hand, are usually less
e-critical and in many cases it will not matter
ou move a job backwards or forwards by as
ch as a month. This is fortunate as it gives you
opportunity to delay a job if the weather is
sh, and to make up for lost time during those
ghter spells.

LEFT: *Azaleas are
popular shrubs, but
they require an acid
soil. You can use a
simple kit to check the
soil acidity.*

RIGHT: *Modern
solidago hybrids are
excellent border
plants for late
summer.*

LEFT: *Varieties of
Anemone x
hybrida and A.
hupehensis come
into their own when
most border flowers
are over.*

LEFT: *The
delightful
evergreen perennial
Liriope Muscari.*

RIGHT: Sorbus
aucuparia *will
sometimes retain its
berries into winter if
birds don't eat them
first.*

SPRING

This is a time when gardeners need no encouragement.
With lengthening days, the air less chilly, and plump buds and birdsong
to stir the imagination, it is the time when gardeners cannot wait to start
propagating and planting. Early spring is a time for caution, however,
as winter seldom comes to a convenient end as spring approaches.
One of the most common causes of disappointment for novice gardeners is
sowing or planting too early – especially outdoors. Often, plants and
seeds put out several weeks later in the season overtake ones planted
earlier because they are less likely to receive a check to growth.

OPPOSITE: *Even small spring flowers make a*
strong display, like this group of narcissi,
pulmonarias, and Anemone blanda.

ABOVE: *Tulips are among the most beautiful*
spring flowers, but they look even better when
interplanted with forget-me-nots.

EARLY SPRING

In cold regions the weather can still be icy in early spring, but in mild climates you can make a start on many outdoor jobs. If sowing or planting outdoors, bear in mind that soil temperature as well as air temperature is important. Few seeds will germinate if the soil temperature is below 7°C (45°F), so use a soil thermometer to check before you sow.

JOBS IN BRIEF

The kitchen garden

- ☐ Apply manures and fertilizers where appropriate
- ☐ Plant onion sets and shallots
- ☐ Warm up the soil with cloches
- ☐ Sow early crops in cold frames or beneath cloches
- ☐ Start sowing vegetables without protection if you live in a mild area – many kinds can be sown from early spring onwards, so check the packets as some varieties are more suitable than others for early sowing
- ☐ Use horticultural fleece or floating cloches for early crops if you don't have conventional cloches
- ☐ Chit 'seed' potatoes
- ☐ Apply fertilizer to fruit bushes if they need it
- ☐ Put cloches over strawberries if you want an early crop
- ☐ Plant new strawberries

BELOW: *Plant strawberries, but make sure they are healthy and disease-free.*

The flower garden

- ☐ Finish planting bare-root trees and shrubs
- ☐ Plant container-grown shrubs
- ☐ Plant herbaceous plants
- ☐ Sow hardy annuals
- ☐ Feed and mulch beds and borders
- ☐ Plant gladioli and summer bulbs

BELOW: *Sow a new lawn when the weather is mild and moist.*

- ☐ Start mowing the lawn, but cut high initially
- ☐ Sow a new lawn or lay a lawn from turf
- ☐ Buy seeds and bulbs if not already done so
- ☐ Sow sweet peas
- ☐ Spring prune shrubs, if applicable
- ☐ Tidy up the rock garden, and apply fresh stone chippings where necessary

The greenhouse and conservatory

- ☐ Take chrysanthemum cuttings
- ☐ Start off begonia and gloxinia tubers
- ☐ Pot up pelargonium and fuchsia cuttings rooted earlier
- ☐ Pot up chrysanthemums rooted earlier

BELOW: *Pot up cuttings as soon as they are growing vigorously.*

- ☐ Take dahlia cuttings
- ☐ Sow seeds of bedding plants and pot plants
- ☐ Prick out or pot up seedlings sown earlier
- ☐ Increase ventilation on warm days
- ☐ Check plants for signs of pests and diseases, which often begin to multiply rapidly as the temperatures rise

PLANTS AT THEIR BEST

Bergenia (non-woody evergreen)
Camellia (shrub)
Chionodoxa (bulb)
Crocus (bulb)
Eranthis hyemalis (bulb)
Garrya elliptica (shrub)
Helleborus orientalis (herbaceous)
Hyacinthus (bulb)
Iris reticulata (bulb)
Magnolia stellata (shrub)
Mahonia (shrub)
Muscari armeniacum (bulb)
Primula × *polyantha*
(herbaceous)
Prunus cerasifera (tree)
Tulipa kaufmanniana (bulb)

ABOVE: *A* Tulipa kaufmanniana *variety.*

LEFT: Iris reticulata.

BELOW: *Chionodoxas and crocuses.*

PLANT ONION SETS

The biggest onions are usually grown from seed, but unless you can give them the dedicated care they need the results will be disappointing. Sets (small onion bulbs) are an almost foolproof way to grow onions, and you should be rewarded with a reasonable crop for very little effort.

1 Take out a shallow drill with the corner of a hoe or rake, using a garden line for a straight row. Space the sets about 15cm (6in) apart.

2 Pull the soil back over the drill, but leave the tips of the onions protruding. If birds are a problem – they may try to pull the onions out by the wispy old stems – protect with netting or keep pushing the bulbs back until rooted.

PLANT SHALLOTS

Shallots are useful for pickling, but also store well for use like onions. They are almost always grown from bulbs, bought or saved from last year's crop.

1 Planted in the same way as onion sets, shallots are spaced about 15cm (6in) apart, but the bulbs are larger, so the drill might have to be a little deeper. Push the bulbs into the base of the drill so that the tip is just protruding. Pull the soil back round them with a hoe or rake.

2 Shallots are useful for an early crop, and you can usually plant them outdoors in late winter, except in very cold regions. If you missed the winter planting but still want to get them growing quickly, start them off in individual pots.

3 Keep the pots in a cold frame or greenhouse until the shoots are 3–5cm (1–2in) high. Then plant the sprouted shallots in the garden, spacing them about 15cm (6in) apart.

SOW EARLY VEGETABLES OUTDOORS

Early sowing can be a gamble. If the weather is cold the seeds may rot before they germinate, and some vegetables tend to run to seed if they are subject to very cold conditions after germinating.

Concentrate early sowings on hardy crops like broad beans and early peas. Try a few short rows of a wider range of vegetables, but be prepared to resow if they don't do well.

1 Peas are best sown in multiple rows so that they can support each other, with walking space between the double or triple rows. Broad beans are also often grown in multiple rows. Take out a flat-bottomed drill 5–8cm (2–3in) deep.

2 Space the seeds by hand. Peas are often sown in three staggered rows, spacing the seeds about 4cm (1½in) apart, but you can double this space and still get a good crop. Broad beans are sown in two rows with each seed about 23cm (9in) apart.

3 Pull the soil back over the drill to cover the seeds. If the ground is dry, water well until the seedlings are through. If seed-eaters such as mice are a problem, netting or traps may be necessary.

AN EARLY START

Peas and beans germinate readily in warm soil, but are less reliable in early spring when the soil temperature fluctuates. You can be more sure of

your early peas if you start the seeds off in a greenhouse or cold frame first, then plant them out when they are growing well.

1 A length of old gutter is ideal for starting off the seeds. Block the ends and fill with soil.

2 Sow the seeds about 5–8cm (2–3in) apart, cover, then keep warm and moist.

3 When ready to plant out, take out a shallow drill with a draw hoe, and gradually slide the peas out of the gutter and into the row.

FERTILIZE THE VEGETABLE PLOT

The vegetable plot needs regular feeding if yields are not to suffer. Unlike beds and borders in the ornamental garden, little natural recycling occurs. The crops are removed and leaves do not naturally fall and decay. Bulky organic manures do much to improve soil structure and increase the nutrient-holding capabilities of the soil, but unless you follow an intensive organic approach and apply sufficient manures and garden compost, some chemical fertilizers are necessary if you want a heavy crop.

INDIVIDUAL BOOSTERS

Throughout the growing season, certain vegetables may need boosters from specific fertilizers or quick-acting general fertilizers whenever growth seems to need encouraging. Spring cabbages often benefit from a light dressing of a nitrogenous fertilizer to stimulate the growth of fresh young leaves now that the weather is improving. Fruit crops, such as tomatoes, benefit from a high-potash feed.

1 The quickest way to apply a general fertilizer to your vegetable plot is with a wheeled spreader that you can adjust to deliver the appropriate amount. Calculate and test the delivery rate first.

2 If applying by hand, measure out the amount of fertilizer required for a square metre or yard, so that you can visualize how much you need. Or pour it into a small container as a measure and note how full it is.

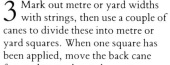

3 Mark out metre or yard widths with strings, then use a couple of canes to divide these into metre or yard squares. When one square has been applied, move the back cane forward to mark out the next area.

4 Use your measure to scoop up the appropriate amount of fertilizer (use the application rates advised on the packet as a guide), then scatter it evenly. Hold the hand about 15–23cm (6–9in) above the soil.

5 Always rake the fertilizer into the surface. This spreads it more evenly and helps it to penetrate more rapidly.

HORTICULTURAL FLEECE

Horticultural fleece is a material that a previous generation of gardeners didn't possess, but the fact that it is now widely used commercially is evidence of its usefulness. The fleece will warm up the soil rather like a cloche, and should provide protection from a degree or two of frost. It also offers protection from animals such as rabbits and pests such as butterflies. You can use it just to start off your seeds, or as protection for a growing crop.

1 Sow your seeds then cover the area with the fleece. Anchor it down loosely with bricks or stones initially, while you secure the edges.

2 You can secure the edges with soil. Make a slit to tuck the end into, or just heap soil over the edges. Water will flow through the fleece, and it will also stretch a little as the plants grow.

3 You can buy various designs of proprietary pegs to hold the fleece in position, and these are preferable to the soil method as they make it easier to lift and replace the fleece for weeding and other cultivation tasks.

FLOATING CLOCHES

Other types of protective covers can also be used successfully. Some are very fine, long-lasting nets (see top), which give little frost protection but effectively keep out most animals and pests, others are perforated plastic films (see above) that let rain through and 'give' enough to rise with the growing crop.

You will have to pull them back to weed and thin. You will find that weeds thrive with the protection as well as the crops!

SOW HARDY ANNUALS

Hardy annuals are among the easiest plants to grow – they are undemanding of soil and are simply sown where they are to grow. Provided you thin overcrowded seedlings and give them a sunny position, the results are almost always bright and pleasing.

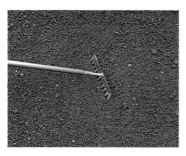

1 It pays to prepare the ground by clearing it of weeds, and raking the surface to a fine, crumbly structure.

2 If you are growing just for cutting, sow in rows in a spare piece of ground, but if you want to make a bright border of hardy annuals, 'draw' your design on the ground with sand and grit.

3 Use the corner of a hoe or rake to draw shallow drills, but change the direction of the drills from one block to the next to avoid a regimented appearance. Check the packet for spacing between rows.

4 Sprinkle the seeds as evenly as possible. If the weather is very dry, run water into the bottom of each drill first and allow it to soak in.

5 Write and insert a label, then cover the seeds by raking the soil back over the drills. Try not to disturb the seeds unnecessarily.

SOWING BROADCAST

Sowing in rows makes thinning and weeding much easier – especially if you don't know what the seedlings look like and find it difficult to distinguish desirable seedlings from weeds. Sometimes, however, the seeds are sown broadcast (scattered randomly) to create a more informal patch of flowers. This is particularly useful for a packet of mixed annuals, for example, where you might want to create the appearance of a wild garden.

Scatter the seeds as evenly as possible (see above), then rake them in – first in one direction and then at right angles.

6 Water thoroughly if the soil is dry and rain is not forecast. Continue to water in dry weather until the seedlings have emerged.

PLANT GLADIOLI

Gladioli are popular, and easy to grow, but their location in the flower garden needs careful thought. Grow them in rows in a spare piece of ground if you want them for cutting, but they look best planted in blocks or clusters when grown among companion plants.

OTHER BULBS TO PLANT

1 If you are growing gladioli for cutting rather than garden display, grow them in rows. Take out a trench as shown deep enough to cover the corms with about 8–10cm (3–4in) of soil. Deep planting reduces the need for staking.

2 Space the corms as recommended on the packet. Planting a double row like this makes supporting easier for tall varieties. Return the soil to the trench to cover them.

Most other summer-flowering bulbs, corms and tubers can be planted in the same way as gladioli, though it is too early to plant any very frost-sensitive plants as the shoots may emerge while frosts are still likely.

As a guide to planting depth, most bulbs should be covered with twice their own depth of soil. If the bulb is 3cm (1in) deep, cover it with 5cm (2in) of soil, though there are a few exceptions.

Some tubers tend to become very dry and shrivelled after a long period in store. You can usually plump them up by soaking in water for a day before you plant, like the anemone tubers shown.

3 If planting in a border among other plants, take out a roughly circular hole, place a group of about five or seven corms in the base, and return the soil. If the ground is heavy, dig in some sand or grit before planting the corms.

4 It is easy to forget where bulbs are planted in a border, so apart from labelling, insert a few small canes around them so that you don't accidentally hoe off the shoots before they emerge.

PLANT SHRUBS

Spring is an ideal time to plant shrubs. You can plant container-grown shrubs in any month provided the ground is not too frozen. However, spring is ideal because the soil is moist and also warm enough for new root growth to help the plant become established quickly.

1 Always clear the area of weeds, and dig out any deep-rooted perennials that will be difficult to eradicate if they grow within the root system of the shrub. Dig in plenty of garden compost or rotted manure.

2 Excavate a large hole, about twice the width of the pot or root-ball. To check the depth, place the plant in position and use a cane or stick across the hole to judge whether the shrub will be at its original depth in the soil.

3 If the roots are dry, water the plant thoroughly then leave for an hour. If roots are wound tightly around the inside of the pot, tease out some of the fine ones to encourage them to grow out into the soil.

4 Place the root-ball in the hole and check that the soil will be level with the potting soil in the root-ball. Return the soil, and firm it well to eliminate large air pockets.

5 To get your shrubs off to a good start, apply a general garden fertilizer at the recommended rate and sprinkle around the plant. Keep away from the stem. Water well.

6 'Balled' or 'root-wrapped' shrubs are sold with their roots wrapped in hessian or a plastic material. Check the depth as before.

7 When the plant is in position, untie the wrapper and slide it out of the hole. Avoid disturbing the ball of soil around the roots.

8 Replace the soil, and firm well to eliminate large pockets of air. Apply fertilizer and water as described for container-grown plants.

9 It is worth mulching the ground after planting. It will conserve moisture and some mulches, such as chipped bark, look attractive too.

PLANT HERBACEOUS PLANTS

Herbaceous border plants can be planted at any time from containers, but most gardeners prefer to get them planted in spring so that they contribute to the summer show.

If you buy plants by mail order they may arrive as small root-wrapped plants, and these should be planted before the new shoots emerge, or are still very short.

ROOT-WRAPPED HERBACEOUS PLANTS

If your herbaceous plants are root-wrapped, keep them in a cool, shady place until you are ready to plant. Make sure that the plants are kept moist at all times.

Remove the wrapping only just before you are ready to plant. Spread the roots out widely within the planting hole before returning the soil.

Root-wrapped plants are more vulnerable than container-grown plants until they become established, so take extra care and keep them well watered.

1 If planting a border, lay the plants out first so that you can visualize the result (don't forget to allow for growth!). It is easier to move them around at this stage, before planting.

2 Water the plants about an hour before you start, and knock them out of their pots only when you are ready to plant.

3 Ensure the ground is clear of weeds before planting, and work methodically from the back of the border or from one end. Most can be planted with a trowel but you may need a spade for large plants.

4 Return the soil, making sure that the plant is at its original depth, and firm well to eliminate any large pockets of air that could cause the roots to dry out.

5 Water the plants thoroughly unless the weather is wet or heavy rain is forecast.

SOW A NEW LAWN

The advantage of a lawn from seed is that it is usually less expensive than turf and you can choose the grass seed mixture. Some turf specialists also offer seed mixtures to suit your specific requirements, but these can be expensive.

Thorough ground preparation is essential for a quality lawn, and this should start several weeks before sowing. If you don't have time to prepare the ground properly this spring, wait and sow in the autumn instead.

1 Dig the ground thoroughly, and make every effort to eliminate difficult or deep-rooted perennial weeds. Then rake the soil level. Use pegs marked with lines drawn 5cm (2in) down from the top as a guide, having checked with a spirit-level on a straight-edge that the pegs are level.

2 Allow the soil to settle for a week, then consolidate it further by treading it evenly to remove large air pockets. The best way to do this is to shuffle your feet over the area, first in one direction then at right angles.

3 Rake the consolidated soil to produce a fine crumbly structure suitable for sowing seeds. If you can, leave the area for a couple of weeks to allow weed seeds to germinate. Hoe them off or use a weedkiller that leaves the ground safe for replanting within days.

4 Use string to divide the area into 1m (1yd) strips, and divide these into 1m (1yd) lengths. Move the canes along the strips as you sow.

5 Use a small container that holds enough seed for a square metre or square yard (make a mark on it if the amount only partly fills the container). Scatter the seeds as evenly as possible with a sweeping motion of the hand.

6 If you have to sow a large area it might be worth hiring a seed/ fertilizer distributor that you can simply wheel over the area. Always check the delivery rate over sheets of paper or plastic first. Lightly rake the seed into the surface. Use a water sprinkler if necessary to keep the soil moist until the seeds germinate.

LAY A LAWN FROM TURF

Turf provides the best method of creating a lawn quickly – you can use it within months – and soil preparation is a little less demanding. You will usually find that it is a more expensive option than seed, but many gardeners are happy to pay a premium for the convenience.

1 Dig and consolidate the soil as described for seed, but there is no need to leave it for a few weeks to allow weed seeds to germinate – the turf will prevent them from germinating. Start by laying the turf along a straight edge.

2 Use a plank to stand on while you lay the next row, as this will help to distribute your weight. Stagger the joints between rows to create a bond like brickwork. If using turf as a long roll there will be fewer joints. Make sure these do not align.

3 Tamp down each row of turf (you can use the head of a rake as shown), then roll the plank forwards to lay the next row.

ABOVE: *A lawn can create a sense of space and is often the central part of the garden. Here an informal shape creates a natural look.*

4 Brush sieved sandy soil, or a mixture of peat and sand, into the joints. This will help to bind the turves together.

5 Shape edges when the lawn is laid. Lay a hose or rope to form the shape for a curved edge, or use a straight-edged piece of wood for a straight edge, and trim with a half-moon edger.

SPRING PRUNE SHRUBS

Only prune shrubs that you know require spring pruning, otherwise you may cut out the shoots that will bear this year's flowers. Advice is given below for some popular shrubs that need spring pruning, but if in doubt about others consult an encyclopedia that gives pruning information.

1 Prune shrubs grown for coloured winter stems shortly before new growth starts. These include *Cornus alba* and *Cornus stolonifera* varieties and *Salix alba* 'Chermesina' (syn. 'Britzensis'). Only prune plants that have been established for a few years.

2 Cut back all the stems to an outward-facing bud about 5cm (2in) from the ground or stump of old, hard wood.

3 Although the pruning seems drastic, new shoots will soon appear and by next winter will make a splendid sight. Prune annually if you feed and mulch the plants, otherwise every second spring.

4 Some popular grey-leaved shrubs, such as *Santolina chamaecyparissus* and *Helichrysum angustifolium*, need regular pruning if they are to remain neat and compact.

5 If you prune the plant regularly from a young age, prune back close to the base to a point where you can see new shoots developing. This may be as low as 10cm (4in) from the ground on some plants, but on old, woody plants you will have to leave a taller framework of woody shoots.

6 The plant will look bare and sparse after pruning, but within a month should be well clothed again.

WHITEWASH BRAMBLES

A few shrubs related to the blackberry are grown for their white winter stems. The shoots arise from ground level like raspberry canes, and these are best cut back every year. Cut all the stems off close to the ground. New shoots will soon grow and the plant will be just as attractive next winter.

7 *Buddleia davidii* produces its flowers at the tops of tall, lanky stems if left unpruned. Each spring, cut back all the shoots to within about two buds of the previous year's growth, close to the old stump.

8 Again, this type of pruning looks drastic but it will greatly enhance the look of the plant later in the year.

PRUNE ROSES

Trials have shown that you can achieve very good results from hybrid tea (large-flowered) and floribunda (cluster-flowered) roses simply by cutting them roughly to an even height with secateurs, or even a hedgetrimmer, without worrying about the detailed pruning shown here. The conventional method is still practised by most rose enthusiasts, however. Don't worry if you make one or two wrong cuts – the roses will probably still bloom prolifically.

1 Moderate pruning is the most appropriate for established hybrid tea roses. Cut back the stems by about half, to an outward-facing bud to keep the centre of the bush open.

2 You can treat floribundas in the same way, but if you prune some shoots severely and others lightly, flowering may be spread over a longer period. Prune the oldest shoots back close to the base, those that grew last year by about a third only.

3 Whichever type of rose you are pruning, cut back any dead or diseased shoots to healthy wood.

START OFF BEGONIA AND GLOXINIA TUBERS

Tuberous-rooted begonias can be grown as pot-plants or in the garden, but wherever they are destined it is well worth starting them into growth now in the greenhouse. This way you will have well-developed plants to put in the garden that will flower much earlier than if the tubers were planted directly into the soil.

Gloxinias, which are suitable only for cultivation in the home or greenhouse, should also be started into growth now.

1 If you are growing your begonias as pot-plants, start them off in small pots to save space in the early stages. Loosely fill the pots with a peat-based or peat-substitute mixture intended for seeds or cuttings.

2 If the tubers have small shoots it will be obvious which is the top, otherwise look for the side with a slight hollow and keep this upwards. Just press the tuber into the compost. Keep in a warm, light place, ideally in a greenhouse.

3 If the begonias are intended for outdoors, perhaps in containers or baskets, start them off in trays instead of pots as this will save space.

LEFT: 'Pin-up' is an outstanding single tuberous-rooted begonia that can be raised from seed to flower in its first year or overwintered as a dry tuber.

4 Gloxinia tubers are started into growth in the same way, but as they will be grown as pot-plants you may prefer to plant them in their final 13–15cm (5–6in) pots. The 'hairy' side (the remains of old roots) is the one to press into the compost.

POT UP AND POT ON CUTTINGS

Pot up cuttings, such as those of pelargoniums and fuchsias, to ensure that their growth rate is not checked. With warmer temperatures they will now be growing vigorously.

1 Pot up the cuttings as soon as they have formed strong root growth. Use an 8–10cm (3–4in) pot and a potting mixture suitable for young plants. Water thoroughly, then keep out of direct sunlight for a couple of days while they recover from the root disturbance.

2 Cuttings that rooted earlier and have already been potted up for a month or more may need moving into larger pots. Check that the roots have filled the potting mixture before you transfer them. If the mixture has lots of white roots, pot on into a larger size.

3 Use a pot a couple of sizes larger, and trickle the same kind of potting mix around the root-ball. Firm well to remove air pockets, and water thoroughly.

ENCOURAGE BUSHY FUCHSIAS

Bush-shaped fuchsias respond well to early 'pruning' and training. You can start as soon as the cuttings have three pairs of leaves.

1 Pinch out the growing tip of your fuchsia cuttings once three pairs of leaves have formed, if you want a bushy shape.

2 New shoots will form after a few weeks, but for really bushy plants pinch out the tips of these sideshoots too. Repeat this process several times throughout spring to encourage well-shaped bushy plants.

SAVING SPACE IN THE GREENHOUSE

Greenhouse space is often a problem at this time of year. If you are growing cuttings for the garden rather than as pot-plants, keep the young plants in small pots rather than potting them on into larger ones. To avoid a check to growth, however, you must feed the young plants regularly to avoid starvation. Move them to a frost-free cold frame as soon as it is warm enough to do so, and allow plenty of space between the plants so that the leaves are not overcrowded.

PRICK OUT SEEDLINGS

Prick out seedlings as soon as they are large enough to handle. If you leave them in their original trays or pots too long, they will quickly become overcrowded and difficult to separate without damage. Some plants are best pricked out into individual pots (see opposite), but this takes up a lot of space and compost, so most bedding plants are pricked out into trays. Instead of pricking out into trays, you can use a modular or cell system, like the one shown here, where each plant has its own pocket of soil, separated from the others. The benefit of this method is that there will be less root disturbance when the plants are eventually put into the garden.

1 Choose a module that suits the size of plant. A small seedling such as ageratum or fibrous-rooted begonia will not need such a large cell as, say, a dahlia. Fill the individual cells loosely with a potting mixture suitable for seedlings.

2 Strike the compost off level with a straight-edge, but do not compress it. It will settle lower in the cells once the seedlings have been inserted and watered.

3 Loosen the seedlings in the tray or pot you are pricking out from, and if possible lift them one at a time by their seed leaves. These are the first ones to open, and they are usually smaller and a different shape to the true leaves.

4 Use a tool designed for the purpose, or improvise with something like a pencil or plant label, to make a hole large enough to take the roots with as little bending or disturbance as possible.

5 Gently firm the compost around the roots, being careful not to press too hard. Water thoroughly, then keep the plants out of direct sunlight for a couple of days.

ABOVE: *The white alyssum and bright golden annual rudbeckias are among many colourful annuals to be pricked out now.*

PRICK OUT INTO POTS

Some plants, such as bedding pelargoniums and pot-plants for the greenhouse and home, are best pricked out into individual pots rather than trays or even modules.

1 Fill small pots with potting mixture and firm it lightly, using the base of another pot.

2 Loosen the compost with a small dibber or transplanting tool. Hold the seedling by its leaves, not the stem.

3 Make a small hole in the centre of the pot, deep enough to take the roots without damage.

PRICKING OUT TINY SEEDLINGS

4 While still holding the seedling by a leaf, very gently firm the potting mixture around the roots, using a small dibber or a finger. Don't press too hard as watering will also settle the mixture around the roots.

5 Water carefully so that the potting mixture is settled around the roots without washing the plant out. Keep the seedlings in a warm, humid place out of direct sunlight for a few days.

Seedlings are almost always pricked out individually, but there are a few special cases when more than a single seedling is used. Lobelia seedlings are tiny, and individual plants not very substantial, so many gardeners prick out a small group of seedlings together, as shown. Prick out about five or six plants at a time, though the number is not critical. Pricking out tiny seedlings in small groups like this also makes the job much quicker and easier, but it is only recommended for certain plants.

By the time these grow into seedlings large enough to plant out they look like one substantial plant.

6 Writing labels for individual pots is tedious and you probably won't want to do it, yet confusion later is highly probable if you have lots of pots containing different varieties. Group individual varieties into trays, and use just one label.

MID SPRING

FOR MANY GARDENERS MID SPRING IS the most exciting as well as the busiest time of the year. The garden looks colourful again by this time, seedlings and cuttings are growing fast, and outdoor sowing and planting can begin in earnest. This is often a time when priorities have to be decided if it isn't possible to keep up with all those urgent jobs. If you don't know whether something can wait, check in the Jobs In Brief notes for late spring: this may enable you to decide what can be delayed. Plants sown or planted in late spring often catch up with those sown a month earlier if the weather happens to be unseasonably cold.

JOBS IN BRIEF

The kitchen garden

- ☐ Apply manures and fertilizers where appropriate
- ☐ Plant onion sets
- ☐ Plant asparagus crowns
- ☐ Continue to sow in cold frames or beneath cloches for earlier crops
- ☐ Start sowing vegetables without protection – many kinds can be sown from mid spring onwards, so check the packets
- ☐ Use horticultural fleece or floating cloches for early crops if you don't have conventional cloches
- ☐ Plant potatoes
- ☐ Plant out vegetable seedlings such as cabbages
- ☐ Apply fertilizer to fruit bushes if they need it
- ☐ Put cloches over strawberries if you want an early crop
- ☐ Plant new strawberries

BELOW: *Plant cabbage and cauliflower plants when the weather is moist and mild.*

The flower garden

- ☐ Plant and stock the pond
- ☐ Divide over-large pond plants
- ☐ Plant container-grown shrubs
- ☐ Plant herbaceous plants
- ☐ Stake herbaceous plants
- ☐ Sow hardy annuals
- ☐ Feed and mulch beds and borders

BELOW: *Aquatics are best planted before growth is advanced.*

- ☐ Plant a hedge
- ☐ Plant gladioli and summer bulbs
- ☐ Mow the lawn regularly from now on
- ☐ Make a new lawn from seed or turf
- ☐ Buy seeds and bulbs if not already done so
- ☐ Plant out sweet peas raised in pots
- ☐ Sow sweet peas where they are to flower
- ☐ Plant ranunculus tubers

The greenhouse and conservatory

- ☐ Sow tender vegetables such as outdoor tomatoes and runner beans to plant out later, and cucumbers for the greenhouse
- ☐ Start begonia and gloxinia tubers into growth
- ☐ Pot up pelargonium and fuchsia cuttings rooted earlier
- ☐ Pot up or pot on into larger pots chrysanthemums rooted earlier
- ☐ Take dahlia cuttings
- ☐ Sow seeds of bedding plants and pot plants
- ☐ Prick out or pot up seedlings sown earlier
- ☐ Take leaf cuttings of saintpaulias and streptocarpus

BELOW: *Softwood cuttings of many shrubs can be taken now, including fuchsias.*

PLANTS AT THEIR BEST

Amelanchier (shrub/tree)
Bergenia (non-woody evergreen)
Cytisus, various (shrub)
Dicentra (herbaceous)
Doronicum (herbaceous)
Forsythia (shrub)
Helleborus orientalis (herbaceous)
Hyacinthus (bulb)
Magnolia × *soulangiana* (tree)
Magnolia stellata (shrub)
Mahonia, various (shrub)
Muscari armeniacum (bulb)
Narcissus (bulb)
Primula × *polyantha* (herbaceous)
Prunus 'Kwanzan' (tree)
Pulsatilla vulgaris (rock plant)
Rhododendron, various (shrub)
Ribes sanguineum (shrub)
Saxifraga, various (rock plant)
Tulipa, various (bulb)

LEFT: *Rhododendrons come in many sizes and colours. Most grow tall, but some are compact enough for a small garden.*

BELOW: *Aubrietas and saxifragas can always be relied upon for a colourful display, set off here by green bergenia and juniper foliage.*

SOW MAINCROP VEGETABLES OUTDOORS

Vegetable sowing begins in earnest now, with crops like beetroot, spinach beet, summer cabbages, salad and pickling onions, scorzonera and turnips, as well as further sowings of lettuces, peas, radishes, spinach, carrots and cauliflowers. Dwarf beans can be sown in mild areas.

1 Break the soil down into a fine crumbly structure, and level with a rake before sowing.

2 Heavy soils may be difficult to break down into a fine structure with the rake, especially if the soil is dry. Treading on the largest lumps usually helps to break them down.

3 Once the soil is reasonably fine, rake it level, and remove any large stones at the same time.

4 Most vegetables grown in rows, such as beetroots and carrots, are best sown in drills. Always use a garden line to make sure the drills – and therefore the rows – are straight.

5 Take out a shallow drill with the corner of a hoe or rake. Always refer to the seed packet for the recommended depth.

6 Flood the drills with water a few minutes before sowing if the weather is dry. Do it before sowing rather than after so that the seeds are not washed away or into clumps.

7 Sprinkle the seeds thinly and evenly along the drill. Do this carefully now and you will save time later when you would have to thin the seedlings if they come up too quickly.

8 Remove the garden line, then use your feet to shuffle the excavated soil back into the drills as you walk along the row. This technique is easy to master.

9 Use a rake to return soil to the drills if you find it easier, but rake in the direction of the row and not across it, otherwise you might spread the seeds and produce an uneven row

FLUID SOWING

Fluid sowing is a technique some gardeners use to get the more difficult seeds off to a flying start. Parsnips, early carrots, onions and parsley are among the vegetables sometimes sown this way.

1 Sow the seeds thickly on damp kitchen paper, and keep in a warm place to germinate. Make sure that they remain moist, and check daily to monitor germination.

2 Once the roots emerge, and before the leaves open, wash the seeds into a sieve and mix them into prepared wallpaper paste (no fungicide) or a special sowing gel.

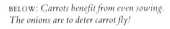

BELOW: *Carrots benefit from even sowing. The onions are to deter carrot fly!*

USING PREPARED SOWING STRIPS

From time to time strips of pre-sown seeds, embedded in a degradable material, may be available. These are an expensive way to buy seeds, but save much time and energy normally spent on spacing and thinning.

Take out a drill as advised and place the strip on edge in the drill. Return the soil to the drill, and keep the ground moist.

Because the seeds receive protection from the material in which they are embedded, and this sometimes also contains nutrients to give the seedlings a boost, you may find it an easy way to achieve a row of well-spaced seedlings.

3 Take out the drill in the normal way, and to the usual depth.

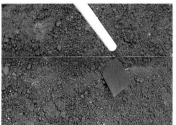

4 Fill a plastic bag with the paste and cut off one corner (rather like an icing bag). Don't make the hole too large. Twist the top of the bag to prevent the paste oozing out, then move along the row as you squeeze out the seeds in the paste.

PLANT POTATOES

It is safe to plant potatoes in most areas, as it will take several weeks before the frost-sensitive shoots emerge from the soil, and these can be protected by earthing up the plants. In cold areas, however, it is best to chit your potatoes (see below) and delay planting for a couple of weeks. The use of cloches, floating cloches or fleece is wise in areas where frost is still likely.

1 Use a draw hoe, spade or a rake head to make wide flat-bottomed or V-shaped drills 10–13cm (4–5in) deep. Space the rows about 43cm (17in) apart for early varieties, 68cm (2¼ft) for second earlies, and 75cm (2½ft) for the maincrop.

2 Space the tubers about 30–45cm (12–18in) apart in the rows. Make sure that the shoots or 'eyes' (buds about to grow into shoots) face upwards. For larger tubers, leave only three sprouts per plant and rub the others off.

CHITTING POTATO TUBERS

Chitting simply means encouraging the potato tubers to sprout before planting. The kind of long shoots that appear when potatoes have been stored in the dark for some time are no use – the shoots must be short and sturdy. Place the tubers in a tray in a light position, perhaps by a window, where there is no risk of frost.

Chitting is useful if you want the tubers to get off to a quick start, as they will usually be through the ground a week or two before unchitted tubers.

3 Cover the tubers by pulling the excavated soil back into the drill.

4 If you don't want the effort of earthing up your potatoes, plant under a black plastic sheet. Bury the edges in slits in the soil and cover with soil to anchor the sheet.

5 Make cross-shaped slits in the plastic with a knife where each tuber is to be planted.

6 Plant through the slit, using a trowel. Make sure that the tuber is covered with 3–5cm (1–2in) of soil. The shoots will find their way through the slits.

PLANT CABBAGES AND CAULIFLOWERS

Cabbages and cauliflowers are not normally sown in their final positions, but started off in seed beds, or sown in late winter and spring in pots or modules in the greenhouse, then transplanted to their growing positions. Buy young plants if you forgot to sow your own.

1 If you have your own seedlings to transplant into the vegetable patch – perhaps growing in a cold frame – water thoroughly an hour before you lift them if the soil is dry.

2 Loosen the soil with a fork or trowel. It is best to lift each one individually with a trowel if possible, but if they have not been thinned sufficiently this may be difficult.

3 Plant with a trowel and firm the soil well. A convenient way to firm soil around the roots is to insert the blade of the trowel about 5cm (2in) away from the plant and press it firmly towards the roots.

4 You can also firm the soil with the handle of the trowel if you don't want to use your hands, but this is not a good idea if the soil is wet as it will dirty the handle. Always water in thoroughly after transplanting.

5 Cabbage and cauliflower seedlings are often raised in modules so that the plants receive less of a shock when transplanted. Many modules are designed so that you can remove the plant by squeezing the base while gently pulling the plant at the top.

PROTECTION FOR EARLY STRAWBERRIES

Strawberries do not need protection from frost, but cloches will bring the crop on earlier and will also help to keep it clean and protect it from birds and other animals.

Cover the plants as soon as possible, but remember to leave access for pollinating insects when the plants are in flower. Most cloches have a system of ventilation that can be used for this on warm days. With polythene tunnel cloches, lift the material along one side to allow for pollination.

ABOVE: *Space cabbages as advised on the packet, as size varies.*

PLANT WATERLILIES

This is a good time to plant up your pond, whether establishing a new one or just adding new plants to an old one. Waterlilies are likely to be much more expensive than the aquatic plants that you plant around the margins of the pool, so it is worth taking special care.

1 Planting baskets are usually used for plants that grow around the edge of a pond, but for deep-water plants like waterlilies a washing-up bowl is ideal. Use a heavy soil that is not too rich in nutrients, available from aquatic specialists.

2 Never add ordinary fertilizers to the soil, as these are likely to encourage a proliferation of algae that will turn the water green. Use a special slow-release fertilizer, preferably one sold specifically for aquatic plants.

USING OXYGENATING PLANTS

Many oxygenating plants, such as elodea, remain below the surface and have little visual appeal. These are used because they are efficient at releasing oxygen into the water, which helps to keep it healthy for fish and wildlife.

Some oxygenating plants are sold as cuttings bundled together, perhaps weighted so that they sink. Just push these into a container of soil and they will soon root.

Some of the more decorative types, such as myriophyllums, which have a feathery growth above the water, are best planted in baskets like marginal aquatics.

3 Remove the waterlily from its container, and plant in the bowl at its original depth.

4 Add a layer of gravel to reduce the chance of fish disturbing the soil. Gravel also helps to keep the soil in place when the container is lowered into the water.

5 Flood the bowl with water and let it stand for a while. This will reduce the chances of the water becoming muddy when you place the bowl in the pond.

6 Place the bowl in a shallow part of the pond initially, especially if new leaves are just developing. Then push it into deeper water a week or two later.

PLANT MARGINAL AQUATICS

There is nothing marginal about the appeal of most plants that come under this description – the term merely indicates that they are planted in shallower water at the margins of the pool. Most ponds are designed with a shelf on which you can grow marginal plants, most conveniently in baskets sold for the purpose, or you can stand the plants on bricks or slabs.

INTRODUCING FISH

Never place fish directly into the pond. First acclimatize them by floating the plastic bag that you transported them in on the surface of the water for an hour, as shown. This will allow the water temperatures to equalize gradually, after which the fish can be allowed to swim out of the bag.

1 Fill a basket sold for marginal plants with garden soil that is not too rich in nutrients, or buy an aquatic compost. Liners are sold to prevent the soil falling through the open sides of the basket.

2 Remove the plant from its container and plant it in the basket at its original depth, using a trowel to add or remove soil as necessary. Firm it in well.

ABOVE: *Always choose waterlily varieties to suit the size of the pond. Some are suitable for a small pool, others demand a lot of space.*

3 Cover with gravel to help keep the soil in place when you place the container in the pond, and to minimize disturbance by fish.

4 Water first to moisten the soil if it is dry, then carefully place on the shelf at the edge of the pool so that the container is covered by 3–5cm (1–2in) of water.

PLANT OR SOW SWEET PEAS

Sweet peas sown in the autumn and overwintered in a cold frame, or sown in a greenhouse in mid or late winter, will have made sturdy plants ready to be put out, but it is not too late to sow now – indoors or out – for a late summer display. To spread the period over which you can enjoy sweet peas, it is a good idea to sow at different times.

1 Insert the supports before you plant. For the best blooms, on long, straight stems, the cordon system is best, but it is very labour-intensive. Insert T-shaped posts at each end of the double row. Stretch wires between the cross-pieces and secure 2.1m (7ft) canes to these at 23cm (9in) intervals, sloping them slightly inwards.

2 For general garden display and a mass of flowers, a wigwam of canes is more satisfactory. Incline the canes inwards and tie at the top, or u a proprietary cane holder.

3 Wire or plastic netting fixed to canes to form a circular tower is another efficient way to support tall sweet peas for general garden decoration at the back of a border.

4 Remove a hole, large enough to take the root-ball with minimal disturbance, at the base of each cane, or about 23cm (9in) apart.

5 Sweet pea plants are sometimes sold with a cluster of seedlings in one pot. Always separate these and plant individually. Spread the roots out, cover, then water thoroughly.

6 Support the plants from an early stage. They can be wound in and out of netting, or attached to canes with string or metal split rings.

7 If sowing directly into the soil, sow two or three seeds at each position, and thin to one later if more germinate.

STAKE BORDER PLANTS

Some border plants are prone to wind damage, and sometimes a potentially beautiful plant is flattened or broken by the weather. Early staking means that the plants will usually grow through or over the support, which will then become almost invisible.

1 Proprietary supports like this are very efficient at supporting border plants that are not very tall but have a mass of tallish floppy or fragile flowering stems.

2 Proprietary supports that link together as shown are useful where you have clumps of varying sizes to support. They can be linked together to suit the individual plant.

3 Twiggy sticks pushed into the ground among and around the plant can be very effective. They may look a little unsightly initially, but once the plant grows you probably won't notice them.

4 Short canes can be used to support plants such as carnations. If you use a stout cane, loop string or twine around it and the plant. Use thinner split canes to keep individual flower stems or groups of stems upright.

ABOVE: *Tall garden canes are an efficient way to support plants with very tall flowering spikes that are vulnerable to wind damage, such as delphiniums. Insert individual canes at an early stage, and tie the spike to it loosely as it grows.*

TAKE SOFTWOOD CUTTINGS

Softwood cuttings, which are taken from the new shoots produced this year, root quickly and easily, and you can multiply many of your plants this way. The list below suggests a selection of some of the more popular garden plants you can propagate in this way.

1 The exact length of a softwood cutting depends on the plant, and some gardeners prefer variations of the basic technique, but typically the stem is cut off below the third or fourth leaf or pairs of leaves.

2 Trim or pull off the lowest pair of leaves (if the plant has scale-like stipules, such as on a pelargonium, pull off these as well). Trim the base of the stem with a sharp knife, cutting just below a leaf joint.

PLANTS TO GROW FROM SOFTWOOD CUTTINGS

The following are just some of the popular plants that can be propagated from softwood cuttings taken now, but there are many more to try. It is always worth experimenting if there is a plant that you want to propagate but are not sure if softwood cuttings are suitable. The chances are that some will root.

Caryopteris
Clematis
Forsythia
Fuchsia
Helichrysum
Kolkwitzia
Lavandula
Pelargonium
Salvia (shrubby types)

3 Dip the end of the cutting into a rooting hormone for speedier rooting, although many softwood cuttings root easily without this aid. Most rooting powders contain a fungicide, however, and this also helps to prevent rotting.

4 Make a hole with a dibber or pencil, then insert the cutting and firm the rooting mixture gently around it. Do not force the cutting in as this may damage it. If you have a lot of cuttings, insert several around the edge of each pot – but don't let the leaves touch.

5 Water and place in a propagator. If you do not have a propagator, enclose the cuttings in a plastic bag secured with a twist-tie or elastic band. High humidity is very important for softwood cuttings. Make sure that the leaves are not in contact with the bag.

PLANT A HANGING BASKET

The best hanging baskets are those planted with fairly small plants that are then grown on in a light, frost-free place until it is safe to put them outdoors – perhaps in late spring or early summer. A greenhouse is ideal, but you might also be able to use an enclosed or protected porch. Giving the baskets protection for a few weeks enables the plants to recover from the transplanting before they have to contend with the winds and drier soil and air outdoors.

1 Stand the basket on a large pot or a bucket to keep it stable while planting. Use a wire basket if you want a traditional display with plenty of plants cascading from the sides as well as the top.

2 Water-absorbing crystals can be added to the potting compost to act as a buffer if you are occasionally forgetful about watering your plants. However, they are no substitute for regular, daily watering during dry and hot weather.

3 You can use proprietary liners and make slits for planting, but if making a traditional basket, line it with moss to the level of the first row of plants. Fill the basket with potting compost up to that level, then insert the plants.

4 Add more moss and potting mix and repeat until just below the rim. Use a bold plant for the centre. It may be necessary to remove a little of the potting soil from the root-ball if the plant has been in a large pot.

5 Finally, fill in with plants around the edges. Encourage cascading plants to trail quickly and effectively by planting the root-ball at a slight angle so that the plant tilts slightly towards the edge.

6 Water thoroughly and keep in a warm, sheltered place until the plants are well established. If you do not have hanging facilities in the greenhouse, keep the basket on the support used for planting it up.

SOW TENDER VEGETABLES

Mid spring is a good time to sow frost-tender vegetables in most areas. If they are sown too early they may be ready to plant out too soon, and they will start to suffer if they are kept in small containers for too long. Vegetables sown now should be ready for planting outdoors after a few weeks of growth in warmth followed by a week or so of acclimatization in a cold frame. In reasonably warm climates all the vegetables mentioned here can be sown outside once the risk of frost has passed. It is only worth sowing indoors if you want an early crop.

1 Sow runner beans about six to eight weeks before the last frost is likely. Fill a 15–20cm (6–8in) pot with sowing compost to within 3cm (1in) of the rim. put three seeds in the pot, cover with about 5cm (2in) of compost and water.

2 Keep the pots in a warm place, and give them good light as soon as the seeds germinate. If all the seeds germinate, pull out the surplus to leave just one or two seedlings.

3 Outdoor and greenhouse cucumbers can be sown now. Use small pots and fill with a seed-sowing mixture to within 3cm (1in) of the rim. Position two or three seeds in each pot, placing them on their narrow edge, cover with compost and water.

4 Keep the pots moist and warm until the seeds germinate. If more than one germinates, thin them at an early stage to leave just one seedling in each pot.

5 Marrows and courgettes can also be started off in pots. Treat like cucumbers, but as the seeds are larger use a bigger pot and plant about 3cm (1in) deep.

6 Sweet corn is best raised in pots to plant out later, except in very mild regions. You can use ordinary pots, but many gardeners prefer to use peat pots. The roots will grow through these once they are planted out. Peat pots are easier to manage if stood in a seed tray lined with a piece of capillary matting.

TAKE LEAF CUTTINGS

Some houseplants – such as saintpaulias and streptocarpus – root readily from various types of leaf cuttings. Two methods are shown here.

Although you can root them at almost any time of the year, spring is a good time as the young plants will grow quickly.

1 The kind of cuttings taken from saintpaulias are known as a leaf petiole cutting and include a length of stalk. Select young but fully grown, healthy leaves, and cut them off cleanly near the base.

2 Trim the stalks about 3cm (1in) below the leaf blade and insert so that the leaf blade sits just in contact with the cutting mixture. Insert individual cuttings in small pots, or several together in larger ones.

4 Streptocarpus can be propagated from leaf sections. Choose a healthy, mature leaf that is not very old, and with a sharp knife cut it into slices 5–8cm (2–3in) wide.

3 Keep the cuttings moist but not wet, and the air humid. If you do not have a propagator, enclose the pot in a plastic bag, but make sure that it does not touch the leaves. Turn the bag regularly to reduce a build up of condensation. Pot up the young plantlets that form once they are growing vigorously.

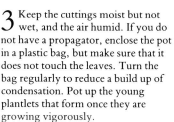

5 Push the sections into the rooting mixture so that about one-third is buried. Make sure that the side originally nearest the leaf stalk forms the base. Keep the cuttings in a warm place in good light but out of direct sunlight.

LATE SPRING

LATE SPRING CAN BE DECEPTIVE. IT often seems as though summer has already arrived, yet in cold areas there can be severe late frosts. Take local climate into account before planting any frost-tender plants outdoors. Even with experience it can be a gamble as an untypical season might produce surprises. Judging when frosts are no longer likely is mainly a matter of assessing risk. A good guide is to watch when summer bedding is put out in the local parks. These gardeners will have amassed generations of local knowledge of your area, which is by far the best guide.

JOBS IN BRIEF

The kitchen garden

- ☐ Plant up a herb pot
- ☐ Apply manures and fertilizers where appropriate
- ☐ Sow sweet corn outdoors in mild areas when further frost is unlikely
- ☐ Sow vegetables without protection – many kinds can be sown now, so check the packets

BELOW: *Plant up a herb pot for a useful as well as a pretty display for the summer.*

- ☐ Plant potatoes
- ☐ Try a collection of mints in a growing bag
- ☐ Plant out vegetable seedlings such as cabbages and cauliflowers
- ☐ Sow seeds of crops such as cabbages, cauliflowers and sprouts in a nursery bed, where they can be grown for later transplanting
- ☐ Put straw down round strawberries or protect fruit with strawberry mats
- ☐ Sow or plant runner beans outdoors

The flower garden

- ☐ Plant and stock the pond
- ☐ Prune forsythia and *Ribes sanguineum*
- ☐ Plant container-grown shrubs
- ☐ Plant herbaceous plants
- ☐ Stake herbaceous plants
- ☐ Plant up a half basket or wall pot
- ☐ Sow hardy annuals
- ☐ Plant gladioli and summer bulbs
- ☐ Mow the lawn regularly from now on
- ☐ Plant out sweet peas raised in pots
- ☐ Sow sweet peas where they are to flower
- ☐ Harden off tender bedding plants

BELOW: *Prune forsythias soon after flowering has finished.*

The greenhouse and conservatory

- ☐ Sow tender vegetables such as outdoor tomatoes and runner beans to plant out later, and cucumbers for the greenhouse
- ☐ Plant greenhouse tomatoes and cucumbers
- ☐ Feed pot-plants and seedlings regularly
- ☐ Pot on young dahlia and chrysanthemum plants if they need it
- ☐ Prick out or pot up late-sown bedding plants
- ☐ Take leaf cuttings of saintpaulias and streptocarpus

BELOW: *Plant greenhouse tomatoes provided there is sufficient warmth.*

PLANTS AT THEIR BEST

Aubrieta (rock plant)
Azalea (shrub)
Bergenia (non-woody evergreen)
Calendula, autumn sown (hardy annual)
Cheiranthus (wallflower)
Choisya ternata (shrub)
Clematis montana (shrubby climber)
Crataegus (tree)
Cytisus, various (shrub)
Dicentra (herbaceous)
Fritillaria (bulb)
Genista (shrub)
Laburnum (tree)
Malus (tree)
Paeonia (herbaceous and shrub)
Phlox subulata (rock plant)
Pulsatilla vulgaris (rock plant)
Rhododendron, various (shrub)
Saxifraga, various (rock plant)
Syringa (lilac)
Tulipa, various (bulb)
Wisteria (shrubby climber)

LEFT: *Alliums beneath a laburnum arch.*

BELOW: Fritillaria meleagris.

PLANT UP A HERB POT

A herb pot makes an attractive feature, but it is best treated as a short-term home to be replanted annually. If you allow shrubby perennial herbs to become large and established, you will find them extremely difficult to remove when it becomes

necessary. Be especially careful of planting a large shrubby plant in the top of a herb pot with a tapering neck. Once the plant has produced a mass of roots, the inward taper makes removal a frustrating task.

1 A herb pot is best filled in stages. Start by adding a good potting compost to the height of the first planting pockets.

2 Using small plants, knock them out of their pots and push the root-balls through the holes in the planting pockets. If necessary, break off some of the root-ball so that you can get it through the hole.

3 Add more potting soil and repeat with the next row of planting holes. Unless the pot is very large, don't try to pack too many herbs into the top. A single well-grown plant often looks much better.

5 In time the shrubby plant may take up all the planting space at the top and you will have an attractive specimen plant, but meanwhile you should be able to fit a collection of smaller herbs around the edge. Avoid mints, which may be difficult to eliminate later.

4 Large earthenware pots can look just as good as herb pots with planting pockets if you plant them imaginatively. If you have an old half-barrel use this instead. Place a bold shrubby herb, such as a sweet bay (*Laurus nobilis*), in the centre.

GROW MINTS

Mints are notoriously difficult to control once they make themselves at home. They send spreading and penetrating shoots beneath the surface which emerge among other plants or even the other side of a path. They are best contained in some way.

1 A growing bag is an ideal home for mints. They will be happy for a couple of seasons, and then are easily removed and replanted for a fresh start. If the mints are in large pots it may be necessary to remove some of the root-ball, but they soon recover.

2 Instead of filling the growing bag with one kind of mint, try planting a collection of perhaps four to six different kinds. This will look good and add to the flavours available for the kitchen.

3 If you want to plant your mint in the border (which avoids the chore of watering frequently), plant it in an old bucket or large pot. Make sure that there are drainage holes in the bottom, and fill with soil or a potting mixture and plant the mint.

4 For a visually pleasing effect, position the rim of the pot just below the level of the surrounding soil, then cover with soil to hide any signs of the pot. Lift, divide and replant annually or every second spring, to maintain vigour.

OTHER HERBS TO RESTRAIN

Although mint is the herb most notorious for being invasive, others can attempt a take-over of the border. Tansy (*Tanacetum vulgare*) and woodruff (*Asperula odorata* syn. *Galium odoratum*) are among the herbs that you may also want to consider planting in a plunged bucket or large pot.

SOW SWEET CORN

Sweet corn is a reliable crop in warm areas, where it can be sown directly into the ground with confidence, but in cold regions with a short growing season, it is best to start the plants off under glass so that they have time to mature before the autumn frosts. In areas where growing conditions are less than favourable, choose a variety specially bred for a cool climate.

1 Sow only when there is no risk of frost and the soil temperature has reached 10°C (50°F). In cold areas, warm up the soil with fleece or cloches for a week or two first.

2 Sow the seeds 3cm (1in) deep and 8cm (3in) apart, and thin to the final recommended spacing later – typically 30cm (12in) apart each way. Sow in blocks rather than single rows.

3 Cover with a fine net floating cloche or horticultural fleece. This can be left on after germination until the plants have pushed the cover up to its limit without damaging the plants.

4 In areas where outdoor sowing is unreliable, raise the plants in modules or peat pots. Plant them out when there is no danger of frost, and after careful hardening off.

PLANT OUTDOOR TOMATOES

Wait until there is little risk of frost before planting your outdoor tomatoes – about the same time as you plant your tender summer bedding. Choose varieties recommended for outdoors.

1 Plant at the spacing recommended for the variety – some grow tall and large, others remain small and compact. Always make sure they have been well hardened off.

2 In cold areas, cover plants with cloches for a few weeks, or use horticultural fleece.

RAISING TOMATOES IN GROWING BAGS

Tomatoes do well in growing bags, and this is a practical way to grow them on a patio as well as in a greenhouse or vegetable patch.

Staking is the main problem if you want to grow tomatoes in growing bags on a hard base. There are many proprietary designs of cane supports intended for crops like tomatoes in growing bags, and most should last for several years.

If the growing bag is positioned on soil you can simply push the cane through the bag, as shown.

3 Once the fleece or protection has been removed, stake the plants immediately. Some small varieties may not require staking.

PLANT RUNNER AND POLE BEANS

In mild areas runner and climbing French beans can be sown in late spring, but in cold areas wait until early summer or start the seeds off indoors. Do not plant out until there is no risk of frost.

1 Sow two seeds 5cm (2in) deep by each cane or support. Thin to one plant later if both germinate. Wait until the soil temperature is at least 12°C (54°F) before sowing.

2 If you raise the plants in pots, plant out once there is no reasonable risk of frost. Use a trowel and plant them just outside the cane. Train them to the cane as soon as they are tall enough.

SUPPORTING RUNNER AND POLE BEANS

Canes and nets are the main methods of supporting runner and pole beans. If you use a net, choose a large-mesh net sold as a pea and bean net, and stretch it taut between well-secured posts. If you use canes, the most popular methods are wigwams (see right) and crossed canes (see far right).

Proprietary supports are also available but, although usually very effective, they can be expensive.

MAKE UP A HALF-BASKET OR WALL POT

Most people love to have a traditional hanging basket, but they can be disappointing unless cared for lovingly. Even though the basket is planted with an all-round view in mind, the side nearest the wall will perform poorly in comparison with the sunny side unless you turn the basket every day or two to even up growth. A half-basket or wall pot fixed against the wall can be just as effective, and because it is planted to look good from the front only, it can be just as bold and striking as a conventional basket. Some wall pots are also decorative in their own right.

1 If the half-basket is small, you may prefer to take it down to plant it. However, drill and plug the holes, fix the hooks or screws and try it out on the wall first.

2 Add a drainage layer, such as broken pots or gravel, then partly fill with a potting mixture.

3 If using a wire half-basket, line it with moss and fill with potting mixture to the height of the first layer of plants.

4 Plant the sides, then add more moss and potting soil.

5 Plant the top of the basket with bold and spectacular plants for an eye-catching display.

6 Choose more restrained plants for a very ornamental wall pot that you want to retain as a feature in its own right.

PUTTING OUT WALL BASKETS

Half-baskets and wall pots are difficult to accommodate in the greenhouse or other sheltered and frost-free position, so it is best to wait until frost is very unlikely before planting. If you can give them a week or two in a greenhouse or cold frame, however, the plants will receive less of a check to growth and the display should be more pleasing.

RIGHT: *A genuine old manger has been used for this lavish display. Well-planted large wall pots can be just as striking.*

HARDEN OFF BEDDING PLANTS

Hardening off is a crucial stage for all plants raised indoors or in a greenhouse. If this is done properly the plants will remain sturdy and healthy, but if you move tender plants straight out into hot, dry conditions or cold biting winds outdoors after a cosseted life on the windowsill or greenhouse, losses could be high.

Plants that you buy from shops and garden centres should have been hardened off before you buy them.

1 Place the plants in a cold frame a week or two before planting-out time. Close the top in the evening and on cold days, otherwise ventilate freely. If frost threatens, cover the frame with insulation material or take the plants into a greenhouse or indoors again.

2 If you don't have a cold frame, cloches can be used instead. Ventilate them whenever possible so that the plants become acclimatized while still receiving protection from the worst winds and cold.

3 If you don't have frames or cloches, group the trays or pots together in a sheltered spot outside and cover them with horticultural fleece or a perforated plastic floating cloche. Take them in again if frost is forecast.

PLANT GREENHOUSE TOMATOES

Greenhouse tomatoes always used to be grown in the greenhouse border, and the soil changed periodically. This was considered risky and ring culture became fashionable. In more recent times growing bags have been in favour. Other methods are used commercially but the three practical and easy methods suitable for amateurs are described here. All three systems have merits and drawbacks, and how well you look after your tomatoes while they are growing can be as important as the system. Choose the one that appeals most or seems the easiest.

1 Always dig in as much rotted manure or garden compost as you can spare and rake in a general garden fertilizer before you plant your tomatoes. Although they can be planted earlier, most amateurs find this is a good time as the greenhouse usually has more space once the bedding plants have been moved out.

2 Most greenhouse varieties grow tall and need support. Tall canes are a convenient method if you have just a few plants, but if you have a lot of plants the string method may be more suitable (see opposite).

3 With ring culture, the water-absorbing roots grow into a moist aggregate and the feeding roots into special bottomless pots filled with a potting compost. Take out a trench about 15–23cm (6–9in) deep in the greenhouse border and line it with a waterproof plastic (this minimizes soil-borne disease contamination).

4 Fill the trench with fine gravel, coarse grit or expanded clay granules. Then place the special bottomless ring culture pots on the aggregate base and fill them with a good potting compost.

5 Plant into the ring and insert a cane or provide an alternative support. Water only into the ring at first. Once the plant is established and some roots have penetrated into the aggregate, water only the aggregate and feed through the pot.

6 Growing bags are less trouble than ring culture to set up, but you still have to feed plants regularly, and watering can be more difficult to control unless you use an automatic system. Insert a cane through the bag or use a string support.

ABOVE: *You can expect crops like this if you plant your greenhouse tomatoes now. For best results, check that the variety is recommended for greenhouse cultivation.*

SUPPORTING TOMATOES ON STRINGS

String is a simple and economical way to support your tomatoes. Fix one wire as high as practical from one end of the greenhouse to the other, aligning it above the border, and another one just above the ground. The lower wire is most conveniently fixed to a stout stake at each end of the row.

Tie lengths of string between the top and bottom wires, in line with each plant.

You don't need to tie the plant to its support, just loop the string around the growing tip so that it forms a spiral.

PLANT AND TRAIN CUCUMBERS

As with tomatoes, there are various ways to plant and train cucumbers.

Try growing cucumbers in growing bags on the greenhouse staging. Insert canes between the growing bags and the eaves, and fix horizontal wires along the length of the roof as shown here. You can then train the growth along the roof and the cucumbers will hang down. A normal growing bag should hold about two cucumbers. Do not over-crowd the plants.

The method shown is easy and convenient, but if you don't want the trouble of ensuring that the growing bags are kept evenly moist, you could plant the cucumbers directly into the border soil and start the horizontal wires on the sides of the greenhouse instead.

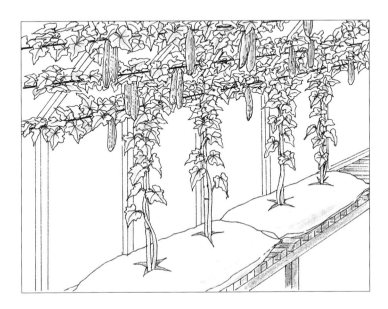

SUMMER

Early summer is a time of intense gardening activity. Everything is growing rapidly, in many areas tender plants can be put out, and weeds seem to grow faster than you ever thought possible.
Mid and late summer are times for enjoying the results of your earlier efforts. There are always jobs to be done, of course, but you should also make time to relax.
During a dry summer water shortages can be a problem, but always water thoroughly, as shallow, impatient watering will encourage surface rooting and make the plants even more vulnerable.

OPPOSITE: *Roses are part of the summer scene, but they have even more impact when used with imagination.*

ABOVE: *By using containers, summer colour can be brought to even the most unpromising corner of the garden.*

EARLY SUMMER

EARLY SUMMER IS A TIME WHEN you can relax a little and enjoy all your efforts of the last few months. But there are still jobs to be done, and pests and diseases are as active as ever. Vigilance and prompt action now will often stop the trouble from spreading out of control, thus avoiding the need for more drastic control measures later.

Although there is always plenty of colour at this time of year, be prepared for a few weeks when the garden is perhaps not looking at its best. Early summer is a transitional period, and there is often an interval between the spring flowering plants dying back and the peak of colour offered by abundant summer bedding.

JOBS IN BRIEF

The kitchen garden

- ☐ Sow sweet corn outdoors in mild areas when further frost is unlikely
- ☐ Sow vegetables – most kinds can be sown now, so check the packets. Make successional sowings of crops such as beetroot, carrots, lettuces and turnips
- ☐ Plant potatoes
- ☐ Plant out vegetable seedlings such as cabbages, cauliflowers, celery, sweetcorn, tomatoes and marrows
- ☐ Sow seeds of crops such as cabbages, cauliflowers and sprouts in a nursery bed, where they can be grown for later transplanting
- ☐ Sow or plant runner and pole beans outdoors
- ☐ Sow French beans
- ☐ Watch out for aphids on broad beans and root flies on cabbages, carrots and onions. Prevention is better than cure

BELOW: *Thin vegetables while still small.*

The flower garden

- ☐ Dead-head border plants regularly
- ☐ Stake herbaceous plants
- ☐ Finish planting up containers and baskets
- ☐ Sow hardy annuals
- ☐ Plant dahlias
- ☐ Finish planting gladioli and summer bulbs

BELOW: *Dead-head lilacs as soon as they have finished flowering.*

- ☐ Prune lilac, philadelphus, spiraea and broom
- ☐ Sow biennials such as wallflowers and forget-me-nots
- ☐ Mow the lawn except in very dry weather
- ☐ Finish hardening off and planting tender bedding plants
- ☐ Pinch out the growing tip from early-flowering chrysanthemums
- ☐ Watch out for signs of mildew and aphids on roses and spray promptly if they are found
- ☐ Apply a rose fertilizer once the main flush of flowering is over

The greenhouse and conservatory

- ☐ Feed pot-plants regularly
- ☐ Take leaf cuttings of saintpaulias and streptocarpus
- ☐ Start to feed tomatoes when the first truss of fruit has set
- ☐ Try biological pest control for greenhouse pests
- ☐ Pot up and pot on seedling pot-plants as it becomes necessary

BELOW: *Check pot-plants regularly to make sure they are receiving enough water.*

BELOW: *Biological pest controls can be very successful if used properly.*

PLANTS AT THEIR BEST

Alchemilla mollis (herbaceous)
Allium (bulb)
Buddleia globosa (shrub)
Calendula (hardy annual)
Cistus (shrub)
Dianthus (carnations and pinks)
Digitalis (biennial)
Geranium (herbaceous)
Godetia (hardy annual)
Iris germanica hybrids (border irises)
Laburnum (tree)
Lupinus (herbaceous)
Paeonia (herbaceous)
Papaver orientale (herbaceous)
Philadelphus (shrub)
Rosa (most types of rose)
Weigela (shrub)

LEFT: *Early summer is full of promise.*

BELOW: Philadelphus *x* lemoinei.

BOTTOM: Dianthus *'Caesar's Bloody Pink.'*

PROTECT AND EARTH UP POTATOES

Potatoes are earthed up to protect the tubers near the surface from light. If they are exposed, their skins will turn green and the tubers will be completely inedible.

1 Potatoes will usually recover from slight frost damage, but if you know that a frost is forecast once the shoots are through the ground try covering the plants with newspaper or horticultural fleece. Peg into position, then remove the next morning or when the frost has gone.

2 Start earthing up the potatoes when the shoots are about 15cm (6in) high. Use a draw hoe to pull up the soil either side of the row.

3 Continue to earth up in stages, as the potatoes grow, until the soil creates a mound about 15cm (6in) high.

THIN SEEDLINGS

Thinning is a tedious but essential task. The final spacing between plants will determine both the size of the individual vegetables and the total yield. Exact spacing will often depend on whether you are more interested in the total crop or large, well-shaped individual specimens.

1 Follow the spacing advice given on the seed packet when sowing. It should also recommend the ideal final spacing between plants after thinning.

2 Thin in stages, pulling up surplus plants between finger and thumb. The first thinning should leave the plants twice as close as their final spacing, to allow for losses after thinning.

3 Before the plants begin to compete with each other, thin once more to the final spacing.

SOWING MINI-CAULIFLOWERS

Mini-cauliflowers are summer varieties sown in spring or early summer but grown at much closer spacing than normal. Sow several seeds every 15cm (6in) where they are to grow, and thin these to one seedling if more than one germinates. The heads are much smaller than normal, but total yield can still be good.

MULTIPLE SOWING

TRANSPLANTING SEEDLINGS

Do not attempt to transplant spare thinnings of root crops such as carrots and turnips, but other crops – like lettuces and cabbages, for example – can transplant satisfactorily.

The secret of success is to water the row thoroughly an hour before you thin or transplant (check to make sure that moisture has penetrated to root level), and to lift the spare seedlings with as much soil as possible around the roots. Always water well until plants recover, and shade from direct sun for a few days.

Some gardeners grow certain vegetables – such as carrots, beetroot, onions and leeks, in small clusters. Four to six seeds are usually sown in each cell of modular trays (see top), and planted out without any attempt to separate them. These are not normally thinned. The vegetables are usually smaller and less well shaped than those sown in rows and thinned normally, but the overall weight of crop may be good if the spacing recommended for this type of cultivation is followed (see above).

LEFT: *The total yield can sometimes be higher from close spacing, even though individual specimens are smaller.*

SUMMER TROUGHS AND WINDOWBOXES

Frost-tender bedding plants can now be planted in all but the coldest areas, but be guided by local conditions. Tubs and troughs packed with summer bedding plants are a sure-fire way to bring pockets of cheerful colour to parts of the garden that would not otherwise be so colourful. Make the most of windowboxes, too, which will brighten the exterior of any home.

1 Windowboxes and troughs can be planted in the same way – but for a windowbox include more trailers than you would for a trough. Always make sure that there are drainage holes, and add a drainage layer such as broken pots or gravel.

2 Half fill the box or trough with a good potting mix – a loam-based one can be used for troughs, but if the windowbox is to be fixed on brackets choose a lightweight mixture based on peat or a peat substitute.

3 Most people prefer a mixed planting, with some trailers and both flowering and foliage plants. Try arranging the plants before actually planting to help visualize how they will look.

SINGLE-SUBJECT PLANTING

4 When the positions look right, insert the plants, firming the compost around each root-ball. Plant more closely than in beds or borders, so avoid using plants that will overpower their neighbours.

Most people plant mixed groups, but sometimes a single-subject planting can look especially striking. Impatiens and begonia are popular plants suitable for this treatment, but be prepared to experiment with others.

Because single-subject plants have an even height, it is important to choose a container that is in proportion to the plants. For example, compact begonias look lost in a deep trough, but are in keeping with a shallow windowbox.

5 Water thoroughly after planting, and make sure that the compost never dries out. In warm weather this means watering daily, sometimes more than once.

PLANT UP TUBS AND PATIO POTS

Although all the plants suitable for windowboxes and troughs can be used in tubs and large patio pots, the greater depth of potting soil offers scope for larger and often bolder plants, and the circular shape generally demands an eye-catching plant as a centrepiece. Trailers will enhance a plain container, but if you have a very ornate or decorative pot, it may be best to plant trailers with restraint so that the pot itself remains a feature in its own right.

1 Filled tubs and pots can be very heavy to move, so plant them up where they are to be displayed. Cover the drainage holes with a layer of broken pots, gravel or chipped bark.

2 A loam-based potting mixture is best for most plants, but if the pot is to be used where weight is a consideration, such as on a balcony, use a peat-based mixture.

3 Choose a tall or bold plant for the centre, such as *Cordyline australis* or a fuchsia, or one with large flowers such as the osteospermum which has been used here.

4 Fill in around the base with some bushier but lower-growing plants. Choose bright flowers if the centrepiece is a foliage plant, but place the emphasis on foliage effect if the focal-point is a flowering plant.

5 Cover the surface with a decorative mulch such as chipped bark or cocoa shells if much of the surface is visible (this is worth doing anyway to conserve moisture). Water thoroughly.

ABOVE: *Even a simple poppy can make an impact if the container itself is interesting.*

SOW BIENNIALS AND HARDY PERENNIALS

Biennials such as wallflowers and forget-me-nots are very easy to raise from seed, and because they can be sown outdoors they need very little attention. Border perennials such as lupins and aquilegias are also easily raised from seed sown now, and some of them may even flower next summer. Others may take another year or so to establish before flowering.

1 Prepare the ground thoroughly, and eliminate as many weeds as possible. Competition from weeds is often the greatest enemy the seedlings face. Break the soil down into a fine, crumbly structure once it has been cleared of weeds.

2 Take out drills with the corner of a hoe or rake to the recommended depth (this varies with the seed, so check the packet). The drills can be quite close together, because the seedlings will be transplanted as soon as they are large enough.

3 Run water into the drill before sowing if the soil is very dry. Space the seeds thinly, and as evenly as you can. This makes thinning and later transplanting much easier.

ABOVE: *Wallflowers are one of the most popular biennials, and really easy to grow from seeds sown now.*

4 Cover the seeds by shuffling the soil back with your feet or carefully ease the soil back with the back of a rake. Remember to add a label.

5 Thin the seedlings as soon as they are large enough to handle easily so that they do not become overcrowded.

PRUNE SHRUBS

Many shrubs thrive without routine annual pruning, but some that flower in spring or early summer benefit from pruning soon after they have finished flowering. These include *Cytisus* (brooms), *Syringas* (lilacs), philadelphus, and spring-flowering spiraeas.

RENOVATING AN OLD LILAC

Very old *Syringa vulgaris* varieties often become tall and leggy, with the flowers very high up. You may be able to rejuvenate a neglected plant by sawing it down to a height of 30–90cm (12in–3ft). This sounds drastic, and it will not flower for a year or two, but it should shoot from the old wood and produce an attractive compact plant again.

1 Philadelphus (illustrated) and spring-flowering spiraeas such as *Spiraea* × *arguta* and *S. thunbergii* become too dense and overcrowded if they are not pruned. Annual pruning keeps them compact and flowering well, and the best time to do this is immediately after flowering.

2 Reduce the shoots by one-third, cutting out the oldest ones. Cut back the old stems to where a new shoot is growing lower down, or to just above the ground if the shoot is very old and the bush very congested.

3 Brooms and genistas tend to become woody at the base with age, with the flowers too high up the plants to look attractive. Prune them as soon as the flowers die and the seed pods are beginning to form.

4 Cut back each shoot to about half way along the new green growth. Do not count dark, old wood, and do not cut back into this as new shoots will be reluctant to grow. You will not be able to make an old neglected plant bush from the base – start regular pruning from an early stage.

5 Lilacs benefit from careful dead-heading. As soon as the flowering is over, cut the dead blooms back to the first pair of leaves below the flower head (no further, otherwise you might remove buds from which new flowering shoots will be produced).

FEEDING AND WATERING IN THE GREENHOUSE

Watering is a year-round chore in the greenhouse, but the summer months are even more demanding. Consider an automatic or semi-automatic watering system to make lighter work of the job. Most pot-plants respond readily to regular feeding during the growing season, but underfeeding is not easy to detect until the plants have been starved for some time.

1 Plants should be watered before they show obvious signs of distress such as wilting. With bushy plants it is not possible to judge by the visual appearance of the potting mixture either, and touch is often the only practical guide. However, this is both time-consuming and only reasonably accurate.

2 Moisture indicators for individual pots can be helpful for a beginner, or if there are just a few plants, but they are not a practical solution if you have a whole greenhouse or conservatory full of plants.

3 Capillary matting is an ideal way to water most pot-plants in summer. You can use a proprietary system fed by mains water, or improvise with a system like the one illustrated. This uses a length of gutter for the water supply. You can keep it topped up by hand, with special water bags or from a cistern.

4 If watering by hand, use the can without a rose unless you are watering seedlings. This will enable you to direct water more easily to the roots rather than sprinkling the leaves. Use a finger over the end of the spout to control the flow, or stick a rag in the end to break the force.

5 An overhead spray system operated automatically or when you turn on the tap is useful for a large greenhouse, either for plants on benches or those planted in the border. Water is not so carefully directed to where it is needed, so it is not ideal for pot-plants, but the spray helps to create a humid atmosphere.

6 Use a liquid fertilizer applied with the water if you can remember to do it regularly. There are both soluble powders and liquids that can be diluted to the appropriate strength.

7 Fertilizer sticks and tablets that you push into the potting soil are a convenient way to administer fertilizer if you don't want to apply liquid feeds regularly. Most of these release their nutrients over a period of several months.

Use a general-purpose fertilizer if you want to avoid using different foods for different plants: this is better than not feeding at all.

Some fertilizers are described as being specially formulated for either foliage plants or flowering plants, however, and these will suit the majority of plants within each category. But if you have to feed both flowering and foliage plants with the one fertilizer, these are unlikely to do any harm.

Some enthusiasts prefer to use special feeds for certain types of plant, such as saintpaulias and cacti, but these will also respond to fertilizers used for other pot-plants.

Fertilizers formulated for strong feeders such as tomatoes and chrysanthemums should only be used on other plants with care – they may be too strong.

BIOLOGICAL CONTROLS

The greenhouse or conservatory is an ideal place to practise biological control methods – the predators will thrive in the protected environment, and should multiply rapidly until control is achieved.

1 Various forms of biological controls are available for a number of greenhouse pests. *Encarsia formosa* is a tiny wasp that parasitizes whitefly larvae and eventually kills them. There are other predatory wasps and mites that will attack red spider, soft scale insects and thrips.

2 If weevil grubs destroy your plants by eating the roots, try controlling them in future with a parasitic eelworm. A suspension of the eelworms is simply watered over the potting soil in each pot.

WORKING WITH BIOLOGICAL CONTROLS

Biological controls usually work best when the weather is warm, and some are unsuitable for use outdoors. Use pesticides with care, as they can wipe out your predators as well as the harmful insects and you will destroy the balance between the two.

With biological controls you will always have some pests – they are essential for the predator to be able to continue to breed – but only at a low population level.

AIR LAYER LEGGY PLANTS

Some hardy plants such as magnolias and rhododendrons can be air layered outside, but the technique is most often used for indoor and greenhouse plants that have become tall and bare at the base. Instead of an unattractive 'leggy' plant you can start off again with a reasonably sized specimen that looks good from top to pot. *Ficus elastica* is commonly treated this way, but other plants, such as dracaenas, are worth trying.

Plants can be air layered at almost any time, but early summer is ideal because they are growing vigorously in the increasing light and warmth.

1 Layer the plant above the bare area, just below the leaves. If you are using the technique on a multi-stemmed plant just to increase stock, remove a few leaves from the point where you want to make the layer.

2 Carefully make an upward slit about 3cm (1in) long, below an old leaf joint. Do not cut more than half-way through the stem, otherwise the shoot may break.

3 Make a sleeve out of plastic sheet. It does not have to form a tube as you can wrap it round the stem then make a seal. Fix the bottom of the sleeve a short distance below the cut, using a twist-tie or adhesive tape.

4 Brush a small amount of rooting hormone (powder or gel) into the wound, to speed rooting. Then pack a little sphagnum moss into the wound to keep it open.

5 Pack plenty of damp sphagnum moss around the stem, to enclose the wound, then cover with the sheet of plastic and secure at the top with another twist-tie or tape. Make sure that the moss is kept moist, and carefully check for roots after a month or so. When well rooted, sever from the parent to pot up.

DIVIDE CONGESTED POT-PLANTS

Once a plant has filled its pot and if it is not practical to move it to a larger one, division may revive it and will also give you a number of extra plants. Not all plants respond to division. Those with a fibrous root system, like calatheas and most ferns, are more likely to divide successfully.

A few flowering plants bloom better if kept slightly pot-bound. Check if a particular plant responds well to division in an encyclopedia.

House and greenhouse plants can be divided throughout the year, but late spring and early summer are particularly good times.

1 Water the plant at least half an hour before you divide it. If the plant will not come out of the pot easily, try inverting the pot while you support the plant and tap its rim on a hard surface.

2 Remove any broken pots used to cover the old drainage hole in a clay pot, and pull away a little potting soil to expose some of the roots and make division easier.

3 Most plants can be pulled apart by hand, but if the root-ball is difficult to break open this way use a hand fork.

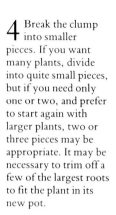

4 Break the clump into smaller pieces. If you want many plants, divide into quite small pieces, but if you need only one or two, and prefer to start again with larger plants, two or three pieces may be appropriate. It may be necessary to trim off a few of the largest roots to fit the plant in its new pot.

5 Replant sections as soon as possible, trickling potting soil around the roots. If possible, use the same kind of potting material as the plant was in before, and firm it well around the roots. Water and keep out of direct sunlight for a few days.

MID SUMMER

MID SUMMER IS MAINLY A TIME to enjoy your garden, rather than do a lot of physical work in it. Most things are already sown or planted, and the emphasis is on weeding and watering. Regular dead-heading will keep the garden looking tidy and benefit the plants too.

JOBS IN BRIEF

The kitchen garden

- ☐ Hoe regularly to keep down weeds
- ☐ Sow more vegetables – including spinach, parsley, and (in cold areas) spring cabbage. Make successional sowings of crops such as beetroot, carrots, lettuces and turnips
- ☐ Continue to thin vegetables sown earlier, before they grow large enough to compete with each other
- ☐ Plant out late cauliflowers, winter cabbages, and leeks
- ☐ Sow more French beans
- ☐ Give plants that need a boost a dressing dose of quick-acting fertilizer, but if using a powder or granules be sure to water in thoroughly
- ☐ Pinch out the growing tips of runner beans when they reach the top of their support
- ☐ Lift shallots if they have finished growing, and leave them on the surface for a few days to dry off
- ☐ Harvest herbs regularly. Don't let the leaves become too old
- ☐ Thin apples
- ☐ Summer prune cordon and espalier apples
- ☐ Tidy up summer-flowering strawberries that have finished fruiting. Cut off old leaves and unwanted runners, remove straw, and control weeds
- ☐ Remain vigilant for early signs of pests and diseases. Caterpillars can devastate a cabbage crop if undetected
- ☐ Water vulnerable crops before they show signs of stress

The flower garden

- ☐ Dead-head border plants regularly
- ☐ Hoe beds and borders regularly to keep down weeds
- ☐ Divide and replant border irises
- ☐ Take semi-ripe cuttings
- ☐ Clip beech, holly, hornbeam and yew hedges towards the end of the period
- ☐ Layer shrubs and carnations
- ☐ Plant colchicums, to flower in the autumn, when they are available
- ☐ Transplant biennials and perennial seedlings to a nursery bed
- ☐ Order bulb catalogues and bulbs for autumn delivery
- ☐ Disbud early-flowering chrysanthemums
- ☐ Mow the lawn except in very dry weather
- ☐ Watch out for signs of mildew and aphids on roses and spray promptly if they are found

BELOW: *Disbud chrysanthemums if you want larger flowers later.*

The greenhouse and conservatory

- ☐ Feed pot-plants regularly
- ☐ Take leaf and semi-ripe cuttings
- ☐ Feed tomatoes and chrysanthemums regularly
- ☐ Remove sideshoots and yellowing leaves from tomatoes regularly
- ☐ Keep a vigilant watch for pests and diseases. Spray promptly or try a biological control for greenhouse pests
- ☐ Pot up and pot on seedling pot-plants as it becomes necessary

BELOW: *Do not forget to feed. Slow-release sticks like this make it a less frequent chore.*

BELOW: *Regularly remove sideshoots from cordon tomatoes (leave them on bush types).*

PLANTS AT THEIR BEST

Alchemilla mollis (herbaceous)
Althaea (herbaceous)
Astilbe (herbaceous)
Cistus (shrub)
Clematis (shrubby climber)
Dianthus (carnations and pinks)
Digitalis (biennial)
Geranium (herbaceous)
Hardy annuals (many)
Helianthemum (shrub)
Hydrangea (shrub)
Hypericum (shrub)
Kniphofia (herbaceous)
Lavandula (shrub)
Lilium (bulb)
Potentilla (shrub)
Rosa (most types of rose)
Summer bedding
Verbascum (herbaceous)

ABOVE: *Lilies like this 'Connecticut King' make stunning border plants.*

BELOW: *Mid summer sees the garden at its most beautiful.*

CONTROL WEEDS

It is never possible to eliminate weeds entirely, but you can control them. Even weeds that are difficult to eradicate can be conquered if you persist, and annual weeds will diminish in numbers if you continue to kill off the seedlings before they can flower and shed more seed.

Once the weed population has been reduced, mulching and prompt action to remove the seedlings that do appear will keep the garden almost weed-free. Be prepared for the battle to be won over a couple of seasons rather than in a few weeks if the garden has been neglected.

1 Deep-rooted perennial weeds that have long, penetrating roots are best forked up. Loosen the roots with a fork, and hold the stem close to its base as you pull up the whole plant. If you don't get all the root out, new pieces may grow.

2 Hoeing is one of the best forms of weed control, but it needs to be done regularly. Slice the weeds off just beneath the soil, preferably when the soil is dry. Keep beds and borders hoed, as well as the vegetable garden.

3 Contact chemical weedkillers are useful if you need to clear an area of ground quickly and easily. Some – which normally only kill the top growth, so are better for annuals than problem perennial weeds – leave the area safe to replant after a day.

4 Some weedkillers kill the whole plant, including the roots. Large areas of ground can be sprayed, but you can paint some formulations onto the leaves to kill the weed without harming neighbouring plants.

5 Mulches are very effective at controlling weeds. In the vegetable and fruit garden various forms of plastic sheeting are a cost-effective method.

6 Where appearance matters, use an organic material such as chipped bark, garden compost or cocoa shells. If the ground is cleared of weeds first, a mulch at least 5cm (2in) thick will suppress most weeds.

SUMMER PRUNE CORDON AND ESPALIER APPLES

Shaped and trained apple trees are normally pruned twice a year – once in summer and again in winter. Summer pruning controls the amount of growth produced each year and maintains the basic shape, winter pruning consists of thinning overcrowded fruiting spurs on old plants. In late spring the new growth at the ends of the main shoots is cut back to its point of origin, but summer pruning is the most crucial in terms of maintaining the trained shape.

ESPALIER

1 Shorten new leafy shoots that have grown directly from the main branches back to three leaves above the basal cluster of leaves. This should only be done once the shoots have dark green leaves and the bark has started to turn brown and is woody at the base. In cold areas it may be early autumn before the shoots are mature enough.

2 If the shoot is growing from a stub left by previous pruning – and not directly from one of the main stems – cut back to just one leaf above the basal cluster of leaves.

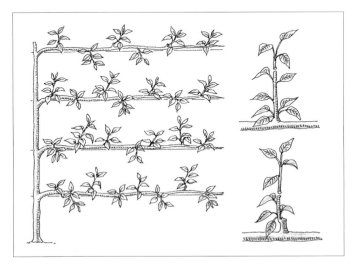

CORDON

1 A cordon is pruned in exactly the same way as an espalier, although, of course, the basic shape of the plant is different. Just cut back shoots growing directly from the main branch to three leaves above the basal cluster of leaves.

2 Cut back shoots growing from stubs left by earlier pruning to one leaf above the basal cluster.

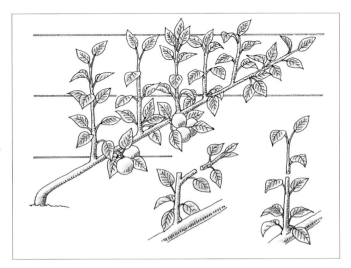

TAKE SEMI-RIPE CUTTINGS

Semi-ripe cuttings – also known as semi-mature cuttings – can be used to propagate a wide range of shrubs, both hardy and tender. If you take them in mid or late summer most will root quickly, and in the case of hardy plants you don't even need a propagator.

1 Choose shoots that are almost fully grown except for the soft tip. The base of the cutting should be hardening, even though the tip may still be soft. Most cuttings are best made 5–10cm (2–4in) long.

2 Strip the lower leaves from each plant to leave a short length of clear stem to insert into the soil.

3 It is well worth using a rooting hormone. Dip the cut end into the powder, liquid or gel, but if using a powder dip the ends into water first so that the powder adheres.

4 Cuttings taken from hardy plants will root outside at this time of year, though they will perform better in a cold frame or propagator.

5 Firm the cuttings to ensure there are no large pockets of air, which might cause the new roots to dry out.

6 Remember to insert a label. This is especially important if you are rooting a number of different kinds of shrubs.

SOME SHRUBS TO PROPAGATE FROM SEMI-RIPE CUTTINGS

Buddleia	*Fuchsia*
Camellia	*Griselinia*
Ceanothus	*Hebe*
Choisya	*Hydrangea*
Cistus	*Philadelphus*
Cotoneaster	*Potentilla*
(illustrated)	*Pyracantha*
Escallonia	*Rosemary*
Forsythia	*Weigela*

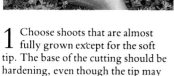

7 Water thoroughly. It is worth adding a fungicide to the water initially, to reduce the chance of the cuttings rotting. Make sure that the soil does not dry out at any time.

LAYER SHRUBS

Layering is usually used for shrubby plants that have low branches easily pegged to the ground, but a few border plants can also be layered – carnations and pinks are often raised this way. In comparison with cuttings, layers usually produce fewer but bigger plants.

1 Find a low-growing shoot that can easily be pegged down to the ground. Trim off the leaves just from the area that will be in contact with the soil.

2 Bend the stem down until it touches the ground. Make a hole 10cm (4in) deep, sloping toward the parent plant but with the other side vertical.

3 Twist or slit the stem slightly to injure it. Peg it into the hole with a piece of bent wire or a peg, using the vertical back of the excavation to force the shoot upright.

4 Return the soil and firm it well. If you keep the ground moist, roots should form and within 12–18 months you may be able to sever the new plant from its parent.

DIVIDE FLAG IRISES

Divide flag irises – hybrids derived from *Iris germanica* – after flowering and if the rhizomes have become very congested.

1 Lift the clump with a fork, and cut away and discard the oldest parts. Use only the current season's growth for replanting.

2 Trim the leaves to stumps about 5–8cm (2–3in) long. Replant the pieces of rhizome on a slight ridge of soil, covering the roots but leaving the tops exposed.

LAYERING CARNATIONS

Border carnations and pinks are layered in a similar way to shrubs, but root much more quickly. Select a few well-spaced, non-flowering shoots and remove all but the top four or five leaves on them. Make a small slit in each one with a sharp knife below the lowest pair of leaves, and peg the shoot – slit down – into good soil. Keep moist.

SUMMER CARE FOR GREENHOUSE TOMATOES

The varieties of tomato usually grown in the greenhouse need regular attention, like the removal of sideshoots, feeding, and tying in.

Keep a watch too for early signs of pests and diseases that could otherwise reduce the quantity or quality of the crop.

1 If the plants are supported by strings, simply loop the string around the top of the shoot whenever necessary. It will form a spiral support that holds the stem upright.

2 To secure the plant to a cane, wrap the string twice around the stake and then loop it loosely around the stem before tying the knot.

3 Snap off sideshoots while they are still small. They will snap off cleanly if you pull them sideways. Do not remove sideshoots if you have a low-growing bush variety.

4 If fruits are failing to form, poor pollination may be the problem. Shake the plants each day, or spray the flowers with water, to spread the pollen.

5 The lowest leaves often turn yellow as they age. Remove these, as they will not contribute to feeding the plant, and letting more light reach the fruits can help to ripen them.

6 'Stop' your plants, by removing the growing tip, when they have formed as many trusses of fruit as are likely to ripen. In an unheated greenhouse this may be as few as four in cold areas; six or seven in warmer regions.

7 Tomatoes respond well to feeding. Some tomato feeds are high in nitrogen for early growth, but now that the fruit is developing, a high-potash tomato fertilizer is best.

OTHER GREENHOUSE CROPS

Greenhouse crops like aubergines, cucumbers and melons also need attention at this time of year if you want to ensure a good, healthy crop.

CARING FOR MELONS

Train the sideshoot of melons to horizontal wires, and pinch back the sideshoots to two leaves beyond each fruit that develops. Melons may require pollinating, in which case transfer the pollen from the male to female flowers with a small paintbrush. It may also be necessary to support developing fruits with nets, as shown.

1 Aubergines make bushier plants if the growing tip is pinched out when the plant is about 30cm (12in) high. Allow only one fruit to develop on each shoot. Pinch out the growing tips of these shoots three leaves beyond the developing fruit. Never let the plants dry out, and feed regularly. Regular misting to provide high humidity is beneficial.

2 Many modern cucumbers produce only female flowers, but there are some varieties you might grow in a greenhouse that produce both male and female blooms (the female flowers have a small embryo fruit behind the petals). Pinch out male flowers before they have a chance to pollinate the female ones, as this can make the cucumbers less palatable.

DAMPING DOWN

Splashing or spraying water over the greenhouse path (traditionally known as damping down) helps to create a humid atmosphere. This is especially beneficial for crops such as aubergines and cucumbers, but most plants appreciate a moist atmosphere on a hot day – including the majority of pot-plants. Do it frequently on very hot days, to create the kind of hot and humid atmosphere that most tropical plants prefer.

LATE SUMMER

LATE SUMMER IS USUALLY A TIME of hot, dry weather, when there is a natural lull in the garden, and the efforts of spring and early summer sowing and planting will have paid dividends. The chores of early autumn can wait until holidays are over and cooler weather begins to return. Most of this month's work in the garden involves watering and routine maintenance tasks like mowing and hoeing, and clipping hedges.

JOBS IN BRIEF

The kitchen garden

- ☐ Hoe regularly to keep down weeds
- ☐ Lift onions and shallots as they become ready
- ☐ Continue to thin vegetables sown earlier
- ☐ Give plants that need a boost a dose of a quick-acting fertilizer
- ☐ Sow cabbages for spring use
- ☐ Pinch out the growing tips of runner beans when they reach the top of their support
- ☐ Pay regular attention to outdoor tomatoes
- ☐ Continue to harvest herbs regularly
- ☐ Summer prune cordon and espalier apples if not already done so and shoots are mature enough
- ☐ Tidy up summer-flowering strawberries. Cut off old leaves and unwanted runners, remove straw, and control weeds
- ☐ Protect fruit against birds if they are troublesome. A fruit cage is ideal

BELOW: *Harvest herbs for a fresh supply of culinary seasonings.*

The flower garden

- ☐ Dead-head plants in borders and containers regularly
- ☐ Feed plants in containers to keep the blooms coming
- ☐ Hoe beds and borders regularly to keep down weeds
- ☐ Take semi-ripe cuttings
- ☐ Clip beech, holly, hornbeam and yew hedges, and most evergreen hedges, if not already done so
- ☐ Plant colchicums, to flower in the autumn
- ☐ Order bulb catalogues and bulbs for autumn delivery
- ☐ Start planting spring-flowering bulbs
- ☐ Take fuchsia and pelargonium cuttings
- ☐ Start sowing hardy annuals to overwinter (only in mild areas or if you can provide winter protection)
- ☐ Prune rambler roses
- ☐ Layer border carnations
- ☐ Mow the lawn except in very dry weather
- ☐ Water the lawn in dry spells, but a few good soaks will be better than many sprinklings that do not penetrate deeply
- ☐ Watch out for pests and diseases on roses and other vulnerable plants
- ☐ Feed and disbud dahlias and chrysanthemums as necessary
- ☐ Transplant polyanthus seedlings into their flowering positions in beds and borders
- ☐ Keep paths and drives weed-free by hand or with a weedkiller

The greenhouse and conservatory

- ☐ Sow spring-flowering plants such as cyclamen, schizanthus and exacums
- ☐ Continue to feed pot-plants regularly
- ☐ Take leaf and semi-ripe cuttings
- ☐ Continue to feed tomatoes and to deal with routine tasks
- ☐ Keep a vigilant watch for pests and diseases
- ☐ Pot up and pot on seedling pot-plants as it becomes necessary
- ☐ Plant hyacinths for early flowering under glass

BELOW: *Plant prepared hyacinths for early flowering as soon as they are available.*

- ☐ Check cinerarias for leaf miners (white 'tunnels' in the leaves). Remove affected leaves or control with a systemic insecticide

PLANTS AT THEIR BEST

Dahlia (bulb)
Erigeron (herbaceous)
Fuchsia (shrub)
Helenium (herbaceous)
Hibiscus syriacus (shrub)
Hydrangea (shrub)
Hypericum (shrub)
Lavatera (shrub)
Lilium (bulb)
Perovskia atriplicifolia (shrub)
Romneya (shrub)
Solidago (herbaceous)
Summer bedding
Verbascum (herbaceous)

RIGHT: *Fuchsias flower throughout the summer and will continue into autumn.*

BELOW: Perovskia atriplicifolia *'Blue Spire' is one of the best blue flowers for late summer, and is undemanding to grow.*

SUMMER CARE FOR OUTDOOR TOMATOES

Outdoor tomatoes demand less attention than greenhouse varieties, especially if you grow the kinds where you leave on the sideshoots. Feeding and watering is a necessary routine if you want a good crop of quality fruits. Regular watering not only ensures a heavy crop but also reduces the risk of fruit splitting through uneven watering. This sometimes happens if dry weather produces hard skins which then can't cope with a sudden spurt of growth following a wet period. Add a liquid fertilizer to the water, at the rate and frequency recommended by the manufacturer. How well your tomatoes crop outdoors depends on a combination of variety, care and climate. In cold areas, outdoor tomatoes can be a disappointing crop, in warm areas you will almost certainly have more fruit than you can cope with.

1 If growing a cordon variety (one that you grow as a single main stem, supported by a cane), keep removing sideshoots as they develop.

2 Regular tying to the support is even more important out-doors than in the greenhouse, as strong winds can break an untied stem and shorten the productive life of the plant.

3 As soon as the plant has set the number of trusses (sprays) of fruit likely to be ripened in your area, pinch out the top of the plant. In many areas you can only reasonably expect to ripen four trusses, but in warm areas it may be more.

4 Many bush varieties have small but prolific fruits. As it is not practical to support all the sideshoots with canes, some branches bend and come into contact with the soil. Place straw beneath these to keep the fruits off the soil. It will keep them cleaner and reduce the risk of them rotting.

LIFT SHALLOTS

Shallots usually stop growing before onions and, if planted early, can be lifted in mid summer.

But if you planted late it may be late summer before they are ready to ripen and harvest.

1 Loosen the clumps with a fork, but leave them exposed on the surface for a few days. This will give the base of the bulb a chance to dry off before being stored.

2 If the weather is damp, leave the bulbs on trays in a light, warm place so that they are not damp when stored. Or leave them on mesh trays outdoors until dry (see onions, step 3).

RIPEN AND HARVEST ONIONS

Harvest onions when the foliage is straw coloured and brittle dry. They will store better if,

when lifted, they are exposed to the sun to ripen and dry first.

1 Ripening can be hastened once the plants are nearing their maximum size by bending over their tops. Bend them so that the bulbs are exposed to as much sun as possible.

2 As soon as the foliage has turned a straw colour and is brittle, lift them with a fork and leave them on the surface for a few days to dry off. Lay with their roots facing the sun.

3 Finish off the hardening and ripening process by laying the bulbs on netting or wire mesh supported above the ground so that air can circulate freely.

4 If the weather is very damp, cover the bulbs with cloches until you can store them.

TAKE FUCHSIA CUTTINGS

Fuchsias are really easy to root, and by taking cuttings now you will have young plants that can be overwintered in a light position in a cool but frost-free room or in a greenhouse. These will make good plants for next summer, or you can use them to provide more cuttings next spring.

1 Softwood cuttings can be taken for as long as new growth is being produced, but at this time of year semi-ripe (semi-mature) cuttings root easily and are simple to take. Pull off sideshoots about 10cm (4in) long, with a 'heel' of old main stem attached.

2 Trim off the lowest leaves and trim the end of the heel to make a clean cut. If you have taken cuttings without a heel, trim the stem straight across beneath a leaf-joint.

3 Although cuttings will usually root without aid, a hormone rooting powder should speed the process. Insert several cuttings around the edge of an 8–10cm (3–4in) pot filled with a rooting mixture.

4 Label the cuttings, water and place them in a cold frame, greenhouse or on a light windowsill. Keep the compost damp, and pot up individually when well rooted. Protect from frost.

TAKE PELARGONIUM CUTTINGS

Pelargoniums (popularly known as bedding geraniums) can be overwintered in a frost-free place to provide cuttings next spring. Many experts prefer to take cuttings now, however, and to overwinter the young plants in a light, frost-free place.

RIGHT: *Pelargoniums, or bedding geraniums, are one of the most popular of summer plants.*

1 Take cuttings from non-flowering shoots (if you have to use flowering shoots, cut off the blooms). A good guide to length is to cut the shoot off just above the third joint below the growing tip.

2 Remove the lowest pair of leaves with a sharp knife, and remove any flowers or buds. Trim straight across the base of each cutting, just below the lowest leaf joint. You can dip the ends in a rooting hormone, but they usually root readily without.

3 Insert about five cuttings around the edge of a 13cm (5in) pot containing a cuttings mixture and firm gently. Keep in a light, warm position but out of direct sun. Be careful not to overwater, otherwise the cuttings will rot. Pot up individually when rooted.

DAHLIA AND CHRYSANTHEMUM CARE

Dahlias and chrysanthemums come into their true glory at the end of summer and into autumn, just as most flowers have passed their best. Some types are simply left to produce masses of blooms with no intervention, but those grown for large flowers are usually selectively disbudded. This produces fewer but larger blooms. Both types of plant need plenty of feeding and a careful watch has to be kept to prevent pests and diseases marring these plants.

1 To produce larger flowers, pinch out the side buds behind the crown (central) flower bud of dahlias, while they are still small. Many chrysanthemums are also disbudded, but how and when you do it depends on the variety, so be guided by a specialist catalogue or publication.

2 The best way to control pests and diseases is to spray at the first signs. Often it may be possible to prevent spread simply by pinching off and destroying the first few affected leaves. This chrysanthemum shows evidence of leaf miner damage.

3 Chrysanthemums and dahlias benefit from regular feeding. Even if you used a slow-release fertilizer to see them through most of the summer, they will probably respond to a boost now. Use a quick-acting general fertilizer or a high-potash feed, but don't boost with too much nitrogen.

PLANT BULBS FOR SPRING

Spring-flowering bulbs are now widely available, but exactly when you plant them will depend largely on whether the ground has been cleared of summer plants. If planting in beds, it is best to let summer bedding flower for as long as possible, and you may prefer not to disturb the last of the summer colour in herbaceous borders just yet, but in vacant ground it is best to plant as soon as possible. Bulbs are always better in the ground rather than in bags and boxes that are probably stored in less than ideal conditions. Bulbs look good in front of shrubs, and you should be able to plant these as soon as they are obtainable. Indoor bulbs that are specially prepared for early flowering should also be planted as soon as they become available.

1 Fork over the ground before planting, and if the plants are to be left undisturbed for some years, try to incorporate plenty of organic material such as rotted garden compost or manure. Many bulbs like well-drained soil but still benefit from plenty of organic material that will hold moisture and nutrients.

2 Avoid adding quick-acting fertilizers in the autumn. Controlled-release fertilizers that provide nutrients according to the soil temperature can be used, but they are best employed in spring. Instead rake a very slow-acting fertilizer such as bonemeal, which contains mainly phosphate, into the surface, or apply it to the planting holes.

3 Where there is space and the plants will benefit from planting in an informal group or cluster, dig out a hole about three times the depth of the bulbs and wide enough to take the clumps.

4 Space the bulbs so that they look like a natural clump. Use the spacing recommended on the packet as a guide. Wide spacing will allow for future growth and multiplication, but if you intend to lift the bulbs after flowering much closer spacing will create a bolder display.

5 Draw the soil back over the bulbs, being careful not to dislodge them in the process.

7 If you are likely to cultivate the area before the shoots come through, mark out where bulbs have been planted with a few small canes. Always insert a label, as it will be months before the bulbs appear and flower, by which time it is often difficult to remember the variety planted.

6 Firm the soil with the back of the rake rather than treading it, which may damage the bulbs.

RECOGNIZING WHICH WAY UP TO PLANT BULBS

Most bulbs have a very obvious top and bottom and present no problem. Others, especially tubers, can cause confusion because they lack an obvious growing point. If in doubt, just plant them on their side – the shoot will grow upwards and the roots down.

A few bulbs that do have an obvious top are planted on their side because the base tends to rot in wet soil, though these are rare exceptions. *Fritillaria imperialis* is sometimes planted this way, and it is always worth planting vulnerable bulbs on a bed of grit or coarse sand to encourage good drainage around the base, as shown.

PLANTING IN INDIVIDUAL HOLES

If you have a lot of bulbs to plant over a wide area, individual planting holes may be more appropriate than creating larger excavations to take a group of bulbs.

There are special long-handled planting tools, but an ordinary long-handled trowel is just as good. You can use a normal trowel with a handle of conventional length, but it makes planting more tedious if the area is large.

Check periodically to make sure that the holes are being made to the correct depth. After checking a few it will be easy to judge by eye.

Make a hole large enough to take the bulb easily (it must not become wedged in the hole, as the roots will then be exposed to dry air).

Return the excavated soil. If planting a large area, you can shuffle it back in with your feet, then rake the surface level.

ABOVE: *Tulips, wallflowers and forget-me-nots, all ideal for spring bedding.*

SOW SPRING-FLOWERING POT-PLANTS

Provided you can keep your greenhouse frost-free during the winter – ideally at a minimum of 7°C (45°F) – it is worth sowing a few flowering plants to bloom next spring. Some suggestions are given in the box below, and those that are hardy, such as calendulas and limnanthes, can even be grown in an unheated greenhouse provided you do not live in a very cold area.

1 As you are only likely to need relatively few plants, sow in pots rather than seed trays. If you don't have a rounded presser to firm the sowing mixture lightly, use the bottom of a jar.

2 Sprinkle the seeds as thinly and evenly as possible over the surface. Large seeds, such as cyclamens, can be spaced individually. Cover with a sprinkling of the sowing mixture if needed (follow the advice on the packet).

3 Stand the pot in a container of water. Letting the moisture seep up from below like this avoids the risk of seeds being washed away or into clumps were you to water the pot from above.

4 Because the outside air temperature is still warm, most seeds will germinate readily without the need for a propagator, but cover with a sheet of glass, or place in a plastic bag, to reduce water loss through evaporation. Seeds that germinate slowly and erratically, such as cyclamen, benefit from being placed in a heated propagator.

SEEDS TO SOW NOW

Browallia
Calendula (choose a very dwarf variety)★
Cineraria
Cyclamen (for home and greenhouse)★★
Exacum affine
Limnanthes douglasii★
Linaria maroccana★
Primula acaulis (cultivated primroses)★
Primula malacoides
Schizanthus

★ These are tough plants that will tolerate some frost and are suitable for an unheated greenhouse in mild areas
★★ Cyclamen should flower in mid winter the following year (ie after about 16 months)

ABOVE: *The pot marigold* (Calendula officinalis), *easy and always cheerful.*

PLANT HYACINTHS FOR EARLY FLOWERING

For early flowering indoors or in the greenhouse, you must choose bulbs that have been 'prepared' or 'treated'. The term may vary, but it simply means that before you receive the bulb it has been stored under specially controlled conditions that make it think more of its resting period has elapsed. It looks no different, but it believes winter is more advanced than in reality and that it needs to grow and bloom quickly.

Ordinary, untreated, hyacinths can be planted now in just the same way, but they will flower later in the season. It is a good idea to pot up some bulbs of both kinds, separately, to spread the flowering period.

1 If using a bowl without drainage, use a special bulb mixture based on peat. If you use a container with drainage holes, any ordinary potting mixture can be used.

2 Place a thin layer of the potting mixture in the container, then space the bulbs close together but make sure they are not touching. An odd number will look better than an even number (three or five bulbs are usually planted in a bowl).

3 Pack more potting mixture around the bulbs, but leave their 'noses' exposed. Water, but be careful not to overwater.

4 Keep the planted bulbs in a cold, dark place indoors, perhaps in the garage, or in a special 'plunge bed' outdoors. Simply stand the bowls in a cool, shady position and cover them with several centimetres or inches of grit, peat or coarse sand. If the containers lack drainage holes, protect from rain to prevent water-logging. Check the containers for progress periodically.

AUTUMN

Be watchful and vigilant as the nights become colder. In some areas quite severe frosts are common in early autumn, and in others light frosts may not occur until mid or late autumn, if at all. Listen to the weather forecasts and take in or protect vulnerable plants if frost is expected. Think seriously about winter protection for plants on the borderline of hardiness, and be prepared to give early winter shelter, perhaps in the form of a windbreak, for newly planted evergreens. A little protection can ensure that many plants survive instead of succumbing to winter winds and cold.

OPPOSITE: *The colourful leaves of* Rhus typhina *'Laciniata', with the white plumes of a cortaderia in the background.*

ABOVE: Liriope muscari, *one of the delights of autumn, is fortunately tough and very easy to grow.*

EARLY AUTUMN

THE WEATHER IN EARLY AUTUMN IS still warm enough to make outdoor gardening a comfortable experience, and although the vibrant flowers of summer may be gone, there are plenty of delights to be enjoyed in the form of bright berries and flaming foliage, not to mention late-flowering gems such as chrysanthemums and nerines. Apart from bulb planting, and protecting frost-tender plants, there are few really pressing jobs at this time of year.

JOBS IN BRIEF

The kitchen garden

- ☐ Lift onions to store
- ☐ Place cloches over lettuces and other low-growing vegetables that will continue to grow for longer with protection
- ☐ Sow a crop of a green manure (such as mustard) to use up nutrients in vacant ground, which will be recycled when the crop is dug in
- ☐ Lift and store maincrop potatoes
- ☐ Protect outdoor tomatoes with cloches or fleece to extend their season and ripen more fruit
- ☐ Summer prune cordon and espalier apples if not already done
- ☐ Clean and store canes and stakes

BELOW: *Extend the vegetable season by covering with cloches.*

The flower garden

- ☐ Plant spring-flowering bulbs
- ☐ Take fuchsia and pelargonium cuttings
- ☐ Sow hardy annuals to overwinter (only in mild areas or if you can provide winter protection)
- ☐ Plant lilies
- ☐ Clear summer bedding and prepare for spring bedding plants
- ☐ Continue to watch for pests and diseases on roses and other vulnerable plants
- ☐ Disbud dahlias and chrysanthemums as necessary
- ☐ Lift and store dahlias after the first frost
- ☐ Lift and store gladioli and other tender bulbs, corms and tubers
- ☐ Take in tender aquatic plants from the pond if frost is threatened

BELOW: *Tulips are best interplanted with spring bedding plants.*

The greenhouse and conservatory

- ☐ Bring in house and greenhouse plants that have been standing outdoors for the summer
- ☐ Sow spring-flowering plants such as cyclamen, schizanthus and exacums
- ☐ Clean off summer shading washes
- ☐ Repot cacti if they need it
- ☐ Check that greenhouse heaters are in good working order. Arrange to have them serviced, if necessary
- ☐ Pot up and pot on seedling pot-plants as it becomes necessary
- ☐ Plant hyacinths for early flowering under glass

BELOW: *Think about repotting your cacti, a prickly job that has to be done at some time.*

PLANTS AT THEIR BEST

Anemone japonica (herbaceous)
Aster novae-angliae (herbaceous)
Aster novi-belgii (herbaceous)
Chrysanthemum, early-flowering
garden type (herbaceous)
Dahlia (bulb)
Hibiscus syriacus (shrub)
Hydrangea (shrub)
Lavatera (shrub)
Nerine bowdenii (bulb)
Pyracantha, berries (shrub)
Rudbeckia (herbaceous)
Sedum spectabile (herbaceous)
Solidago (herbaceous)
Sorbus, berries (tree)
Sternbergia lutea (bulb)

RIGHT: *The autumn-flowering* Sedum
spectabile *is a highlight of autumn.*

BELOW: Rudbeckia fulgida *'Goldsturm' is
one of the stars of the autumn border.*

PUT CLOCHES IN PLACE

If you have cloches that you normally use to protect your crops in spring, make the most of them by extending the end of the season as well as the beginning.

Save large barn cloches for large crops such as tomatoes (see opposite), if wished, and use tent and plastic tunnel cloches for low-growing crops such as lettuces.

1 Winter radishes and mooli radishes are frost-hardy, but you can encourage further growth before bad weather sets in by covering them with cloches. If you failed to sow them earlier, you may be able to start them off under cloches now in a mild area, provided you do so while the soil is still warm.

2 Try sowing lamb's lettuce and winter purslane as a cold month crop. They don't need cloche protection except in cold areas, but the cover will ensure a better supply of more succulent leaves.

ABOVE: *Put cloches in place now to warm up the soil for early crops such as lettuces.*

RIGHT: *Beetroot can also be sown earlier if you first warm the soil with cloches.*

3 Put the cloches in position before the cold weather checks growth. With a little protection like this the plants will crop more freely.

PROTECT OUTDOOR TOMATOES

Green tomatoes can be ripened indoors provided they have reached a reasonable stage of maturity, but it makes sense to ripen as many as possible on the plant. As soon as a severe frost is forecast, however, harvest the remaining fruit and ripen as many as possible indoors.

1 Frost will kill tomatoes, but you can often extend their season by a few weeks and ripen a few more fruits on the plant with protection. Bush plants that are already low-growing are best covered with a large cloche. Packing straw beneath the plants first will also provide a little insulation.

2 Cordon-trained tomatoes must be lowered before they can be protected with cloches. Untie the plant and remove the stake.

3 Lay a bed of straw on the ground, then carefully lower the plants onto this. If you lay all the stems in the same direction, you will have a neat row of tomatoes that are easily covered with cloches.

5 Fleece can also be used to protect cordon tomatoes while still staked. Sheets of fleece can be wrapped round, or you may be able to buy fleece produced as a tube. Simply cut off the required length, slip it over the plant, and secure at the top and bottom.

4 Fleece can be used to offer wind protection and enough shelter to keep off a degree or two of frost, though it does not warm the air during the day in the same way as glass or some rigid plastics. Drape several layers over low-growing varieties, and peg it down securely along each side, and at the ends.

PLANT UP A SPRING WINDOWBOX WITH BULBS

Spring bulb displays are less predictable than summer flowers, and it can be especially disappointing when different bulbs planted in the same windowbox flower at different times. The consolation is that this does at least extend the interest. A good alternative is to plant single-subject displays which, although often brief, are frequently bolder.

1 Make sure that there are drainage holes, and add a layer of material to aid quick drainage, such as broken pots or pieces of chipped bark (sold for mulching).

2 Add enough potting soil to cover the bottom couple of centimetres (about an inch). As the bulbs do not need a lot of nutrients during the winter, you can often use some of the potting mixture previously used for summer bedding.

3 You can pack in more bulbs by planting in layers. Place large bulbs such as daffodils or tulips at the lower level.

4 Add more potting soil, then position the smaller bulbs, such as crocuses and scillas. Try to position them so that they lie between the larger bulbs. Be careful about the bulbs that you mix – small crocuses will be swamped by tall daffodils, so choose miniature or dwarf daffodils, to keep a suitable balance.

5 Top up with more potting soil, but leave 2–3cm (¾–1in) of space at the top for watering and perhaps a decorative mulch. As the windowbox will look bare for some months, a few winter pansies will add a touch of interest. Don't worry about the bulbs beneath – they will find their way through the pansies.

BULBS AND SPRING BEDDING

Some of the best container displays for spring combine bulbs with spring-flowering bedding plants such as forget-me-nots (*Myosotis*), double daisies (*Bellis*) and cultivated primroses. This is often more effective than filling the container with bulbs alone. It means that the container looks less bleak after planting, and the period of flowering is greatly extended.

Put the plants in first, then the bulbs between them. If you plant the bulbs first, it will be difficult to remember the positioning and they are likely to be disturbed when you insert the plants.

LEFT: *Even common plants like tulips and pansies can look stunning in the right combination and setting.*

PLANT UP A TUB OR PATIO POT WITH BULBS

Tubs, large pots, and urns can be planted in the same way as windowboxes – with bulbs in multiple layers or combined with spring-flowering plants – but bulbs also make good companions for shrubs and small trees in tubs.

They make the most of space around the edge of the container that is usually wasted, and if the shrubby plant sheds its leaves in winter, the bulbs will complete the important parts of their annual cycle before there is competition for light.

1 If planting an empty container, try placing a small conifer in the centre to provide winter interest. A few ivies positioned so that they trail over the edge will usually improve the appearance in winter.

2 Position the bulbs on the surface first so that they are evenly spaced around the edge. Small plants that multiply freely, such as *Muscari armeniacum*, scillas, chionodoxas, and *Anemone blanda*, are among the plants that can usually be depended upon to improve year by year.

3 Plant with a trowel, being careful to disturb the roots of an established plant as little as possible.

PLANT BEDS AND BORDERS FOR A SPRING DISPLAY

Beds normally used for summer bedding can be replanted with spring bedding – a combination of plants and bulbs will create a better display than bulbs alone. Plants like forget-me-nots and double daisies help to clothe the ground between the bulbs during the winter, and in spring fill in around the base of tall bulbs such as tulips that can otherwise look rather stalky.

It is a good idea to see what your local parks department does for plant combinations. It is better to modify an existing combination that you like, even if you don't want to copy it exactly, rather than experiment if you don't know much about the plants. A failure will mean that you will have to wait another year for the next attempt.

1 Fork over the ground after clearing it of summer bedding plants. Fertilizer is not normally needed, but bonemeal, which is very slow-acting, is worth adding if the soil is impoverished. Apply bonemeal after forking over and rake it in.

2 If you have raised the plants yourself, and have them growing in a nursery bed, water well about an hour before lifting them. Lift with as much soil round the roots as possible.

3 Spring bedding plants bought from garden centres are usually sold in trays or strips. These are usually disposable, so don't be afraid to break them if this allows you to release the root-ball with as little damage as possible.

ABOVE: *Tulips usually look better if underplanted with wallflowers or forget-me-nots.*

4 Space the plants out on the surface, allowing for the bulbs, before planting. Space the bulbs out, then begin planting from the back or one end.

PLANT LILIES FOR SUMMER

Lilies are often planted in spring, but you can also plant them now except in very cold areas. The bulbs are less likely to dry out, which can result in failures. Most lilies prefer a slightly acid soil (pH6–6.5), but some – including *Lilium candidum* – will do well in alkaline soils.

1 Lilies demand a well-prepared site, so dig the soil deeply and work in as much well-rotted manure or garden compost as you can spare. Add plenty of grit to improve drainage if the soil tends to be wet.

2 Lilies look best in groups rather than as isolated specimens, so excavate an area of soil to a depth of about 20cm (8in), large enough to take at least four or five bulbs. Add coarse grit or sand unless the soil is very well drained.

3 Add a sprinkling of bonemeal or a controlled-release fertilizer, as lilies are usually left undisturbed until overcrowded and therefore feeding is more important than with bedding bulbs used for a single season.

4 Space the bulbs about 15cm (6in) apart and make sure that they are deep enough to be covered with about twice their own depth of soil. Sprinkle more grit or coarse sand around the bulbs to deter slugs and reduce the risk of waterlogging.

5 Place small canes or sticks around the planting area before you return the soil. These remind you to avoid damaging the emerging shoots when you hoe. Remember to label.

ABOVE: *Lilies are real eye-catchers, as this drift of the compact 'Little Girl' proves.*

CLEAR SUMMER BEDDING

If frosts have not put an abrupt end to your summer bedding display, the plants will undoubtedly be looking sad and dejected by now.

Even if you do not plan to replant with spring bedding, the garden will look tidier if the old plants are cleared away and the ground dug over.

1 Plants like this will do more good on the compost heap than left on show. Bare soil can look neat and tidy provided you eliminate weeds.

2 Bedding plants generally have shallow roots and are easy to pull up by hand. If some are deep-rooted, just loosen the roots with a fork.

3 Old bedding plants are ideal for the compost heap. Being non-woody they rot down easily.

4 Dig over the ground, and remove any large weeds. Use a spade if the ground is very weedy so that most of them can be buried as the soil is turned, otherwise use a fork.

5 Whether or not you are replanting with spring bedding, rake the ground level so that it looks neat and tidy.

PRESERVE AND STORE GARDEN CANES

Bamboo canes deteriorate after a season or two in use, especially where they have been in the ground. Extend their life by cleaning and preserving them. Store in a dry place, rather than leaving them exposed in the garden.

1 Knock most of the soil off, then scrub the canes with a stiff brush and garden or household disinfectant. Pay special attention to the ends, and make sure any soil is removed.

2 Wipe the scrubbed canes with a cloth to dry them, then stand the ends that have been in the soil in a bucket or container partly filled with a wood preservative. Leave overnight to allow the preservative to penetrate.

3 Bundle the canes to keep them tidy, and store in a dry place until needed next year.

LIFT AND STORE GLADIOLI

Gladioli can only be left in the ground in mild areas where frosts are always light and do not penetrate far into the soil. In cold areas gladioli will be killed if they remain in the soil, so lift them before there are penetrating frosts.

Gladioli flower reliably from year to year, so they are almost always worth saving. The cormels (small corms) that form around the base will reach flowering size within a couple of years if looked after.

1 Loosen the soil with a garden fork before attempting to lift the plants.

2 Trim off most of the foliage, leaving just a stub to dry off. Shake off most of the soil.

3 Leave the lifted plants in a dry place for a few days to dry off. When the remains of the old stems have shrivelled, trim them off, and remove the cormels that have grown around the base. Store these if you want to save them, otherwise discard. Pull off the remains of the old corm to leave just the healthy new corm. Lay the corms in trays and keep in a frost-proof place for a day or two for further drying.

4 Dust with fungicide and store in paper bags away from frost.

REPOT CACTI AND SUCCULENTS

Cacti and succulents can be repotted at any time of the year, though spring or the end of the growing season are convenient times. Many succulents present no special handling problems, but prickly cacti have to be treated with respect.

If possible, choose a soil mix formulated for cacti, as this will be well drained and have the right sort of structure and nutrient level. A soil-based potting mixture is a practical alternative. Some commercial growers use peat-based potting mixtures, but these are best avoided. Apart from the difficulty in keeping the water balance right, peat-based potting mixtures do not have the weight and structure to support large cacti and succulents.

Large specimens do not need regular repotting. Simply remove about 3cm (1in) of soil from the top and replace with fresh cactus soil.

1 To handle a prickly cactus, fold a strip of newspaper, thick paper or thin card to make a flexible band that you can wrap around the plant.

2 Tap the pot on a hard surface to loosen the root-ball. You can then often lift the plant out with the improvised handle. If it refuses to move, try pushing a pencil through the drainage hole to break the bond.

3 If the plant has been in the same soil for a long time, crumble away a little of it from the base and around the sides of the root-ball. But be careful to minimize damage to the roots. Just shake off loose compost.

4 The majority of cacti and succulents are best in pots that are quite small in proportion to the size of the top growth. It is usually best to move the plant into a pot only one size larger. If using a clay pot, cover the drainage hole with pieces of broken pot or other material.

5 While holding the plant with the improvised handle, trickle compost around the old root-ball. With some cacti, their shape makes this difficult to do without your hand touching the spines, in which case you can use a spoon.

6 Tap the bottom of the pot on a hard surface to settle the soil around the roots. This is especially important as it is often difficult to firm the soil with your fingers if the cactus is prickly. Wait for a couple of days before watering.

BRING IN POT-PLANTS FROM THE GARDEN

Many winter and spring-flowering houseplants, such as schulmbergeras, zygocactus, and solanums grown for their winter berries, even orchids, can spend the summer outdoors as they look uninteresting at this stage. Make sure these are brought in before the first frost threatens.

1 Clear away the mulching material if the pots have been plunged into the ground and mulched to reduce the need for regular watering.

2 If the pots do not come up easily, insert a garden fork a little distance away and lever them gently to avoid damaging the pots.

3 Remove leaves and debris from the surface of the potting soil, which will almost certainly have become contaminated. Wipe the pot clean with a damp cloth, and be especially careful to clean the bottom of the pot so that it does not make a mess indoors.

4 Always check for pests and diseases before taking the plant indoors or into the greenhouse. Look on the backs of the leaves too, which is where snails will often be found. Even a small snail can do a lot of damage if left undetected. If the plant has thick or glossy leaves, wipe them over with a proprietary leaf shine to improve their appearance. Plants left outdoors almost always become splashed with mud and dirt.

GREENHOUSE SHADING

Plants now need all the light they can get, so remove greenhouse shading as soon as possible. If you applied a shading wash earlier in the year, clean it off now. Most can be rubbed off with a duster when the glass is dry. Internal or external shading material such as blinds or nets can also be removed now, as shown here. You may be able to use the same internal fixings to secure winter insulation.

MID AUTUMN

THIS IS AN UNPREDICTABLE TIME OF the year. In cold regions quite severe frosts are not uncommon, while in mild climates some plants are still growing and tender plants may not be brought to an abrupt end for another month or more. This is a time to listen to the weather forecast and to be on the alert, in particular, for frost warnings if you haven't yet had the first frost. Be flexible and garden with an eye to the weather as well as the calendar.

JOBS IN BRIEF

The kitchen garden

- ☐ Plant cabbages for spring harvesting
- ☐ Thin late-sown lettuces for winter harvesting
- ☐ Continue to earth up celery and leeks
- ☐ Lift and store potatoes
- ☐ Protect late cauliflowers from frost by bending surrounding leaves over the heads
- ☐ Cut the dead tops off asparagus
- ☐ Use cloches to protect vulnerable vegetables
- ☐ Start winter digging on heavy soils
- ☐ Pot up some herbs for winter use
- ☐ Pick and store apples when ready
- ☐ Take black currant cuttings
- ☐ Prune black currants, gooseberries and raspberries
- ☐ Cover late-fruiting strawberries with cloches to extend the season
- ☐ Plant bare-root fruit bushes and trees
- ☐ Apply greasebands to apple trees

BELOW: *Greasebanding is a non-chemical method of controlling some fruit pests.*

The flower garden

- ☐ Make a new lawn from turf
- ☐ Give an established lawn autumn lawncare treatment
- ☐ Plant roses
- ☐ Plant bare-root and balled trees and shrubs
- ☐ Plant herbaceous plants
- ☐ Divide over-large herbaceous plants
- ☐ Clear summer bedding
- ☐ Plant spring bulbs
- ☐ Take in tender fuchsias and pelargoniums
- ☐ Protect vulnerable plants

BELOW: *Bare-root plants can be dug in temporarily if you are not ready to plant.*

- ☐ Cut down and lift dahlias blackened by frost
- ☐ Lift and take in chrysanthemums not hardy enough to overwinter outside
- ☐ Lift gladioli corms
- ☐ Plant lilies
- ☐ Sow sweet peas in pots
- ☐ Plant hedges
- ☐ Prepare the pond for winter
- ☐ Collect and compost fallen leaves
- ☐ Remove leaves that have fallen on rock plants

The greenhouse and conservatory

- ☐ Clean and disinfect, ready for winter
- ☐ Insulate
- ☐ Remove yellowing and dead leaves from plants – pick them off the pot as well as the plant
- ☐ Check that heaters are working properly
- ☐ Check minimum temperatures being achieved (if you don't have a minimum–maximum thermometer, buy one)
- ☐ Ventilate whenever the weather is mild enough

BELOW: *Bubble insulation will save money if you heat your greenhouse in winter.*

PLANTS AT THEIR BEST

Acer, colourful foliage (tree/shrub)
Anemone japonica (herbaceous)
Aster novi-belgii (herbaceous)
Berberis, colourful foliage and berries
(shrub)
Fothergilla, colourful foliage (shrub)
Liriope muscari (herbaceous)
Parthenocissus, colourful foliage
(climber)
Pernettya, berries (shrub)
Pyracantha, berries (shrub)
Schizostylis coccinea (herbaceous)

LEFT: *Apples are very decorative fruits, and some will be ready to harvest.*

BELOW LEFT: Parthenocissus tricuspidatus *ends its season with brilliant autumn colour.*

BELOW: *'Audrey' is one of many varieties of* Aster novi-belgii, *ideal for autumn colour.*

LIFT AND STORE POTATOES

Early and mid-season varieties are best eaten soon after harvesting, but the late varieties are grown mainly for storing for winter use. If you grow a small quantity they are best stored in paper sacks kept indoors, but if you grow a lot and indoor storage space is limited, try using the traditional clamping method. It looks primitive but works except where winters are very severe.

1 Lift the tubers with a fork once the foliage has died down. You can leave them in the ground for longer if penetrating frosts are not likely to be a problem, but lift promptly if pests like slugs appear.

2 Leave the potatoes on the surface for a couple of hours so that the skins dry off and harden.

3 Sort the potatoes before storing. It is sufficient to grade them into four sizes: very small, small, medium and large. Discard or use up very small ones immediately, keep small ones for use soon, and only store the medium and largest.

RIGHT: *Potatoes are best left to dry off for a couple of hours before sorting and storing.*

4 Place the largest potatoes in sacks to store in a cool but frost-proof place. Paper sacks are best, but if you can't obtain them, use plastic sacks in which case make slits with a knife to provide some ventilation.

5 If you have too many potatoes to store in sacks, or don't have space indoors, make a clamp in the garden. Excavate a shallow depression and line it with a thick layer of straw.

6 Pile the potatoes on to the bed of straw, as shown.

7 Heap a thick layer of straw over the top. It must be thick enough to provide good insulation.

8 Mound earth over the straw, but leave a few tufts of straw sticking out of the top for ventilation.

PROLONGING HERBS

Parsley is one of the herbs that will continue to provide leaves for harvesting throughout the winter if you protect the plants with cloches. Make sure that the end pieces are tightly secured.

STRAW PROTECTION

Vegetables such as celery (shown here) and beetroot benefit in cold areas if you protect the stems with straw. Pack the straw among and between the plants in the blocks or rows. It does not matter if the tops of the leaves are exposed – you are only protecting the edible part.

Mature celery will usually survive some frost, but the protection is useful if it turns very cold before you are ready to lift it. In mild areas you can leave beetroot unprotected, but the straw does help to keep plants in better condition for longer in cold areas.

NATURALIZE BULBS IN GRASS

Naturalizing bulbs is a good way to enjoy a trouble-free display each spring, and one that should improve each year. You will need an area of grass that you don't mind leaving unmown until early summer, to allow bulb foliage to die back naturally.

1 If you have a lot of small bulbs, such as crocuses and eranthis, to plant in a limited area, try lifting an area of turf. Use a spade or half-moon edger to make an H-shaped cut.

2 Slice beneath the grass with a spade until you can fold the turf back for planting.

3 Loosen the ground first, as it will be very compacted. If you want to apply a slow-acting fertilizer such as bonemeal, work it into the soil at the same time.

4 Avoid planting in rows or regimented patterns. You want them to look natural and informal, so scatter them and plant where they fall.

5 If you plant large bulbs this way, you will have to make deeper holes with a trowel. Plant them so that they are covered with about twice their own depth of soil.

6 Firm the soil then return the grass. Firm again if necessary to make sure it is flat, and water if the weather is dry to ensure that the grass grows again quickly.

7 Large bulbs such as daffodils are easier to plant using a bulb planter that takes out a core of soil. Scatter the bulbs randomly so that the display will look natural.

8 Push the bulb planter into the soil, twisting it a little if the ground is hard, then pull it out with the core of soil. Release the core of soil and place the bulb at the bottom of the hole.

9 First pull off a little soil from the base of the core (to allow for the depth of the bulb), then replace core in the hole. Firm gently.

RIGHT: *Try naturalizing bulbs, like these anemones, at the edge of the lawn, where you can leave the grass long until the plants die down.*

LIFT AND STORE DAHLIAS

Do not discard your dahlias – lift the tubers before frosts penetrate the ground, and store them for next year. Even seed-raised plants will have formed tubers that you can store.

1 Lift the dahlia tubers once the first frosts have blackened the foliage. Use a fork to lift the tubers, to minimize the risk of damaging them. Cut off the old stem to leave a stump about 5cm (2in) long.

2 Stand the tubers upside down so that moisture drains easily from the hollow stems. Using a mesh support is a convenient way to allow them to dry off. Keep in a dry, frost-free place.

3 After a few days the tubers should be dry enough to store. Remove surplus soil, trim off loose bits of old roots and shorten the stem to leave a short stump. Label each plant.

4 Pack the tubers in a well-insulated box with peat, vermiculite, wood shavings, or crumpled newspaper placed between them. Keep in a frost-free location.

WINTER QUARTERS

A spare bedroom or cool but frost-free garage are sensible places to store overwintering bulbs, corms and tubers such as dahlias. Avoid a very warm place, as roots will spread more rapidly if they become established, and the bulbs or tubers are more likely to dry out. Keep bulbs, corms and tubers where you can easily check them about once a month, to ensure they are all still sound. Any that start to rot must be removed immediately.

PREPARE THE POND FOR WINTER

Although ponds need little routine maintenance, there are a few end-of-season tasks that are essential if you want to keep your plants and fish in good condition.

1 Protect the pond from the worst of the leaf fall with a fine-mesh net. Anchor it just above the surface of the pond. This is not practical for a large pond, but it is useful for a small one. Remove the leaves regularly, and eventually take the netting off.

2 If you are not able to cover your pond with a net, or don't like the appearance of one, use a fish net or rake to remove leaves regularly – not only from the surface, but also from below the surface as well. Too many leaves in the water can pollute the pond.

3 Submerged oxygenating plants, such as elodea and rampant growers like myriophyllum, will eventually clog the pond unless you net or rake them out periodically. This is a good time to thin them simply by raking out the excess.

4 Trim back dead or dying plants from around the edge of the pond, especially where the vegetation is likely to fall into the water.

5 To divide overgrown water plants, first remove the plants from their containers. It may be necessary to cut some roots to do so.

6 Some plants can simply be pulled apart by hand, but others will have such a tight mass of entangled roots that you need to chop them into smaller pieces with a spade.

7 Discard any pieces you don't want for replanting, then pot up the others in planting baskets. Cover the top of the baskets with gravel to prevent soil disturbance.

TAKE IN TENDER AQUATICS

Some aquatic plants, such as the water lettuce (*Pistia stratiotes*) and *Salvinia auriculata*, will be killed by frost, even though they can multiply rapidly outdoors in summer. The fairy moss (*Azolla caroliniana*) sometimes survives a mild winter in favourable areas, but as an insurance policy a few plants should be overwintered in a frost-proof place.

LEFT: *A pond can look perfect in summer, but if you have tender pond plants, now is the time to take them in.*

1 Net a few plants in good condition. They may already be deteriorating in the cooler weather, so don't save any that appear to be rotting or badly damaged.

2 Put a handful of the plants into a plastic container – such as a lunch box or ice cream container. Don't cram them in so that they are overcrowded. Use extra containers rather than have them all touching. Some gardeners put a little soil in the bottom to provide nutrients.

3 Keep the plants in a warm, light place, such as a greenhouse. You might also be able to keep them on a light windowsill. Top up or change the water occasionally to prevent the water becoming stagnant.

CARING FOR MINIATURE WATERLILIES

With the exception of tropical waterlilies, which are usually only grown by enthusiasts with heated pools, waterlilies are very hardy and are usually planted deep enough not to come to any harm.

Miniature waterlilies are sometimes used for raised miniature pools, in a half barrel or shrub tub for example, and these are vulnerable. Because the container is raised above the ground, in very severe weather the water can freeze solid throughout. This can lead to winter losses. Try wrapping your raised miniature pool in several layers of bubble insulation material, or move it into a cool greenhouse for the winter.

AUTUMN LAWNCARE

Autumn is a good time to prepare your lawn for the year ahead, and the best time to tackle any long-term improvements. Tasks, such as raking out lawn debris, eradicating moss, feeding and aerating, will improve the quality of your lawn greatly if carried out on a yearly basis.

1 Over the years, grass clippings and debris form a 'thatch' on the surface of your lawn. This affects growth of the grass and should be removed with a lawn rake. Raking also removes moss.

2 If grass growth is poor, aerate the lawn. You can do this by pushing the prongs of a fork about 15cm (6in) into the ground.

3 Brush a soil improver into the holes made by the fork. Use sand or a mixture of fine soil and sand if the ground is poorly drained. Alternatively, use peat, a peat-substitute or very fine, well-rotted compost if the ground is sandy.

4 If your lawn is in poor condition and needs reviving, apply an autumn lawn feed. It is essential that you use one formulated for autumn use, as spring and summer feeds will contain too much nitrogen.

5 If the grass contains a lot of moss, apply a moss killer. Use one recommended for autumn use – the mixture known as lawn sand, sometimes used to kill moss, contains too much nitrogen.

6 You can tidy an uneven edge at any time, but doing it in autumn will relieve the pressure at busier times of year. Hold a half-moon edger against a board held in position with your feet. This is not an annual job.

COLLECT AND COMPOST LEAVES

Never waste leaves: they will make excellent garden compost if you rot them down; and, if left on the ground, they can damage areas of grass and smother small plants.

1 Don't let leaves lie for long on your lawn. The grass beneath will turn yellow and be prone to disease. On a small lawn, rake them up with a lawn rake.

2 Leaves on paths and drives are best brushed up with a broom or besom.

4 Leaves can be added to the compost heap or bin, but some leaves rot down slowly, so it is best to compost a large amount on their own. Rotted leaves are a useful addition to potting soils.

3 You can buy special tools to lift the leaves without too much bending, but two pieces of wood are also an effective way to lift them once they have been brushed into a heap.

MECHANICAL AIDS

Raking out thatch and moss from your lawn by hand is tiring. If you have a large lawn, invest in a powered lawn rake. This will do the job rapidly and efficiently. Take the drudgery out of aerating your lawn by using a hollow-tined aerator that removes a core of soil effortlessly and efficiently. Equally, you could invest in a powered lawn rake or a special leaf sweeper to clear large lawns of leaves.

DON'T LET LEAVES SMOTHER SMALL PLANTS

If you let leaves lie for long on small plants, such as alpines, they may begin to rot due to the lack of light and free movement of air. The leaves will also provide a haven for slugs and other pests that may eat your plants. Wait until most of the leaves have fallen from the trees, then go round and pick them off vulnerable plants, as shown.

PROTECT VULNERABLE SHRUBS

Many shrubs on the borderline of hardiness can be coaxed through the winter with a little protection. There are several methods you can use to provide shelter.

1 A little protection from cold winds and snow is all that many cold-sensitive shrubs require in areas where they are of borderline hardiness. Push cut branches of evergreens, such as conifers, into the soil around the plant.

2 If the shrub is tall, you may also need to tie cut branches of evergreens, or bracken, so that they remain in position.

3 If you don't have a supply of evergreen shoots or bracken, use horticultural fleece or a woven mesh for protection. For extra protection, fold these over to give more than one thickness before tying into position.

4 Some shrubs are damaged by cold winds as much as low temperatures, and for these a windbreak will prevent wind scorch. Insert canes or stakes around the plant, then fix several layers of wind-break netting or plastic sheeting to these.

RIGHT: *Always knock heavy falls of snow off your conifers before the weight can damage the branches and spoil the shape of the tree.*

PROTECT NEWLY PLANTED EVERGREENS

An evergreen planted in late summer or the autumn may not have grown new roots out into the soil, and if not watered regularly, it will not be able to absorb water as rapidly as it is lost. A windbreak for the first winter will reduce moisture loss and help a vulnerable plant to survive.

2 If you don't want to erect a shield, perhaps on aesthetic grounds, water in very dry spells to keep the roots moist, and cover the plant with a large plastic bag, pegged to the ground, when very severe weather is forecast. Remove it afterwards.

1 Insert three stout canes or stakes around the plant, then wrap a plastic sheet or several layers of horticultural fleece around the edge. Peg down the bottom.

PROTECT DELICATE ALPINES

Some alpines with hairy leaves are likely to rot if they become too wet and waterlogged during the cold months.

SNOW PROTECTION

1 If you know that a particular alpine needs winter wet protection, cover it with a sheet of glass or rigid plastic substitute supported on special wires.

2 You can also use bricks to support and weight the pane. If you have a spare cloche, perhaps not needed until spring, you might be able to use this to protect alpines. Leave the ends open, but make sure that the cloche is firmly anchored and not likely to be lifted by strong winds.

Conifers with an attractive or formal shape can be disfigured by a heavy fall of snow that pulls down or breaks the branches. If you live in an area of heavy snowfall, tie the branches, as shown. Green or brown twine is less conspicuous than string.

PLANT A HEDGE

Shrubs can be planted at almost any time of the year if you buy them in containers, but this is an expensive way to plant a hedge as you need so many plants. Most garden centres stock bundles of bare-root hedging plants at this time, so plant now if you want to create a hedge economically.

1 Prepare the ground thoroughly, as a hedge will be there for a long time and this is your only opportunity to improve the soil. Clear it of weeds, and dig deeply, especially if the soil is shallow or compacted.

2 Take out a trench about 25cm (10in) deep, using a garden line to ensure that the row will be straight.

3 Add as much garden compost or rotted manure as you can spare, then fork it into the base of the trench to improve the soil and encourage deep rooting.

4 Return the soil to the trench, adding more organic material as you do so. Then apply bonemeal and rake it in. Don't apply fast-acting fertilizers at this time of year.

5 You may find bare-root hedging simply bundled together, with their roots in a bed of peat or soil. If not, and if you will not be planting it out immediately, dig the hedging into a spare piece of ground.

6 Dig large holes at the appropriate spacing. A typical spacing is 38–45cm (15–18in), but it may be different for some plants, so always check the recommended spacing first.

7 Firm the plants in well, treading around them to remove any large air pockets that may cause the roots to dry out.

8 Water thoroughly, and be prepared to water regularly in dry spells for the first year.

PLANT A ROSE

Nowadays roses get planted throughout the year because most are grown in containers. Those ordered from specialist nurseries by mail order may arrive bare-root, however, and some garden centres and other shops also sell them like this in the autumn, perhaps with their roots wrapped in moss and a protective sleeve. These are plants that have been lifted from the field; they are often less expensive than those grown in containers, and can be just as good if planted promptly.

PLANTING A CLIMBING ROSE

Never plant a climbing rose too close to a wall or fence. Try to position the root-ball about 35cm (15in) away, and angle the stem slightly towards the support. In this way, the shoots can be trained normally, yet the roots will not be in the driest area of soil.

LEFT: *Roses always add charm to a garden, and now is a good time to plant.*

1 Dig a hole large enough to spread all the roots out, and fork in as much garden compost or rotted manure as you can spare. It is especially important to break up any compacted soil.

2 Trim off any broken or damaged roots, and if they appear dry, soak the roots in a bucket of water for an hour or two.

3 Trickle soil back around the roots, remembering to give the plant a shake occasionally to settle the soil around them.

4 To ensure the rose is planted firmly, with no large pockets of air, and that the bush cannot be rocked by wind, firm the soil with your feet. Rake over and water thoroughly.

5 If the plant was unpruned when bought, cut back all the shoots to about 15–20cm (6–8in) above the ground. This will also reduce the risk of winds loosening the rose.

INSULATE THE GREENHOUSE

Insulation will cut down heating costs. Even if you don't heat your greenhouse during the winter, insulation will afford extra protection for those not-quite-hardy plants.

1 There are many proprietary fasteners for securing polythene to the inside of a metal greenhouse. Details may vary, but they slot into the groove in the metal moulding and can be secured in position with a twisting motion.

2 With the main part of the clip in place, the top is pushed or twisted into position, clamping the polythene liner. If using thick bubble polythene, you may need to buy clips designed for the extra thickness.

3 You may find it easier to line the sides and roof separately. If you decide to do this, be prepared to use a draught proofing strip if there is a gap at the eaves.

4 You can fix the insulation to a timber-framed greenhouse with drawing pins, or special pins sold for the purpose.

5 If you don't want to fix the insulation directly to the wooden frame, suction fixers can be attached to the glass. These can also be used for metal-framed greenhouses. Moisten the plastic before pressing into place.

7 Whichever method of fixing you choose, you should always insulate the ventilators separately. Although you need to conserve heat as much as possible, some ventilation is essential when it's warm enough. You must be able to open at least one ventilator if necessary.

6 Secure the liner to the cup with the special pin provided (or use a drawing pin).

8 To avoid too much warmth being lost between the sheets where they join, seal joins with a transparent tape.

RIGHT: *Bubble insulation will keep the temperature up and your bills down.*

SCREENS AND DIVIDERS

Thermal screens made of clear plastic or special translucent fabrics are widely used commercially to conserve heat. Fixed horizontally over the plants, they seal off the space at the top of the greenhouse. They are usually pulled across at night, and drawn back during the day. A similar technique can be used in your own greenhouse by stretching supporting wires along each side of the greenhouse, over which the fabric can be draped or pulled (see below left).

If you have a large greenhouse, it may be more economic to heat just part of it. Use a vertical screen to partition off the end (see below right) to reduce the area to be heated.

INSULATION MATERIALS

Proper double glazing is not very practical or cost-effective for most amateur greenhouses where very high temperatures are not normally maintained. Polythene sheeting is the most practical choice as it can be taken down at the end of the heating season and used again if stored carefully for the summer.

Single thickness, heavy-duty polythene lets through plenty of light, and is cheap to buy, but it is not the most effective material for conserving heat.

Bubble polythene is more efficient because air trapped in the bubbles cuts down heat loss. If possible, choose bubble polythene that is thick, with large pockets of air. It lets through less light, but is more efficient at reducing heat loss.

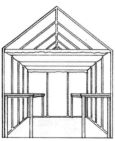

OVERWINTER TENDER FUCHSIAS

Most fuchsias are killed by frost, so unless you know that a particular variety is hardy enough to be left outdoors for the winter in your area, overwinter them in a frost-proof place.

1 If your fuchsias have been grown in pots during the summer, lift them to take into the greenhouse. If planted in the open soil, lift with a fork and remove excess soil.

2 Pot up the plants individually, or in large boxes if you have a lot of plants, then put them in a frost-free place, such as in the greenhouse or on a light windowsill indoors.

3 Tidy up the plants by removing old leaves and pinching out any soft green tips. You must keep the plants cool but frost-free, with the soil almost dry.

OVERWINTERING FUCHSIAS OUTDOORS

If you don't have a greenhouse or space indoors, try this method instead of throwing the plants away. Dig a trench about 30cm (12in) deep, line with straw, then lay the plants on this, as shown above. Cover the plants with more straw and then return the soil.

Dig them up in spring, pot them up and keep in warmth and good light to start into growth again. If the winters are not too harsh, many of the plants should survive.

PROTECTING HARDY FUCHSIAS

Hardy is a relative term, and although some fuchsias are tough enough for the roots not to be killed by frost where winters are not too severe, in cold areas they may succumb without a little extra protection.

Leave the old stems on, even though these will be killed, as this may afford the plant some additional shelter. To reduce the depth to which severe frosts penetrate, cover the crown with a thick layer of bracken, straw or peat, as shown here. Remove the protection in spring when the new shoots appear.

In mild areas, extra protection is not necessary for tough species such as *Fuchsia magellanica*.

OVERWINTER PELARGONIUMS

Pelargoniums, otherwise known as bedding geraniums, should be overwintered in a light and frost-free environment. If you have a lot of plants, a greenhouse is the best place to keep them, but if you do not have a greenhouse you may have space for a few plants indoors.

1 Lift the plants before the first frost if possible, though they will often survive a light frost if you take them in promptly afterwards.

2 Shake as much of the soil off the roots as possible, to reduce the size of the plant.

3 Trim the longest roots back to about 5–8cm (2–3in) long, to make potting up easier.

4 Shorten the shoots to about 10cm (4in), and trim off any remaining leaves. Although this looks drastic, new shoots will grow in spring, which you can use for cuttings if you want more plants.

5 The most effective way to store pelargoniums for the winter is in large trays at least 15cm (6in) deep. Half fill with soil or sowing compost, position the plants and add more compost to cover the roots. Water well initially, then only when the soil becomes almost dry.

DEALING WITH YOUNG PLANTS

Fuchsias and pelargoniums can be rooted from cuttings taken in spring or autumn. If you are overwintering old plants, you can use them to provide plenty of cuttings in spring.

If you took cuttings in late summer or the autumn, however, your young plants will still be growing actively. Make sure that you keep these plants in good light and reasonably warm, in which case they will probably retain their foliage. If conditions are favourable, pelargoniums may even flower during the winter months.

6 If you want to overwinter your pelargoniums on a windowsill indoors, you may find it more convenient to use large pots instead of trays.

LATE AUTUMN

A LAST-MINUTE SPURT OF ACTION IS often needed at this time of year, to get the garden ready for winter and ensure protection for plants that need it. In cold areas winter will already have taken its grip, but in warmer climates there are still many mild days to be enjoyed. Take advantage of them before colder temperatures and strong winds drive you indoors.

JOBS IN BRIEF

The kitchen garden

- ☐ Protect late cauliflowers from frost by bending surrounding leaves over the head
- ☐ Use cloches to protect vulnerable vegetables
- ☐ Winter dig, especially heavy soils
- ☐ Pot up some herbs for winter use
- ☐ Prune black currants, gooseberries and raspberries
- ☐ Plant bare-root fruit bushes and trees

BELOW: *Pot up a few mint roots to prolong the season and for early leaves next spring.*

The flower garden

- ☐ Cut down the dead tops of herbaceous perennials
- ☐ Get rid of garden refuse by burning or composting
- ☐ Remove pumps from the pond and store for the winter
- ☐ Plant roses
- ☐ Plant bare-root and balled trees and shrubs
- ☐ Clear summer bedding if not already done so
- ☐ Finish planting spring bulbs as soon as possible
- ☐ Protect vulnerable plants that will remain in the garden
- ☐ Lift and take in chrysanthemums not hardy enough to overwinter outside
- ☐ Take hardwood shrub cuttings
- ☐ Plant hedges
- ☐ Prepare the pond for winter
- ☐ Collect and compost fallen leaves
- ☐ Remove leaves that have fallen on rock plants
- ☐ Cover alpines that need protection from winter wet with a pane of glass
- ☐ Protect the crowns of vulnerable herbaceous plants such as delphiniums and lupins from slugs by sprinkling coarse grit around them

The greenhouse and conservatory

- ☐ Clean and disinfect, ready for winter
- ☐ Insulate
- ☐ Check the minimum temperatures being achieved (if you don't have a minimum-maximum thermometer, buy one)
- ☐ Ventilate whenever the weather is mild enough
- ☐ Except with winter-flowering plants that are still in strong, active growth, gradually give plants less water. Most will then tolerate low temperatures better and disease should be less of a problem

BELOW: *This is a good time to wash and scrub all those dirty pots.*

PLANTS AT THEIR BEST

Acer, colourful foliage (tree/shrub)
Berberis, colourful foliage and berries (shrub)
Cotoneaster, berries (shrub)
Fothergilla, colourful foliage (shrub)
Gentiana sino-ornata (alpine)
Liriope muscari (herbaceous)
Nerine bowdenii (bulb)
Pernettya, berries (shrub)
Pyracantha, berries (shrub)
Schizostylis coccinea (herbaceous)

LEFT: *Forthergillas are uninspiring for most of the year, with white flowers in late spring and early summer, but in autumn they take centre stage with brilliant leaf colouring.*

BELOW: Schizostylis coccinea *is always an eye-catcher in late autumn, when most other border plants have finished flowering.*

PRUNE BLACK CURRANTS

Black currants fruit best on year-old branches, so in pruning an established bush the aim is to remove the oldest shoots and encourage new ones. Prune while the plant is dormant.

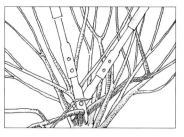 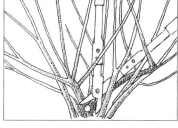 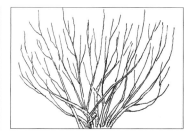

1 Only start pruning once they are old enough to fruit reliably. Cut back one-third of the shoots close to the base, choosing the oldest.

2 Cut back to their point of origin any diseased, damaged or badly placed shoots.

3 This is what the bush should look like after pruning, with plenty of well-spaced young shoots.

PRUNE RED AND WHITE CURRANTS

Unlike black currants, these fruit on shoots that are at least two years old. They are usually grown on a 'leg' (a short length of clear stem) as shown, but can be grown as a bush or trained as cordons.

1 If it was not done in the summer, start by removing any crossing or over-crowded shoots, to allow plenty of light into the centre of the bush.

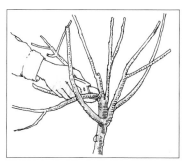

2 When badly placed shoots have been removed, shorten last summer's growth at the tip of each main shoot by half.

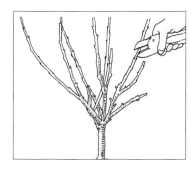

3 Finally, cut back the side-shoots to within one or two buds of the main stems. This will encourage fruiting.

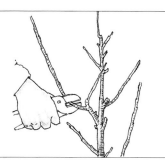

4 On an old bush it may be necessary to cut out a few very old shoots that no longer fruit well, but try to leave a vigorous young sideshoot to replace each one.

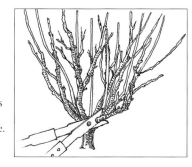

PRUNE RASPBERRIES

Autumn-fruiting raspberries bear fruit on canes grown that year, so pruning is easy. Summer-fruiting raspberries fruit on shoots that are a year old, so be careful not to prune last summer's shoots.

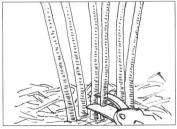
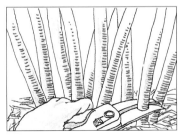

1 Provided you are sure the variety is autumn-fruiting, simply cut all the canes down to ground level while they are dormant.

2 On summer-fruiting raspberries cut the old canes (dark stems) that fruited this summer to just above the ground. Tie in the remaining shoots to support wires if necessary.

3 If the raspberries have been growing undisturbed for several years, the clumps may have become congested. Thin out surplus canes to leave them about 8cm (3in) apart.

PRUNE GOOSEBERRIES

Gooseberries fruit on shoots that are a year or more old, and continue to fruit quite well even if you neglect pruning. But with spiny stems, the fruit is difficult to harvest if not pruned annually.

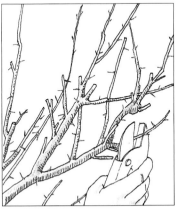
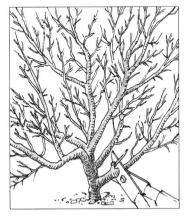

1 If the job was not done after harvesting, cut out any low branches near the soil to an upward-pointing bud, and also eliminate any badly placed and crossing branches. Try to ensure that the centre of the bush is left open.

2 While the bush is dormant, reduce the length of new summer growth at the tips of the main shoots by about half. Then go along each main branch and prune back the sideshoots to two buds from the old wood.

3 If the plant is old, cut out one or two of the oldest shoots, to a point where there is a younger replacement to take over.

PLANT SOFT FRUIT

Nowadays most soft fruits – with the exception of cane plants such as raspberries – are usually sold in containers. They can be planted at almost any time, but late autumn is ideal when there is a good choice of plants in garden centres. Bare-root plants must be planted while dormant.

1 Excavate the soil for an area at least twice the size of the root-ball or container so that you can improve the soil over an area that the roots are likely to explore later.

2 Although it is not essential, your fruit will do much better if you can add plenty of humus-making material to the soil. Dig in as much rotten manure or garden compost as you can spare.

3 Soak the roots of bare-root plants in water for an hour before planting, and water container-grown plants for at least half an hour before planting. Place a plant in the hole and use a cane to make sure that it will be at its original depth.

4 Firm the plant in well, pressing with the heel of the foot to remove any large pockets of air around the roots.

5 After firming the soil, hoe and rake the ground to remove footprints, then water thoroughly.

6 Although it seems drastic, most bushes grown on stems that sprout from the base, such as black currants and raspberries, are best cut back to about 23–30cm (9–12in) after planting. This will stimulate new shoots to grow from the base.

POT UP HERBS FOR WINTER USE

You don't have to make do with dried or frozen herbs just because it is winter. Some herbs, such as mint, chives, parsley and marjoram, can be potted up to grow indoors or in the greenhouse for a fresh supply of winter leaves. The supply will be modest, but no less welcome.

1 Mint is an easy plant to force indoors, or in a cold frame or greenhouse. Lift an established clump to provide a supply of roots to pot up.

2 Be careful to select only pieces with healthy leaves (diseased leaves are common by the end of the season). You can pull pieces off by hand or cut through them with a knife.

3 Plant the roots in a pot if you want to try to keep the plant growing indoors for a month or so longer. Three-quarters fill a 20–25cm (8–10in) pot with soil or potting soil, then spread the roots out and cover with more soil.

4 If you want a supply of tender fresh leaves early next spring, cut off the tops and put the roots in seed trays or deeper boxes, then cover them with soil. If you keep them in a greenhouse (or even a protected cold frame) you will be able to harvest new mint much earlier.

5 Chives also respond favourably to lifting for an extended season. Lift a small clump to pot up. If it's too large, you should be able to pull it apart into smaller pieces.

6 Place the clump in a pot of ordinary garden soil or potting soil, firm well, and water thoroughly. It should continue to provide leaves after those outdoors have died back, and will produce new ones earlier next spring.

PARSLEY AND MARJORAM

If you cut down and pot up marjoram, it will usually spring into new growth provided warmth and light are right.

Parsley is always a dependable winter herb if grown from a late summer or autumn sowing and kept on a windowsill.

LIFT AND PROTECT CHRYSANTHEMUMS

Not all autumn-flowering chrysanthemums have to be lifted (see box), but many do. The roots are potted into boxes, which means that you can start them off in warmth in spring.

1 Lift the roots after the plants have finished flowering and before severe frosts arrive.

2 Shake surplus soil off the roots before removing from the garden.

3 Trim the tops off and cut any long, straggly roots back to keep the root-ball compact.

4 Place a layer of soil or potting soil in a box or tray about 10cm (4in) deep. Position the roots and cover them with about 3cm (1in) of soil, firming lightly. Don't forget to label the plants. Keep the box in a cool, light place, such as a cool greenhouse, light garage windowsill, or a cold frame. For most types of chrysanthemum it does not matter if they receive a touch of frost. Keep the soil slightly damp but not wet.

BELOW: Chrysanthemum *'Countryman'*, is a reflexed early-flowering outdoor variety.

OVERWINTERING CHRYSANTHEMUMS

There are many kinds of chrysanthemum, but it is only the autumn-flowering chrysanthemums that are likely to cause confusion regarding overwintering.

In mild, frost-free climates they can all be left in the ground, and many of the species like *Chrysanthemum rubellum*, are hardy even in cold areas.

But in temperate climates the highly bred early-flowering autumn chrysanthemums are best lifted and stored, and even those outdoor ones that flower later are best treated this way. Even those that tolerate some frost are more likely to survive if kept fairly dry. Wet and cold is the combination to avoid.

PROTECT POND PUMPS

If you leave a pump in your pond over winter, ice may damage it. Don't just take it out of the pond and leave it where moisture can enter – store it in a dry place.

1 Remove submersible pumps from the water before penetrating frosts cause the water to freeze deeply.

2 Clean the pump before you put it away. It will probably be covered with algae which can be scrubbed off.

3 Remove the filter and either replace it or clean it. Follow the manufacturer's instructions.

4 Make sure all the water is drained from the pump. If your pump is an external one, make sure the system is drained.

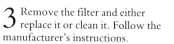

5 Read the manufacturer's instructions, and carry out any other servicing that is necessary before storing the pump in a dry place. It may be necessary to send it away for a service, in which case do it now instead of waiting until spring.

DISPOSE OF YOUR RUBBISH . . . WISELY

Gardeners always acquire a lot of rubbish and debris in the autumn, but there is no one simple way to deal with it all. Be environmentally friendly and recycle as much as possible through composting.

To improve the chances of good compost, add a layer of manure or a proprietary compost activator after every 15cm (6in) of kitchen and garden refuse. Woody material such as hedge clippings and pruning will rot down too slowly to put straight on to the compost heap. These are best put through a shredder, then composted or used as a mulch. Some things are best burnt – diseased material and pernicious perennial weeds for instance, as well as woody material if you don't have a shredder. An incinerator that will burn the rubbish quickly is preferable to a traditional smoky bonfire.

A large quantity of leaves is better composted separately. Some leaves rot down slowly, but the end product is particularly useful for adding to potting mixtures.

TAKE HARDWOOD CUTTINGS

Hardwood cuttings root more slowly than most of the softwood or semi-ripe cuttings that you can take during the spring and summer, but they need much less attention. They don't need heat, and because you plant them in the open ground (or in a cold frame), watering won't be an onerous chore.

Many shrubs, and even trees, can be raised from hardwood cuttings. Some of them are suggested in the box below.

 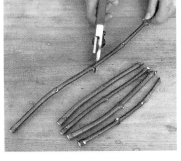 

1 Choose stems that are firm and hard but not old and thick (pencil thickness is about right). With shrubs like this dogwood you should be able to make several cuttings from one shoot. The length of the cutting will depend on the plant, but about 15cm (6in) is appropriate for most. Make a cut straight across the stem, just below a node.

2 Make the second cut about 15cm (6in) above the first, and above a node, but this time at an angle so that you will know which is the top and which the bottom of the cutting.

3 Although a rooting hormone is not essential, it should increase the success rate, especially with plants that are difficult to root. Moisten the bases of the cuttings in water.

SHRUBS TO PROPAGATE

The list below is just a selection of the shrubs that usually root easily from hardwood cuttings, but there are many others. Be prepared to experiment, or consult a specialist book to see which plants are normally rooted by this method.
Aucuba japonica (spotted laurel)
Buddleia (butterfly bush)
Cornus alba (dogwood)
Cornus stolonifera (dogwood) – illustrated
Forsythia
Ligustrum ovalifolium (privet)
Philadelphus (mock orange)
Ribes sanguineum (flowering currant)

Roses (species and hybrids)
Salix (willow)
Spiraea
Viburnum (deciduous species)

4 Dip the moistened ends into a rooting powder. You can also use liquid and gel rooting hormones, in which case you should not dip the end in water first. Treat only the base end of each cutting.

5 Make a slit trench with a spade, a little shallower than the length of the cuttings. Choose a position where the cuttings can be left undisturbed for a year.

6 Sprinkle some grit or coarse sand in the base of the slit if the ground is poorly drained. This will help to prevent water-logging around the cuttings.

7 Insert the cuttings 8–10cm (3–4in) apart, upright against the back of the slit, leaving about 3–5cm (1–2in) above the ground.

8 Firm the soil around the cuttings, to eliminate the pockets of air that would cause the cutting to dry out.

9 Water the cuttings and label. Remember to water them in dry weather.

TREES FROM HARDWOOD CUTTINGS

Some trees can also be propagated from hardwood cuttings, and those below are particularly easy.

If propagating trees, decide whether you want a multi-stemmed tree or one with a single main stem. If the latter, set the cuttings deeper in the trench so that the top bud is just below the surface of the soil.

Platanus (plane)
Populus (poplar) – illustrated
Salix (willow)

AUTUMN CLEAN THE GREENHOUSE

Autumn is an ideal time to clean the greenhouse. It is likely to be less full than in spring, and it is important to start the season of cold, dull days with clean glass to allow in all available light, and an environment as free as possible of pests and diseases.

1 If you have not already removed the remains of summer shading, do it as soon as possible. Shading washes like this are easy to wipe off with a duster if dry.

2 Whether or not summer shading has been used, clean the glass. The easiest way to clean the outside is with a brush or cleaning head on a long handle. Spray with water, adding a little detergent if necessary, and rub clean. Rinse with clean water.

LEFT: *Even if the greenhouse is still filled with colour, autumn is a good time to give the structure, shelves and benches a thorough clean.*

3 A proprietary glass cleaner will be very effective in removing dirt and grime, but is usually only practical for a small greenhouse where you can easily reach the glass. Clean the glass inside as well as out.

4 Algae often grow where the panes of glass overlap, an area that also traps dirt. Try squirting a jet of water between the panes, then dislodge the dirt with a thin strip of rigid plastic (a plastic plant label usually works well).

5 Finally, squirt another jet of water between the panes to move the loosened dirt and algae.

7 Fumigation is a good way to control a number of pests and diseases that may be lurking in nooks and crannies around the greenhouse. You may be able to keep some or all of the plants in, or you can fumigate an empty greenhouse. Check the label.

6 Dirt and soil also accumulates where the glass joins the base, and this can be a breeding ground for pests and diseases. Use a label or a small tool to lift the soil out of the crevice, then douse with a garden disinfectant (keep away from plants).

9 Diseases are easily carried over from one plant to another on old pots and seed trays. When you have a moment between now and spring, wash them all in a garden disinfectant, scrubbing them well. The inside is as important as the outside.

8 It is worth disinfecting the frame and staging, whether or not you fumigate the greenhouse. Rather than use a household disinfectant, use one sold for the garden and greenhouse.

WINTER

*A well-planned garden will not be devoid of colour or interest in the
winter months, and working outdoors can be a real pleasure.
There are always jobs to be done, and tackling them now relieves
the pressure in spring.
Sometimes there is no choice but to become an armchair gardener.
This is the time to scan your gardening books and plant encyclopedias
for ideas, perhaps plan minor improvements or even totally redesign
your garden, and of course fill in your seed order – perhaps one of the
most pleasurable jobs of all.*

OPPOSITE: *The red-stemmed* Cornus alba
*remain bright and interesting throughout
the winter.*

ABOVE: *Focal points like this ornament can
help to compensate for the lack of colour during
the cold months.*

EARLY WINTER

THE ONSET OF WINTER INEVITABLY MEANS fewer jobs to do in the garden, but it is a good idea to get outdoors whenever the weather is favourable. There is always tidying-up to be done, and things like broken fences to be mended. It makes sense to get jobs like this finished before the more severe winter weather makes them less appealing. This is an especially good time to take a critical look at how you can improve your soil in time for the next growing season.

JOBS IN BRIEF

The kitchen garden

- ☐ Test your soil
- ☐ Apply lime to your soil if the test shows it is necessary
- ☐ Dig over the vegetable plot
- ☐ Prune black currants, gooseberries and raspberries
- ☐ Plant bare-root fruit bushes and trees
- ☐ Check the condition of canes and stakes, and clean them up if necessary. Stand the ends in a wood preservative for a day if not already done so
- ☐ Finish picking late apples
- ☐ Lift leeks and parsnips as required for use. If the weather is severe, lift leeks in a mild period and heel in so that they are easy to lift when the ground is frozen
- ☐ Start forcing rhubarb

BELOW: *Warm up with some winter digging. Here the ground is being marked out.*

The flower garden

- ☐ Check bulbs, corms and tubers in store
- ☐ Get rid of garden refuse by burning or composting
- ☐ Service your mower or have it done professionally

BELOW: *Service your mower and prepare it for winter storage.*

- ☐ Plant bare-root and balled trees and shrubs
- ☐ Check bulbs being grown in pots for early flowering
- ☐ Protect vulnerable plants that will remain in the garden
- ☐ Order seeds
- ☐ Take hardwood shrub cuttings
- ☐ Take root cuttings
- ☐ Plant hedges
- ☐ Install a pond heater if you live in a cold area where thick ice is a problem
- ☐ Remove leaves that have fallen on rock plants
- ☐ Cover alpines that need protection from winter wet with a pane of glass
- ☐ Protect flowers of winter plants that might be spoilt by the weather

The greenhouse and conservatory

- ☐ Once a week check all plants and pick off any dead or dying leaves before they start to rot
- ☐ Ventilate on warm days, especially if the greenhouse is well insulated. Lack of air movement can encourage diseases
- ☐ Except with winter-flowering plants that are still in strong, active growth, gradually give plants less water. Most will then tolerate low temperatures better and diseases should be less of a problem

BELOW: *When indoor hyacinths are over, cut off the dead flower heads.*

- ☐ Clear out the gutters, which may have become clogged with autumn leaves
- ☐ Clean the glass to make the most of the poor winter light

ABOVE: Jasminum nudiflorum, *one of the delights of winter.*

LEFT: Pyracantha *'Watereri', brilliant even in the grip of winter.*

PLANTS AT THEIR BEST

Chimonanthus praecox (shrub)
Erica carnea (shrub)
Erica × *darleyensis* (shrub)
Hamamelis mollis (shrub)
Iris unguicularis (syn. *I. stylosa*) (herbaceous)
Ilex, berries (hollies)
Jasminum nudiflorum (wall shrub)
Liriope muscari (herbaceous)
Mahonia 'Charity' (shrub)
Nerine bowdenii (bulb)
Pernettya, berries (shrub)
Prunus × *subhirtella* 'Autumnalis' (tree)
Pyracantha, berries (shrub)
Sarcococca (shrub)
Viburnum × *bobnantense* (shrub)
Viburnum farreri (syn. *V. fragrans*) (shrub)
Viburnum tinus (shrub)

WINTER DIG THE VEGETABLE PLOT

If you have a vegetable plot, or other large area of ground that requires digging, this is a good time to do it. If the soil is a heavy clay, leaving it rough-dug over the winter will allow frost and the weather to help break down large clods. This will make it easier to rake level and to produce a seedbed of fine, crumbly soil in spring. You may prefer to leave digging a light, sandy soil until spring, as this type of soil tends to become flattened and compacted by winter rain if dug too early. New weed growth may also be a problem by spring and can be dealt with at the same time.

1 Divide the space to be dug in half lengthways, marking the area with string. Dividing the plot like this avoids moving excavated soil from one end of the plot to the other.

2 Take out a trench the depth and width of a spade blade. Pile the soil at the end of the other half of the plot, as shown.

3 When you remove the next trench, throw the soil forward into the space left by the first. Digging is easier if you first 'cut' a slice the width of the bite of soil to be dug.

4 Push the spade in parallel to the trench, taking a slice of soil about 15–20cm (6–8in) deep. Larger bites may be too heavy to lift comfortably.

5 Loosen the soil by pulling back on the handle, while trying to keep the bite of soil on the spade.

6 Flick the soil over with the wrist, inverting the clod of earth so that the top is buried. Lift with your knees, not your back.

7 When the end of the plot is reached, fill the trench with soil taken from the first row of the return strip.

8 Finally, fill the trench left when digging has been completed with the soil put on one side from the initial excavation.

DOUBLE DIGGING

Single digging is adequate for most plants, and adding manure or garden compost in this top layer is likely to do more good for short-rooted plants like lettuces and cabbages than burying it deeply. However, for certain deep-rooted crops, such as runner beans, or to break up neglected ground, double digging can be useful. Bear in mind that it also doubles the effort!

1 Divide the plot up in the same way as described for single digging, and deal with the soil from the end of each strip in the same way. But this time make the trenches about 40cm (16in) wide and 25cm (10in) deep.

2 Spread a generous layer of well-rotted manure or garden compost – or other bulky organic material that will retain moisture and add humus – over the bottom of the trench.

3 Fork this thick layer of manure or organic material into the bottom of the trench. A fork is better than a spade because it will penetrate the harder lower layer more easily and will mix the material into the soil better.

4 Move the garden line to the next position, maintaining the same 40cm (16in) spacing, or thereabouts. Cut and slice the soil and throw it forward as before, but take several bites per strip, otherwise the soil will be too heavy.

TEST YOUR SOIL

Many people garden successfully without ever testing their soil, but they are probably fortunate in gardening on ground that is not deficient in nutrients, is neither too acid nor too alkaline, and receives plenty of nutrients anyway as part of normal cultivation. If things don't seem to be growing well, a soil test is the best starting point for putting things right, and keen growers test their soil routinely once a year.

Professional soil testing is the most accurate for nutrients, but you can get a reasonable idea of the major nutrients in your soil with simple indicator kits. Testing for pH (see the box opposite) is quick and effective.

Bear in mind that kits vary from one manufacturer to another, so always follow the manufacturer's instructions if they vary from the advice given here.

1 Collect the soil sample from about 5–8cm (2–3in) below the surface. This gives a more typical reading of nutrient levels in the root area. Take a number of samples from around the garden, but test each one separately.

2 With this kit one part of soil is mixed with five parts of water. Shake together vigorously in a clean jar, then allow the water to settle. This can take between half an hour and a day, depending on the soil.

3 Draw off some settled liquid from the top few centimetres (about an inch) for your test.

4 Carefully transfer the solution to the test and reference chambers in the plastic container, using the pipette provided.

5 Select the appropriate colour-coded capsule (different ones are used for each major nutrient) and empty the powder it contains into the test chamber. Replace the cap, then shake vigorously.

6 After a few minutes, compare the colour of the liquid with the shade panel that forms part of the container. The kit contains an explanation of the significance of each reading, and what – if anything – to do.

WHAT IS pH?

The term pH is a scientific way of stating how acid or alkaline something is. Soils vary in their degree of acidity or alkalinity. The scale runs from 0 (most acid) to 14 (most alkaline), with 7 as neutral. Soils never reach these extremes, and horticulturally, 6.5 can be considered neutral in that it is the pH at which most plants will grow happily. Acid-loving plants, such as rhododendrons, camellias, peonies (see above) and heathers, need a lower pH

and may develop chlorosis – a yellowing of the leaves – if grown on chalky soil. Chalk-loving plants like dianthus and lilacs prefer a pH of 7 or above.

These differences may sound small, but on the pH scale 1 point represents a ten-fold increase in acidity or alkalinity.

TESTING THE pH

Collect your samples and mix with water as described for nutrient testing, but for the pH test you don't have to

wait for the mixture to settle, and only the test chamber is filled with the solution. Clean tap water is used for the reference chamber. Add the indicator chemical provided with the kit, then put the top on and shake vigorously. Compare the colour with the shade panel on the container for the nearest pH value.

USING PROBE METERS

Probes that measure the pH on a dial are very quick and easy to use, but some people consider them less accurate than colour indicator tests. To ensure an accurate reading, follow the instructions and keep the tip clean.

Push the probe into the soil, and take the reading once the needle seems to have settled. Take several readings from the same area to check results, then move on to another part of the garden.

ADDING LIME TO THE SOIL

Never add lime unless you have tested your soil first and know that it is necessary. Too much lime applied regularly can be harmful for your plants. Always check that you are applying the

right sort of lime at the appropriate application rate. Your testing kit should contain advice about how much lime (which will vary with type) to apply to your soil to adjust the pH.

1 Hydrated lime, often used for gardens, should not be handled unnecessarily. Always use gloves, and goggles to protect your eyes. Ground limestone is safer to handle.

2 Rake the lime into the surface, whichever kind of lime you use.

PROTECT WINTER HELLEBORE FLOWERS

Winter-flowering hellebores such as *Helleborus niger* (Christmas rose) are frost-hardy, but their pale blooms are often only just above soil level.

If you want to cut the flowers to take indoors, covering the plants will reduce mud splashes and keep the blooms clean and in good condition.

1 Protect low-growing winter-flowering plants such as *H. niger* with a cloche if you want perfect blooms to cut for indoors. Though frost-hardy, the flowers tend to become splashed with mud and damaged by the weather.

2 If you don't have a cloche, improvise with a piece of polythene over wire hoops, or a pane of glass supported on bricks.

ABOVE RIGHT: Helleborus argutifolius *is a tall species that will not need protection.*

RIGHT: Helleborus orientalis *may benefit from protection for early cut blooms.*

CHECK BULBS AND CORMS IN STORE

Don't wait until it is time to plant your tender overwintering bulbs before checking them for

rot. Storage rots are common, and easily spread from affected bulbs or corms to healthy ones.

1 Bulbs, corms and tubers being over-wintered in a frost-free place should be checked once a month. By eliminating diseased or soft bulbs or corms, you will prevent the rot spreading to others.

2 If you discover soft or diseased bulbs in store, it's worth dusting the others with a fungicide. Check with the label to ensure that it is suitable for the purpose, and be careful not to inhale the dust.

SERVICING YOUR MOWER

Winter is the best time to have your mower serviced. The chances are you won't bother once it is in regular use during the summer. You may prefer to have the servicing done professionally, which is often cheaper at this time than in spring, but you can do some of the simple tasks yourself. The advice below should be followed in conjunction with your handbook.

1 Remove accumulated clippings and dirt from around the blade housing of a rotary mower, being certain that any power supply is disconnected. Use an abrasive paper to clean metal blades.

2 Wipe the blade with an oily rag or spray with an anti-rust aerosol. If the blade is in poor condition, replace it with a new one. On appropriate models you may consider replacing it with a plastic blade for safety.

3 If you have a petrol mower, drain the fuel and oil before storing the machine for the winter.

4 Remove the spark plug, clean it and reset the gap if necessary. If the plug is in poor condition, replace with a new one.

5 Pour a table-spoonful of oil into the cylinder and pull the starter to turn the engine over half a dozen times before you return the spark plug, thus coating the engine.

6 Brush or wipe away accumulated clippings from a cylinder mower. If the mower is electric, disconnect the power supply before you start.

7 Wipe the mower with an oily rag, or spray with an anti-rust aerosol, before you store it.

8 Oil the chain if your mower is fitted with one. You may have to remove the chain guard to reach it.

BRING ON FORCED BULBS

Whether your bulbs flower at Christmas, or on any particular date, depends partly on whether you used prepared bulbs in the first place. However, timing also depends on how cold you have kept the bulbs and at what point you bring them out from their resting place into light and warmth.

1 Check bowls of bulbs plunged outdoors beneath sand, peat or grit used to keep them cool and dark while roots develop. If the shoots are about 3cm (1in) high, it is time to bring them indoors.

2 If you have kept bulbs in a cool, dark place indoors, in a cupboard or loft, check these periodically too. Bring them into the light when the shoots are 3–5cm (1–2in) tall.

ABOVE: *Moss provides a more instant way of improving the appearance of a bowl or basket of bulbs. Lift clumps of moss, with roots intact, from your garden and cover the surface.*

3 Wipe the container clean if it has been plunged outdoors, then place in a light but cool position indoors or in a conservatory. Only put in a warm place once the buds have emerged and are beginning to show colour, else the stems may be too long and weak.

4 If you sow grass seed on the surface as soon as you bring the bulbs into the light, you should have an attractive carpet of grass by the time they flower.

5 Just before the bulbs come into full flower, cut the grass to a height of about 3–5cm (1–2in), to make it look even and neat.

WHEN FLOWERING IS OVER

Never attempt to grow the same bulbs indoors for a second year, with the exception of indoor plants like amaryllis (*Hippeastrum*) – see the box below for more information. Forcing hardy bulbs to flower indoors drains their reserves and results are almost always disappointing a second time. But there is no need to discard them. Plant them in the garden where they should gradually recover over a few seasons.

1 If you plan to keep your bulbs to grow in the garden, dead-head them as soon as the display is over. This will avoid energy being wasted on seed production.

3 In spring, plant the bulbs out in a border or other spot where they can be left undisturbed to grow as a natural group. Some types of bulb may not produce flowers the following season, but probably will do so in subsequent years.

KEEPING AMARYLLIS TO FLOWER AGAIN

The houseplant popularly known as amaryllis is really a *Hippeastrum*. Many are sold in flower during the winter, or as bulbs that grow with phenomenal speed once started. You should be able to keep them so that they flower another year if you follow this advice.

- Cut the flower stalks close to their point of origin once the flowers fade.
- Keep watered, and feed occasionally.
- From late spring onwards keep in a greenhouse or conservatory if possible.
- If you don't have a greenhouse or conservatory, stand the plant outside for the summer.
- Let the foliage die down in late summer or the autumn.
- Start into growth again in late autumn or early winter.

2 Do not plant directly into the garden, but acclimatize them gradually by placing in a cold frame or other cool but protected place. Regular watering and a dose of liquid feed will help them recover.

ABOVE: *Amaryllis should flower the following year – the box, left, tells you how.*

MID WINTER

IF YOU MADE AN EARLY START with winter jobs like digging and tidying beds and borders, mid winter is a time mainly for indoor jobs like ordering seeds and plants, writing labels, and designing improvements for the year ahead.

These are not unimportant tasks, and by attending to them in good time you are more likely to make the right decisions and have everything ready for late winter and early spring when gardening begins again in earnest.

JOBS IN BRIEF

The kitchen garden

- ☐ Test your soil
- ☐ Apply lime if your soil needs it
- ☐ Continue winter digging
- ☐ Force rhubarb
- ☐ Sow broad beans under cloches in mild areas

BELOW: *Winter is a good time to test your soil, and kits like this make it easy.*

BELOW: *This is the time to start thinking about forcing rhubarb.*

The flower garden

- ☐ Check bulbs, corms and tubers in store
- ☐ Service your mower or have it done professionally
- ☐ Check bulbs being grown in pots for early flowering
- ☐ Order seeds, bulbs and plants for the coming season
- ☐ Take hardwood shrub cuttings
- ☐ Take root cuttings
- ☐ Keep an area of water open in an iced over pond if there is a prolonged freeze. If you don't have a pond heater, try standing a pan of boiling water on the ice until it melts through
- ☐ Protect flowers of winter plants that might be spoilt by the weather
- ☐ Knock heavy snow off hedges and conifers if the branches start to bend under the weight. If you leave it, the shape may be spoilt
- ☐ Insulate the cold frame for extra protection against the coldest weather

BELOW: *Fish will appreciate it if you melt a hole in the ice during a prolonged freeze.*

The greenhouse and conservatory

- ☐ Once a week check all plants and pick off any dead or dying leaves before they start to rot
- ☐ Ventilate on warm days
- ☐ Start off overwintered chrysanthemum stools (roots) to provide cuttings
- ☐ Start sowing seeds if you can provide sufficient warmth to germinate them and a very light position in which to grow the seedlings afterwards

BELOW: *Chrysanthemum cuttings are easy to root, and now is a good time to take them.*

PLANTS AT THEIR BEST

Chimonanthus praecox (shrub)
Eranthis hyemalis (bulb)
Erica carnea (shrub)
Erica × darleyensis (shrub)
Galanthus nivalis (bulb)
Garrya elliptica (shrub)
Hamamelis mollis (shrub)
Iris unguicularis (syn. *I. stylosa*)
(herbaceous)
Ilex, berries (hollies)
Jasminum nudiflorum (wall shrub)
Lonicera fragrantissima (shrub)
Prunus × subhirtella 'Autumnalis'
(tree)
Sarcococca (shrub)
Viburnum × bodnantense (shrub)
Viburnum farreri (syn. *V. fragrans*)
(shrub)
Viburnum tinus (shrub)

LEFT: Garrya elliptica.

BELOW LEFT: Viburnum x bodnantense *'Dawn', in bloom in mid winter.*

BELOW: Hamamelis mollis.

FORCE RHUBARB

Rhubarb is one of those crops that almost looks after itself, and if you have an established clump, forcing tender young stems is very easy. There are many methods of forcing rhubarb, and they all seem to work well. Just choose a technique that you find convenient.

ABOVE: *Rhubarb is a useful early crop that you can start forcing now. A terracotta forcing pot is shown in the background.*

1 Choose a method of excluding light. Special pots were once used for this, but now most people improvise. An old tea chest, bucket, or barrel are simple but effective alternatives. If you don't have these, make a frame from wire-netting and canes as shown here.

2 Pile straw into the wire-netting cage, pressing it well down, to provide warmth and protection.

5 Replant your chilled crown for outdoor forcing, or bring it into the greenhouse. If you have a warm greenhouse, place it under the bench, screened with black plastic. Alternatively, pot it up and put in a plastic bag to take indoors. Make sure there is plenty of air in the bag by keeping it loose and making a few small air holes, then place the bag in a warm yet convenient place – under the stairs or in a kitchen cupboard. Check progress periodically.

3 Another simple way to make a rhubarb forcer is with a plastic dustbin. If you don't mind cutting the bottom out of it, use it the right way up with a lid on, otherwise use it inverted without a lid.

4 For really early crops many gardeners lift a well-established root to leave on the surface for a few weeks. This gives the root a cold spell that makes it think winter is more advanced than it is.

FORCE CHICORY

Chicons, the forced and blanched new shoots produced from chicory roots, are an enjoyable winter vegetable when fresh produce is scarce. It is best if you grow your own roots from plants sown in late spring or early summer, but you may be able to buy roots for forcing.

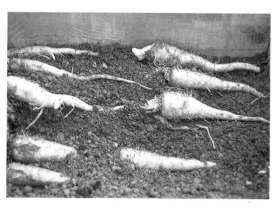

1 To produce chicons, you should choose a variety of chicory recommended for the purpose – 'Witloof' is an old and traditional variety. Lift the root from mid autumn onwards, and leave on the surface for a few days.

2 When the roots have been exposed for a few days, which helps to retard growth, trim the tops off to leave a 3–5cm (1–2in) stump of growth. You can pot them up now or store them in a box of sand, peat or dry soil for use later.

3 To force, place three roots in a 23cm (9in) pot, using a moist potting soil or ordinary garden soil. You may have to trim the ends of the roots to fit them in the pot. Leave the crowns exposed.

Cover the pot with a second pot with the drainage holes blocked (use a piece of kitchen foil for this), and keep in a temperature of 10–18°C (50–65°F). Keep the compost just moist. The chicons will be ready in about three weeks.

WRITING LABELS IN ADVANCE

It makes sense to do as many jobs as you can in winter that will save time later when you are busy sowing and planting. Instead of waiting, write your labels on a day when you can't get into the garden. You will probably make a neater job of it by doing it more leisurely, and it will take pressure off the time when you're busy in the garden.

TAKE ROOT CUTTINGS

Nearly everyone takes stem cuttings at some time, but surprisingly few gardeners bother with root cuttings. Some useful plants can be propagated this way (see the box opposite for examples), and it is an interesting and relatively simple winter job, because root cuttings are only likely to be successful if taken during the dormant season.

1 Lift a young but well-established plant to provide the cuttings. If you don't want to use the whole plant for cuttings, and prefer to leave the parent plant largely undisturbed, just remove soil from one side to gain access to the roots.

2 If the plant has large, fleshy roots, cut some off close to the main stem or root. You should be able to make several cuttings from one root by cutting it into sections later.

3 Cut each root into lengths about 5cm (2in) long. To help you remember which way up they are, cut them horizontally at the top and diagonally at the bottom.

4 Fill a pot with a gritty potting mixture and insert the cuttings using a dibber or pencil to make the hole. The top of the cutting should be flush with the top of the potting soil.

5 Sprinkle a thin layer of grit over the surface. Label, as nothing will be visible for a few months, and it's easy to forget what the pot contains. Place in a cold frame or greenhouse and keep the potting soil just moist.

6 Some plants, such as border phlox and rock plants like *Primula denticulata*, have thin roots. These can be laid horizontally, so don't make sloping cuts to indicate the bottom. Just cut into 3–5cm (1–2in) lengths.

7 Fill a seed tray with a gritty compost and firm it level.

8 Space the cuttings out evenly over the surface, then cover them with a layer of the gritty potting mix. Keep moist but not too wet, in a cold frame or greenhouse.

SOME PLANTS TO GROW FROM ROOT CUTTINGS

Acanthus
Echinops
Gaillardia
Phlox (border)
Primula denticulata
Pulsatilla vulgaris
Romneya coulteri

LEFT: *Border phlox can be propagated from root cuttings. This one is* Phlox paniculata 'Flamingo'.

INSULATE COLD FRAMES

Old-fashioned cold frames with brick or timber sides were not as light as modern aluminium and glass or plastic cold frames, but they were warmer. Glass sides let in more light, but also lose heat rapidly. Have the best of both worlds by insulating your glass-sided cold frame during the coldest weather, while taking full advantage of the glass sides in spring and summer.

COVERING COLD FRAMES

1 Sometimes there are small gaps between the glass and an aluminium frame. This does not matter in hot weather, but for winter warmth it's worth sealing the gaps with draught-proofing strip sold for windows and doors.

2 Insulate the glass sides with sheets of expanded polystyrene. Cut it with a knife or saw. Measure accurately, allowing for the thickness of the material where sheets join at the ends. Push sheets into place so that they fit tightly.

Cold frames of any kind benefit from a warm blanket thrown over them on very cold nights. A piece of old carpet is an ideal alternative (see above). Put it in place *before* the temperature drops, and remember to remove it the next morning unless it remains exceptionally cold. Your plants need light and warmth.

TAKE CHRYSANTHEMUM CUTTINGS

Chrysanthemums that are overwintered in a greenhouse or cold frame are usually propagated from cuttings once the old stool (clump of roots) starts to produce shoots. It is better to raise vigorous young plants from cuttings than simply to replant the old clump. Chrysanthemums that have been boxed or potted up in the autumn, and kept frost-free and just moist, will soon start producing new shoots. Stimulate growth now with plenty of light and warmth.

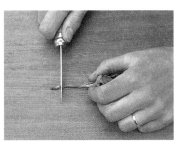

1 When your boxes or pots of chrysanthemum stools have produced shoots about 5cm (2in) long, it is time to take cuttings.

2 If possible, choose shoots coming directly from the base of the plant. Cut them off close to the base.

3 Pull off the lowest leaves and trim the ends of the cuttings straight across with a sharp knife.

4 Dip the ends in a rooting hormone. If using a powder, dip the end in water first so that it adheres. Hormone treatment usually improves the rate and speed of rooting.

5 Insert the cuttings around the edge of a pot containing a mixture suitable for cuttings.

6 If you don't have a propagator, cover the pot with a plastic bag, but inflate it to ensure it is not in contact with the leaves. Turn the bag regularly to avoid condensation dripping onto the leaves. Remove when the plants have rooted.

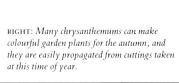

RIGHT: *Many chrysanthemums can make colourful garden plants for the autumn, and they are easily propagated from cuttings taken at this time of year.*

SOW SEEDS FOR SUMMER FLOWERS

It is too early to sow seeds outdoors, and it is likely to be too soon to sow most tender bedding plants in the greenhouse or on a windowsill. But it is not too soon to sow summer flowers that need a long growing period before they flower, such as fibrous rooted begonias (*Begonia semperflorens*). If in doubt, check the seed packet to see whether a particular flower needs early sowing or not.

Because it is difficult to provide the necessary warmth economically at this time of year, especially in a greenhouse, it is best to start the seeds off in a propagator, and move them out once they have germinated. By sowing in pots you will be able to germinate more kinds of seeds in your propagator at the same time. Sowing in pots is also sensible for seeds where only a few plants are needed, such as for trees and shrubs.

1 Fill the pot with a seed sowing compost, and gently firm and level it. Using the base or top of a jar is a convenient way of doing this.

2 Sow thinly, and as evenly as possible. Bear in mind that you have to handle the seedlings later, and very close spacing will make this difficult. Most can be sprinkled easily between finger and thumb, like salt.

3 Large seeds are best spaced individually. If they are very large, you can insert them into small holes made with a dibber.

4 Most seeds should be covered with a light sprinkling of the same soil mix. Use a sieve to spread the soil evenly. Some seeds germinate best in light and should not be covered – check the sowing instructions.

5 To avoid disturbing the evenly distributed seeds, water the pot initially by standing it in shallow water. Remove the pot and let it drain when the surface looks moist.

6 If you don't have a propagator, cover the pot with a sheet of glass or plastic until the seeds germinate. Turn the covering periodically if condensation is heavy. Don't forget the label!

LATE WINTER

In FAVOURABLE AREAS LATE WINTER CAN be almost spring-like, especially in a mild winter, but don't be lulled into sowing and planting outdoors too soon. If the weather turns very cold, seeds won't germinate, and seedlings and plants may receive such a check to growth that they do not do as well as those sown or planted later.

Concentrate your efforts on indoor sowing, but make the most of frames and cloches, too, for early crops.

JOBS IN BRIEF

The kitchen garden

- ☐ Finish winter digging
- ☐ Apply manures and fertilizers where appropriate
- ☐ Force rhubarb
- ☐ Sow broad beans under cloches
- ☐ Plant shallots
- ☐ Place cloches in position to warm up the soil
- ☐ Sow early crops in cold frames or beneath cloches
- ☐ Prepare runner bean and celery trenches
- ☐ Chit 'seed' potatoes (small tubers) of early varieties
- ☐ Plant new fruit trees

BELOW: *Mulching fruit bushes now will give them a good start for the season.*

- ☐ Mulch established fruit trees and bushes with garden compost or rotted manure
- ☐ Put cloches over strawberries if you want an early crop
- ☐ Spray peaches and nectarines with a fungicide recommended for peach leaf curl if this disease is a problem where you live

The flower garden

- ☐ Plant climbers
- ☐ Check bulbs, corms and tubers in store
- ☐ Feed and mulch beds and borders
- ☐ Service your mower or have it done professionally
- ☐ Order seeds, bulbs and plants for the coming season
- ☐ Keep an area of water open in an iced-over pond if there is a prolonged freeze
- ☐ Insulate the cold frame for extra protection against the coldest weather
- ☐ Sow sweet peas
- ☐ Pinch out growing tips of autumn-sown sweet peas
- ☐ Tidy up the rock garden, and apply fresh stone chippings where necessary

BELOW: *Take time now to tidy up the rock garden.*

- ☐ Check labels on shrubs and border plants and renew if necessary
- ☐ Lay a new lawn from turf, provided the ground is not frozen

The greenhouse and conservatory

- ☐ Take chrysanthemum cuttings
- ☐ Pot up chrysanthemums rooted earlier
- ☐ Take dahlia cuttings
- ☐ Sow seeds of bedding plants and pot plants
- ☐ Prick out seedlings sown earlier
- ☐ Increase ventilation on warm days
- ☐ Make sure glass is clean so that the plants receive plenty of light

BELOW: *Many summer bedding plants can be sown now.*

BELOW: *Many summer bedding plants sown earlier will be ready to prick out.*

PLANTS AT THEIR BEST

Crocus (bulb)
Daphne mezereum (shrub)
Eranthis hyemalis (bulb)
Erica carnea (shrub)
Erica × *darleyensis* (shrub)
Galanthus nivalis (bulb)
Garrya elliptica (shrub)
Helleborus niger (herbaceous)
Helleborus orientalis (herbaceous)
Iris unguicularis (syn. *I. stylosa*)
(herbaceous)
Iris reticulata (bulb)
Jasminum nudiflorum (wall shrub)
Muscari armeniacum (bulb)
Prunus cerasifera (tree)
Prunus × *subhirtella* 'Autumnalis'
(tree)
Sarcococca (shrub)
Viburnum × *bodnantense* (shrub)
Viburnum tinus (shrub)

RIGHT: *Varieties of* Erica carnea *flower in winter and often into spring.*

BELOW: *In mild areas,* Muscari armeniacum *will put in an appearance at the end of winter.*

SOW EARLY CROPS IN YOUR COLD FRAME

If your cold frame is not packed with over-wintering plants, make use of it for early vegetable crops. Radishes and turnips are among the crops that grow quickly and mature early in a cold frame, but you can also try forcing varieties of carrot. Suitable varieties of lettuce also do well.

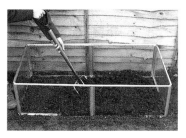

1 Dig over the ground in the frame, working in as much organic material as possible. Farmyard manure is useful for enriching the soil for these early crops. Do not apply powerful artificial fertilizers at this time.

2 Rake the soil level, and make shallow drills with the rake or a hoe. You can sow the seeds broadcast (scattered randomly), but this makes weeding and thinning more difficult.

3 Sow the seeds thinly, then rake the soil back over the drills. Water thoroughly, then keep the frame closed until the seeds germinate. Once they are through, ventilate on mild days, but keep closed, and if possible insulated, at night.

WARM UP THE SOIL

If you have a kitchen garden, start warming up the soil with cloches to get your vegetables off to an early start. Although most early vegetables are not sown until early spring, you need to have your cloches in position several weeks before you plan to sow.

1 Cloche designs vary considerably, but most can easily be made into long runs the length of the row. Make sure that they are butted close together and that plastic cloches are well anchored to the ground.

2 End pieces are essential, otherwise the cloches will just become a wind tunnel. Make sure they are fixed firmly in place.

3 Polythene tunnel cloches are inexpensive to buy, and although they need to be re-covered after a few seasons, a replacement sheet is inexpensive. Fix the hoops first, then stretch the sheet over them.

4 Use the special fixing wires to hold the sheet in position.

5 Secure the ends with sticks or pegs, pulling the plastic taut.

6 Heap a little soil over the edges to anchor the cloches.

PREPARE BEAN AND CELERY TRENCHES

You can grow a satisfactory crop of beans without special soil preparation, and achieve a respectable crop of self-blanching celery by planting on ground that has not been specially enriched. But if you want an especially heavy and impressive crop, it is worth preparing the trench.

1 Take out a trench 25–30cm (10–12in) deep and 60cm (2ft) wide for runner beans, 38cm (15in) wide for celery. Heap the soil to one or both sides of the trench.

2 Add as much rotted manure or garden compost as you can spare. This will add some nutrients and benefit the structure and moisture-holding capacity of the soil.

3 Fork the manure or garden compost into the soil at the bottom of the trench – don't leave it as a layer. Finally, rake the soil back into the trench.

APPLY SLOW-ACTING FERTILIZERS

Apply slow-acting fertilizers such as bonemeal and proprietary controlled-release fertilizers when the vegetable plot has been dug and levelled, ready for sowing from early spring onwards. Controlled-release fertilizers release their nutrients only when the soil is warm enough for the plants to use them. Fertilizers should always be applied evenly and at the recommended rate.

1 Divide the area into strips 1m or 1yd wide with string, and space canes at the same interval to form a square. Scatter the measured dose, then move the canes. Rake into the soil.

TAKE DAHLIA CUTTINGS

If you require just one or two more dahlia plants, you can simply divide the tubers before planting them in late spring, making sure that each piece has an 'eye' or bud. For more plants, it is best to take cuttings after starting the tubers into growth early in the greenhouse.

1 Plant the tubers in deep boxes of compost. You will not be able to bury the tubers, but that does not matter so long as you trickle as much soil as possible around them. Keep the boxes in a light, warm place.

2 Take the cuttings when they have two or three pairs of leaves. If you take a tiny piece of the parent tuber, they should root quickly without a rooting hormone.

3 **You can take larger cuttings if you miss the earlier stage, but try not to let them become longer than 8cm (3in). Cut off with a sharp knife just above the tuber.**

4 Remove the lowest pair of leaves to leave a clear stem. Pull the leaves off carefully or cut them off with a sharp knife. If some of the leaves have grown large, cut these in half and discard the tips. This will reduce the area of leaf through which moisture can be lost while the cutting is rooting.

5 To increase the number of cuttings likely to root successfully, dip the cut ends into a rooting hormone. Insert the cuttings around the edge of a pot, label, then place in a propagator to root.

6 **If you don't have a propagator, enclose the pot and cuttings in a plastic bag. Try to keep the leaves out of contact with the bag. They should root in a matter of weeks if you keep them in a warm, light position.**

PLANT CLIMBERS

You can plant container-grown climbers at almost any time of the year provided the ground is not frozen or waterlogged. However, it is much easier to train in new shoots as they grow than it is to untangle them from their temporary support and attempt to retrain them.

1 Excavate a hole about twice the diameter of the root-ball. The centre of the plant should be at least 30cm (12in) away from the wall or fence, otherwise the roots will be too dry.

2 Dig in a generous amount of rotted manure or garden compost. This is particularly important when planting a climber near a wall or fence, as you need material that will hold moisture around the roots.

3 Tease out some of the fine roots from around the edge of the rootball, to encourage the plant to root out into the surrounding soil. Return and firm the soil around the plant, and apply a slow or controlled-release fertilizer.

4 Loosen the stems first if they have been tied to a cane, then tie them to the support. Spread them out evenly, and don't be afraid to spread them wide and low – new shoots will grow upwards to fill the space.

5 Water thoroughly after planting, and be prepared to water regularly in dry weather for the first year. Climbers are usually planted where walls or other plants shield them from most of the rain.

6 Apply a mulch at least 5cm (2in) thick around the plant after the ground has been soaked thoroughly. This will reduce water loss as well as suppress weeds.

SOW BEDDING PLANTS

Late winter is a good time to sow the majority of frost-tender plants used for summer bedding if you have a heated greenhouse, although a few such as pelargonium (bedding geraniums) and *Begonia semperflorens* are best sown earlier to give them a long period of growth before planting out in late spring or early summer. Quick-growers, such as alyssum and French marigolds (*Tagetes*

patula), will soon catch up even if you sow in early or mid spring.

Because you usually need quite a lot of each kind for bedding, it is normally best to sow the seeds in trays rather than pots. However, you may prefer to use pots for the more difficult seeds that need to be germinated in a propagator, as you can pack more in.

1 Fill a seed tray with a sterilized compost suitable for seeds and seedlings. A potting mix could inhibit germination or harm some seedlings. Strike the compost off level with the rim of the tray.

2 Use a presser board (a scrap of wood cut to the right size will usually do the job) and press the compost gently until it is firmed about 1cm (½in) below the rim.

3 Water the tray now, before you sow. This should provide enough moisture for the seeds initially, and won't wash fine seeds away or to one side of the tray.

4 Very large seeds can be spaced by hand, but most medium-sized seeds are easily scattered with a folded piece of stiff paper. Tap it with a finger as you move it over the surface.

5 Unless the packet advises not to cover the seeds (a few germinate better if exposed to light), cover them by sifting more of the sowing mixture over the top.

6 Unless you are placing the tray in a propagator, cover it with a sheet of glass, or place it in a plastic bag. Turn the glass over or the bag inside out regularly (it may be necessary to do this every day) to prevent condensation drips.

7 Remove any covering when the first seeds start to germinate. If you don't, the seedlings may succumb to diseases. It may be possible to reduce the amount of warmth needed once the seeds have germinated, but good light is essential.

SOWING FINE SEEDS

Very tiny seeds, like lobelia and begonia, are difficult to handle and to spread evenly. Mix them with a small quantity of silver sand to provide greater bulk, then sprinkle the sand and seed mix between finger and thumb as you move your hand over the surface of the tray.

PRICK OUT BEDDING PLANTS

Seeds sown in mid winter may be ready for pricking out, and even those sown in late winter may be ready to move on soon. Never let seedlings become overcrowded after germination.

1 Fill seed trays with a potting mixture recommended for seedlings. Strike the compost off level, then firm it with fingers or a pressing board.

2 Prick out a seedling by loosening the soil and lifting up the plant by its seed leaves (the first ones that open, which usually look very different from the proper leaves).

3 Make a hole in the potting mix, deep enough to take most of the roots without curling them. Gently firm the compost round the roots.

4 To help produce an evenly spaced box of plants, first prick out a row along the end and one side. When you have this spacing right, fill in the rest of the tray.

5 Exact spacing will depend on the type of plant you are pricking out. Large ones need more space than small ones. You are unlikely to fit more than 40 plants in a seed tray.

6 If you find it more convenient, use a modular tray system. This makes spacing easier, and there is less root disturbance when the plants are put in the garden later.

INDOOR GARDENING

INTRODUCTION

TO GET THE BEST OUT OF your houseplants, you need to appreciate them as plants as well as decorations and some understanding of the different plant groups will help you to display them appropriately and grow them more successfully. In the first part of the section you will find advice on how to recognize and use all the major plant groups around the home, along with tips on selecting the best plants for different positions and particular conditions.

Be prepared to experiment with plants, accept that there will be failures, and look beyond the commonplace to discover the range of interesting or more unusual plants that you can grow in the home. Growing houseplants will then become an even more stimulating hobby.

The second part of the section will give you the advice and guidance you need to keep your plants in tip-top condition. Houseplants do, of course, demand time and attention. If you forget to water them, few will forgive the lapse. If you don't feed them, most will look weak and starved. None of this should deter anyone from growing them, for there are plants and techniques that you can choose to suit the time you can devote to your plants.

For example, if watering is something you just can't remember to think about every day, or regular

travel takes you away from home and there's nobody to plant-sit for you, there are simple solutions: concentrate on cacti and succulents that are naturally adapted to this kind of deprivation, or grow ordinary houseplants in special containers. Self-watering planters are ideal for groups of plants and you only need to top up the reservoir every week or so. Hydroculture is another excellent option if you want to minimize the watering chore. Feeding is also easy, with slow-release tablets and sticks that you can push into the compost to release nutrients over a long period.

All these aids for the busy person are extremely useful, but caring for

your plants is pleasurable in itself. By grooming them you not only notice whether pests are about to attack, you also get to know your plants better, and often you will see things that would otherwise go unnoticed. If you do no more than slosh a bit of water onto your aspidistra you will soon take it for granted. But if you groom it by removing a dying leaf, or wiping the leaves over with a moist cloth to bring back the sparkle and gloss, you may suddenly notice a curious-looking purple flower sitting at compost level, a gem that you would otherwise miss. Houseplants are full of surprises, many of which only reveal themselves when you *really* care for them.

OPPOSITE: *A large specimen plant, such as this majestic palm, will make a statement in any home.*

RIGHT: *Plant groupings, such as these ferns displayed in a basket, create a stronger visual impact than single plants dotted around a room.*

DEPENDABLE EVERGREENS

Choose some of the easiest and most dependable evergreens as the backbone of your displays. Many of them are tough enough for the more difficult positions around the home, and most of those suggested here are bold enough to be focal point plants too.

The glossy evergreens such as dracaenas, fatsias, ficus, scheffleras, palms and philodendrons generally make excellent stand–alone plants, but they can also be used as the framework plants for groups and arrangements. They will be far more robust than plants with thin or papery leaves, feathery and frondy ferns, or even those with hairy leaves. You need these other leaf textures, as well as flowering plants, to add variety of shape and form, and a touch of colour, but it makes sense to use the toughest evergreens as the basis of your houseplant displays.

Indoor 'trees'
Even the plainest room can be brought to life and given a sense of design and character with a large

specimen plant that has the stature of a small tree. Some houseplants grow into real trees in their natural environment, but indoors you need plants that are in proportion with the dimensions of your room, and that won't quickly outgrow their space.

Large palms are ideal for this purpose, but many of the ficus family do just as well. The common *Ficus elastica*, once so popular, but now often passed by as unexciting, is a good choice, and there are many excellent variegated varieties that are far from dull. If you want an all-green one (and these have the merit of growing more quickly than the variegated kinds), 'Robusta' is a good variety to choose. If you don't like the upright and sometimes leggy appearance of this plant, cut

TOP: Ficus elastica *was once a very popular houseplant, and is still well worth growing. The variety usually grown is 'Robusta', an improvement on the species that used to be grown years ago.*

ABOVE: Ficus lyrata *is a bold 'architectural' plant that can easily reach ceiling height.*

FAR LEFT: Philodendron scandens *is effective both as a trailing plant and grown up a moss pole, as here.*

LEFT: Yucca elephantipes *is a justifiably popular houseplant. It makes a bold focal point and is a really tough plant that should survive for years.*

out the tip when it is about 1.5–1.8m (5–6ft) feet high, to stimulate low branching.

Other ficus to look for are *F. lyrata* (very large leaves with a distinctive shape), *F. benghalensis*, and the widely available *Ficus benjamina*. This is especially beautiful because it grows tall with a broad crown and arching branches. There are also beautiful variegated varieties of this species such as 'Starlight'.

Bushy plants that will give height and spread include *Schefflera arboricola* (syn. *Heptapleurum arboricola*) and *Schefflera actinophylla*. Both have finger-like leaflets radiating from a central point.

When a tough plant is needed
If you need a tough, glossy evergreen for a cold or draughty spot, perhaps for a hallway or near the back door, consider using some of the hardy foliage plants that have to cope with frost and gales when planted outdoors!

Fatsia japonica is another glossy evergreen with fingered foliage, rather like the palm of a hand (look for a variegated variety if you don't like the plain green leaves). Closely

related is × *Fatshedera lizei*, a bigeneric hybrid between *Fatsia japonica* and an ivy. Grow it as a shrub by pinching out the growing tips each spring, or let it show its ivy parentage and grow more upright.

Others to look for are variegated varieties of *Aucuba japonica*, and *Euonymus japonicus* varieties such as 'Mediopictus', 'Microphyllus Albovariegatus' and 'Microphyllus Aureovariegatus'.

Ivies are ideal if you need a tough climber or trailer, and there are lots of varieties to choose from, with a wide choice of leaf shape, size and colour.

Philodendron scandens   P. 'Blue Mink'   P. 'Xanadu'

P. bipinnatifidum   P. 'Pink Prince'

Philodendron leaves
ABOVE: *Some genera have species and varieties with very different leaves. The five philodendron leaves shown here are typical of the variation you can find within one group of plants.*

TOP RIGHT: Monstera deliciosa *is one of the most striking focal point foliage plants that you can grow. The leaves are big and shapely, and the plant will grow large.*

RIGHT: Aspidistra elatior *is a tough plant that seems to tolerate all kinds of neglect. If you look after it properly, however, you will have a fine foliage plant. There is also a variegated variety.*

ABOVE RIGHT: Radermachera *combines tough, glossy leaves with a 'loose' and almost ferny appearance; a refreshing change to most of the glossy evergreens.*

ABOVE: Scindapsus aureus, *often sold under its other name of* Epipremnum aureum, *is a useful climber or trailer. This is the golden variety 'Neon'.*

ELEGANT PALMS

Palms are the epitome of elegance and will add a touch of sophistication to your home. They bring to mind images of a tinkling piano in the palm court of a grand hotel, yet some can look just as elegant and imposing in an ultra-modern home interior.

Many palms are slow-growing, and, consequently, large specimens are often expensive. But don't be deterred from trying palms; if you provide the right conditions, even small plants will gradually become impressive specimens.

Not all palms grow large, and many are compact enough for a table-top or for pride of place on a pedestal. Some are even small enough to use in a bottle garden while young.

How to grow healthy palms

The most common mistake is to regard all palms as lovers of hot sunshine and desert-dry air. They often have to cope with both in countries where they grow outdoors, but as houseplants you want them to remain in good condition with unblemished leaves.

- Keep cool in winter, but not less than 10°C (50°F).
- Keep out of direct sunshine unless you know that your palm revels in sunshine (a few do).
- Use a loam-based compost and ensure that the drainage is good.
- Only repot when absolutely essential as palms dislike root disturbance. Always ensure that the new compost is firmly compacted if you do repot.
- Water liberally in spring and summer, sparingly in winter.
- Mist the plants frequently with water and sponge the leaves occasionally with water.
- Do not use an aerosol leaf shine.

WHAT WENT WRONG

- **Brown leaf tips** are usually caused by dry air. Underwatering and cold are other likely causes.

- **Brown spots on the leaves** are probably caused by a disease, encouraged by overwatering or chills. Cut off all affected leaves.

- **Yellowing leaves** are most likely to be caused by under-watering, though they could also indicate that the plant needs feeding.

- **Brown leaves** are nothing to worry about if they are few in number and only the lowest ones are affected.

LEFT: *Washingtonia palms have fan-like leaves that create a striking effect.*

CHOOSING A PALM

• Tall and tough

Chamaerops humilis Can be grown outdoors where frosts are only mild; suitable for a cold position indoors.

Howeia forsteriana (syn. *Kentia forsteriana*) and *H. belmoreana* (syn. *K. belmoreana*) Associated with the old palm courts. Will survive in a dark situation, but growth is very slow.

Phoenix canariensis This one enjoys full sun (but beware of leaf scorch through glass) and can sit on the patio for the summer. Keep in a cool room – minimum about 7°C(45°F) – in winter.

• Table-top and easy

Chamaedorea elegans (syn. *Neanthe bella*) Can be used in a bottle garden when small. Insignificant flowers often appear on young plants.

• Difficult but worth the effort

Cocos nucifera This is the coconut palm, and it is usually grown as a novelty with the large nut clearly visible at the base. Even a young plant can be 1.8m (6ft) tall, and it is difficult to keep in the home.

Cocos weddeliana A slow-grower. Can be used in a bottle garden.

ABOVE RIGHT: Howeia belmoreana *is sometimes sold under its other name of* Kentia belmoreana.

FAR RIGHT: Chamaedorea elegans *is a palm to choose if you want one that is easy and dependable. It will remain compact enough to use on a table-top.*

RIGHT: Cocus nucifera *is a big palm that is quite difficult to keep in the home.*

Dealing with brown leaves

It is natural for the lower leaves on palms to turn brown and die in time. To keep the plant looking smart, cut these off close to the point of origin (TOP). Secateurs are adequate for most palms, but a saw may be required for specimens with very tough leaves. If the tips of the leaves turn brown, trim them off with scissors, but avoid actually cutting into the healthy leaf (ABOVE).

VARIEGATED PLANTS

Variegated foliage plants will bring colour and a touch of the exotic into a dull corner or bright windowsill, depending on the type. Unlike flowering plants, most remain colourful for twelve months of the year.

Variegation has evolved for several reasons, and the two main ones are important to understand if you want to grow healthy-looking plants with good variegation.

Many variegated houseplants are derived from forest-floor dwellers in which variegation is useful where they occur in lighter areas, such as on the edge of clearings, because it reduces the area of functional leaf. This type of variegation is frequently white and green, the white areas cutting down the area that is reactive to sunlight. This group of plants often has the best variegation when positioned away from direct light.

Others are light-demanding species and have acquired colours and patterns for other reasons. Red and pink leaves are able to absorb light from different parts of the spectrum to green leaves, for example, and many different colours in the one leaf may make it more efficient. The variegation on these plants is often better if positioned in good light.

A few plants have colourful leaves to attract pollinators. The common poinsettia (*Euphorbia pulcherrima*), and bromeliads such as neoregelia, are able to change the colour of the leaves that surround the insignificant flowers from green to bright colours such as reds and pinks.

There are other reasons for variegation, such as being a warning to predators, so there can be no simple rules that apply to all colourful foliage plants.

Potential problems

Some plants lose their strong variegation if the light is too strong, others if it is too weak. If the plant seems unhappy, move it to a lighter or shadier position as appropriate.

If any isolated, all-green shoots appear on an otherwise satisfactorily variegated plant, cut them back to the point of origin. Some plants will 'revert' and the all-green part of the plant will eventually dominate unless you remove the offending shoots.

Coloured bracts (the modified leaves that frame a cluster of flowers) will lose their colour or intensity of colour outside the flowering period. You can do nothing about this.

Begonia rex leaves

Although they are unlikely to be labelled as specific varieties, you can collect a whole range of Begonia rex *with different variegations. Two other types of foliage begonias are shown here:* B. masoniana (TOP LEFT) *and, to the right,* B. 'Tiger'.

GOING FOR A COLLECTION

● There are so many variegated houseplants that some people like to start a collection of a particular group of them. This makes it easy to provide the right conditions for all of them, and the searching out of new species or varieties to add to the collection adds another dimension to the hobby.

Good plants to collect are begonias (there are many variations among *B. rex*, but lots of other begonias have interesting variegation), caladiums (if you like a challenge), codiaeums, dracaenas and cordylines, marantas and calatheas, and pileas. Named varieties of vegetatively propagated coleus are difficult to obtain, but a packet of seeds will give you an amazing range of colours and variegation from which to select those to keep.

OPPOSITE TOP: Begonia rex *varies in leaf colouring from one plant to another, but all are attractively variegated and make bold foliage plants.*

OPPOSITE RIGHT: Dracaena marginata *is a popular houseplant, and there are varieties with attractively variegated leaves.*

OPPOSITE LEFT: Cordyline terminalis, *also sold as* Dracaena terminalis, *comes in many varieties, the difference being in the colouring and variegation.*

TOP RIGHT: *Ivies (varieties of* Hedera helix*) are versatile plants that can be used as climbers or trailers.*

TOP LEFT: Ficus benjamina *'Starlight' is an outstanding houseplant with brightly variegated leaves on a plant that will eventually make a tall specimen with attractively arching shoots.*

RIGHT: *Codiaeums, also known as crotons, can be demanding to grow well, but they make spectacular plants. Leaf hue and shape vary greatly according to variety, but all are bright and colourful.*

GRACEFUL FERNS

Ferns are fascinating plants that will add a special charm to any room in which you want to create a feeling of cool tranquillity and green lushness. They bestow a relaxed atmosphere in contrast to the vivid colour of brighter foliage plants and the brashness of some flowers.

Ferns are grown mainly for the grace and beauty of their fronds, and their elegance compensates for their lack of flowers.

The majority of ferns will thrive in shade or partial shade, conditions that are easily provided in any home. Unfortunately they also require lots of moisture and high humidity, both of which are in short supply in the average living-room. If you want ferns to thrive, you will have to choose easy and tolerant varieties (see the *Fern Selector* above right) or provide them with the humidity and moisture that is so vital. Although most of the ferns sold as houseplants come from tropical regions and

benefit from warmth, central heating spells death to many of them unless you counteract the dry air by taking measures to increase the humidity, at least immediately surrounding the plants.

The ideal place for ferns is in a conservatory, porch or garden room where it is easier to establish a moist atmosphere.

Not all ferns need coddling, however, and some have adapted to dry air or cool temperatures. There are sure to be some ferns that you can grow successfully, and if you are determined to grow the delicate types with thin, feathery fronds, try planting them in a bottle garden or terrarium where they will thrive.

FERN SELECTORS

- **Good for beginners**
Asplenium nidus
Cyrtomium falcatum (syn.
   Polystichum falcatum)
Nephrolepis exaltata
Pellaea rotundifolia

- **For the more experienced**
Adiantum capillus-veneris
Platycerium bifurcatum
Polypodium aureum
Pteris cretica (and its varieties)

- **Difficult but interesting**
Asplenium bulbiferum
Davallia fejeenis

Starting with ferns

If you haven't grown ferns before, start with the easy ones. As you gain experience, add some of the more exotic and difficult species.

The commonest ferns are inexpensive, and even the more unusual kinds are usually cheap if you choose small specimens.

Florists and garden centres sell the most popular houseplant ferns, but you may have to buy the less common ones from a specialist nursery.

Propagating ferns

The simplest way to increase your ferns is to divide a large clump, or to remove offsets. Some, like *Davallia fejeenis*, send out rhizomes that root and can be used to grow new plants, others produce small bulbils or even plantlets on the leaves (*Asplenium bulbiferum* is one). These will usually root into moist compost if pressed into the surface.

LEFT: *Most of the aspleniums are much easier to care for than the ferns with very thin and finely divided leaves.* Asplenium nidus (LEFT) *has broad leaves that radiate from a central well or 'nest' and is a particularly good houseplant.*

These are interesting and fun ways to grow more ferns.

Growing your own ferns from spores is possible but slow, and you may find it difficult to obtain fresh spores of houseplant species with good germination.

Don't be deceived!

Many plants commonly regarded as ferns simply masquerade under that name. Some, like the selaginellas, are also primitive plants, other such as asparagus 'ferns' are more evolved flowering plants that simply have fine, feathery-looking foliage – an attribute associated with ferns. The asparagus fern belongs to the lily family, though you would hardly recognize the connection from its insignificant flowers.

Selaginellas are pretty, low-growing plants that like the same conditions as indoor ferns: damp shade and moderate warmth. They will happily grow alongside ferns in a bottle garden.

Asparagus ferns are available as houseplants, all of them tougher and more tolerant of neglect than the majority of true ferns.

Mounting a stag's horn

The Platycerium bifurcatum *is a native of Australia and unlike most ferns it does not mind a dry atmosphere. One of the most spectacular ways to display it is mounted on bark. Keep the root-ball damp and mist the plant regularly.*

1 Find a suitably sized piece of bark such as cork bark. Start with a small plant and remove it from the pot. If necessary, remove some of the compost to reduce its bulk, then wrap the roots in damp sphagnum moss. Secure with wire.

ABOVE RIGHT: Cyrtomium falcatum *is the one to choose if you find ferns generally too demanding. This one will tolerate a much drier atmosphere than most, and does not need a lot of warmth.*

RIGHT: Nephrolepis exaltata *is one of the best ferns for a pedestal or table-top display. There are several varieties, with variation in leaf shape, some being more 'ruffled' than others.*

ABOVE: Adiantum capillus-veneris, *like most of the maidenhair ferns, demands a humid atmosphere to do well. However, this is a truly graceful species.*

2 Bind the mossy root-ball to the cork bark, using florists' wire or plastic-covered wire to hold it.

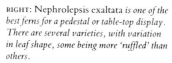

CACTI AND SUCCULENTS

Some people are fascinated by cacti and they become a passionate hobby, others dismiss them as being not quite 'real' houseplants. Whatever you think of them, cacti and succulents are some of the easiest plants to look after and make the ideal choice if you often have to leave your houseplants unattended.

Cacti can be very beautiful in flower, and a huge epiphyllum bloom can be almost breath-takingly beautiful, but you will probably decide whether or not to grow cacti depending on whether you like or dislike their overall shape and form. It has to be admitted that a few, like the epiphyllum just mentioned, can be ungainly and unattractive when out of bloom, but the vast majority are neat, compact and in the eyes of most people have a fascinating beauty of their own. There are species that creep and cascade, others which have hairy or cylindrical spiny columns, some with flat jointed pads, and others with globular or candelabra shapes.

Succulents are just as diverse: some are grown for their flowers, others for shape or foliage effect. There are hundreds of them readily available, and many more can be found in specialist nurseries.

Flowers of the desert

These need minimal water between mid-autumn and early spring, but plenty of sunshine at all times. As a rule, keep them cool in winter (about 10°C/50°F) to encourage flowering. Repot annually when young, but later only repot when really necessary as a small pot also hastens flowering.

Not all cacti will flower when young, so if you want some that flower freely on young plants, look for species of echinopsis, lobivia, mammillaria, notocactus, parodia and rebutia.

Forest cacti

The forest cacti, which have flattened, leaf-like stems, are the most popular type of cacti. To keep them flowering well each year remember not to treat them like ordinary cacti, and follow these basic guidelines.

Exact treatment depends on the species, but they will require a resting period, when they are kept cool and watered only infrequently, usually mid-autumn to mid-winter

LEFT: *Cacti often look better in small groups rather than as isolated specimens. In the group shown here, a grafted cactus (to the left of the arrangement) has been used to add additional interest.*

BELOW: *Epiphyllums have huge flowers and are among the most spectacular cacti in bloom. Unfortunately they look ugly and ungainly out of flower, so for most of the year you will want to relegate them to an inconspicuous spot.*

or late winter to early spring, followed by a period of warmth when they are watered freely. They will also benefit from spending the summer in a shady spot outdoors.

Succulents

Succulents vary enormously in their requirements – some, such as sempervivums, are tough and frost-tolerant, others are tender and temperamental. Always look up the specific needs for each plant, but as a rule they need very good light and little water in winter.

Displaying and collecting

Few cacti and succulents make good focal point plants – though a large epiphyllum in a porch can be a real stunner – and they are generally best displayed as groups in dish gardens or troughs. Cascading cacti, however, like the forest cacti already mentioned, are almost always displayed in isolation and look good on a pedestal while they are in bloom. But if you have a conservatory, you can try planting several of them in a hanging basket.

Handling cacti

Repotting a cactus can be a prickly job. Make it easier on your hands by folding up a strip of newspaper or brown paper (TOP). Wrap this around the plant, leaving enough paper at each end to form a handle (ABOVE).

CACTUS OR SUCCULENT?

● Succulent simply means a plant that has adapted to dry conditions and can retain moisture with minimal loss from its leaves, which are often plump and fleshy. Cacti are also succulents, but in all except a few primitive species the leaves have become modified to spines or hairs and the stems have taken over the function of leaves – being thick, fleshy and with the ability to photosynthesize.

Although most cacti have their natural home in warm, semi-desert regions of America, some grow as epiphytes on trees in the forests of tropical America. Some of these, such as zygocactus, schlumbergera and rhipsalidopsis, have produced hybrids and varieties that are popular flowering houseplants in winter and spring.

ABOVE: Crassula ovata, *like most succulents, is undemanding and will thrive with just a modicum of care.*

FAR LEFT: Euphorbia trigona *is an easy-to-grow succulent with distinctive three- to four-sided branches.*

LEFT: Sansevieria trifasciata *'Laurentii' is an attractive variegated plant that is really tough and needs minimal attention.*

BROMELIADS

Bromeliads are strange plants. Some have leaves that form water-holding vases, others have brightly coloured leaves that make a substitute for colourful flowers, and a few actually grow on air and need no soil.

Some bromeliads – aechmeas, vrieseas and guzmanias for example – are grown for their attractive flower heads as well as for their foliage. A few – billbergias, for example – have individual flowers that are both strange and beautiful. The vast majority are best considered as foliage plants. Some, such as neoregelias, form a rosette of leaves that becomes brightly coloured in the centre when the plants flower, others like cryptanthus are prettily variegated. The pineapple is the best-known bromeliad, but it is the variegated forms such as *Ananas comosus* 'Variegatus' that are generally grown as houseplants.

Air plants

A large group of tillandsias are known as air plants because they grow without soil. In nature they drape themselves over branches or even wires, or cling to rocks. One of the most attractive ways to display them is on a bromeliad tree (see opposite), but you can buy them displayed in shells, baskets, or even attached to a mirror with glue.

- Mist the plants regularly, especially from spring to autumn. This is the only way that they can receive moisture if the air itself is not sufficiently humid.
- Feed by adding a very dilute liquid fertilizer to the misting water, perhaps once a fortnight, when the plants are actively growing.

CARING FOR BROMELIADS

- Bromeliads need special care. The following advice applies to most kinds, but see the separate instructions for air plant tillandsias.

- Most kinds need only moderate warmth (about 10°C/50°F), but some need 24°C/75° to flower.

- Give them good light, out of direct sun (a few, such as cryptanthus and pineapples, will tolerate full sun).

- Grow in small pots as they don't need much compost and water only when the compost becomes almost dry.

- Use a peat-based compost rather than one with loam, and if possible mix in perlite or sphagnum moss.

- For those that form a 'vase', keep this topped up with water (rain-water in hard-water areas).

- Mist the leaves in summer, and add a foliar feed occasionally. Vase types can have a one-third strength fertilizer added to the vase water every couple of weeks.

OPPOSITE LEFT: Ananas bracteatus striatus *is a variegated version of the pineapple that makes a striking houseplant.*

LEFT: Neoregelia carolinae *is typical of the 'vase' bromeliads. The central leaves colour when the small flowers appear in the central vase formed by the rosette of leaves.*

ABOVE LEFT: *Most tillandsias are popularly known as air plants because they do not need planting in compost. They are very ornamental when mounted on a piece of bark or driftwood.*

OPPOSITE RIGHT: *Most guzmanias, like G.* lingulata, *have long-lasting flower heads.*

BELOW: Aechmea
fasciata *has weird but
beautiful flowers, set off
by bold, greyish foliage.*

MAKE A BROMELIAD TREE

● The size and shape of your 'tree' will depend on the space that you have available, a suitable container, and the size of your branch. Choose a forked branch from a tree and saw it to size.

Anchor the branch in the container with stones, bricks or beach pebbles – this will add weight and stability as well as holding the branch upright. Then pour in plaster of Paris or a mortar or concrete mix, to within a couple of centimetres (an inch) of the top of the container. You can set a few empty pots into the plaster or concrete to allow for planting into the base later.

When the plaster or concrete has set, wire your bromeliads to the tree. Remove most of the compost from the roots, and pack some sphagnum moss around them. Secure the roots to the tree with plastic-covered or copper wire. Make sure that you take advantage of any forks in the branch to hold an attractive bromeliad.

Air plant tillandsias such as *T. usneoides* can simply be draped over the branches; other species may have to be wired or glued on.

FLOWERING HOUSEPLANTS

Flowering houseplants are usually short-lived in the home, but they bring a splash of colour and vibrancy that not even coloured foliage can achieve. They also add an element of seasonal variation that foliage plants lack.

The most rewarding flowering houseplants are those that grow bigger and better each year, with each subsequent blooming crowning another year of good cultivation and care. Flowers that you should be able to keep growing in the home from year to year include beloperones, bougainvilleas, *Campanula isophylla*, clivias, gardenias, hoyas, *Jasminum polyanthum*, *Nerium oleander*, pelargoniums, saintpaulias, spathiphyllums and streptocarpus.

The disposables

Many flowering pot plants are difficult to keep permanently in the home and are best discarded when flowering has finished (or in some cases placed in a greenhouse if you have one). They are no less valuable indoors, and should be regarded rather like long-lasting cut flowers. A lot of them are annuals and can,

LEFT: Begonia elatior *hybrids can be in flower for most months of the year, but plants like the dwarf narcissus 'Tete-a-Tete' are especially welcome because of their seasonal nature.*

BELOW LEFT: *Varieties of* Kalanchoe blossfeldiana *are available in flower the year round.*

BELOW: *Pot-grown lilies make striking houseplants, but it is usually better to buy them in flower rather than try to grow your own from bulbs. Commercial growers can ensure that suitable dwarf varieties are used, and chemicals are often employed to keep the plants compact. Plant them in the garden to flower in future years.*

therefore, be inexpensively raised from seed: try browallias, calceolarias, cinerarias and exacums, which are all bright and cheerful, inexpensive to buy and not difficult to raise from seed yourself.

Annuals die after flowering and have to be discarded, but others are just not worth the effort of trying to save in home conditions: impatiens are often leggy if saved, and easy to raise or cheap to buy; Hiemalis begonias quickly deteriorate and are difficult to keep healthy; furthermore, they are so cheap to buy that it's hardly worth taking up valuable space with them once flowering is over. Garden bulbs like hyacinths may bloom beautifully if forced for early flowering, but they will fail to give an acceptable repeat performance and are therefore best put out in the garden to recover and give a garden display in future years.

Hardy border plants such as astilbes are sometimes sold as pot plants. They look magnificent in flower, but the pot of large leaves left afterwards is hardly attractive, and the plant is almost sure to deteriorate if kept indoors. By planting it in the garden after

RIGHT: *Saintpaulias are among the most popular flowering plants, and there are so many variations in flower shape, size and colour that you can easily form an interesting collection of them.*

BELOW LEFT: *Hydrangeas make attractive houseplants if bought in flower, but they do not make easy long-term residents in the home. Try planting them in the garden when they have finished flowering.*

BELOW RIGHT: *Impatiens have always been popular houseplants, but the New Guinea types have bolder foliage than the older types usually grown. Some also have striking variegated leaves, as a bonus to the pretty flowers.*

flowering you will have enjoyed plumes of beauty for a few weeks after purchase, then years of pleasure in the garden afterwards.

Tricked into flowering

Some plants are tricked into flowering at a particular time, or into blooming on compact plants. You won't be able to reproduce these conditions in the home. Year-round chrysanthemums are made to bloom every month of the year by having their day length adjusted by special lighting and by blacking out the greenhouse. They will probably be blooming on compact plants because they have been treated with dwarfing chemicals, the effects of which gradually wear off. If you manage to keep them going, they will become taller and probably flower at a different time. Try planting them in the garden – some varieties will thrive as garden plants if the winters are not too severe.

BRIGHT BERRIES

● Don't overlook plants with bright berries. These will often remain attractive for much longer than flowers; some of the most popular ones are easily raised from seed and are relatively inexpensive if you have to buy them. Annual peppers (*Capsicum annuum*) have cone-shaped fruits in shades of yellow, red, and purple. *Solanum capsicastrum* has orange or red berries shaped like small tomatoes – and with luck you can keep the plant going for another year, placing it outdoors for the summer. Remember to keep the air humid by misting periodically to prevent berries dropping prematurely.

OPPOSITE ABOVE: *Year-round chrysanthemums make excellent short-term houseplants. They are best bought in bud or flower then enjoyed for a few weeks before being discarded.*

OPPOSITE BELOW: *Berries can be as bright as flowers, and often last for much longer. Those of* Solanum capsicastrum *and* S. pseudocapsicum *and their hybrids look like cherry-sized tomatoes. The plants are usually discarded after flowering but can be kept for another year.*

TOP LEFT: Beloperone guttata *is easy to grow, long-lasting in flower, and you should be able to keep it from year to year.*

TOP RIGHT: Primula obconica *is a delightful houseplant when it is in flower. However, some people have an allergic reaction to the leaves.*

CENTRE RIGHT: *The azalea most commonly sold as a pot plant, and sometimes called* Azalea indica, *is botanically* Rhododendron simsii.

RIGHT: Euphorbia pulcherrima, *the so-called poinsettia, has insignificant true flowers, but really spectacular and colourful bracts to surround them.*

GARDEN ANNUALS

- If you have a few spare plants after planting out the summer bedding, it might be worth potting some of them up into larger pots to use indoors. Among those that can make attractive short-term houseplants if the position is light enough are ageratums, lobelias, salvias and French marigolds.

SCENT IN THE AIR

Scent adds another dimension to your plants, and it's not only flowers that are fragrant. Take another journey of discovery with some of the aromatic houseplants that will make you wonder why you ever used chemical air fresheners.

ABOVE: *The flowers of* Gardenia jasminoides *are pure white in full bloom, darkening to a creamy-yellow with age, and are richly fragrant.*

BELOW LEFT: Datura suaveolens *(syn.* Brugmansia suaveolens*) is a large and magnificent plant, with huge bell-like flowers and a strength of scent that matches the size of the blooms. This variety is* 'Grand Marnier'*, sometimes listed as the variety* D. x candida.

Perception of scent is an individual experience, and one that is more developed in some individuals than in others. Our ability to detect scents can be affected by the way in which our scent receptors are genetically determined. Some people are scent blind in the same way in which some people are colour blind. They can detect most smells but have a deficiency in certain types: someone who can smell a rose or a sweet pea might be unable to appreciate the equally potent perfume of the freesia. This makes it difficult to recommend specific plants to others without qualification: the plants suggested here have a smell readily detected by most people, but you may find a particular scent weak or even indiscernible.

Scent is further complicated by individual reactions to a scent when it is detected. Sometimes this may be for biochemical reasons, but it may even be that some scents are associated with pleasant or unpleasant experiences. There are scented-leaved geraniums (pelargoniums) that might remind one person of the tangy fragrance of lemons while another may detect a thymol smell in them that reminds them of an earlier visit to a dentist.

The only way to discover whether you like the scent of a particular plant is to grow it and

sniff it. You will almost certainly like those suggested below, but if you don't, simply cross them off your list for the future.

Placing scented plants

Plants that have a delicate fragrance, which you have to sniff at close quarters, such as an exacum, need to be positioned where sniffing is easy – perhaps on a table or shelf that you pass in the hall, or as a centrepiece for the dining table.

Plants with a dominant scent, like gardenias and hyacinths, can be so potent that one plant will fill the whole room with scent. It doesn't matter where you place these in the room, but avoid other fragrant plants that may conflict with them; place these in another room where you can appreciate their own distinct fragrances in isolation.

ABOVE: Stephanotis floribunda *is a very fragrant climber that can be grown as a pot-plant while young.*

ABOVE CENTRE: *A bowl of hyacinths will fill a room with scent. Although they are at their best for perhaps a week, by planting different varieties, and using ordinary bulbs and those specially treated for early flowering, you can enjoy them over a period of months.*

ABOVE RIGHT: *Scented-leaved geraniums (pelargoniums) usually have insignificant flowers. Grow them for their aromatic foliage and position them where you might accidentally brush against them, or can touch the leaves to release their pungent fragrance. This is* Pelargonium graveolens, *with a scent reminiscent of lemons.*

BELOW: *Oranges make superb conservatory plants, and can be brought into the house for short spells.*

FRAGRANT FOLIAGE

- Some of the best plants to grow for fragrant foliage are the scented-leaved geraniums (pelargoniums). These are just of few of them:

P. capitatum (rose-scented)
P. crispum (lemon-scented)
P. graveolens (slightly lemony)
P. odoratissimum (apple-scented)
P. tomentosum (peppermint-scented)

Plants that you have to touch or brush against to release the scent, like scented-leaved geraniums (pelargoniums), should be placed where you might come into contact with them as you pass: alcoves or windows by a flight of stairs and on the kitchen table, for example.

SCENTED FLOWERS

- Citrus (fragrant flowers, citrus-scented foliage and fruit)
Datura suaveolens
Exacum affine
Hyacinths
Hymenocallis × festalis, H. narcissiflora
Jasminum officinale
Narcissus 'Paperwhite'
Stephanotis floribunda

Orchids and Other Exotics

Add a touch of class to your collection of houseplants by growing a few orchids, along with other exotics, such as strelitzia, the 'bird of paradise flower'.

Orchids have a reputation for being difficult to grow and, consequently, many people are deterred from trying them as houseplants. If you choose the right types, however, they are relatively undemanding and should make larger and more impressive clumps each year.

The drawback to orchids is the contrast between the beauty of their exotic flowers and the rather ungainly foliage with which you have to live for the other ten or eleven months of the year. The best way to grow them is to stand the plants in a sheltered and partially shaded spot in the garden during the summer – or better still in a conservatory if you have one – and then to bring them indoors for the winter or when they are coming into flower.

Easy orchids

The best orchids to start with are cymbidium hybrids, which are easy to grow, readily available and inexpensive to buy if you are not fussy about a particular variety.

Miltonias are a better choice if you want a more compact plant. The large, flat, pansy-like flowers come in a range of brilliant colours, and will often last for a month.

Cypripediums (paphiopedilums) are another group of distinctive and easy orchids to try. Sometimes called slipper orchids, the bottom petals form a slipper-shaped pouch.

Other orchids can be grown indoors, especially if you are able to create a special area for them, perhaps with artificial light, but it is best to gain experience first with the easy genera described above.

Other exotics

Try some of the following exotic-looking flowering plants that will bring some of the brilliance and flamboyance of the tropics to your home.

Anthuriums have vivid pink, red or orange 'flowers' that will never be ignored. The 'flower' is actually a spathe and it is the curly tail-like spadix that contains the true flowers. The 'flowers' are long-lasting and the foliage is attractive.

Bougainvilleas are at their best climbing into the roof of a conservatory, but you could try one in a porch or light window. The bright 'flowers' are actually papery bracts. Prune after flowering and keep cool but frost-free for the winter.

Grooming orchids

With age, orchid leaves often become blemished. If the damage is towards the end of the leaf, try cutting it away. Angle the cut to make the end a more natural shape than if cut at right-angles.

Daturas are big plants, really at their best in a conservatory, although you can use small plants indoors. The huge bell-like flowers are usually white, pink or yellow, depending on the species and variety. The heady scent matches the magnificence of the blooms – a single flower can fill a small house with scent in the evening.

Hibiscus rosa-sinensis grows into quite a large shrub but can be bought as a small plant. The blooms are big and beautiful: 10cm (4in) or more across, in shades of red, yellow and almost orange.

Strelitzias are sometimes called 'bird of paradise flowers' because the orange and blue flowers resemble the head of an exotic-looking bird. The leaves are often 1m (3ft) or more tall, and a large plant is truly spectacular.

HOW TO GROW ORCHIDS

- It is best to check the specific requirements for each species, but the following rules apply to most:

- Place them in a very light position, but not in direct, strong sunlight.

- Provide plenty of humidity. Stand the pots on a gravel tray, or mist regularly. Small plants do well in an enclosed plant case.

- Avoid draughts, but provide plenty of ventilation. Move them away from a cold window at night.

- Repot only when the pot is full of roots. Always use a special potting mixture recommended for orchids (you may have to buy it from a specialist nursery).

- Feed regularly during the summer.

- Stand the plants outdoors in a sheltered position for the summer if you don't have a conservatory to put them in.

- Water only when the compost is almost dry.

OPPOSITE TOP: Strelitzia reginae, *the 'bird of paradise flower', never fails to impress with its flamboyant flowers.*

OPPOSITE CENTRE: *The red or pink 'petals' that surround the insignificant proper flowers of the striking anthuriums are in fact modified leaves.*

TOP: *Bougainvilleas have a really exotic look, and although they are climbers can be used as a houseplant while small. Larger plants are best in a conservatory.*

ABOVE: *Phalaenopsis orchids will flower in most months of the year, but they are not easy plants to grow in the home.*

ABOVE RIGHT: *Cymbidiums are among the easiest orchids to grow in the house, but even so they usually benefit from a spell outdoors or in the greenhouse during the summer months.*

RIGHT: Hibiscus rosa-sinensis *blooms are big, bold and bright; they seldom fail to attract attention.*

Fun Plants

Some plants are entertaining or educational rather than beautiful. They are a good way to instill children with an appreciation of plants, and make interesting houseplants.

Carnivorous plants always fascinate children. Few of them are beautiful, though some have quite pretty flowers. *Pinguicula grandiflora* has pretty pink flowers like violets on long stalks that seem to last for weeks. Most have uninteresting flowers, however, and their attraction lies solely in the various forms of trap.

Some cannot be grown satisfactorily in the home, but the following are worth trying: *Dionaea muscipula* (a snap trap), *Drosera capensis* (an adhesive trap), *Pinguicula grandiflora* (a 'fly paper' trap), and *Sarracenia flava* (a pitfall trap). Enthusiasts grow dozens of different kinds, but these represent four different types of trap and all make quite acceptable houseplants, though they must be treated with care if they are not to be short-lived.

Sensitive plants
Several plants are sensitive to touch, collapsing on contact. The most widely available one is *Mimosa pudica*, which makes quite a pretty plant with its sensitive leaflets and attractive flowers like pink balls. It's easy to raise from seed if you can't find plants in local nurseries or garden centres.

Leaves that bear 'babies'
Some plants have the ability to produce small plantlets on the leaves, which eventually fall and root (or you can speed things up by removing them and potting them up).

Two that are quite widely available are *Kalanchoe daigremontiana* (syn. *Bryophyllum daigremontianum*), which has miniature plants all around the edge of the leaf, and *K. tubiflora* (syn. *Bryophyllum tubiflorum*), which produces them in clusters at the ends of the leaves.

Other plants that produce ready-made 'babies' are the fern *Asplenium bulbiferum* and *Tolmiea menziesii*.

Bulbs that flower without soil

For a novelty, try flowering colchicums 'dry'. For stability, place them on a saucer of sand. Usually within weeks, the large crocus-like flowers emerge from the dry bulb.

An unusual bulb called *Sauromatum venosum* (syn. *S. guttatum*) is sometimes sold as a novelty for flowering 'dry' (treat like the colchicums). The tube-like flower that emerges is a sinister greenish-purple. This strange flower will soon make its presence known by the awful stench of carrion – fascinating for children, but not something to have in your living-room for long!

OPPOSITE ABOVE: Colchicum autumnale *can be grown 'dry'. Either stand the corms directly on a windowsill or place them in a saucer of sand or pebbles for stability, and wait just a few weeks for the large crocus-like flowers to emerge.*

OPPOSITE BELOW: Dionaea muscipula *is a carnivorous plant with a snap trap that quickly closes over its prey.*

TOP RIGHT: Sarracenia flava *is a carnivorous plant with a pitfall trap.*

CENTRE RIGHT: Drosera capensis *is an example of an adhesive trap, and makes an interesting addition to a collection of carnivorous plants.*

LEFT AND ABOVE: Kalanchoe daigremontiana *(syn.* Bryophyllum daigremontianum*) produces plantlets along the edges of its leaves (*LEFT*). These often fall and root into the compost around*

CARING FOR CARNIVOROUS PLANTS

● Don't use an ordinary potting compost. It needs to be acidic and low in soluble minerals. A suitable compost (medium) usually includes peat, sand, sphagnum moss, and sometimes perlite or finely chipped bark.

● Grow a collection of them in a plant case or old aquarium. Cover it if possible, to create a humid environment.

● Provide good light.

● Stand the pots on trays of gravel filled with water to provide humidity if not in an enclosed environment.

● Some species prefer a constantly wet compost and you can stand these in a saucer that is kept topped up with water (not advisable for normal houseplants).

● Only ever use soft water (distilled or deionized would do, but rainwater is best).

● It is best not to use a fertilizer. Most may be harmful, and if you think the plants really do need feeding, try misting them with a foliar feed made up at quarter strength, about once a fortnight during the period of active growth.

● These plants catch prey to obtain nutrients, but indoors the number of insects available to them will be limited. Some people release fruit flies near them or feed them with fly maggots (often available from fishing tackle shops).

*the parent plant, but you can easily remove them to pot up for a supply of plants to give to friends (*ABOVE LEFT*).*

SHOPPING FOR HOUSEPLANTS

Shopping for new and interesting houseplants can be fun, but be wary about where and when you buy. A plant that has been poorly treated before you buy it may only reveal the ill-treatment after you get it home.

Choosing houseplants requires as much thought and care as the purchase of anything else for the home. Indeed, some plants will be with you for much longer than many household items.

You can buy a plant simply because you like the look of it, then try to find a suitable spot; or decide what you need to fill a particular niche in the home, before going out to buy an appropriate plant. The latter is undoubtedly the theoretical ideal, but it overlooks reality.

Except for the most common houseplants, the chances of finding a particular plant, even over several shopping trips, is not great. Although advance planning is desirable, never be deterred from the impulse buy of something interesting or unusual, especially if you are prepared for a few failures along the way.

Where to buy

For everyday houseplants, a garden centre is often the best place to buy: there is likely to be a reasonable selection of 'basic' houseplants, and usually a few uncommon kinds. Importantly, they will be in conditions similar to a greenhouse: good light, warmth (ventilated in summer), with a buoyant and humid atmosphere. Staff are usually knowledgeable, but beware of assuming that part-time or temporary staff know more than you do!

Florists also sell pot plants but, except for the very largest shops, the range is limited and conditions are seldom good.

Some large stores sell a limited

ABOVE: *Try to buy your houseplants from a nursery or garden centre where they have excellent growing conditions in good light.*

GETTING THEM HOME

- Buy your plants last, immediately before you go home.

- Don't put plants in a hot car boot, especially if you don't plan to drive straight home, or if the drive is a long one.

- Make sure that they are wrapped in a protective sleeve if carrying them home by public transport. This will protect them from cold and wind, and guard against knocks.

range of plants. At the best of them the quality is excellent, with the plants well looked after and removed from sale if not bought within a certain time. In others they can languish in poor light and with inadequate care, slowly deteriorating until they reach the point of death. The quality and condition of plants sold by ordinary shops or home-improvement stores vary enormously. Go through the *Buyer's checklist* below carefully before buying from these sources.

Market stalls often sell plants at very competitive prices, and they are usually sold quickly, so it is possible to obtain quality plants cheaply if you don't mind the limited range. Beware of buying in cold weather – especially in winter. The chill plants receive, having come out of hot-house conditions, may not be obvious until a few days after you get them home, when the leaves start to drop. Even in the summer, houseplants displayed outdoors can suffer a severe check to growth if the weather is cold or windy.

Buyer's checklist

- Check the compost. If it has dried out the plants have been neglected. Don't buy.
- Lift and check the base of the pot. If lots of roots are coming out of the bottom, the plant should have been repotted sooner. A few small roots through the bottom of the pot is not a sign of neglect, and is normal where the plants have been grown on capillary matting.
- If buying a flowering plant, make

sure that there are still plenty of buds to open, otherwise the display may be brief.

- Look critically at the shape. If growth is lop-sided, or the plant is bare at the base, choose another.
- Make sure the plant is labelled. A label should tell you how to care for the plant, and unlabelled plants suggest a lack of concern for plants and customers.
- Avoid plants with damaged or broken leaves.
- Don't be afraid to turn the leaves over. Look for signs of pests and diseases. If you find any, leave them in the shop!
- If the plants are displayed in a protective sleeve, don't buy unless you can remove your potential purchase for inspection. Display sleeves can hide rot and disease, pests, and even a sparse or poorly shaped plant.

Root check

It is natural for a few roots to grow through the bottom of the pot, especially if a capillary watering system has been used (which is normal in plant nurseries), but a mass of roots growing through the pot is probably a sign that it needs repotting.

Flowering plants

When buying a flowering plant, make sure that there are plenty of buds still to open. A plant in full flower may be more spectacular initially, but the display will be shorter.

Pests and diseases

Examine the undersides of a few leaves to make sure they are free of pests and diseases before you buy.

Houseplants look better, and will grow better, if they are in a pot of an appropriate size. The plant in the picture at the top of the page is in a pot that's too large – it dominates the plant. The one shown above is in a pot that's too small; not only is it top-heavy and unstable, but the amount of compost in the pot is unlikely to be sufficient to sustain the plant.

Protective sleeves

These can be useful: they help to get the plant home with minimum damage and offer some protection from cold winds in winter. But make sure they don't hide damaged or diseased leaves. Be prepared to remove the sleeve to examine a plant if they are displayed in this way.

CREATING THE RIGHT ENVIRONMENT

It's impossible to recreate the atmosphere of a South American rainforest or the semi-desert conditions of the world's more arid regions in our homes. Yet we expect orchids and bromeliads to thrive alongside cacti and succulents, plants from the world's warmest regions to coexist with hardy plants such as ivies and aucubas. Creating the right conditions to suit such a diversity of plants, whilst keeping a home that's also comfortable to live in, calls for ingenuity and a dash of compromise.

Use the advice on labels and in books as a guide to the best conditions in which to keep your plants. In reality you may not be able to accommodate all the conditions listed as desirable, but most plants will still survive even if they do not thrive. Take recommendations for humidity seriously: a plant that requires very high humidity is likely to die soon in very dry air. Recommendations regarding light and shade are important but if you get this slightly wrong the consequence is more likely to be poor variegation, perhaps scorch marks on the leaves, or drawn and lanky plants, rather than dead ones. You can usually correct the problem by moving the plant.

Temperature is the most flexible requirement, and most plants will tolerate a wide fluctuation above or below the suggested targets.

Temperature
Treat with caution advice in books and on labels that gives a precise temperature range. Most plants will survive temperatures much lower than the ones normally recommended, and, in winter when the light is poor, a high temperature may stimulate growth that can't be supported by the light levels. Upper temperature figures are meaningless unless you have air conditioning. In summer the outside temperature

often rises above those recommended for particular plants, and unless you have some way of cooling the air, the plants will have to suffer the heat along with you. They will almost certainly come to no harm if shaded from direct sun and provided that the humidity is high enough.

Once the temperature drops towards freezing, however, most houseplants are at risk. Even in a centrally heated home, temperatures can drop very low if heating is turned off at night.

Light and shade
The best position for most plants is in good light but out of direct sun. Even plants that thrive in sun outdoors may resent the strongly magnified rays through glass, which will often scorch the leaves. Be especially wary of positioning plants behind patterned glass in full sun: the pattern can magnify the sun's rays.

Only plants that normally grow in deserts, on steppes, high mountains and barren moors grow in areas devoid of shade. And even these may not like the sun's rays intensified through glass. If possible, fit shades that you can use for the hottest part of the day. Even net curtains are useful in screening out some of the strongest rays.

The so-called shade plants do not like any direct sun, but that does not

necessarily mean that they will grow in gloom. The eye is deceptive when it comes to judging light levels. Use a camera fitted with a light meter, and measure the light in different parts of the room. You might discover that the light is as poor immediately above or below a window as it is in the centre of the room. If the windows are high, experiment with the light meter to see how much better the light might be if you raised a plant on a pedestal or positioned it on a low table.

ABOVE: *Leaf scorch (brown marks or blotches that leave the areas looking thin and papery) is a common problem on plants placed on a very sunny windowsill. Unless they are adapted to this kind of intense heat, the tissue of the leaves can be damaged. The problem is most likely if drops of water are left on the foliage in bright sunlight (the water acts like a magnifying glass) or where patterned glass intensifies the sun's rays.*

ABOVE: *Plants like schizanthus and cinerarias will make a super show if you can provide good light and moist, humid conditions.*

KEEPING THEM INSULATED

The greatest dangers to plants are cold draughts, especially at night when the temperature drops and the heating is turned off, and frost. Take precautions to keep them insulated:

Move plants into the room when you pull the curtains – don't leave them trapped between curtains and glass, where the temperature can drop dramatically.

If you have to leave plants by a window on a cold night, try insulating them with sheets of styrofoam placed against the lower half of the window.

Humidity

Humidity – or the amount of moisture present in the air at a given temperature – is important to all plants, but especially those with thin or delicate leaves, such as ferns, selaginellas and caladiums. Grow those plants that need a very humid atmosphere in a bottle garden or plant case, or mist the plants frequently (at least once a day, more often if possible).

For less demanding plants that still need high humidity, grow them in groups to create a microclimate or stand the plants on gravel, pebbles or marbles in a shallow dish containing water. Provided that the bottom of the pot is not in direct contact with the water the air will be humid without the compost becoming waterlogged. Misting is still desirable, but if the plants are in flower shield the blooms while you do so, otherwise the petals may become marked or begin to rot.

Simple humidity trays to place over radiators are inexpensive and help to create a more buoyant atmosphere for houseplants.

ABOVE: *It can be difficult to create a humid environment in the home, but a small microclimate can be created around the plant. Standing the plant over a dish containing water will increase the humidity, but the pot must be stood on small pebbles or marbles to keep it above water level and avoid waterlogged potting soil.*

ABOVE: *The majority of houseplants will benefit from misting with water. If you can do it daily the plants will almost certainly grow better. Delicate ferns that need a very high humidity may need misting several times a day for really good results.*

ABOVE: *Although the foliage benefits from misting, water can damage delicate flowers. Simply protect the blooms with a piece of paper or cardboard if the plant is in flower.*

WINDOWSILL PLANTS

Windowsills are a favourite position for houseplants, but you need to choose plants appropriate to the aspect. Not all plants appreciate a baking in the sunshine.

It is a good idea to analyse the amount of direct light coming through each window before deciding on the best spots for various plants with different light needs. Large windows obviously let in most light, but it will still be less than outdoors, and the larger the area of glass, the more rapidly temperatures drop at night.

The majority of plants flourish best when placed in good light in a position that is shaded from the direct rays of the sun. There are bound to be some rooms that receive little direct light, but most will receive some sun at least in the morning or evening. Except for shade lovers that are particularly vulnerable to direct sun, the majority of plants will benefit from this as the strength of the sun is generally weaker in the early morning and evening, so leaf scorch is less likely.

Very sunny windows can still be packed with interest if you select the plants carefully, but be prepared to keep the compost well watered in warm weather. Avoid splashing the leaves when the sun is on them, however, as the droplets of water can act like a further magnifying glass and scorch the leaves.

The lists of suggested plants given here are not definitive, but an example of what can be grown. Be prepared to experiment with many more, especially on a light windowsill that does not receive fierce direct sun.

Where only the genus is mentioned, all the widely available species sold as houseplants should be successful.

Many plants will grow in sun or partial shade and a few will do well in both direct sun and indirect light.

Plants for a very sunny window
Ananas, cacti, ceropegia, chlorophytum, coleus, geraniums (pelargoniums), regal, zonal, scented-leaved, gerbera, hippeastrum, *Hoya carnosa*, hypocyrta, impatiens, iresine, *Kalanchoe blossfeldiana* and hybrids, nerium, *Plectranthus fruticosus*, sansevieria, setcreasea, stapelia, succulents (most), yucca and zebrina.

Plants for a window that receives early or late sun
Aechmea, aglaonema, anthurium, aphelandra, begonia, beloperone, billbergia, caladium, calathea, capsicum, chlorophytum, chrysanthemum, cocos, codiaeum, coleus, *Cordyline terminalis* (syn. *C. fruticosa*) and varieties, crossandra, cuphea, ficus (most), gardenia, gynura, hoya, impatiens, maranta, nertera, *Plectranthus oertendahlii*, rhipsalidopsis, saintpaulia, sansevieria, sinningia, solanum, spathiphyllum, tolmiea, tradescantia, zebrina.

Plants for a light window out of direct sunlight
Adiantum, aglaonema, anthurium, asparagus, aspidistra, asplenium, billbergia, calathea, chlorophytum, clivia, dieffenbachia, dracaena, ferns, *Ficus deltoidea*, *Ficus pumila*, hydrangea, maranta, orchids, saintpaulia, sansevieria, selaginella, soleirolia (syn. helxine), spathiphyllum.

ABOVE: Hoya carnosa *is a pretty climber or trailer for a sunny position. It is usually grown for its white flowers, but the variegated 'Tricolor' also makes an attractive foliage plant.*

ABOVE: Aphelandra squarrosa *needs good light but not direct summer sun. Grow it where it just receives early or late sun in the summer and in the best light possible in winter.*

ABOVE: *Gerberas will tolerate a very sunny position, but if you plan to discard the plant after flowering you can use it to brighten up dull spots too.*

ABOVE: Mammillaria elongata, *like most cacti, will thrive in a hot, sunny position.*

ABOVE: Aglaonema *'Silver Queen' grows well in semi-shade or bright light, but avoid direct midday sun.*

ABOVE: Sansevieria trifasciata *'Laurentii' is one of those tough plants that will do well on any windowsill, in shade or full sun.*

ABOVE: Yucca elephantipes *benefits from as much light as possible. It will enjoy a hot, sunny position.*

BELOW: Zygocactus (Schlumbergera) *hybrids are forest cacti, best grown in good light shaded from direct sunlight.*

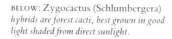

RIGHT: Kalanchoe blossfeldiana *hybrids do well on a sunny windowsill.*

ABOVE: Calathea zebrina *is best in a light position that receives early or late sun, but not direct midday sun.*

ABOVE: Aechmea fasciata *is grown mainly for its fascinating flower spike. Because it grows naturally in trees, it is not adapted to life on a very hot, sunny windowsill. Position it where it receives early or late sun.*

SHADY SPOTS

Plants that tolerate shade are particularly useful, especially if you need focal point plants for difficult positions within the room. Large specimen plants are usually too large for a windowsill so these have to combine size with shade tolerance.

It is a mistake to position a plant purely for decorative effect, and you should always choose a spot that the plant will at least tolerate even if it doesn't thrive. For really inhospitable corners where it's just too dark even for shade lovers, use disposable flowering plants, or even ferns if you are prepared to discard them after a couple of months.

In winter, plants are unlikely to tolerate a light intensity less than 1,000 lux, and 5,000 lux in summer is about the minimum for foliage plants such as aspidistras and *Cissus rhombifolia* (syn. *Rhoicissus rhomboidea*). These are meaningless figures unless you have a way of measuring light, but fortunately there is a simple rough-and-ready way that can be used. Two methods of judging light levels are described in *How to Assess Light* (opposite).

ARTIFICIAL LIGHT

● Artificial light can be used to highlight plants in dull spots, and can also be used to help plants thrive where natural light is inadequate.

Even ordinary light bulbs can help plants to grow by providing localized warmth and a degree of increased illumination. However, fluorescent tubes are better for plant growth and, because they generate less heat, they can be used closer to the plant. Light sources need to be close, and if possible the tubes should be specially balanced for plant growth (you can buy these at some gardening shops and also at aquarium suppliers). Otherwise use the tubes in pairs with one 'daylight' and one 'cool white' used together.

ABOVE: Aglaonema *'Silver Queen' is undemanding and useful for low-light areas.*

ABOVE: Aucuba japonica *varieties are not only shade-tolerant but cold-tolerant too. They are frost-hardy, so choose them for a position that has both low light levels and low temperatures in winter.*

ABOVE: Fatsia japonica *is a garden shrub hardy enough to grow outside except in very cold regions, but indoors the variegated form is more attractive. Choose it for a low light area where temperatures also drop in the winter.*

ABOVE: Philodendron scandens *is a useful trailer for a low-light area.*

ABOVE: Ficus pumila *is a low-growing trailer that would soon die on a sunny window. The variegated varieties are more attractive than the all-green species.*

ABOVE: Helxine soleirolii, *also sold as* Solcirolia soleirolii, *is a tough carpeter that will tolerate low light and cool temperatures (it will even stand some frost). There are green, silver and golden forms.*

ABOVE: *Ivies (varieties of* Hedera helix) *grow happily in the wild in sun or shade, and they will do the same in the home. If possible provide bright conditions in winter and avoid direct sunlight in summer.*

ABOVE: Fittonia verschaffeltii *is one of the more difficult foliage plants to try. It will be short-lived in direct sunlight.*

ABOVE: Pellaea rotundifolia *does not demand such a humid atmosphere as most ferns; a light window out of direct sunlight is ideal.*

ABOVE: Adiantum capillus-veneris *will not tolerate a hot, sunny position for long. It will be much happier in a humid and shaded conservatory.*

ABOVE: Scindapsus aureus, *also sold as* Epipremnum aureum, *is a trailer or climber that will do well in low-light areas. This golden form is particularly bright, but in time the leaves become more green and less colourful.*

ABOVE: Asplenium nidus *is one of the easiest ferns to grow.*

HOW TO ASSESS THE LIGHT

● Use a camera with a built-in light meter, and set it to a 100 ISO (ASA) film speed and 1/125 second shutter speed. Take the reading at about midday on a bright day in late spring or early summer. Position the camera where you want to place the plant, and point it towards the window.

Read off the aperture setting then use the following as a rough guide to the light level:

f16 or more = Strong light, suitable for those plants that need the best light.

f8–11 = Equivalent to screened daylight, and suitable for those plants that like good light but not strong direct sunlight.

f4–5.6 = Poor light, only suitable for those plants adapted to shade.

f2.8 = Suitable for only the most shade-tolerant species, and plants may not survive in the winter months.

● Another test is to try reading a newspaper where you plan to position the plant. Assuming that you have good eyesight, the position is too dark for plants if you can't read the newspaper comfortably.

● **Plants for poor light**
Aglaonema, araucaria, asplenium, aspidistra, aucuba, bulbs (such as hyacinths), but keep in good light until flowering starts, *Cissus rhombifolia* (syn. *Rhoicissus rhomboidea*) × Fatshedera, fatsia, ferns (most), *Ficus pumila*, fittonia, *Hedera helix* (ivy), palms (most), *Philodendron scandens*, pteris, sansevieria, *Scindapsus aureus* (syn. *Epipremnum aureum*, *Rhaphidophora aurea*), but be prepared for it to lose most of its variegation, *Soleirolia soleirolii* (syn. *Helxine soleirolii*).

WATERING

No plant can survive without water, yet more plants probably die from overwatering than from underwatering. Getting to grips with this apparently simple procedure is one of the essentials of good plant care.

Meters and indicator strips that are pushed into the compost help to put some kind of measurement to the amount of moisture available in the compost, but are impractical if you have a lot of houseplants. You will soon tire of pushing a probe into each pot or reading indicators left in each one. These devices are best used by beginners still gaining experience of how to judge the moisture content by other means.

How much water?
There are no fixed rules about watering. How much a plant needs, and how often, depends not only on the plant but also the kind of pot (clay pots need watering more often than plastic ones), the compost, (peat-based composts retain more water than loam-based), and the temperature and humidity.

Watering is an acquired skill, and one that needs to be practised on an almost daily basis, otherwise it is best to switch to self-watering containers or hydroponically grown plants.

Useful techniques
Examine the pots daily if possible, using whichever of the following techniques you find the most convenient:

- Appearance alone can be a guide. Dry, loam-based composts look paler than when they are moist. A dry surface does not mean that the compost is dry lower down, but if it looks damp you know that you don't need to water. If the plant is placed in a saucer, see

if there is any standing water. Apart from bog plants, never add more water if there is any trace still left in the saucer.
- The touch test is useful for a peat-based compost. Press a finger gently into the surface – you will know immediately if it feels very dry or very wet.
- The bell test is useful for clay pots, especially large ones containing specimen plants and that hold a large volume of compost. Push a cotton reel onto a short garden cane and tap the pot: a dull thud indicates moist compost (although it could also indicate a cracked pot!), a clear ring suggests dry compost. This

Watering from above
A small watering-can is still the most popular way to water houseplants. Choose one that is well-balanced to hold and with a long, narrow spout that makes it easy to direct the water to the compost rather than over the plant.

Compost check
If you use a clay pot, it will ring with a hollow sound if you tap it with a cotton reel on a cane or pencil and the compost is dry. If the compost is still moist the sound will be duller. With a little experience you will be able to detect the difference.

doesn't work well with peat-based composts, and not at all with plastic pots.
- With practice you can tell when the compost is dry simply by lifting the pot slightly: a pot with dry compost will feel much lighter than one with moist compost.

How to water
When you water, fill the pot to the brim – dribbles are not sufficient. If

the root-ball has completely dried out, water may run straight through, down the inside of the pot, in which case stand the pot in a bucket of water until the air bubbles stop rising.

After watering, always check whether surplus water is sitting in the saucer or cache-pot. This will not matter if there are pebbles or marbles to keep the bottom of the pot out of contact with the moisture, but otherwise you must tip out the extra water. *Failure to tip out standing water is the most common cause of failure.* With just a few exceptions, if you leave most ordinary houseplants standing in water for long, they will probably die.

A long-necked watering-can is the most convenient way to water the majority of houseplants. The long neck makes it easy to reach among the leaves, and a narrow spout makes it easier to control the flow, which is also less forceful and unlikely to wash the compost away.

Watering with a can means that you may wet the leaves and crown of ground-hugging plants such as saintpaulias, and unless you are careful this can encourage rotting. For plants like this you may prefer to stand them in a bowl with a few centimetres (inches) of water in the bottom. Remove and allow to drain as soon as the surface of the compost becomes moist.

Special needs

Tap water is far from ideal, but the vast majority of houseplants will tolerate it. If the water is hard (has a high calcium or magnesium content), however, you need to make special arrangements for plants that react badly to alkaline soil or compost. These include aphelandras, azaleas, hydrangeas, orchids, rhododendrons and saintpaulias. Rain-water is usually recommended for these plants, but a good supply is not always available throughout the year, and in some areas it can be polluted.

If your tap water is only slightly hard, simply filling the watering cans the day before and allowing the water to stand overnight may be sufficient. For harder water, try boiling it: part of the hardness will be deposited in the form of scale, and you can use the water once it has cooled.

Many water softeners work on a principle that unfortunately does not help the plants: if you want to benefit the plants, a demineralization system is necessary, which removes all the minerals and leaves distilled water. However, it is only worth the expense if you have a lot of plants.

Underwatering

If a plant wilts or collapses like this (TOP) it can usually be revived by standing the pot in a bowl of water for a few hours, then leaving it in a cool, shady position for a day. By the next day it will probably be as perky as before (ABOVE). Always make sure that the compost is dry before doing this, as an overwatered plant will also wilt.

Watering the outer pot

Just a few plants tolerate standing with their roots in water, like this cyperus. With these you can add water to the saucer or outer container, but never do this unless you know the plant grows naturally in marshy places.

Self-watering pots

If you find watering a chore, self-watering pots may be the answer. The moisture is drawn up into the compost through wicks from a reservoir below, and you will need to water much less frequently.

Overwatering

Before an overwatered plant reaches the stage of collapsing, it will probably begin to look sickly. The plant on the left has been overwatered, the one on the right has received the correct amount of water.

FEEDING

Feeding can make the difference between a plant that simply exists and seems to 'stand still', and one that looks healthy and vigorous and really flourishes. Modern fertilizers have made feeding really easy, and now it isn't even a chore that you have to remember on a regular basis.

Houseplants are handicapped simply by being contained in a pot. The volume of soil or compost that the roots can explore is strictly limited, and sometimes we expect the same compost to support a large plant for many years.

With a few exceptions, your plants will look better if you feed them. You can buy special fertilizers for flowering plants, foliage plants and even special groups such as saintpaulias, but if you want to keep things simple and use one type of feed for all your plants they will still respond better than if they hadn't been fed at all.

When to feed

If in doubt about a particular plant, check the label or look it up in a book. As a general rule, plants should be fed only when they are growing actively and when light and temperature are such that they can actually take advantage of the additional nutrients. This generally means between mid-spring and mid-autumn, but there are exceptions – notably with winter-flowering plants.

Cyclamen are fed during the winter as well as before, and the winter- and spring-flowering forest cacti are fed during the winter but rested in summer. The rule of 'active growth' is more important than the time of year.

Controlled-release fertilizers are useful for houseplants, but bear in mind that they are influenced by temperature, so they won't stop releasing nutrients in winter as they would outdoors.

How often to apply

Some trial and error is inevitable. Books and plant labels often give advice like 'feed once a fortnight', but with so many formulations available such advice may be inappropriate. It assumes a typical liquid houseplant feed. Do not follow this advice too closely if you use one of the other types.

Controlled- and slow-release fertilizers

These are widely used commercially, especially for outdoor container-grown plants and pot plants. Unlike ordinary fertilizers, the nutrients are released over a period of months, so a couple of applications in a year is all that most plants require.

Controlled-release fertilizers are most useful for outdoor plants because they release the nutrients only when the soil temperature is high enough for the plants to make use of them.

Why feed?

These two Rhoicissus rhomboidea *are the same age and were the same size when bought. The plant on the left has been fed regularly and repotted once; the one on the right has not been fed and shows typical signs of starvation.*

Slow-release fertilizers

Slow-release fertilizers are worth adding to the compost because they sustain the plants over a period of perhaps six months. The nutrients in many peat-based or peat-substitute composts may become depleted within weeks or perhaps a couple of months.

Slow-release fertilizers are most useful for houseplants as a compost additive when potting up an established plant.

Liquid feeds

Liquid fertilizers are quick-acting, and useful for an immediate boost. Strengths and dilutions vary, so *follow the manufacturer's advice* for rate and frequency of application.

Pellets and sticks

There are various products designed to take the chore out of regular feeding. These will save you a lot of time and trouble in comparison with liquid feeds, although they may work out more expensive in

---

DON'T OVER-FEED

● Because some feeding is good does not mean that more feeding is better. Do not apply more than the manufacturer recommends, otherwise you might kill your plants. Salts build up in the compost and can affect the intake of water and nutrients which, coupled with an over-stimulation of the plant, can end in collapse.

Fertilizer sticks and pellets

Pot-plant fertilizers are also available in sticks (TOP) and pellets (ABOVE) that you push into the compost. Many people find these more convenient to use than having to mix and apply liquid feeds.

the long run. Some are tablet-shaped, others stick-shaped, but the principle is always the same: you make a hole in the compost, push in the fertilizer stick or pellet, then leave it to release its nutrients slowly over a period of a month or so (check the instructions).

Slow-release sachets

Slow-release fertilizers are available in sachets that you place inside the pot at the bottom. These are most appropriate when repotting.

Soluble powders

These work on the same principle as liquid feeds, but you simply dissolve the powder in water at the appropriate rate. They often work out less expensive than liquid fertilizers.

Granular fertilizer

If you have to add a granular or powder fertilizer to the compost, use a fork to stir it into the surface, then water it in thoroughly.

Benefits of feeding

To appreciate the benefits of feeding try starting with two plants of the same age and size, then feed just one of the plants regularly. The two Pilea cadierei (TOP) are the plants as bought. The same plants (ABOVE) show the effect a couple of months later after the one on the right was given just one dose of slow-release fertilizer.

CHOOSING A COMPOST

Your plants will only be as good as the compost they grow in. Feeding will help to overcome nutritional deficiencies, but the structure of the compost is also important if the roots are to get the right balance between moisture and air, so vital for healthy growth. Commercially, composts are chosen that make capillary watering easy, and that are light to transport, but in the home they may not be the most appropriate growing medium.

Compost does more than simply anchor the plant, it acts as a reservoir for nutrients and if the structure is right achieves the right balance between moisture and air. It also acts as a host to many beneficial micro-organisms.

Earlier generations of gardeners used to formulate special potting mixtures for different types of plant, but nowadays composts are available that suit the majority of plants, and only a few have special requirements.

The main choice is between loam-based composts and those based on peat or a peat substitute. Most plants will grow well in either type, but there are pros and cons that may make one more or less appropriate for a particular plant.

Loam-based composts use sterilized loam as the main ingredient, with added sand and peat to improve the structure, and fertilizers to supplement the nutrients already present in the loam.

Loam composts have weight, a useful attribute for a large plant with a lot of top growth, such as a big palm, as it provides stability to the pot.

Peat-based composts are light and pleasant to handle, and many plants thrive in them. Sand or other materials are sometimes added, but all of them depend on the addition of fertilizers to support plant growth. Often the fertilizers present in the compost run out quickly, and the plants will almost certainly suffer unless you begin supplementary feeding as soon as the plants show signs of poor growth.

Peat composts are very easy to manage on a commercial scale, with automatic watering systems, but in the home they demand more careful watering than loam composts. They can dry out more completely and become difficult to re-wet, and they are also more easily overwatered.

Some gardeners are reluctant to use peat-based composts on the grounds of depleting wetland areas where peat is excavated. For that reason many alternative products are now being introduced, including composts based on coir (waste from coconuts) and finely pulverized bark. Some use a mixture of materials. Results from these alternative composts can be very variable, depending on the make and formulation. Try a number of plants in several different makes – potting up the same types of plants in each – then decide which is best.

SPECIAL MEDIUMS

● A few plants have particular needs that make a general-purpose compost inappropriate. Lime-hating plants, such as azaleas, many begonias, ericas and saintpaulias, are the most common group, and they will grow poorly in ordinary composts. Even peat-based composts are generally alkaline, because they have lime added to make them suitable for the majority of houseplants. For lime-hating plants you need an 'ericaceous' compost widely available at garden centres.

Bromeliads, cacti and orchids are other groups that have special needs, and you can buy specially formulated composts suitable for these from many specialist nurseries and good garden centres.

Perlite

Gravel

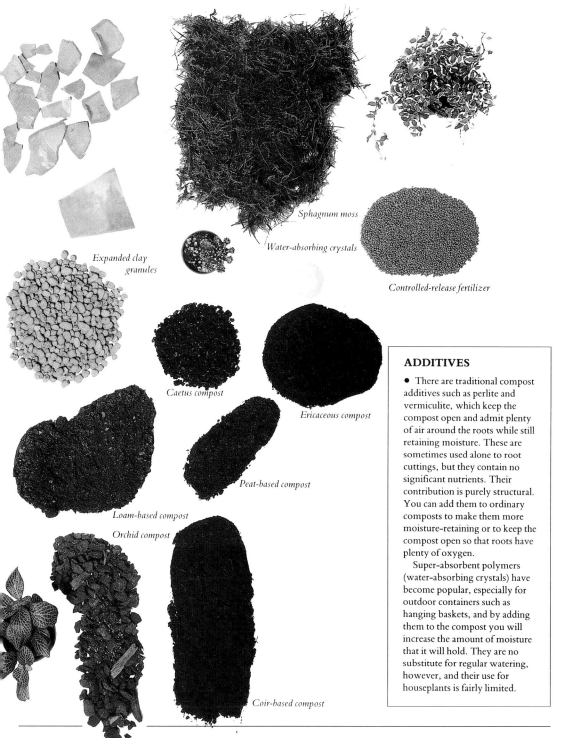

Expanded clay
granules

Sphagnum moss

Water-absorbing crystals

Controlled-release fertilizer

Caetus compost

Ericaceous compost

Peat-based compost

Loam-based compost

Orchid compost

Coir-based compost

ADDITIVES

● There are traditional compost additives such as perlite and vermiculite, which keep the compost open and admit plenty of air around the roots while still retaining moisture. These are sometimes used alone to root cuttings, but they contain no significant nutrients. Their contribution is purely structural. You can add them to ordinary composts to make them more moisture-retaining or to keep the compost open so that roots have plenty of oxygen.

Super-absorbent polymers (water-absorbing crystals) have become popular, especially for outdoor containers such as hanging baskets, and by adding them to the compost you will increase the amount of moisture that it will hold. They are no substitute for regular watering, however, and their use for houseplants is fairly limited.

POTS AND CONTAINERS

Pots needn't just be practical, they can be pretty or interesting too. But whatever type you choose, their size and proportion in relation to the plants contained will affect how they are perceived, and the pot can make or mar a plant.

Ordinary clay or plastic pots lack visual appeal, and most people hide them in a more decorative cache-pot that is slightly larger. If you do this, put gravel, expanded clay granules or a few pebbles in the base to keep the bottom of the pot from contact with the surplus water that collects in the base. Alternatively, pack the space between the inner and outer pots with peat to absorb most of the moisture, at the same time helping to create a more humid microclimate around the plant. Only use the latter method if you are very methodical about watering and are unlikely to overwater or leave stagnant water sitting at the base of the container. It will be difficult to detect and tip out once the space between the two pots has been filled.

Some plants do look good in clay pots, especially cacti and some succulents. But half-pots are often more appropriate as cacti do not have a large root system, and a shallower pot will usually look more in proportion to the plant. Half-pots have the same diameter as a full pot, but stand only about half the height. Seed pans, which are uncommon now, are similar but shallower; although intended for seed-sowing they can also be used for low or prostrate plants.

Many other plants look better in a half-pot, including azaleas, most begonias, saintpaulias and the majority of bromeliads. Be guided by the type of pot the plant is in when you buy it: if it's a shallow one, use another half-pot when you need to repot.

Some of the better quality plastic pots are coloured and come with a matching saucer, and these can look as attractive as a cache-pot, especially if you choose a colour that is co-ordinated with the room.

You can decorate ordinary clay or plastic pots by painting them freehand or using a stencil. For clay pots use masonry paint, for plastic pots use acrylic artists' paints.

Square pots are more often used in the greenhouse than indoors, but they are space-saving if you have a collection of small plants such as cacti.

PLASTIC OR CLAY?

• The vast majority of the plants on sale are grown in plastic pots: evidence that commercial growers find them satisfactory. Plastic pots are clean, light, easy to handle, remain largely free of algae and are inexpensive. They retain moisture better and the compost is less likely to dry out.

Perhaps surprisingly, clay pots will usually last longer than plastic ones. Plastic pots become brittle with age and even a slight knock is sometimes sufficient to break them. A clay pot won't break unless you actually drop it onto a hard surface. The extra weight of a clay pot will also be of benefit if a plant is large and rather top-heavy.

ABOVE: *This zinc container creates just the right atmosphere for an old-fashioned kitchen setting. If a container is large enough, try using a couple of compatible plants, like the adiantum and pellaea ferns.*

ABOVE: *Rush baskets can be very effective for small spring bulbs or compact plants like saintpaulias. Always line them or use them simply as a cache-pot.*

ABOVE: *Ceramic pots look stylish, and so much more colourful than an ordinary clay or plastic pot.*

ABOVE: *Bark baskets look good for houseplants that you would normally associate with trees, such as an ivy.*

ABOVE: *In a modern setting you may want a stylish type of container, like this small zinc one. The purple gynura does not detract from the container, which is a feature in its own right.*

ABOVE: *Terracotta hanging pots look more attractive than the plastic versions for a semi-cascading plant like this nephrolepis fern.*

ABOVE: *This china cache-pot picks up the colour of the cyclamen flowers to create a co-ordinated look.*

ABOVE: *Moss baskets make a nice setting for a few spring plants like primroses, and crocuses. Do not plant directly into this type of container unless you can ensure the surface is protected from drips.*

ABOVE: *Keep an eye open for the unlikely or unexpected. This distinctive container is made from dried fungi! The plant in it is a variegated* Ficus pumila.

ABOVE: *Stoneware pots are appropriate for plants in a kitchen. This one has been planted with* Helxine soleirolii *(syn.* Soleirolia soleirolii*), which reflects the rounded shape of the pot.*

ABOVE: *Terracotta wall planters can be used indoors as well as out. This* Philodendron scandens *will be trimmed after a few months to retain the container as a feature.*

ABOVE: *This metal planter is the kind of container that would look stunning in the right setting. You can line it with moss, rather like a hanging basket.*

ABOVE: *Matching drip trays are useful, and this one is particularly attractive because it takes three ceramic pots.*

ABOVE: *All kinds of decorative cache-pots are available in stores and garden centres, so it should be easy to choose those that appeal to your own tastes.*

ABOVE: *Sometimes old hand-made clay pots can be used effectively. The white deposit that often appears on old pots adds to the impression of age. These have been planted with ivies.*

POTTING PLANTS

Sooner or later most plants need repotting, and it can give an ailing plant a new lease of life. But not all plants respond well to frequent repotting, and some prefer to be in small pots. Knowing when to repot, and into which sized pot, is a skill that develops with experience.

Never be in too much of a hurry to pot on a plant into a larger container. Plants do not appreciate having their roots disturbed, and any damage to them will result in some check to growth.

Repotting should never simply be an annual routine. It's a job to be thought about annually, but not actually done unless the plant needs it.

Young plants require potting on much more frequently than older ones. Once a large specimen is in a big pot it may be better to keep it growing by repotting into another pot of the same size, by topdressing, or simply by additional feeding.

When repotting is necessary
The sight of roots growing through the base of the pot is not in it itself a sign that repotting is necessary. If the plants have been watered through a capillary mat, or the pot has been placed in a cache-pot, some roots will inevitably grow through the base to seek the water.

If in doubt, knock the plant out of its pot. To remove the root-ball easily, invert the pot and knock the rim on a hard surface while supporting the plant and compost with your hand. It is normal for a few roots to run around the inside of the pot, but if there is also a solid mass of roots it's time to pot on.

There are several ways to repot a plant, but the two described here are among the best.

When to repot

A mass of thick roots growing through the bottom of the pot (TOP) is an indication that it's time to move the plant into a large one. Equally, a mass of roots curled around the edge of the pot (ABOVE) is another sign that it's time for a larger container.

1 Prepare a clay pot as described in the *Traditional method.* However, don't cover the drainage hole at all if using a plastic pot and a capillary watering mat.

POTTING ON, POTTING UP, REPOTTING

• Although some of these terms are commonly used interchangeably, their true meanings are specific:

• **Potting up** is what happens the first time a seedling or cutting is given its own pot.

• **Potting on** is the action of replanting the root-ball in a larger pot.

• **Repotting** is sometimes taken to mean replacing the plant in a pot of the same size, but with most of the compost replaced. This is only necessary if the plant cannot be moved into a larger pot.

2 Place a little dampened compost over the base material then insert the existing pot, ensuring that the level of the soil surface will be about 1cm (½in) below the top of the new pot when filled.

3 Pack more compost firmly between the inner and outer pots, pressing it down gently with your fingers. This creates a mould when the inner pot is removed.

4 Remove the inner pot, then take the plant from its original container and drop it into the hole formed in the new compost. Gently firm the compost around the root-ball, and water thoroughly.

TRADITIONAL METHOD

1 Prepare a pot that is one or two sizes larger than the original and, if the pot is a clay one, cover the drainage hole with a piece of broken pot or a few pieces of chipped bark.

2 Make sure that the plant has been watered a short time beforehand, and knock the root-ball out of the old pot. Remove it by pulling gently on the plant, or invert the pot and tap the rim.

3 Place a small amount of compost in the base of the new pot, then position the root-ball so that it is at the right height.

4 Trickle more compost around the sides, turning the pot as you work. Use the same kind of compost – peat- or loam-based – as used in the original pot.

5 Gently firm the compost. Allow a gap of about 1–2.5cm (½–1in) between the top of the compost and the rim of the pot, for watering. Water thoroughly.

TOPDRESSING

● Once plants are in large pots, perhaps 25–30cm (10–12in) in diameter, continual potting on into a larger pot may not be practical. Try removing the top few centimetres (inches) of compost, loosening it first with a small hand fork. Replace this with fresh potting compost of the same type. This, plus regular feeding, will enable most plants to be grown in the same pot for many years.

PRUNING AND GROOMING

Grooming your plants occasionally not only keeps them looking good, it also enables you to check them for early signs of pests and diseases before these become a problem.

Some pruning and grooming tasks simply keep the plants looking fresh and tidy, others actually improve them by encouraging bushier growth or promoting further flowering.

Apart from picking off dead flowers, which is best done whenever you notice them, grooming is only a once-a-week task. Most jobs need doing less frequently than this, but by making a routine of tidying up your plants you will almost certainly detect pest, disease and nutritional problems that much earlier. One also learns to appreciate the plants more by close examination, so you will benefit as well as the plants.

Deadheading

This keeps the plant looking tidy, and in many cases encourages the production of more flowers. It also discourages diseases: fungus infections often start on dead or dying flowers, before spreading to the leaves.

Plants with masses of small flowers, such as fibrous-rooted begonias (*B. semperflorens*) are difficult to deadhead often enough, but unless you make some effort the flowers that fall often make a mess of the furniture or sill that they fall on, as well as spoiling the appearance of the plant itself.

Apart from where the flowers appear in a spike, remove the flower stalks as well as the flowers. Sometimes the stalks are most easily removed by hand, using a pulling and twisting motion at the same time.

If the flowers appear in spikes or large heads, such as a hydrangea, cut the whole head or spike back to just above a pair of leaves when the last blooms have finished.

Leaves

Dust and dirt accumulate on leaves as well as on furniture, but this is not always obvious unless the foliage is naturally glossy. This accumulation not only implies neglect, it also harms the plant slightly by cutting down on the amount of light falling on the leaf and thereby hindering photosynthesis, the process by which the plant produces energy for growth.

Wipe smooth leaves with a soft, damp cloth. Some people add a little milk to the water to produce a shine on glossy foliage. The alternative is to use a commercial leaf shine. Some leaf cleaners come as aerosols

Removing leaves
Sooner or later all plants have a few dead leaves. Even evergreens drop old leaves from time to time. Don't let them spoil the appearance of the plant; most are easily removed with a gentle tug, but tough ones may have to be cut off.

TOOLS FOR THE JOB

● Most of the equipment you need in order to care for houseplants you will probably already have around the home. You might want to try commercial leaf shines or buy secateurs, but a sponge or soft cloth and kitchen scissors will usually do the job just as well.

It is worth keeping a small grooming kit handy, perhaps in a small box that you can carry around during grooming sessions. It should contain:

● Sharp, pointed scissors, or a small pair of secateurs or flower-gathering scissors.

● A supply of split canes for supports.

● A ball of soft garden string, preferably green, or metal split rings. For some jobs, a reel of green plastic-covered wire is useful.

● A sponge for wiping glossy leaves.

● A small paintbrush for cleaning hairy leaves.

Leaf wipes

You might find commercial leaf wipes more convenient to use. They leave large, glossy leaves looking shiny and bright.

or sprays, others as impregnated wipes. If you are using an aerosol, follow the manufacturer's instructions carefully and pay particular attention to the recommended spraying distance.

Cloths and sprays are no use for cleaning hairy leaves. Instead, use a small paintbrush as a duster. You can dust cacti in the same way.

Compact non-flowering plants that don't have hairy leaves – aglaonemas for example – can be cleaned by swishing the foliage in a bowl of tepid water. But make sure that the plant dries off out of direct sunlight, otherwise the leaves may be scorched.

Shaping and training

You can improve the shape of many houseplants by pinching out the growing tips to prevent them from becoming tall and leggy. Removing the tips of the shoots makes the plant bushier. Impatiens, hypoestes, pileas and tradescantias are among the many plants that benefit from this treatment.

Climbers and trailers need regular attention. Tie in any new shoots to the support, and cut off any long shoots that spoil the shape.

Deadheading

Removing dead flowers will keep the plant looking smart, and reduce the chance of dead petals encouraging the growth of moulds and other diseases. Some plants also make a mess of the table or windowsill if the flowers are simply allowed to drop.

Sponging

Glossy-leaved plants like this ficus will look smarter if you wipe over the foliage with slightly soapy water occasionally. The plants also benefit because dust can reduce the amount of light received and also clog some of the pores through which the plant 'breathes'.

Immersing foliage

If the plant is small enough to handle conveniently, try swishing the foliage in a bowl of tepid water. Do not do this if the plant has hairy or delicate leaves.

Brushing leaves

Plants with hairy leaves, like this saintpaulia, should not be sponged or cleaned with a leaf wipe. Instead, brush them occasionally with a soft paintbrush.

Pinching out

If you want a bushy rather than a tall or sprawling plant, pinch out the growing tips a few times while it is still young. This will stimulate the growth of sideshoots that will produce a bushier effect. Most plants will respond to this treatment, but beware of doing it to slow-growing plants.

HOLIDAY CARE

Short-term holiday care
If you have to leave your plants unattended for a while, try grouping them together in a large container. Place them on wet capillary matting and make sure the compost is moist too. If leaving them for more than a few days, you may need to arrange a system to keep the mat moist.

Holidays are good for us, but not for plants. Unless you have a friendly neighbour who can plant-sit for you, you will have to devise ways of keeping your plants watered while you are away.

Most houseplants will survive in winter for a few days, or even a week, if they are well watered beforehand, especially if the central heating is turned down. In hot summer weather, special arrangements will have to be made for your plants if you are leaving them for anything more than a long weekend.

If you can't arrange for a neighbour to pop in every couple of days to water your houseplants, take the following precautions:

- If it is summer, stand as many as possible outdoors. Choose a shady, sheltered position, and plunge the pots up to their rims in the soil. Then apply a thick mulch of chipped bark or peat over the pots to keep them cool and to conserve moisture. Provided that they are watered well before you leave, most plants will survive a week like this, even without rain.
- Move those that are too delicate to go outdoors into a few large groups in a cool position out of direct sunlight.
- Stand as many as possible on trays of gravel, watered to just below the level of the pot bases. Although this will not moisten the compost, the humid air will help to keep the plants in good condition.
- Ensure that all of the most vulnerable plants have some kind of watering system.

Proprietary watering devices
Many kinds of watering devices can be bought, and new ones – usually variations on an old theme – appear each year. Most work on one of the following principles:

Porous reservoirs are pushed into the compost and filled with water. The water slowly seeps though the porous walls over a period of a few days to a week. These are useful for one or two pots for a short period of time, but as you need one for each pot and the reservoir is small, their use is limited.

Ceramic mushrooms work on a similar principle, but the top is sealed and there is a connecting tube for insertion into a large reservoir of water (such as a bucket). As the water seeps through the porous shaft, the pressure in the sealed unit drops and fresh water is drawn from the reservoir. This simple but effective device will keep a plant happy for a couple of weeks, but again, you need one for each pot!

Wicks are sold for insertion into the base of the pot, which is then stood above a reservoir of water. This is a good method if you only have a handful of plants, otherwise too tricky to set up.

Drip feeds, sold for greenhouse and garden use, are a good solution. They can be expensive, and if you use a portable bag reservoir they are not very elegant for the home – but that will not matter while you are away.

Improvising
Two reliable systems use the kitchen sink or bath and capillary matting, which is available at all good garden centres and home improvement stores.

Improvised wicks
Make your own porous wicks by cutting capillary matting into strips. Make sure the wicks and compost are moist before you leave, and that the wick is pushed well into the compost.

Conserving moisture
Placing a plant in an inflated plastic bag like this will conserve the moisture for quite a long time, but if left too long there is a risk of leaves rotting. Try to keep the bag out of contact with the leaves if possible.

For the sink, cut a length of matting that fits the draining area and is long enough to dip into the basin part. Fill this with water as a reservoir, or leave the plug out but let the tap drip onto the mat to keep it moist. If you leave the tap dripping, have a trial run

beforehand to make sure that it keeps the mat moist without wasting water.

If you want to leave water in the bath, place the mat and plants on a plank of wood supported on bricks, to leave space beneath for the water.

Bear in mind that compost in clay

pots with broken pots over the drainage holes will not benefit from the capillary action efficiently (though you could insert small wicks though the holes). The system works best for houseplants kept in plastic pots, with nothing placed over the drainage holes.

Hardy plants
Many of the tougher houseplants can stand outdoors with their pots plunged in the ground. Choose a shady spot, water the plants thoroughly and cover the tops of the pots with a thick layer of chipped bark.

Porous irrigators
Porous irrigators can be useful if you only leave your plants for a few days. Make sure the compost is moist, then fill the irrigators with water.

Porous wicks
Use a large needle to pull the wicks through the compost and out of the drainage hole at the base of the pot.

Ceramic mushrooms
Ceramic mushrooms can be very effective. As water seeps through the porous container the pressure drops, and more water is sucked up from the reservoir. Provided the reservoir is large enough, you should be able to leave your plant for a week or more.

Using the bath
The bath is a good place to keep plants moist on capillary matting; you can also stand the plants on porous bricks without the mat. Have a trial run to make sure the plug retains the water without seepage.

HYDROCULTURE

Hydroculture – also known as hydroponics – is a method of growing plants without soil or compost. Watering is normally only necessary every couple of weeks, and feeding is only a twice-yearly task. Hydroculture will give you successful plants with the minimum of attention.

Hydroponics can be a highly scientific way to cultivate plants, with nutrient solutions carefully controlled by expensive monitoring equipment. However, the system usually used in homes by amateurs – and generally referred to as hydroculture – is designed to be simple and can be used successfully even by the complete beginner.

You can buy plants that are already growing hydroponically, and these are the best way to start as you would in any case have to buy suitable containers, clay granules and a special fertilizer. But once you realize how easy hydroculture plants are to look after, you will probably want to start off your own plants from scratch.

Routine care

Wait until the water indicator registers minimum, *but do not water immediately*. Allow an interval of two or three days before filling again. Don't keep topping up the water to keep it near the maximum level – it is important that air is allowed to penetrate to the lower levels.

Always use *tap* water because the special ion-exchange fertilizer depends on the chemicals in tap water to function effectively.

Make sure that the water is at room temperature. Because there is no compost, cold water has an immediate chilling effect on the plant, and this is a common cause of failure with hydroculture plants.

Make a note of when you replace the fertilizer, and renew it every six

HOW HYDROCULTURE WORKS

● Plants can grow different kinds of roots: ground roots and water roots. If you root a cutting in water it will produce water roots, but once you pot it into compost it almost has to start again by producing ground roots. This makes the transition between compost and water cultivation tricky in either direction. But once the plant has passed through the transitional phase, a hydroculture plant can draw its moisture and nutrients from the solution at the base of the container, while those above can absorb the essential oxygen.

The level of the nutrient solution is crucial. If you fill the tank with too much water there will not be enough air spaces left for the roots to absorb sufficient oxygen and the plant will die.

1 Choose a young plant and wash the roots free of compost, being careful not to damage them. Place the plant in a container with slatted or mesh sides.

5 Pack with more clay granules to secure the inner pot and water indicator.

months. Some systems use the fertilizer in a 'battery' fitted within the special hydroculture pot, but otherwise you can just sprinkle it on to be washed in with a little water.

Just like plants in compost, hydroculture plants gradually grow larger. Because the roots do not have to search for moisture and nutrients the root system is usually smaller than for a comparable plant

in compost, but in time the plant will need repotting, especially if the top growth looks out of proportion with the container.

Remove the plant as carefully as possible. It may be necessary to cut the inner container to minimize damage to the roots, but sometimes you can leave the plant in the inner container and just use a larger outer one. If a very large and tangled root system has formed, some judicious pruning may be called for. Both roots and top growth can often be trimmed back successfully, but much depends on the type of plant.

2 Pack expanded clay granules around the roots, being careful to damage them as little as possible.

3 Insert the inner pot into a larger, watertight container, first laying clay granules on the base to raise the inner pot to 1cm (½in) below the rim.

4 Insert the water level tube. If you cannot find one to indicate the water level, use one that indicates how moist the roots are.

6 Sprinkle the special hydroculture fertilizer over the clay granules.

7 Wash the fertilizer down as you water to the maximum level on the indicator. If the indicator does not show a level, add water equal to one-quarter the capacity of the container. Water again when the indicator shows dry. Always fill with tap water.

8 A few months on and the houseplant is flourishing.

Suitable plants

Not all plants respond well to hydroculture, so some experimentation may be necessary. The range is surprisingly wide, however, and includes cacti and succulents (with these it is essential to ensure an adequate 'dry period' before topping up with more water, and not to let the water level rise too high), as well as orchids.

As a starting point, try some plants from the following list, or be guided by what you see planted in commercially-produced hydroculture units. Then experiment further as you gain more experience – *Aechmea fasciata*, aglaonema, amaryllis, anthurium, asparagus, aspidistra, beaucarnea, *Begonia manicata*, *Begonia rex*, cacti★, cissus, clivia, codiaeum, dieffenbachia, dizygotheca, dracaena, *Euphorbia pulcherrima*, ficus, gynura, hedera, hibiscus, hoya, maranta, monstera, nephrolepis, philodendron, saintpaulia, sansevieria, schefflera, *Spathiphyllum wallisii*, stephanotis, streptocarpus, tradescantia, *Vriesea splendens*, yucca.

★ Most cacti can be grown hydroponically, but it is essential that the water level is regulated carefully. If the water level is too high the plants will soon die.

DISORDERS AND DEFICIENCIES

Not all troubles are caused by pests and diseases. Sometimes physiological problems such as chills and cold draughts, or nutritional deficiencies, can be the case.

Tracking down a physiological problem calls for a bit of detective work. The descriptions of some common problems described here will help to pinpoint some potential causes, but be prepared to look for anything that has disturbed the usual routine. By piecing together the various clues you can often deduce probable causes, and thereby work out what you can do to avoid a repetition.

Temperature
Most houseplants will tolerate cool but frost-free temperatures if they have to. It is sudden changes of temperature or icy draughts in a warm room that cause most problems.

If leaves drop it may be due to low temperature. This often happens with newly bought plants that have been on display outdoors or chilled on the way home. Leaves that look shrivelled and slightly translucent may have been touched by frost.

Hardy plants like *Euonymus japonicus* may drop their leaves if kept too warm in winter. Berries are also likely to fall prematurely if the temperature is kept too high.

Light and sun
Plants that need a high light intensity will become elongated and drawn if the illumination is poor. Lop-sided growth is another indication of inadequate light. If you can't move the plant into a lighter position, try turning the pot round by 45 degrees each day (put a tiny mark on the pot as a reminder of whether you've turned it).

Light is a good thing, but direct sunlight, intensified through glass, will often scorch leaves – the effect will be brown, papery areas on the leaf. Patterned glass is a particular problem as it acts like a magnifying glass, causing dry brown patches where the rays are concentrated.

Humidity
Dry air can cause leaf tips to go brown and papery on vulnerable plants.

Watering
Too little water is the most likely cause of wilting and collapse, if the compost feels very dry to the touch. If the plant collapses and the compost feels very wet, or water is standing in the saucer or cache-pot, suspect overwatering.

Neglect
This plant is clearly showing signs of stress and lack of nutrients. It may be best to discard a plant in this state.

Sun scorch
Plants that are not adapted to grow in very strong light are easily scorched by strong sunlight intensified by a glass window. This dieffenbachia is suffering from scorch.

Effects of overwatering
Yellowing lower leaves are often a sign of overwatering, but may also be due to a chill if it happens in winter. This is a Fatshedera lizei showing signs of overwatering.

Aerosol scorch

A plant can also be damaged by aerosol sprays (even one containing an insecticide intended for houseplants). This dieffenbachia has dropped many of its leaves, and others are scorched, because an insecticidal aerosol was used too close to the plant.

Feeding

Pale leaves and short, stunted growth may be due to lack of fertilizer in the compost. Try liquid feeding for a quick boost. Specific plants, such as citrus fruits and rhododendrons, may show signs of iron deficiency (yellowing leaves) if grown in an alkaline compost. Feed with a chelated (sequestered) iron and next time you repot use an ericaceous compost (specially developed for lime-hating plants).

Bud drop

Bud drop is often caused by dry compost or dry air, but sometimes it is due to the plant being moved or turned once the buds have formed. The plant resents having to re-orientate its buds to light from a different direction.

Effects of dry air

Dry air is a particular problem for most ferns. This adiantum is showing the signs of low humidity.

Dehydration

This thunbergia shows the classic symptoms of a dehydrated plant. The very dry compost is confirmation of the cause. The best treatment is to stand the pot in a bowl of water for several hours, until the compost is thoroughly wet. Peat composts are particularly difficult to rewet once they have dried out completely, but a few drops of mild household detergent added to the water will help to rewet it.

Bud drop

Bud drop is often caused by dry root, overwatering, or by moving a plant once the flower buds have formed.

Index